SOCIAL WORK

SOCIAL WORK
A Profession of Many Faces

NINTH EDITION

Armando T. Morales

University of California at Los Angeles

Bradford W. Sheafor

Colorado State University

Allyn and Bacon

Boston   London   Toronto   Sydney   Tokyo   Singapore

To my wife, Cynthia,
and my children: Christina Mia, Roland, Gary, and Soo
—ATM

To my wife, Nadine,
and my children: Christopher, Perry, Brandon, and Laura
—BWS

Senior Editor: Judy Fifer
Editor in Chief, Social Sciences: Karen Hanson
Editorial Assistant: Alyssa Pratt
Marketing Manager: Jacqueline Aaron
Editorial Production Service: Raeia Maes, Maes Associates
Manufacturing Buyer: Julie McNeill
Cover Administrator: Linda Knowles
Electronic Composition: Omegatype Typography, Inc.

Copyright © 2001, 1998, 1995, 1992, 1989, 1986, 1983, 1980, 1977, by Allyn & Bacon
A Pearson Education Company
160 Gould Street
Needham Heights, MA 02494

Internet: www.abacon.com

Between the time web site information is gathered and published, some sites may have closed. Also, the transcription of URLs can result in typographical errors. The publisher would appreciate notification where these errors occur so that they may be corrected in subsequent editions.

Library of Congress Cataloging-in-Publication Data

Morales, Armando.
   Social work : a profession of many faces / Armando T. Morales,
Bradford W. Sheafor. — 9th ed.
      p.   cm.
   Includes bibliographical references and indexes.
   ISBN 0–205–31740–5
   1. Social service—United States.   2. Social work education—United States.   3. Social
service—Vocational guidance—United States.   4. Social work with minorities—United
States.   I. Sheafor, Bradford W.   II. Title.
HV91.M67 2001
361.973—dc21   00-027635
                                                                     CIP

Printed in the United States of America

10 9 8 7 6 5 4 3 2 1   RRD-VA   05 04 03 02 01 00

Photo Credits:
Photo credits are found on page 618, which should be considered an extension of the copyright page.

CONTENTS

PREFACE

There are many different expressions of social work. When someone wants to learn about this profession, it is often difficult to discern the common threads that unite social workers into a single profession. Since we began writing this book nearly thirty years ago, we have carefully reported the evolution of this profession and attempted to provide a book that would allow our readers to better understand social work.

In the ninth edition of *Social Work: A Profession of Many Faces,* we present an overview of social work, introducing many of the terms, concepts, people, professional organizations, and critical events that have shaped this profession. We have also described factors that help a reader to understand what it is like to be a social worker, including the education and experience required for different jobs, the places where social workers are employed, and the values and competencies required for effective practice. In this edition, we have added four new chapters, including the topics of suburban gangs, children and youth, Asian Americans, and social work as it is practiced in other parts of the world. Finally, we have incorporated materials—some were prepared by persons other than ourselves who have unique expertise on these topics—that describe the social problems experienced by vulnerable population groups and identify some ways that social workers can assist them.

It is our goal to help the reader to appreciate the relevance of social work to today's social issues. Far from being on the periphery of critical events that shape the quality of life for people in this society, social workers are on the front lines, developing social programs that are responsive to such human needs as homelessness, poverty, family breakup, mental illness, physical and mental disabilities, alcohol and substance abuse, domestic violence, and many other problems. At the same time, social workers directly help people who are victims of these problems so that they can change their own lives or change the aspects of their environments that are part of the problem. Social workers operate from values that recognize each person as relevant to society and believe that, when needed, society should help each person to achieve his or her fullest potential. Social workers also work from the perspective that the society is often a cause of, or at least a contributor to, most social problems. Our social institutions must be helped to become more just in their operation and more adaptable to changing human needs. In this way, social workers perform a critical role in the improvement of the well-being of all people and therefore in the maintenance of society itself.

During the years we have worked on this book, we have seen dramatic changes in the human services programs that social workers and other helping professionals are employed to deliver. Never during this period, in our estimation, has there been sufficient investment in improving the social conditions of *all* Americans. Two facts illustrate our concern. During this period, we have seen the number of persons living in poverty vary from a low of 11.2 percent in 1974 to a high of 15.2 percent in 1983 and, even with the strong economy of the late 1990s, we continue to have 35.5 million people or 13.3 percent of the population living in poverty.[1] A more close examination of these data reveals that these rates are more than twice as high for minority group members and female-headed families. The second fact is that national social policy is tipped in favor of the rich, and the rich are getting richer. To illustrate, when the value of the dollar is adjusted for inflation, the average income for the poorest 20 percent (quintile) of the population increased only 2 percent between 1975 and 1997. During that same period, income increased 7 percent for the next quintile, grew 10 percent for the middle quintile, improved 18 percent for the fourth quintile, and expanded by 44 percent for the richest quintile.[2] In 1997, the richest 20 percent of the households possessed 49.4 percent of the income. We would argue that this nation is moving in the wrong direction to bring about a just and equitable distribution of its wealth and, therefore, the opportunity for many to be full participants in U.S. society.

We have also seen rather dramatic shifts in social work practice during this time. Many social workers have moved away from social work's historic mission of serving the most vulnerable members of society and have increasingly engaged in private practice, practice in industry, or employment with for-profit organizations primarily serving the middle class. Where social workers once were on the front lines of social change movements, whether advocating women's right to vote, creating child labor laws, or demonstrating for civil rights, social workers today are more involved in helping people *adapt* to existing social conditions than participating in efforts to *change* these conditions.

It is our hope that this book will help new social workers to understand the necessity of both attending to clients' personal problems and resolving social issues that will prevent these problems from occurring in the first place. Throughout its history, social work has adapted its emphasis to focus either on social treatment or social change in response to the prevailing philosophy regarding human services. It is our deep conviction that the identity of social work should center on maintaining a balance between these two functions, that is, helping people to interact more effectively with the world around them *and* working to change that world to prevent problems and improve the quality of life for all.

The title, *Social Work: A Profession of Many Faces,* reflects another central feature of social work. This profession is made up of people from widely diverse backgrounds who serve people with a range of social problems, work under the auspices of a wide variety of human services agencies, and use varied knowledge and techniques to help people to change their situations. Social work can look very different depending on what expression of its practice one is observing. Nevertheless, the focus of this book is on the many common features that help to bind social workers together into one profession.

The authors themselves reflect some of the different faces of social work. One has devoted most of his practice experience to working with individuals, families, and groups, whereas the other has worked mostly with organizations and communities. Both are employed by universities. However, one is primarily engaged in direct clinical practice with the poor and in teaching and training psychiatric residents and psychology and social work interns in a department of psychiatry in a school of medicine. The other is engaged in teaching baccalaureate- and master's-level students in professional social work education. One is a member of a minority group, and the other is part of the majority. One has always lived in a large urban area on the West Coast; the other is a product of smaller communities in the midwest and Rocky

Mountain regions. One has filled prominent leadership positions with the National Association of Social Workers and the other with the Council on Social Work Education. Both, however, are enthusiastic about the role that social workers play in U.S. society and are committed to promoting the profession of social work.

We view this book as a way to point out to new social workers what we perceive to be the fundamental nature of this profession, and we believe it important to confess some biases that we will exhibit about what social work is and should become. For example, we frankly seek to appeal to the social conscience of those who read these pages. We hope that our readers will be deeply concerned by the evidence of inequality and the social injustices reported on these pages. Also, as we have already indicated, we strive to project the social worker as one who works simultaneously with both the person *and* the environment. In addition, our view of the social worker is that of the generalist—a practitioner who can serve multilevel clients (that is, individuals, families and other households, groups, organizations, and communities) with a range of interventive approaches. Furthermore, we attempt to communicate a disciplined approach to social work practice, characterized by an informed passion for improving the quality of life for all people, especially for the most vulnerable members of our country. Our clients deserve the best service that we can provide, and this requires social workers who are knowledgeable, ethical, and skillful. Finally, we are convinced that social work has an essential role to perform in helping people to deal more effectively with the world around them, and we conclude that few occupations can offer the personal satisfaction that a social worker experiences when successfully helping people. We are proud of our identification with social work.

A note to our readers. Through our many revisions to this textbook, we have sought to clarify, extend, and reorganize the material to make the content more interesting and accessible to our readers and more teachable for instructors who adopt this as a classroom text. We have appreciated the constructive feedback from our own students, our colleagues who teach this material, and our editors at Allyn and Bacon, Inc. All have helped this book to grow into nine editions and, we hope, to influence to some degree the practice orientation of many social workers. The most difficult task for us has been to make the material interesting to students who typically are more interested in "doing social work" than learning about social work. Without compromising the important content that one must understand to become a competent professional, we have adopted two strategies that should help our readers to maintain interest in learning about social work.

First, we know from experience that the motivation for most beginning social work students is simply to get into a career where they can help people to lead more fulfilling lives. It is a second step to select the career that they will follow—medicine or nursing if their primary concern is with health, teaching if concerned with intellectual development, or social work if interested in helping people and communities to improve their social functioning. Furthermore, we also are aware that the opportunity to be helpful as a social worker depends on the nature of the issues that people experience and the programs available to provide assistance. Therefore, the organization of the book begins with a broad view of U.S. society, the human issues that people confront on a daily basis, and the social programs, agencies, and helping professions that have emerged to help people to improve their lives. Of course, our most elaborate description of a profession relates to social work and how it has evolved to become one of the most dynamic and vital professions today. In Part Two, we begin to narrow our focus to examine social work career patterns, the different human needs that are addressed, and the kind of structures (for example, organizations and private practice) from which social workers deliver their services to clients. Next, in Part Three, we become even more specific by introducing the reader to the values and ethical prescriptions that guide social work practice, the competencies expected of a social worker, and the special contributions that can be added through prevention efforts and we look at the transferability of U.S. social work knowledge and skills to other countries. In Part Four, we provide considerable information about a number of subgroups within the society that are especially vulnerable to social issues and take a look at what social workers do to provide assistance to them. Finally in Part Five, a very timely and relevant high school intervention model is presented, which mental health practitioners at the Columbine High massacre found helpful.

Our second strategy has been to intersperse historical material, relevant data, and case examples throughout the book. The process of learning requires that a person obtain a certain amount of basic information that admittedly is not always interesting to acquire. To assist in this learning, we have presented information both in a narrative form and, where possible, have used the graphics found in the tables, figures, and boxes in the text. Also, in a field of study where the science will ultimately be applied to helping people, it is important to consider how the information is used when working with people. Therefore, we have included case vignettes in many of the chapters and devoted the final chapter to an extensive description of a social worker dealing with a complex case situation. Some readers, particularly those who have not had much exposure to providing human services, may want to start by reading that case example as background for fitting the academic content into a practice perspective.

A note to our instructors. We want to be sure that those who teach from this book are aware of the *Instructor's Manual/Test Bank* that accompanies it. In the *Manual* we share teaching techniques developed over many years of teaching this material. For each chapter in *Social Work: A Profession of Many Faces,* the *Manual* gives a synopsis of the most important content; lists key concepts and terms that the student should master; offers sample exercises for teaching the materials; and provides sample discussion, essay, and multiple-choice questions. A computerized version of the test bank is available from Allyn and Bacon that is formatted for both Macintosh and IBM personal computers. Also, please visit our web site (http://www.abacon.com/books/ab_020527224x.html) for other useful information.

The Baez Family Fire case continues to be available for teaching purposes in the *Instructor's Manual,* as well as on our web site. We have organized the material so that the case unfolds a few pages at a time, allowing an instructor to process the content with students before continuing to the next events in the case. We believe this format provides the necessary flexibility for using this case material in discussion groups, assigning term papers, and even providing a context for examination questions. Instructors are free to use this case material without seeking permission from Allyn and Bacon. Also, Allyn and Bacon sends copies of this book to Recording for the Blind (20 Rosel Road, Princeton, New Jersey 08540) when the first copies are printed in anticipation that an audio version will be available for persons who are visually impaired as soon as it is needed for classroom instruction.

Many people directly or indirectly influenced our ideas and gave support to make the preparation of this work possible. We wish to acknowledge our universities, the University of California at Los Angeles and Colorado State University, as well as our colleagues and students who have in countless ways helped by sharing ideas and offering critical reviews of these materials. Their critiques have often led to revisions that improved the quality and readability of this material. A special thanks are particularly in order to Karen Hanson, Judy Fifer, and other staff members at Allyn and Bacon who have nurtured this book through two decades of publications. We appreciate their combination of professional competence and personal warmth and regret that we have not yet recruited them to social work. In addition, the members of the social work office staffs at UCLA and Colorado State University deserve special recognition for their assistance in helping us manage our other commitments in order to complete this manuscript.

Finally, thanks to our families and loved ones—and especially our wives Cynthia and Nadine—for sacrificing some of our precious time together so that the activity of planning and preparing this edition could be included in our already busy lives. Their love, support, and encouragement provide meaning to our work and enhance the quality of our lives. Thanks also to the reviewers who provided helpful feedback and comments for this edition: Carmen A. Aponte, SUNY College at Brockport; Carol J. Bridges, East Central University; and Leon F. Burrell, University of Vermont.

ENDNOTES

1. Joseph Dalker and Mary Naifeh. *Poverty in the United States: 1997.* Current Population Reports, Consumer Income, P60–201. Washington, D.C.: U.S. Department of Commerce, September 1998, Table C-1.
   [http://www.census.gov/ hhes/www/povty97.html]
2. U.S. Bureau of Census. *Money Income in the United States: 1997.* Current Population Reports, P60–200. Washington, D.C.: U.S. Department of Commerce, September 1998, Table B.
   [http://www.census.gov/hhes/income/income97/in97dis.html]

Social Work in U.S. Society

If the world were a perfect place, it would provide for everyone warm and safe housing, an adequate supply of nutritious food, challenging jobs, good health care, and love and caring from friends and family. It would be a world with minimal stress, crime, and suffering. All people would find their lives satisfying and fulfilling. Social work exists because the world is less than perfect. Social workers serve people and the institutions of society as they confront this imperfection.

The social worker is not satisfied with this imperfect world that sends too many children to bed hungry at night, has effectively declared too many older people useless, restricts too many physically disabled people from productive living, allows too many women and children to be physically and sexually abused, deprives too many members of minority groups of the full opportunity to share in the benefits of this affluent society, has too many single parents trying to raise children in substandard housing without enough money for proper nutrition and food, and deprives too many emotionally and intellectually impaired people of satisfying lives because they behave or learn differently from the majority in the society. In fact, when even one person suffers from loneliness, hunger, discrimination, poor housing, domestic violence, or emotional upset, there is a need for social work.

Social work emerged during the twentieth century as an important profession in U.S. society. Its development has paralleled a seeming roller coaster of public interest in human welfare and social services. At times, when the national political climate placed a high priority on human welfare, social work jobs became plentiful and the number of bright and socially concerned people entering social work increased dramatically. However, the tides of the political climate periodically yield a conservative orientation more concerned with economic prosperity than human welfare, with big business than human rights, and with reducing taxes for the wealthy than maintaining or improving social programs. In such times, the appeal of social work to many young people tends to decline, and the supply of competent social workers is reduced. Clearly, social work is closely tied to the political and social philosophy that dominates at any period of time.

Although the supply of social workers may increase or decline from time to time, it is likely that there will always be a strong demand for this profession. The places of employment or the type of services needed from social workers may change, but the need for social work services will undoubtedly continue. It has become a central part of the fabric of U.S. society.

Why is social work important to U.S. society? Social workers provide important services to help people solve problems that limit their social functioning and services to enhance the quality of their lives. Social workers provide these services in a variety of ways.

Sometimes social workers offer a *direct service* or help individuals, families, or other groups on a face-to-face basis. In some situations they help people solve specific problems, while at other times they counsel people to solve problems or engage in activities that will enhance the quality of their lives—whether or not they experience an identifiable problem.

Services might also be provided indirectly on behalf of individuals or groups of people. These *indirect services* help to make social institutions such as organizations, neighborhoods, communities, or even the policies of a government or laws of a country more responsive to the needs of people.

Providing needed human services and contributing to improvement of the quality of life for all people are personally rewarding experiences. Each social worker can enjoy the satisfaction of knowing that he or she makes a small but important contribution to the well-being of society.

This book presents an overview of social work for the person considering this profession as a possible career choice. It does not attempt to "sell" social work but to portray it honestly, with its strengths and limitations in clear view. Because we are interested in recruiting qualified people to our profession—a profession in which we take great pride—we hope this book will enable people to discover whether social work is for them. Social work is not easy work. It can be as emotionally draining as it is rewarding. It can be as frustrating as it is satisfying. The prerequisite to developing the knowledge, values, and skills necessary for competent social work practice must be a basic commitment to social betterment and a willingness to invest oneself in facilitating the process of change.

To understand the current status of social work in the United States, one must first understand the historical context in which it developed. Chapter 1 begins with a quotation from the Preamble to the U.S. Constitution that commits this nation to "promoting the general welfare" of its people. Although there has been considerable fluctuation in the degree to which members of the society choose to share their resources to fulfill that commitment and continuing disagreement about how meeting social needs

should be accomplished, a fundamental strength of this nation has been its basic assurance that at least the minimum needs of all people would be met. In Chapter 1 we examine the efforts of U.S. society to respond to the needs of its members. A summary of some of the important events and philosophies that have shaped society's social programs and its methods of delivering human services is presented. In addition, some of the continuing issues regarding the provision of human services are highlighted because, as it will later become evident, they affect the tools that social workers have available to serve their clients.

Within the framework of an evolving social welfare institution that today combines public, voluntary, and for-profit forms of service delivery, a profession concerned with helping people interact more effectively with the world around them, and simultaneously change that world to make it more supportive of human welfare, has emerged. An overview of that profession, social work, is the substance of Chapter 2. Social work is presented as a profession characterized by breadth and versatility. While the central focus of social work is seemingly obscured when one looks at the many different expressions of social work in the wide range of human service organizations and the varied practice activities in which social workers engage, its central feature—attending to the quality of people's social functioning—makes it an important profession in fulfilling society's commitment to the welfare of its people.

Building on the concept of social work as a comprehensive helping profession concerned with enhancing social functioning, Chapter 3 charts its evolution as a profession from well-meaning volunteers to a recognized and respected helping profession. Of particular note is Table 3-1; it presents major events in the history of the United States and displays parallel events in the evolution of the social welfare institution and the social work profession in an effort to integrate the historical information found throughout the book.

Part One, then, establishes the position of social work in U.S. society. Like all professions, social work exists because it fulfills important social needs and because this society sanctions its role in meeting those needs. That is not true everywhere. In certain parts of the world societies do not take on that responsibility. Those societies leave such efforts entirely to friends, family, and neighbors, and these informal efforts may or may not prove helpful.

CHAPTER 1

Social Welfare: A Response to Human Need

Prefatory Comment

To understand social work and the activities of social workers, we must begin with an examination of U.S. society's commitment to the well-being of its members. How a society responds to the Biblical question, "Am I my brother's (and sister's) keeper?" is perhaps the acid test of that society's real interest in its people. Individuals and political parties regularly disagree about when our society should accept responsibility for assisting our brothers and sisters, as well as who should pay for it and how much money or other resources should be invested in meeting their needs. Nevertheless, it is evident that in a complex industrialized society such as the United States, a formalized battery of social programs and human services is required if minimum standards of living are to be achieved by most (if not all) citizens. Those programs and services make up an essential element of U.S. society—its social welfare institution.

What social workers do and the resources they have available to help people meet their social needs are highly dependent on the degree to which the society supports its human service programs. Therefore, we have initiated this book's exploration of social work with a chapter that examines the evolution of U.S. society's social welfare institution.

From its very beginning the United States has been committed to "promoting the general welfare" of its people:

> We, the people of the United States, in order to form a more perfect Union, establish justice, insure domestic tranquility, provide for the common defense, promote the general welfare, and secure the blessings of liberty to ourselves and our posterity, do ordain and establish this Constitution for the United States of America.
>
> —Preamble to the Constitution

During the ensuing years since the Constitution was adopted, there have been continuing debate and changing public policy about how to fulfill this promise.

How is a nation to promote the welfare of its citizens? Clearly, a first step is to meet their basic needs. To achieve that objective, programs must be provided that ensure at least minimum levels of safety, health, and personal well-being. The design of such programs, however, requires sufficient flexibility to respond to changing needs. For example, moving from an agriculture-based economy to one based on machines and then to one based on electronic technology radically altered the structure of the workforce and the opportunity for many to hold meaningful jobs. Similarly, the movement from an agricultural to an industrial society influenced the ability of the primary social institution, the family, to perform many of its traditional functions in meeting the needs of its members. Extended family members are often scattered geographically where jobs are located, and many cannot readily interact with other family members when they need help. Also, the effect of such factors as racism, sexism, and ageism has created large groups of citizens who do not have equal access to many of the established ways of having needs met (e.g., rewarding jobs, police protection, quality housing), making them especially vulnerable. These and other trends have moved social welfare programs from a relatively minor role in U.S. society to an increasingly central place.

To reach people in need, social programs must be designed to serve the people for whom they are intended and delivered in such a manner that those people can benefit from them. In most cases, these programs require skilled professionals to serve the people needing assistance. Depending on the need being addressed, the helpers must have various kinds of knowledge and unique competencies to effectively serve their clients. As the knowledge and skill requirements have become more than any one person can master, a division of labor has occurred and several helping professions have evolved to provide these programs. One of these professions is social work. Social work's unique contribution among the helping professions is to assist individuals to interact more effectively with the people and social institutions (e.g., family members, neighbors, schools, hospitals, courts, nursing homes, and even whole communities) that are important parts of their lives.

Some Social Workers in Action

Examining the day-to-day work of several social workers helps one to appreciate how social workers serve their clients and the kind of human needs they address. Consider the following case examples of social workers as they go about their tasks:

In twenty minutes, Nadine Harrison, a social worker with the local public social services department, has an appointment with Ms. Kim Lee. Ms. Lee is terribly worried about her future and that of her two small children. Her husband was killed two months ago in a robbery at the neighborhood market where he worked. In addition to her grief and loneliness, Ms. Lee found that, after paying funeral expenses, little money was left for raising the children. She asks Ms. Harrison for help.

Laura Jackson is executive director of the Council on Aging in her community. This council identifies and seeks solutions to problems experienced by older people in that community. As executive director, Ms. Jackson provides leadership to the citizen board as it considers new programs. Tonight the board will consider initiating a new program for older people: a telephone hook-up between shut-ins.

Brandon Ford is a social worker employed in a psychiatric hospital. Although he works with some patients individually, this afternoon he will meet with a group of adolescent boys who expect to be released from the hospital in a few weeks. Mr. Ford will help the boys explore their feelings about leaving the hospital and their friends, and will discuss the problems they may face when they return to their homes. He will also help to connect them and their parents with a local mental health clinic where they can receive support after their hospitalization is ended.

Perry Garcia is a social worker at a storefront neighborhood center in a large city. His job is to help residents rectify substandard housing conditions in the area. Tonight Mr. Garcia is helping a group from the neighborhood plan a strategy for pressuring some of the landlords to improve the quality of housing.

This afternoon Christopher Warren will testify before a committee of the state legislature that is considering the need for new laws and programs related to the state parole system. After seven years as a probation officer, Mr. Warren is well prepared to provide the Senate committee with expert testimony about problems with the existing approach to parole and probation.

Each of these social workers is either carrying out a social program intended to meet some human need or, in the case of Christopher Warren, is attempting to improve a program. All are employed by human service agencies—some are *public* or tax-supported organizations created by government, while others are *private* agencies supported through donations and governed by a volunteer board. Some of these social workers serve an area as small as a neighborhood, while others have a whole state as their service area. Most work directly with individuals and families, although some work primarily through committees or other groups in an effort to achieve a high quality of life for all.

In short, the many faces of social work reveal a profession serving a wide range of people by assisting them to improve their general well-being. Social workers play a central role in helping the society realize its commitment to promoting the general welfare of its citizens.

Identifying Human Needs

Each individual has his or her own special needs. The configuration of these needs, the intensity with which they are felt, and the ability to discover ways to meet them are part of what makes humans unique. Individuals vary, for example, in the degree of need for expressions of affection, for approval from friends and family, and for intellectual stimulation. Some people can manage pain and illness or limited financial resources quite satisfactorily, while others suffer greatly. Some can ignore the many injustices that prevail, while others are motivated to action when they observe injustices.

It is not necessary for a society to develop programs that respond to each and every human need. People are expected to develop their own means of satisfying most of their needs without help from others. If that fails, they typically look to family and friends and natural helpers in the community. If they still are unable to find help, only then will they turn to the various human services to meet these needs. Social programs, then, are often a "resource of last resort."

There are fundamental differences of opinion about the appropriate role of human services in U.S. society. A *conservative* philosophy argues for placing primary responsibility on the individual and family; a *liberal* position favors a more substantial role for social programs in meeting those needs. The society must ultimately determine the degree to which its function is to provide for people's needs and/or wants. At any time, that decision is determined by the society's prevailing philosophy regarding social responsibility. As the political climate moves between conservative and liberal philosophies, the human services are impacted—sometimes dramatically.

Although each of us has his or her own unique constellation of needs, there are some common needs that affect all people. Romanyshyn described these as needs of the flesh (survival and creature comforts), needs of the heart (love, intimacy, and exchange of tenderness), needs of the ego (sense of adequacy and self-assertiveness), and needs of the soul (transcending self to define the meaning of life beyond one's own biological existence).[1] Which of these needs should the society attempt to serve? Logically an effort should be made first to address the most basic needs and then, if there is sufficient interest, to deal with those of lesser priority. Maslow suggests the following priorities, or *hierarchy of human needs*, beginning with the most basic:[2]

- *Physiological survival needs:* nourishment, rest, and warmth

- *Safety needs:* preservation of life and sense of security

- *Belongingness needs:* to be a part of a group and to love and be loved

- *Esteem needs:* approval, respect, acceptance, and appreciation

- *Self-actualization needs:* opportunity to fulfill one's potential

The more basic the need, the more likely it is that society will make some provision for assisting people to meet that need. Thus, human service programs that respond to the hungry child or homeless family (i.e., physiological survival need) are more likely to be supported than marital counseling (i.e., belongingness need) or programs that offer growth-enhancing experiences for the "normal" or "healthy" person (i.e., self-actualization need).

Social Welfare Programs

Some of society's efforts to meet human needs are labeled "social welfare programs." The term *social,* when applied to humans, addresses the interactions of individuals or groups with other people, groups, organizations, or communities. The term *welfare* implies concern for the "well-being" of people. Social welfare programs, then, are developed to help people function more satisfactorily in their interactions with others and thus lead more fulfilling lives.

Social welfare programs take many forms. Some, for example, are income-transfer programs intended to achieve greater economic equity in the society by taxing the more wealthy and providing financial assistance to the poor. Other social programs are intended as society's efforts to prevent physical, psychological, or sexual abuse, for example, those programs that protect children from harmful parental behavior. Still other social welfare programs might be found in hospitals where patients are helped to adjust to changed capacities or to obtain needed resources to deal with a medical problem. These programs are not intended to replace individual caring, but rather to express formal (or institutionalized) social concern.

How individual and institutionalized caring should interact has been an issue in U.S. society from its founding. In the early years of this "land of opportunity" with its abundant resources and vast, unsettled lands, the "rugged individualist mentality" prevailed. It was thought that individuals and families should take care of themselves and, if that failed, neighbors or churches and synagogues should take care of their members. Only when those sources failed to meet the need would the community and more formal social programs be used to serve those in need.

While the spirit of caring about those in need is inherent in the U.S. historical commitment to the ethics embodied in Judaism and Christianity, it has not played out as unrestrained willingness to provide services. In practice, most human service programs have been limited to problem solving. The emphasis has been on "fixing" problems or "curing" harmful conditions. Thus, programs aimed at enhancing social functioning or preventing emerging problems generally have been neglected.

It is evident that society holds different views about the people who are the recipients of various social programs. For example, in relation to financial aid programs it is considered quite acceptable to assist the farmer facing fluctuations in the price of crops by providing price supports. It is similarly acceptable for small business owners or college students to receive government-subsidized grants or loans. However, it is much less acceptable, even for single mothers and their children, to receive food stamps or direct cash assistance as indicated by the passage of the Personal Responsibilities and Work Opportunity Reconciliation Act in 1996, popularly known as the "welfare reform law." Financial aid is even more unacceptable when it is provided to the alcoholic or substance abuser who cannot hold a job, though the person's need may be just as great as in many other situations. These examples demonstrate an important point: The conditions that create the need for human services affect the willingness of society to provide social programs to address those needs.

The Evolution of Social Programs

An index of the nation's continued commitment to its people is its investment in social programs. These programs are the mechanisms by which public concerns are translated into methods of serving individual people. They are expressed in laws and other policies that represent the society's plans to provide for selected needs. Social programs not only include giving tangible resources (i.e., food, housing, and clothing), but also incorporate a variety of activities like counseling or group facilitation provided by skilled professionals. To make these services available to clients, programs must be delivered by an organization where clients and service providers can come together to address the need.

In the United States, social welfare programs have been subject to ever-changing philosophies and, therefore, support for these programs has increased and decreased at various periods. A brief review of the emergence of social welfare in the United States provides an important context for understanding the social programs offered today and the place of social work among the helping professions.

COLONIAL TIMES TO THE GREAT DEPRESSION

Picture life in the rural United States in the 1700s when land was plowed and families worked to tame the wilderness. Although there were many trials and tribulations in an agricultural society, the person with average intelligence and a willingness to work hard could usually succeed. Given an open frontier and liberal government policies for staking a claim to fertile land, an individual could readily acquire property and produce at least the necessities of life. Because the family was strong and each member had sharply defined roles that contributed to the family's welfare, people survived and, in time, usually prospered. The "American Dream" could become a reality for most (unless one was of African, Asian, Mexican, or Native American background) in this simple agrarian society.

The family was not usually alone or completely self-supporting. All members of the family (i.e., grandparents, children, and other relatives) were supportive and, perhaps as important, were needed. Even the mentally or physically disabled person could find meaningful ways to contribute. For mutual protection, social interaction, and opportunity to trade the goods they produced, families would band together into loosely knit communities. Trade centers eventually emerged as small towns; a market economy evolved; and merchants opened stores, bought and sold products, and extended credit to people until their products were ready for market.

Efforts to meet human needs in this environment can best be characterized as *mutual aid*. When special problems arose, neighbors and the community responded. The barn that burned was quickly rebuilt, widows and orphans were cared for, and the sick were tended to. People shared what they had with needy friends and neighbors, knowing that the favor would be returned some day. In this preindustrial society, the quality of life depended on the "grace of God" and hard work. Society rarely needed to respond to unmet human needs; but when it did, churches and synagogues usually provided that service.

Conditions began to change in the 1800s and early 1900s when industrialization and urbanization created rapid and dramatic changes in both the family and the market system. People congregated in cities where there were jobs, the individual breadwinner rather than the family unit became the key to survival, and interactions with others were increasingly characterized by impersonality. Those from the vulnerable population groups (e.g., immigrants, the aged, minorities, women, persons with disabilities) in particular experienced reduced opportunity for employment or, if employed, access to meaningful and personally rewarding jobs. Not only were social problems increased, but with the changed roles of the family and market system, society had to create new means of responding to human needs.

Early social welfare programs were heavily influenced by the *Puritan ethic* that argued that only those people with a moral defect failed. According to Puritan reasoning, those who failed must suffer from a moral weakness and were viewed as sinful and ethically weak. It is not uncommon even today for clients to feel that their troubles represent God's means of punishing them for some sin or act of immoral behavior. Following the same philosophy, grudging taxpayers often resent contributing to human services when they believe the client is at fault for needing assistance. This view, however, does not take into consideration the structural factors in the society that contribute to or even may cause an individual's problems.

The United States was not settled by wealthy people—the wealthy had no reason to leave Europe. When social needs were addressed by this developing society, small voluntary organizations were formed to provide services. Puritan judgmentalism was evident in the names of organizations such as the "Home for Intemperate Women" or the "Penitent Females Refuge." If voluntary organizations did not meet needs, town meetings were held and actions taken to provide assistance, thus creating the first public social services. Any assistance was considered charity, not a right. Requests for help were either supported or rejected, depending on the judgments made by the townsfolk.

The philosophy derived from the *French Enlightenment* of the eighteenth century contradicted the Puritan view. It argued that people are inherently good and that need for assistance is not necessarily tied to morality. People needing help were considered worthy of that assistance depending on the causes of their problems. Persons with limited income, for example, were classified as worthy poor and unworthy poor. The *worthy poor* were viewed as good people who required help because they were afflicted with an ailment or were women and children left destitute by the death or desertion of the breadwinning husband and father. The *unworthy poor* were thought to have flaws of character. In one attempt to better understand the factors that contributed to the presence of the unworthy poor, a report of the Society for the Prevention of Pauperism in the City of New York in 1818 identified the following causes of poverty: ignorance, idleness, intemperance in drinking, want of economy, imprudent and hasty marriages, lotteries, pawnbrokers, and houses of ill fame.[3] That one's plight may have been caused by others, by chance, or even by structural conditions in the society was only beginning to be recognized.

There were, of course, those who held a more sympathetic view of persons in need and attempted to reform the punitive and uncaring approaches to providing services. For example, as early as 1776, in Philadelphia, the Society for Alleviating the Miseries of Public Prisons was formed. Later, one of the first great social reformers, Dorothea Dix, chronicled the deplorable conditions in prisons and almshouses (also referred to as "poor farms") and sought to establish government responsibility for meeting human needs. Her effective lobbying contributed to the passage of a bill in the U.S. Congress to grant federal land to states to help them finance care for the mentally ill. The veto of that bill in 1854 by President Franklin Pierce established a precedent that was to dominate thinking about society's responsibility for social welfare for the next three-quarters of a century—that the federal government should play no part in providing human services. As late as 1930, President Herbert Hoover relied on the precedent established by the Pierce veto when he approved an appropriation of $45 million to feed livestock in Arkansas during a drought while opposing an additional $25 million to feed the farmers who raised that livestock.[4]

Other social reformers, too, began to advocate for programs to meet needs— mostly through voluntary associations such as the Charity Organization Societies,

Settlement Houses, the Mental Hygiene Movement, and programs to assist former slaves to integrate into the dominant society. When the federal government refused to engage in providing human services, the states sporadically offered services, with several states creating state charity boards or public welfare departments. However, not until the Great Depression of the 1930s led to severe economic crisis and the ensuing New Deal programs of President Franklin D. Roosevelt was it recognized that private philanthropy, even in combination with limited state and local government support, could not adequately address the major human needs.

The human services would never again be the same. New partnerships and a division of responsibility among local, state, and federal governments had to be forged, and it was necessary for the ensuing social programs to be articulated with programs offered by the private sector.

THE GREAT DEPRESSION TO THE PRESENT

The Great Depression was also the great equalizer. People who had previously been successful suddenly required help. These were moral, able-bodied people who needed assistance. Could they be blamed for their condition or did other factors contribute to their troubles? Did they have a right to some form of assistance when they were in trouble? In this case it was the deterioration of the worldwide economy that forced many people into poverty. U.S. society began to recognize that indeed there were structural factors in modern society responsible for many social problems. Thus began an unprecedented period of expansion in social welfare in the United States.

World War II rallied the United States to a common cause and helped people recognize their interdependence. Each person was counted on to contribute to the common good during wartime conditions, and the nation could ill afford to create "throwaway" people by failing to provide for their basic needs. By the 1960s economic recovery was complete, and a brief period of prosperity and responsiveness to human needs followed. The Kennedy and Johnson administrations fostered the War on Poverty and Great Society programs, and the Human Rights Revolution was in its heyday. These activities focused public concern on the poor, minorities, women, the aged, the mentally and physically disabled, and other population groups that had previously been largely ignored. Legislation protecting civil rights and creating massive social programs was passed; court decisions validated the new legislation, and a vast array of new social programs emerged. For example, poverty rates, the prime indicator of social well-being, dropped by half, from 22.4 percent in 1959 to a low of 11.1 percent in 1973. [5]

With the exception of the cost of the Vietnam War and the military buildup during the Reagan and Bush administrations, examination of federal expenditures reveals a continuous decline in expenditures on national defense. At the same time, only the conservative Reagan era has countered the trend for the United States to increasingly invest in its human resources. Even the George Bush presidency saw a rather dramatic increase in human resource spending. At the beginning of the Kennedy Administration in 1962, almost twice as much was spent on defense as on human resources. By the end of the Clinton Administration, the amount of money invested in national defense was only slightly more than one-fourth of that spent on human resources. Figure 1-1 reflects the annual expenditures in billions of dollars from the federal budget on human resources and national defense with the value of the dollar held constant (i.e., all years translated to the value of the dollar in 1992).

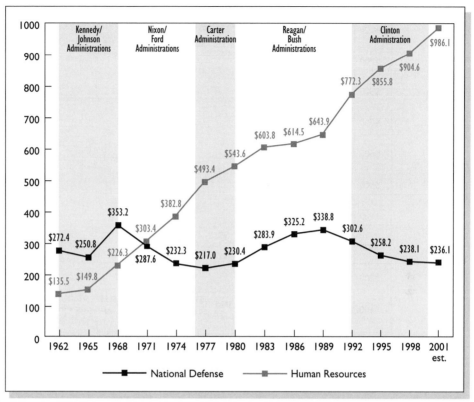

FIGURE 1-1 **U.S Expenditures on National Defense and Human Resources (in billions of constant FY 1992 dollars): 1962–2001 (est.)**

Source: U.S. Office of Management of the Budget, "The Budget for Fiscal Year 2000," Historical Tables, Table 3.1. http://www.access.gpo.gov/usbudget/fy2000/buddocs/html budget

The bloom on social programs began to fade in the middle of the 1970s, and public apathy replaced public concern. A deteriorating economy was accompanied by a growing political conservatism, and the continued commitment to human services was placed in direct competition with military buildup and the maintenance of U.S. superpower status. By the 1980s, the time was ripe for conservatives to attempt to dismantle the social programs that had developed over the last two decades. Echoing the political rhetoric based on the distrust of government that had characterized the philosophies of Presidents Franklin Pierce and Herbert Hoover, and mixed with punitive, moralistic views regarding the recipients of human services that revealed vestiges of the Puritan philosophy, President Ronald Reagan set out to limit the federal government's social programs. As reflected in Figure 1-2, the Reagan administration had only moderate influence over expenditures for mandated social programs such as Social Security, but was able to decrease by almost 15 percent the expenditures on discretionary social programs.

The Reagan administration set out not only to cut federal expenditures, but also to shift responsibility to state and local governments or, where possible, to the private sector of the human services. However, the combination of a more liberal Congress

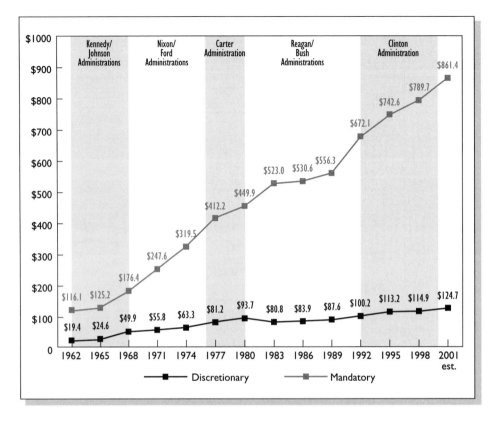

FIGURE 1-2   **Mandatory and Discretionary U.S. Government Expenditures on Human Resource* (in billions of constant FY 1992 dollars): 1962–2001 (est.)**

*U.S. Budget areas included in these data are mandatory and discretionary outlays for (1) education, training, employment, and social services; (2) health; (3) Medicare; income security and housing; and (5) veteran's benefits.

Source: U.S. Office of Management of the Budget, "The Budget for Fiscal Year 2000," Historical Tables, Table 3.1. http://www.access.gpo.gov/usbudget/fy2000/buddocs/html budget

and a series of Supreme Court decisions that protected the gains made in human services and civil rights during the prior two decades partially blunted the radical changes that President Reagan had promised. With per capita expenditures remaining somewhat constant during this period at about $2,500 per person, the 1983 poverty rate* reached the highest point (15.2 percent of the population) in

---

*The poverty level is adjusted annually to reflect the amount of money required by families of different sizes to be able to provide a minimum level of nutritious food, obtain adequate housing, sufficiently clothe family members for work and school, and provide needed health care. The poverty threshold in 1998 was approximately $8,200 for a single-person household; $11,200 for two persons; $13,000 for a family of three including one child; $16,600 for a family of four with two children; and so on. As a reference point, median income for all families in the United States in 1997 was $45,347. Poverty thresholds for households of varying sizes can be found at http://www.census.gov/hhes/poverty/threshold/threshold98.html.

twenty years, began to decline in the late 1980s, and then bounced back to another high point (14.8 percent) at the end of the Bush era (see Figure 1-3). Implementation of President Clinton's moderate social agenda, although blunted somewhat by a very conservative Congress, resulted in a small increase in per capita human resource expenditures and a slight decrease in the poverty rate to 13.3 percent.

A major piece of the Clinton social agenda was to strengthen the health care system and make some form of health care available to all citizens. Meaningful health care reform was not accomplished during the Clinton era, but a second central agenda item, welfare reform, was passed and signed by the president in 1996 in the form of the Personal Responsibilities and Work Opportunity Reconciliation Act. The upbeat title of the act belied its more mean-spirited intent, which was to roll back key provisions of the Social Security Act and drive people off welfare—even if their condition might worsen. Under this act the unconditional guarantee of cash aid

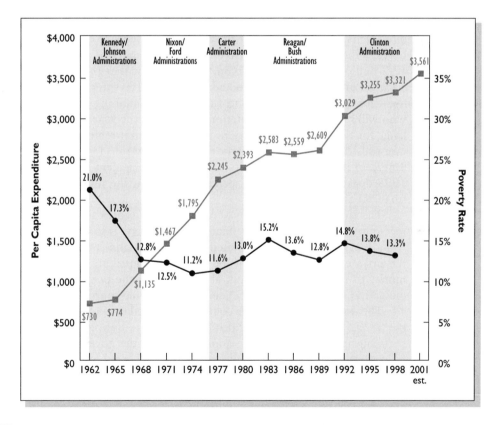

FIGURE 1-3   **Per Capital U.S. Government Expenditures on Human Resources* (in constant FY 1992 dollars) and Poverty Rate: 1962–2001 (est.)**

*U.S. Budget areas included in these data are mandatory and discretionary outlays for (1) education, training, employment, and social services; (2) health; (3) Medicare; (4) income security and housing; and (5) veteran's benefits.

Sources: Joseph Dalaker and Mary Naifeh. *Poverty in the United States: 1997.*
Current Population Reports, Consumer Income, p. 60–201. Washington, D.C.: U.S. Department of Commerce, September 1998: 55–58. http://www.census.gov/hhes/www/poverty97.html

for persons in need (i.e., an entitlement) was eliminated. Aid to Families with Dependent Children (AFDC) was replaced by Temporary Assistance to Needy Families (TANF), reflecting the expectation that the help was only temporary (i.e., a maximum of five years in a family's life). In addition, many legal immigrants became ineligible for services; the definition of disabilities was narrowed, making many previously eligible people ineligible for continuing aid; and there was a work requirement that limited families to two consecutive years of assistance if job training has not been secured and employment not obtained. The states and various American Indian tribes were given the authority and funds ($16.5B) per year in the form of block grants to design and implement the TANF program within their jurisdictions.[6] The result has been little consistency in these programs across the United States.

For clients, it is fortunate that TANF was implemented at the time of a booming economy and the labor market was able to absorb the large number of persons seeking employment, usually with limited job skills. In fact, before the implementation of TANF, the economy had improved and the number of people receiving public assistance had begun to decline. With government funds used to reward businesses that hired welfare recipients and the provision of assistance to clients with child-care costs, by 1998 the number of people receiving financial aid had declined substantially, from 12.3 million in 1996 to 8 million.[7] It is thought that the first two years of TANF creamed off the recipients who had the potential to enter and remain in the employment market. Finding a way to support the remaining less employable recipients who will have used up their lifetime benefits by the year 2001 will be a major challenge for the next administration. It is evident that removing people from the welfare rolls does not necessarily mean that they are no longer living in poverty. The 3 percent decline in the poverty rate from 13.7 percent in 1996 to 13.3 percent in 1998 does not match the 35 percent decline in the number of persons receiving financial aid.

The emphasis on federal government expenditures should not detract from the recognition that considerable financial investment is made to support the general welfare of the people of the United States. Local and state governments, as well as the private/nonprofit sector of the economy, contribute a considerable amount of money to the health, education, and welfare of the people. Table 1-1 provides an indication of the amounts expended by these three sources of funds.

The dollars reported in the column for the federal government in Table 1-1 omit the $329.5B Social Security expenditures that are derived from employee/employer social insurance taxes and are administered by the government. Shoring up Social Security is another serious challenge facing the United States. High on the political agenda for the next few years must be the development of a plan to assure the survival of Social Security, because at the current rate by the year 2014 the revenues generated by the Social Security Trust Fund will not equal the expenditures required by the retired population.[8] Nevertheless, it is important to note that people in the United States contribute almost $1,392 billion each year to improve the general well-being of the people. For those of us more accustomed to dealing in $100 increments, the billions of dollars invested in these services is sometimes difficult to comprehend. In 1997, for example, an average of approximately $5,179 from tax-generated and voluntary funds was spent to support each of the 269 million people in the United States.

TABLE 1-1	Government and Private Sector Allocations to Health, Education, and Social Welfare (in billions of dollars)			
	Federal Govt. (1998)	State/Local Govt. (1995)	Private/Nonprofit (1997)	Total
Health, hospitals, Medicare	$342.2B	$108.8B	$14.0B	$465.0B
Elementary, secondary, higher education and training programs	37.5	358.8	21.5	417.8
Human services (social services, recreation, housing, community planning)	55.8	41.8	21.7	110.3
Income security (cash assistance and other public welfare)	204.5	195.5	0	400.0
TOTAL	$640.0B	$704.9B	$48.2B	$1,393.1B

Note: The dates in Table 1-1 are derived from the latest reports for each source. It takes considerable time for the federal government to secure and summarize data from each of the state and local governments. Also, categories for reporting (e.g., health, education, human services) are not identical for each source and the above data should be viewed as approximate.

Sources:
(Federal Government) U.S. Office of Management and Budget, "The Budget for Fiscal Year 2000," Historical Tables, Table 3.1. http://www.access.gpo.gov/usbudget/fy2000/buddocshtml#budget
(State and Local Governments) U.S. Bureau of the Census [http://www.census.gov/govs/estimate/96stlus.txt].
(Private/Nonprofit) Ann E. Kaplan, ed., *Giving USA: The Annual Report on Philanthropy for the Year 1997.* New York: American Association of Fund-Raising Counsel Trust for Philanthropy, 1998, p. 23.

Further examination of Table 1-1 reveals that the major financial responsibility for health care rests with the federal government and that state and local governments are the primary contributors to education and training programs. These two sources almost equally fund the income security programs. It is also noteworthy that human services receive only limited funding from any source. Had the philosophy of the Pierce Doctrine that government should not be involved in human services prevailed, it is clear that, generous as it is, the private sector voluntarily contributes only 3 percent of the funds to support health, education, and social welfare would not meet the need. Without a substantial tax base, the United States could not begin to adequately assist in carrying out the mandate of the Constitution to promote the general welfare of the people.

Continuing Issues in Social Welfare

It is within the context of changing philosophies of social welfare that the social work profession emerged and established its role among the helping professions. The manner in which the following issues are resolved when establishing the various social programs affects the type of work performed by social workers and their ability to respond to client needs.

PURPOSES AND GOALS FOR SOCIAL PROGRAMS

Social programs are created to accomplish three general purposes. First, most are designed for the *remediation* of a social problem. When a sufficient number of people experience difficulty in a particular aspect of social functioning, social programs are created to provide services intended to correct that problem—or at least to help the clients deal with it more effectively. Remediation programs include services such as income support for the poor, counseling for the mentally ill, and job training for the displaced worker. Remediation has historically been the central form of human service.

A second general purpose of human services has evolved more recently—the *enhancement* of social functioning. In this form of social program the emphasis is on the growth and development of clients in a particular area of functioning without a "problem" having necessarily been identified. Well-baby clinics, parent-effectiveness training, and various youth recreation programs are all examples of social programs designed for personal enhancement.

Finally, the purpose of some social programs is the *prevention* of social problems. As opposed to treating symptoms, prevention programs attempt to identify the basic causes of difficulties in social functioning and seek to stimulate changes that will keep problems from ever developing. Prevention programs, for example, might include helping parents learn appropriate ways to discipline children or conducting community education to make the public aware of the negative impact racism or sexism has on the growth and development of children.

Social programs have been created to serve at least four specific goals: socialization, social integration, social control, and social change. Each goal responds to different human needs—some programs are focused on the needs of individuals or families and others address the needs of the society.

One goal of social programs is to facilitate the *socialization* of people to the accepted norms and behaviors of society. Such programs are designed to help people develop the knowledge and skills to become full participating and contributing members of society and include, for example, such programs as scouting, Boys Clubs and Girls Clubs, and YMCA or YWCA activities. A goal of other social programs is to assist in *social integration* where people are helped to become more successful in interacting with the world around them. Counseling, therapy, and rehabilitation programs, for example, attempt to achieve this goal. A third goal of social programs is, at times, to provide *social control* by removing people from situations when they might place themselves or others at risk or when they require some period of isolation from their usual surroundings in order to address problems. Examples of these programs are found in mental hospitals and correctional facilities. Finally, some programs are intended to achieve *social change,* that is, to express the conscience of society by stimulating changes that will enhance the overall quality of life. For example, public education to encourage the practice of safe sex to reduce the risk of AIDS and the solicitation of employers to hire the developmentally disabled are activities that help to bring about social changes that benefit the society.

RESPONSIBILITY FOR MEETING HUMAN NEEDS

A somewhat controversial issue affecting human services is the assignment of responsibility for meeting basic needs. Our historical review of social programs indicated that the expectation in the most simple form of U.S. society was that the individual would take care of himself or herself or, if not, that families would see that their members' needs were met. Laws in the United States have placed primary responsibility on the family unit for caring for its members and, to a larger extent than in many societies, have protected the sanctity of the family's decisions about how to achieve this goal. It is only in cases where family members are being damaged (e.g., child abuse or neglect, domestic violence, elder maltreatment) that society reluctantly intervenes.

Although some important human services are provided under the auspices of religious organizations, a second level of responsibility for addressing unmet needs increasingly has been assigned to secular nonprofit human service organizations. U.S. society first looked to these voluntary organizations, such as those associated with a local United Way, to meet needs that the family could not provide. Today the most conservative viewpoint would argue that even this auspice for service provision inappropriately relieves families of their responsibility to care for their members. Most people, however, recognize that private human services are an important means of promoting the general welfare in today's mobile and complex society.

As massive social problems persisted, such as the continuing high poverty rate, it became evident that voluntary donations would not be sufficient to achieve even minimal levels of well-being for a large number of people. Therefore, it became necessary for government to enter the business of providing social programs where taxes could be levied to ensure the availability of sufficient funds to meet the most basic needs. One perspective about government-sponsored programs is that they should be developed locally where they can respond to the uniqueness of the region—whether that be a city, county, state, or some other governmental unit. Those supporting the other side of this issue seek a strong federal role in social programs and argue that the causes of many human problems are such factors as chronic unemployment, institutionalized discrimination, inflation, an international trade deficit, and even the volatile price of goods and services on the worldwide market. They argue that individuals and local areas have little, if any, influence over these factors and that it is necessary to create national programs to equalize the burden of responding to the victims of these largely uncontrollable events.

Finally, what had been a sharply increasing role of government in human services was blunted during the 1980s and early 1990s when government agencies initiated a pattern of contracting with private for-profit sources to provide services. The conservative viewpoint contends that it is inefficient for government agencies to commit to employment of staff and construction of facilities where social programs are offered. Instead, they argue it is better to allow the competition of private enterprise to shape service provision by allowing government-funded programs to contract with private practitioners and for-profit corporations. Opponents of this argument for privatization, in contrast, contend that this activity has allowed private enterprise to "cream off" the clients most amenable to help, leaving the more hard-core problems for public and voluntary (nonprofit) human service agencies.

The presence of diverse and sometimes contradictory social programs has resulted in a complex and confusing patchwork of programs and services. For most people seeking help, finding one's way through the network of services with differing sponsorship and differing eligibility requirements is virtually impossible. Professional assistance is often required to negotiate the human services system.

HUMAN SERVICE AS A RIGHT

Regardless of the auspices (i.e., sponsorship) of a social program, the problem of whether clients have a right to receive or refuse the services must be addressed. Historically, social services were viewed as charity—that is, benevolent gifts that a righteous public bestowed on the worthy poor and begrudgingly provided for the not-so-worthy. When human services are based on charity, the recipient is expected to be grateful for any help given, and the donors expect to be appreciated for their contributions to these good works.

A contrasting view is that any member of the society may someday be a victim of factors beyond his or her control and, therefore, has a right to receive services. Given this perspective, some clients have taken the position that they are entitled to services and increasingly have organized or sought legal remedy to ensure that help is provided when needed. Groups advocating for the rights of the poor, the aged, the developmentally disabled, and the physically disabled are found throughout the United States. Once the view is adopted that one has a right to service, the matter of one's having the right to refuse service also arises. For example, should the homeless be required to accept shelter? Or, is it the right of a mental patient to refuse medication? The answers to these questions affect the manner in which professions provide human services.

SOCIAL PROGRAM CONCEPTIONS

The design of social programs also reflects differing philosophical views about who should be served and when services should be given. Programs based on the *safety net approach* are planned as a way for the society to assist people when other social institutions have failed to resolve specific problems. An alternative conception of social programs, the *social utilities approach,* views human services as society's frontline manner of addressing common human needs.

THE SAFETY NET APPROACH.   One conception views human services as a safety net that saves people who have not had their needs met by their primary resources such as the family or employment/economic systems. This approach begins with the presumption that a predefined problem exists—for example, that a family's income is too low, that a person's behavior is deviant, that a child is at risk. Services are then provided to address the problems, and, when a satisfactory level of problem reduction is achieved, the services are terminated. One negative aspect of such programs is that to be eligible for a safety net program, a client must also take on the stigma of having failed in some aspect of social functioning. Further, at times clients must be terminated from service because they have reached a predefined level of functioning, even though the service providers recognize that the clients would benefit from additional assistance.

Safety net programs are thought of as *residual* because they are designed to deal with the residue of human problems—that is, those problems that are left after all other processes of helping are exhausted. Programs based on this approach are also *selective* in the sense that they are designed to serve a specific population experiencing a specific need. Finally, safety net programs are *time-limited* in the sense that services are terminated when a problem is solved (or at least reduced) or a predetermined level of functioning is achieved.

THE SOCIAL UTILITIES APPROACH.   The social utilities conception of human services views social programs as one of society's first-line social institutions for meeting needs. Like public utilities for water and electricity, these social utilities are available to all people who wish to make use of them. They do not assume that the person who receives services is at fault or has necessarily failed if he or she requires services. Rather, this concept recognizes that society creates conditions where all people can benefit from social programs, whether the program is designed to help people solve problems or enhance already adequate functioning.

Social utility programs are *universal* in the sense that they do not have strict eligibility requirements. Such programs are also based on an *institutional* conception of human services that considers social programs a regular or institutionalized way of meeting human needs. They do not assume that the individual, family, or any other social institution has failed if, for example, parents place a child in day care, if a young person joins a scouting program, or if a senior citizen takes advantage of a senior center's lunch program.

Different social programs in the United States reflect the safety net and social utilities philosophies. Some human service agencies provide programs representing both philosophies. For example, a public human services department might administer safety net programs such as financial assistance and child protection services and, at the same time, carry responsibility for Medicare and adoption services that are based on the social utilities concept.

HUMAN SERVICE PROGRAM CATEGORIES

Finally, it is useful to recognize that social programs can be divided into three distinct categories: social provisions, personal services, and social action. Each category serves an important function in promoting the general welfare of persons in U.S. society.

SOCIAL PROVISIONS.   This category of social programs is designed to meet the most fundamental needs of the population, and such programs are typically viewed as part of the safety net. *Social provisions* are the tangible resources given to persons in need, either as cash or as direct benefits, such as food, clothing, or housing.

Social provisions are the most costly programs in outlay of actual dollars. As social programs have evolved, governmental agencies have assumed the primary responsibility for providing these services, and the private sector has taken the role of providing backup for those people who slip through the mesh of the public safety net. Such major social provision programs as Temporary Assistance to Needy Families (TANF), Supplemental Security Income (SSI), Food Stamps, Low-rent Public Housing, and many others are provided under governmental auspices. Meals and lodging for transients and the homeless, emergency food programs, financial aid in response to crisis situations, shelters for battered wives, and many other social provision programs, however, are offered by voluntary social agencies.

PERSONAL SERVICES. The personal services category of programs includes both problem-solving and enhancement programs. Unlike social provisions, *personal services* are intangible services that help people resolve issues in their social functioning. Examples of personal service programs are marriage and family counseling, child protection services, client advocacy, family therapy, care for the disabled, job training, family planning and abortion counseling, foster care programs, human service brokering and referral activities, and many other programs aimed at helping clients strengthen their social functioning.

SOCIAL ACTION. When one works with people, it quickly becomes evident that it is often inadequate just to help a person or group cope with an unjust world. Efforts must be made to create a more just and supportive environment. For example, it is not enough to help a woman understand and cope with discrimination in the workplace. Although these activities may be important for her ability to keep her job, they do not resolve the basic problem, and they place the burden of change and adjustment on the victim. *Social action* programs help change conditions that create difficulties in social functioning. They require specialized knowledge and skill to effect change in organizations and communities. These efforts involve fact finding, analysis of community needs, research and interpretation of data, and other efforts to inform and mobilize the public to action in order to achieve change.

Concluding Comment

Nearly two hundred and twenty-five years ago the United States of America was formed with a goal of joining people to promote, among other things, the general welfare of all. To achieve that purpose, a variety of programs have been created to meet basic human needs. As the society has changed, so have the programs.

Programs that address needs related to people's social functioning have increasingly been created. Beginning with the expectation that families would take care of their members and, if not, then voluntary associations or local government would make needed provisions, the period since the Great Depression has seen the evolution of a welfare state where public programs primarily support the basic social provisions of food, clothing, and housing. Yet, private philanthropy remains an important resource for personal services and social action programs. Although a considerable share of the nation's resources has been applied to the human services, the principal indicator of its social health, poverty, remains at a high level—particularly for households headed by single mothers and members of minority groups. The passage of the Personal Responsibilities and Work Opportunity Reconciliation Act in 1996 by the U.S. Congress—and the action by President Clinton to sign it into law—represents a major step backward in the society's taking responsibility for its poorest and most vulnerable members.

More effective provision of social programs will require skilled professionals to help clients achieve more desirable levels of social functioning. A group of professional helpers who are central to the efforts to improve the general well-being of people are social workers. Chapter 2 examines that profession and its evolution from a group of concerned volunteers to its role today as a critical part of U.S. society.

KEY WORDS AND CONCEPTS

Hierarchy of needs

Social welfare programs

Human services

Mutual aid philosophy

Puritan philosophy

French Enlightenment philosophy

Conservative/liberal philosophies

Social problem

Social program purposes (i.e., remediation, enhancement, prevention)

Social program goals (i.e., socialization, social integration, social control, social action)

Social program conceptions (i.e., safety net, social utilities)

Human service program categories (i.e., social provisions, personal services, social action)

SUGGESTED READINGS

Axinn, June, and Leven, Herman. *Social Welfare: A History of the American Response to Need*, 4th Edition. New York: Longman, 1997.

Chelf, Carl P. *Controversial Issues in Social Welfare Policy: Government and the Pursuit of Happiness*. Newbury Park, CA: Sage, 1992.

Day, Phyllis J. *A New History of Social Welfare*. Englewood Cliffs, NJ: Prentice Hall, 1989.

Miringoff, Marc, and Miringoff, Marque-Luisa. *The Social Health of the Nation: How America Is Really Doing*. New York: Oxford University Press, 1999.

O'Looney, John. *Redesigning the Work of Human Services*. Westport, CT: Quorum, 1996.

Trattner, Walter I. *From Poor Law to Welfare State*, 6th Edition. New York: Free Press, 1999.

ENDNOTES

1. John Romanyshyn, Victor Baez, and Bradford W. Sheafor, "Social Welfare, Organizational Structure, and Professionals" (Fort Collins: Colorado State University, 1976), videotape.
2. Abraham H. Maslow, *Motivation and Personality* (New York: Harper & Row, 1970), pp. 25–58.
3. Ralph E. Pumphrey and Muriel W. Pumphrey, eds., *The Heritage of American Social Work* (New York: Columbia University Press, 1961), p. 60.
4. Harold L. Wilensky and Charles N. Lebeaux, *Industrial Society and Social Welfare* (New York: Free Press, 1965), p. 42.
5. U.S. Census Bureau, "Poverty 1997" (Washington, D.C.: The Bureau, 1999). http://www.census.gov/hhes/poverty/poverty997/pv97/est1.html
6. U.S. Department of Health and Human Services, The Administration for Children and Families, June 30, 1999. http://www.acf.dhhs.gov/programs/opa/facts/majorpr.htm.
7. Ibid.
8. George W. Church, "How We Can Fix Social Security," *Time* 123 (18, May 10, 1999), unnumbered special insert.

CHAPTER 2

Social Work: A Comprehensive Helping Profession

The human services have become a central part of the fabric of U.S. society. Founded on the goal of promoting the general welfare of its members, society has gradually assumed considerable responsibility for ensuring that its people have access to assistance in meeting their basic needs. One way society provides such assistance is through social programs that make available both tangible resources and various social services to aid people in solving problems or enhancing their social functioning.

The provision of social programs requires people who possess a variety of helping skills. Such helping is often rewarding to both the recipient and the provider of the services. From ancient times to the present all civilized societies have placed great value on helping others. Even in the most simple societies, family, friends, members of the clan or tribe, and other personal acquaintances were expected to care for people in need. As societies became more complex and social programs were created to respond to the more severe needs of people, volunteers associated with churches and community service agencies began to play an active role in providing assistance. In today's industrial and technological society the resolution of many social problems is quite complicated, requiring that human services be provided by highly trained professionals. It is within this context that social work was born.

Social work is one of several professions that has evolved to offer these human services. This chapter provides a general description, an overview, of social work with many of its elements to be revisited and examined in greater depth in subsequent chapters.

What is perhaps the most basic form of helping has been termed *natural helping*. Before reaching a social worker or other professional helpers, clients often have been counseled or assisted in some way by family, friends, neighbors, or volunteers. Natural helping is based on a mutual relationship among equals, and the helper draws heavily on intuition and life experience to guide the helping process. The complexity of social issues and the extensive knowledge and skill required to effectively provide some human services exceed what natural helpers can typically accomplish. This has resulted in the emergence of several occupations that deliver more complicated services to people in need.

Professional helping is different from natural helping in that it is a disciplined approach focused on the needs of the client and it requires specific knowledge, values, and skills to guide the helping activity. Both natural and professional helping are valid means of assisting people in resolving issues related to their social functioning. In fact, many helping professionals first became interested in these careers because they were successful natural helpers and found the experience rewarding. Social workers often work closely with natural helping networks both during the change process and as a source of support after professional service is terminated. However, natural helpers are not a substitute for competent professional help in addressing serious problems or gaining access to needed services.

Social work is the most comprehensive of human service occupations and, through time, has become recognized as the profession that centers its attention on helping people improve their social functioning. In simplest terms, social workers help people strengthen their interaction with various aspects of their world—their children, parents, spouse or other loved one, family, friends, coworkers, or even organizations and whole communities. Social work is also committed to changing factors in the society that diminish the quality of life for all people, but especially for those persons who are most vulnerable to social problems.

Social work's mission of serving both people and the social environment is ambitious. To fulfill that mission, social workers must possess a broad range of knowledge about the functioning of people and social institutions, as well as have a variety of skills for facilitating change in how individuals, organizations, and other social structures operate. This comprehensive mission has made social work an often misunderstood profession. Like the fable of the blind men examining the elephant with each believing that the whole elephant is like the leg, trunk, ear, and so on that he examined, too often people observe one example of social work and conclude that it represents the whole of professional activity. To appreciate the full scope of this profession, it is useful to examine its most fundamental characteristics—the themes that characterize social work.

The Central Themes Underpinning Social Work

Five themes can be identified that reflect the character of social work. No one theme is unique to this profession, but in combination they provide a foundation on which to build one's understanding of social workers and their practice.

A COMMITMENT TO SOCIAL BETTERMENT

Belief in the fundamental importance of improving the quality of social interaction for all people, that is, *social betterment,* is a central value of the social worker.

The social work profession has taken the position that all people should have the opportunity for assistance in meeting their social needs. The source of that assistance might be family, friends, or more formal social programs.

Social work has maintained an idealism about the ability and responsibility of this society to provide opportunities and resources that allow each person to lead a full and rewarding life. It has been particularly concerned with the underdog—the most vulnerable people in the society. This idealism must not be confused with naivete. Social workers are often the most knowledgeable people in the community about the plight of the poor, the abused, the lonely, and others who for a variety of reasons are out of the mainstream of society or experiencing social problems. When social workers express their desire for changes that contribute to the social betterment of people, it is often viewed as a threat by those who want to protect the status quo.

A GOAL TO ENHANCE SOCIAL FUNCTIONING

The commitment to social betterment precludes a narrow focus on specific social problems. In fact, social work takes the position that social betterment involves more than addressing problems—it also involves assisting those who want to improve some aspect of their lives, even though it may not be considered as problematic. Social work, then, is concerned with helping people enhance their *social functioning*, that is, the manner in which they interact with people and social institutions.

Social workers help people and social institutions change in relation to a rapidly changing world. The technology explosion, information explosion, population explosion, and even the threat of nuclear explosion dramatically impact people's lives. Those who can readily adapt to these changes—and are not limited by discrimination due to race, cultural background, gender, age, or physical, emotional, or intellectual abilities—seldom use the services of social workers. Others who have become victims of this too rapidly changing world and its unstable social institutions, however, are likely to require professional help in dealing with this change.

AN ACTION ORIENTATION

Social work is a profession of doers. Social workers are not satisfied just to examine social issues. Rather, they take action to prevent problems from developing, attack problematic situations that can be changed, and help people deal with troublesome situations that cannot be changed. To do this, social workers provide services that include such activities as individual counseling, family and group therapy, linking people to the network of services in a community, fund raising, and even social action. Indeed, social work is an applied science.

AN APPRECIATION FOR HUMAN DIVERSITY

To deal effectively with the wide range of individual and institutional change to which social work is committed, it has become a profession characterized by *diversity*—diversity of clientele, diversity of knowledge and skills, and diversity of services provided. In addition, social workers themselves come in all shapes, colors, ages, and descriptions.

Social workers view diversity as positive. They consider human difference desirable and appreciate the richness that can be offered a society through the culture, language, and traditions of various ethnic, racial, and cultural groups. They value the unique perspectives of persons of different gender, sexual orientation, or age groups, and they recognize and develop the strengths of persons who have been disadvantaged. What's more, social workers view their own diversity as an enriching quality that has created a dynamic profession that can respond to human needs in an ever-changing world.

A VERSATILE PRACTICE PERSPECTIVE

The wide range of human problems with which social workers deal, the variety of settings in which they are employed, the extensive scope of services they provide, and the diverse populations they serve make it unrealistic to expect that a single practice approach could adequately support social work practice. Rather, the social worker must have a comprehensive repertoire of knowledge and techniques that can be used to meet the unique needs of individual clients and client groups.

The versatile social worker, then, must have a solid foundation of knowledge about the behavior of people and social institutions in order to understand the situations their clients bring to them. He or she also needs to understand that differing beliefs may affect the way people will interpret and react to those situations. And, finally, the social worker must have mastered a number of helping techniques from which he or she can imaginatively select and skillfully use to help individuals, families, groups, organizations, and communities improve their social functioning.

How do these themes affect social work practice? The following case example* is just one of many situations where a social worker might help a client:

> Karoline Truesdale, a school social worker, interviewed Kathy and Jim Swan in anticipation of the Swans' oldest son, Danny, beginning school in the fall. The Swans responded to Ms. Truesdale's invitation to the parents of all prospective kindergartners to talk over any concerns they might have about their children's schooling. When making the appointment, Kathy Swan indicated that her son, Danny, was near the cut-off age for entering school and may not be ready yet for kindergarten. When questioned further, Kathy expressed considerable ambivalence indicating that having him in school would help to relieve other burdens at home, but may be too much for Danny.

> Karoline's notes from the interview contained the following information:

> *Kathy Swan is 20 years old and about to deliver her third child. She indicates that they certainly did not need another mouth to feed at this time, but "accidents happen" and she will attempt to cope with this additional child when it is born (although she already*

---

*Sonia Nornes and Bradford W. Sheafor originally developed this case material for the Fort Collins (Colorado) Family Support Alliance.

appears physically and emotionally depleted). Jim is 21 years old and holds a temporary job earning minimum wage. He moved the family to the city because "money in agriculture has gone to hell" and a maintenance job was available at a manufacturing plant here. However, he was laid off after three months when the plant's workforce was reduced. Jim is angry that he moved the family for this job, yet the company felt no obligation to keep him on. He stated that "people in the country don't treat others like that." He is also worried that his temporary job will last only a few more weeks and commented that Kathy "spends money on those kids like it was going out of style." Jim said in no uncertain terms that he did not want and they could not afford another baby, but Kathy had refused to even consider an abortion.

The children are quite active and Danny pays little attention to Kathy's constant requests that he calm down. When Jim attempts to control Danny, Kathy accuses him of being too physical in his discipline. When questioned about this, Jim reported that his Dad "beat me plenty and that sure got results." Kathy complains that Jim does not appreciate the difficulty of being home with the children all of the time, and she objects to the increasing amount of time he is away in the evenings. Jim replied rather pointedly that "it is not much fun being at home anymore." Tension between Kathy and Jim was evident.

When questioned about their social contacts since moving to the city, both Kathy and Jim reported that it had been hard to make friends. They knew "everyone in town" before they moved, but it is different now. With his changing employment, Jim has not made any real friends at work, and Kathy feels isolated at home since Jim takes the car to work each day and the bus is her only means of transportation. She did indicate that one neighbor has been friendly, and they have met two couples they liked at church.

When asked specifically about Danny, Kathy reported that he has been ill frequently with colds and chronic ear infections. She hesitantly described his behavior as troublesome and hoped the school's structure would help him. Kathy described a Sunday school teacher who called him hyperactive and suggested that she not take him to Sunday school anymore. Kathy wondered if there was some kind of treatment that would help Danny and allowed that she was "about at the end of her rope with that child."

It was clear to Karoline that both Kathy and Jim wanted Danny to begin school. But was Danny ready for school—and would the school be ready for Danny? Would Danny's entering school be best for him? Would it resolve the family's problems? Are there other things that could be done to help this family and, perhaps, prevent other problems from emerging?

Within the strict definition of her job, Ms. Truesdale could assist the Swans in reaching a decision about school attendance and complete her service to this family. With her "social betterment" concern, however, resolution of only the question about Danny's entering school would not be sufficient. As a social worker, Karoline would hope to help the Swan family address some of the more basic issues they face in order to improve the overall quality of their lives.

Social workers are not experts on all problems clients may experience. Ms. Truesdale's experience, for example, would not prepare her to make judgments about Danny's health and the possible relationship between his chronic colds and ear infections and his behavior problems. She might refer the Swans to a low-cost medical clinic where a diagnosis of Danny's health problems can be made. She is, however, an expert in "social functioning" and can help Jim and Kathy Swan work on their parenting skills, strengthen the quality of their communication, assist them in developing social relationships in the community, and, perhaps, help Jim obtain job training and stable employment. Karoline's "action orientation" would not allow her to procrastinate. She would be anxious to engage this family in assessing the issues it faces and would support Kathy and Jim as they take action to resolve them.

The Swan family represents at least one form of "human diversity." They are a rural family attempting to adapt to an urban environment. Ms. Truesdale knows that it will take time and probably some help to make this adjustment. She will explore strengths that may have been derived from their rural background. Perhaps Jim's skills in gardening and machinery repair would prove to be an asset in some lines of employment. Also, their rural friendliness may prove beneficial in establishing new social relationships, and they might be helped to build friendships through their church or neighborhood, or to use other resources where they can find informal sources of support (i.e., natural helping).

Service to the Swan family will require considerable practice "versatility." Ms. Truesdale will need to assist the family in problem solving around whether or not to send Danny to school. She will hopefully engage them in more in-depth family counseling. She might invite them to join a parents' group she leads to discuss child-rearing practices, link them with medical and psychological testing services for Danny, and help Mr. Swan obtain job training. If Danny does attend school next year, Karoline might work closely with his teacher and Mrs. Swan to monitor Danny's progress and address any problems in his social functioning that may arise. If he does not attend school, an alternative program might be found where he can develop the socialization skills required in the classroom. Clearly, a wide range of practice activities would be needed and Karoline must be versatile in her practice to apply them.

The Mission of Social Work

While social work practice requires considerable variation in activity, at a more abstract level the profession has consistently maintained that its fundamental *mission* is directly serving people in need and, at the same time, making social institutions more responsive to people. Although this unique mission has been steadfastly held for more than a century, it has been difficult to develop public understanding of its uniqueness among the helping professions. Carol Meyer accurately sums up the situation:

> All enduring professions adapt to social change and pursue their interests, but they maintain the same purposes at the core. Architects design buildings, doctors deal with sickness and health, lawyers practice law, and educators teach. Social workers are concerned with _____ ? With what? Fill in the blank. With people? Psychological functioning? Delivery of social services? Management of human service agencies? Policy analysis? Social change? . . . All of these or some of these?[1]

One way to identify the boundaries of social work is to examine its three primary purposes: caring, curing, and changing.

CARING

Throughout their history social workers have sought to improve the quality of life for the most vulnerable groups in the population. At times the best knowledge we can muster is inadequate to prevent or cure the many problems encountered by the disabled, elderly, terminally ill, and other persons with limited capacity for social functioning. From Dorothea Dix's concerns about the plight of people in mental hospitals in the mid-1800s to today's concerns about the negative experiences of people in some nursing homes, social workers have recognized that certain conditions in life cannot be corrected. Yet, the victims of these conditions deserve not only humane but high-quality care.

Caring that makes people comfortable and helps them cope with their limitations is frequently the most valuable service a social worker can provide. Sometimes caring takes the form of making social provisions available to people such as arranging for meals to be delivered or for income to be supplemented, and ensuring that adequate housing is provided. At other times, the person and/or family may require caring in the form of personal services such as counseling to better adjust to an unchangeable situation like a disability or terminal illness. There is an important leadership role for social work in helping communities create the necessary services to provide such care. The fundamental intention of caring for those in need continues to be a central purpose of social work practice.

CURING

Another thrust of social work practice has been to provide treatment for individuals and families experiencing problems in social functioning. Depending on client needs, direct service practices ranging from psychosocial therapy to behavioral modification, reality therapy, crisis intervention, and various group and family therapy approaches are used by social workers.[2] These approaches do not automatically cure social problems in the same way a physician might prescribe a medication to cure an infection. In fact, most social workers would argue that at best they can only help clients cure themselves. The contribution the social worker makes is the ability to engage the client in actively working toward change, to accurately assess the individual and societal factors that have created the need for change, to select appropriate techniques for a given client and situation, and to use these techniques effectively in conjunction with the clients to accomplish the desired results.

CHANGING THE SOCIETY

Social change is the third primary purpose of social work. Social workers are committed to reforming existing laws, procedures, and attitudes until they are more responsive to human needs. Many pioneer social workers were active reformers who worked to improve conditions in slums, hospitals, and poorhouses. Today, they actively influence social legislation in an effort to create new social programs or to change factors that contribute to damaging social conditions such as racism, sexism, and poverty.

Social workers also seek to change negative public attitudes about the more vulnerable members of society by providing public education and facilitating the empowerment of the affected members of the population to advocate for their own interests. Social workers, then, bring about change in the society by representing the interests of their clientele and/or helping clients convince decision makers at the local, state, or national levels to respond to human needs.

Defining Social Work

Three concerted efforts have been made to arrive at a clear definition of social work. The first occurred in the 1920s when the American Association of Social Workers convened a series of meetings of key agency executives in Milford, Pennsylvania. These representatives from a range of practice settings identified several factors that appeared to be common to all social work practice, but they could not agree on a concise definition of social work. However, the Milford Conference encouraged further efforts at articulating a definition of social work when it concluded that social work's common features were more substantial than the differences related to practice in different settings.[3]

The 1950s brought a second surge of interest in developing a clear conception of social work. The merger of several specialized social work practice organizations (e.g., American Association of Hospital Social Workers, National Association of Visiting Teachers, American Association of Psychiatric Social Workers, and the more generic American Association of Social Workers) into the National Association of Social Workers (NASW) was completed in 1955. For a time, a spirit of unity dominated the social work profession, and the effort to find a definition of social work that would reflect the commonality in diverse practice activities began in earnest. A critical step was the publication of the "Working Definition of Social Work Practice" in 1958. Although not yet providing a comprehensive definition of social work, the document established an important basis for subsequent definitions by identifying three common goals of social work practice:[4]

1. To assist individuals and groups to identify and resolve or minimize problems arising out of disequilibrium between themselves and their environment.
2. To identify potential areas of disequilibrium between individuals or groups and the environment in order to prevent the occurrence of disequilibrium.
3. To seek out, identify, and strengthen the maximum potential of individuals, groups, and communities.

Thus, the "Working Definition" established that social workers are concerned with curative or treatment goals, as well as emphasizing the importance of social change or prevention. In addition, the definition recognized the focus of social work on the interactions between people and their environments and the responsibility of social workers to provide services to people as individuals, as parts of various groups, and as members of communities.

Third, in the 1970s and 1980s, NASW published three special issues of its major journal, *Social Work,* that generated substantial debate and discussion, although not conclusions, about the nature of social work.[5] This activity enhanced understanding of the central features that characterize social work but did not lead to a definitive description of this profession.

Although NASW has never adopted a definition of social work, a one-sentence definition developed by one of its committees has gained widespread acceptance.

> Social work is the professional activity of helping individuals, groups, or communities enhance or restore their capacity for social functioning and creating societal conditions favorable to that goal.[6]

This statement provides a concise one-sentence "dictionary definition" of the profession. It draws important boundaries around social work. First, social work is considered professional activity. Professional activity requires a particular body of knowledge, values, and skills, as well as a discrete purpose that guides one's practice activities. When practice is judged professional, community sanction to perform these tasks is assumed to be present, and the profession, in turn, is expected to be accountable to the public for the quality of services provided.

Second, this definition captures a uniqueness of social work. It makes clear that social workers serve a range of client systems that include individuals, families or other household units, groups, organizations, neighborhoods, communities, and even larger units of society. For social work, the identification of one's client is tricky because a client or target of practice activity may range from an individual to a state or nation. The unique activities of the social worker are directed toward helping all of those systems interact more effectively and require professional education as preparation.

Finally, the last part of the definition concerns social work's dual focus on person and environment. Social workers help people enhance or restore their capacity for social functioning. At the same time, they work to change societal conditions that may help or hinder people from improving their social functioning. Herein lies another uniqueness of social work. Whereas some professions focus on change in the person and others on changing the environment, social work's attention is directed to the connections between person and environment.

When working with clients, social workers must take into consideration both the characteristics of the person and the impinging forces from the environment. In contrast, the physician is primarily prepared to treat physical aspects of the individual, and the attorney is largely concerned with the operation of the legal system in the larger environment (although both the physician and attorney should give secondary attention to other, related systems). Social work recognizes that each person brings to the helping situation a set of behaviors, needs, and beliefs that are the result of his or her unique experiences from birth. Yet it also recognizes that whatever is brought to the situation must be related to the world as that person confronts it. By focusing on transactions between the person and his or her environment, social interaction can be improved.

Figure 2-1 depicts this unique focus of social work. Social workers operate at the boundary between people and their environment. They are not prepared to deal with all boundary matters. Rather, they address those matters that are judged problematic

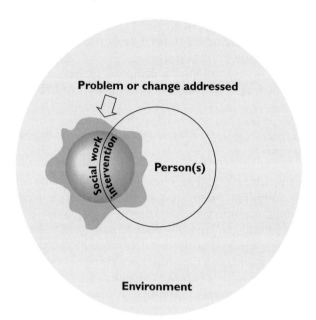

Problem or change addressed

Social work intervention

Person(s)

Environment

FIGURE 2-1   **Focal Point of Social Work Intervention**

or have been selected as a way to contribute to the enhancement of social functioning. In sum, social workers temporarily enter the lives of their clients to help them improve their transactions with important elements of their environment.

Social Work Practice Approaches

Arriving at a practice approach that is sufficiently flexible and encompassing to relate to this complex profession has proven difficult. In fact, social work might be characterized during much of its history as a profession in search of a practice approach. That search included the development of several distinct practice methods.

TRADITIONAL PRACTICE METHODS

As part of the drive to become a unique profession, social work sought to identify a distinctive method of practice that would distinguish it from other helping professions such as law, medicine, and psychology. The first practice method to develop, *social casework,* was first described in the 1917 classic social work book, *Social Diagnosis.*[7] In this book, Mary Richmond focused on the requirements for effective practice with individuals and families, regardless of the type of problem presented. The book filled an important void in social work by introducing a practice literature. The principles of social casework identified by Richmond were enthusiastically adopted by social workers, and the profession moved its primary focus to work with individuals and families. The popularity of Freudian psychology in the 1920s and 1930s also directed social work toward individual practice, rather than to the more controversial activities associated with changing social institutions that had previously characterized much of social work practice. Edith Abbott noted that Richmond later expressed concern over this trend to emphasize the person side of the person-environment mission of social work:

> The good social worker, says Miss Richmond, doesn't go on helping people out of a ditch. Pretty soon she begins to find out what ought to be done to get rid of the ditch.[8]

Social workers concerned with providing services to groups took longer to develop a set of guiding principles, partially because those social workers disagreed as to whether they should identify professionally with the emerging field of social work or with recreation or continuing education. This disagreement among *social group workers* was resolved in the 1930s in favor of identifying with social work, and thus a second distinct method evolved.

The third practice method to develop was *community organization*. With many social agencies and social programs evolving in each community, their coordination and the evaluation of their effectiveness became important and, to meet that need, another distinct practice area emerged. Community organization became the practice method primarily concerned with the distribution of financial resources and building linkages among existing services.

In addition to using one of these three primary practice methods in their work, many social workers found themselves responsible for administering social agencies and conducting research on the effectiveness of social programs. Their experience and education usually left them with little preparation for these indirect service activities. By the late 1940s *administration* and *research* had evolved as practice methods in social work. Viewed as secondary methods, they were seen as a supplement to a person's ability as a caseworker, group worker, or community organizer.

MULTIMETHOD PRACTICE APPROACH

Concurrent with the development of these five distinct practice approaches was the growing commitment to the evolution of social work as a single profession with a unifying practice method. A major study of social work and social work education, the Hollis–Taylor Report, was concluded in 1951. It recommended that, because the breadth of social work practice required social workers to intervene at more than one level of client system, social work education should prepare students with a beginning level of competence in each of the five practice methods.[9]

The multimethod practice approach proved a good fit with the varied demands for social work practice, but failed to yield the unifying practice theme the profession needed. Practitioners typically identified with a dominant method and used the others sparingly. Elitism based on practice method and setting persisted (e.g., it was preferable to be a psychiatric caseworker rather than "just" a social worker), creating an attitude that interfered with the search for commonality and unity within social work.

GENERALIST PRACTICE APPROACH

Supported by concepts drawn from social systems theory, the generalist approach to practice began to emerge in the late 1960s. As Balinsky stated, "The complexity of human problems necessitates a broadly oriented practitioner with a versatile repertoire of methods and skills capable of interacting in any one of a number of systems."[10] The generalist model provided that versatility and met the requirement for a flexible approach to social work practice demanded by the increasing complexity and interrelatedness of human problems.

Generalist practice contains two fundamental components. First, it provides a perspective from which the social worker views the practice situation. Social systems theory helps the social worker to maintain a focus on the interaction between systems—that is, the person–environment transactions—and to continually look for ways to intervene in more than one relevant system. Second, rather than attempting to make the client's situation fit the methodological orientation of the social worker, the situation is viewed as determining the practice approach to be used. Thus, the social worker is required to have a broad knowledge and skill base from which to serve clients or client systems and to have the ability to appropriately select from that base to meet the needs of the clients.

Although many social workers contend that the generalist approach has been part of social work practice since its inception, only recently have there been analysis and explication of this practice approach. With the accreditation requirement that both baccalaureate- and master's-level social workers be prepared as generalist practitioners, there has been a resurgence of activity aimed at clarifying the nature of generalist practice in recent years. In their article entitled "Milford Redefined: A Model of Initial and Advanced Generalist Social Work," Schatz, Jenkins, and Sheafor delineate the key elements of generalist social work at both the initial and advanced generalist levels.[11] Their model is based on research that documented areas of agreement among experts who have written about generalist social work practice or administered educational programs that prepared students as generalists.

This model recognizes that there is a *generic foundation* for all social work, whether generalist or specialist, that includes such factors as knowledge about the social work profession, social work values, the purpose of social work, ethnic/diversity sensitivity, basic communication skills, understanding of human relationships, and others.

The *generalist perspective,* according to the Schatz–Jenkins–Sheafor model: (1) is informed by sociobehavioral and ecosystems knowledge; (2) incorporates ideologies that include democracy, humanism, and empowerment; (3) requires a worker to be theoretically and methodologically open when approaching a practice situation; (4) is client-centered and problem-focused; (5) involves both direct and indirect intervention awareness; and (6) is research-based.

At the *initial generalist* level of practice, the social worker builds on the generic foundation and, using the generalist perspective, must at least be capable of: (1) engaging effectively in interpersonal helping; (2) managing change processes; (3) appropriately selecting and utilizing multilevel intervention modes; (4) intervening in multiple-sized systems as determined by the practice situation; (5) performing varied practice roles; (6) assessing and examining one's own practice; and (7) functioning successfully within an agency.

The *advanced generalist* social worker engages in more difficult practice tasks and, therefore, operates from an expanded knowledge base about individuals, groups, organizations, and communities. The advanced generalist must also develop increased skills to intervene in direct service provision with individuals, families, and groups at one end of the multiple-level practice spectrum, and, at the other end, address more complex indirect practice situations such as supervision, administration, and policy or program evaluation. Finally, the advanced generalist is expected to approach social work practice from an eclectic, but disciplined and systematic, stance and to simultaneously engage in both theoretical research and practice evaluation.

SPECIALIST PRACTICE APPROACH

In contrast to the generalist, a number of specialized practice approaches have emerged. *Specialist* social work practice is characterized by the application of selected knowledge and skills to a narrowed area of practice based on practice setting, population served, social problems addressed, and/or practice intervention mode used. In other words, this practice approach begins with a preference about the knowledge and skills required for practice in that specialized area and fits the client into those more narrow, but in-depth, worker competencies.

While education for generalist practice usually is offered in baccalaureate programs or the early part of master's-level programs, specialist education has increasingly been designated as the prerogative of the latter part of a master's degree. The Curriculum Policy Statement of the Council on Social Work Education that guides the accreditation of these programs identifies the following categories of specializations that schools might offer:

Fields of Practice: for example, services to families, children, and youth; services to the elderly; health; mental health; developmental disabilities; education; business and industry; neighborhood and community development; income maintenance; employment.

Problem Areas: for example, crime and delinquency; substance abuse; developmental disabilities; family violence; mental illness; neighborhood deterioration; poverty; racism; sexism.

Populations-at-Risk: for example, children and youth; the aged; women; single parents; ethnic populations; persons in poverty; migrants; gay and lesbian persons; the chronically mentally ill.

Intervention Methods or Roles: for example, specific practice approaches with individuals, families, and groups; consultation; community organization; social planning; administration; case management; social policy formulation; research.

Practice Contexts and Perspectives: for example, industry; hospitals; rural or urban areas.[12]

Today, like many disciplines, social work embraces both generalist and specialist approaches to practice. The generalist viewpoint supports the commonality that unites social work into one profession; the specialist approach helps to delineate unique areas for in-depth social work practice.

Social Workers: Their Many Faces

Three factors help to explain what it is like to be a social worker: career patterns at different educational levels; knowledge, values, and skills used in practice; and personal characteristics of social workers. For each factor there is considerable diversity expressed in the practice activities of social workers.

CAREER PATTERNS OF SOCIAL WORKERS

Varying career patterns have evolved as the practice of social work has changed over time. The early social workers were volunteers or paid staff who required no specific training or educational program to qualify for the work. When formal education programs were instituted at the turn of the century, they were training programs located in the larger social agencies. In fact, it was not until 1939 that accreditation standards required that all recognized social work education must be offered in institutions of higher education. There was also controversy over whether appropriate social work education could be offered at the baccalaureate level as well as at the more professionally respectable master's level. The reorganization of social work into one professional association (the National Association of Social Workers, NASW) and one professional education association (the Council on Social Work Education, CSWE) in the 1950s yielded a single-level profession. At that time, only the master's degree from an accredited school of social work was considered "legitimate" social work preparation. Today, the MSW degree still is considered the "terminal practice degree" in social work, but other professional practice levels are now recognized. In 1998, 13,660 persons received the MSW degree from one of the 126 accredited programs, making it the dominant qualification for social work practice.[13]

Another level of professional recognition was established in 1961 by the NASW—the Academy of Certified Social Workers (ACSW). The ACSW was the first step in creating a multilevel career pattern and represented the profession's method of identifying its more experienced practitioners. To be recognized as a member of the Academy, one must have completed an MSW, have at least two years of supervised practice experience, have favorable references, and pass a test on practice knowledge.

Increasingly, social workers are also completing doctoral degrees in social work, either the Doctor of Social Work (DSW) or the Doctor of Philosophy (Ph.D.). In 1998, for example, about 266 persons completed a doctorate in social work from sixty-two schools in the United States.[14] In addition, a number of other social workers also completed doctorates in related disciplines. Most doctoral-level social workers are employed in teaching or research positions, but an increasing number of doctoral programs aimed at preparing people for direct social work are emerging. Doctoral programs, however, are not subject to accreditation by CSWE and are not recognized as professional preparation for social work practice. Thus, the MSW continues to be viewed as the terminal practice degree.

It was not until 1970 that the NASW recognized baccalaureate-level (BSW) social workers as members of the Association. The Council on Social Work Education subsequently created accreditation standards, and, by 1998, 410 schools throughout the United States graduated 11,435 persons with the BSW (at times this may be a BA or a BS degree) from an accredited social work education program.[15] Another career level had been recognized.

By 1981, NASW found it necessary to develop a classification system that would help to clarify the various entry points to social work and define the educational and practice requirements at each level. This system sorts out the somewhat mixed career levels in social work:[16]

Basic Professional	Requires a baccalaureate degree from a program accredited by CSWE.
Specialized Professional	Requires a master's degree from a program accredited by CSWE.
Independent Professional	Requires an accredited MSW and at least two years of post-master's experience under appropriate professional supervision. (Requirements for the ACSW match this standard.)
Advanced Professional	Requires special theoretical, practice, administrative, or policy proficiency or ability to conduct advanced research or studies in social welfare, usually demonstrated through a doctoral degree in social work or a closely related social science discipline.

NASW's classification scheme has several benefits. First, it identifies and clarifies the practice levels existing in social work and, in general terms, spells out the competencies that both clients and employers can expect from workers at each level. Second, it describes a continuum of social work practice with several entry points based on education and experience. Finally, it suggests a basis for job classification that can increasingly distinguish among the various levels of social work competence and assist agencies in selecting appropriately prepared social workers to fill their positions.

THE SOCIAL WORKER'S KNOWLEDGE, VALUES, AND SKILLS

To practice social work effectively, specific knowledge and mastery of a variety of intervention approaches are needed. The social worker not only must be able to work directly with a client or clients, but also should be prepared to understand and work to change the environment of these clients. He or she must understand the culture in which the practice occurs, the background of the people served, and the functioning of the social agency where the services are provided. The social worker must also know what other services are available in the community, know the causes of the client's problems in social functioning, and have the means to effectively provide human services. It takes rigorous professional education to master the knowledge, values, and skills required for social work practice.

What basic competencies are fundamental to social work practice? Depending on the particular job, the type of agency where one works, client capabilities, problems being addressed, and resources available, the social worker will need to have differing competencies. Yet, any profession must have some common features in the tasks performed by its members. A comprehensive task analysis of social workers conducted by Teare and Sheafor has provided an empirically based description of the work of social workers and identifies competencies required to perform that work. This study is the basis for Chapter 8, which details a set of competencies required for social work practice. One finding of that study is that there are several tasks regularly performed by virtually all social workers. These tasks are related to interpersonal helping (i.e., basic interviewing and communication with clients), case planning and maintenance, professional competence development and workload planning, and the ongoing acquisition of knowledge about the human service delivery system.[17]

CHARACTERISTICS OF TODAY'S SOCIAL WORKERS

Who are the people who have elected a career in social work? It is difficult to accurately determine the characteristics of today's social workers because a single data source that includes all social workers does not exist. The U.S. Bureau of Labor Statistics (BLS) estimates that in 1996 there were 585,000 employed social workers in the United States who had completed a social work degree. Unfortunately, the BLS data provide little information about these social workers and it is necessary to examine only the characteristics of those social workers who are members of the National Association of Social Workers to gain more detail about the members of this profession. The NASW membership data are heavily skewed toward the specialized or independent, that is, the MSW-level workers (85.5%). For several reasons, such as the cost of NASW membership compared to salaries, the relative emphasis of NASW programs on the concerns of master's-level social workers, and the large portion of the BSW workers later going on to complete an MSW degree, only 9.9 percent of the NASW members are baccalaureate-level social workers.[18] Nevertheless, the NASW membership data summarized in Table 2-1 yield the most accurate depiction of social workers at bachelor's, master's, and doctoral educational levels that is currently available.

Although social work is highly committed to diversity, it is clear that the ranks of social workers are largely white females. It is evident from the NASW mem-

TABLE 2-1   **Characteristics of Baccalaureate-, Master's-, and Doctoral-level Social Workers**

Social Worker Characteristic	BSW	MSW	DSW
Gender: Female	89.7%	78.5%	58.5%
Minority Group Member	13.7	11.3	13.6
Annual Income from Full-time Employment			
Less than $15,000	10.0	1.4	1.0
$15,000 to $19,999	20.1	2.6	0.4
$20,000 to $29,999	46.4	26.6	8.3
$30,000 to $39,999	16.6	38.0	25.5
$40,000 or more	6.8	31.5	64.7
Primary Employment Setting			
Social services agency	33.7	20.5	10.1
Health/mental health facility (hospital and outpatient)	26.6	38.9	20.0
Residential care facility	21.1	6.4	2.2
School (preschool through grade 12)	3.8	7.1	3.2
Private practice	3.1	20.2	24.1
Courts/justice system	2.6	3.9	0.6
College/university	2.6	2.6	37.2
Other	6.3	3.0	2.5
Primary Auspices of Employment			
Federal/state/local government	41.6	33.0	41.0
Private (nonprofit) agency	40.4	38.6	31.6
Private (for-profit) agency	18.1	28.3	27.5
Primary Practice Area			
Children-families	29.2	24.9	19.6
Mental health	18.3	39.6	40.7
Medical health	17.0	13.2	7.7
Aging	16.7	4.2	3.7
Schools	2.6	5.4	4.1
Criminal justice	2.5	1.1	1.1
Other	13.2	10.8	22.2
Primary Job Function			
Clinical/direct service	65.5	71.1	40.4
Administration/management	10.6	15.7	16.7
Teaching/training	5.9	2.8	32.1
Supervision	4.6	5.7	2.3
Other	13.5	4.2	8.4

Source: Margaret Gibelman and Philip H. Schervish, *Who We Are: A Second Look* (Washington, D.C.: NASW Press, 1997), pp. 54, 59, 71, 86, 103, 114, and 134.

bership data that the pay for social work is moderate with the median annual full-time employment income for BSW workers typically ranging from $20,000 to $30,000. Income increases about $10,000 per year for social workers practicing at the master's level, and for those at the doctoral level, it increases to well above $40,000 per year. Educational level is clearly the most significant factor influencing salary. However, other factors that are often associated with job access at the different educational levels also reflect substantial salary variations. For example, social workers working primarily with older people and children and youth (except for schools) are at the lowest pay levels, while those working in mental health, in business and industry, or at colleges and universities earn the most. Further, when auspices of the employing agency are considered, social workers employed by nonprofit agencies earn the least and those working for for-profit organizations earn considerably more. Finally, workers in direct practice (clinical) jobs average the least income, while those in administrative or management positions earn the most.[19]

Examination of the NASW membership data in Table 2-1 reveals substantial differences in the settings in which social workers are employed. Baccalaureate-level (or basic) social workers are most likely to be employed in social services agencies such as a public human services department or a small nonprofit community agency, followed by employment in a health/mental health agency, or a residential facility such as a group home or nursing home. Clearly the feature that distinguishes the basic social worker from the specialized or independent social worker is the concentration in practice positions working with older people and the relatively small proportion employed in mental health.

Master's-level workers, by contrast, are considerably more likely to work in mental health (particularly the for-profit agencies) or to maintain their own private practice in which they independently contract with their clients to provide services. The specialized- or independent-level social workers also report that they are somewhat more likely than basic workers to serve in administrative and management positions.

The doctoral-level social workers are most likely to be employed by a college or university, although about one-fourth of them are in private practice and another one-fifth are employed in health/mental health settings. Social workers at this advanced level are primarily direct service clinicians or social work faculty members and, to a lesser extent, agency administrators.

Concluding Comment

Since its inception more than a century ago, social work has emerged as a comprehensive helping profession. From the beginning, social workers sought that elusive common denominator that would depict this profession as clearly as possible and help social work form into a cohesive entity.

Recognition of the common mission of working simultaneously with both people and their environments to improve social functioning has consistently served as social work's primary mission and thus differentiates social work from the other helping professions. In addition to helping people deal with their environments, social workers also consider it their mission to bring about social change in order to prevent problems or to make social institutions more responsive to the needs of people—especially the most vulnerable members of the society. With this person and environment focus, social workers provide a combination of caring, curing, and changing activities that help people improve the quality of their lives and, therefore, help the society accomplish its goal of promoting the general welfare.

When carrying out their professional service activities, social workers are typically employed in public or nonprofit voluntary human service agencies that provide services ranging from child protection to family counseling to assisting the aged. An increasing number, particularly those with master's and doctorate degrees, are employed in for-profit agencies or as private practitioners where they contract directly with clients to provide services. Some are generalists and approach their practice in a manner like the physician who is a general practitioner, while others are specialists and provide in-depth services related to particular helping activities. As Chapter 8 will amplify, there is a core of competencies required of all social workers regardless of setting, educational level, practice area, or job function.

Social work has evolved a career ladder that recognizes professionals at four levels: basic, specialized, independent, and advanced. This classification scheme recognizes that at each of the four levels somewhat different job activities occur. The two entry levels (i.e., basic and specialized professional levels) require that the worker complete the requisite educational preparation represented in the accreditation standards of the Council on Social Work Education. At the latter two levels, additional practice experience and expertise and/or advanced education warrant the recognition.

KEY WORDS AND CONCEPTS

Natural and professional helping

Social betterment

Social functioning

Human diversity

Caring/Curing/Changing

"Working Definition" of social work

"NASW Definition" of social work

Dual focus on person and environment

Generalist social work practice

Advanced generalist social work practice

Specialist social work practice

Traditional practice methods

NASW classification of practice levels (basic, specialized, independent, advanced)

SUGGESTED READINGS

Bartlett, Harriet M. "Toward Clarification and Improvement of Social Work Practice," *Social Work* 3 (April 1958): 3–9.

Corey, Mariane Schneider, and Corey, Gerald. *Becoming a Helper,* 3rd Edition. Belmont, CA: Brooks/Cole, 1998.

Gordon, William E. "A Critique of the Working Definition," *Social Work* 7 (October 1992): 3–13.

National Association of Social Workers. *Social Work* 19 (September 1974); 22 (September 1977); and 26 (January 1981). (These three issues are devoted to conceptual frameworks for the profession.)

Reid, P. Nelson, and Popple, Philip R., eds. *The Moral Purposes of Social Work: The Character and Intentions of a Profession.* Chicago: Nelson-Hall, 1992.

Specht, Harry, and Courtney, Mark E. *Unfaithful Angels: How Social Work Has Abandoned Its Mission.* New York: Free Press, 1994.

Wagner, David. *The Quest for a Radical Profession: Social Service Careers and Political Ideology.* Lanham, MD: University Press of America, 1990.

ENDNOTES

1. Carol H. Meyer, "Social Work Purpose: Status by Choice or Coercion?" *Social Work* 26 (January 1981): 71–72.
2. For a brief description of a number of practice approaches, see Bradford W. Sheafor, Charles R. Horejsi, and Gloria A. Horejsi, *Techniques and Guidelines for Social Work Practice,* 5th Edition (Boston: Allyn and Bacon, 2000), Chapter 6.
3. American Association of Social Workers, *Social Casework: Generic and Specific: A Report of the Milford Conference* (New York: National Association of Social Workers, 1974), p. 11. (Original work published in 1929.)
4. Harriet M. Bartlett, "Towards Clarification and Improvement of Social Work Practice," *Social Work* 3 (April 1958): 5–7.
5. See *Social Work* 19 (September 1974); *Social Work* 22 (September 1977); and *Social Work* 26 (January 1981).
6. National Association of Social Workers, *Standards for Social Service Manpower* (Washington, D.C.: NASW, 1973), pp. 4–5.
7. Mary E. Richmond, *Social Diagnosis* (New York: Russell Sage Foundation, 1917).
8. Edith Abbott, "The Social Caseworker and the Enforcement of Industrial Legislation," in *Proceedings of the National Conference on Social Work, 1918* (Chicago: Rogers and Hall, 1919), p. 313.
9. Ernest V. Hollis and Alice L. Taylor, *Social Work Education in the United States* (New York: Columbia University Press, 1951).
10. Rosalie Balinsky, "Generic Practice in Graduate Social Work Curricula: A Study of Educators' Experiences and Attitudes," *Journal of Education for Social Work* 18 (Fall 1982): 47.
11. Mona S. Schatz, Lowell E. Jenkins, and Bradford W. Sheafor, "Milford Redefined: A Model of Initial and Advanced Generalist Social Work," *Journal of Social Work Education* 26 (Fall 1990): 217–231.
12. Council on Social Work Education, "Curriculum Policy Statement for Master's Degree Programs in Social Work Education" (Alexandria, VA: Council on Social Work Education, 1992), p. 10.
13. Todd N. Lennon, ed., *Statistics on Social Work Education in the United States: 1998* (Alexandria, VA: Council on Social Work Education, 1999), p. 45.
14. Ibid.
15. Ibid., p. 44.

16. Reprinted with permission from *NASW Standards for the Classification of Social Work Practice,* Policy Statement 4 (Silver Spring, MD: National Association of Social Workers, 1981), p. 9.

17. Robert J. Teare and Bradford W. Sheafor, *Practice-Sensitive Social Work Education: An Empirical Analysis of Social Work Practice and Practitioners* (Alexandria, VA: Council on Social Work Education, 1995).

18. Margaret Gibelman and Philip H. Schervish, *Who We Are: A Second Look* (Washington, D.C.: NASW Press, 1997), p. 23.

19. Ibid., pp. 134–145.

Social work pioneer Jane Addams visits with children at Chicago's Hull House.

CHAPTER 3

The Emergence
of Social Work as a Profession

Prefatory Comment   In order to understand and appreciate social work more fully, it is useful to trace its emergence and identify key historical events and professional actions that have shaped the profession. While one could gain insight into the emergence of social work by examining the influence of external events, this chapter is guided by an examination of social work's efforts to become a recognized profession. It begins with a review of the nature of professions, particularly the helping professions, in U.S. society. It traces the emergence of social work during the past century, with emphasis on the choices made that affected its acceptance as a profession, and concludes with an analysis of its current professional status.

The growth and development of social work has not been a planned event. It just happened. It was a response to human suffering that began in several different parts of American society and eventually coalesced into a single, diverse profession.

Because its development has not been guided by a clear master plan, social work has been heavily influenced by a variety of factors. It has been pushed in one direction by forces such as periods of political and economic conservatism, the stress of wars and other major international events, and by competition from other emerging helping disciplines. At the same time, social work has been pulled in other directions by its own goals and aspirations, such as the need for a coherent concept of the profession that could incorporate its different roots and its intense desire to be recognized as a profession.

The Nature of Professions

A field of sociological inquiry is devoted to the definition and description of the nature of professions. One of the central figures in this field, Wilbert Moore, concluded that "to have one's occupational status accepted as professional or to have one's occupational conduct judged as professional is highly regarded in all post industrial societies and in at least the modernizing sectors of others."[1]

Professions are highly regarded, in part, because they have been granted sanction to perform essential services that ensure survival and help people enhance the quality of life. Professionals use specialized knowledge and skillfully provide services to people in need of assistance in sensitive areas of their lives. The knowledge and skills required exceed that expected of volunteers and other natural helpers. For individual members, being part of a profession is usually personally satisfying and financially rewarding, and yields high social status. From the client's point of view, the designation of professionalism signals those persons who are qualified to provide particular services and provides at least a minimum level of protection against incompetent and unethical behavior by practitioners. For the professions, this recognition is essential because it enhances the ability to recruit qualified people and ensures the respect of other professions and the general public. Recognition as professional, then, has been an important motivation driving many occupations.

How is it determined whether an occupation is a profession? One approach to the study of professions, known as the *absolute approach,* has been to examine the traditional professions of medicine, law, and higher education to isolate their fundamental elements. These studies revealed that professions could be characterized by such factors as their requirements for specialized skill and training, a specific base of knowledge, the formation of professional associations, and the development of codes of ethical behavior governing professional practice. Other occupations were then evaluated to determine whether they, too, contained these elements and could be considered professions. Using this approach, occupational groups were classified in one of two categories: professional or nonprofessional.

More recently, the prevalent approach to the study of professions has been to identify the key attributes common to professions and assess the degree to which any other occupational group possesses these attributes. This *relative approach* to professionalism allows for the placement of any occupational group along a continuum from nonprofessional to professional. Using this approach, Moore, for example, identifies the primary characteristics of a profession as a full-time occupation, commitment to a calling, identification with peers, specified training or education, a service orientation, and autonomy restrained by responsibility.[2] Using such criteria, it is possible to place each occupational group on a scale of professionalism relative to other occupations. The point at which an occupation sufficiently meets the criteria to be considered a profession is not absolute but determined by judgment.

As more has been learned about professions, three elements have been delineated to help explain the unique characteristics of the occupations that are considered to be professions. First, professionals must be free from constraints that might limit their ability to act in the best interests of their clients. The protection of this *professional autonomy* has been most successful in professions that contract directly with clients to provide services. In these situations few constraints are imposed on the manner in which practice is conducted. In agency-based professions, however, the organizations employ the professionals and contract with the clients to provide service. The agency's rules and regulations, intended to improve the organizations' efficiency and accountability, limit the professional's autonomy to exercise independent judgment regarding the manner in which services are provided.

Second, society has granted *professional authority* to a few people who have acquired the necessary knowledge and skills to provide the needed services in a given area of professional practice. Society grants this authority because it has, in effect, determined that it is inefficient, if not impossible, for every person to acquire all the knowledge and skill needed to meet complex human needs. Thus, these professionals are given the exclusive right to make judgments and give advice to their clients. In granting this professional authority, society, in essence, gives up the right to judge these professionals except in extreme cases of incompetent or unethical practice. Society depends on the members of that profession to determine the requisite entrance preparation and to be sure those who are practicing as members of that profession do so competently.

To be able to operate within the authority of a given profession, each member must master the knowledge and skills the profession has determined to be essential. Through the accreditation of its educational programs and the content of examinations that govern certification by a profession, the technical information and competencies fundamental to that profession are assured. However, human problems typically extend beyond the purview of any one profession. To be of maximum effectiveness, it is important that the professional not only has the technical training required for his or her profession, but also possesses a fund of general knowledge gained from the study of history, literature, philosophy, theater, and other fields that will help to provide a broad understanding of the human condition. In short, professionals must be both technically and generally educated.

Third, when the right to judge practice is relinquished by granting professional authority, the public becomes vulnerable and rightfully expects the professions to protect them from abuses that may accrue from the professional monopoly. Hughes indicates that the motto of the professions must be *credat emptor* ("buyer trust"), as opposed to the motto of the marketplace, *caveat emptor* ("buyer beware").[3] For example, where the layperson would rarely question the prescription of a physician, that same person might be very cautious when buying a used car and might have it thoroughly tested by an independent mechanic before making a purchase. To maintain this buyer trust, the professions must be accountable to the public that has granted them the sanction to perform these services. In order to establish and maintain this *professional responsibility*, professions develop codes that identify the expected ethical behavior of practitioners and establish mechanisms for policing their membership regarding unethical or incompetent practice.

In a sense, the professions and society struck a deal. In exchange for responsible service in sensitive areas of life, the professions were granted exclusive authority, that is, a professional monopoly, to offer these services.

Helping Professions: A Response to Human Need

All helping professions began as a response to unmet human need. As people experienced suffering or insufficient development in some aspect of life, when natural helping networks were not sufficient to meet the resulting needs, various forms of professional help emerged. Physicians, teachers, clergy, and other professional groups began to appear and to be given approval by the society to perform specific helping functions. The buyers', or clients', vulnerability was intensified in the area of helping services because they dealt in especially sensitive areas where unwitting persons could be harmed by the incompetent or improper actions of the professional. In addition to the codes of ethics and bodies established to investigate situations where abuses of this monopoly were alleged, the helping professions also characteristically have had external sources of client protection. For many professions, this additional protection has taken the form of licensing professional practice, while clients of agency-based professions are usually considered to have adequate supplemental protection through the monitoring of practice by the agencies and organizations.

It was soon realized that the effectiveness of these helpers was increased when their skills were supported by specific knowledge and values that could guide their interventions into the lives of clients or groups of clients. As this professional knowledge expanded through the development of theories and concepts, as well as through experience, trial and error, or practice wisdom, the professions expanded their technical knowledge requirements and their membership became increasingly exclusive. There was a time when each profession could respond to a number of human needs. However, the increasingly specialized knowledge necessary to provide effective helping services has led to a proliferation of helping professions, each with its own specializations.

What are these needs to which the helping professions have responded? Brill's description of needs helps to clarify the primary focus of the several helping professions as they exist today:[4]

- *Physical needs:* functioning of the physical structures and organic processes of the body (Physicians and Nurses)

- *Emotional needs:* feelings or affective aspects of the consciousness that are subjectively experienced (Psychologists)

- *Intellectual needs:* capacity for rational and intelligent thought (Teachers)

- *Spiritual needs:* desire for a meaning in life that transcends one's life on earth (Clergy)

- *Social needs:* capacity for satisfying relationships with others (Social Workers)

While the helping professions have tended to organize around a single need, there are exceptions, such as psychiatry, in which both emotional and physical needs—and their interaction—are the focus of professional service.

The increase of helping professions from few to many, and their overlap when providing services to people who experience more than one problem, has inevitably led to difficulty in defining professional boundaries. As professions like social work, occupational therapy, and music therapy have emerged, they have devoted considerable energy to staking out their professional boundaries. That activity is important because it identifies for each profession, the other professions, and the public the unique contribution made by each to meeting human needs. It also helps to focus their education and training programs, research activities, and the development of appropriate professional knowledge.

How a profession stakes out its professional boundaries has significant influence on that profession. The more elitist professions limit the people they claim as their target of service to those with narrowly defined problems, typically charging high fees to the few people who require that service. These professions usually require extensive and highly technical training and few people acquire the credentials to be recognized as part of that profession. This limited supply of professionals yields high prestige and financial reward for those who hold the proper qualifications. Other professions have been far more open in their membership requirements and more general in the type of issues for which they provide service. This lack of exclusiveness has at times been viewed as less professional and has resulted in lower prestige and less financial remuneration for the persons identified with these professions.

Two models of professionalism have developed in the United States. One is the *private model,* where the individual client contracts directly with the professional for service. Law and medicine are clear examples of professions that have followed this model. A second model, typified by teachers and city planners, is the *public model* in which the professionals primarily operate under the auspice of formal organizations and direct their services to the common good.

How, then, has social work emerged? Where does it fit among the helping professions?

Social Work as a Profession: A Historical Perspective

Social work did not evolve in a vacuum. A series of events affected its development and will continue to shape social work in the future. Some of those events are represented by major factors in the history of the United States such as settlement patterns, wars, international conditions, economic fluctuations, the philosophy of elected political leaders, and others. These events influenced decisions about the extent to which this society would respond to its members' social needs and, subsequently, to the social programs that would be supported.

Table 3-1 identifies some of the important events that affected the evolution of U.S. society's approach to the human services and shows selected mileposts in the development of social work. In columns 1 and 2 the table lists dates and events that identify a historical event that had a direct influence on a social program or social work such as the Civil War or the Great Depression. Column 3 identifies important historical events that shaped social programs (e.g., the Pierce Veto), and column 4 lists some critical events in the development of the social work profession—for example, publication of *Social Diagnosis* in 1917.

FROM VOLUNTEERS TO AN OCCUPATION (PRIOR TO 1915)

The roots of social work may be found in the extensive volunteer movement during the formative years of the United States. In the colonial period, for example, it was

TABLE 3-1 **Timetable of Selected Events in Social Welfare and Social Work History**

Approximate Date	U.S. History Event	Social Welfare Event	Social Work Event
Founding of United States	Agriculture-based society Open frontier	Family responsibility Mutual aid Puritan ethic Town meetings Orphan homes and first charitable societies First general hospital (Pennsylvania Hospital) Poorhouses First public mental hospital	
1776	Declaration of Independence Revolutionary War Act for the Gradual Abolition of Slavery (Pennsylvania)	Growth of voluntary social agencies based on special needs Society for Alleviating the Miseries of Public Prisons	
1789	George Washington inaugurated	Merchant philanthropists	
1800	United States prohibits importation of slaves War of 1812 Child labor laws Anti-Slavery Movement Treaty of Guadalupe–Hidalgo Chinese immigration began	Elizabeth Seton founds Sisters of Charity Mass. General Hospital Gallaudet School for Deaf Society for the Prevention of Pauperism NY House of Refuge (for juveniles)	Dorothea Dix begins crusade for improved conditions in "insane asylums"
1850	Emergence of industrial society Rise of cities and urbanization	Pierce Veto Children's Aid Societies Orphan Trains YMCA movement	
1863	Civil War	Freedman's aid societies Mass. Board of Charities Tenement (housing) reforms	U.S. Sanitary Commission (first paid social workers)
1877	Reconstruction Era Chinese Exclusion Act Dawes Act (Indian Land Allotment Act)	Buffalo Charity Aid Society	National Conference on Charities and Correction Friendly visitors
1889		Hull House	Settlement workers
1898	Japanese immigration began Spanish-American War Immigration peaks	First Juvenile Court	NY School of Philanthropy

TABLE 3-1	(Continued)		

Approximate Date	U.S. History Event	Social Welfare Event	Social Work Event
1910	World War I	White House Conference on Children	Introduction of medical social work
		U.S. Children's Bureau	Introduction of psychiatric social work
		Community Chest (federated fund raising)	Introduction of school social work
1915	Progressive Era	NAACP National Urban League	Flexner, "Is Social Work A Profession?" Richmond, *Social Diagnosis* National Social Workers Exchange Association of Training Schools for Prof. SW
1920	Women's Suffrage (19th Amendment)	County and state relief agencies Freudian influence Smith–Fess (Rehabilitation) Act	American Association of Social Workers Milford Conference
1930	Stock market crash The Great Depression "Great Migration" from Puerto Rico	American Public Welfare Association Indian Reorganization Act Federal Emergency Relief Act Civilian Conservation Corps (CCC)	American Association of Schools of Social Work
1935		Social Security Act Works Progress Administration (WPA)	American Association of Group Workers
1941	United States enters World War II Japanese relocation centers	U.S.O. organized National Social Welfare Assembly	National Association of Schools of Social Administration Association for the Study of Community Organization Social Work Research Group
	End of WW II Postwar recovery period		Council on Social Work Education (merger of AASSW and NASSA)
1949 1952 1955	Korean Conflict Civil Rights Movement Women's Movement	U.S. Department of Health, Education, and Welfare Indian Health Service Juvenile Delinquency Act	National Association of Social Workers (merger of six professional specialization groups and American Association of Social Workers)

(Continued)

| **TABLE 3-1** | Timetable of Selected Events in Social Welfare and Social Work History (Continued) |

Approximate Date	U.S. History Event	Social Welfare Event	Social Work Event
1960	Kennedy administration	Herrington, *The Other America* Equal Pay Act	Greenwood, "Attributes of a Profession" NASW "Working Definition of Social Work Practice"
1963	Kennedy assassination Johnson administration Vietnam War	Community Mental Health Act Food Stamp Act Civil Rights Act of 1964 Economic Opportunity Act Appalachian Regional Development Act	NASW "Code of Ethics"
	Black Power Movement		
1965		Older American Act	Academy of Certified Social Workers (ACSW)
	Watts, Chicago, Detroit race riots Welfare Rights Movement Martin Luther King, Jr. assassination	Indian Civil Rights Act Immigration Act of 1965 Medicare Act Medicaid Narcotic Addict Rehabilitation Act	
	Nixon administration	Supplemental Security Income (SSI) approved	NASW recognition of baccalaureate social worker as professional
1970	East LA police riots; Stonewall "Riot" and Gay Liberation Movement		
1972	*Roe v. Wade* decision	Child Abuse Prevention & Treatment Act	CSWE begins BSW accreditation process (generalist emphasis)
1974	Watergate and Nixon resignation		CSWE approves advanced standing for BSWs
	Ford administration		NASW "Conceptual Frameworks" series
1977		Education of All Handicapped Children Act	
	Carter administration	Indian Child Welfare Act	
1980		Privatization of human services expanded	
	Reagan administration	Social Security Block Grant Act (decentralize some programs to states)	Expansion of private practice
		AIDS Epidemic Tax Equity and Fiscal Responsibility Act of 1982 (cutbacks in human service provisions by federal government) Equal Rights Amendment (ratification fails)	Expansion of doctoral social work education (GADE)

TABLE 3-1	(Continued)		
Approximate Date	U.S. History Event	Social Welfare Event	Social Work Event
1988	Bush administration		Academy of Certified Baccalaureate Social Workers (ACBSW)
	Persian Gulf War	Americans with Disabilities Act Individuals with Disabilities Education Act	
1992	Clinton administration	Health care reform fails	Social workers licensed in all states, D.C., and some territories
	Los Angeles police riot (in the wake of the Rodney King verdict)		ACBSW terminated
	Republican "Contract for America"	Family and Medical Leave Act	
1996	Oklahoma City federal building bombing		
1999	Clinton impeachment Columbine High School gang massacre	Personal Responsibility and Work Opportunity Reconciliation Act	"Code of Ethics" revised

assumed that individuals and families would care for themselves, but if further difficulties existed, one could depend on *mutual aid*. Friends, neighbors, or other representatives of the community could be counted on to help out when needed. Volunteer activities involved interaction with the poor, the ill, and those experiencing other social problems. As social agencies began to develop, they soon learned how to train volunteers in constructive ways to relate to clients and improved their ability to be helpful.

Developing out of this background came social work as an *occupation*. The first paid social work-type positions in the country were jobs in the Special Relief Department of the United States Sanitary Commission. Beginning as a voluntary agency and then receiving public support as the Civil War progressed, the Special Relief Department and its agents served Union soldiers and their families experiencing social and health problems due to the war. Wartime needs temporarily opened the door to providing social services, and the outstanding performance of these workers helped pave the way for other positions in social work. Several women involved in the war effort performed important leadership roles in the development of human services. For example, Dorothea Dix (Superintendent of Nurses in the U.S. Sanitary Commission) previously had provided leadership in an attempt to secure federal government support for mental hospitals; Clara Barton later founded the American Red Cross; Josephine Shaw Lowell helped start the Charity Organization Society in New York City and also headed the Consumers' League, which worked to protect shopgirls from exploitation; Sojourner Truth gave leadership to the National Freedman's Relief Association; and Harriet Tubman, a central figure in the Underground Railroad, subsequently established a home for elderly African Americans. Following the war the Special Relief Department was closed.

Social work also appeared when the Massachusetts Board of Charities was established in 1863. Founded under the leadership of Samuel Gridley Howe, an advocate for the physically and mentally disabled, this agency coordinated services in almshouses, hospitals, and other institutions of the state. Although its powers were limited to inspection and advice, the Board gained wide acceptance under the leadership of Howe and its paid director, Frank B. Sanborn. The concept of boards overseeing state services spread to other states in the 1870s and became the forerunners to today's state departments of social services and institutions.

The Massachusetts Board of Charities also introduced social research into human service delivery. An 1893 report, for example, identified the causes of poverty as "first, physical degradation and inferiority; second, moral perversity; third, mental incapacity; fourth, accidents and infirmities; fifth, unjust and unwise laws, and the customs of society."[5] Although the approach was perhaps more moralistic than would be found in social work today, the report reflected the understanding that both personal and societal factors contribute to poverty.

Another significant development leading to the emergence of social work was the establishment of the Charity Organization Society (COS) of Buffalo, New York, in 1877. Modeled after an organization in London, charity organization societies sprang up in a number of communities with the dual purposes of finding means to help the poor and preventing the poor from taking advantage of the numerous uncoordinated social agencies that provided financial assistance. Leaders in social work from the COS movement included Mary Richmond, who helped identify a theory of practice in her books *Friendly Visiting Among the Poor* (1899) and *Social Diagnosis* (1917); Edward T. Devine, a founder of the New York School of Philanthropy in 1898 and its first director; and Porter Lee, who was instrumental in founding the American Association of Schools of Social Work in 1919.

Another important development that contributed to the emergence of social work was the Settlement House Movement initiated in 1886. Patterning settlement houses after London's Toynbee Hall, settlements were established in New York and Chicago. Within fifteen years, about one hundred settlement houses were operating in the United States. The settlements helped the poor learn skills required for urban living and simultaneously provided leadership in political action efforts to improve the social environment. Bremner sums up the impact of the settlement movement:

Where others thought of the people of the slums as miserable wretches deserving either pity or correction, settlement residents knew them as much entitled to respect as any other members of the community. Numerous young men and women who lived and worked in the settlements during the 1890s carried this attitude with them into later careers in social work, business, government service, and the arts.[6]

The residents of Chicago's Hull House are a good example. Its founder, Jane Addams, won the Nobel Peace Prize in 1931; Julia Lathrop became the first director of the U.S. Children's Bureau and was succeeded by other Hull House alumnae Katherine Lenroot and Grace Abbott, thus contributing to the protection of children and youth for several decades.

The efforts to integrate the African American population into the mainstream of U.S. society following the Civil War also contributed to the development of social work. George Haynes, the first African American graduate of the New York School of Philanthropy, for example, helped found the National Urban League, while Mary McLeod Bethune, who gave leadership to the education of African American women, was a founder of the National Council of Negro Women and was influential in making New Deal policies more equitable for the African American population.

Social work expanded into another setting in the early 1900s when Richard Cabot and Ida Cannon opened a social work program at the Massachusetts General Hospital. These social workers provided services for patients experiencing health-related social problems and also worked to strengthen the services of related health and welfare agencies throughout the community. Lubove identifies the significance of this development for the professionalization of social work:

> The enlistment of medical social workers marked an important stage in the development of professional social work. A casework limited to the charity organization and child welfare societies provided too narrow a base for professional development, associated as it was with problems of relief and economic dependency. Medical social work added an entirely new institutional setting in which to explore the implications of casework theory and practice.[7]

Medical social workers became interested in professional education as a means of moving beyond social work's "warm heart" image and into a more disciplined understanding of the psychic or social conditions as the base of patient distress. In 1912, with Ida Cannon's participation, a one-year training program in medical social work was established in the Boston School of Social Work.

Through these years, social work jobs were also springing up in other practice areas such as mental hygiene (mental health), prisons, employment and labor relations, and schools. Beginning in 1873 an organization designed to draw together members of this diverse occupation was formed, the National Conference on Charities. Later renamed the National Conference on Charities and Correction, this organization brought volunteer and professional staff members of social agencies together to exchange ideas about the provision of services, discuss social problems, and study the characteristics of effective practice. By the time World War I began social work was an established occupation distinguishable from the many volunteer groups and other occupations concerned with the well-being of the most vulnerable members of U.S. society.

PROFESSIONAL EMERGENCE (1915–1950)

With social work firmly established as an occupation, attention then turned to its development as a profession. At the 1915 meeting of the National Conference on Charities and Correction, Abraham Flexner addressed the subject, "Is Social Work a Profession?" Dr. Flexner, an authority on graduate education, had previously done a penetrating study that led to major changes in medical education. The organizers of this session of the National Conference apparently hoped Flexner would assure them that social work was, or was about to become, a full-fledged profession. However, that was not in the cards. Flexner, using an "absolute approach" to his study of professions, spelled out six criteria that an occupation must fully meet to be considered a profession:

1. Professions are essentially intellectual operations with large individual responsibility.
2. They derive their raw material from science and learning.
3. This material is worked up to a practical and clear-cut end.
4. Professions possess an educationally communicable technique.
5. They tend to self-organization.
6. They become increasingly altruistic in motivation.[8]

Based on these criteria Flexner concluded that social work had not yet made it into the professional elite. Following Flexner's admonition to "go forth and build thyself a profession," social workers busily attended to these functions over the next thirty-five years.

One effort was to develop a code of ethics. In 1921 Mary Richmond indicated that, "we need a code; something to abide by, or else we will have low social standing."[9] One code, the "Experimental Draft of a Code of Ethics for Social Case Workers," was discussed at the 1923 meeting of the National Conference on Social Welfare. Although this proposed code was never acted on, it represented a beginning effort at formulating a statement of professional ethics.

Probably the greatest amount of effort was devoted to self-organization. The National Social Workers Exchange was opened in 1917 to provide vocational counseling and placement and later became actively involved in the identification and definition of professional standards. In 1921 its functions were taken over by the broader American Association of Social Workers, which made significant efforts to develop a comprehensive professional association. This effort was later weakened by attempts of some specialties to develop their own professional organizations. A chronology of the development of these specialized groups follows:[10]

- 1918 American Association of Hospital Social Workers
- 1919 National Association of Visiting Teachers
- 1926 American Association of Psychiatric Social Workers

- 1936 American Association for the Study of Group Work

- 1946 Association for the Study of Community Organization

- 1949 Social Work Research Group

It was not clear whether social work was one or many professions.

Another development during this period concerned the required preparation to enter the social work profession. Social work education had begun as agency-based training, but a concerted effort was made during this period to transfer it to colleges and universities, where other professions had located their professional education. In 1919 the Association of Training Schools for Professional Social Workers was established with seventeen charter members—both agency and university affiliated schools. The purpose of that organization was to develop standards for all social work education. By 1927 considerable progress toward that purpose had been made, and the Association of Training Schools reorganized into the American Association of Schools of Social Work (AASSW). Although education programs had been offered in agencies, as well as at both undergraduate and graduate levels in colleges and universities, the AASSW determined that by 1939 only university affiliated programs with two-year graduate programs would be recognized as professional social work education.

That action led to a revolt by schools whose undergraduate programs prepared professionals to meet the staffing needs of the social agencies in their states. A second professional education organization was formed in 1942, the National Association of Schools of Social Administration, made up largely of public universities in the midwest that offered baccalaureate- and one-year graduate-level professional education programs. Harper described this development as "a protest movement against unrealistic and premature insistence upon graduate training and overemphasis upon professional casework as the major social work technique."[11]

With leadership from governmental and voluntary practice agencies, the two organizations were later merged (1952) into the Council on Social Work Education (CSWE) following the landmark Hollis–Taylor study of social work education.[12] The outcome of that decision favored the two-year master's program as the minimum educational requirement for full professional status. Undergraduate social work education temporarily faded from the scene.

Another important area of concern that was given only limited attention during this period was strengthening the knowledge and skill base of social work practice. Richmond's rich contribution, *Social Diagnosis,* was the first effort to formalize a communicable body of techniques applicable to the diverse settings in which social caseworkers were found.[13]

Momentum from this thrust, however, was lost as social work slipped into the grasp of the popular psychoanalytic approach. Cohen comments, "The search for a method occurred just at the time the impact of psychoanalysis was being felt. Did social work, in its haste for professional stature, reach out for a ready-made methodology for treating sick people, thus closing itself off from the influence of developments in the other sciences?"[14] This question must be answered in the affirmative. By adopting the helping methodology that was currently in vogue, social work embraced firmly, but perhaps inappropriately, the private model of professionalism. Writing in *Harper's Monthly* in 1957, Sanders accurately criticized social work for "floating with the ghost of Freud."[15] One might speculate about what would have happened if the model adopted had been the one for public education or public health.

CONSOLIDATING THE GAINS (1950–1970)

The move to consolidate the accrediting bodies for the schools of social work into the CSWE set an important precedent for the field and was part of a broad movement to treat social work as a single and unified profession. In 1950 the several specialized associations and the American Association of Social Workers agreed to form the Temporary Inter-Association Council of Social Work Membership Organizations (TIAC). The purpose behind the formation of TIAC was to bring these specialized groups into one central professional association. After considerable efforts by the specialties to maintain their identities, TIAC proposed a merger of the several groups in 1952. By 1955 this was accomplished, and the National Association of Social Workers (NASW) was formed.

NASW membership rose from 28,000 to 45,000 between 1961 and 1965, largely because of the formation of the Academy of Certified Social Workers (ACSW), which required both NASW membership and a two-year period of supervised experience. Many job descriptions were revised to require membership in the Academy, forcing social workers to join the NASW and obtain certification.

The late 1950s were a time of great introspection, and the professional journal, *Social Work,* was filled with articles such as "The Nature of Social Work,"[16] "How Social Will Social Work Be?"[17] and "A Changing Profession in a Changing World."[18] Perhaps the most significant work was Ernest Greenwood's classic article, "Attributes of a Profession," in 1957.[19] Greenwood, using the "relative approach" to the study of professions, identified five critical attributes of professions that, depending on the degree to which they have been accomplished, determine the degree of professionalism for any occupational group:

1. A systematic body of theory
2. Professional authority
3. Sanction of the community
4. A regulative code of ethics
5. A professional culture

He related the development of social work to each of these five criteria and concluded that social work was a profession. He observed:

> When we hold up social work against the model of the professions presented above, it does not take long to decide whether to classify it within the professional or nonprofessional occupations. Social work is already a profession; it has too many points of congruence with the model to be classifiable otherwise.[20]

To the credit of social workers, they were as stimulated by Greenwood's declaration that they had become a profession as they were by Flexner's conclusion that they were not yet in the select circle. In 1958 the NASW published the "Working Definition of Social Work Practice," a valuable beginning to the difficult task of identifying professional boundaries.[21] This was followed by Gordon's excellent critique, which helped strengthen and clarify some parts of the working definition, particularly in relation to knowledge, values, and practice methodology.[22] In 1960 the NASW adopted a Code of Ethics to serve as a guide for ethical professional practice,[23] thus completing the steps to become a fully recognized profession.

At what price has professional status been attained? Sanders pointedly noted that social work had become a profession but had lost a mission. She indicated that social work had avoided controversial issues to keep its image clean, had become rigid in efforts to control service provision, and had developed jargon to maintain exclusiveness.[24]

TURNING AWAY FROM THE ELITIST PROFESSIONAL MODEL (1970–PRESENT)

From the turn of the twentieth century to the late 1960s, social work displayed a pattern typical of an emerging profession. It created a single association to guide professional growth and development; adopted a code of ethical professional behavior; provided for graduate-level university-based professional schools and acquired recognition to accredit those educational programs; successfully obtained licensing for social work practice in some states; conducted public education campaigns to interpret social work to the public; achieved recognition for social work among the helping professions; and moved in the direction of other professions by increasing specialization and limiting access to the profession. Indeed, social work was on its way to carving its niche among the elite group of helping professions.

However, social work did not vigorously pursue the path that would lead to even greater professional status. Perhaps influenced by a renewed spirit of concern emanating from the Civil Rights, Welfare Rights, and Women's Rights movements, the development of social work as a profession during the 1970s and 1980s was marked by ambivalence over following the more traditional format of the established professions.

First, there was a resurgence of social change activity on the part of social workers. A legacy from Lyndon Johnson's Great Society programs was federal support, in the form of jobs and other resources, toward efforts to eliminate social problems and alleviate human suffering. Social work was already committed to those goals, and social workers were prepared to move away from their clinical orientation and onto the front lines of social action.

For social workers bent on achieving higher professional status, activist social workers were sometimes unpopular. Their somewhat controversial activities at times created an unwelcome public image of a profession characterized by activists on the front lines of social change. This change in the balance of activities performed by social workers, however, helped to bring social work back to its roots and reestablish the "change" orientation in its purposes of caring, curing, and changing the society. The more liberal political climate that supported social work activism was short-lived. Federal support for programs encouraging social change dwindled and was nearly nonexistent under the Reagan and Bush administrations.

Next, in 1970 NASW made a dramatic move by revising its membership requirements to give full membership privileges to anyone who had completed a baccalaureate degree in social work from an undergraduate program approved by CSWE. In opposition to the pattern of professions becoming more exclusive, social work opened its membership to more people, and a generalist approach to practice was embraced. Beginning in 1970, professional qualifications could be gained by obtaining professional education at the undergraduate level. However, social work has been uneasy about operating as a multilevel profession, and, although the NASW classification system is clear about the "basic social worker" being viewed as professional, the social worker at this level has never been fully accepted by many MSW social workers. Some advocates for the baccalaureate social worker contend that NASW has not devoted sufficient attention to this practice level and that its program priorities in the 1980s "centered too much on licensing, vendor payments, private practice and other issues that were not sufficiently relevant to the baccalaureate worker."[25] NASW's creation of the Academy of Certified Baccalaureate Social Workers in the early 1990s represented movement away from that overemphasis on the interests of master's-level social workers, but the discontinuance of that certification in 1996 was a retreat from that position.

With NASW's formal recognition of baccalaureate social work as fully professional, in 1974 the Council on Social Work Education began accrediting baccalaureate social work education (BSW) programs. Initially, 135 schools met the undergraduate accreditation requirements, and by 1999 that number had increased to 415 schools in the United States and Puerto Rico with another 31 schools in candidacy for accreditation.[26] Of particular importance was the accessibility of these programs to persons wishing to become social workers. Whereas most MSW programs were located in urban areas, undergraduate programs were located in both urban and rural communities. A study of BSW practitioners in 1989 found that 43.9 percent of the "basic social workers" worked in communities of 40,000 or fewer (as compared to approximately 22% of the U.S. population), and 16.7 percent were employed in communities of 10,000 or fewer.[27] These data suggest that the professionalization of baccalaureate social work opened educational opportunities to people who could not attend schools in urban areas and who have enriched the provision of services in smaller communities by filling human service jobs in these areas.

Similarly, the emergence of professionally sanctioned baccalaureate-level social work education increased the opportunity for members from minority and lower socioeconomic backgrounds to enter social work, as they could complete the requisite education preparation without needing both baccalaureate and master's degrees. To illustrate, in 1998, 33.6 percent of the 35,816 full-time baccalaureate majors were of minority background, as compared to 25.5 percent of the 20,409 full-time MSW students.[28]

The return of a conservative political climate in the United States during the 1980s created a perception that few jobs would be available in social work when the Reagan Administration completed its objective of dismantling the Great Society programs. When it became evident that such mass destruction of human service programs was not going to occur, interest in careers in social work revived and social work education programs experienced a resurgence of student interest. After peaking at nearly 28,000 undergraduate social work majors in the late 1970s, that number declined by more than one-fourth in 1983, returned to the 28,000 level in 1990, and increased to nearly 36,000 in 1998. For the MSW programs a similar pattern occurred. Full-time enrollment declined by one-fifth between 1978 and 1983, but increased to nearly 20,500 in 1998.[29]

Concluding Comment	In the past century, social work has developed in a manner that meets the generally accepted criteria for professions. Consensus about its unique purpose among the professions has been reached, and social work has achieved sanction as the appropriate profession to help people resolve problems in their interaction with their environments. Social workers have been granted the professional authority to provide the necessary helping services for people in need, although they are constrained by the fact that most are employed in social agencies that sometimes limit their professional autonomy. Increasingly, they are entering private practice where the constraints are less severe.

Social work has taken its authority to provide these professional services seriously. Its national professional organization, the National Association of Social Workers, has worked through the decades to clarify social work's knowledge, value, and skill base. Social work has developed educational programs that prepare new people to enter this profession and has established a process for accrediting the programs that meet qualitative educational standards at both the baccalaureate and master's levels. Accredited programs exist in more than 442 colleges and universities and enroll approximately 74,000 full- and part-time students each year.[30]

Social work has also adopted a comprehensive Code of Ethics and has established procedures for dealing with social workers who might violate that code. A process has been established through the National Association of Social Workers that allows the profession to carry out its professional responsibility to protect clients and the general public from abuses that might arise from the monopoly it has achieved.

One might expect social workers to feel satisfied with these accomplishments. Yet, within this profession of many faces, there are inevitably varied opinions. While most social workers believe the progress made in becoming a recognized profession is desirable, some believe that it has become too elitist and is targeting its services too much to the white middle class. Others believe that it has lowered professional standards by opening its membership to those with less than graduate-level credentials. Some believe it should become more entrepreneurial like the private professions, and still others believe it should more fully embrace the agency-based model of the public professions where the most vulnerable members of the society are likely to be served. Some also believe that social work's unique role in interprofessional practice should be that of the case manager who orchestrates or coordinates the client services provided by several disciplines, while others view social work's role as providing more specialized social treatment services on a parallel with the other helping professions as they respond to clients' physical, emotional, spiritual, and intellectual needs. These issues must continue to be on social work's agenda.

KEY WORDS AND CONCEPTS

Profession	State boards of charities
Relative vs. absolute professions	Charity organization societies
Professional autonomy	Settlement houses
Professional authority	*Social Diagnosis*
Professional responsibility	Council on Social Work Education
Public vs. private professions	National Association of Social Workers
U.S. Sanitary Commission	

SUGGESTED READINGS

Brieland, Donald. "History and Evolution of Social Work Practice," in Anne Minahan, ed., *Encyclopedia of Social Work,* 18th Edition. Silver Spring, MD: National Association of Social Workers, 1987, pp. 739–754.

Greenwood, Ernest. "Attributes of a Profession," *Social Work* 2 (July 1957): 45–55.

Howe, Elizabeth. "Public Professions and the Private Model of Professionalism," *Social Work* 25 (May 1980): 179–191.

Leigninger, Leslie. *Social Work: Search for Identity.* Westport, CT: Greenwood, 1987.

Lowe, Gary R. "Social Work's Professional Mistake: Confusing Status for Control and Losing Both," *Journal of Sociology and Social Welfare* 14 (June 1987): 187–206.

Lubove, Roy. *The Professional Altruist.* Cambridge, MA: Harvard University Press, 1989.

Trolander, Judith Ann. *Professionalism and Social Change: From the Settlement House to Neighborhood Centers, 1886 to the Present.* New York: Columbia University Press, 1987.

ENDNOTES

1. Wilbert E. Moore, *The Professions: Roles and Rules* (New York: Russell Sage Foundation, 1970), p. 3.
2. Ibid., pp. 5–6.
3. Everett C. Hughes, "Professions," *Daedalus* (Fall 1963): 657.
4. Naomi I. Brill, *Working with People: The Helping Process,* 3rd Edition (New York: Longman, 1985), pp. 24–28.
5. Cited in Ralph E. Pumphrey and Muriel W. Pumphrey, eds., *The Heritage of American Social Work* (New York: Columbia University Press, 1961), p. 12.
6. Robert H. Bremner, *From the Depths* (New York: New York University Press, 1956), p. 66.
7. Roy Lubove, *The Professional Altruist* (Cambridge, MA: Harvard University Press, 1965), p. 32.
8. Abraham Flexner, "Is Social Work a Profession?" in *Proceedings of the National Conference on Charities and Correction, 1915* (Chicago: National Conference on Charities and Correction, 1916): 576–590.
9. Pumphrey and Pumphrey, *Heritage,* p. 310.
10. John C. Kidneigh, "History of American Social Work," in Harry L. Lurie, ed., *Encyclopedia of Social Work,* 15th Edition (New York: National Association of Social Workers, 1965), pp. 13–14.

11. Herbert Bisno, "The Place of Undergraduate Curriculum in Social Work Education," in Werner W. Boehm, ed., *A Report of the Curriculum Study* Vol. II (New York: Council on Social Work Education, 1959), p. 8.

12. Ernest V. Hollis and Alice L. Taylor, *Social Work Education in the United States* (New York: Columbia University Press, 1951).

13. Mary E. Richmond, *Social Diagnosis* (New York: Russell Sage Foundation, 1917).

14. Nathan E. Cohen, *Social Work in the American Tradition* (New York: Holt, Rinehart, & Winston, 1958), pp. 120–121.

15. Marion K. Sanders, "Social Work: A Profession Chasing Its Tail," *Harper's Monthly* 214 (March 1957): 56–62.

16. Werner W. Boehm, "The Nature of Social Work," *Social Work* 3 (April 1958): 10–18.

17. Herbert Bisno, "How Social Will Social Work Be?" *Social Work* 1 (April 1956): 12–18.

18. Nathan E. Cohen, "A Changing Profession in a Changing World," *Social Work* 1 (October 1956): 12–19.

19. Ernest Greenwood, "Attributes of a Profession," *Social Work* 2 (July 1957): 45–55.

20. Ibid., p. 54.

21. Harriet M. Bartlett, "Towards Clarification and Improvement of Social Work Practice," *Social Work* 3 (April 1958): 5–7.

22. William E. Gordon, "Critique of the Working Definition," *Social Work* 7 (October 1962): 3–13; and "Knowledge and Values: Their Distinction and Relationship in Clarifying Social Work Practice," *Social Work* 10 (July 1965): 32–39.

23. National Association of Social Workers, *Code of Ethics* (Washington, D.C.: The Association, 1960).

24. Sanders, pp. 56–62.

25. Bradford W. Sheafor and Barbara W. Shank, *Undergraduate Social Work Education: A Survivor in a Changing Profession* (Austin: University of Texas School of Social Work, 1986), Social Work Education Monograph Series 3, p. 25.

26. Nancy Randolph, "Report of the Division of Accreditation," *The Social Work Education Reporter* (Spring 1999): 22.

27. Robert J. Teare and Bradford W. Sheafor, *Practice-Sensitive Social Work Education: An Empirical Analysis of Social Work Practice and Practitioners* (Alexandria, VA: Council on Social Work Education, 1995), p. 35.

28. Todd N. Lennon, ed., *Statistics on Social Work Education in the United States, 1998* (Alexandria, VA: Council on Social Work Education, 1999), pp. 44–45.

29. Ibid.

30. Ibid.

PART

TWO

Social Work
Career Options

In Part One we identified two characteristics of Western societies. One is the tendency to create programs to meet the basic social needs of its citizens. The second is the tendency to create professions to deliver those programs to the people in need. Within that framework social work has emerged during the past century as a central feature of U.S. society. Its emergence has been uneven and confusing because, in fact, social work is an umbrella profession that includes many and varied practice activities.

For the person entering social work, the vagueness about social work's focus is offset by the flexibility it permits. Compared to the schoolteacher, for example, who has relatively few career options within the education profession, the social worker has many choices. One can practice as a professional social worker at the baccalaureate, master's, or doctoral level. A social worker's potential fields of practice include working with older people, addressing physical or mental health problems, practicing in schools or the correctional system, or even being part of the staff of a major corporation. Although increasingly social workers independently open an office and engage in their own private practice, most are employed by some form of human service organization ranging, for example, from public welfare agencies to safehouses for battered women.

Each social worker must make certain decisions that will affect his or her career path in social work. One important decision concerns one's level

of educational preparation. Chapter 4 summarizes a considerable amount of data about social workers at different educational levels and highlights the employment opportunities at each. In essence, the baccalaureate-level social worker works in direct services with clients and is most likely to serve either children and youth or older people. The master's-level social worker, in contrast, has much more job flexibility. Many hold administrative and supervisory positions, and those in direct service positions are most likely to address medical, mental health, and school-related issues with the breadwinning adult population, their most frequent clients. Some doctoral-level social workers can be found scattered throughout advanced administrative and direct practice jobs, but the majority are concentrated in teaching positions.

A second decision concerns the practice area one chooses to enter. Chapter 5 surveys thirteen unique fields in which social workers apply their trade. The potential practice areas from which a social worker might select vary from social work with children to social work in business and industry, from corrections to mental health, and from hospitals to residential treatment centers. Despite the differences in these fields of practice, a basic pattern emerges of the social workers helping people interact more effectively with the world around them.

Finally, a social worker must decide if he or she is to work in a human service organization or engage in private practice. Chapter 6 examines those public and private human service agencies where most social workers are employed. Factors affecting agency structure and functioning are discussed, with special attention given to the inherent conflicts that exist between the professional practice model and the bureaucratic model of organization usually found in social agencies. In addition, this chapter addresses the fact that some social workers have adopted an entrepreneurial approach to their work and have opted for private practice. Private practice presents a different set of problems than are experienced by those social workers employed in human service organizations.

By understanding the various career options in social work and the issues surrounding each, the prospective social worker can make informed decisions about important career choices. There are fundamental values and competencies, as Part Three will identify, that are transferable among the various expressions of social work. Thus, the social worker has considerable job mobility and any career choice can be altered.

CHAPTER 4

Entry to the Social Work Profession

Prefatory Comment

Selecting a career is one of the most important decisions a person must make. Whether that decision is to become a homemaker, physician, salesperson, teacher, chemist, or social worker, it should be based on a thorough understanding of the physical, emotional, and intellectual demands of the field and a close look at one's own suitability for that type of work. Whatever the choice, it will dictate how a person spends a major part of each day. It will also spill over into other aspects of life, including lifestyle, general satisfaction with self, and quality of life.

The decision to enter a particular profession does not lock a person into that occupation for a lifetime, but it does represent a substantial commitment of time, energy, and resources to prepare for professional practice and obtain the requisite credentials. After entering a profession, a person's job consumes a major part of his or her daily activity, and, if that was a good career choice, one's job can be an exhilarating and stimulating experience. However, if there is a poor fit between a person and their chosen occupation, work can be frustrating and unrewarding. If the career choice is one of the professions, the work will not typically result in an 8:00 AM to 5:00 PM job that is left at the office when the workday ends. Rather, the calling to the profession requires a commitment to clients and concern about their welfare that cannot readily be turned off when one goes home. Further, the complexity of human situations requiring professional assistance and the growing knowledge about effective helping obligates the professional to a career of continued learning and skill development. Unless a person is willing to make such a commitment, a professional career should not be pursued.

For the person considering the social work profession, it is useful to have a clear perception of the career opportunities this profession affords. Social work has evolved a four-level career ladder that has two entry points (i.e., the basic and specialized social worker) and two additional levels based on more advanced experience and education. Determining one's niche in social work requires careful investigation. This chapter describes the educational preparation and practice experience required for each practice level and identifies factors that shaped the evolution of social work practice at those levels.

Making a career choice is difficult because of the wide range of careers to choose from but, more importantly, because of the problems an outsider experiences in gaining an adequate and accurate understanding of a career. Too often, only after a person has made substantial commitments in time, energy, and money or has cut off other opportunities by taking steps to enter a career does he or she find that it is not what was expected or wanted. Another difficulty lies in having a clear perception of one's own needs, interests, and abilities. Personal introspection, occupational preference testing, guidance counseling, and experience in activities related to the career are all resources for making this choice.

The person contemplating a career in social work must consider a number of factors.[1] It is evident that social work is extremely broad in scope—ranging from social action to individual therapy—and is constantly changing, with a knowledge base that is far from stable or well developed. Thus, explicit guidelines for social work practice do not exist, leaving the social worker with the responsibility for exercising a great deal of individual judgment. Furthermore, the skills demanded of the social worker vary widely and require a flexible, creative, and introspective person to practice them. The pressures of a social work job create a degree of stress because the outcome of the work is critically important to the clients. In addition, social workers are regularly criticized by both clients and the general public, frequently in regard to programs social workers administer but over which they have little policy-making influence.

If a person can tolerate the ambiguity, responsibility, pressures, and criticism that are a part of social work; if the values, skills, and interests required of social workers are compatible; and if it is rewarding to work constructively to help people improve their level of social functioning, social work offers a rich and satisfying career. Before selecting social work as a career, one needs a general knowledge of this profession. In addition, volunteer experience, summer or part-time jobs in social agencies, and personal interaction with social workers may also help to determine one's suitability for a career in social work. The information contained in this chapter provides an orientation to a social work career.

Issues in Social Work Preparation and Employment

Membership in any profession requires that the persons aspiring to enter it acquire the specified qualifications. The very act of defining professional membership is inherently elitist in that whenever qualifications are established, some persons who operate with similar knowledge and values but lack the identified qualifications will be excluded. In social work, for example, completion of the education and practice experience specified by the National Association of Social Workers (NASW) in its membership qualifications is necessary to gain professional recognition. However, social workers are cognizant that many other helping people with different educations and experiences make important contributions to the delivery of human services. For the person entering social work, or considering becoming a member of this profession, it is important to be aware of several issues that relate to professional qualifications.

EDUCATION AND ACCREDITATION

The social work profession contends that a person must have a formal social work education; that is, either a baccalaureate degree with a major in social work or a master's degree in social work (MSW) from an accredited social work education program, as a minimum for professional recognition. The *accreditation* process is administered by the Council on Social Work Education (CSWE) and has become a significant factor in social work because the graduate of the accredited program is assumed to be prepared to enter practice as a beginning-level professional social worker—ready to apply the appropriate knowledge, values, and skills in the service of clients. For all practical purposes, education is the primary gatekeeper of the profession. This does not mean that all graduates are equally prepared to enter practice, that some people who do not have all the required social work courses are unable to perform many tasks of the social worker, or even that all schools offer the same opportunity for learning the essentials of social work. Rather, accreditation attests to the fact that the public can have confidence that graduates are at least minimally prepared for beginning-level social work practice because they have completed an instructional program that is soundly designed and taught by competent faculty.

PROFESSIONAL CERTIFICATION

The National Association of Social Workers provides confirmation to clientele and employing human services agencies that some social workers have demonstrated the requisite knowledge and competence to engage in practice, that is, *professional certification*. Where accreditation is testimony to the quality of an educational program, certification is the profession's testimony regarding the individual's knowledge, values, and skills.

In 1960 NASW initiated its first professional certification by creating the Academy of Certified Social Workers (ACSW). This credential was intended to recognize the "independent" social worker who had completed an MSW degree from an accredited college or university, had practiced a minimum of two years under the supervision of an ACSW social worker, had earned a satisfactory score on a national examination, and had received favorable evaluation of practice competence by peers. Today, the ACSW is a required credential for many social work jobs and 60,000 social workers are members of the Academy.[2]

In 1990 NASW created a similar credential for the baccalaureate-level social worker, the Academy of Certified Baccalaureate Social Workers (ACBSW). However, few agencies required the ACBSW as a job credential, and thus relatively few workers sought this professional credential. As a result, the ACBSW was discontinued in 1996.

Three other professional certifications created by NASW, however, have succeeded: the Qualified Clinical Social Worker (QCSW), Diplomate in Clinical Social Work, and the School Social Work Specialist. Each requires graduation from an accredited master's program in social work, adherence to NASW's Code of Ethics, and two or more years of post-master's practice experience. The Diplomate further requires an additional three years of full-time clinical social work experience. The two clinical certifications are designed to interface with the ACSW and/or state licensing requirements. These credentials are designed to serve as indicators of competence for specialized positions in schools and social agencies or as evidence to clients and insurance companies that offer reimbursement for social workers' services that these workers have the profession's stamp of approval.

LICENSING OR STATE REGULATION OF SOCIAL WORK PRACTICE

The social work profession, through the Council on Social Work Education, has shaped its educational programs through accreditation requirements and, through NASW, has sought to identify its competent and experienced practitioners by creating its certification programs. However, over the past two decades perhaps the most dominant issue on NASW's agenda has been to encourage the licensing of social workers throughout the United States.

As described by the American Association of State Social Work Boards, *licensing* is:

> . . . a process by which an agency of state government or other jurisdiction acting upon legislative mandate grants permission to individuals to engage in the practice of a particular profession or vocation and prohibits all others from legally doing so. By ensuring a level of safe practice, the licensure process protects the general public. Those who are licensed are permitted by the state to use a specific title and perform activities because they have demonstrated to the state's satisfaction that they have reached an acceptable level of practice.[3]

The intent of licensing is to have neutral sources, that is, state governments, identify those social workers who are properly prepared through professional education and experience to provide client services. Both consumers of service (particularly in private practice settings) and health insurance companies that reimburse for the cost of social work services have looked to licensing as a desirable way to determine a social worker's practice competence. In order to attract clients and to be eligible for payments from insurance companies, social workers have embraced state licensing for social work. All fifty states, the District of Columbia, Puerto Rico, and the Virgin Islands license (or certify) social workers. Thirty-four offer specialized forms of certification to experienced MSWs and thirty-three recognize the basic social worker.[4] Where professional certification is national in scope, licensing is conducted on a state-by-state basis with each state having somewhat unique standards and requirements. Because of these differences, a license from one state may not be accepted by another.

PROFESSIONAL STANDARDS

A profession is required by society to protect the public from those members who abuse the professional monopoly. To conduct this self-policing, every profession must establish standards and develop procedures for evaluating complaints and imposing negative sanctions if a member engages in incompetent or unethical practice. State licensing, too, performs this client protection function by withdrawing the legal right to practice as a social worker if such violations occur.

NASW has been granted authority by the social work profession to establish appropriate standards of conduct and maintain a process to ensure the public that recognized professional social workers meet those standards. The standards for social workers are embodied in NASW's *Code of Ethics*. The Code spells out in some detail the social worker's ethical responsibilities to clients, colleagues, practice settings, other professionals, the profession of social work, and the broader society.[5] When a social worker becomes a member of NASW, he or she must profess willingness to practice within the guidelines prescribed by the Code of Ethics, and the Code, in turn, becomes the baseline for evaluating the professional behavior of social workers.

Because social work is primarily an agency-based profession, NASW has also established standards for appropriate personnel practices in agencies that employ social workers. These guidelines describe personnel standards and practices that uphold the fair treatment of social workers in the hiring process, assure necessary working conditions for social work practice, and identify proper procedures for the termination of a social worker's employment.[6] These standards serve as the basis for judging the validity of claims by social workers that they have been wrongfully treated by their employers.

The process established for complaints begins with the local chapter of NASW. An individual or organization may lodge a formal complaint about the practice of a social worker or the personnel practices of an agency. A committee of the chapter will then conduct an investigation of the complaint and make a determination that the complaint is or is not substantiated. Either party has the right to appeal to the NASW National Committee on Inquiry, which reviews the charges and makes a final judgment. If the Committee on Inquiry concludes that standards have been violated, a plan to correct the behavior through training or treatment may be developed or the individual's membership in NASW may be suspended. Action taken against either an individual or agency is published in the *NASW News*. The sanctions remain in effect until the terms established by the Committee on Inquiry are satisfied.

Options for Human Service Practice

Addressing complex human needs requires a range of service providers equipped with a variety of knowledge and skills. The human services, therefore, are made up of many people—from volunteers to members of related disciplines—who provide many different forms of helping. The person considering a career in a helping profession should carefully compare social work with other human service providers to determine if serving as a social worker would be the most satisfying way to spend one's work life.

VOLUNTEERS

One cannot fully examine the human services without recognizing the important role played by volunteers. For many people who have other vocations, one way to be involved with human services is to volunteer. The willingness to give of oneself, without monetary reward, in order to help others is characteristic of human societies and is expressed in the activity of millions of people who give their time, energy, and talents to make this a better world. It was from efforts to prepare volunteers to provide more effective human services that social work became a paid occupation and, later, a significant helping profession.

Today, social workers work closely with volunteers in many agencies. Their jobs often include the recruitment, selection, training, and supervision of volunteers. Although most commonly found in youth-serving agencies, such as scouting organizations or the YMCA, volunteers also serve on the boards of, or in a direct working capacity in, every human service agency imaginable—from nursing homes to crisis hotlines to mental hospitals.

The qualifications of volunteers vary from activity to activity. At times professionals volunteer their services beyond their jobs in their own agencies or to help in other agencies. These volunteer activities may use their professional abilities but may also require skills unrelated to professional training. Like any other good citizen, the social worker has an obligation to donate his or her talents in order to improve social conditions.

NONPROFESSIONAL SERVICE PROVIDERS

Not all human service practice requires the competencies of a social worker or someone with related professional skills. Many important services can be provided by persons who bring to the helping situation the perspective of the client population. These people have been referred to in the literature as *indigenous workers*. They may be clients, former clients, or others who have rapport with low-income or other client groups based on having similar experiences to the client population. At times indigenous workers can build relationships with clients when professionals have difficulty establishing rapport. Indigenous workers can be found in human service organizations ranging from neighborhood centers to welfare agencies. His or her life experience and knowledge of the individuals or groups being served are the most important qualifications.

Another important source of nonprofessional personnel for human service agencies are *graduates of community colleges*. These Associate of Arts (AA) degree programs vary considerably from school to school but focus on preparing for very specific human service jobs with titles such as mental health technician, community service aide, case aide, or eligibility worker. The AA degree programs usually include the study of human growth and behavior, social problems, the social service delivery system, personal values and self-awareness, and basic communication skills. These programs may provide field experiences so students have an opportunity to apply knowledge acquired in the classroom. The tasks the AA graduate can be expected to perform are very concrete and require limited individual judgment. They include such activities as fact finding relative to specific cases, interviewing to obtain data, locating sources of assistance, organizing community groups around specific issues, making social provisions (e.g., money, food stamps, and housing) available to people, and screening applicants for service.

OTHER BACCALAUREATE-LEVEL DISCIPLINES

Several disciplines offer majors in colleges and universities that are closely related to social work. Completing these degrees can serve as helpful preparation for some human service jobs and can also be good preparation for a subsequent degree in social work. However, these programs of study should not be confused with social work degree programs that, if accredited, carry professional recognition.

SOCIAL SCIENCE DISCIPLINES.   Social work has traditionally had a close relationship with the social science disciplines for two reasons. First, social work has drawn on basic knowledge from the disciplines of psychology, sociology, anthropology, economics, and political science, while developing its theoretical base for understanding the individual, family, group, organization, community, and the impact of culture on all these. Second, in higher education, social work has had close administrative ties with these disciplines at the baccalaureate level. It is not uncommon to find a baccalaureate-level social work education program housed in a sociology department or in a multidisciplinary social science department.

Most positions for social scientists involve research or teaching, and, thus, a Ph.D. is necessary to be competitive in the job market. With the exception of the small branch of applied sociology, social scientists do not typically engage in the provision of human services. Their purpose is to develop and test theories that will increase understanding of the people or places they study, but they do not intend to intervene to help people or social institutions change.

RELATED HELPING PROFESSIONS.   When making a career choice within the helping services, a person should examine a range of helping professions that might fit his or her individual talents and interests. The more established professions are medicine, law, nursing, teaching, dentistry, and psychology. Other helping professions, such as physical therapy, music therapy, speech pathology and audiology, occupational therapy, recreation therapy, urban planning, and school counseling, also offer challenging and rewarding careers.

Each of these is an established profession and has prescribed and accredited educational programs a person must complete to be recognized as a member of that profession. Like social work, these professions identify standards for competent and ethical practice and take responsibility for policing the membership for compliance with these standards. The clientele of these professions, then, have some protection from the possible misuse of professional authority. Employment opportunities in these professions vary considerably, but most jobs are defined as requiring the requisite professional education for entry.

It is instructive to compare estimates of the demand for social workers with that of other helping professions. Table 4-1 provides a comparison of selected helping professions based on the projections of the U.S. Bureau of Labor Statistics (BLS). The supply estimate is derived from BLS data reporting the number of persons who completed professional preparation for that discipline. In social work, for example, graduates of BSW and MSW programs are compared to the number of social workers needed to fill new positions and replace workers who are permanently leaving the labor market. These data overstate the supply of "new" social workers by about 10 percent[7] because some who have completed a BSW return to school for a master's education and therefore are not new social workers. It is clear from these data that social work's supply and demand are about equal.

TABLE 4-1	**Employment Projections among the Helping Professions: 1996–2006**

Profession	Estimated Workers, 1996[a]	Estimated Annual Growth Rate[i] %[a]	Total New and Replacement Workers Needed Annually[a]	Estimated Annual Supply[b]	Annual Supply as % of Demand
Lawyers	622,000	1.9	29,000	41,067[c]	141.6
Occupational Therapists	57,000	6.6	4,400	3,641[d]	82.8
Physical Therapists	115,000	7.1	9,400	6,320[d]	67.2
Physicians	560,000	2.1	19,700	15,786[c]	80.1
Psychologists	143,000	0.8	2,500	4,027[e]	116.1
Registered Nurses	1,971,000	2.1	68,300	96,893[f]	141.9
Social Workers	585,000	3.2	27,700	28,888[d]	104.3
Speeh Pathology/Audiology	87,000	5.1	5,400	4,670[g]	86.5
Teachers					
Administrators	386,000	1.6	14,600	13,335[d]	91.3
Preschool and Kindergarten	499,000	2.0	19,000	9,373[h]	49.3
Elementary	1,491,000	1.0	43,800	60,984[d]	139.2
Secondary	1,406,000	2.2	73,000	67,645[d]	92.7
Special Education	407,000	5.9	29,900	20,621[d]	69.0
School Counselors	175,000	1.9	7,300	12,288[g]	168.3
Urban and Regional Planners	29,000	0.5	600	1,806[d]	301.0

[a]George T. Silvestri, "Occupational Employment to 2006," *Monthly Labor Review* 120 (November 1997), pp. 58–67.

[b]Bureau of Labor Statistics, *Occupational Projections and Training Data, 1998–99 Edition* (Washington, D.C.: U.S. Department of Labor, 1998), pp. 37–51.

[c]Includes professional degree (e.g., law, medicine) only.

[d]Includes bachelor's and master's degrees.

[e]Includes doctoral degree only (an increase of master's-level jobs is developing in psychology).

[f]Includes associate and bachelor's degrees.

[g]Includes master's degree only.

[h]Includes associate, bachelor's and master's degrees.

[i]Growth Rate Definitions

  Increase 3.6% or more = grow much faster than average

  Increase 2.1% to 3.5% = grow faster than average

  Increase 1.0% to 2.0% = grow about as fast as average

  Increase 0% to .9% = grow more slowly than average

EMERGING HUMAN SERVICE OCCUPATIONS.   During the 1970s a new occupational group began to emerge, known generally as *human services* or *human development*. The human services occupations differ from the helping professions we have reviewed because they intend to be nonprofessional. Most people giving leadership to these occupations are professionally trained in other disciplines and have been largely involved in corrections and mental health services—although they branch into every aspect of the social services.

The development of the human services field was stimulated by dissatisfaction with the service delivery system. Fundamental to the philosophy behind this field are two viewpoints.[8] First, the human services have been fragmented into problem areas (e.g., public welfare, corrections, mental health) that create barriers to good service because many clients experience complex problems and must deal with multiple agencies, programs, and service providers. Second, the integration of services into "umbrella agencies" and the creation of a broad discipline that can provide a wide range of services is preferable to the more focused professional orientation.

Social workers would agree that the fragmented methods of delivering social services often make it difficult for clients to locate help. However, the profession does not regard service integration as a solution (division lines can exist just as rigidly within one large agency as in several smaller ones) and believe that the professional model, with all its limitations, continues to be the most valid means of identifying the people who are prepared with the knowledge, values, and skills to respond to specific human needs. Social work would argue that clients are better served through greater efforts at *interdisciplinary practice,* rather than the emergence of new human service disciplines that have no clear service focus or practice approach, no established standards for ethical conduct, no professional responsibility for quality control, and no standardized educational preparation subject to professional accreditation.

Professional Social Work Practice

Social work's evolution as a profession has been uneven, and the career paths one might follow as a social worker can be confusing. Figure 4-1 portrays the various career options available to the professional social worker. It recognizes that before a person decides to begin the educational preparation required to become a professional social worker, he or she will typically have had some positive experiences that have motivated this decision. This future social worker will typically have been a good natural helper or volunteer, the client of a social worker who received useful services, or perhaps a human services provider who did not have professional preparation. If he or she has not already completed a bachelor's degree, the most likely place to begin would be in a BSW program. However, if this is a person who has a degree in another discipline, a second entry point is available—an MSW program.

To make appropriate career development decisions, it is useful for the potential social worker to understand what is expected of a social worker at each of the four practice levels and how that practice level has emerged historically. The following materials, based on NASW's classification system,[9] briefly describe each level, identify the qualifications, and trace the manner in which its central characteristics have emerged.

THE BASIC PROFESSIONAL

Description: Practice as a basic social worker requires professional practice skills, theoretical knowledge, and values not normally obtainable in day-to-day experience

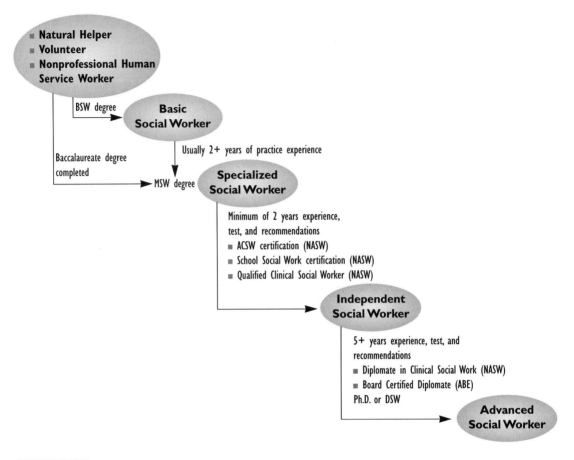

FIGURE 4-1 **Career Options for the Professional Social Worker**

but that are obtainable through formal social work education. This knowledge is distinguished from experiential learning by being based on conceptual and theoretical knowledge of personal and social interaction and by training in the disciplined use of self in relationship with clients.

Qualifications: Requires a baccalaureate degree from a social work program accredited by the Council on Social Work Education.

Characteristics: Practice at this first level has been formally recognized as professional only since 1970, when the NASW first admitted to full membership persons with a BA or BSW from a social work program approved by the Council on Social Work Education. This recognition not only reflected a movement away from professional elitism but also increased the quantity and quality of undergraduate social work programs.

A few schools offered baccalaureate-level social work courses as early as the 1920s.[10] However, the thrust of social work was toward graduate education. In 1932 the American Association of Schools of Social Work (AASSW) declared that, to be recognized as professional, a social worker must graduate from a four-year college and complete at least one year of graduate education. In 1937 this position was revised to establish two years of graduate education as the minimum level for professional practice.

In response to the AASSW policy, in 1942 several schools created a competing organization, the National Association of Schools of Social Administration (NASSA), for the purpose of having undergraduate programs recognized as professional preparation. After several years of conflict over the legitimacy of undergraduate education, thirteen organizations interested in the resolution of this issue and in the overall enhancement of social work education formed the National Council on Social Work Education. As an initial activity of this organization, the Hollis–Taylor study of social work education was commissioned.

The Hollis–Taylor report, released in 1951, urged that undergraduate education maintain a broad focus and avoid teaching social work skills or preparing students for social work practice on graduation.[11] However, the process by which this study was conducted created harmony between the AASSW and the NASSA, which then merged with the National Council to create what is now the single accrediting body for social work education: the Council on Social Work Education (CSWE).

The CSWE offered membership to both undergraduate and graduate schools and undertook a thirteen-volume curriculum study of social work education at both levels. One volume of this study recommended establishment of professional social work education at the undergraduate level with a continuum developed from undergraduate to graduate programs.[12] This recommendation was initially rejected by the CSWE. During most of the 1960s, undergraduate programs operated under CSWE guidelines that might best be described as a traditional liberal arts education oriented toward social welfare.[13] They were usually taught in departments of psychology or sociology, offered no more than three or four social work courses, and sometimes had no social workers as faculty. With little independent identity on their campuses, and with the failure of both employers and graduate social work programs to give preference or credit for completion of these programs, they were not popular—even among students who planned to enter social work.

Disenchantment of students, employers, and professional social workers with undergraduate education contributed to the establishment of a joint CSWE–NASW Ad Hoc Committee on Manpower Issues in 1968. The Committee's recommendations contributed to concurrent actions in 1970 by NASW members to grant full membership to graduates of approved undergraduate programs and by the CSWE to establish standards for approval of these programs. The first standards adopted were essentially structural: they contributed to the visibility of social work programs, required that social workers be included in faculty, and demanded specification of educational objectives.[14]

CSWE "approval" was granted to 220 schools by 1973, but was at best a limited and informal type of accreditation. Its primary concern was that the schools have an adequate structure for the growth and development of a baccalaureate program.

Specification of curriculum content was slower to develop because a workable division between baccalaureate- and master's-level education had not yet evolved.

In 1973 CSWE took the second step to complete legitimate accreditation: it adopted much more substantial standards for baccalaureate degree programs, placing the primary focus on preparation for professional social work practice. Some previously "approved" programs could not meet the new standards, but most were able to secure the necessary resources to upgrade their programs and achieve accredited status. The number of BSW programs gradually increased, and by 1980 a total of 261 met the accreditation requirements.[15]

In 1984 another significant step to upgrade the quality of baccalaureate social work education was taken when the CSWE operationalized a new set of accreditation standards and a much more substantive Curriculum Policy Statement. These standards spelled out the expectations for each program relative to its purpose, structure, and resources, and also required that each school's curriculum be consistent with the Curriculum Policy Statement.[16] While the standards did not dictate how a school should organize its curriculum, they were considerably more explicit than the 1974 accreditation standards about the content of the student's learning experience. Rigorous application of the accreditation standards did not deter colleges and universities of all sizes in all states from building and maintaining undergraduate social work education programs. As of 1999, 446 colleges and universities had BSW programs that were fully accredited or in candidacy status.[17]

With NASW recognition came the gradual acceptance of baccalaureate-level social work, both by employers as preparation for practice and by the graduate programs as preparation for advanced standing. Increasingly, jobs were defined to recognize the competence and abilities of social workers who had completed this type of educational program, and salary and work assignments were differentiated from those without this preparation. Furthermore, in 1972 CSWE granted approval for graduate schools to accept up to one year's credit for special groups of students. By 1998, 85 percent of the graduate programs offered some form of *advanced standing* to graduates of accredited programs that typically amounted to waiving one to two terms of graduate work.[18]

Clearly, the developments in the 1970s and 1980s enhance the conclusion that the social worker who has completed an accredited undergraduate social work program should be prepared with the competencies for the level of professional practice. Perhaps the most valid test of the acceptance of baccalaureate or basic social workers is whether they find employment as social workers. One study of 5,228 graduates of BSW programs found that 71.4 percent found their first job in social work; 86.8 percent secured employment within six months after graduation. Over time 84.3 percent of the BSW graduates were employed as social workers. These data suggest that the human service agencies found baccalaureate-level social workers attractive, especially in direct service positions, in which 90.2 percent were employed in their first social work job.[19]

THE SPECIALIZED PROFESSIONAL

Description: Practice at this level requires the specific and demonstrated mastery of therapeutic techniques in at least one knowledge and skill method, as well as general knowledge of human personality as influenced by social factors. Specialized practice also requires the disciplined use of self in treatment relationships with individuals or groups, or a broad conceptual knowledge of research, administration, or planning methods and social problems.

Qualifications: Requires a master's degree (MSW) from a social work program accredited by the CSWE.

Characteristics: Prior to the reemergence of baccalaureate-level social work education and the basic social worker, the generally accepted level of preparation for social work practice was that of the specialized social worker. Although it is expected that the MSW social worker, too, will make use of professional supervision, he or she should have sufficient competence to appropriately exercise independent judgment and initiative.

Historically, master's-level social work education began much like the more sophisticated in-service training programs of today. The first formal education program, known as the New York School of Philanthropy (now the Columbia University School of Social Work), was a six-week course offered under the auspices of the New York Charity Organization Society in 1898. The early curricula of the evolving schools incorporated preparation for a range of services, from individual helping approaches to economic and reform theory. They included a heavy investment in internships or field experiences as tools for learning practice skills and tended to be organized around practice settings, such as hospital social work and school social work. The MSW programs' greatest emphasis was on preparation for the services offered by private social agencies, and they tended to neglect the growing demand for social workers in the public social services.

By the 1940s the two-year MSW had become the minimum requirement for professional practice, although a few schools with strong undergraduate programs were resisting that requirement. The two-year programs were typically organized around what was known as the "Basic Eight," in reference to what at that time were considered the eight primary divisions of social work practice: public welfare, social casework, social group work, community organization, medical information, social research, psychiatry, and social welfare administration.

The period from 1950 through 1965 was one of rapid growth in the number of MSW programs and the relative standardization of these programs. By 1965 there were sixty-seven accredited graduate schools and nearly 9,000 students.[20] The schools had largely abandoned programs structured on the basis of practice setting and instead organized curricula around the practice methods of casework, group work, community organization, administration, and research.

Three factors have significantly influenced social work education at the graduate level in the past quarter-century. First, the reemergence of baccalaureate-level social work forced some reorientation of master's education; it was necessary to adapt to the student who entered the MSW program with a substantial social work education already completed. For this student, provision was made for advanced standing in the graduate-level program, which typically meant waiving or testing out of up to one year of graduate work. A continuum of education between the baccalaureate and master's programs began to emerge.

Second, the Council on Social Work Education's Standards for Accreditation and Curriculum Policy Statement allowed individual schools increased flexibility in determining curriculum content. As the typical two-year MSW program evolved, it offered a general orientation to social work practice during the first year and then provided more specialized content based on population served, social problem addressed, practice intervention approach, or client group served during the second year. Prior to that development, students attending MSW programs could expect pretty much the same basic curriculum regardless of which school they attended. Today, this selection is based on the specialization the student desires to develop and the interests and capacity of the school's faculty. In a real sense, graduate social work education has become what traditionally was the expectation of graduate-level work; that is, it is more substantive and specialized than that which one would find at the baccalaureate level.

Finally, the conservative philosophy that dominated the United States during the 1980s initially eliminated some social work jobs and created a tighter job market in the human services. Student interest shifted toward the clinical aspects of social work, and particularly to private practice, where one could avoid the risks of employment in an agency that might lose its funding as a result of a conservative administration. The data on applications for first-year and advanced standing admission to MSW programs provide clear evidence of potential students' fears that the human services would be diminished. In 1979, for example, the number of applications had peaked at 33,978 and 59.9 percent of these students were accepted to admission. Applications then dropped precipitously until 1984 when there were only 22,158 applications of which 78.9 percent were accepted. After hitting bottom in 1984, the applications began to increase and by 1990 the losses were recouped. In 1994 an all-time high of 51,668 applications for the first year of study or advanced standing were received by the graduate programs and an all-time low percentage (46.7%) were accepted for admission.[21] By adjusting acceptance rates, the schools avoid a decline in the number of new social workers being prepared at the master's level, which would create a shortfall when the market for social workers rebounded.

How do basic and specialized social workers differ in the expected abilities they bring to their jobs? The 1992 revisions to the CSWE's Curriculum Policy Statement provide guidelines that social work education programs must follow when preparing students at the two entry levels of social work practice. Table 4-2 compares these two levels and indicates that, while many of the same abilities are expected at both levels, there are uniquenesses that reinforce the perception of the master's-level graduate as a specialized practitioner (i.e., one who has a particular area of concentration) and the basic social worker as one who functions under the supervision of an experienced worker. The social worker with the more advanced degree, according to the Curriculum Policy Statement, is also expected to have greater ability to synthesize and analyze knowledge, to influence policy formulation, and to engage in empirical practice research.

TABLE 4-2 Expected Abilities of Basic and Specialized Social Workers upon Graduation from Accredited Educational Programs

The Basic Social Worker	The Specialized Social Worker
Graduates of a baccalaureate social work program will be able to:	Graduates of a master's social work program are advanced practitioners who can analyze, intervene, and evaluate in ways that are highly differentiated, discriminating, and self-critical. They must synthesize and apply a broad range of knowledge as well as practice with a high degree of autonomy and skill. They must be able to refine and advance the quality of their practice as well as that of the larger social work profession. These advanced competencies must be appropriately integrated and reflected in all aspects of their social work practice, including their ability to:
1. Apply critical-thinking skills within the context of professional social work practice.	1. Apply critical thinking within professional contexts, including **synthesizing and applying appropriate theories and knowledge to practice interventions.**
2. Practice within the values and ethics of the social work profession and within an understanding of and respect for the positive value of diversity.	2. Same as BSW standard.
3. Demonstrate the professional use of self.	3. Same as BSW standard.
4. Understand the forms and mechanisms of oppression and discrimination and apply the strategies and skills of change that advance social and economic justice.	4. Same as BSW standard.
5. Understand the history of the social work profession and its current structures and issues.	5. Understand **and interpret** the history of the social work profession and its current structures and issues.
6. Apply the knowledge and skills of generalist social work to practice with systems of all sizes.	6a. Apply the knowledge and skills of **a generalist perspective** to practice with systems of all sizes. 6b. **Apply the knowledge and skills of advanced social work practice in an area of concentration.**
7. Apply knowledge of bio-psycho-social variables that affect individual development and behavior, and use theoretical frameworks to understand the interactions among individuals and between individuals and social systems (i.e., families, groups, organizations, and communities).	7. **Critically analyze** and apply knowledge of bio-psycho-social variables that affect individual development and behavior, and use theoretical frameworks among individuals and between individuals and social systems (i.e., families, groups, organizations, and communities).
8. Analyze the impact of social policies on client systems, workers, and agencies.	8. Analyze the impact of social policies on client systems, workers, and agencies **and demonstrate skills for influencing policy formulation and change.**
9. Evaluate research studies and apply findings to practice, and, **under supervision,** evaluate their own practice interventions and those of other relevant systems.	9a. Evaluate research studies and apply findings to practice, **and demonstrate skills in quantitative and qualitative research design, data analysis, and knowledge dissemination.** 9b. **Conduct empirical evaluations** of their own practice interventions and those of other relevant systems.
10. Use communication skills differentially with a variety of client populations, colleagues, and members of the community.	10. Same as BSW standard.
11. Use supervision appropriate to **generalist** practice.	11. Use supervision **and consultation** appropriate to **advanced practice in an area of concentration.**
12. Function within the structure of organizations and service delivery systems and, **under supervision,** seek necessary organizational change.	12. Function within the structure of organizations and service delivery systems and seek necessary organizational change.

Source: Council on Social Work Education, *Handbook of Accreditation Standards and Procedures* (Alexandria, VA: CSWE, 1994), pp. 99, 138.

THE INDEPENDENT PROFESSIONAL

Description: The independent practice level is based on appropriate specialized training beyond the MSW and continued professional development under supervision that is sufficient to ensure dependable, regular use of professional skills in independent private practice. A minimum of two years post-master's experience is required to demonstrate this direct practice, administration, or training competence.

Qualifications: Requires an accredited MSW and at least two years of post-master's experience under appropriate professional supervision.

Characteristics: The independent social worker is expected to have developed and integrated the knowledge, values, and skills of social work in at least one practice area. From this experience, he or she should be able to develop sufficient expertise in that field to function independently and skillfully in sensitive situations and should be prepared to practice outside the auspices of a social agency. Furthermore, the independent social worker should be able to provide leadership in at least one practice arena and to supervise and consult with other social workers.

One indicator of reaching the independent professional level is membership in the *Academy of Certified Social Workers* (ACSW). The ACSW was established in 1960 to protect clients from the abuses and incompetence of inadequately prepared practitioners. The Academy also was intended to establish a more favorable public image, to obtain societal sanction, and to increase confidence and understanding in social work. Requirements for becoming a member of the Academy include maintaining membership in NASW, having a minimum of two years full-time practice experience, providing reference letters from professional peers, and achieving a sufficient score on the ACSW exam (a multiple-choice test).

As Figure 4-1 further indicates, NASW has developed two other certification programs intended to certify that workers are prepared to practice independently in specialized areas. To earn the *Qualified Clinical Social Worker* credential, a social worker must have had at least two years of post-MSW clinical practice experience in an agency that was supervised by an experienced clinical social worker. In addition, he or she must hold either the ACSW or a state license and receive favorable references from social work colleagues. The *School Social Work Specialist* must meet similar qualifications and achieve a passing score on the School Social Worker Specialty Area Test, which is a specialty area of the National Teacher's Examination.

THE ADVANCED PROFESSIONAL

Description: Practice at the advanced level is that which carries major social and organizational responsibility for professional development, analysis, research, or policy implementation, or is achieved by personal professional growth demonstrated through advanced conceptual contributions to professional knowledge.

Qualifications: This level requires proficiency in a special theoretical, practice, administration, or policy area, or the ability to conduct advanced research studies in social welfare; usually demonstrated through a doctoral degree in social work or another discipline—in addition to the MSW.

Characteristics: This classification is reserved for the most highly experienced practitioners as well as for social workers who have obtained a doctoral in social work or a related field. In contrast to many professions, relatively few social workers seek or achieve the advanced professional level.

For direct service or clinical practitioners who aspire to the advanced level, two indicators have been developed that provide national identification of the person's competence. One is the *Diplomate in Clinical Social Work* (DCSW) offered by NASW. To be recognized as a diplomate in clinical social work, a person must have completed an accredited MSW program, possess an advanced or clinical state license, have a minimum of five years of post-master's clinical experience, perform satisfactorily on a case-based essay examination, and receive a favorable comprehensive supervisory evaluation. A similar recognition with similar requirements, the *Board Certified Diplomate,* is offered by the independent American Board of Examiners in Clinical Social Work (ABE).

Doctoral education represents the second route to the advanced social work level. The purposes for doctoral degrees (DSW or Ph.D.) in social work have not followed a consistent pattern. Most devote their efforts to preparing the researcher and teacher, but increasingly there as been some focus on preparation for the advanced practitioner. Since the doctorate is not viewed as an entry degree for the social work profession and it is not accredited by the profession, the doctoral programs receive their sanction only from their universities. Therefore, the schools have considerable flexibility to determine the focus of their curricula and have taken on unique identities. By the late 1990s, sixty-two doctoral programs in social work were available throughout the United States enrolling about 1,000 full-time and slightly fewer part-time students. In 1998, 266 doctoral degrees in social work were awarded.[22] These numbers do not, however, reflect the total number of social workers completing doctoral degrees because some complete doctoral work in related fields such as sociology, psychology, higher education, and public administration.

At this time the advanced social worker represents a very small part of social work and is rarely recognized in job-classification schemes or state licensing provisions. This level might best be viewed as a means of holding a classification title for this gradually developing aspect of social work.

Concluding Comment

Through the years of its emergence, social work has gradually evolved four distinct practice levels. The professional membership association, the National Association of Social Workers, has codified these levels into a classification system with expectations for the practitioner at each level defined and education and experience qualifications specified. This classification system embraces two problems in terminology—both created by the acceptance of the concept of an advanced generalist social worker (see Chapter 2). First, the MSW graduate prepared as an advanced generalist is qualified under the classification system as a "Specialized Social Worker." Can one be a specialized generalist? Also, an advanced generalist social worker is not the same as an Advanced Social Worker in NASW's classification system. Persons new to social work should be aware of this confusing terminology.

Nevertheless, the NASW classification of social work practice levels is a useful tool for both social agencies wanting to match workers with job demands and for persons considering a career in social work. For the latter, the selection of a particular practice level as a career goal requires that one assess his or her desire to provide the particular types of service for which that level offers the necessary preparation and the ability to arrange one's personal life to acquire the requisite professional education and experiences. In social work, in contrast to some of the other helping professions, one can change directions after entering the profession. A person might enter social work in a particular field of practice, such as providing services to the aged or developmentally disabled, and later transfer the skills used in that job to employment in mental health or corrections. Or the direct service worker (usually with a master's degree) might transfer into a job involving agency administration or move away from agency-based practice and into autonomous or private practice.

KEY WORDS AND CONCEPTS

Accreditation (of educational programs)

Professional certification

Academy of Certified Social Workers

Licensing (state regulation of practice)

Volunteers

Indigenous workers

Social science professions

American Association of Schools of Social Work

National Association of Schools of Social Administration

Advanced standing

Basic social worker

Specialized social worker

Independent social worker

Advanced social worker

SUGGESTED READINGS

Biggerstaff, Marilyn A. "Licensing, Regulation, and Certification." In Richard L. Edwards, ed., *Encyclopedia of Social Work,* 19th Edition. Washington, D.C.: NASW Press, 1995, pp. 1616–1624.

Gibelman, Margaret, and Schervish, Phillip H. *Who We Are: A Second Look.* Washington, D.C.: NASW Press, 1996.

Teare, Robert J., and Sheafor, Bradford W. *Practice-Sensitive Social Work Education: An Empirical Analysis of Social Work Practice and Practitioners.* Alexandria, VA: Council on Social Work Education, 1995.

ENDNOTES

1. For suggestions of issues one might examine when considering social work as a career choice, see Bradford W. Sheafor, Charles R. Horejsi, and Gloria A. Horejsi, *Techniques and Guidelines for Social Work Practice,* 5th Edition (Boston: Allyn and Bacon, 2000), Chapter 2.

2. Ruth R. Middleman, *A Study Guide for ACSW Certification,* 4th Edition (Washington, D.C.: NASW Press, 1996), p. v.

3. Robert R. Wohlgemuth and Thomas Samph, *Summary Report: Content Validity Study in Support of the Licensure Examination Program of the American Association of State Social Work Boards* (Oak Park, IL: The Association, 1983), p. 2.

4. Donna DeAngelis, *State Comparison of Laws Regulating Social Work* (Washington, D.C.: National Association of Social Workers, 1993).

5. *NASW News* 42 (January 1996): 19–22.

6. National Association of Social Workers, *Standards for Social Work Personnel Practices: Policy Statement No. 2* (Washington, D.C.: The Association, 1971).

7. Todd M. Lennon, *Statistics for Social Work Education in the United States: 1994* (Alexandria, VA: Council on Social Work Education, 1995), p. 30.

8. Joseph Mehr, *Human Services: Concepts and Intervention Strategies,* 6th Edition (Boston: Allyn and Bacon, 1995), pp. 11–20.

9. National Association of Social Workers, *NASW Standards for the Classification of Social Work Practice* (Washington, D.C.: The Association, 1981).

10. A comprehensive analysis of the evolution of baccalaureate-level social work can be found in Bradford W. Sheafor and Barbara W. Shank, *Undergraduate Social Work Education: A Survivor in a Changing Profession* (Austin: University of Texas at Austin School of Social Work, 1986).

11. Ernest V. Hollis and Alice L. Taylor, *Social Work Education in the United States* (New York: Columbia University Press, 1951).

12. Herbert Bisno, *The Place of Undergraduate Curriculum in Social Work Education,* Social Work Curriculum Study Vol. 2 (New York: Council on Social Work Education, 1959).

13. Council on Social Work Education, *Social Welfare Content in Undergraduate Education* (New York: The Council, 1962), pp. 3–4.

14. Council on Social Work Education, *Undergraduate Programs in Social Work* (New York: The Council, 1971).

15. Allen Rubin, *Statistics on Social Work Education in the United States: 1980* (New York: Council on Social Work Education, 1981), p. 1.

16. Council on Social Work Education, *Handbook of Accreditation Standards and Procedures* (Washington, D.C.: The Council, 1984).

17. Nancy Randolph, "Report from the Division of Standards and Accreditation," *The Social Work Education Reporter* 49 (Spring–Summer 1999): 22.

18. Council on Social Work Education, *Summary Information on Master of Social Work Programs: 1997–98* (Alexandria, VA: Council on Social Work Education, 1998).

19. Robert J. Teare, Barbara W. Shank, and Bradford W. Sheafor, "Career Patterns of the BSW Social Worker." Unpublished manuscript, Colorado State University, Fort Collins.

20. Raymond DeVera, ed., *Statistics on Social Work Education, 1965–66* (New York: Council on Social Work Education, 1966), p. 6.

21. Allen Rubin, *Statistics on Social Work Education in the United States: 1983* (New York: Council on Social Work Education, 1984), p. 49; Elaine C. Spaulding, *Statistics on Social Work Education in the United States: 1987* (Washington, D.C.: Council on Social Work Education, 1988), p. 36; and Todd M. Lennon, *Statistics on Social Work Education in the United States: 1998* (Alexandria, VA: Council on Social Work Education, 1999), p. 45.

22. Lennon, *Statistics,* 1999, pp. 1, 45.

CHAPTER 5

Fields of Social
Work Practice

**Prefatory
Comment**

One factor that makes social work different from many other professions is the opportunity to help people deal with a wide range of human problems without needing to obtain specialized professional credentials for each area of practice. During his or her lifetime, for example, one social worker might organize and lead self-help groups in a hospital, deal with cases of abuse and neglect, develop release plans for persons in a correctional facility, plan demonstrations protesting racist or sexist injustices, arrange for foster homes and adoptions for children, secure nursing home placements for older people, supervise new social workers, and serve as executive director of a human service agency. Regardless of the type of work performed, the social worker always has the same fundamental purpose—to draw on basic knowledge, values, and skills in order to help achieve desired change to improve the quality of life for the persons involved.

Although there are similarities in the tasks performed by social workers regardless of the nature of the services provided, there are also unique aspects of their practice with each population group. For example, services to children and youth differ from services to the elderly, the needs of a disabled adult differ from those of a person about to be released from a correctional facility, or the assistance required by a pregnant teenager differs from that needed by a teenager engaged in gang activity or substance abuse. Each of these fields of practice typically uses at least some specialized language, emphasizes specific helping approaches and techniques, or may be affected by different laws or social programs. Therefore, what a social worker does and needs to know will vary to some extent from field to field.

The human services system is indeed complex, and the layperson cannot be expected to negotiate this system alone. As the profession with the primary responsibility for helping people in need to gain access to the services in a community, the social worker must not only know what services are available, but must also be prepared to interpret them to their clients and help these clients gain access to the resources they need. To reduce the client's sense of "getting the runaround" in securing services, and perhaps reduce the chance of the client becoming discouraged and not getting to needed help, the social worker must carefully check that the referral is to an appropriate resource. In addition, the professional, at times, may need to provide a variety of supports, such as encouragement, telephone numbers, names of individuals to contact, or even transportation to facilitate the client's getting to the correct resources. Thus, the social worker must not only work within a single practice field but should also be prepared to help clients negotiate services among practice fields.

This chapter identifies some of the features of the primary fields of social work practice to familiarize the beginning worker with the range of places where a social worker might be employed. *Field of social work practice* is a phrase used to describe a group of practice settings that deal with similar client problems. Each field may include a number of different agencies or other organized ways of providing services. For example, in any community, the social agencies concerned with crime and delinquency might include a juvenile court, a residential center or halfway house, a community corrections agency, a probation office for adult offenders, and/or a correctional facility where offenders are incarcerated. All fields work with people who have come to the attention of the legal system and would be considered part of the practice field of corrections. Although the fields discussed in the remainder of this chapter do not exhaust the full range where social workers might practice, those identified suggest the great variety of settings in which the social worker is prepared to provide services.

Below, when each of the thirteen selected fields of social work practice is described, data are presented in a table that reports percentage of BSW and MSW social workers who are employed in that field, that is, their *primary practice area*. In addition, where data are available, information is included in the table that indicates the percentages of social workers who consider the client problems in this field one of the three most prevalent client needs they address in their practice—even if addressing that need is not their primary practice activity.* For example, as reported in the following section, 16.5 percent of the basic social workers report that their primary practice area is providing services to aged persons. However, 23.6 percent indicate that one of the three most dominant client needs they address in their work relates to some problem associated with aging. Thus, in addition to those who consider aging their primary practice area, another 7.1 percent of the basic social workers also work extensively with the aging population.

---

*All data reported in this chapter are from Robert J. Teare and Bradford W. Sheafor, "National Task Analysis of Social Work Practice." A description of the method of data collection appears in Robert J. Teare and Bradford W. Sheafor, *Practice Sensitive Social Work Education: An Empirical Analysis of Social Work Practice and Practitioners* (Alexandria, VA: Council on Social Work Education, 1995).

Aging

	Primary Practice Area	Prevalent Client Need
Basic Social Worker	16.5%	23.6%
Specialist/Independent Social Worker	3.7	10.2

Many social workers provide services to older people, both those requiring support to remain in their own homes and those residing in long-term care facilities such as nursing homes and congregate-care centers. Basic social workers are the primary service providers for older people, although many workers at the specialized and independent levels also regularly serve older people as part of their social work practice.

With increased industrialization and technological development in U.S. society, meaningful roles for older people have decreased. Improved medical care that extends life and inflation that reduces the buying power of savings and retirement funds have made the elderly a vulnerable population (see Chapter 14). Today more than 12.7 percent of the U.S. population (34.1 million people) are age sixty-five or over, and nearly four million of these older persons are over age eighty-five—an age at which it is estimated that approximately one-half need assistance with everyday living activities.[1] Those who are able to remain in their homes or the homes of family members experience more physical and social problems than the general population. For example, 3.4 million older people live in poverty, 6 percent live in housing with severe physical problems, 37 percent deal with one or more chronic illness, many are lonely due to the loss of a mate (42.3% of the women are widows and 15% of the men are widowers), and many find it difficult to adapt to a changing life style caused by retirement or a health condition.[2]

A number of programs are available to help older people remain in their own homes as long as doing so is a safe and satisfying experience. Social workers help older people make links to community programs that bring health care, meals, and home-maker services into their homes; provide transportation services; and offer day care or recreation programs. Increasingly, when older people are faced with a terminal illness, social workers help them deal with their impending death through counseling or referral to a hospice program.

For approximately 4 percent (1.4M) of the older people, some form of long-term care in a nursing home or other group living facility becomes a necessity. Social workers frequently help the individual and/or family select the facility and make moving arrangements; some are even staff members of the facility.

While much attention in a long-term care facility is directed toward meeting the basic physical and medical needs of the residents, social workers in these facilities contribute to the quality of life for residents by helping them maintain contact with their families and friends when possible, develop meaningful relationships with other people within the facility, and engage in a variety of activities both within and outside the facility. They also facilitate access to other social services when needed and help residents secure arrangements that protect their personal rights and ensure quality care while living in the long-term care facility.

Alcohol and Substance Abuse

	Primary Practice Area	Prevalent Client Need
Basic Social Worker	3.2%	20.1%
Specialist/Independent Social Worker	2.2	14.8

Considering the size and scope of alcohol and drug problems in U.S. society, relatively few social workers have this field as their primary practice area. Those who do are primarily employed in alcohol and drug treatment centers or are engaged in private practice. However, the interrelationship between substance abuse and other social problems is evident in the fact that these problems were prevalent in the work of between 15 and 20 percent of all social workers. Social workers employed by virtually every type of human service organization, from mental health and correctional facilities to schools and hospitals, deal with the effects of substance abuse on social functioning. Between nine and twelve million individuals in the United States are alcoholics or drug abusers, and each individual usually affects at least four other persons in some negative, unhealthy, or destructive manner.[3] The social implications of alcohol and substance abuse are significant as they are highly correlated with murders, suicides, accidents, health problems, and domestic violence.

In recent years social workers have increasingly found success in working with alcohol and substance abusers. Much of the credit for this success has come as social workers and other professionals have moved from viewing alcoholism not "as a moral weakness, requiring only a strong will and determination to 'reform,' "[4] toward viewing it as a disease. This has been beneficial not only for enlisting an alcoholic in his or her own recovery but also for approaching the problem from a sounder scientific basis.

Using current scientific understanding of these problems, Lawson and Lawson have identified three primary factors that should be considered in treating and preventing alcoholism and substance abuse. First, they recognize that physiological factors such as physical addiction, disease or physical disorders, medical problems, inherited risk, and/or mental disorders with physiological causes may contribute to the problem. Second, Lawson and Lawson identify several sociological factors, such as ethnic and cultural differences, family background, education, employment, and peer relationships, as also related to alcoholism and substance abuse. Finally, they note that psychological factors, including social skills, emotional level, self-image, attitude toward life, defense mechanisms, mental obsessions, judgment, and decision-making skills all can be contributors to this disease.[5] Growing understanding of these associated and interrelated factors has provided the helping professions with an opportunity to apply their knowledge and skills to helping clients prevent and resolve their problems. Social work plays a particularly important role, as the addictions inevitably have a significant effect on family, friends, coworkers, and others who are in contact with the person experiencing the addiction. Both the person and the environment must be helped to change when this disease is treated.

Children and Youth

	Primary Practice Area	*Prevalent Client Need*
Basic Social Worker	18.8%	63.6%
Specialist/Independent Social Worker	13.1	66.1

From work in the almshouses in the 1800s to work with street gangs today (see Chapter 13), social workers have devoted a major part of their effort to creating conditions that improve the quality of life for children and youth. This work is the largest primary practice area for basic social workers and follows only mental health and family services among the specialist and independent social workers. Further, nearly two-thirds of both groups work with children and youth as a primary part of their social work practice.

The U.S. society has entrusted the family with full responsibility for the care and nurturing of children. Law and custom mandate that other social institutions must not interfere with the rights and responsibilities of the family to care for its children. Historically, it has been assumed that parents would make choices that were in the best interest of both themselves and their children. For example, if parents thought it more important for children to work in a factory or to help with farm work than to attend school or have time for play, that decision was honored. That authority, however, left children vulnerable. Legislation permitting other social institutions (e.g., child protective services, police, and courts) to intervene in family situations that were potentially harmful to children was reluctantly adopted. Today, children and youth continue to be somewhat hidden within families with only limited protection when abusive situations are present.

In most situations social workers seek to work with both the parents and children. Children can often be helped most if parents are assisted in obtaining needed resources and/or developing effective ways to raise their offspring. In addition, social workers have not only provided services directly to parents and children but have also actively promoted laws, programs, and public understanding of the needs of children and youth. Examples of some of the practice areas in which social workers serve children and youth follow.

ADOPTION AND SERVICES TO UNMARRIED PARENTS

The adoption process begins with the expectant mother, often unmarried, who faces the difficult decision of whether to keep her baby or place the child for adoption. A few of the factors to be considered in this decision include the mother's plans for the future, such as continuing school or securing employment and child care, the attitudes of the mother's family about the pregnancy, the feelings of the father and the mother's relationship with him, and where the mother will live while pregnant and after the baby arrives. Social workers use both individual and group counseling to help women consider the implications of their decisions. They also, at times, offer counseling to unmarried fathers to help them deal with this situation.

If the decision is made to place the child for adoption, the social worker must screen and select adoptive parents carefully. Matching parents and children is a difficult task that requires considerable knowledge and skill. To gain the best information possible on which to base these decisions, the social worker might conduct group orientation meetings and develop thorough social histories of the prospective adoptive parents. Detailed information on the child's background and even special interests of the natural mother for the child's future (religious affiliation, for example) become part of the basis for final adoptive placement.

There has always been an abundance of prospective adoptive homes, and recent trends making it more socially acceptable for single parents to raise children have reduced the supply of infants available for adoptive placement. However, it continues to be difficult to secure satisfactory adoptive homes for older children or those who are physically or mentally disabled. An important function of the social worker is to recruit parents for these hard-to-place children.

FOSTER CARE

At times children may need to be removed from their own homes, but it is not possible, nor desirable, to permanently sever the relationship with their natural parents, as in placing them for adoption. In these cases, temporary (sometimes long-term) foster care is required. The social worker must work with the parents, the child, and the courts to obtain a decision to remove a child from his or her own home and make a foster home placement. This process involves a careful assessment and a plan whereby the child can return home if conditions improve.

The social worker is also responsible for developing a pool of good quality foster homes. He or she must recruit, select, train, and monitor those families that are entrusted with the care of foster children. The placement of a child in a foster home often creates severe stress on the child, the natural parents, and the foster parents. Considerable practice skill by the social worker is required if he or she is to help resolve these problems.

RESIDENTIAL CARE

At times the appropriate placement for a child is a residential care facility, that is, a group home or a residential treatment center. These facilities are most likely to be chosen when the child exhibits antisocial behavior or requires intensive treatment to change behaviors that may create problems for him- or herself or others.

In these situations, one role of the social worker is to select an appropriate residential care facility, which involves working with the child, the family, and, often, the courts. In addition, other social workers are usually staff members of such a facility, providing care and treatment for the children who are placed there. They are especially involved in helping maintain positive contact between the child and the family and in making plans for the child to return home when appropriate. The fact that these residential care facilities require licensing creates another role for the social worker—evaluating facilities for the purpose of licensing.

SUPPORT IN OWN HOME

Much work with children and youth involves providing support services in order to keep children in their own homes. These support services can take the form of counseling or linking clients with outside resources.

Counseling may involve one-to-one consultation with a parent or child to resolve a particular problem with the child–parent relationship. It may also involve family consultation in which all the family members work with the social worker in an attempt to improve some aspect of their functioning. Family members may also participate in group counseling with other parents or children experiencing similar problems. The social worker guides the participants as they address the issues relevant to their problems.

In work with children and youth, the most common outside resources are day care and homemaker services. Day care centers can provide a stimulating environment for children and relieve parents of the stress created by the child's continual presence in the home. The social worker must know the strengths and limitations of various day care centers and match children with appropriate resources. Homemaker services help parents learn homemaking skills and reduce the pressures of caring for the children and the household.

PROTECTIVE SERVICES

Some children are abused or neglected by one or both parents. Abuse, whether it is physical, sexual, or emotional, is an active mistreatment or exploitation of the child. Neglect is a more passive mistreatment of the child but can be just as damaging. It can take the form of inadequate food and shelter, unwholesome conditions, failure to have the child attend school, or inadequate provision of medical care.

The social worker, as an agent of society, seeks to protect the child without infringing on the rights of the parents. When a referral is received, the social worker must determine if the child is in immediate danger, assess the ability of the parents to resolve the problem, and make a judgment about the risks of working with the family while keeping the child in the home. If the child is removed from the home (with approval of the courts), the social worker continues to work with the family in an effort to eliminate the difficulties that led to the referral. This process may involve individual, family, or group counseling; the provision of support services; or education of family members in the areas of their incompetence.

YOUTH SERVICES

Very early in U.S. history a number of human service programs were developed to provide educational and recreational opportunities for people of all social classes. These services were aimed at character-building among youth, with organizations such as the YMCA, YWCA, Boys and Girls Clubs, and various scouting groups developing. Later, with the growth of settlement houses, programs were broadened to serve other age groups. Although other disciplines also provide staff for these organizations, this field of practice continues to be a small but important area of social work.

These services seek to enhance the growth and development of all interested participants, from the poor to the well-to-do. Through the use of such activities as crafts, sports, camping, friendship groups, drama, music, informal counseling, and other forms of group participation, the members are guided toward personal development. The role of the social worker might be to administer these agencies, to lead the group process, or to provide individual counseling.

Community/Neighborhood

	Primary Practice Area	Prevalent Client Need
Basic Social Worker	0.5%	No data
Specialist/Independent Social Worker	1.5	No data

Relatively few social work jobs are primarily related to helping communities improve their functioning. These data suggest that neighborhood and community change activity, when it does occur, is most likely to be a secondary part of a social work job. As Chapter 8 indicates, analysis of the tasks performed by social workers in all fields of practice does not support the conclusion that they do, in fact, engage in a substantial amount of social action or community change activity. These data raise a question about the degree to which social workers are fulfilling their mission of addressing issues of *both* person and environment.

Beginning with the Charity Organization Societies and the Settlement House Movement in the late 1800s, social workers clearly saw the need both to coordinate the multiple human services that existed in a community and to stimulate change in these communities to make them more responsive to the needs of people or change patterns of operation that have negative effects on people. When social workers do provide neighborhood or community services today, three forms of intervention are typically applied: community organization, community planning, and community development.

COMMUNITY ORGANIZATION

A traditional practice area for social work has been working within the network of human services to increase their effectiveness in meeting human needs. This activity involves collecting and analyzing data related to the delivery of services, matching that information with data on population distribution, securing funds to maintain and enhance the quality of services, coordinating the efforts of existing agencies, and educating the general public about these services. The principal agencies in which social workers are employed to do this type of work are community planning councils, United Way agencies, and other federations of agencies under the auspices of religious groups, such as the Jewish Welfare Federation.

COMMUNITY PLANNING

A few social workers with specialized training join physical, economic, and health planners in the long-range planning of communities. This work requires the ability to apply planning technology in order to project and plan the growth and development of communities. The special contribution of the social worker is to analyze the needs for human services as towns, cities, or regions undergo change. These contributions might range from anticipating "boom-town" developments in energy-impacted areas of Colorado or Wyoming to helping an urban ghetto plan for an increase in human service needs brought about by businesses moving to the suburbs, leaving the central city with an eroding tax base.

COMMUNITY DEVELOPMENT

Social work joins a number of disciplines in giving assistance to people in communities as they seek to improve conditions. This approach is based on a self-help philosophy that encourages members of the community to mobilize their resources in order to study their problems and seek solutions. In rural areas, the social worker contributes to this "grass roots" approach by guiding those involved toward a sound process that maximizes the participation of many concerned citizens. The social worker or other professional also serves as a resource for obtaining technical consultation in areas where there is not expertise among the community members. In urban areas this process, sometimes known as an "asphalt roots" approach, is used to help neighborhoods or special population groups (such as the poor, minorities, or older people) work together to improve the quality of their lives.

Corrections/Criminal Justice

	Primary Practice Area	*Prevalent Client Need*
Basic Social Worker	2.7%	6.4%
Specialist/Independent Social Worker	1.3	4.0

Another small but important part of social work practice occurs in the area of corrections and criminal justice. Correctional social workers are employed in courts, parole and probation offices, and correctional facilities. Social workers often find corrections a perplexing field of practice because the structure of services is usually based on punishment and taking custody of the lives of offenders, which conflicts with many social work values and principles. Yet, because the nature of the problems experienced by persons who come to the attention of professionals in this field are basically those of social functioning, the social worker has a valuable contribution to make.

The corrections field embraces offenders from all aspects of society—youth and adults, males and females, rich and poor, members of dominant population groups and minorities, and even former politicians. In correctional settings, the poor, especially minorities, are very much overrepresented. The social worker's involvement with the criminal justice system can begin at the time of arrest and terminate at the person's release. Some social workers serve as, or work with, juvenile officers in diversionary programs, where they provide crisis intervention or referral services at the time of arrest. These programs divert people from the criminal justice system and into more appropriate community services. Social workers also prepare social histories and make psychosocial assessments of individuals charged with crimes as part of the data a judge uses in making decisions about a case. If the person is placed on probation, a social worker might be the probation officer providing individual, family, or group counseling and helping the convicted person make changes in behavior that will satisfy the terms of probation and prevent additional problems from developing.

Social workers are also found in correctional facilities. In these facilities they provide counseling and serve as a link to the outside world, which encompasses the family, potential employers, and the community service network that will provide support to that person at the time of release. If parole is granted, a social worker might serve as the parole officer or work in a halfway house where the person may live prior to a completely independent re-entry to the community.

Disabilities (Physical/Mental)

	Primary Practice Area	Prevalent Client Need
Basic Social Worker	10.4%	33.4%
Specialist/Independent Social Worker	4.1	34.0

Assisting persons with physical, mental, and developmental disabilities is a field of practice in which basic social workers are most likely to be the primary service providers. Yet helping people deal with disabling conditions affects most fields of social work (see Chapter 15). Social workers are concerned with such disabling conditions as mental retardation, visual and hearing impairment, communication disability, learning disability, and cerebral palsy, which affect not only the person's physical and intellectual functioning but also interaction with others, that is, social functioning. The special role of social work is to help these persons and their families learn to live as successfully as possible in a society structured for the more fully functioning individual.

Disabling conditions are about equally divided among mental retardation, behavioral disorders, and sensory and/or physical disorders. In addition, some persons experience more than one form of disability with a few experiencing the "dual diagnosis" of both a developmental disability and emotional illness.

What is a *developmental disability?* The term has evolved to include a rather broad range of disabling conditions that affect the physical, social, and intellectual development of a person. The Developmental Disabilities Assistance and Bill of

Rights Act (Public Law 95-602) provides the following definition of a developmental disability:

> . . . a severe chronic disability of a person which: a) is attributable to a mental or physical impairment or combination of mental or physical impairments; b) is manifested before the person attains age 22; c) is likely to continue indefinitely; d) results in substantial functional limitations in three or more of the following areas of major life activity, including self-care, receptive/expressive language, learning, mobility, self-direction, capacity for independent living, and economic self-sufficiency; and e) reflects the person's need for a combination and sequence of special, interdisciplinary, or generic care, treatment, or other services which are individually planned and coordinated.[6]

While the definition of a disabled person contained in PL 95-602 does not include all physically and intellectually disabled people, it does encompass a large share of the most seriously disabled. In an effort to enhance the quality of life for all people, social workers serve clients who experience both mild and severe disabilities. To accomplish this goal, social workers help people find suitable living arrangements (either with their families or in community facilities), assist in the alleviation of problems associated with the disability, contribute to public education efforts about the causes and society's responses to these disabilities, and help individuals gain access to needed services.

Education and Training

	Primary Practice Area	Prevalent Client Need
Basic Social Worker	0.3%	10.5%
Specialist/Independent Social Worker	3.4	9.8

Some social work practice does not involve directly serving clients, but rather teaches others to provide services needed by individuals, families, groups, organizations, and communities. Most of these social workers are employed by colleges and universities, while others provide training programs for volunteers or employees of human service organizations. Rarely is education or training the primary function of either a basic or specialized social worker. This function is usually performed by advanced workers.[7] However, it is noteworthy that about 10 percent of all social workers devote a part of their practice to various education and training activities.

Education and training require a wide range of skills. Much of the work involves classroom, workshop, or seminar formats for providing instruction. However, training also involves more individualized forms of instruction found in the direct observation and coaching of volunteers, students, professionals, or other staff members of social agencies. The communication skills and group interaction skills used in many aspects of social work practice have made social workers particularly effective in conducting education and training activities.

Family Services

	Primary Practice Area	*Prevalent Client Need*
Basic Social Worker	13.7%	38.3%
Specialist/Independent Social Worker	13.7	45.1

Social workers at all levels are likely to be involved in helping families address issues in their social functioning, both as their primary practice area and as a client need they frequently address when employed in other fields of practice. Why are family services such a substantial part of social work practice? Changing marital arrangements, child-rearing practices, and patterns of employment in the United States have placed considerable strain on the nuclear family. A growing number of single-parent families, reconstituted families (often involving her children, his children, and their children), duo-breadwinner families, and gay/lesbian households, for example, have dramatically affected social structures that were established for the older family pattern of a mom, a dad, and their children. Social workers have a key role in helping society address these changes and in assisting individual families and households to adapt to these newer conditions or resolve problems associated with them. Three broad service areas capture the bulk of the activities in which social workers engage: family counseling, education, and planning.

FAMILY COUNSELING

Social work employs three approaches to family counseling in an effort to help the family adjust to its changing role and deal with the problems it experiences. One is *family casework*. This approach emphasizes helping individual members of the family change their behaviors in order to make them more productive contributors to the family. It draws on techniques used in individual casework and is strongly influenced by psychosocial treatment approaches and a problem-solving orientation.

A second approach is termed *family group work*. Recognizing that the family is a special form of a small group, this approach incorporates much of the theory of social work practice with groups. It emphasizes the process by which the family examines its relationships. The social worker helps family members work together to resolve their problems.

The third approach is *family therapy*. This approach seeks to change the structure of the family to make it more supportive of its members. The family, then, is regarded as a unit that can contribute to the well-being of its individual members and is encouraged to perform this function. Family therapy requires advanced skills and training to prepare properly for this therapeutic activity.

FAMILY LIFE EDUCATION

The quality of family life can sometimes be strengthened through activities that fall under the label of family life education. This social work practice activity recognizes that all families face certain kinds of stress, and it seeks to prevent family breakdown by educating family members to cope with anticipated problems. It teaches about interpersonal, family, and sex relationships to help people to have more satisfactory and fulfilling lives. Family life education is a preventive approach to human services that has the potential for reaching a large number of people.

FAMILY PLANNING

Social workers have long been sensitive to the fact that both an unwanted child and his or her parents often experience problems. Adequately carrying out the responsibilities of raising a child is difficult under the best of circumstances, and an unwanted pregnancy makes it even more difficult. Most social workers contend that each child should have the right to begin life as a wanted person. Helping families to plan the number, spacing, and timing of the births of children to fit with their needs improves the chance of achieving the goal of bearing wanted children.

Family planning does not imply that there should be a minimum or maximum number of children in a family or that any specific birth control method should be used. Rather, from the social work perspective, the family is helped to make decisions about their patterns of reproduction in order to maximize the quality of life for all family members.

The social worker does not have medical training and cannot replace the important role of physicians and nurses in teaching the physiological aspects of family planning. However, he or she must have a minimal understanding of human reproduction, contraception, and abortion to help families with the decisions they must make. Because the issue of family planning can arise in many counseling situations, social workers in hospitals, public welfare agencies, mental health clinics, family services, health departments, schools, family planning clinics, and private practice must be prepared to help clients when the need for family planning decisions arise.

Income Maintenance

	Primary Practice Area	Prevalent Client Need
Basic Social Worker	3.1%	14.9%
Specialist/Independent Social Worker	1.5	7.1

Once the primary discipline engaged in income maintenance, today relatively few social workers report employment in public assistance positions. Many more, however, indicate that financial issues are one of the most common problems experienced by their clients. Therefore, it is important for social workers to be knowledgeable about poverty and the various income maintenance programs available to assist poor people.

Social workers have learned that living in poverty is much more than just not having a sufficient supply of cash. Poverty is much more complex and insidious. It is associated with the quality of housing in which one lives, the safety of the neighborhood, the quality of meals, the person's health and thus regularity of school and work attendance, and many other factors. Experience indicates that financial assistance, at least at the levels U.S. society has been willing to make available, will not, in itself, break the cycle of poverty. Yet, sufficient income is a prerequisite for addressing many other problems in social functioning.

Despite the many factors that contribute to poverty, lack of income is an unmet need that brings poor people to the attention of the social worker. A number of government-sponsored and voluntary social programs have been developed to provide assistance to, or reduce financial demands on, the poor. The two dominant areas of the income maintenance field are public assistance and social insurance programs, although there are other programs that serve this area of human need.

The reasons that people require financial assistance vary, and so do the programs designed to meet these needs. For some, help with the purchase of food is enough, and providing families with *food stamps* is adequate to reduce hunger. For others, the federal government provides funds through *Temporary Assistance for Needy Families (TANF),* which offers more substantial financial aid that will help to pay for housing, clothing, and other daily living costs. Some of these families may also receive food stamps to supplement the TANF income. States supplement these programs from their revenues by providing *general assistance* to give temporary support to people who, for varying reasons, are not eligible for other financial aid programs. A more specialized program is *Social Security Income (SSI),* which is intended to provide a minimum level of income for some of the most vulnerable members of the society—the aged, blind, and disabled. Finally, the *Medicaid* program provides for hospital and medical care for the poor in an effort to minimize the financial impact of a serious illness on people who cannot afford medical insurance. These programs reflect the "safety net" concept of human services, requiring that the recipient experience serious problems before the services become available.

Other basic social services are provided through individual and employer contributions to a specific program, rather than through direct tax revenues. These *social insurance* programs are "universal" because they are available without the stigma of demeaning eligibility tests. Assistance is viewed as a right, not charity. The major social insurance program is *Old Age, Survivors, Disability, and Health Insurance (OASDHI),* better known as Social Security. It provides income and other benefits to the worker, worker's spouse, and dependent children of a retired or disabled worker. *Medicare* is a federal health insurance program directed at persons over age sixty-five, who are especially vulnerable to serious illnesses that can quickly deplete financial resources and place them permanently in need of public assistance. Other important social insurance programs are *Unemployment Insurance* and *Worker's Compensation Insurance.* The former provides temporary benefits to eligible persons who have lost their jobs, and the latter furnishes income and medical expenses to people who have been injured on their jobs.

Finally, a wide range of cash and in-kind benefits is also provided through a variety of private sources in people's own communities. Local churches and social agencies usually have small amounts of emergency support funds, food banks, food kitchens, and other resources from which the poor can obtain help in meeting their basic needs. These resources are so indigenous to local areas that local human resources directories or local experts on the services such as social workers must be consulted to locate needed sources for assistance.

Medical and Health Care

	Primary Practice Area	*Prevalent Client Need*
Basic Social Worker	12.8%	26.8%
Specialist/Independent Social Worker	13.5	18.3

Medical social work was initiated in the early 1900s, with social workers playing a peripheral role to physicians and nurses in health and medical settings. With increased understanding that illnesses can be caused or exacerbated by social factors, social workers gained a more central role in providing medical and health care. Today, social work in hospitals, outpatient clinics, and other health-related organizations is one of the largest practice fields for both basic and specialist/independent social workers.

A primary place for social work practice in this field is in hospitals. In these settings, for example, social workers address social and psychological factors that are either contributing causes of medical ailments or are side effects of a medical condition that must be dealt with to facilitate recovery and prevent occurrences of nonfunctional dependence. Social workers help to link patients, perhaps with changed levels of functioning due to a medical problem, with their environments by providing individual, group, and family counseling; serving as patient advocates; and working with self-help groups of patients experiencing similar medical or social problems. Social workers also might be engaged in counseling terminally ill patients and their families.

In addition, social workers are involved in other health and medical care facilities besides hospitals. They work in public health clinics and private physicians' offices providing counseling and referral services to people who have sought medical treatment related to family planning, prenatal care, child growth and development, venereal disease, and physical disability, for example. They have also taken an active role in health maintenance and disease prevention programs in local communities. With the skyrocketing costs of medical care, it is even more important that these efforts be continued by the social work profession.

Mental Health and Illness

	Primary Practice Area	*Prevalent Client Need*
Basic Social Worker	9.9%	No data
Specialist/Independent Social Worker	28.3	No data

It has long been recognized that one's mental health and capacity for social functioning are highly correlated. A person who is depressed, hyperactive, hallucinating, or experiencing any of the other symptoms of mental illness is likely at some time to become the client of a social worker. It is estimated that 15 percent of the general population experience emotional disturbance at any one time, creating a high demand for social workers in this field. In fact, social workers are twice as prevalent as psychologists and psychiatrists in the mental health field. Most social workers serving mentally ill persons are at the specialist or independent social worker level; however, 15 to 20 percent of the BSWs report dealing extensively with mental health problems such as anxiety and depression, interpersonal relations, character or behavior disorders, and, more generally, mental illness.

Social workers in mental health settings work with people experiencing these difficulties by treating those who have the potential for change. They help them learn to cope with problems in their social functioning and, at the same time, work to change factors in their environment to promote better mental health or eliminate social conditions that have a negative effect on their functioning. There are three practice settings where social workers are most likely to engage in psychiatric social work, outpatient mental heath clinics, inpatient psychiatric hospitals, and in private practice.

About 8.7 percent of the BSW and 17.9 percent of the MSW workers provide mental health services on an outpatient basis in a mental health center, sheltered workshop, or counseling center. They provide clinical or therapeutic services to individuals and families or to small groups of clients. They may also consult with a variety of organizations, such as group homes, or work with the mass media, in an effort to create an environment that is conducive to the health, growth, and development of all people—both clients and the public.

A much smaller number of social workers (4.4% of the BSW and 2.9% of the MSW workers) provide mental health services on an inpatient basis in psychiatric hospitals. These services are given to people of all ages experiencing severe mental health problems requiring the full-time care and structure available at a hospital or other living situation. Whereas the MSW workers may provide a variety of treatment activities, the BSW workers are more likely to serve as liaisons to the patient's outside world and help the patient and family or friends maintain contact while the person is hospitalized. The social worker might also assess the impact of family, friends, employer, school, and so forth on the client's situation and offer assistance in helping these significant others change in ways that will benefit the client. Finally, when patients are ready to return to the community, social workers become the key professional people helping them to make arrangements for returning to school or work, securing an appropriate living situation, connecting with support programs in local human service agencies, and developing and maintaining needed social relationships.

Occupational Social Work

	Primary Practice Area	*Prevalent Client Need*
Basic Social Worker	0.6%	8.1%
Specialist/Independent Social Worker	1.1	12.4

Social work has been practiced in business and industrial settings since the late 1800s. Social workers have been employed both by management and labor unions to offer services and provide consultation through employee assistance programs. In recent years, with businesses increasingly realizing that worker productivity is closely related to the workers' general satisfaction with the quality of their lives, an investment in helping employees resolve problems in social functioning is seen as simply good business. This perspective has created a small but growing field of practice known as occupational or industrial social work. With more than 131 million people in the civilian labor force,[8] the workplace is an opportune setting in which to identify social problems and provide needed services. Often, early intervention at the location of one's employment can prevent more serious problems from developing later.

Shank and Jorve identify three models of social work practice in business and industry: the employee service model, the consumer service model, and the corporate social responsibility model.[9] An explanation of each follows.

The *employee service model* of occupational social work focuses on activities that provide direct service to the employees of a business or industry. The social worker using this model might develop and implement employee assistance programs and various supervisory training programs. In addition, the social worker might provide counseling to individuals or families in relation to marital, family, substance abuse, aging, health, and retirement problems; offer referral to other community agencies or self-help groups such as Alcoholics Anonymous; and consult with management on individual problems. Typical problems the social worker might also address would be the identification of job-related factors such as boredom or stress, an employee's desire to find resources to upgrade his or her job skills, the need for preretirement planning, or a linkage to Worker's Compensation or unemployment insurance programs.

The occupational social worker following the *consumer service model* might serve as the company's representative to various consumer groups and focus on identifying consumer needs and methods of meeting them. Typically found in banks, public utilities, and government agencies, these social workers help to provide a liaison between consumer groups and social service agencies, develop outreach programs, and provide counseling to customers to meet unique needs.

The third model of practice, the *corporate social responsibility model,* places the social worker in the role of assisting corporations and businesses to make a commitment to the social and economic well-being of the communities in which they are located. The social workers consult with management on their policies concerning human resources, their donations to nonprofit organizations, and social legislation they may wish to support. In addition, social workers may administer health and welfare benefit programs for employees, represent the company in research and community development activities, and provide linkage between social service, social policy, and corporate interests.

Schools

	Primary Practice Area	Prevalent Client Need
Basic Social Worker	1.4%	8.4%
Specialist/Independent Social Worker	6.3	13.6

Just as places of employment are important locations for identifying and addressing problems of social functioning for the employed population, schools are an important place to serve children and youth. Although individual and family problems directly affect a child's ability to learn, relatively few school social workers are employed to help parents, teachers, and the children themselves address these complex issues. Most of these social workers are prepared at the specialist or independent worker level.

The traditional approach of social workers in schools has been to counsel the child and confer with the family. They have depended on the cooperation of teachers to make referrals when problems are evident and have had varying degrees of effectiveness, depending on the willingness of teachers and school systems to use them as a resource. Problems of truancy, suspected child abuse, inadequate nutrition, substance abuse, parental neglect, and inappropriate behavior are often referred to the social worker.

Recently this practice field has undergone a marked change with the school being approached as a primary setting where social problems should be identified and addressed. Social workers have, under this approach, become more aggressive in their practice activities, serving as a link between school, family, and community. Some activities that school social workers typically perform include offering counseling to children, their families, and teachers related to factors that affect the child's performance at school; serving as an advocate for children with school administrators and community agencies when specialized services are needed; organizing parent and community groups to strengthen school and community relationships; and coordinating teams that draw on different disciplines' expertise and parent's interests to assess a child and develop a plan to assist a child's development.

Concluding Comment

For the person considering a career in social work, it is important to have an understanding of the many different fields of practice open to the social worker. It is evident that the attention social workers give to helping people and their environments interact more favorably makes an important contribution to resolving social problems or enhancing social functioning in many areas.

The most current data about social work practitioners indicate there are some practice areas where substantial numbers of both basic and specialist/independent social workers are employed, and this includes such areas as work with children and youth, families, and health care. BSW-level workers are much more likely than their MSW counterparts to be engaged in providing services to the aged and working in the disabilities area, while the primary practice area for the MSWs, by a substantial margin, is mental health.

A clear picture of client needs addressed by social workers emerges from data presented in this chapter. Helping clients resolve problems in family functioning stands well above all others. A second and often interrelated tier of issues are those of client functioning that have been affected by mental illness or retardation, character disorders or behavior problems, health-related matters, anxiety or depression, difficulties in interpersonal relations, and problems associated with alcohol and substance abuse.

The knowledge and skills acquired when obtaining a baccalaureate or master's degree in social work are intended to prepare one to engage in social work practice in any of these practice fields. The ability to transfer these competencies from field to field gives the social worker considerable flexibility in selecting where he or she will work and what type of client issues will be the focus of practice. This job flexibility has long been an attractive feature of social work.

KEY WORDS AND CONCEPTS

Field of practice

Primary practice area

Prevalent client need

Community organization

Community planning

Community development

Developmental disability

Occupational or industrial social work

Public assistance

Social insurance

SUGGESTED READINGS

Literally hundreds of books and articles are published each year on the various fields of practice described in this chapter. The two books listed below are recommended as resources for beginning the process of acquiring additional information about these and other fields of social work. One book, the 2,600-page *Encyclopedia of Social Work,* is a valuable resource for investigating most topics relevant to social workers. The author(s) of each chapter is selected by the *Encyclopedia*'s editorial board as highly respected experts on the subject matter. These authors, then, provide a "state-of-the-art" summary of the topic and a bibliography of the seminal literature on that subject. In the second recommended book, Gibelman provides another useful way to examine social work. Her book, *What Social Workers Do,* is packed with short chapters describing more than fifty different examples of social work practice. Each contains a short case vignette that helps the reader gain insight into what the social worker actually does when serving clients.

Edwards, Richard L., editor-in-chief. *Encyclopedia of Social Work,* 19th Edition. Washington, D.C.: NASW Press, 1995. (Available in hardcopy and CD-ROM versions.)

Gibelman, Margaret. *What Social Workers Do.* Washington, D.C.: NASW Press, 1995.

ENDNOTES

1. U.S. Bureau of the Census, "Profile of Older Americans: 1998." (http://www.aoa.dhhs.gov/aoa/stats/profile/default.htm#older)
2. Ibid.
3. Ronald E. Herrington, George R. Jacobson, and David G. Benzer, eds., *Alcohol and Drug Abuse Handbook* (St. Louis: Warren H. Green, 1987), p. xiii.
4. David Cook, Christine Fewell, and John Riolo, eds., *Social Work Treatment of Alcohol Problems* (New Brunswick, NJ: Rutgers School of Alcohol Studies, 1983), p. xiii.
5. Gary W. Lawson and Ann W. Lawson, *Alcoholism and Substance Abuse in Special Populations* (Rockville, MD: Aspen Publishers, 1989), pp. 5–7.
6. Robert L. Schalock, *Services for Developmentally Disabled Adults* (Baltimore: University Park Press, 1982), p. 12.
7. Robert J. Teare and Bradford W. Sheafor, *Practice-Sensitive Social Work Education: An Analysis of Social Work Practice and Practitioners* (Alexandria, VA: Council on Social Work Education, 1995).
8. U.S. Bureau of the Census, "USA Statistics in Brief." [http://www.census.gov/ftp/pub/statab/USAbrief/part2.txt]
9. Barbara W. Shank and Beth K. Jorve, "Industrial Social Work: A New Arena for the BSW." Paper presented at the National Symposium of Social Workers, Washington, D.C., 1983, p. 14.

CHAPTER 6

Settings for Social Work Practice

Prefatory Comment

Our society's commitment to the welfare of its members is played out through an extensive array of social programs that are delivered by several different helping professions—including social work. For people to gain access to these programs and professionals, there must be some form of organizational structure that serves as a vehicle for delivering human services. Usually that is a formal organization that operates under the auspices of a federal, state, or local government, or it is a private human services agency that is structured as either a nonprofit or for-profit agency. Increasingly these services are also offered by social workers who are private practitioners, that is, social workers who contract directly with their clients for services in the same manner as the private physician or attorney contracts with his or her clients.

These differing practice settings influence the nature of the problems a social worker addresses, the clients served, the amount of red tape and paperwork required, the salary earned, and many other factors that affect one's work activity and job satisfaction. This chapter examines the advantages and disadvantages for both social workers and their clients in the different practice settings.

Throughout its history, social work has been an agency-based profession. Like teaching, nursing, and the clergy, social work practice emerged primarily within organizations, and today, as in the past, most social workers are employed in some form of human service organization. Accreditation standards require that all students complete a substantial learning experience in a social agency, and the profession does not consider social workers ready for the independent level of practice, that is, private practice, until they have a period of supervised work in an agency after completing the MSW.

In recent years there has been a shift in the employment patterns of social workers. Where once virtually all social workers were employed in either government or nonprofit human services agencies, a whole new sector of employment has opened for social workers today. As indicated in Table 6-1, the public or *government sector* is the largest employer of basic social workers and encompasses nearly one-third of the master's-level social workers. The basic and specialist/independent social workers are about evenly divided in the *voluntary sector* with nearly 40 percent of both groups working in nonprofit agencies. However, a substantial portion of the MSW-level social workers (28.3%) work in the *business sector* where they are employed in for-profit agencies or are engaged in private practice. This chapter examines the practice conditions and issues social workers typically face when working in each of these three primary sectors of the society.

Characteristics of Practice Settings

When social programs are created, a decision must be made about how the program will be delivered. Whether it offers a direct benefit, such as food stamps, or depends on a third-party payment, such as Medicare, the program must be provided under the auspices of a human service organization or by an independent practitioner.

When programs are provided by human service organizations, the agencies establish the necessary policies and supply the administrative structure to make the program available to recipients. Clients then contract with that agency to provide the needed service and the agency employs staff to deliver the program. The organization is responsible for determining who is eligible for service and how that service will be performed, for screening and selecting its staff, assigning the work to various staff members, monitoring the quality of the work, and securing funds to pay the costs of providing the service.

TABLE 6-1   **Sector of Primary Employment for NASW Members: 1995**

Employment Sector	Basic	Specialist/Independent
Government Sector	41.6%	33.0%
Local	21.4	17.3
State	16.8	12.1
Federal	2.7	2.7
Military	0.7	0.9
Voluntary (nonprofit) Sector	40.4%	38.6%
Business (for-profit) Sector	18.1%	28.3%

Source: Margaret Gibelman and Philip H. Schervish, *Who We Are: A Second Look* (Washington, D.C.: NASW Press, 1997), p. 71.

When the service is delivered by a social worker in private practice, the client contracts directly with the social worker or the private practice group with which the worker is associated. The client then pays directly for the service or draws on insurance, Medicare, or other funds to pay for the service. Certification and licensing help the clients or companies paying for this service to determine if the practitioner is qualified to perform this service. One reason NASW requires two years of supervised practice experience beyond the MSW in order to be recognized as an "independent social worker" (see Chapter 4) is that the person engaged in private practice does not have an agency structure to monitor the quality of service given, and, NASW has concluded, this requirement provides greater protection to clients against the possibility of contracting with an inexperienced or incompetent worker.

The type of practice setting, whether agency or private practice, partially determines who will be clients, how clients will be protected against incompetent practice, and the degree of flexibility the worker has in providing services to clients. Thus, it is useful to examine the several types of organizational structures that serve as the settings for social work practice.

GOVERNMENT SECTOR SETTINGS

Government organizations are established and funded by the general public with the intent to provide services that preserve and protect the well-being of all people in the community. These agencies reflect city, county, state, and federal governmental efforts to respond to human needs and are limited by the provisions of the laws under which they were established.

Most government sector social programs are created by lawmakers in Washington, D.C., or a state capital. These policy makers are usually geographically distant from the clients and service providers alike and, too often, are unfamiliar with the issues that arise when these laws are implemented by local agencies. For this reason social workers often find their practice in government agencies frustrating. There is inherent inflexibility in these settings because laws are difficult to change, budgeting and auditing systems are highly structured, cumbersome civil service or personnel systems are mandated, and coordination among the different governmental levels is difficult. Further, these organizations are subject to political manipulation, and financial support and program development can be significantly influenced by a changing political climate. Except through substantial political action efforts, those who must carry out these programs have limited opportunity to influence their structure and funding.

On the positive side, although sometimes client fees are required, public agencies are financed almost completely by taxes, and the regular flow of tax money offers some stability to the programs. Legislative bodies are authorized to levy taxes so human needs can be met, and, in times of economic difficulty when voluntary contributions may be reduced, legislators have the power to tax and, therefore, maintain the services. Also, the larger amounts of money potentially available to public agencies allow for experimentation with various methods of service provision. Research and demonstration grants sponsored by government agencies have, in recent years, been the most significant factor in developing new and creative approaches to meeting human needs.

It should be recognized that government sector agencies provide services that are likely to meet the most basic human needs such as food, clothing, and shelter. It simply is not possible to adequately respond to the fundamental needs of the poor, homeless, disabled, aged, and others through voluntary and for-profit human services.

VOLUNTARY (NONPROFIT) SECTOR SETTINGS

Out of the history of providing assistance for persons needing help, a number of *mutual aid organizations* have been created to facilitate members of a group providing services for other members of that group. Churches, labor unions, and civic clubs are examples of this type of voluntary organization. Although civic and fraternal organizations such as Rotary, Soroptimist, and Kiwanis Clubs and various Masonic and ethnic group-focused organizations support some human service programs, they rarely employ professional staff.

Religious groups, however, have created *sectarian programs* staffed by social workers and limited to members of that denomination or faith. A substantial amount of human services from counseling to social provisions are provided to group members by synagogues and various denominational groups on a daily basis. Most of this service is not documented and largely goes unrecognized. These church-sponsored human service agencies that restrict their services to members, however, are only a small part of the social programs supported by religious groups. Many organized religions believe that a part of their responsibility is to serve persons in need, whether a member of that faith or not. Most human service programs sponsored by religious organizations (e.g., hospitals, group homes, retirement centers, and family counseling agencies), therefore, are *nonsectarian*. As such, they are designed to fulfill a religion's responsibility to serve the whole community.

Labor unions represent another mutual aid setting where social workers might be found. Although relatively few social workers are employed by labor unions, they have expanded their social services in recent years. Unions historically have been successful in organizing workers who are underpaid and undervalued by management. Like social workers employed in business and industry, the labor union setting presents an exceptional opportunity to intervene with people at the place they work, and therefore improve the likelihood of resolving problems before they reach a crisis level. Social workers in these settings typically help union members with such work-related problems as finding child care, dealing with family problems related to work schedules, and addressing stress created by changed family roles when both spouses are employed.

A second type of practice setting in the voluntary sector of human services is the *private nonprofit agency*. Private agencies traditionally have depended on voluntary individual and corporate support for their operation. Their sources of funds have included gifts and bequests, door-to-door solicitations, membership dues, fees for service, and participation in federated campaigns such as a United Way or a Jewish Welfare Federation. More recently, however, private agencies have begun receiving a substantial share of their funding through contracts with government agencies to provide specific direct services, conduct research and demonstration projects, or to support their programs through block grants or revenue sharing. Government agencies have increasingly found this a desirable arrangement because it has allowed them to bypass much of the rigidity of the large bureaucratic organizations in favor of the more flexible private agency structures.

Although there has been an intermingling of taxes and donated funds in the budgets of these private agencies, they are classified as part of the voluntary sector because they operate with policies established by a governing board made up of community volunteers. In the structure of their governance, then, nonprofits differ dramatically from government agencies that have elected officials responsible for making basic policy decisions. In most instances, these agencies have the advantage of being small and primarily concerned with the provision of local services. Thus, the board members are able to become directly exposed to the agency and are more capable of responding to changing conditions and needs for services in a local community.

A board, however, does not have complete autonomy in developing policies and programs for the agency. Many nonprofit agencies receive a part of their funding from a local United Way, and that participation as part of a federation of agencies inevitably requires some loss of autonomy. Also, some agencies are affiliated with a national organization such as the Child Welfare League of America or the Family Service Association of America, which may impose some limitations on agency functioning.

The term *nonprofit* indicates that if the agency should end a year with any funds remaining, those resources are allocated to enhance the agency's operation and not paid to staff, board, or any other parties. Since no one profits financially from the operation of the agency and it serves the public good, the Internal Revenue Service has created a process to approve agencies [Section 501 (c) (3) of the Internal Revenue Code] as nonprofit organizations. With this designation, persons who donate funds to support the agency can deduct the contribution from their income taxes. In this way, the government is underwriting the voluntary sector human services.

BUSINESS SECTOR SETTINGS

The most rapidly growing setting for social work practice is the for-profit or business sector. This category of practice includes both private practice and employment in large organizations that exist to earn a profit for their owners.

The term *private practice* is used to indicate a practice situation where a contract for the provision of service is made directly between the worker and the clients. Usually this term is applied in reference to social workers who provide clinical services, but sometimes private practice involves nonclinical activities such as consulting, conducting workshops or training programs, or contracting to perform research or other professional service for a fee.

With direct client–worker contracts, the practitioners have considerable autonomy in determining how the practice situation will be addressed and what intervention approaches will be used. However, without the monitoring of services that human services agencies provide, clients are more vulnerable to incompetent or unethical practitioners. It is fundamentally for client information and protection that all 50 states license or certify social workers and the NASW has created credentialing processes for workers at the independent level.

For some social workers, private practice is an attractive alternative to agency-based practice. Usually there is less paperwork to manage, more flexibility in scheduling, and, often, the elimination of unnecessary supervision. In addition, private practice is among the highest-paying settings for social workers. The downside of private practice is that it is a small business and, like many small businesses, is difficult to sustain. A practice must attract a sufficient number of clients who can pay high fees to support the ongoing operating costs (e.g., space, utilities, clerical staff) and also provide a wage for the social worker. For this reason, many social workers engage in private practice on a part-time basis and maintain their primary employment in a human services agency.

Another emerging entrepreneurial setting for social work is in *for-profit organizations*. During the past decade there has been a transformation in the funding of human service programs. From the 1930s through the 1970s a pattern emerged in which legislative bodies allocated substantial funds for government agencies to provide services directly to clients. Therefore, a relatively large public sector developed. Later, that pattern shifted to purchase-of-service agreements with nonprofit agencies rather than governmental agencies providing these services themselves. A second, and perhaps even more dramatic, shift known as *privatization* is now occurring. Governmental agencies have begun to invest a substantial amount of their funds in the purchase of service from for-profit organizations that are owned and operated as any other business. In fact, many are owned and operated by large corporations.

Several fields of practice have rapidly increased their reliance on these businesses to provide human services. For example, a national study of child welfare services found that proprietary firms were used as vendors for services for 51 percent of all residential treatment, 49 percent of institutional care, and 58 percent of the services provided in group homes.[1] To a lesser degree public agencies rely on contracts with proprietary organizations to provide day care, day treatment services, nursing home care, correctional facilities, and health care.

Social work, as well as other professions, is uneasy about the growing amount of for-profit practice. The trend toward the privatization of human services threatens to replace the service orientation of professions with the profit motive. Privatization risks making the bottom line the amount of return to the shareholder, rather than the quality of service to the client. When the shareholder is also the professional, serious ethical issues arise that can erode public trust in the professions.

One development that has affected all social workers in the business sector, whether in private practice or employed by for-profit organizations, is the evolution of *managed care*—or perhaps more accurately, managed costs. Stimulated by the escalating cost of health and mental health services, a variety of plans have been developed to provide health care consumers with needed services at controlled costs.[2] On the positive side, these plans require greater accountability for the quality of services offered, which ultimately should enhance the services clients receive. However, analysts of managed health care programs conclude that many decisions about the nature and extent of services provided are being shifted from the professionals and clients to the managers of the insurance companies. These are not typically people with the qualifications to determine an individual's need for professional services. Although social workers continue to provide a substantial part of the direct services delivered under managed care plans, they increasingly play an active role as advocates with insurance companies or government agencies for clients who do not receive the services they require.

Social workers have a central role to play in all three sectors of the economy—government, voluntary, and business. The ability of these professionals to perform their function depends at least partially on their ability to effectively work within a human services organization or manage a private practice. Understanding several issues typically experienced in each of these settings can help future social workers anticipate difficulties they may face and be prepared to deal with them head on.

Issues Affecting Agency-Based Practice

When considering a social work job, it is important to address issues that are likely to be experienced when working in a formal organization. Potential employing agencies should be examined in relation to their relative compatibility with professional values and standards and the autonomy workers have to exercise their professional judgment in performing the job tasks. The manner in which a human service organization deals with the following issues will affect the work of its professional staff, and they are, therefore, useful to recognize.

ACCOMMODATING HORIZONTAL AND VERTICAL INFLUENCES

Social workers employed in most human service organizations, as well as those in private practice, often find they cannot successfully work in isolation from other agencies. Clients' needs are not necessarily experienced in the same way as social agencies identify their mission, and often clients must address multiple issues simultaneously—some extending beyond the programs offered in any one agency.

At the local level, social workers often lead efforts to coordinate the services provided to clients by the full array of social agencies in that community. This coordination requires that interagency networks, or *horizontal affiliations,* are developed among the agencies. The form of these horizontal networks may range from informal discussions among agency representatives regarding human service programs to the formal creation of human resources planning organizations that study the local service network, encourage efforts to fill gaps in the services, and facilitate cooperation among the agencies. The ability of a social worker to effectively perform his or her professional tasks is enhanced when there is a strong interagency network in a community and the social worker's employing agency supports his or her participation in these activities.

Social agencies and social workers are also influenced by *vertical affiliations,* that is, those organizations external to the community that have the authority to at least partially shape the services or operating procedures of a local agency. Voluntary agencies, for example, might affiliate as chapters or members of a national organization, which can immediately give the agency name recognition, provide the community with some assurance that at least minimum standards acceptable in that practice field are being met, make staff development opportunities available through national meetings, and sometimes help secure financial resources. At the same time, these agencies give up some local autonomy as they are committed to operate within the guidelines of the national organization. Vertical affiliation with the American Red Cross, Boy or Girl Scouts of America, the YWCA or YMCA, the American Heart Association, the Salvation Army, or the Family Service Association of America are typical examples of such affiliations. Further, many local voluntary agencies must meet state licensing requirements or other state standards if they are vendors of services to public agencies. This also limits their discretion.

Public agencies typically have more direct and formal vertical relationships. A local governmental agency may be implementing programs that have been created and partially funded at the federal level, further defined and partially funded at the state level, and finally modified and also funded by county government. Thus, a county social services department, for example, is constrained by requirements imposed by federal, state, and county governments. Although these vertical affiliations add considerably to the complexity of tailoring service programs to local needs, they have the advantage of fostering greater equality in the benefits and services provided to people throughout a region and the nation. In addition, vertical affiliation creates a larger geographic area for securing funds to support the services, making it possible to more adequately meet needs in a local or regional area that lacks its own resources.

BALANCING EFFICIENCY AND EFFECTIVENESS

A fundamental goal of all human service agencies, whether they are public or private, is to use the scarce resources available to provide the most and best service possible. To achieve this goal agencies must operate both efficiently and effectively. An agency that leans too far in favoring one over the other ultimately creates problems for the staff members employed in that agency.

Efficiency represents the efforts of the agency to achieve the maximum output of services with a minimum input of resources. The goal of efficiency places the emphasis on the quantity of services provided and often attracts most of the attention of lawmakers, governing boards, and local media. Yet, quantity must be related to quality if an agency is to find a balance that represents the maximum level of service. The qualitative aspects of service are represented in an agency's *effectiveness,* or the degree to which the agency achieves its goals.

The governance of most social agencies has been dominated, in both the public and voluntary sectors, by people who have given leadership to thriving business and industrial enterprises. They often bring a strong bias toward efficiency; and, although some degree of effectiveness in producing goods was necessary, low cost-per-unit production was clearly the most valued goal. That orientation is especially evident in managed care and the for-profit human service organizations. Thus, the social worker considering agency employment should carefully examine the agency's effectiveness orientation lest the quality of his or her work be seriously compromised in favor of overemphasis on efficiency.

How can efficiency be attained in human service organizations? Successful managers from business and industry have transferred one proven tool in their work to the human services—bureaucratic structure. And why not? Bureaucracy had worked to build automobiles and appliances at a fraction of the cost of handmade products. Weber created the clearest statement of bureaucratic theory. His "ideal-type" description of the characteristics of a bureaucratic organization was intended to reflect a pure, but extreme, statement of the characteristics of a bureaucracy:[3]

1. *Division of Labor.* Each person in the organization has a clearly defined and specialized assignment in the organization.
2. *Hierarchy.* Specific lines of authority exist in which every person in the administrative structure is not only responsible for his or her own assignments but is also responsible for the performance of subordinates.
3. *Consistent System of Rules.* Every task in the organization is governed by an explicit set of rules which specify the standards of performance and the relationships among tasks.
4. *Spirit of Impersonality.* Work is to be performed without favoritism or prejudice entering official decisions.
5. *Employment Constitutes a Career.* Persons are employed only on the basis of technical qualifications required by the organization, with rewards provided to encourage loyalty and offer opportunity for a career in that organization.

With some modifications, when applied to the assembly line that produces automobiles in Detroit or toasters in New Jersey, bureaucratic principles led to a high degree of organizational efficiency. This model yielded good results when the product was made from standardized parts. In fact, the greater the standardization, the more effective the bureaucratic organization becomes. A person could quickly be trained to perform a very specific function, for example, installing a fuel pump as an automobile passes on the assembly line. With a line supervisor to check for quality control and enforce the rules established for efficiency (the worker cannot be taking a break when the engine arrives for a fuel pump), the company usually produced a good-quality product. Under this system there could be no allowance for the worker's personal problems, nor could the boss play favorites. Bureaucratic theory assumes that the rewards of seniority, salary increases, and promotion are sufficient to keep the successful employee satisfied with the organization.

When these principles are applied to human services agencies, social workers and other professionals often find that bureaucratization has both positive and negative consequences. Indeed, the application of bureaucratic principles can ensure equity for both clients and workers, facilitate efficiency in operation, and enhance public support of the organization.

Accommodating the Professional Model

Rigid application of bureaucratic principles, however, is in direct conflict with the very nature of professions. As opposed to manufacturing products, in human services the parts being worked with are people who are constantly changing, and the product (attaining maximum client well-being) differs to some degree in each situation. It is simply not realistic to provide narrow technical training, to create highly specialized assignments, or to establish an inflexible system of rules that a staff must follow regardless of the uniqueness of the client or practice situation.

When the professional model (see Chapter 3) is compared to the bureaucratic model, inherent conflicts emerge. These conflicts have been identified by Scott as: (1) the professional's resistance to bureaucratic rules; (2) the professional's rejection of bureaucratic standards; (3) the professional's resistance to bureaucratic supervision; and (4) the professional's conditional loyalty to the bureaucratic organization.[4] These conflicts are present in varying degrees in any organization where the professional social worker, or any other professional, is employed.

Bureaucratic rules present a constant dilemma for professionals. When a division of labor exists, each person provides only a part of the work for the agency. Procedures, or rules, must then be established to facilitate interaction among the workers and coordinate their activities. Those rules are inherently arbitrary and somewhat inflexible, making it difficult for professionals to respond to unique client needs, thus limiting their autonomy in delivering client services.

Bureaucratic standards also present difficulties for the professional. Standards are ordinarily based on a perception of the "typical client," but in reality, clients present great variability and require services that may not fit the profile that was followed when a social program was created. The professional model suggests that social workers will serve clients as long as service is needed, but bureaucratic standards such as agency eligibility requirements, limits on length of service, access to specialized services, and so on may limit the ability of the professional to fulfill the professional obligation to provide needed services.

In bureaucratic systems, authority is assigned to a position. Conversely, professional authority is generated from competence as judged by one's peers. It is no wonder that professionals resist *bureaucratic supervision,* which is based on authority derived from a person's place in the organization. By definition a professional is considered competent to perform his or her job without the requirement of someone constantly monitoring that performance—particularly when the person monitoring may be from another profession or an administrator with no professional preparation at all.

Finally, professionals typically display a *conditional loyalty,* rather than a strong commitment to the employing organization. Professionals are prepared with general competencies that are transferable from one organization to another, making it relatively easy to leave an unsatisfactory work environment. A professionally educated social worker, for example, can move from juvenile court to a hospital without additional educational preparation. Any additional knowledge about the specific setting or field of practice can be obtained by reviewing the literature on the subject, through supervision, and by attending various workshops and seminars. People wedded to a bureaucratic organization, however, do not have that degree of flexibility and can experience job mobility primarily by moving up in the organization. At times, the person who is too dependent on the organization must compromise service to clients, as well as professional integrity, in order to succeed as a member of the organization and receive the rewards (e.g., salary increases, promotions) the organization offers its employees.

DETERMINING THE STATUS OF SOCIAL WORK

One final factor to consider when selecting a place of employment is the centrality of social work to the mission of that particular setting. The status of social work in an agency influences the manner in which a social worker spends much of his or her time and affects the opportunity of clients to have the full benefit of the perspective that social work brings to the helping situation. When the policies and procedures of the organization are designed to maximize social work services, social workers can most effectively serve their clientele. However, in a practice setting where another discipline is dominant, social workers often spend considerable effort educating others about the contributions social work can make to the agency's clientele.

In some practice settings social work is the *primary discipline*. The primary services provided call for social work expertise, most key jobs require social work training, and social workers hold the major administrative jobs. In practice fields such as child welfare, family services, and income maintenance, social work has traditionally been the primary discipline. In these settings other disciplines may be involved to provide specialized expertise or consultation, but the services are organized to maximize the contributions of the social worker.

In other practice settings the social worker is an *equal partner* along with members of one or more other disciplines. The services are organized to maximize interdisciplinary cooperation, and a member of any of the disciplines might provide administrative leadership to the agency. The fields of aging, mental health and retardation, and community and neighborhood services are examples of practice fields that are shared by several disciplines.

In still other settings social work might provide supporting services to another profession. As the *secondary discipline* in these agencies, social work is, in one sense, a guest of the primary discipline. The agency is organized to allow the primary discipline to work as effectively as possible, and the needs of social work or other professions receive lower priority. The role of the social worker in a medical setting illustrates social work as a secondary discipline. Hospitals, a setting for medical practice, are geared to the needs of the physician. Social services are provided at the physician's referral and are organized so they do not compete with the schedule and work of the medical profession. A similar role would be assumed by the social worker in corrections, school, and industrial settings.

SUCCEEDING AS A SOCIAL WORKER IN AN AGENCY STRUCTURE

Clearly, an employee is obligated to work within the legitimate requirements of his or her employer, and a social worker cannot ethically ignore the rules and regulations of the agency. However, it is not sufficient to be merely a passive employee who unquestioningly accepts and carries out the rules and regulations of the agency. Client services can be compromised if social workers do not actively work to promote agency flexibility in service provision and, when warranted, be willing to challenge the agency's methods of operating. At times, this may mean taking some risks that may affect one's evaluations, pay increases, or even employment in the agency. Thus the successful agency-based social worker must be smart about organizational change efforts.

Many times constricting agency rules and regulations do not need to be changed. Creative interpretations that stretch the rules to fit client needs are often possible and frequently can be applied with the full support of one's supervisor. Some regulations, however, may not lend themselves to this flexibility, and it may be necessary to attempt to initiate a process to change these rules. Change, especially in large public agencies, takes considerable time and effort. The social worker who has attempted to bring about such change can identify with the adage, "The change agent must have the time sense of a geologist." With skill, patience, and perseverance, such change can be accomplished and the professional obligation of the worker to provide the best services possible fulfilled. If this effort fails, however, the worker must either learn to live with the existing regulations or make the decision to seek employment elsewhere.

Assuming that satisfactory conditions exist in an agency for performing social work practice, it becomes important for the worker to discover ways to be responsible to the agency and at the same time maximize the ability to provide services to clients. Pruger suggests four helpful tactics that a worker might employ.[5] First, it is important to understand the agency's (or supervisor's) legitimate authority. Within the guidelines of responsible behavior, the social worker seeks to discover the limits of the discretion that a worker has in providing services to clients. Second, because organizations often present demands (e.g., paperwork, staff meetings) that divert the worker's time and energy from the work of providing services, the worker should be cautious about overcommitting to these activities that are of secondary importance. Third, the worker should develop supplemental competencies that are needed by the agency. Professional work involves more than carrying out the routine job duties. It involves making a commitment to expand one's contributions by learning, for example, new practice techniques, skills in grant writing, knowledge of computer applications in practice, or methods of interpreting the agency and its services to the public. Finally, the worker should not yield unnecessarily to agency requirements established for administrative convenience. For instance, it may be convenient to have clients come to the worker's office to receive services so that back-to-back interviews can be scheduled and the worker's time used efficiently. However, for some clients the requirement of arranging transportation, leaving work, or the unfamiliarity with the agency may discourage them from keeping the appointment. In such a case, a home visit by the worker may be far more successful. Although challenging unproductive regulations may not help the social worker win popularity contests, this action can be a valuable contribution to the organization's effectiveness.

Another contribution that a social worker can make to an employing agency is to prepare to move into a supervisory role or to assume an executive or high-level administrative position in the agency. Making such a transition is difficult. A study (reported in more detail in Chapter 8) that compared the tasks performed by social workers in direct practice positions and administrative positions revealed two very different sets of activities, although some skills overlapped the two job functions.[6] As compared to direct service practitioners, the social workers who were administrators were much more involved in activities such as making staff assignments and conducting evaluations of their work, representing the agency and helping to build the service delivery system in the community, engaging in program development, and carrying various tasks (e.g., budget development, expense approval, staff coordination) that help to maintain the organization's daily operations.

Finally, a worker should be prepared to engage in teamwork and interprofessional practice. Agency practice typically draws together persons from varying professions who have their own unique areas of expertise, volunteers with their basic talents, and other staff members in an effort to respond to human needs. In theory the unique roles and capacities of each discipline appear clear and workers need only coordinate their efforts. In reality, however, there is considerable blurring of lines between the various helping disciplines. Turf problems inevitably emerge that, if not resolved, can jeopardize good client service. Thus, interprofessional collaboration and teamwork are essential.

Human services agencies continue to seek means of improving interprofessional cooperation through various administrative structures, team approaches to case situations, the development of protocols that spell out the functions to be performed by each discipline, and the use of case managers charged with coordinating the services an individual or family might require. Social workers, with their mission to facilitate the interface of clients with their environments, have a particularly important leadership role to perform in facilitating interprofessional collaboration.

ADVANTAGES OF AGENCY-BASED PRACTICE

Given the complexities of agency practice, why does social work continue to function as an agency-based profession? Why not adopt the private practice model of other successful professions? Most social workers recognize that agency-based practice offers several advantages.

First, it makes the services more visible and, therefore, more accessible to all persons in need. The existence of agencies in a community over time and the attendant publicity about their operations typically make both their programs and their locations familiar to all members of the community. As opposed to nonagency practice, which caters to those who can pay the full cost of services, public and private human service agencies are more likely to have as clients the most vulnerable members of society. For the social worker committed to serving the part of the population experiencing the most serious social problems, agency practice is the only game in town.

Second, agencies survive because they have received the sanction, or approval, of the community for the services they provide. Clients approach the helping situation with a greater trust in the quality of services they will receive because of the agency's implied responsibility to ensure that quality services are delivered. In private practice situations the client must place full trust in the individual practitioner to perform high-quality practice.

Third, clients have the benefit of an extra layer of protection against possible misuse of professional authority in social agencies. Clients in any setting are protected by both the professional ethics of the workers and, in many cases, the legal regulation or licensing of that practice. In agencies, however, they are also protected by the agency's selection of staff and ongoing monitoring of the quality of services.

Fourth, human service agencies tend to have a broad scope and often employ persons from several different professions, which provide clients with ready access to the competencies of multiple professions and give the worker the opportunity for interdisciplinary practice activities. In addition, as opposed to the more limited service focus found in private practice, agencies typically offer a broad range of services, from direct practice to social action. Thus, they provide the social worker with the stimulation of engaging in a range of different practice activities and make it possible to change the focus of one's practice area or move into supervisory or management positions without changing employers.

Fifth, most agencies offer staff development opportunities that stimulate professional growth among workers. Characteristically, social agencies employ a large enough number of staff members that workers do not feel isolated and, in fact, typically carry out programs that contribute to the continued professional growth and development of other members. The rapidly changing knowledge and skill base of the helping professions makes continuing professional development important to the services the clients receive and adds to the intellectual stimulation of the staff.

Last, agencies have the ability to raise funds from the community, whether from taxes or voluntary contributions, and to offer a stable salary to employees. Agencies do not face as great a risk of a fluctuating income as is experienced by persons in private practice settings.

Issues in Private Practice

The principal alternative to agency-based practice for the social worker is private practice. The remarkable expansion of this setting in the past decade is an important feature of social work today. It is useful for future social workers to be aware of the issues that surround this practice setting.

Why is private practice gaining such popularity among social workers? From the vantage point of the social worker, private practice is attractive partially because of the greater opportunity for financial gain, but more importantly, for the freedom to exercise professional autonomy in the conduct of social work practice. The bureaucratic constraints of many human service agencies have placed restrictions on practice activities that compromise the ability of social workers to effectively use their professional competencies for the benefit of clients. Thus, some social workers have actively sought a different practice setting that would not restrict their work.

Although private practice avoids many of the limitations that accrue from practice within a bureaucratic structure, it also places greater responsibility on the social worker to follow the ethical guidelines of the profession. There is no professional monitoring of private practice, although complaints can be filed with a state licensing board or the local NASW chapter. NASW has rightfully been concerned about establishing guidelines that will identify for the public those social workers who have the requisite preparation and experience to conduct autonomous practice.

THE ORGANIZATION OF PRIVATE PRACTICE

What does a social worker do in private practice? In his study of clinically oriented private practice, Wallace found that the average for these social workers was "63 percent of private practice time in individual treatment, 19 percent devoted to work with marital couples, 8 percent to group therapy, 7 percent to family treatment, and 2 percent to joint interviews with clients other than married couples."[7] For the delivery of these clinical services, three organizational approaches are used.

In the first approach, the social worker engages in multidisciplinary practice. In this arrangement the social worker participates with members of other disciplines (for example, psychiatry and psychology) to provide a *group practice* that can meet a broad range of client needs. The social worker is an equal partner with the other disciplines and, in fact, is a co-owner of the business.

In the second form of private practice, the social worker provides a *supportive practice* for a member of another profession. For example, some physicians are hiring social workers to help patients deal with social problems related to specific illnesses. The social worker might also provide more general services in the physician's office such as educating expectant parents about child development, counseling families that need help with child-rearing practices, or referring people to appropriate community resources for help with other problems.

In the third form, social workers are the *sole owners* of their private practice. Sole ownership involves securing office space, hiring staff, advertising services, making contacts to acquire referrals, overseeing the determination and collection of fees, and doing everything related to the management of a small business. Like any other business, private practice is a "sink or swim" proposition with no guarantee of income equivalent to expenses. The main problems for full-time private practitioners are generating sufficient referrals to be able to keep the business solvent, handling the business details including securing payment from third-party vendors, obtaining competent consultation, minimizing the inherent isolation, arranging for backup in managing crisis situations, and protecting practitioners against their vulnerable position if there should be malpractice charges.

It is estimated that two to three times as many social workers are engaged in part-time as are in full-time private practice. Many of these social workers are employed by a social agency but maintain a small private practice as well. Kelley and Alexander identify four groups of social workers who elect to engage in part-time private practice:[8]

1. Agency practitioners who welcome the independence and additional income,
2. Social workers in supervisory or administrative positions who wish to maintain client contact and clinical skills,
3. Educators who wish to have sufficient practice activity to remain sufficiently current with a practice to effectively teach clinical courses, and
4. Social workers who are parents of young children and need to control their hours of work.

Part-time private practitioners experience many of the same problems as those in full-time practice. Kelley and Alexander's study of part-time private practitioners indicates that the most serious problems they face in getting a practice started are generating referrals and handling the practical business issues such as locating office space, securing financing, keeping records, and the like. Although these matters continue to be problems, they are somewhat transitional and become less consuming once a practice is established. Later, and particularly unique to the person in part-time private practice, time management problems become the most difficult part.[9]

Some social workers in private practice provide indirect services such as consultation. Consultation might be provided to another social worker or to a member of another helping profession concerning the handling of a case. For example, a social worker might consult with a lawyer about a divorce or child custody case. He or she might also be involved in working with a social agency, such as helping a nursing home with staff–patient relations, administrative procedures, or program development.

Another form of indirect private practice involves the training of social workers, or members of other disciplines, in special skills. The increasing demand for experienced social workers to provide workshops, seminars, or other forms of training is contributing to the growing demand for private practice.

CONCERNS RELATED TO PRIVATE PRACTICE

The private practice approach represents a substantial departure from social work's historical agency orientation. It has not been without controversy in the profession and has experienced problems in becoming accepted and appreciated in the general community. Four issues have emerged concerning this practice mode.

First, private clients do not have an agency monitoring system to provide protection against incompetence or abuses of the professional monopoly. Therefore, social work has been careful to specify more extensive education and experience as minimum preparation for the private practitioner than for the agency-based practitioner. The standards established by NASW call for completion of a master's degree in social work from an accredited school of social work, two years of full-time or 3,000 hours of part-time practice experience, and successfully passing the examination required for membership in the Academy of Certified Social Workers (ACSW). To be listed in both the *National Registry of Health Care Providers in Clinical Social Work* and NASW's *Register of Clinical Social Workers,* a social worker is required to have completed at least two years of full-time, post-master's employment as a social worker.

Second, because many private practitioners work on a part-time basis, some agencies are concerned that private practice will detract from agency practice. They fear the social worker will place self-interest above the needs of the agency. A study of twenty voluntary agencies yielded the following common concerns about private practice.[10]

1. That the worker will not do justice to his or her agency responsibilities because of the amount of time and energy that may go into private practice.
2. That the worker may take clients from the agency or gain clients in the community who may otherwise have gone to the agency.

3. That the staff person will become more his or her own agent instead of being an enabler for the agency.

4. That the staff person may not meet the minimum standards set by the National Association of Social Workers for private practice.

On the other side of this issue, it is argued that private practice offers different professional stimulation than is found in agency practice and also provides a supplemental income to agency salaries that keeps workers satisfied with their agency employment. Some agencies even encourage social workers to engage in some part-time private practice by allowing them to use their agency offices in the evenings or by arranging schedules to allow a day off each week for this purpose. Such arrangements, however, are ripe for conflict of interest issues.

Finally, some critics have accused private practitioners of diverting social work from its mission of serving the most vulnerable members of society. There is little argument that clinical private practice represents a deviation from social work's philanthropic roots. Barker states, "Undoubtedly, the major dilemma is that private practice services are less accessible to the very people who have historically been social work's traditional clientele—the disadvantaged."[11] Moreover, private practice has been accused of failing to perform the social action responsibilities that are central to social work's mission of person and environment change. Teare and Sheafor confirmed this accusation, but additionally found that most other direct service practitioners also failed to engage in social change activities.[12]

ADVANTAGES OF PRIVATE PRACTICE

There are also arguments in favor of social work's movement toward private practice. First, in most human service agencies clients have little opportunity to exercise individual choice in regard to which professionals will provide services. Clients typically cannot select their individual social workers nor can they fire them if unsatisfied with the services received. Clients exercise considerably more control in a private setting.

Second, from the social worker's perspective, agency rules and regulations place constraints on the worker's ability to conduct a practice in the manner he or she believes would be most effective. Professional autonomy is inherently compromised. For example, agency-based social workers cannot choose their clients; are not completely free to determine the amount and type of service to be given; and are almost always supervised, at times by one who interferes with the professional judgment of the worker.

Third, agency salaries tend to be lower than those of the private practitioner. Further, as opposed to the market-driven income of the private practitioner that is, at least theoretically, based on competence, agency salaries are based to a greater degree on seniority and position within the agency.

Last, few agencies avoid the pitfalls that plague most bureaucratic organizations, in which workers find that a disproportionate share of their time is devoted to meetings and paperwork. The less elaborate mechanisms required for accountability in private practice free the worker from much of the less people-oriented activity found in agency practice.

For both clients and social workers, there are gains and losses from both agency and private practice. These factors influence the nature and quality of services provided as well as the social worker's satisfaction with his or her employment.

Concluding Comment

Social work practice has permeated U.S. society to the extent that it occurs in every sector of society: government, voluntary, and business. Although the roots of social work are in agency-based practice, where public concerns for people in need took the form of creating human service agencies, social work now is offered through both agency and private practice modes.

Most social workers continue to be employed in agency settings, and thus they must be able to work effectively within agency structures if they are to maximize their ability to serve clients. Understanding the principles on which agencies are organized and the problems social workers commonly experience in matching their professional orientation with agency requirements is, therefore, important for providing quality services.

An increasing number of social workers have entered private practice to avoid some of the problems experienced by the agency-based practitioner and to increase potential income. However, private practice is certainly not trouble-free. Social work is beginning to address the important issues related to private practice: adequate preparation for the responsibilities of independent practice, the lessening quality of agency practice, the move away from the social work mission of focusing services on the poor and other vulnerable population groups, and public sanction and client protection for this relatively new method of service delivery.

It appears, at this point in history, that the trend in social work is toward an increasingly entrepreneurial approach to practice. However, it is clear that some critical social programs can never be made available through the mutual benefit organizations and entrepreneurial human services in sufficient quantity to meet the needs of the most vulnerable members of this society. Thus, it is reasonable to conclude that social work will continue to be primarily an agency-based profession and that social workers must continue to devote attention to making these organizations more responsive to the requirements for effective professional practice.

KEY WORDS AND CONCEPTS

Government sector	Managed care
Voluntary sector	Horizontal/vertical influences
Business sector	Efficiency vs. effectiveness
Mutual aid organization	Bureaucracy
Nonprofit agencies	Bureaucratic vs. professional model
For-profit organizations	Interprofessional teamwork
Private practice	Social work as: primary discipline, equal
Privatization	partner, secondary discipline

SUGGESTED READINGS

Barker, Robert L. *Social Work in Private Practice: Principles, Issues, Dilemmas,* 2nd Edition. Washington, D.C.: NASW Press, 1991.

Kamerman, Sheila, and Kahn, Alfred J., eds. *Privatization and the Welfare State.* Princeton, NJ: Princeton University Press, 1989.

O'Looney, John. *Redesigning the Work of Human Services.* Westport, CT: Quorum Books, 1996.

Salamon, Lester M. *Partners in Public Service: Government-Nonprofit Relations in the Modern Welfare State.* Baltimore: Johns Hopkins University Press, 1995.

ENDNOTES

1. Catherine E. Born, "Proprietary Firms and Child Welfare Services: Patterns and Implications," *Child Welfare* 62 (March–April 1983): 112.

2. Golda M. Edinburg and Joan M. Cotter, "Managed Care," in Richard L. Edwards, ed., *Encyclopedia of Social Work,* 19th Edition (Washington, D.C.: NASW Press, 1995), *The Social Work Reference Library* (CD-ROM).

3. Peter M. Blau and Marshall W. Meyer, *Bureaucracy in Modern Society,* 2nd Edition (New York: Random House, 1973), pp. 18–23.

4. W. Richard Scott, "Professionals in Bureaucracies—Areas of Conflict," in Howard M. Vollmer and Donald L. Mills, eds., *Professionalization* (Englewood Cliffs, NJ: Prentice-Hall, 1966), pp. 264–275.

5. Robert Pruger, "The Good Bureaucrat," *Social Work* 18 (July 1973): 26–27.

6. Robert J. Teare and Bradford W. Sheafor, *Practice-Sensitive Social Work Education: An Analysis of Social work Practice and Practitioners* (Alexandria, VA: Council on Social Work Education, 1995), pp. 180–182.

7. Marquis Earl Wallace, "Private Practice: A Nationwide Study," *Social Work* 27 (May 1983): 265.

8. Patricia Kelly and Paul Alexander, "Part-Time Private Practice: Practical and Ethical Considerations," *Social Work* 30 (May–June 1985): 254.

9. Ibid., p. 255.

10. Janice Proshaska, "Private Practice May Benefit Voluntary Agencies," *Social Casework* 59 (July 1978): 374.

11. Robert Barker, "Private Practice Primer for Social Work," *NASW News* 28 (October 1983): 13.

12. Teare and Sheafor, Ibid., p. 117.

THREE

The Practice of Social Work

The payoff in social work is in the services rendered to clients or improvements made to problematic social conditions in society that affect the quality of life for some or all people. That activity is commonly referred to as social work *practice*. In order to most effectively carry out the practice of social work, the social worker must know *what* he or she is doing, *why* it is done, and *how* to do it. Parts One and Two of this book addressed the what and the why. In Part Three we turn to how.

It has long been recognized that social work practice requires attention to *values* (what we believe ought to be), *knowledge* (our perception of how things are), and *skills* (our ability to use knowledge and intervention techniques effectively in our practice). It is the latter part of social work practice that is most visible to clients. The competence with which the worker draws together his or her professional knowledge, values, and skills and joins them to his or her personal practice style directly affects the quality of services the client receives.

Chapter 7 examines the value base of social work. The profession of social work is founded upon adherence to certain values. Central among these values are beliefs that all people are inherently worthy of being treated with respect and should be assisted in meeting their social needs; that people have a need to belong and should be helped to have meaningful interaction with others; that people are interdependent and must take responsibility for providing for

themselves, for assisting their fellow human beings, and for improving the society; and that the society has a responsibility for helping its members lead fulfilling lives. Without adhering to those values, the social work profession would be unable to perform its role in U.S. society. Additionally, social workers must be highly ethical in their work, as they are involved with highly personal and sensitive aspects of the lives of vulnerable people. Attention is given in this chapter to the NASW Code of Ethics and its important place in shaping how a social worker practices.

Chapter 8 describes the basic competencies required of most social workers. The chapter is organized around the tasks most frequently performed by social workers as identified in the National Task Analysis Study of Social Work Practice. Eighteen clusters of activity performed by social workers who were direct service providers, administrators, or supervisors are identified and the knowledge and skill required to perform them described. It is evident from these data that there is a core of activity in social work practice that includes interpersonal helping, workload management, professional development, and gaining expertise regarding the human service delivery system. The competence to perform these activities effectively is at the heart of social work.

The limited activity by social workers in the community change area revealed in the National Task Analysis Study of Social Work Practice represents a deviation from social work's historical mission of working to facilitate change related to both people and the environment. In an effort to provide readers with an illustration of how social workers might prevent social problems from developing or creating opportunities for large groups of people to improve their well-being, Chapter 9 examines prevention as an area of increased emphasis for social work intervention. Prevention intervention models are presented, including ways of preventing gang homicide.

Another challenge is to advance social work as a global profession. Some of the most serious problems throughout the world (e.g., hunger, inadequate housing, assistance to people experiencing mental and physical disabilities, child and spouse abuse, violations of human rights) are all addressed by social workers—either by treating the victims or seeking ways to prevent these problems. As Chapter 10 indicates, social work is relatively new or currently not recognized in many countries, but the social work perspective is nonetheless needed. Although the practice of social work must be modified to respect cultural variations, its potential to positively affect the quality of life throughout the world is important.

CHAPTER 7

Values and Ethics in Social Work

Prefatory
Comment

At the heart of social work is its values. Values assist the social worker and the social work profession in setting goals related to both clients and society. Of course, like any other population group, every social worker does not have identical values. Yet, there are some common themes in social work that suggest that, by and large, social workers hold some fundamental beliefs in common. As opposed to many other groups of people, for example, social workers tend to believe that society has the responsibility to assist people in meeting their needs, that people should be included in making decisions that affect their lives, that positive change in people's lives can be attained through professional help, and so on. This chapter examines these and other values that are central to social work's belief system.

The most concrete expression of social work's ethical guidelines are embodied in the NASW Code of Ethics. This Code helps social workers to make the inevitable moral choices that arise in their daily practice and is intended to assure clients that the professional monopoly given to social workers will not be abused. If such abuse (i.e., unethical practice) is suspected, the Code also becomes the criteria by which the social worker's ethical behavior is evaluated.

From formulating social programs to helping clients, values affect social work practice. It is evident the social programs created to "promote the general welfare" of the people are influenced by the values held by legislators, board members, or owners of for-profit organizations who created or maintain those programs. Beliefs about who should be responsible for meeting human needs, what role government or private charity should play, and how much of the nation's wealth should be invested in meeting people's social needs are just three examples of factors that have shaped human services programs.

Also, values affect the manner in which human service organizations operate. Values, at least partially, determine the answers to important questions: Should potential clients be encouraged or discouraged from asking for help? Should clients

be required to pay for services? Should volunteers, staff with no specific preparation, or professionals provide services? To what extent should an agency attempt to
make services readily accessible to clients and assure that the surroundings are comfortable and pleasant? Should a social worker be allowed to terminate services
before a client's insurance benefits are exhausted when the agency needs the funds
to meet its financial obligations? Should services be terminated just because the
client can no longer pay yet continues to need help? In short, the dominant values
of an agency can have a direct impact on social work practice.

The values of a social worker's clients, too, affect practice. If a client feels stigmatized, demeaned, or embarrassed to ask for assistance in addressing a social problem, the client's ability to productively use the service is affected. If the client is
unnecessarily demanding of a worker's time and attention or resents being required
to use social services (i.e., an involuntary client), that, too, affects the way a social
worker assists the client. Further, much of practice involves helping clients identify,
clarify, and resolve value issues that are almost always present in human interactions.

As members of a profession that has based many of its practice approaches and
principles on certain beliefs about people and how they can best be served, social
workers must be cognizant of the profession's values. Further, since social work must
protect the public from potential abuses of the professional monopoly, it has
adopted a code of ethical practice that prescribes certain professional behaviors
related to interactions with clients, colleagues, employers, and the community. Each
social worker must be prepared to adhere to the NASW Code of Ethics.

Finally, the social worker must be clear about how the profession's values and
ethical standards interact with his or her own belief system. Therefore, understanding one's own values becomes critical for the social worker. R. Huws Jones, a British
social work educator, is quoted as saying, "A man's values are like his kidneys: he
rarely knows he has any until they are upset."[1] Indeed, most of us do not typically
contemplate our values unless they somehow are upset or create problems for us as
we address the issues we confront in life. This chapter, however, asks the reader to
consider the nature of values, their place in promoting people's welfare through
shaping social programs, the values and ethics of social workers, and, finally, the fit
between social work's values and one's own. Understanding the central place of values and ethics in social work is another important factor in making a career choice
or preparing to enter the social work profession.

The Nature of Values

Unlike knowledge, which explains what is, values express what ought to be. Rokeach
more precisely defines a *value* as "a type of belief, centrally located in one's total
belief system, about how one ought or ought not to behave, or about some end-state
of existence worth or not worth attaining."[2] In short, values guide our thinking about
how we should behave and what we want to accomplish.

Values are much more than emotional reactions to situations or doing what
feels right. Values are the fundamental criteria that lead us to thoughtful decisions. It is important to recognize, however, that people do not always behave in

a manner consistent with their values. Values guide decisions but do not dictate choices. People can and do make decisions contrary to their values. Such decisions might be made when other factors are given priority ("I know that I shouldn't have done that, but when will I ever get another chance to make that kind of money?"), the person acts on emotion ("I was just so angry, I hit her without thinking"), or when one fails to adequately think through and understand the value issues in a situation ("It just didn't occur to me that my quitting school would make my parents think that they have failed").

Each person values a variety of things in life. Differences in the strength with which one holds any particular value and the priority a particular value will have among the whole constellation of that person's values, that is, the person's *value system,* is a part of what makes individuals unique. For example, for many people the most important value is feeling secure in their relationships with loved ones. For some, generating income is the driving force in their lives. For others, giving service or maintaining relationships dominates their value system. Still others attempt to maintain some balance among these values.

Dealing with values is particularly difficult for several reasons. First, values are such a central part of our thought processes that we often are not consciously aware of them and therefore are unable to identify their influence on our decisions. The social worker should constantly be alert to values in practice situations as these values may subtly influence the thoughts, feelings, attitudes, and behaviors of both the client and the social worker.

Second, a person may be forced to choose among values that are in conflict with one another. Who can avoid wrestling with a *value conflict* when confronted by a person on the street asking for money to buy something to eat? We may value responding to people in need, but we may equally value encouraging people to use the organized system for receiving financial assistance that does not put the person into the degrading position of panhandling.

Third, addressing values in the abstract may be quite different from applying them in a real-life situation. The social worker must recognize, for example, that clients may not act on the basis of value choices selected in a counseling session when they are confronted with the actual people and conditions where this value must be operationalized.

Finally, values are problematic because they change over time. Various events, experiences, and even new information can lead clients to adapt their system of values to more closely fit their current situation. A person whose job is eliminated, for instance, may be much more supportive of a universal health insurance program than when he or she was employed and receiving health insurance benefits from the employer.

The Place of Values in Social Work

Helping people to be clear about their individual values, that is, *values clarification,* and facilitating their understanding of how the particular set of values they hold influences their goals and decisions is an important aspect of social work practice. At times, clients also must be assisted in recognizing and understanding the values of others. Taking into consideration the values of family members, friends, employers, teachers, or others in that person's environment may be prerequisite to making appropriate and workable decisions. The matter becomes more complicated when social work practice involves more than one person, as it is likely that each will have a somewhat different value system. In that case the social worker may need to help resolve issues that stem from differences in values.

Further, the social worker must be concerned with his or her own values and control for their inappropriate intrusion into practice situations. Value choices that may be viable personally for the social worker may not coincide with the needs, wants, priorities, or realities the client experiences. Ultimately, the client must live with the decisions that are made, and they should be consistent with his or her own value system—not the value system of the social worker. Learning to suspend one's own values (i.e., *value suspension*) to keep the focus of helping on the client or client group is an important, yet difficult task for every social worker.

People are attracted to particular helping professions because they perceive that the work they do will be consistent with their personal values and, therefore, the job will be satisfying. The way a profession views its role in society, its attitudes toward the clients it serves, the knowledge it selects as the basis for its practice, its requirements for ethical practice behavior, and so forth are all influenced by the profession's values.

With social work practice focused at the interface between person and environment, the social worker must simultaneously address several sets of values. It is no wonder that social work has perhaps devoted more attention to values than has any other helping profession. Yet it has not developed a sufficiently clear and adequately tested statement of its core values to offer a definitive description of its central beliefs. At best, there is only rather general agreement that some values are fundamental to social work practice.

Social Values in U.S. Society

Values differ from *needs*. The latter refers to people's basic biological or psychological urges, while values reflect what people hope to get out of life and how this should be accomplished. The choice of which needs a society will attempt to meet depends on what it values. The most predominant feature of Western values is the central place of the individual; that is, the society exists to help individuals lead satisfying and productive lives.[3] Like other parts of Western culture, the values that guide choices in U.S. society focus on the individual. These values have their roots in at least four different sources, all of which are concerned with the responsibilities of the individual toward self and society and/or the society's responsibility to the individual.[4] These sources include:

1. Judaism and Christianity with their doctrine of the integral worth of humans and their responsibilities for their neighbors;
2. The democratic ideals that emphasize the equality of all people and a person's right to "life, liberty, and the pursuit of happiness";

3. The Puritan ethic, which says that character is all, circumstances nothing, that the moral person is the one who works and is independent, and that pleasure is sinful;

4. The tenets of Social Darwinism, which emphasize that the fittest survive and the weak perish in a natural evolutionary process that produces the strong individual and society.

It is evident that much of the disagreement in the United States over the provision of human services results from value conflicts inherent in the U.S. public's value system. Brill points out:

> Even the casual reader will see that a dichotomy exists within this value system. We hold that all men are equal, but he who does not work is less equal. . . . We hold that the individual life has worth, but that only the fit should survive. We believe that we are responsible for each other, but he who is dependent upon another for his living is of lesser worth.[5]

In carrying out the commitments of the social welfare institution to respond to human needs, the social worker becomes an intermediary between people in need and society's value judgments about what needs are to be met. As one cynic phrased it, the social worker stands "between the demanding recipient and the grudging donor." Therefore, the social worker must be particularly knowledgeable about the values that are dominant in U.S. society.

What constellation of values are held by the U.S. population? In this nation of people with widely diverse backgrounds and interests, it is not surprising that there is considerable variation in belief systems. The answer to the question "Am I my brother's (or sister's) keeper?" is not a categorical "yes" or "no." Protecting a woman's "right to choose" in regard to abortion in one person's value system, for example, is viewed as a "license to kill" in another's system of beliefs. Efforts to document preferred values held by the U.S. public are the basis for considerable political debate, but rarely identify a clear consensus on issues.

Kahle's carefully constructed study of the social values held by Americans suggests that value preferences differ substantially for different segments of the population.[6] The study asked respondents to indicate which of eight fundamental social values was the most important for a person to achieve in life.* The data reveal that the more vulnerable groups consistently hold two values, security and being respected, at much higher levels than the general population. Perhaps that is not surprising. If one is poor, has a limited education, is a minority group member, or is old, he or she is likely to worry about having basic health insurance, sufficient income, and safety. It is also likely that he or she is regularly treated with some

---

*The eight social values, in order of numbers of times it was selected as most important, were (1) having *self-respect* (feeling good about oneself and what has been accomplished in life); (2) attaining a *sense of security* (feeling safe and comfortable about the future); (3) having *warm personal relationships* (maintaining satisfying interpersonal relations with friends and family); (4) feeling *successful* in life's undertakings; (5) being *respected by others;* (6) feeling *fulfilled* by the quality of life experiences; (7) experiencing *a sense of belonging* to valued groups of people; and (8) finding *fun, enjoyment, and excitement* in life's activities.

degree of disrespect by other members in the society as many do not have the education and experience to compete well for jobs, are considered "too old" to take on meaningful work, suffer various forms of discrimination, and so forth. Under these conditions, one values highly what he or she does not have—security and respect. From the vantage point of social work, these data reinforce the view that it is important to support the development of social programs that increase people's security and to deliver those programs in a manner that treats the recipients with dignity. With those two basic social values achieved, people are then ready to address other areas of need that can enhance the quality of their lives.

Social workers and other professionals must be particularly alert to what the clients value because those values are not likely to be held with the same strength by the professionals themselves. The data from the Kahle study indicate that attaining such basic values as security and being respected by others were not of high priority to professionals. After all, they really don't need to worry about those basics. Professionals are highly educated, usually have secure jobs with relatively high income, don't typically experience discrimination, and can feel pretty safe about their futures. Their value preferences are related to items that enhance the quality of life such as achieving self-respect, having a sense of accomplishment, and experiencing fulfillment.[7] It takes discipline and commitment to avoid the trap of seeing the world only through one's own eyes and actively seeking to understand and appreciate the value preferences of others.

Values Held by Social Workers

We have seen that the social worker must relate to the values of both the client or client group and the society. In order to avoid imposing personal values on the client or making inappropriate judgments about a client's values, the social worker must have a clear understanding of his or her own personal values. In addition, the social worker must be fully aware of, and guided by, the fundamental values of the social work profession.

What, then, are the values commonly held by social workers? When developing its classification scheme for different levels of practice, the National Association of Social Workers identified ten basic social work values.[8] These statements express the basic values that underpin the profession of social work.

1. *Commitment to the primary importance of the individual in society.* In this value statement social work reaffirms its commitment to the most basic cultural value in Western society—the primacy of the individual. Social work accepts the position that the individual is the center of practice and that every person is of inherent worth because of his or her humanness. The social worker need not approve of what a person does but must treat that person as a valued member of society. Each client should be treated with dignity.

Commitment to the centrality of the individual has also led social workers to recognize that each person is unique and that practice activities must be tailored for that person's or group's uniqueness. Such individualization permits the worker to determine where and how to intervene in each helping situation, while at the same time communicating respect for the people being served.

2. *Commitment to social change to meet socially recognized needs.* Giving primacy to the individual does not minimize the commitment of the social worker to achieve societal change. Rather, it suggests that the social worker recognizes that the outcome of change activities in the larger society must ultimately benefit individuals.

Social work evolved as the primary profession responsible for helping society fulfill its commitment to meet the social needs of people, that is, to operationalize the social welfare institution. The obligation of social work is not only to deliver social provisions and social services to people in need, but also to serve as instruments of social change as a means of allowing each person to realize his or her fullest potential.

Social workers, then, are committed to the belief that the society has a responsibility to provide resources and services to help people avoid such problems as hunger, insufficient education, discrimination, illness without care, and inadequate housing. While social workers accept the primacy of the individual, they also hold the society responsible for meeting social needs. Social workers serve both the person and the environment in responding to social needs.

3. *Commitment to social justice and the economic, physical, and mental well-being of all in society.* The obligation of social workers is to attempt to improve the quality of all people's lives. Social workers believe that social justice must be achieved if each person is to have the opportunity to develop his or her unique potential and, therefore, make his or her maximum contribution to society. Thus, social workers believe that each person should have the right to participate in molding the social institutions and the decision-making processes in U.S. society so that programs, policies, and procedures are responsive to the needs and conditions of all.

Of course, when needs are competing in a diverse society and when resources are limited, choices must be made. Not every person can have all needs met. When they are making choices, the values held by social workers emphasize the importance of responding to the needs of the most vulnerable members of the society. Typically, these vulnerable people are children, the aged, minority group members, the disabled, women, and others who have been victims of institutionalized discrimination. Social workers are committed to ensuring that social justice is achieved for these persons, individually and as a population group.

4. *Respect and appreciation for individual and group differences.* Social workers recognize that there are common needs, goals, aspirations, and wants that are held by all people. In some ways we are all alike. However, social workers also recognize that in other ways each individual's life experience and capacities make him or her different from others. Where some may fear differences or resist working with people who are not like themselves, social workers value and respect uniqueness. They believe that the quality of life is enriched by different cultural patterns, different beliefs, and different forms of activity. As opposed to efforts to assimilate persons who are in some way different from the general population, social workers value a pluralistic society that can accommodate a range of beliefs, behaviors, languages, and customs.

The title of this book, *Social Work: A Profession of Many Faces,* is intended to suggest that social work not only includes people of many backgrounds performing a wide variety of human services but that social workers also provide services to people from virtually all backgrounds and walks of life. The chapters in Part Four,

"Social Work Practice with Special Populations," elaborate on some of these differences and their impact on social work practice.

5. *Commitment to developing clients' ability to help themselves*. If clients are to change their social conditions, their actions that contributed to the conditions must ultimately change. Unlike medicine, where an injection may solve a patient's problem, social change requires that the people affected become personally engaged in the change process and actively work to create the desired change. Underpinning social work practice, then, must be the social worker's belief that each person has an inherent capacity and drive that can result in desirable change.

Social workers do not view people as static or unchanging, nor is anyone assumed to be unable to engage in activities that may produce a more satisfying and rewarding life. Rather, social workers view people as adaptable. Although there are conditions that some people face that cannot be changed, the people themselves or the world around them can be helped to adapt to these conditions. For example, the terminally ill patient cannot be made well, the blind child cannot be made to see, and the severely retarded person cannot be made self-sustaining. Yet in each case the person involved can be helped to adjust to these conditions, and the person's environment can be adapted to more adequately accommodate special needs. Within the individual's or group's capacities, the social worker places high value on helping people take responsibility for their own decisions and actions.

6. *Willingness to transmit knowledge and skills to others*. Perhaps the most important function performed by the social worker in helping clients accomplish the change they desire is to effectively guide the change process. A significant part of this guidance involves helping clients understand the situation they experience from both a personal perspective and the perspectives of others, as well as helping them develop the skills to resolve their problems.

Effective helping avoids making clients dependent on helpers and prepares them to address other issues that arise in their lives. Thus, it is important that social workers assist clients in identifying strengths that can be mobilized for solving the immediate problem and to help them learn how to use these strengths in solving problems that may arise in the future.

A second application of this value concerns the commitment of professionals to share knowledge with colleagues. Knowledge or skills developed by a social worker are not to be kept secret or limited to clients who work only with that social worker. Rather, the social worker is obligated to transmit this information to other social workers so that they might bring the best knowledge and skill possible to their clients.

7. *Willingness to keep personal feelings and needs separate from professional relationships*. It is important for the social worker to recognize that the focus of practice must be maintained on the client—not on the social worker. Because social workers care about the people they work with, it is easy to become overidentified with clients' lives or even to develop personal relationships with them. If that happens, the client loses the benefit of an objective helper, the social worker can be placed in a compromising position, and the quality of the helping process is diminished because the relationship has changed from professional to personal.

As opposed to the many personal relationships that each person has throughout life, professional relationships require that a degree of professional objectivity be maintained. If a social worker becomes too closely identified with a client, the ability to stand back from the situation and view it from a neutral position is minimized. Sheafor, Horejsi, and Horejsi argue the importance of maintaining an appropriate degree of personal distance from clients:

> By the time most clients come into contact with a professional helper, they have attempted to resolve their troublesome situation themselves—by struggling alone or seeking assistance from family, friends, or other natural helpers.
>
> The professional adds a new dimension to the helping process by operating with a degree of emotional neutrality. Maintaining this neutrality without appearing unconcerned or uncaring is a delicate balancing act. The worker who becomes too involved and too identified with the client's concerns can lose perspective and objectivity. At the other extreme, the worker who is emotionally detached fails to energize clients or, even worse, discourages clients from investing the emotional energy necessary to achieve change.[9]

8. *Respect for the confidentiality of relationship with clients.* Although it is rare that the social worker can guarantee "absolute confidentiality" to a client, social workers value achieving the maximum possible protection of information received in working with clients. The very nature of a helping relationship suggests that there is sensitive information that must be shared between the person being helped and the helper. For example, the social worker must learn the reasons a client has been fired from a job, why a person who is chronically mentally ill has failed in a community group home placement, what keeps a homeless person from being able to secure resources to pay rent, why an alcoholic has not been able to stop drinking, or why a couple involved in marriage counseling has not been able to solve problems without fighting, and the like. In each case, some information typically passes between client and worker that could potentially be emotionally or economically damaging if it is inappropriately revealed to other parties. Social workers consider it of critical importance to respect the privacy of this communication.

9. *Willingness to persist in efforts on behalf of clients despite frustration.* Situations that require social work intervention typically do not develop quickly and usually cannot be resolved readily. Recognizing the frustration that they experience when change is slow to occur, social workers have come to value tenacity in addressing both individual problems and the problems that affect groups of people, organizations, communities, and society in general.

When providing direct services, a social worker may become frustrated with a client who, at a given time, is unable or unwilling to engage in activities the social worker believes would improve the situation. Or, when advocating on behalf of a client with another agency to provide needed services, the social worker may also experience frustration when the client is denied service or is placed on a waiting list. Advocacy for classes of clients or in relation to broad social issues can also prove quite frustrating. If delay tactics or the length of the change process is extended, the social worker may understandably become discouraged. Social workers must be persistent.

10. *Commitment to a high standard of personal and professional conduct.* The final value on the NASW list directs the worker to use the highest ethical standards in his or her practice. It suggests that the worker must conduct professional activities in a manner that protects the interests of the public, the agency, the clients, and the social worker.

This value has been operationalized in the form of the NASW Code of Ethics, which is perhaps the single most important unifying element among social workers. Loewenberg and Dolgoff identify the following five functions served by an ethical code:[10]

1. Provide practitioners with guidance when faced by practice dilemmas that include ethical issues.
2. Protect the public from charlatans and incompetent practitioners.
3. Protect the profession from governmental control; self-regulation is preferable to state regulation.
4. Enable professional colleagues to live in harmony with each other by preventing the self-destruction that results from internal bickering.
5. Protect professionals from litigation; practitioners who follow the Code are offered some protection if sued for malpractice.

Shortly after its founding, the NASW began the development of a Code of Ethics that could serve the needs of this profession. The Code was originally approved in 1960 and experienced major reorganization and revisions in 1979 and 1996. During periods between these comprehensive reviews of the Code, incremental revisions are made as complaints of Code violations are reviewed and the need for clarification is recognized or ethical issues not explicitly covered by the Code are identified.

With a clearly explicated Code of Ethics in place, NASW members can be clear about expectations for competent and ethical practice and the profession has a standard against which to assess complaints that the public has been violated. To join NASW, the social worker must sign a statement agreeing to abide by the ethical standards contained in the Code and to participate in the adjudication process if a complaint is made. By renewing one's membership each year, he or she reaffirms the commitment to adhere to NASW's Code of Ethics. NASW has created an elaborate procedure for hearing grievances at the local or chapter level with appeal to the national level possible for all parties to the complaint. A member found to have violated the Code of Ethics can be asked to take corrective actions, may be listed on a published report of Code violators, or may have his or her NASW membership revoked.

A study of a sample of 300 formal complaints filed with NASW between 1982 and 1992 reveals that about one-third of the complaints claiming violation of the Code of Ethics were substantiated (upheld) during the process of review and appeal. In 61 percent of the cases the person making the complaint was another social worker and in another 34 percent it was the client or a member of the client's family.[11] It appears that social workers take seriously the responsibility to file a complaint when they believe a colleague is not abiding by the Code of Ethics. Of those complaints that were substantiated, the most prevalent Code violation related to workers engaging in sexual activity with their clients (29.2%). Other frequently violated provisions in the Code of Ethics were concerned with the social worker having relationships or commitments that were in conflict with the interests of the client (16.9%), withdrawing services without efforts to minimize possible adverse affects for the client (16.7%), and exploiting professional relationships for personal gain (16.4%).

Areas of Practice Addressed by the NASW Code of Ethics

The *NASW Code of Ethics* has evolved from its 1960 format of ten general statements to guide ethical considerations in practice to its 1996 format that consumes twenty-seven pages of ethical prescriptions. Mastering the specifics of the *Code* and interpreting its provisions in actual practice situations is an ongoing challenge for all social workers. This process begins by recognizing the general areas of practice activity that the *Code* addresses.* The following statements summarize the main sections of the 1996 version of NASW's *Code of Ethics*.

1. **Standards related to the social worker's ethical responsibilities to clients.** This section of the *Code of Ethics* is concerned with such factors and principles as the following: the worker's primary responsibility is to the client; respect for client self-determination; securing client's informed consent; the worker's competence to provide needed services; the worker's cultural competence; avoiding conflict of interest; respecting clients' rights to privacy and confidentiality; the prohibition of sexual involvement, sexual harassment, inappropriate physical contact, and abusive or derogatory language; special considerations when clients lack decision-making capacity; avoiding the interruption of services; and the planful termination of services.

2. **The social worker's ethical responsibilities to colleagues.** Section 2 is concerned with the social workers' responsibility to treat colleagues with respect; concern for maintaining confidentiality among professionals; appropriate collaboration and teamwork; proper handling of disputes and disagreements; developing appropriate consultation relationships; proper referral of clients to colleagues; the prohibition of sexual harassment and sexual involvement with one's supervisees or students; and the requirement for responsible action in relation to a colleague who is impaired, incompetent, or unethical in his or her practice.

3. **The social worker's ethical responsibilities in practice settings.** This section of the *Code of Ethics* relates to services performed in relation to social workers and other professionals and only indirectly relates to clients. The items addressed include the competence required for providing supervision, consultation, education, and training; responsible evaluation of the performance of other workers; maintaining proper client records and billing properly; carefully evaluating client needs before accepting transfers; assuring an appropriate working environment and providing ongoing education and training in human services agencies; demonstrating commitment to agency employees; and guidelines for acting responsibly in labor disputes.

4. **The social worker's ethical responsibilities as a professional.** Section 4 includes items related to the social worker accepting employment and job assignments when

---

*The full text of the *NASW Code of Ethics* can be obtained from the National Association of Social Workers, 750 First Street, NE, Washington, DC 20002-4241, or can be downloaded from NASW's web site (http://www.naswdc.org). The Canadian code of ethics (which contains similar provisions) can be obtained from MYROPEN Publications, 383 Parkdale Ave., Suite 402, Ottawa, ON K1Y 4R4, and additional information on this code can be obtained from the Canadian Association of Social Worker's web site (http://www.ca/~casw-acts/code2-e.htm).

he or she may not be competent to perform that work; prohibition from practicing, condoning, or participating in any form of discrimination; engaging in private conduct that compromises the ability to fulfill professional responsibilities; restriction from engaging in dishonesty, fraud, and deception; the responsibility to address one's own problems if impaired; the requirement to be clear in public statements regarding whether acting as a professional or a private citizen; prohibiting uninvited solicitations for business; and properly acknowledging any contributions to one's written or other work made by others.

5. The social worker's ethical responsibilities to the social work profession. The *Code of Ethics* is also concerned with issues related to the social worker promoting high standards for social work and contributing time and energy to the profession's growth and development, as well as addressing items related to social workers continuously monitoring and evaluating social policies, programs, and their own practice interventions.

6. The social worker's ethical responsibilities to the broader society. In its final section the *Code of Ethics* charges social workers with promoting the general welfare of the society and seeking to assure social justice for all people; participating in public debate to shape social policies and institutions; providing services in public emergencies; and actively engaging in social and political action.

The maintenance of a code of ethics helps to satisfy social work's obligation to be responsible in performing its duties as a recognized profession. It provides guidance to social workers as they make ethical decisions in their day-to-day practice, spells out expected behaviors in areas where ethical compromises may arise, and provides clarity to the general public, employers, and other professionals who may feel that a social worker has violated the principles of ethical practice and wish to have NASW and/or the courts determine if a social worker has violated the public trust granted to professions.

An Illustration of Values and Ethics Operating in Social Work Practice

For most social workers, theoretical or abstract discussion of values and ethical dilemmas is not a daily event. It is usually when these issues are experienced when working with clients that they take on full significance. Hokenstad notes that "half of professional decision making requires ethical rather than scientific judgment. . . . Such judgment requires the capability to make moral precepts operational in specific situations and calls for tolerance or ambiguity in some cases and the ability to resolve conflicts between principles in others."[12] It is through consideration of a case example describing a social worker in action that the reader may be able to extend his or her more applied understanding of how values and ethical decisions affect social work practice.

In her book *Never Too Old*, Twente presented a case illustration of a social worker providing service to an aged widower who was unsuccessfully attempting to establish a new life with his son and his son's family.[13] In the following excerpt from this case, some value and ethical issues become evident:

> When Miss Jones visits Mr. Brandon, Sr., he at first seems determined not to enter into any kind of a discussion. He answers with a curt "no" or "yes" or "hmmm." Some reference to an old chair in which he sits brings forth the comment that it belonged to "mom and me." It was bought secondhand when they "set up housekeeping."
>
> "How long ago was that?" asks Miss Jones.
>
> "Fifty-one years last February," Mr. Brandon is struggling with tears.
>
> "It must be hard to go on without her," comments Miss Jones quietly. Mr. Brandon nods. There is a sob. Miss Jones rises, walks to the bedtable and looks closely at a photograph. "Is this she?"
>
> "Yes." Miss Jones sits down again. There is a silence. "There never was a better wife or mother than she." Miss Jones nods sympathetically.
>
> "Is the other picture on the table of your granddaughter?" she asks. "There seems to be a resemblance."
>
> "There is," responds Mr. Brandon, and for the first time his face lights up. "She is like my wife, Peggy is. Sometimes she comes into my room and asks me questions. All kinds of fool questions. She'll say, 'Grandpa, how did you meet grandma?' or 'What did you do when you took her out?' or 'Did you and grandma dance at parties?' And when I'll say, 'Yes, but not the kind of dances you kids dance,' she'll get up and do some funny turns and say, 'Was it like this, Grandpa?' I tell her, 'No. We waltzed and sometimes I jigged.' 'Show me, Grandpa,' she says. And I get up, but these stiff hips of mine won't move like they ought to." Then he becomes silent again.

The gentle probing of Miss Jones in this part of the case allows her to understand some of the things that Mr. Brandon values, such as the satisfaction from the warm relationship he had with his wife and the joy he gets from his granddaughter. The social worker reflects her value of the worth of Mr. Brandon and treats him with dignity by listening carefully and showing interest in his experiences and feelings. She also allowed him the privilege of only minimally participating in the discussion until he was ready to become involved. Mr. Brandon is important not because of his charm or good looks but because of his humanness. The case continues:

> "You aren't very happy here, are you?"
>
> The next comments come like the rush of water through a broken dam. "No, I'm not happy. How can I be? I am just an old man in everybody's way. Oh, perhaps that is not quite true of Peggy. She likes to visit me, I think. But she has many friends. You know how popular young girls are. Tom is a good son. He works hard, and sometimes he comes in to talk to me. But I can tell he would rather read about sports or look at TV."
>
> "How about Tom Junior?" prods Miss Jones.
>
> "Oh, young Tom is like all young fellers. He is so busy going off on hikes and playing ball and the likes, he doesn't know I exist. I have his room. That should not be. The boy needs his own room to keep things like rocks and frogs and snakes." Again, there is that impish expression. Now there can be no mistaking it. "Margaret doesn't like them things in the house, and she's put her foot down about bringing them alive into the basement.

She says she has to do the washing down there and she doesn't want the critters around her feet."

"You don't get along too well with Margaret," said Miss Jones.

"Oh, Margaret's all right. She is just too persnickity. When I first came I said, 'Now, Margaret, you let me do the dishes.' She said it would be hard for me to get them clean because I don't see so well. Well, I washed them, and then I saw her wash them over again. I don't see so bad, but I could see what she did." Then, after a short pause, "I am just in the way. I am an old farmer, and I am what I am. Margaret doesn't like the way I eat. When they had fancy company, she said to me, 'Grandpa, would you prefer to eat in your own room? I can fix your dinner on the card table.' I knew the score. She just didn't want me."

In this passage Mr. Brandon reflects his loss of a sense of self-respect. He views himself as an unimportant old man who doesn't suit the tastes of his daughter-in-law and is a burden for the rest of the family. Like many older people, he feels that he is of little use in a society that values work and productivity. While his life may have been fulfilling before and there was a real sense of achievement when he was managing the farm, life was hollow for Mr. Brandon now. Miss Jones communicates genuine concern about his well-being and seeks to understand the roots of the problem. The story goes on:

After a while Miss Jones asks him if he knows anyone in town besides Tom and his family. "No, all of my friends are out in the country, what is left of them. I can't go out there and they can't come in. Too far."

"And how about church?" asks Miss Jones.

"Mom and I always went to the Methodist Church. Tom and Margaret go to the Christian. Disciples of Christ, they call it. That was Margaret's church. Tom had to be 'ducked' before he could belong." Mr. Brandon does not want to be baptized again. "Once is enough." And he doesn't know anybody. So he stays at home and listens to the radio. Anyhow, his stiff hips can't do those steps very well.

"Did you ever like fishing or hunting?" asks Miss Jones.

"No, you know, where we lived there was no water for miles around. And as to hunting, there are jackrabbits and prairie dogs, but I was never one to shoot except to protect the crops."

"When you and your wife had company on Sunday afternoons, what did you men do?" Miss Jones continues her questions.

"Oh, we talked politics and things like that, and looked at crops; and sometimes we played horseshoe," replies Mr. Brandon. "Horseshoe was fun, then, but with these hips, it's out of the question."

"How about Sunday afternoons in the winter?" Miss Jones is not giving up.

"Well, we played checkers and dominoes and sometimes Flinch."

"Did you enjoy that?" asks Miss Jones.

"Yes." His face brightens. "Hank Brown and I used to play checkers. We played to win. Maggie, that was my wife, and Elizabeth, Hank's wife, had to remind us that the stock had to be fed and we had to go home."

"Would you care to play checkers now, that is, if there were someone to play with you?"

"No. Anyhow, there's nobody to play with."

"There is a Center on Elm Street and retired men get together for checkers and cards. They seem to have fun."

Here Miss Jones moves the conversation to understand better the uniqueness of Mr. Brandon. Although he faces problems experienced by other old people, Mr. Brandon is a unique individual with his own interests and abilities. Miss Jones responds to his need to belong and searches for interests that match community resources that would provide him with an opportunity to make new friends. She knows that men in Mr. Brandon's age group especially need to have warm relationships with a group of friends. Miss Jones reflects the belief that people can change in a new environment and that Mr. Brandon could once again enter the mainstream of life, yet she is ethically bound to present options and let Mr. Brandon determine what, if any, changes he will make in his life. She is persistent and does not let his despair frustrate her efforts to help find a solution:

Mr. Brandon shakes his head. "I've heard about the Center but it does not appeal to me. Anyhow, I won't be in town very long. I overheard Tom and Margaret discuss me. They want me to go into a home." He seems resigned.

"And do you want to go?" Miss Jones keeps on digging.

"Hell, no. But what can an old man like me do? I don't want to stay where I am not wanted. Not me."

"I am not sure that you are not wanted," says Miss Jones. "Why don't you talk it over with Tom and Margaret and tell them how you feel?"

"I couldn't do that," says Mr. Brandon. "Anyhow, what's the use? I shouldn't have blabbered so much to you. I wasn't going to, and then I went and did it anyhow."

"Do you want me to talk to Tom and Margaret and perhaps with Peggy and young Tom present, too?" asks Miss Jones.

"What would Peggy and young Tom have to do with it?" He is almost shouting. "They are not responsible for me. Not them young kids."

"No, they aren't, but they are a part of the family and they know whether they want you to stay or to leave. I think Peggy, especially, would hate to see you go to a home."

"Well, I'm going and that is that." Mr. Brandon is trembling. "Like I told you, I am not going to be in anybody's way."

Miss Jones asks for at least a minimum level of informed consent. Mr. Brandon, now that he knows there may be some options, is in a position to judge if he wants to continue with this service from the social worker.

"Do you want me to tell you about the homes nearby?" asks Miss Jones.

The answer sounds something like assent. Miss Jones lists the four different kinds of institutions in the county and briefly describes each one. Mr. Brandon is silent. After a while he says, "You sure know about all these things, don't you?"

"It's my business to know," says Miss Jones.

There is another pause. This time it is a long one. "Does Tom know about all of this, I mean all of these homes?"

"Yes," replies Miss Jones. "I told them when they came in to see me."

"And they want me to go?"

"Only Tom and Margaret and Peggy and Tom Junior can answer that," says Miss Jones. "I do think they would like to see you happier than you have been here."

"Well, I would be! A damn sight happier!" Then, in quite another voice, "Can family visit you in those places? I mean, can young kids come too?"

"Yes, they can, especially during visiting hours."

"What do you have to do with all of this?" he then asks.

"Really very little, Mr. Brandon. We do give information when it is wanted and needed, and sometimes we help with the finances. Most of all we are interested in trying to help families find the best solutions in situations like yours. Tom and Margaret told us they were concerned about you. They know you are lonely and unhappy. They thought a home might be a solution and they asked for information."

"Did they also ask you to come and talk with me?" Mr. Brandon is shouting again.

"Yes, but they understood that I would not try to persuade you to go to a home or do anything else you don't want to do. I think this is up to you and your family."

"And that includes Peggy and Tom Junior?"

"To me it would seem so."

Soon after that, Mr. Brandon comments, "Well, I've got something to think about."

We find Miss Jones reflecting the social work value of helping the clients help themselves. She recognizes that people must be permitted to determine what is best for them and take responsibility for these decisions. Miss Jones is also aware that Mr. Brandon said some things he would not want her to report back to Tom and Margaret. She is ethically obligated to protect the confidentiality of their conversation by asking if he wants her to talk with the family about his views. Yet she refuses to be drawn into the role of an interpreter for the family and, instead, helps them come together to talk about the problems and possible solutions. The final decision, however, is left to them. Although frustrated at times, she continues to pursue working with the family until a satisfactory solution is achieved.

Examples of Ethical Issues in Social Work Practice

What are the ethical dilemmas one faces in social work practice? The Code violations substantiated by NASW described previously center around social workers making judgments in practice situations in which they placed their own wants and needs above their obligation to serve their clients. Within the expectations of a profession, those decisions were clearly wrong. Most ethical decisions, unfortunately, are not so clear. They require the social worker to make choices when, sometimes, none of the alternatives are desirable. The worker must weigh one choice against others and make a decision about which option is best or, too often, which is least harmful.

Consider the following examples of a range of decisions a social worker must make that have ethical elements to them:

- What should a social worker do if a client announces the decision to return to an abusive spouse when the worker fears for the client's safety?

- Is it ethical for a social worker to attempt to provide specialized therapeutic services for which he or she is not trained if the worker doubts the competence of the only credentialed person with that expertise in the area where the client lives?

- Should a social worker accept a personal gift from a client beyond the fee the client pays for the professional service? In lieu of a fee for professional service?

- Should a social worker report a colleague to NASW or the state licensing board if that colleague reveals that he or she has developed a sexual relationship with one of his or her clients?

- What should a social worker do if a grand jury requests a client's file that contains case notes that may be damaging to the client?

- What should a social work intern do if a field instructor is touching him or her inappropriately in the course of field instruction activities?

- Is a social worker obligated to do anything if he or she believes a colleague has developed a substance abuse problem?

- If requested by the agency's executive director, is it okay for a social worker to provide supervision to another staff member in a practice area in which the worker has limited knowledge and competence?

- What should be done if a client asks a social worker in a probation setting to overlook (and not mention in the case record) a violation of a condition of parole—promising not to repeat the activity?

- Is it okay for a social worker not to record information given by a client in confidence in the case file when the agency's administrative procedures require recording all pertinent information to the case? If state law requires reporting that information to a central registry or a protective services agency?

- What should a social worker in private practice do if a local company considering a substantial service contract with the worker requests the names and addresses of current clients to contact in order to assess their satisfaction with the worker's performance?

- If the administrator in a nursing home directs the social work staff to transfer out of the agency all patients who do not have insurance or other benefits because the nursing home is experiencing financial difficulty, should the social workers abide by this directive?

- Is it ethical for a social worker who develops a successful helping technique to obtain a patent and market the technique for a profit to other social workers?

- Is a social worker obligated to engage in social and political action when his or her job description does not specify such activity?

The NASW Code of Ethics offers some guidance on each, but at times more than one Code provision applies, and, even more frustrating, sometimes if the worker follows one Code guideline another may be violated.

Concluding Comment

One cannot understand social work without being sensitive to values. Values represent a highly individual and personal view that must be constantly examined during practice.

The social worker must be aware of the value system of the client or client group and the values held by society that impinge upon the client. Research reported in the chapter identifies the dominant values in U.S. society that form the context in which social programs are formulated and in which social workers and their clients engage in the helping process. These values, however, are not held equally by all people, and client groups can be expected to vary in the intensity with which they hold particular values.

The social worker must be especially cognizant of his or her personal values, lest they intrude into the helping process. Certainly it would be unrealistic to expect, or even desire, that the helping process occur in a value-free environment. Yet the social worker must attempt to avoid imposing personal values inappropriately on the client or client groups. In order to practice social work, one must be prepared to accept and understand people who hold values that are different from their own.

The social worker also must be guided by the values and ethics of the social work profession. These beliefs are not held exclusively by social workers. Some overlap with the values of other professions, and there is indication that professionals hold distinctly different values from the general population.[14] Social work's constellation of core values, however, is unique. Roberts, for example, has identified five areas where the values of physicians and those of social workers are quite different, including attitudes about such factors as saving life versus quality of life, the professional's control versus patient autonomy in establishing treatment plans, and so on.[15] Further, Abbott's research identified areas of significant difference in the values held by social workers, physicians, nurses, teachers, psychologists, and business people. Of these groups, psychologists were most like social workers in their beliefs.[16]

In many ways, values or beliefs about how things ought to be or how people ought to behave are the cornerstone of social work. Even when the knowledge available to guide practice is limited, the social worker who falls back on the values of the profession cannot go far wrong in guiding the helping process. When the worker is value-sensitive and effectively supplies the competencies of social work practice, clients receive the quality of services they should expect from a professional.

KEY WORDS AND CONCEPTS

Values	Value suspension
Ethics	Western society's values
Knowledge versus values	U.S. society's values
Value conflict	Social workers' values
Value system	Social workers' ethics
Values clarification	NASW Code of Ethics

SUGGESTED READINGS

Bullis, Ronald K. *Clinical Social Worker Misconduct: Laws, Ethics, and Personal Dynamics.* Chicago: Nelson-Hall, 1995.

Gambrill, Eileen, and Pruger, Robert. *Controversial Issues in Social Work Ethics, Values, and Obligations.* Boston: Allyn and Bacon, 1997.

Levy, Charles S. *Social Work Ethics on the Line.* New York: Haworth, 1993.

Reamer, Frederic G. *Social Work Values and Ethics,* 2nd Edition. New York: Columbia University Press, 1999.

Wells, Carolyn Cressy, with Masch, M. Kathleen. *Social Work Ethics Day to Day: Guidelines for Professional Practice,* 2nd Edition. Prospect Hills, IL: Waveland Press, 1991.

ENDNOTES

1. R. Huws Jones, "Social Values and Social Work Education," in Katherine A. Kendall, ed., *Social Work Values in an Age of Discontent* (New York: Council on Social Work Education, 1970).

2. Milton Rokeach, *Beliefs, Values, and Attitudes: A Theory of Organization and Change* (San Francisco: Jossey-Bass, 1968), p. 124.

3. Shepard B. Clough, *Basic Values of Western Civilization* (New York: Columbia University Press, 1960), p. 5.

4. Naomi I. Brill, *Working with People: The Helping Process,* 4th Edition (New York: Longman, 1990), p. 29.

5. Ibid., p. 12.

6. Lynn R. Kahle and Susan Groff Timmer, "A Theory and a Method for Studying Values," in Lynn R. Kahle, ed., *Social Values and Social Change: Adaptation to Life in America* (New York: Praeger Publishers, 1983), pp. 47–108.

7. Ibid., p. 110

8. National Association of Social Workers, *NASW Standards for the Classification of Social Work Practice, Policy Statement 4* (Silver Spring, MD: The Association, September 1981), p. 18.

9. Bradford W. Sheafor, Charles R. Horejsi, and Gloria A. Horejsi, *Techniques and Guidelines for Social Work Practice,* 5th Edition (Boston: Allyn and Bacon, 2000), p. 70.

10. Frank Loewenberg and Ralph Dolgoff, *Ethical Decisions for Social Work Practice,* 5th Edition (Itasca, IL: F. E. Peacock, 1996), p. 35.

11. National Association of Social Workers, "Overview of a Decade of Adjudication," mimeo (Washington, D.C.: The Association, 1995).

12. M.C. Hokenstad, "Teaching Practitioners Ethical Judgment," *NASW News* 32 (October 1987): 4.

13. Esther E. Twente, *Never Too Old: The Aged in Community Life* (San Francisco: Jossey-Bass, 1970), pp. 151–158.

14. William C. Horner and Les B. Whitebeck, "Personal versus Professional Values in Social Work: A Methodological Note," *Journal of Social Service Research* 14 (Issue 1/2 1991): 21–43.

15. Cleora S. Roberts, "Conflicting Professional Values in Social Work and Medicine," *Health and Social Work* 13 (August 1989): 211–218.

16. Ann A. Abbott, *Professional Choices: Values at Work* (Silver Spring, MD: National Association of Social Workers, 1988), pp. 74–75.

CHAPTER 8

Competencies Required for Social Work Practice Today

Prefatory Comment Equipped with adequate social programs to meet client needs, sanction to perform professional services, a suitable agency or private practice environment, and the requisite professional values and ethical guidelines, the social worker is prepared to deliver helping services. Little of this background for practice is usually recognized or even of interest to clients, although the absence of any one of these factors would minimize the social worker's ability to be helpful. Instead, the clients' primary concern is with the social worker and the social worker's competence to be of maximum assistance in addressing their needs and enhancing their general well-being.

To understand social work, then, it is important to be familiar with the competencies needed to perform this professional activity. In this chapter, a major national study of social work practice serves as the basis for describing the competencies typically required of a social worker.

The term *competence* is a particularly useful descriptor for professional practice, because it not only includes the expertise to perform a function but also suggests the capability to translate that expertise into useful actions. Synonyms for competence include skill and knowledge, art and science, as well as talent and proficiency. Competence, then, requires the worker to not only have the requisite information, but he or she must be able to use that knowledge to effectively assist clients in changing their social functioning or bringing about change in the functioning of some part of their environment.

What must a social worker be competent to do? As a profession with a mission to facilitate change in both people and the environment, a wide range of competencies are required. The requisite knowledge and abilities appear quite different depending on which part of social work one is exploring. One might wonder if there is sufficient similarity in the activity performed by social workers in the various fields of practice (e.g., criminal justice, family services, community planning), social work practice settings (e.g., schools, nursing homes, private practice), and professional education levels (i.e., BSW, MSW, DSW) to fit under the umbrella of a single profession. Indeed, throughout most of social work's evolution from volunteerism to a recognized profession it has sought to identify the characteristics that all social workers have in common. As Chapter 2 indicated, social work found such a common theme at the rather lofty conceptual level of its mission, that is, to help people simultaneously address both person and environment. But are there competencies that most social workers use on a day-to-day basis that indicate the presence of a single profession at a more concrete level?

The Competencies Required for Social Work Practice

In the most comprehensive study of social work practice to date, a representative sample of 7,000 social workers from throughout the United States indicated how often they performed 131 different tasks as part of their jobs and how important each task was for successfully doing their jobs.* The sample was made up of approximately 21 percent basic social workers, 75 percent who had the MSW as their highest degree, and the remainder were doctoral-level social workers. Through a statistical procedure commonly referred to as cluster analysis, the tasks were statistically grouped into eighteen distinct clusters of work activity. The mean (or average) score for each cluster could range from a low score of 1.00 (the cluster is not a part of the social worker's job activity) to a high of 5.00 (the activities in the cluster are almost always performed).

To identify the competencies required for various career paths in social work, the task analysis data provide a useful structure. First, the mean scores for each of the eighteen clusters can be compared to determine which are tasks most likely to be performed by social workers and which are the least common activities. In the remainder of this chapter the clusters are presented in that order with the mean score for the composite sample ($n = 7,000$) indicating the frequency with which the typical social worker performs those tasks.

---

*All data reported in this chapter, as well as the eighteen cluster descriptions, are from Robert J. Teare and Bradford W. Sheafor, "National Task Analysis Study of Social Work Practice." (Unpublished materials. School of Social Work, University of Alabama, Tuscaloosa.) The most complete description of the methodology used in collecting and analyzing the data and the most comprehensive published report of the full study can be found in Robert J. Teare and Bradford W. Sheafor, *Practice-Sensitive Social Work Education: An Empirical Analysis of Social Work Practice and Practitioners* (Alexandria, VA: Council on Social Work Education, 1995).

Second, the data indicate that the most significant factor that affects the task a social worker performs is his or her *primary job function*. With some variation, the profile of activities is similar for *direct service* practitioners (i.e., social workers who work primarily in face-to-face contact with clients) regardless of field of practice or employment setting. Social workers who are agency *administrators* also do similar things wherever they are employed. As will become evident when examining the data in this chapter, with the exception of a few clusters administrators have a very different set of activities to perform when they carry out the job of managing human services agencies than do social workers in direct practice jobs. The third job function analyzed, *supervision,* reflects the need for a blend of direct service and administrative competencies. Each job function offers a challenging career track for a social worker.

Third, a significant factor in one's career decision relates to whether he or she will prepare for practice by obtaining the BSW degree or secure the MSW to practice at the specialized or independent levels. Thus, it is useful to compare the activities of BSWs with those of MSWs. Because relatively few BSW-level social workers are engaged in supervision and administrative jobs, only the mean scores for direct service practitioners from the task analysis study are presented for each cluster of activity. Examination of the data will indicate that the profiles for practice levels are similar with the exception of MSW-level practitioners being more treatment oriented (e.g., individual and family treatment, group work) and the BSWs more likely to engage in more concrete and tangible activities such as case planning and ongoing case maintenance, dispute resolution, and connecting clients into the service delivery system.*

Finally, knowing what social workers do leads to the identification of the competencies one needs to carry out those job activities. These competencies, although not empirically derived as part of the task analysis study, help the prospective social worker recognize the knowledge and skills one must master to become a social worker. They also assist social work education programs to identify content they should include in their curricula.

THE UNIVERSAL SOCIAL WORK COMPETENCIES

Two clusters of tasks, interpersonal helping and professional competence development, were consistently performed by most social workers at all levels of practice, in all job functions, and in all practice areas and settings. They represent the most clear indication of a common set of work activities that help to bind social workers into a single profession.

---

*Preliminary results from a 1997 update of the task analysis data from all MSW-level social workers (n = 4,266) indicate little change in the cluster scores. In general, there was a slight increase in direct service activities and a decrease in indirect services over the intervening twelve years.

INTERPERSONAL HELPING.   The cluster of tasks most frequently performed by all social workers requires the worker to engage in interpersonal helping. To perform this set of activities the social worker must be prepared to use basic helping skills (e.g., interviewing, questioning, counseling) to assist individuals and/or families in understanding the problems they experience in social functioning and in helping them to examine possible options for resolving those problems. In carrying out these activities, the worker actively involves individuals and families in discussions designed to explore options for solving problems. The worker encourages people to express their points of view and share their feelings. Throughout this process the worker attempts to communicate an understanding of other people's points of view and establish a relationship of trust with clients.

The high frequency with which social workers use interpersonal helping, especially in direct practice jobs, is indicated by the mean scores achieved in the task analysis study. Box 8-1 reveals the universal application of these skills.

What competencies are needed to carry out these interpersonal helping tasks? Different social workers would, no doubt, approach practice situations in a manner that reflects their individual ways of working with clients. However, most social workers would probably include at least the following items in a list of interpersonal helping competencies:

1. *Self-awareness and the ability to use self in facilitating change.* The primary tool for helping by a social worker is the social worker himself or herself. The social worker cannot give a client an injection that will cure a social problem or surgically remove some impediment to healthy social functioning. To use oneself effectively, a social worker must be sensitive to his or her own strengths and limitations, be aware of areas of knowledge and ignorance, and recognize the potential to be both helpful and harmful when serving clients.

2. *Knowledge of the psychology of giving and receiving help.* Often a part of the motivation for entering a helping profession is the desire to give of oneself to improve the lives of others. It is rewarding to help others, but social workers must take care to focus the helping process on what is needed by the client. Also, social workers must remember that clients are often uncomfortable when receiving help— both because our society suggests that one has somehow failed if he or she needs assistance and because we sometimes offer social programs in a manner that is demeaning to clients.

BOX 8-1   **Mean Scores for Interpersonal Helping Tasks**

All Social Workers: 3.98	
BSW Direct Practitioners: 4.27	MSW Direct Practitioners: 4.40
	MSW Supervisors: 3.77
	MSW Administrators: 3.35

3. *Ability to establish professional helping relationships.* Prerequisite to all successful helping is the establishment of a positive helping relationship. Whether working directly with clients, coworkers, or others in the community, the social worker must establish a relationship characterized by mutual respect and trust. Personal characteristics of the worker that have been found to be critical for creating such a helping relationship include empathy, positive regard, warmth, and genuineness. Research has further indicated that the social worker whose interaction with clients is characterized by concreteness, objectivity, and the ability to introduce and maintain structure in the helping process further improves the worker's success rate.

4. *Understanding differing ethnic and cultural patterns, as well as the capacity to engage in ethnic-, gender-, and age-sensitive practice.* One's social functioning, and even perceptions of what is positive social functioning, is affected by a person's appreciation of variations in cultural background experienced by various subgroups of the population. The various ethnic and racial minority groups in the United States have had a very different experience, both in cultural background and in their experience with the dominant white culture, than have members of the majority. Similarly, women have had more limited opportunities than men, and older people often have a quite different place in society than when they were younger. To engage in effective interpersonal helping the social worker must not only be aware of these different life experiences but must also be aware of how they affect the social functioning of individual clients. In short, the effective social worker engages in ethnic-, gender-, and age-sensitive practice. That same sensitivity should be applied to other population groups such as the physically and mentally disabled, gay and lesbian persons, persons of varied religious backgrounds, and so on.

5. *Knowledge and application of the Code of Ethics as a guide to ethical practice.* Inherent in the practice of any profession is the expectation that the public trust evident in granting professional sanction is rewarded by the professional mandate to engage in ethical practice. Each social worker is expected to conduct his or her practice in a manner that attempts to bring the best services possible to clients and, at a minimum, does no damage. The NASW Code of Ethics represents social work's effort to spell out the minimum requirements for ethical social work practice. Adhering to the Code of Ethics must be part of carrying out every practice task from interpersonal helping to research and policy analysis.

6. *General understanding of individual and family behavior patterns.* Interpersonal helping must be underpinned by knowledge of people, both individually and as part of families or other households. Effective interpersonal helping requires doing more than just what feels right. The social worker needs a thorough grounding in expected human growth and development patterns throughout the life cycle, understanding of different family structures and their influence on family members, and sufficient knowledge of human physiology and anatomy to recognize biological factors that may affect one's social functioning. It requires synthesizing knowledge from the disciplines of biology, psychology, and sociology to understand the bio-psycho-social functioning of clients.

7. *Skill in client information gathering.* Interpersonal helping requires a set of specific skills for gathering information that will help determine the social worker's course of action in regard to the client's situation. Perhaps the most fundamental skill a social worker must have is the ability to conduct an interview that not only reveals important information but also facilitates a continuing professional relationship. A substantial and rich literature on interviewing is available to the social worker.[1] Skills such as focusing an interview, listening, questioning, reflecting feeling and content, interpreting meaning, confronting, and many other techniques are necessary for the social worker to master. Information-gathering skills are used by social workers in virtually every setting, practice area, and job function and apply to work with individuals, couples, families, and even professional teams and committees.

8. *Ability to analyze client information and identify both the strengths and problems evident in a practice situation.* Once information is collected about a client situation, the social worker must interpret its meaning and arrive at an assessment about its effects on the client's situation. This assessment often will be based on a combination of the social worker's experience or practice wisdom, as well as on various assessment tools that have been developed for social work practice.[2] Arriving at an accurate understanding of the problems in a case situation is central to most interpersonal helping. Yet the identification of problems does not provide a sufficient basis to resolve or overcome them. Social workers must also seek to identify client strengths as essential resources for problem resolution.

9. *Capacity to counsel, problem solve, and/or engage in conflict resolution with clients.* Interpersonal helping also includes basic skills in assisting clients to understand, accept, and come to grips with the issues in their lives that brought them to the social worker. Skills in counseling, values clarification, problem solving, and conflict resolution, for example, must be a part of the social worker's equipment. When working with clients, social workers should avoid, where possible, actions that take over aspects of clients' lives. Instead, they should attempt to maximize a client's participation in the change process and leave final decisions in the client's hands. After all, it is the client who must live with the results of those decisions.

10. *Possession of expertise in guiding the change process.* When engaged in interpersonal helping, social workers attempt to help their clients to bring about some kind of change in their lives. The social worker has a particularly important role in guiding that change process through its various phases. Typically, a helping situation is initiated by a client requesting service or being referred either to a human services agency or private practitioner. The worker must first *engage* the client in addressing and clarifying the situation and determine if the agency is the proper source of help. The latter is known as making an *intake* decision. Second, the worker and client cooperate in *data collection* and *assessment* of the information obtained so that both fully understand the nature of the problem or situation, as well as the various factors that may have contributed to it. Here, especially, the social worker must direct the process carefully, as the tendency is to move too quickly to action.

Third, the worker and client must develop a *plan* for accomplishing the agreed-upon change and reach agreement (i.e., a formal or informal *contract*) about how to address the issues and choose the activities each will carry out. Fourth, the actual *intervention(s)* will occur, and the social worker will *monitor* the change activities to determine if they indeed are helping. Finally, when the helping activity has run its course, the process will be *terminated* with the expectation that the client's social functioning has been stabilized at an appropriate level. Ultimately, the social worker should *evaluate* the overall process and apply what is learned from this evaluation to future practice activities. It is evident that the competence required for assisting clients in changing their social functioning is substantial and requires a social worker who is both knowledgeable about that process and skilled at moving through its several phases.

PROFESSIONAL COMPETENCE DEVELOPMENT. To their credit, all social workers devote a considerable amount of energy to improving the quality of their practice. To maintain high-quality practice the social worker in every position must carefully monitor his or her own work and continually engage in activities that will improve their job performance. To accomplish these goals, the social worker must regularly engage in activities that strengthen one's own practice effectiveness and expand one's professional competence. Some of the tasks involve self-assessment, that is, periodically taking stock of one's performance by evaluating actions and decisions made within the context of practice. Other tasks involve attendance at workshops, seminars, or professional meetings, as well as reading professional journals, magazines, and newspapers in order to keep abreast of new developments. The focus of the cluster is the perception of professional development as an ongoing process.

In their task analysis study, Teare and Sheafor found little variation among social workers in their commitment to the careful examination of their practice and the pursuit of increased knowledge and skill (see Box 8-2).

Professional development is a lifelong process. It includes both learning about practice and making contributions back to the profession through sharing one's own learning. Among the competencies required for professional development are the following:

1. *Ability to be introspective and critically evaluate one's own practice.* At the heart of professional development is self-assessment. One must be willing to critically

Box 8-2 **Mean Scores for Professional Competence Development**

All Social Workers: 3.64	
BSW Direct Practitioners: 3.72	MSW Direct Practitioners: 3.61
	MSW Supervisors: 3.63
	MSW Administrators: 3.68

examine his or her own work and engage regularly in reflective thinking about practice events. When limitations are evident, there must be an effort to correct them. It is important in a profession to focus on both ethical aspects of practice and the quality of services provided. A thorough understanding of the *NASW Code of Ethics* is an important prerequisite to addressing ethical issues, while the availability of professional supervision and/or consultation provides a valuable perspective for recognizing and resolving professional issues. The social worker should also develop the capability to engage in ongoing practice evaluation wherein one's practice activities can be tracked and compared to service results.

2. Ability to make use of consultation. Effective professional practice requires that the worker obtain regular consultation regarding his or her service provision activities. While a professional is expected to practice with considerable autonomy and has final responsibility for his or her practice decisions, the social worker is not expected to conduct these activities alone. The use of consultation from peers is a hallmark of professions. Sometimes this consultation is provided by a supervisor, while at other times consultation from persons outside the administrative structure of the agency is obtained. In either case, the purpose is to offer guidance in making practice decisions or to provide a second opinion regarding decisions that have already been made.

3. Ability to consume and extend professional knowledge. The social worker must be committed to participating in a range of external activities that build his or her base of practice knowledge and skills. This might include attending staff training sessions and professional workshops and conferences, and regular reading of the professional literature. In addition, as social workers gain experience and insights from their practice, they are expected to share their understanding with others in the social work profession. The NASW Code of Ethics, for example, indicates that "the social worker should contribute to the knowledge base of social work and share with colleagues knowledge related to practice, research, and ethics."[3] That means contributing to social work's knowledge base and involves being competent to make conference presentations and prepare articles for publication in professional journals.

FREQUENTLY UTILIZED SOCIAL WORK COMPETENCIES

Six additional clusters of activity were regularly performed by most social workers, but were especially emphasized in work in one or more of the job functions. The competencies to perform these tasks, however, are sufficiently important for all social workers to master.

CASE PLANNING AND MAINTENANCE. The tasks included in the case planning and maintenance cluster require the worker to be competent to perform ongoing case planning, coordinate any additional services the client requires, monitor and evaluate case progress, obtain case consultation when appropriate, and complete required paperwork for case records. Tasks include preparing and reviewing case materials to assess progress, coordinating service planning with agency staff and providers from other agencies, and carrying out appropriate procedures (e.g., obtaining consent, explaining rights, and maintaining security in order to ensure that client's rights are protected).

As Box 8-3 indicates, this cluster of activities is most prominent among the direct service worker and supervisors—and is especially important for the basic social workers.

In addition to using the basic interpersonal helping skills required to perform these tasks, the particular competencies required for case planning and monitoring include the following:

1. *Expertise in service planning and monitoring.* Social work practice often involves oversight of a battery of services being offered to an individual or family. With the client, the social worker identifies the services already being provided and those still needed, and helps to develop plans for clients to gain access to resources that might prove helpful. Once the service plan is in operation, the social worker may then shift emphasis to monitoring the progress of the case to ensure that the plan, in fact, is working. This may include reviewing case records, consulting with other service providers both within the employing agency and elsewhere, and maintaining a professional relationship with the client to assess his or her ongoing perception of the helpfulness of the services being provided.

2. *Ability to carry out the employing agency's programs and operating procedures.* Agency-based social workers are agents of the organizations that employ them. Whether the programs are social provisions, social services, or social action, they are important tools for helping, and the social worker must know how to access those resources to benefit their clients. Often agencies require a frustrating amount of paperwork, but it is, nevertheless, essential to complete the required forms and recording. Human services agencies typically have a variety of procedures in place that must be followed by the worker so that information is recorded that will, for example, ensure that funds continue to be generated by the agency, continuity can be achieved should the social worker assigned to a case change positions, and appropriate monitoring by supervisors can take place.

3. *Knowledge of client background factors.* In conjunction with the case assessment that is part of one's interpersonal helping competence, the social worker involved in case planning must gather specific background information that can be

Box 8-3   **Mean Scores for Case Planning and Maintenance**

All Social Workers: 3.46	
BSW Direct Practitioners: 4.02	MSW Direct Practitioners: 3.79
	MSW Supervisors: 3.45
	MSW Administrators: 2.89

used in creating a comprehensive approach to helping. Included among this information is the identification of such resources as friends, family, neighbors, coworkers, teachers, clergy, and other personal contacts that may offer assistance. The social worker must also obtain information from the client about current or past experiences with the human services delivery system in order to make judgments about the merits of connecting clients to particular resources as part of a package of helping services. Finally, the social worker serving as a case manager is responsible for ensuring that clients are informed of their rights and that confidentiality regarding their situation is properly protected even though services are being provided by several agencies.

4. *Skill in interagency coordination.* The social worker, as orchestrator of a battery of services and service professionals, must be knowledgeable about the availability of various resources and the requirements for gaining access to them and be capable of making sound professional judgments about their potential helpfulness. Further, the social worker must be skilled in communicating with persons with various professional backgrounds and creating networks among agencies and professionals to facilitate a coordinated approach to client services. This may mean exchanging information among agencies, planning and leading case conferences, securing case consultation when needed, and negotiating decisions about who will provide which services to an individual or family—and, importantly, who will pay for them.

5. *Ability to engage in case advocacy.* Ideally, services will be given to clients when they are needed. In reality, that is not always possible. At times, clients in crisis are placed on an agency's waiting list, an agency's eligibility requirements are rigidly interpreted in a way that does not fit the uniqueness of a particular client's situation, or many other factors may interfere with clients receiving needed services. In those cases, the social worker may become an advocate for the client and make appeals to his or her own or another human services agency to help clients obtain needed services. This may involve activities such as informing clients about an agency's appeal process, making a personal appeal to a social worker in another agency, or even representing a client before an agency's appeal board.

INDIVIDUAL AND FAMILY TREATMENT.   Another set of tasks frequently performed by social workers in direct service positions involves providing treatment to individuals and families. Individual and family treatment requires that the social workers select and use clearly defined formal treatment modes or models to help individuals and/or families improve their social functioning or resolve social problems. Activities include the use of any of a wide array of interventive techniques and strategies ranging from nondirective to confrontational approaches.

This set of activities, as would be expected, is used mostly by direct service practitioners and especially by the specialized and independent-level practitioners as indicated in Box 8-4.

Box 8-4 **Mean Scores for Individual and/or Family Treatment**

All Social Workers: 3.24	
BSW Direct Practitioners: 3.35	MSW Direct Practitioners: 3.61
	MSW Supervisors: 3.14
	MSW Administrators: 2.89

Certainly the social worker engaged in treatment activities mixes the specific treatment approach selected with the basic interpersonal helping skills. However, the worker must also possess the following:

1. *Sufficient knowledge of human development to make in-depth psychosocial assessments.* The social worker engaged in clinical or treatment activities with individuals and families is required to have considerable knowledge about human functioning. He or she must be prepared with sufficient information about expected functioning for persons at different developmental levels to make a valid psychosocial assessment on which treatment plans can be developed. In addition to knowledge of normal development, the social worker must have sufficient knowledge to diagnose pathology, recognize deviance, and help clients recognize their own or others' dysfunctional behaviors.

In some settings the social worker is required to identify client issues according to the categories of the *Diagnostic and Statistical Manual for Mental Disorders* (DSM–IV).[4] This manual, developed by the American Psychiatric Association, describes symptoms, suggests criteria for making a diagnoses, and so on, for more than 200 mental disorders. Although it is not specifically intended for the diagnosis of problems in social functioning, many agencies utilize the DSM–IV, making it necessary for social workers employed in those agencies or in private practice to be knowledgeable about these diagnostic categories.

2. *In-depth knowledge of family functioning.* Just as the social worker must be skilled at assessing normal and problematic individual social functioning, one must also be prepared to diagnose factors affecting the functioning of families and other households. A rather substantial literature exists that identifies various types of family structures including the two-parent, single-parent, postdivorce, remarried or blended, and gay/lesbian households. Each has particular issues it must address if it is to attain stability and offer a positive environment to its members. Clinical social workers, especially, need to recognize that interactional patterns of families can have a profound and lasting impact on family members and that, with professional help, harmful patterns can often be corrected.

3. *Skill in the selection and application of individual and/or family treatment modalities.* To engage in individual and family treatment, the social worker must have mastered one or more specific treatment approaches. The range of specific approaches that a social worker might draw from is quite broad. Sheafor, Horejsi, and Horejsi, for example, identify the following as some of the practice frameworks social workers typically use:[5]

Psychosocial therapy	Task-centered model
Behavior modification therapy	Addictions model
Cognitive–behavioral therapy	Clubhouse model
Person-centered therapy	Self-help approach
Reality therapy	Family systems approach
Interactional model	Family therapy approach
Structural model	Family problem-solving approach
Crisis intervention	Family preservation model

This list would be extended considerably if one were to compile a list of all of the specialized individual and family treatment models and approaches that might be a part of a clinical social worker's repertoire. A social worker will typically begin by developing the necessary skill to carry out one or two approaches and later add to his or her repertoire as subsequent practice experience indicates the need for additional approaches.

DELIVERY SYSTEM KNOWLEDGE DEVELOPMENT. Among the helping professions it is social workers who are most likely to help clients manage the complex web of human services that exists in most communities. The tasks included in the delivery system knowledge development cluster suggest that the social worker must learn about the community's service delivery system and develop an understanding of various regulations, policies, and procedures that affect social programs. The focus of this cluster is on the gathering of information about the network of services and service resources within the social worker's geographic area. Activities include visiting agencies, attending meetings, and making contacts in order to become acquainted with or keep up-to-date with changes in the services provided, developing cooperative service arrangements among agencies, and keeping current on regulations, organizational policies, and agency guidelines.

Developing knowledge about the human services delivery system is an *indirect service*. It is work that develops important background information when serving clients, but it is usually conducted outside the presence of clients and is done without reference to a single client or group of clients. Engaging in interagency contact that yields this valuable information is a function performed by all social workers. However, as indicated in Box 8-5, the work of creating service agreements and participation in interagency coordination meetings is primarily the responsibility of supervisors and administrators. To carry out these activities the social worker must have the following competencies:

Box 8-5 **Mean Scores for Delivery System Knowledge Development**

All Social Workers: 3.09

BSW Direct Practitioners: 2.97	MSW Direct Practitioners: 2.89
	MSW Supervisors: 3.32
	MSW Administrators: 3.48

1. *Ability to maintain up-to-date knowledge of a variety of human services programs.* The effective social worker cannot be agency-bound. He or she must know the community—or at least the human services delivery system in the community. The worker must read about local, state, and national programs, visit human services agencies to gain in-depth knowledge of their programs and procedures for gaining access to those services, and regularly attend interagency meetings where one can be updated about changing programs.

2. *Skills in building interagency coordination and linkage.* Rarely is merely acquiring information sufficient for social work practice. Social workers must be prepared to act on that knowledge. In the case of knowledge about human services, social workers often develop linkage arrangements to facilitate information-sharing processes among agencies that regularly interact when serving clients. Sometimes that takes the form of interagency teams, such as a domestic violence team, where social workers must be skilled at interagency and interprofessional team building.

STAFF INFORMATION EXCHANGE. As an agency-based profession, social workers must also be thoroughly versed about the programs and operating procedures in their own agencies. In addition, a worker must be prepared to contribute to the effective operation of that organization by working to resolve problems in agency functioning and contributing to decisions that strengthen the agency. This exchange of information among staff members is another indirect service activity of social workers. To be effective in information exchange, the social worker must be prepared to organize and/or participate in meetings or use other means of communication to exchange information with staff members, resolve job-related problems, and/or make decisions that affect agency functioning. The essence of the tasks in this cluster is the presentation and receiving of information, with individuals and in group meetings, in order to accomplish task-centered objectives.

Box 8-6 indicates that almost all social workers participate in this intra-agency exchange of information and decision making to some degree, although MSW-level private practitioners are an exception. However, the primary responsibility for facilitating this exchange falls to the supervisors and agency administrators.

To achieve effective intra-agency communication, all members of the staff must regularly participate in the giving and receiving of information. The following competencies are required of the social worker when performing these tasks:

1. *Ability to prepare and consume written and oral presentations regarding agency programs.* Much of the information about agency operation is transmitted

Box 8-6 **Mean Scores for Staff Information Exchange**

All Social Workers: 2.94	
BSW Direct Practitioners: 2.72	MSW Direct Practitioners: 2.56
	MSW Supervisors: 3.40
	MSW Administrators: 3.48

through written communication or formal staff meetings. This activity can consume considerable time, and, if it is not to detract from client services, the social worker must learn to read and write such materials quickly and accurately. Oral communication skills, too, are important. Knowing how to make formal presentations that are interesting and lively, yet emphasize the important content, facilitates effective communication of in-house materials. The bottom line, however, is that all staff members must have thorough knowledge of the employing agency's policies, programs, and operating procedures.

2. *Capacity to facilitate staff members' ability to make decisions and resolve problems.* In addition to sharing information, the members of an agency staff must regularly engage in activities that help the agency resolve problems and find ways to function more effectively. Typically this activity occurs through staff meetings, committee assignments, or team meetings. Knowledge of group dynamics, parliamentary procedure, and skill in moving group processes ahead all help to facilitate this activity. At times, the social worker may be required to use skills in consensus building, mediation, or negotiation in order to complete the work in this cluster of tasks.

3. *Ability to facilitate interdisciplinary collaboration.* In agencies that use the talents of several professions or disciplines in delivering their social programs, problems in interdisciplinary collaboration inevitably occur. Although the professions have carved out their boundaries or unique missions in general terms, in practice there are overlapping areas. Further, individual practitioners often drift in their practice activities toward the orientation of their colleagues, blurring even further the boundaries between the disciplines. When professional drift becomes excessive, clients lose the advantage of the perspective that each discipline offers and, sometimes, services are given by persons without sufficient preparation. Professionals, including all social workers, must be vigilant regarding interdisciplinary collaboration—facilitating appropriate collaboration and guarding against inappropriate professional drift.

RISK ASSESSMENT AND TRANSITION SERVICES.   All direct service providers must carefully assess a variety of case situations. They regularly have to make judgments about the urgency for services or the consequences of not providing services. Based on that assessment they determine the type of services needed, facilitate the transition of clients from one service to another, and/or decide on the appropriateness of terminating the helping process. To perform these tasks, the worker must have the competence to assess a case situation to determine its difficulty (i.e., risk, urgency, or need) and engage clients either in making use of services or preparing them for transition or termination of services. Tasks include the observation of individuals and the gathering of information in order to decide if specialized services are required. In certain circumstances the worker will be expected to deal with hostile or unco-operative clients.

Sound assessment is prerequisite to all change efforts. However, as Box 8-7 suggests, the assessment of changing client conditions is more associated with the activities of basic social workers. Their work often places them in the role of making intake decisions and planning for clients' transition from agency services to other agencies or, hopefully, providing them with the ability to maintain themselves without the support of social workers or human services programs.

It takes considerable knowledge to accurately assess a practice situation. The social worker must learn the client's perception of the reasons services are required, the viewpoints of significant people in the client's immediate environment, and, if working as part of an interdisciplinary team, obtain information others have collected. To engage in these assessment activities, the social worker should have the following competencies:

1. *Ability to apply general systems and/or ecosystems theory when assessing factors affecting a practice situation.* It is evident that the perspective one brings to the assessment process will affect the conclusions that are eventually reached. Due to the need for social workers to assess both personal and environmental factors, social workers have increasingly found various system-based theories particularly valuable because they allow the social worker to address interactions between systems (e.g., individual, family, neighborhood). The focus of the ecosystems perspective, for example, is on interaction among five elements in a practice situation: (1) individual(s) characteristics; (2) family life-style and dynamics; (3) cultural values and beliefs; (4) environmental-structural factors such as racism, sexism, or ageism; and (5) historical experiences that have contributed to the client's situation. Meyer notes that the ecosystems perspective allows "social workers to look at psychological phenomena, account for complex variables, assess the dynamic interplay of these variables, draw conceptual boundaries around the unit of attention of the case, and then generate ideas for interventions."[6]

Box 8-7   **Mean Scores for Risk Assessment and Transition Services**

All Social Workers: 2.79	
BSW Direct Practitioners: 3.20	MSW Direct Practitioners: 2.99
	MSW Supervisors: 2.85
	MSW Administrators: 2.43

2. *Skill in engaging clients in examining problems in social functioning.* An important part of social work practice involves helping clients explore the severity and intensity of the situation being addressed and determining if routine or emergency service is required. The most critical source of information for making such judgments is the client. The worker must be skilled in engaging clients in problem analysis. In some cases clients are involuntarily receiving services and sometimes are hostile or resistant to providing such information. In such cases, it is especially important that the social worker is skilled in recognizing client resistance and engaging clients in problem assessment.

3. *Skill in utilizing social work assessment techniques.* The ability to use specific assessment tools effectively is critical if a social worker is to make valid judgments about the severity of a particular case situation or is to make a decision about terminating service and/or helping clients with transition to other services. Examples of competencies a social worker might possess to accurately assess a client situation include mastery of assessment techniques such as ecomaps, genograms, or life history grids; the competence to help clients accurately identify and specify the problems to be addressed; and the ability to prepare clear and concise social functioning assessment reports for agency records and communication with other professionals.

4. *Skill in the use of crisis intervention.* If a risk assessment determines that a client (i.e., individual or family) is in crisis, the social worker must be prepared to act immediately. Meaningful change frequently occurs when the client is experiencing a crisis and the opportunity to be helpful is missed if the worker is not prepared to act. Crisis intervention requires rapid response over a limited time that is focused on a specific client emergency. The worker's focus is on helping the client make decisions that will resolve the crisis, and, if necessary, crisis intervention may require taking action that will protect the client as well as others.

5. *Ability to facilitate client transitions between services and/or to terminate service.* Helping clients make transitions from one service to another also requires considerable care and planning. Transitions might involve, for example, moving from one's own home to a foster home, from a hospital to a nursing home, from one agency to another, or simply from one social worker to another. Workers must be sensitive to the difficulty of such transitions for clients and carefully prepare them for these changes. When the service activity is completed, or if for some reason a different social worker is assigned to a case, clients must be prepared for the termination of the professional relationship. At times clients can feel that a meaningful person in their lives is lost, making termination a painful event.

STAFF SUPERVISION. Agency-based human services practice requires an additional indirect service competence—supervision of a variety of personnel with differing qualifications and job assignments. Some may be volunteers who provide various helping services, others may be staff members such as custodians and clerical staff, and still others are other social workers or human services providers. To provide staff supervision, one must be prepared to guide the day-to-day work of staff members (e.g., professional and clerical employees, volunteers, and/or students) by orienting them to the organization and its requirements, by assigning work and teaching them to perform their jobs, as well as by monitoring and assessing their performance. The tasks in this cluster encompass the array of tasks typically associated with supervision including the provision of job orientation and training by means of regular case review and critique, clarification of job duties and work expectations with individuals and groups, and the evaluation, interpretation, and feedback of job performance evaluations.

As Box 8-8 reveals, the oversight and direction of the work of agency personnel is not a significant responsibility of direct service practitioners, although it is not uncommon for either a BSW- or MSW-level social worker to direct the work of volunteers. Supervision is, however, a substantial part of the job of social workers who perform management roles in human services agencies—either as supervisors or agency administrators.

Many of the skills required for interpersonal helping are also important for supervising employees and volunteers. One must be skilled at collecting pertinent information, developing productive working relationships, assessing situations, and so on. In addition, the social worker engaged in staff supervision must have the following competencies:

1. *Knowledge of the literature regarding the supervisory process.* A rather abundant literature has emerged that can be of assistance to social workers who assume supervisory responsibilities.[7] This literature, for example, helps supervisors recognize that there is an administrative or monitoring component to supervision, a role in providing professional support to the worker, and an educational component through which the worker is helped to grow and develop in practice competence. This literature also suggests ways to structure supervisory learning processes so that it is of maximum value to the worker and yet is efficient in terms of the time invested by both the worker and supervisor.

2. *Capacity to facilitate the work of supervisees.* The ultimate payoff from good supervision is having supervisees who can perform their work efficiently and effectively. The supervisor must be clear about the job assignments of the workers and able to assess their strengths and limitations related to performing various assignments. Of critical importance is the ability to provide a sound orientation to the agency and job requirements when the worker (or student) begins the supervisory process. When necessary, supervisors also teach the workers practice skills and/or

Box 8-8 **Mean Scores for Staff Supervision**

All Social Workers: 2.62	
BSW Direct Practitioners: 1.97	MSW Direct Practitioners: 2.28
	MSW Supervisors: 3.98
	MSW Administrators: 3.14

facilitate their attendance at training sessions or professional seminars in which their competence can be enhanced.

3. *Ability to conduct worker evaluation and professional development.* For the protection of both clients and the agency, the work of supervisees must be constantly monitored to ensure that high-quality service is provided and agency policies and procedures are appropriately carried out. In addition, the supervisor must be prepared to formally evaluate worker performance on a periodic basis, discuss that overall evaluation with the worker in a manner that will enhance professional growth, and supply the results of the evaluation for the agency's personnel records. Since these evaluations often become the basis for job promotion and salary increments, or possibly even job termination, they require accurate, fair, and sensitive interpretation and feedback from the supervisor.

COMPETENCIES OCCASIONALLY NEEDED BY SOCIAL WORKERS

The following seven task clusters of social work practice activity are occasionally performed by most social workers and more regularly required in one or more specialized job functions or practice areas. The competencies required to perform these activities should be a part of each social worker's repertoire of knowledge and skill, but one would not expect to use them on a daily basis in most social work jobs.

GROUP WORK.   A cluster of tasks that have been a part of social work from the initial days of the Settlement House Movement are those associated with working with groups of clients. Although a powerful and efficient tool in both treatment and teaching activities, the use of group-centered techniques has diminished in recent years. Group work requires the social worker to use small groups as an environment for teaching clients skills for effective performance of daily living tasks, communicating information to enhance social functioning, or for facilitating problem resolution or therapeutic change. In these tasks, the worker consciously uses the group process in order to teach individuals how groups work and how to act as a member of the group. These tasks involve the worker in therapeutic groups as well as task-oriented work groups in organizations and communities.

The mean scores for the groups of social workers reported in Box 8-9 indicate that work with groups is at least a small part of all social workers' practice. However, it is the direct service practitioners at the specialized or independent levels that are most likely to apply group techniques as a part of their practice approach.

Like the individual and family treatment cluster, group work activities require the conscious selection of group processes as a means to address a practice situation. Group skills appear to be used most as a method of treatment by MSW-level social workers, but they also have application when teaching skills to clients or staff and in team meetings or other agency-related activities. Competencies required to perform these tasks include the following:

1. *Knowledge of group structure and function.* A sizable body of theory exists about the nature of groups and the dynamic nature of their functioning. Groups may

Box 8-9   **Mean Scores for Group Work**

All Social Workers: 2.43	
BSW Direct Practitioners: 2.36	MSW Direct Practitioners: 2.85
	MSW Supervisors: 2.37
	MSW Administrators: 2.16

be formed in social work practice for such varied purposes as therapy, training, mutual support, or social action. Some will be structured to maximize members' input into deliberations, while others will be focused on accomplishing specific tasks or making decisions. All, however, will be concerned with interaction among members as they engage in their work. The social worker needs knowledge of the phases of group development and skills in handling the power issues that characteristically arise in groups.

2. *Capacity to perform the staff role within a group.* Social workers are often responsible for constructing groups. They must be able to identify the criteria for selecting clients or others to participate in the group, recruit and screen potential members, and conduct the initial planning activities (e.g., arrange time and place to meet, invite members) that allow the group to come together. Depending on its purpose, when the group does meet, the social worker is most likely to perform such functions as helping the group determine its goals, providing information, teaching particular skills to the members, building consensus, discouraging those who tend to dominate and encouraging those who are reluctant to become involved, supporting group leaders, and so on.

3. *Ability to engage in group therapy.* In therapeutic groups, a social worker is likely to be particularly active in guiding the group's process. The worker should have considerable knowledge about each member and guide the process to ensure that his or her goals for being in the group are met while, at the same time, the group's goals are being attained. In this capacity the social worker is typically viewed as the group leader and an expert in facilitating group interaction. Yet the process belongs to the members, and the worker helps them to clarify their own issues by discussing them with each other and by using the group as a sounding board for decision making.

DISPUTE RESOLUTION.   Like every form of organization, disputes inevitably arise in human services agencies. At times those disputes are between clients and the agency. A client may have been judged ineligible for service or may have expected resources that were not provided in a timely manner. Or a staff member may have been viewed as discourteous or unhelpful. It is within a client's rights to dispute these matters or even to file a formal grievance. Disputes may also exist between staff members or between a staff member and the administrator or board of an organization. Such disputes must be resolved if the agency is to devote maximum attention to client services. To be prepared to help resolve disputes, the social worker should be prepared to use advocacy, negotiation, and mediation to resolve interpersonal problems among staff members or between client/staff and the organization. These tasks involve interpersonal interactions in a "charged" organizational climate. The worker is expected to then listen to dissatisfied parties and mediate disputes at various levels in the organization.

As the person in the chain of command to whom a client would complain about a worker's actions and as the link between workers and agency administration, it is not surprising that supervisors are more likely to engage in dispute resolution than social workers in other jobs (see Box 8-10). It is also not surprising that the MSW direct practitioners are less involved in dispute resolution because those in private practice are not a part of an agency and therefore would not be expected to assist in such disputes.

In addition to using basic interpersonal helping skills to assist in dispute resolution, a social worker must also have the following two additional competencies:

1. *Understanding of agency procedures and its decision-making structure.* To address disputes, the social worker must not only be thoroughly familiar with the client's concerns but must be prepared to accurately relate those concerns to the agency's functioning. If a client's rights have been violated, the worker must understand how that relates to agency policies and procedures in order either to correct the problem or explain why it occurred. The worker also needs to understand the agency's structure so that the correct person or persons can be approached to address the problem or a strategy can be developed to correct agency procedures and prevent similar problems from occurring in the future.

2. *Skill in advocacy, negotiation, and mediation.* The social worker involved in dispute resolution is often in a position to help resolve the issue by advocating for the client's or another worker's interests, mediating the problem between the affected parties, or helping to negotiate a resolution of the matter. These skills should be a part of the repertoire of all social workers, but most specifically those who hold administrative or supervisory positions.

SERVICE CONNECTION.   The maze of human services that has evolved is often confusing and difficult for clients to utilize. Social workers engaged in direct practice, in particular, must be able to help clients obtain the services they want or need. As brokers for the human services who link clients with community resources, social

---

BOX 8-10 | **Mean Scores for Dispute Resolution**

All Social Workers: 2.30	
BSW Direct Practitioners: 2.41	MSW Direct Practitioners: 2.07
	MSW Supervisors: 2.71
	MSW Administrators: 2.50

workers must be prepared to employ techniques that help clients to connect with established services and take action to eliminate barriers that prevent them from receiving those services. Activities in this cluster center on the linkage function, although some advocacy on the part of the worker may be required. Tasks include arranging transportation, following up by phone, and carrying out intake procedures.

It is the front-line workers who are most likely to spend time linking clients with services. Therefore, as Box 8-11 indicates, it is the BSW direct practice positions that make the heaviest demand on the service connection competency.

Service connection tasks overlap with some of those used in case planning and maintenance, but they differ to the extent that the worker engaging in service connection helps the client make the desired connection with a community service and then drops out of the picture. Service connection also overlaps somewhat with interpersonal helping, because those basic helping skills must be used to assist clients in determining the services needed. Additional competencies that are particularly important in this cluster of activity are the following:

1. *Maintaining an ongoing critical assessment of the battery of social programs in the community and region.* Social programs change rapidly. Printed and computerized directories are available in most communities, but they still do not provide the quality of information that a social worker needs to communicate to clients. When making service connections, social workers must be careful to provide accurate information because clients can become frustrated and discouraged if a referral is inappropriate and may not follow through and thus not receive needed assistance.

2. *Ability to make an accurate intake assessment of a client's needs and to skillfully refer clients to appropriate resources.* When clients enter the human services delivery system they often are not clear about just what services they need or where to get them. A familiar agency is sometimes the starting point, and the social worker must be prepared to help clients gain clarity about the issues that concern them and the services they require. Sometimes the social worker or others in the agency can provide the needed services, but at other times referrals must be made elsewhere. A social worker must make judgments regarding how directive to be when making a referral and might use techniques ranging from giving the client the name and telephone number of an agency, to making an appointment for the client, to arranging for transportation, or even to taking the client to the appointment. Research into the referral process indicates that fewer than one-half of all referrals actually result

---

Box 8-11   **Mean Scores for Service Connection**

All Social Workers: 2.30	
BSW Direct Practitioners: 3.08	MSW Direct Practitioners: 2.20
	MSW Supervisors: 2.16
	MSW Administrators: 1.95

in the client receiving service.[8] Human service brokering requires considerable care if a social worker is to successfully connect clients with other human services.

3. *Expertise in advocating for clients with human service programs.* Efforts to connect clients with services often fail because clients are placed on lengthy waiting lists or agencies are unwilling to make flexible interpretations of eligibility requirements that might permit serving the client that has been referred. It is important that social workers follow-up with clients who have been referred elsewhere to be sure that the connection was made. If the client has not received service, the worker may elect to actively advocate for that client with that agency. At times agencies will respond more favorably to the request of another helping professional than to the application of the client.

PROGRAM DEVELOPMENT.   Social workers who hold administrative or management positions often carry responsibility for either modifying existing programs or creating new ones. They must have the competence to document and interpret the need for additional human services programs, develop working relationships with relevant resources for program support (e.g., boards, funding sources, legislative bodies, referral sources), oversee implementation of new programs, and evaluate program success. The tasks in this cluster focus on the development of *new* programs or the *alteration* of existing ones. Workers convert program goals and concepts into specific plans, develop budgets and staffing plans, "sell" the program(s) to funding sources and other decision makers, and compile data for evaluation purposes. In this cluster, workers meet with resource people, explain needs, and encourage resource contributions.

As evidenced in Box 8-12, direct practice workers are usually only minimally involved in program development. A social worker in a supervisory position could expect some involvement, but it is the administrators who must possess the ability to assess community needs, design programs, garner support from funding agencies, install the new program in the agency, and evaluate its success.

The competencies required to successfully carry out this indirect service activity include:

1. *Skill in community and organizational data collection and analysis.* Program change or the creation of new social programs can be quite time consuming and expensive. Social workers engaged in program development must do their homework carefully to ensure that client services are not jeopardized by the enthusiasm for innovation. The skills required for program development include collecting and analyzing data about the adequacy of programs offered in their own agencies, as well as the ability to conduct community needs assessments that will help to place their programs in the context of the battery of human services in the community.

2. *Skill in the design and implementation of social programs.* Once a careful analysis of information regarding existing programs is completed, the social worker engaged in program development must develop a plan for new or revised programs that will more adequately respond to the community's needs. The program must be carefully designed and issues addressed as to who will be eligible, where services will

Box 8-12   **Mean Scores for Program Development**

All Social Workers: 2.27	
BSW Direct Practitioners: 1.87	MSW Direct Practitioners: 1.82
	MSW Supervisors: 2.44
	MSW Administrators: 3.19

be provided, what it will cost, who will deliver the service or social provision, what practice approach will be used, and how its effectiveness will be evaluated. The social worker must then develop a budget identifying the anticipated income and expenditures required to start the operation of the program and describe specific plans for its implementation.

3. *The capacity to obtain agency and/or community support for new or revised programs.* Gaining support for change requires considerable effort. The social worker promoting either program modification or the creation of a new program must have the support of the staff and board (or responsible legislative body) where it will be located. Securing such support requires knowledge of organizational change processes and skill in presenting and interpreting the merits of the proposed programs. Typically, this does not happen without a long period of planning and involvement of board and staff members in the process of developing the proposal for change.

Obtaining support for new programs from the community requires additional skills. It often requires coalition building among human services agencies and other interested parties. The coalition can then select a strategy and create an action plan to develop support for the program. Program development, at times, involves the social worker in the preparation of grant applications for initial support of the program, and in public education activities such as speaking before community groups, preparing news articles, conducting radio and TV interviews, and lobbying individuals for support.

INSTRUCTION.   Most social workers engage in a certain amount of teaching. Much of their teaching is in informal work with clients to help them learn skills for addressing the issues they face in life. However, many social workers also engage in instructional activities in which a planned curriculum is delivered to groups of clients, agency staff members or volunteers, students, or community groups. To provide instruction effectively, the social worker must be prepared to plan, arrange, conduct, and evaluate programs that enhance the knowledge or increase the skills of staff members, students, agency volunteers, or participants in community groups. This cluster deals with formal instruction rather than the kind of informal teaching associated with orientation or on-the-job training. Activities involve course planning, syllabus design, test construction, and course evaluation.

Formal instructional activities are typically a relatively minor part of the direct practitioner's workload (see Box 8-13) but are a more substantial part of the work

Box 8-13   **Mean Scores for Instruction**

All Social Workers: 2.20	
BSW Direct Practitioners: 1.80	MSW Direct Practitioners: 1.81
	MSW Supervisors: 2.32
	MSW Administrators: 2.50

of supervisors and administrators. These experienced agency staff members are the persons usually designated to perform the more advanced teaching roles in both the agency and the community.

Several special competencies are required to fulfill the formal teaching roles of social workers and include the following:

1. *Capacity to develop curriculum for instruction or training programs.* Sound instruction requires a carefully developed curriculum. Whether helping parents learn more effective ways to deal with the inevitable problems their children experience or teaching foster parents about expected phases of child development, the curriculum must be based in the best available literature and delivered in a carefully sequenced and organized manner. Unfortunately, it is rare that a social work education program, even at the doctoral level, teaches how to develop curriculum. On some topics prepackaged curricula are available, but more typically social workers are on their own to develop a curriculum.

2. *Skill in planning workshops, seminars, or classroom sessions.* Once a curriculum is developed, it must be delivered. The logistics of announcing the meetings, recruiting the participants, ensuring that there is a quiet and comfortable meeting space with plenty of parking, arranging for refreshments, having the necessary instructional materials available, and so on, all call for careful planning. Failure to attend to these planning matters can negate even the best content.

3. *Ability to engage students, trainees, or groups of clients in learning activities.* Social workers are usually skilled in engaging their audience in learning. Their skills in group work, adapting to client interests, and basic communication skills serve them well when teaching. Because the content is typically aimed at helping the audience learn how to do something, the teaching style is likely to be more interactional than the styles used in standard classroom instruction where the goal is more oriented to transmitting information to students.

4. *Capacity to assess and evaluate instructional activities.* Instructional programs tend to be repeated and, while good instruction requires adapting to each audience, critique of instructional activities provides an important base for the next round of instruction. The competent instructor, therefore, must develop or adopt instruments that accurately assess the students' learning experience and invite suggestions for ways to improve the value of the experience for participants.

STAFF DEPLOYMENT.   Human services agencies are labor intensive, that is, they work with relatively few tangible products and most of their resources are invested in people. Therefore, an important indirect service activity for some social workers is the deployment of staff in a way that makes efficient use of staff time (the most valuable commodity for an agency) and ensures that the appropriate personnel are available to serve clients. To perform this set of tasks effectively, a social worker must recruit and select staff (e.g., professional and clerical employees, volunteers, and students), arrange staffing patterns and workload assignments, monitor staff productivity, and oversee compliance with organizational policies. Tasks in this cluster concentrate on the ensurance of staff coverage and equitable workload distribution, along with scheduling and coordinating working hours, leave, and vacation, and monitoring service demands.

The data in Box 8-14 make it clear that direct service practitioners rarely engage in staff deployment activities. This work, however, is a substantial part of the activity of supervisors and administrators who are charged with the responsibility to implement the programs of the agency in a way that is both efficient and effective.

As opposed to most other supervisory tasks that are focused on the development of the staff members, staff deployment tasks are primarily concerned with the functioning of the agency. These tasks require the following competencies:

1. *Capacity to match personnel with job assignments.* To accurately select and assign staff and volunteers to the various tasks that must be performed, it is necessary for the supervisor or administrator to have considerable knowledge of the work to be done and the capacities of available staff members. If needed skills are not present, it is important to then seek that competence through additional personnel and, at times, the replacement of existing personnel. Thus, the social worker in this capacity must be skilled at personnel selection and recruitment, as well as in appropriately matching the resources to the needs of the agency.

2. *Ability to create a clear organizational structure for conducting the work of the agency and a fair means of assigning the workload.* Human services workers are known for their dedication and willingness to extend well beyond the typical expectations for a job. They are equally known for their intolerance of time wasted due to organizational inefficiencies. It is, therefore, important that those social workers involved in personnel deployment are skilled at maintaining an equitable plan for

---

Box 8-14   **Mean Scores for Staff Deployment**

All Social Workers: 2.08	
BSW Direct Practitioners: 1.48	MSW Direct Practitioners: 1.57
	MSW Supervisors: 3.18
	MSW Administrators: 3.14

assigning workload, a clear and fair set of personnel rules and regulations that provides for both professional autonomy and agency responsibility, and a reasonable plan for monitoring the performance of the staff members. Specific activities that might be performed to accomplish these goals include assigning tasks, coordinating working hours, planning vacation time, making arrangements when personnel are on sick leave, and so on.

3. *Skill in the development of instruments for the evaluation of worker performance.* Supervisors are responsible for the evaluation of those staff members they supervise. The staff deployment personnel, additionally, are responsible for assessing the broader picture of how well all of the personnel mesh their talents to meet the agency's goals. To make those judgments, it is important to monitor changing service demands and worker competencies in order to determine staffing requirements. Worker performance evaluation requires carefully constructed performance measures that can be applied to workers throughout the organization and will yield valid information for assessing the agency's effectiveness.

PROTECTIVE SERVICES. The very young and the very old are among the most vulnerable members of U.S. society, and social workers are often in a position to protect both children and older people from potential physical, mental, or economic abuses. Some social workers are employed for the primary function of serving as agents of the society to offer protective services when there is suspected abuse. To provide those services, the social worker is required to collect and analyze data to be used in assessing at-risk clients and presenting information to appropriate authorities if clients are judged to be in danger of physical and emotional maltreatment or of having their basic rights violated. This includes the observation and assessment of children and/or adults to determine whether they have been abused or neglected. As part of this process, the worker may be expected to start legal proceedings and testify or participate in court hearings involving custody, competence, outplacement, or institutionalization.

Box 8-15 provides evidence that the provision of protective services is not a universal activity of social workers, despite the amount of television time devoted to social workers removing children from abusive situations. It is primarily basic social workers working on the front lines of public human services agencies that deal with the complex family situations that require protective services.

The following are examples of special competencies required to provide effective protective services. These specific competencies need to be used in addition to the competencies already described, especially those associated with interpersonal helping, individual and family therapy, case planning and maintenance, and risk assessment:

1. *Capacity to identify at-risk factors such as physical and emotional maltreatment.* Abusive situations are difficult to identify because abuse often occurs within a family or other living situation and is not readily evident to outsiders. The abusers attempt to conceal the maltreatment, and the persons being abused are often intimidated to the point they are fearful of reporting or even admitting they

Box 8-15 **Mean Scores for Protective Services**

All Social Workers: 2.03	
BSW Direct Practitioners: 2.39	MSW Direct Practitioners: 1.98
	MSW Supervisors: 2.15
	MSW Administrators: 1.71

have been abused. A variety of literature and workshops are available to help social workers providing protective services develop the needed competencies to work in these situations.

2. *Knowledge of the law and legal processes concerning protective services.* In most states it is mandatory that any helping professional report suspected abuse or maltreatment. When abuse is suspected, the legal and human services systems join together to investigate and, when appropriate, take action to prevent further abuse and resolve issues that contribute to the abuse. To perform this service the social worker not only needs good clinical skills but must also be thoroughly familiar with the relevant laws and legal processes that apply.

3. *Knowledge of local resources to be contacted if clients are in danger.* In some abusive situations the client is in immediate danger and the social worker must be prepared to seek police protection, make arrangements for temporary placement outside the home, or take other needed actions to protect the client. The worker engaged in child protection work must be thoroughly informed about the available resources and how to gain access to them.

4. *Ability to deal with conflictual situations.* People are typically frightened and angry when a social worker enters an abusive situation. The worker must be able to diffuse situations where high levels of conflict are present and assist clients to attempt resolution of issues in a calm and peaceful manner.

ORGANIZATIONAL MAINTENANCE. A certain amount of effort in every organization is devoted to carrying out its programs as efficiently as possible. Organizational maintenance activities require a social worker with the necessary knowledge and skills to manage the ongoing operation of a program or administrative unit to ensure its efficient and effective functioning by securing, allocating, and overseeing the utilization of its resources (e.g., staff, funds, supplies, space) and marketing its services. This cluster includes a wide array of tasks concerned with the operation of an existing program or unit. Some of the tasks center on financial operations, for example, estimating budgets, documenting and reviewing expenditures, and compiling billings, cost reimbursement, and cost control documents. Other tasks deal with the maintenance of a physical plant, control of inventory, and working with staff and vendors in order to ensure smooth program operations.

This day-to-day detail work is not usually the responsibility of a social worker unless he or she serves in an administrative role in the agency. For administrators (see Box 8-16), however, organizational maintenance tasks are a key part of the work to be done.

The following competencies are necessary to conduct the activities associated with organizational maintenance:

1. *Understand the operation of basic business systems and the requirements for oversight of agency resources.* The administrator must see that the scarce resources available to most human services organizations are used prudently. Public scrutiny of these agencies is typically high, requiring that administrators create and implement carefully developed measures of accountability. Systems must be developed for such activities as estimating budgets, documenting and reviewing expenditures, compiling billings, managing funds, maintaining the physical plant, securing necessary supplies, and so on. These administrative activities are essential for the efficient operation of the agency.

2. *Skill in creating and managing agency paperflow.* At times the excessive demand for accountability in human services agencies creates an enormous amount of paperwork, and administrators must attempt to protect workers from devoting excessive time to this administrative detail. To plan programs that maximize staff efficiency, social work administrators should possess knowledge of computer word processing and data analysis, should be able to create systems for the collection and storage of agency records, and should be skilled in implementing cost control programs.

3. *Skill in marketing and fund-raising for human services organizations.* Organizational maintenance also requires that the social worker be prepared for the continuing activity of making the services of the agency known in the community. Potential clients need to be made aware of the services that might be secured from the agency, and the general public needs to be informed on a regular basis about the important role the agency plays in enhancing the quality of life in the community. This public relations activity is a prerequisite for another important activity, that is, securing funds to operate the agency's programs. In addition to documenting, justifying, and monitoring the regular flow of funds from client fees, tax sources, and/or United Way allocations, effort must also be made to generate supplemental funds through such sources as foundation grants, agency benefit events, and personal bequests.

Box 8-16 **Mean Scores for Organizational Maintenance**

All Social Workers: 1.82	
BSW Direct Practitioners: 1.56	MSW Direct Practitioners: 1.42
	MSW Supervisors: 2.00
	MSW Administrators: 2.64

LOW UTILIZATION COMPETENCIES FOR MOST SOCIAL WORKERS

The final two task clusters, research and policy development and tangible service provision, were not a central part of the activity of any group of social workers. Both sets of activity were central to social work in its historical development but appear to be at best a secondary activity for social workers today. The low scores for research and policy development, when combined with somewhat low scores for program development and public education (i.e., instruction), generates an important question for social work. Has this profession abandoned its mission to address the societal, as well as the individual, causes of social dysfunctioning? The even lower scores for tangible service provision also raises a question. Has social work abandoned its commitment to the most vulnerable members of the society, that is, those who are in need of the most basic resources of food, clothing, and housing?

RESEARCH AND POLICY DEVELOPMENT.   From its early development in the state boards of charity, settlement houses, and charity organization societies, research and social policy development has been an integral part of social work practice. If social workers are to assist communities to improve social conditions or contribute to improved social conditions through influencing laws or regulations at the state or federal levels, they must be skilled at collecting data about those social conditions and assist policy makers as they apply that knowledge to various social policies and programs. In short, the worker must be prepared to collect, analyze, and publish data; present technical information to the general public, legislators, or other decision makers responsible for changes in human services programs or community conditions; and/or interact with community groups. While the tasks in this cluster involve a wide assortment of research, public relations, and community outreach activities, most of them are concerned with influencing public opinion, public policy, or legislation. The worker may collect and compile information, conduct surveys, present or publish findings from studies, testify as an expert witness, or organize and take part in campaigns or demonstrations.

The data presented in Box 8-17 indicate that for the typical social worker it is very rare to engage in this activity. Even the MSW-level administrators (Mean = 1.99) who are in roles where they are most likely to interface with community decision makers are not regularly involved in research and social policy development activities. The data may, however, underrepresent the full involvement of social workers

---

Box 8-17   **Mean Scores for Research and Policy Development**

All Social Workers: 1.72	
BSW Direct Practitioners: 1.48	MSW Direct Practitioners: 1.51
	MSW Supervisors: 1.66
	MSW Administrators: 1.99

in this area. The job function data do not report the social work educators (5.6% of the sample) who conduct the major part of social work research. These university-based social workers had a 2.63 score on this cluster of tasks.

What competencies does a social worker need to perform the research and policy development tasks? The following are necessary:

1. *Ability to develop and implement program and needs assessment research.* Sound policy development begins with valid information. Much discussion of social policy is highly tinged with emotion and political rhetoric. An important mechanism for minimizing the effect of political manipulation in policy and program decisions is fact. If social workers simply bring more or different emotion to the bargaining table, helpful social policy is unlikely to emerge. Thus, social workers must be prepared to collect accurate data to serve as the foundation for social policy analysis.

2. *Skill in social policy analysis and influencing decisions of policy makers.* With a sound data base, social workers are then prepared to assess existing and proposed social policies to determine a proposed policy's potential for resolving social problems and/or enhancing the overall quality of life for members of the society. For most social policy changes, some people will gain and some will lose. Social workers must be prepared to use one or more of the available policy analysis techniques to arrive at their conclusions and develop defensible positions on the proposals. Armed with a solid analysis, the social worker then calls on an additional set of competencies as he or she carries out a strategy to influence the outcome through actions intended to influence the decisions of those who finally establish the policy or program.

3. *Capacity to inform the public regarding social problems and potential solutions.* A part of influencing social policy is public education. An uninformed public is unlikely to support any significant change. Social workers are often in a position to see the effects of existing social policies as they affect their clients in positive or negative ways and, therefore, it is important for them to share that knowledge through speaking to public groups, working with the media, and so forth.

TANGIBLE SERVICE PROVISION. At the heart of social work's self-image is its concern that the poor and most at-risk members of the society have their basic needs met through the provision of adequate food, housing, clothing, and fundamental social supports. To provide these basic human services, social workers must be prepared to deliver a variety of "hard" tangible services designed to assist people coping with problems or activities associated with daily living. These activities focus on meeting the basic needs of clients as they cope with everyday life. Tasks include teaching budgeting, money management, food preparation and homemaking skills; helping clients find jobs and housing; and putting clients in touch with people of similar backgrounds and experience. Workers may visit clients to assess the suitability of living arrangements and take part in leisure activities to help them reduce loneliness.

The scores from the task analysis study contained in Box 8-18 suggest that most social workers are not meaningfully involved in delivering tangible services. Only

Box 8-18   **Mean Scores for Tangible Service Provision**

All Social Workers: 1.60	
BSW Direct Practitioners: 1.98	MSW Direct Practitioners: 1.56
	MSW Supervisors: 1.51
	MSW Administrators: 1.49

the BSW direct practitioners report even a limited amount of practice activity that involves assisting clients to receive basic social provisions.

Those social workers who are involved in tangible service provision need to be competent in the following areas:

1. *Knowledge of local resources that provide clients with social provisions such as shelter, food, clothing, money, and employment.* In virtually all communities and in most legislation creating social programs, the responsibility for implementing programs is assigned to several different human services agencies. For example, financial assistance, housing, job counseling and placement, and a food bank would usually be located in different agencies in different locations. "One-stop shopping" is rare in the human services. The social worker, then, must be familiar with the social provisions that are available and know how clients can gain access to them.

2. *Ability to develop positive helping relationships with clients requiring basic social provisions.* Social stigma is often attached to needing these basic services. To help clients make use of these provisions and, where possible, become self-supporting, social workers need to establish good working relationships characterized by empathy and trust. Such a relationship can become both supportive and a motivating factor in bringing about lasting change.

3. *Competence in teaching clients to use resources effectively.* It is said that the successful social worker works himself or herself out of a job. Indeed, the competent social worker can teach clients to do many things for themselves—including how to gain access to resources when needed and how to use those resources in a way that helps them achieve independence from the human services.

Concluding Comment

For a profession with the broad mission of helping people interact more effectively with their environments, it is not surprising that the identification of common features that bind social work practitioners into one profession has proven difficult. It is only at the somewhat general level of defining its mission that social workers have gradually moved toward consensus. Agreement at this broad conceptual level, however, does not necessarily indicate that at the more concrete level of day-to-day practice there is sufficient similarity in the work performed to consider this a single profession.

Drawing on data from a national task analysis study of social work and examining the clusters of work activity regularly performed by social workers, it has been possible to obtain a reasonably clear picture of social work practice. It is evident from these data that there is a core of helping tasks that most social workers regularly perform, as well as some that only a relatively few perform. One can reasonably conclude that in practice, as well as in theory, social work can stand as a single profession. Many tasks are regularly performed by most social workers, supporting the view that a common core of activities exists in the many expressions of practice.

In the preceding pages a set of competencies social workers are expected to possess are identified. These expressions of the tasks associated with each cluster provide a relatively clear overview of social work practice and represent one of the first data-based descriptions of what social workers need to be able to do to carry out their professional obligations.

KEY WORDS AND CONCEPTS

Competence

Mean

Task analysis

Cluster of practice activity

Universal practice competencies

Primary job function

Direct practice

Supervision

Administration

Indirect service activities

SUGGESTED READINGS

Raymond, Ginny Terry, Teare, Robert J., and Atherton, Charles R. "Is 'Field of Practice' a Relevant Organizing Principle for the MSW Curriculum?" *Journal of Education for Social Work* 32 (Winter 1996): 19–30.

Sheafor, Bradford W., Horejsi, Charles R., and Horejsi, Gloria A. *Techniques and Guidelines for Social Work Practice,* 5th Edition. Boston: Allyn and Bacon, 2000.

Teare, Robert J., and Sheafor, Bradford W. *Practice-Sensitive Social Work Education: An Empirical Analysis of Social Work Practice and Practitioners.* Alexandria, VA: Council on Social Work Education, 1995.

ENDNOTES

1. For example, see Laura Epstein, *Talking and Listening: A Guide to the Helping Interview,* 3rd Edition (New York: Macmillan, 1991); Alfred Kadushin, *The Social Work Interview,* 3rd Edition (New York: Columbia University Press, 1990); Bradford W. Sheafor, Charles R. Horejsi, and Gloria A. Horejsi, *Techniques and Guidelines for Social Work Practice,* 5th Edition (Boston: Allyn and Bacon, 2000), pp. 134–170; and Lawrence Shulman, *The Skills of Helping: Individuals, Families, and Groups,* 3rd Edition (Itasca, IL: F. E. Peacock, 1992).

2. Sheafor, Horejsi, and Horejsi, pp. 301–396.

3. National Association of Social Workers, *Code of Ethics* (Washington, D.C.: National Association of Social Workers, 1996).

4. American Psychiatric Association, *Diagnostic and Statistical Manual of Mental Disorders,* 4th Edition (Washington, D.C.: American Psychiatric Association, 1994).

5. Sheafor, Horejsi, and Horejsi, pp. 97–113.

6. Carol H. Meyer, "What Directions for Direct Practice?" *Social Work* 24 (July 1979): 271.

7. See, for example, Douglas R. Bunker and Marion J. Wijnberg, *Supervision and Performance: Managing Professional Work in Human Service Organizations* (San Francisco: Jossey-Bass, 1988); Alfred Kadushin, *Supervision in Social Work,* 3rd Edition (New York: Columbia University Press, 1992); Bradford W. Sheafor and Lowell E. Jenkins, eds., *Quality Field Instruction in Social Work* (New York: Longman, 1982); and Carlton Munson, *An Introduction to Clinical Social Work Supervision,* 2nd Edition (New York: Haworth, 1993).

8. Laura Epstein, *Brief Treatment and a New Look at the Task-Centered Approach,* 3rd Edition (New York: Macmillan, 1992), p. 137.

CHAPTER 9

Prevention as a New Direction: The Future of Social Work

Prefatory Comment

The nature of social work practice has been able to demonstrate flexibility based on public needs within the context of political and economic opportunities and constraints. The latter appears to be the case in the late 1990s and as we enter into the twenty-first century. Assisting social work practice in this regard are intervention concepts such as *prevention*, originally developed by the medical and public health professions. The social work profession is challenged to develop its own prevention theories grounded on psychosocial concepts as demonstrated in this chapter. Following an in-depth discussion of *prevention*, the remainder of the chapter will examine the topic areas of: (1) the role of social workers ensuring a person's right to treatment, or nontreatment, and even preventing treatment abuse with involuntary clients; (2) the potential role of social work intervention in the prevention of violence and homicide in gangs; (3) the application of advocacy and empowerment concepts in working with clients as a foundation to develop primary prevention strategies for nonclient populations; and (4) the continued development and testing in the courts or *class action social work* as a primary mental health prevention tool.

Prevention: An Evolving Concept Going into the Twenty-First Century

As human services budgets were drastically reduced during the 1980s and into the 1990s, an increasing number of people continued to need services. Substance abuse, child abuse, crime and delinquency, homelessness, AIDS, and the breakdown of the family are social problems that also continue to increase. Even in the most favorable economic periods for the human services, the mental health needs of the U.S. population have far surpassed the nation's financial and manpower resources to meet these needs. For example, it is estimated that there are anywhere from 1 to 2 million children in the United States each year who suffer physical or sexual abuse or neglect. Considering that each case could cost society $7,000 to treat, the total treatment expenditure might amount to $14 billion. The Department of Health and Human Services, however, spends less than $30 million per year for the treatment of child abuse and neglect. Federal and state agencies spend approximately $500 million per year for alcohol treatment services and yet treat less than 10 percent of all addicted alcohol abusers.[1] To live with increasingly limited financial and professional personnel resources while not losing sight of the potential of progressive health and welfare policies, were they to be someday passed by Congress, could result in less costly interventive approaches impacting larger numbers of people. Theories of *prevention*, therefore, have to be developed and applied to practice.

PREVENTION

Contemporary mental health conceptual formulations of prevention have as their foundation public health prevention theories and practice. In public health terms, prevention, as previously noted, has three stages. *Primary prevention* indicates actions taken prior to the onset of a problem to intercept its cause or to modify its course *before* a person is involved. It is the elimination of the noxious agent at its source. Through systematic spraying of affected ponds, for example, malaria-carrying mosquitoes, their eggs, and larva are destroyed before they have the opportunity to infect humans. *Secondary prevention* involves prompt efforts to curtail and stop the disease in the affected persons and the spreading of the disease to others. *Tertiary prevention* involves rehabilitative efforts to reduce the residual effects of the illness, that is, reducing the duration and disabling severity of the disease. In its most succinct form, therefore, prevention has three stages: prevention, treatment, and rehabilitation.

In 1977, the National Institute of Mental Health established an Office of Prevention to stimulate and sponsor large-scale programs of research on prevention. This office has also assisted the Council on Social Work Education to prepare curriculum materials about prevention.[2] The director of the Office of Prevention developed the following definition of primary prevention within a mental health context:

> Primary prevention encompasses activities directed towards specifically identified vulnerable high risk groups within the community who have not been labeled psychiatrically ill and for whom measures can be undertaken to avoid the onset of emotional disturbance and/or to enhance their level of positive mental health.[3]

Primary preventive programs were for the promotion of mental health, as educational rather than *clinical* in conception and practice, with their ultimate goal being to help persons increase their ability for dealing with crises and for taking steps to improve their own lives.[4] Goldston identifies two goals in primary prevention: (1) to prevent needless psychopathology and symptoms, maladjustment, maladaptation, and "misery" regardless of whether the end point might be mental illness; and (2) to promote mental health by increasing levels of wellness among various defined populations.[5] This places an emphasis on strength and positive qualities, in contrast to the problem-centered focus found in the medical model.

In applying primary prevention to child abuse, for example, intervention program efforts can be developed at three different levels. On a macro, social-reform level, prevention interventions may include legislation to protect children's rights, abolishment of corporal punishment, advocacy for abortion, and a more equitable economic distribution of resources. A second level of primary prevention intervention, also macro in impact, may utilize educational approaches aimed at a variety of audiences. This may include, for example, educating and sensitizing society to basic issues in child abuse and its deterrents, the use of newsletters and "crash courses" to provide helpful information to young families, and teaching adolescents in public schools essential skills needed in their future parental roles. A more focused primary prevention practice strategy, which is directly concerned with the operation of intrafamilial variables, involves utilizing homemaker and home visitor services to provide support and crisis assistance to at-risk families with young children. The visitors could be hospital-based personnel, day care, child support workers, or community volunteers.[6]

Preventing Treatment Abuse with At-Risk Populations

An at-risk population group with whom social workers should be concerned is juveniles who in fact have *not* committed crimes, yet are involuntarily coming to the attention of private psychiatric hospitals and the public juvenile justice system. Congress enacted the Juvenile Justice and Delinquency Prevention Act of 1974 as a decriminalization and deinstitutionalization effort designed to prevent young people from entering a "failing juvenile justice system," and to assist communities in developing more sensible and economical alternatives for youths already in the juvenile justice system.[7] The Act was successful; arrests for status offenses or "crimes" which, had they been committed by adults, would not have been considered crimes (such as truancy, running away, or incorrigibility), declined 15.8 percent (569,481 arrests to 466,885 arrests) between 1974 and 1979.[8] The 1980s presented a mixed picture, as juvenile crime nationally was decreasing yet more juveniles were institutionalized. In Minnesota, for example, even though there was a decrease in institutionalization in public juvenile training institutions, there was a tremendous growth in the numbers of youths admitted "voluntarily" to inpatient psychiatric settings in private hospitals.[9]

Many allege that poor adolescents who are genuinely mentally ill but whose parents do not have the economic resources or insurance coverage are not receiving the specialized treatment that affluent youths with less severe problems receive, and the poor are tracked instead into the public juvenile justice system.[10] Setting aside the potential economic conflict-of-interest issue for private hospitals and the double standard of treatment for the affluent and the poor, are the rights of hospitalized, affluent adolescents being abused?

Saul Brown, head of psychiatry at Cedars-Sinai Medical Center in Los Angeles, believes the issue of patients' rights is a misguided one and that giving adolescents the right to decide whether they need treatment abrogates a certain kind of parental reason. The United States Supreme Court ruled in 1979 that parents had the right to commit their children to a psychiatric facility if qualified medical professionals did the admitting. However, the ruling applied *only* to state hospitals. This situation has been referred to as a *legal twilight zone*. The California Supreme Court has asked the legislature to conduct an inquiry into psychiatric facilities being used by parents as "private prison hospitals for their incorrigible children."[11]

On the one hand, while some affluent white adolescents expressing behavioral disorder symptoms are being involuntarily committed by their parents to private psychiatric hospitals, risking the long-term psychosocio-political consequences of a psychiatric label, some poor adolescents—mostly minorities—who have not committed any crimes and are expressing behavioral disorder symptoms are being labeled criminal by law enforcement officials and tracked prematurely into the public juvenile justice system. They will have to suffer the long-term consequences of a criminal label. The U.S. Department of Justice has developed and funded the SHODI (Serious Habitual Offenders—Drug Involved) program in five cities: Oxnard and San José, California; Portsmouth, Virginia; Jacksonville, Florida; and Colorado Springs, Colorado. The purpose of the SHODI program, according to Oxnard Police Chief Robert Owens, is to (1) identify the most serious offenders, ages thirteen to seventeen; (2) ensure they receive stiff sentences; and (3) keep the youths off the streets for the longest period of time. The criteria to be labeled a SHODI is three arrests in the past year and two previous arrests (three of the five arrests must be for felonies); or three arrests in the past year and seven previous arrests (eight of the ten arrests must be for petty theft, misdemeanor assault, narcotics, or weapons violations).[12] The most controversial aspect of the program is that a juvenile who has never been convicted of a crime (or allegations found to be true and sustained in a juvenile court proceeding) could be classified by police as a habitual offender because criteria are based on arrests, *not convictions!*

With reference to the affluent white and poor minority adolescents being prematurely labeled and tracked into the private psychiatric hospitals and public juvenile justice systems, the values social workers place on self-determination, right to nontreatment, opposing discrimination, and treatment abuse may require them to assume a position and take action. Those adolescents who are definitely a danger to themselves or others, who are severely psychiatrically disabled, or who chronically damage property or commit acts of violence, based on *convictions*, may indeed have to be institutionalized for their and/or society's protection. Social workers must support these detentions and make sure the youths receive proper treatment rather than punishment. This role would be consistent with *tertiary prevention*. However, for those youngsters whose acting out is not harmful or who have numerous arrests that are related more to police deployment practices rather than predelinquent behavior of poor minority adolescents, social workers should assume a *secondary prevention* role as advocates encouraging intervention at the family and community level rather than harsher measures such as institutionalization. *Primary prevention* intervention involving educational and employment alternatives for at-risk families and youths might consist of evening workshops or seminars for affluent families concerning the stresses and pressures some affluent adolescents suffer; for example, the fear that they will not be able to achieve as well as their parents in a tight economy that places the cost of a home out of reach for many. For poor communities, primary prevention community education programs could focus on helping families learn to cope with the stresses of migration, urbanization, gangs, and drugs. Youths would be provided assistance in school or helped to obtain employment if they chose not to remain in school.

Gang Violence and Homicide Prevention

Numerous polls show that the nation's number one problem is youth violence. In addition to pending crime bills, President Clinton is advocating proposals that limit the availability of guns and is attempting to influence the media to show less violence on the screen. U.S. Attorney General Janet Reno has threatened a "crackdown" on Hollywood over television violence.[13] Reno goes even further when she states that the United States has passed white South Africa as having the highest number of people in jail per capita. She is described as being "remarkably" interested in *preventing* crime rather than just punishing it, reflecting a shift in priority that, if she succeeds, could leave a lasting mark on law enforcement nationally.[14]

Youth violence is increasing dramatically. According to the Department of Justice between 1987 and 1991 the number of adolescents arrested for homicide in the nation increased by 85 percent. In 1991 youths from ten to seventeen accounted for 17 percent of *all* violent crime arrests. Youths are not only the perpetrators, they are also the victims. Violent youth gangs, which are now present in 126 cities across the nation, are responsible for many of these homicides.[15] Like the nation, the president, and the U.S. attorney general, the profession of social work has to be concerned and challenged and has to address this national problem of gang violence and homicide with its own psychosocial-based theories of prevention. What follows is one approach in addressing this problem, first anticipated and reported in social work in this text in the late 1980s.

A seventeen-year Chicago study involving 12,872 homicides reported that more than half of Hispanic youth victims were killed in gang-related altercations.[16] In 1985, 10.5 percent of 2,781 homicide victims in California were killed by gangs, and in Los Angeles 24 percent of 1,037 homicides were gang-related.[17] Other large urban areas with gangs also have significant numbers of persons being assaulted and/or killed by gangs. This violence exacts an extremely high toll in injuries, death, and emotional pain and adversely impacts the quality of life for thousands of poor residing in the inner cities.

The public health profession, with its focus on epidemiologic analysis and prevention, believes it can make a substantial contribution to solving problems of interpersonal violence. Former Surgeon General C. Everett Koop stated that "violence is every bit a public health issue for me and my successors in this century as smallpox, tuberculosis, and syphilis were for my predecessors in the last two centuries."[18] The health professions are making their initial bold entry into this major problem area, following in the footsteps of criminology, sociology, and the criminal justice system. Psychiatry and psychology have been investigating the issue primarily from a biological (brain chemistry) and behavioral (modifying the behavior of *individuals*) perspective. Chapter 17 demonstrates how the social work profession, with its micro- to macrolevel knowledge and skills base, is ideally suited to apply its techniques with individual gang members, gang groups, and the community to reduce urban gang violence and homicide. In addition to employing social work's traditional approaches in dealing with the problem, the present task is to devise ways in which prevention theory, with corresponding intervention models, can be applied.

It was stated earlier that *primary prevention* in a public health context involves averting the initial occurrence of a disease, defect, or injury. Primary prevention in homicide requires national efforts directed at the social, cultural, educational, technological, and legal aspects of the macro environment which facilitate the perpetuation of the country's extremely high homicide rate—indeed a tall order. A national strategy would involve public education on the seriousness and ramifications of violence, contributing factors, high-risk groups, and need for social policy as a physical health and mental health priority in the United States. The topic must become a higher priority in medical schools and schools of nursing, social work, and psychology. At the community level community self-help groups, social planning councils, and other civic groups need to work toward educating U.S. citizens about the causal relationship of alcohol, illegal drugs, firearms, and television violence to homicide and violence.[19] In theory these strategies, when directed at high-risk populations, are supposed to reduce those conditions that are seen as contributing to violence and homicide.

Secondary prevention in a public health context concerns the cessation or slowing down of the progression of a health problem. It involves the early detection and case finding by which more serious morbidity may be decreased. Applying this concept to homicide, such case finding requires the identification of persons showing early signs of behavioral and social problems that are related to increased risk for subsequent homicide victimization. Variables such as family violence, childhood and adolescent aggression, school violence, truancy or dropping out of school, and substance abuse are early indicators of many persons who later become perpetrators of violence and homicide. Secondary prevention intervention strategies with individuals already exhibiting these early symptoms interrupts a pattern that may later result in serious violence or homicide.[20]

Tertiary prevention pertains to those situations in which a health problem is already well-established, but efforts can still be made to prevent further progress toward disability and death. In the case of homicide, the problems of greatest concern are those of interpersonal conflict and nonfatal violence, which appear to have a high risk for homicide. Aggravated assault is one early significant predictor related to homicide.[21] In a study in Kansas, in 25 percent of the homicides either the victim or the perpetrator had previously been arrested for an assault or disturbance.[22] Victims of aggravated assault, such as spouses or gang members, are at especially high risk for becoming homicide cases.

Attempts have been made to develop program models aimed at preventing youth violence and homicide, although some of these programs are not specifically aimed at *gang* homicide prevention. These educational-, court-, and community-based programs seem to be functioning mainly at the primary (reducing conditions contributing to homicide) and secondary (identifying persons showing early signs of sociobehavioral problems) prevention levels. A few of these programs, as examples of prevention models, will be discussed.

EDUCATIONAL PREVENTION MODELS

The *Boston Youth Program* instituted in four Boston high schools had a curriculum on anger and violence. The ten-session curriculum provided (1) information on adolescent violence and homicide; (2) the discussion of anger as a normal, potentially constructive emotion; (3) knowledge in developing alternatives to fighting; (4) role-playing and videotapes; and (5) the fostering of nonviolent values. Following the completion of the program, an evaluation of a control group (no curriculum) and an experimental group (curriculum) revealed that there was a significant, positive change of attitude in the experimental group. The researchers cautioned, however, that further study had to delineate the actual impact the curriculum would have on actual *behavior,* and the longevity of the impact.[23] The Boston Youth Program was directed at minority students, but it was not indicated whether any of these students were gang members.

Peer Dynamics is another school-based program, sponsored by the Nebraska Commission on Drugs, which was designed to reduce the incidence of destructive risk-taking behaviors associated with juvenile delinquency and substance abuse among high school adolescents in fifty-six public schools. With the goal of developing improved self-esteem and better communication skills, the program trained and supervised students who participated in group interaction activities with other students. A follow-up evaluation found that in relationship to other students, program participants showed a noticeable drop in discipline referrals. The final evaluation noted that Peer Dynamics affected both sexes equally and that the greatest changes were noted in eighth-, tenth-, and eleventh-grade students. No significant change in attitude toward themselves or others was reported in the control group.[24] Again, this was not a program designed specifically for gang youths, although some gang members may have been participants. The question remains, however, whether improved *attitudes* result in less violence and homicide.

A third school-based prevention program functioning in the city of Paramount in Los Angeles County is called the *Paramount Plan.* This was designed to be a "gang-prevention" model and, unlike the Boston Youth Program and Peer Dynamics that target high school youths, it is an educational model directed at *all* fifth and sixth graders in the school district. The program consists of neighborhood parent meetings and an antigang curriculum taught to students in school for fifteen weeks. Prior to the program, 50 percent of students were "undecided" about joining gangs. After the fifteen weeks, 90 percent said they would not join gangs.[25] No mention was made of the 10 percent of students who did not change their minds about joining gangs. In poor urban areas where there are gangs, only 3 to 5 percent of youths become delinquents and/or join gangs. In other words, at least 95 percent of youths do not join gangs even without a gang-prevention program such as the Paramount Plan. Further research is needed to determine if those in the 10 percent who did *not* change their minds about joining gangs actually do, and second, whether they later become either perpetrators or victims of gang homicide. Perhaps one of the major research challenges is to be able to measure what was prevented.

COURT- AND COMMUNITY-BASED PROGRAMS

In Baltimore, Maryland, *Strike II* was developed as a court-based program linking juvenile justice with health care. Its "clients" were court adjudicated first-time offenders (secondary prevention) for violent crimes, assault, robbery, arson, and breaking and entering. Noninstitutionalized probationers were eligible for the program, which was a probation requirement. This multidisciplinary program employed paralegal staff, counselors, social workers, and psychiatrists. The juvenile probationers were involved in five programs: recreation, education, job readiness, and ongoing counseling and medical care as needed. These services were in *addition* to traditional probation supervision.

The recidivism rate for Strike II clients was only 7 percent, compared to 35 percent statewide and 65 percent for those leaving corrections institutions. The basic cost (excluding medical and job readiness services) was $100 per client.[26] With impressive results, the Strike II program dealt largely with violent juveniles in a physical health/mental health, educational, employment, juvenile justice program. Although gang members were not mentioned specifically, it would appear that with a reduction in recidivism these perpetrators would also have been at reduced risk for becoming violence/homicide victims.

Another community-based program, aimed specifically at gangs, was called *House of Umoja*. It was developed in Philadelphia by two inner-city black parents whose son had joined a gang. His fellow gang members were invited to live with the family, following the model of an extended African family. In response to increased gang-related homicides in 1974 and 1975, the House of Umoja spearheaded a successful campaign to reduce gang violence by obtaining peace pledges from eighty youth gangs. From this experience evolved a community agency called Crisis Intervention Network that worked toward reducing gang violence through communication with concerned parties and organizational efforts.[27] This approach later was called the *Philadelphia Plan*.

In 1978 the state of California Youth Authority reported its findings concerning its *Gang Violence Reduction Project* in East Los Angeles. The project's basic strategy was to (1) promote peace among gangs through negotiation; and (2) provide positive activities for gang members. Directors maintain they reduced gang homicides in East Los Angeles 55 percent, from eleven homicides in seven months of one year down to five homicides during a similar seven-month period the following year. The project researchers admitted that "any judgment that a relationship exists between the changes in gang-related homicide and violent-incident statistics and the activities of the Gang Violence Reduction Project must be based on inference."[28]

Another community-based peace-treaty program targeting high-risk gang youth, patterned after the Philadelphia Plan, is the *Community Youth Gang Services Corporation* in Los Angeles. CYGS counselors in fourteen street teams were able to convince forty-four of 200 gangs they worked with to come to the table to develop a "peace treaty." During the period the peace agreement was in effect, from Thanksgiving of 1986 through the New Year's holidays of 1987, there was only *one* act of violence among the forty-four gangs. The peace-treaties model can "buy time" for all concerned, but if society does not respond with the needed resources (employment, job training, physical health/mental health services, education), peace treaties are very difficult to maintain. Obviously, *all* the above approaches are needed.

GANG HOMICIDE PSYCHOSOCIAL PREVENTION MODELS

Continuing efforts have to be made in further refining homicide prevention models in order for them to correspond more closely with the specific type of homicide one wishes to prevent. There are different types of homicide that vary according to circumstances. Robbery, spousal, and gang homicide are all different and require different prevention strategies. If, for example, Asian Americans are at extremely high risk for being robbed and murdered at 2 AM in Uptown, U.S.A., through a community education effort Asian Americans would be informed about the high homicide risk in visiting Uptown at 2 AM. Adhering to the warning could immediately reduce the number of Asian American homicide victims.

In addition to attempting to get a "close fit" between the prevention model and the specific type of homicide, it is equally important that the high-risk person be clearly identified in order to maximize the impact of the prevention model. In the educational- and community-based violence prevention models previously discussed, the focus of intervention appeared to be more on the perpetrator or the "pre-perpetrator" (the person showing early behavioral signs indicating he or she *might* become a perpetrator) who was at high risk for committing a violent act. In theory all potential victims in an *unspecified* population are spared victimization when the perpetrator ceases to be violent. Furthermore, there did not seem to be specific prevention programmatic strategies focusing on the violence *victim* or the person most likely to become a victim. What seems to be needed is a guideline or framework that assists in the identification of high-risk gang members.

Using California as an example, Table 9-1 represents a "general to specific" profile framework for identifying and "zeroing in" on the high-risk gang members who will be the target population for homicide prevention.

For our purposes, we will attempt to develop a hospital-based and community-based youth gang psychosocial homicide prevention model in which social workers play a key intervention role. The focus of these prevention models will be on the gang member who actually becomes a violence or homicide victim of a gang and goes or is taken to the hospital. In Table 9-1 these victims would be the gang members found in items 2b and 2c. In this respect the prevention models are largely tertiary in nature. However, they become primary prevention models when intervention strategies are aimed at younger children and latency-age siblings of the victim who are not yet gang members. By preventing children in high-risk families from becoming future gang members, the likelihood of the children being killed may be significantly reduced, because gang members are nearly sixty times more likely to be killed than persons in the general population (519/100,000 versus 10/100,000).

TABLE 9-1	**Area and Demographic Characteristics Related to Homicide Risk**
I. United States	One of the most violent countries in the world, ranked no. 5 out of 41 countries
II. California	Along with Southern states, ranks among the most violent states
III. Los Angeles	Among the more violent cities in the U.S.
IV. Inner City (L.A.)	The poorest areas, often the scene of most violent crime
A. Minority Groups	Overrepresented among the disadvantaged, poor, and those residing in the inner city
1. Profile of Perpetrators and Victims	
a. Males	4 to 5 times more likely than females to be killed
b. Age	15–25 age category at highest risk
c. Substance Abuse	Found in 50 to 66 percent of cases
d. Low Education	50 percent school drop-out rate not uncommon
e. Low Income	High unemployment, many living in poverty
2. Gangs	Quite prevalent in inner city and a product of social disorganization
a. Minor Assaults	Gang members are at high risk for being assaulted
b. Aggravated Assaults	Gang members are at high risk for being victims of aggravated assault; occurs 20 to 35 times more often than homicide
c. Homicide	Gang members are at high risk for becoming homicide victims, rate being 519 per 100,000 in the 150,000 gang-member population

Sources: M. L. Rosenberg and J. A. Mercy, "Homicide: Epidemiologic Analysis at the National Level," *Bulletin of the New York Academy of Medicine* 62 (June 1986): 382; H. M. Rose, "Can We Substantially Lower Homicide Risk in the Nation's Larger Black Communities?" *Report of the Secretary's Task Force on Black and Minority Health,* Vol. 5 (Washington, D.C.: U.S. Department of Health and Human Services, January 1986); I. A. Spergel, "Violent Gangs in Chicago: In Search of Social Policy," *Social Service Review* 58 (June 1984): 201–202; A. Morales, "Hispanic Gang Violence and Homicide," Paper presented to the Research Conference on Violence and Homicide in Hispanic Communities, Los Angeles, September 14–15, 1987, p. 13; *Los Angeles Times,* Wednesday, October 5, 1995, p. B-9; A. Morales, "Homicide," in Richard L. Edwards, ed., *Encyclopedia of Social Work,* 19th Edition (Washington, D.C.: NASW Press, 1995).

HOSPITAL-BASED MODEL. Health professionals in community clinics and hospitals are actually in the "trenches," dealing with thousands of violence and homicide casualties related to gang violence. These professionals are usually the first to touch these bodies, and in medical settings they function in a tertiary prevention role, literally trying to control bleeding and save lives. Wounded gang victims of gang violence are in reality a "captive audience," which creates an excellent intervention opportunity for secondary prevention.

Through the physician, social worker, nurse, or other health practitioners on the hospital emergency room team inquiring *how* the victim was injured (which may be confirmed by police, family members, or interested parties), professionals could ascertain if the incident was gang-related. Through in-service staff training concerning gangs and their culture, health staff would be able to determine whether the victim was a gang member. Specifically, dress codes, mannerisms, graffiti, language, tattoos, and other gang symbols could help establish or rule out the gang identity of the victim. Police, family members, peers, and/or witnesses could also be good sources for gang identity confirmation.

If the injuries were caused by gang members and the victim is a gang member, a designated health team member (the social worker) would be responsible for referring the matter to the hospital's SCAN Team. "SCAN Team" refers to Suspected

Child Abuse and Neglect, or in some hospitals, Supporting Child Adult Network.[29] SCAN Teams, which are found in many hospitals, are composed of multidisciplinary health staff in which at least one member is a social worker. SCAN Teams were originally developed to investigate suspected child sexual or physical abuse or neglect cases coming to their attention in medical settings. In cases of suspected child abuse, for the protection of the child SCAN Teams are required to take immediate action by involving law enforcement and the child-welfare department.

Our gang-homicide prevention model would require that gang violence victims also become a SCAN Team intervention priority. However, one additional social worker on the SCAN Team would be a gang "specialist" and have primary treatment-coordinating responsibility with the gang victim, his or her family, and the community.

Although not intentional, the emergency room provides access to a high-risk population (victims and families) that is often too embarrassed, frightened, or reluctant to seek assistance from traditional social work agencies. The anonymity of a large, busy, impersonal hospital can be less threatening.[30] Additionally, medical crises may make some persons psychologically vulnerable, hence more amenable to change during the crisis period.

In working with gang members who have been seriously injured as the result of gang assault, the author has found that often this is when their psychological defenses are down because they are suffering adjustment disorder or posttraumatic stress disorder symptoms (PTSD). In the acute stage of PTSD symptoms, victims may have recurrent, intrusive, distressing recollections of the event, including nightmares, flashbacks, intense stress at exposure to events resembling the traumatic event, persistent avoidance of stimuli associated with the event, sleeping problems, hypervigilance, anxiety, and fear. They are sometimes reluctant to leave the home and even become fearful of their own friends in gang "uniform."

During this acute stage, which may last about six months, they are quite motivated to abandon "gang banging" (gang fighting). If the social worker is not the primary therapist, arrangements should be made for the youth to receive prompt treatment for PTSD while hospitalized, as untreated PTSD may become chronic and last for years. It is at this point that the social worker can also obtain needed employment, educational, recreational, or training resources for the vulnerable gang member. The parents may also be emotionally vulnerable, having just gone through an experience in which they almost lost their son or daughter. They may be more willing to accept services for themselves, if needed, and/or for younger siblings who might be showing some early behavioral signs of problems (deteriorating school performance, truancy, aggressiveness). Helping the family and young siblings is a *primary prevention* role, as these efforts may prevent future gang members (perpetrators or victims) from developing in this at-risk family.

There also may be situations in which the gang member arrives deceased at the hospital or dies during or after surgery. These cases would still be referred to the SCAN Team social worker for service. The focus of help would be—with the family's permission—helping the parents and other children deal with grief and providing any additional assistance they may need in burying their loved one. If there are adolescent gang members in the family, they may be quite angry and want to get even for their brother or sister's death. If not already involved, the social worker would call on community gang group agencies to assist in reducing further conflict. If there are younger siblings in the family, an assessment would be made of their needs, and efforts would be made to mobilize resources to meet these needs. These intervention strategies would have the objective of preventing future homicides in a high-risk family.

The preceding gang homicide prevention model operating from a medical-based agency is presented to illustrate how social work may be able to have intervention impact on a very serious problem shortening the life of many poor, inner-city youths. Figure 9-1 illustrates the various intervention strategies of the hospital-based gang homicide intervention model. Other models can be developed, such as the community agency-based model described in the following paragraphs.

COMMUNITY AGENCY-BASED MODEL.   An example of an inner-city community agency-based model that the author is currently developing and implementing with the help of a full-time social worker and a second-year clinical social work intern, is a clinical program funded by the Kellogg Foundation. The agency, Challengers Boys and Girls Club, founded in 1968 by Lou Dantzler, is located in South Central Los Angeles, a poor, predominantly African American area. This community was the hardest hit in all of Los Angeles as a result of the April 29, 1992, riot, which was this nation's most destructive and deadliest riot, resulting in sixty deaths and nearly a billion dollars of damage.

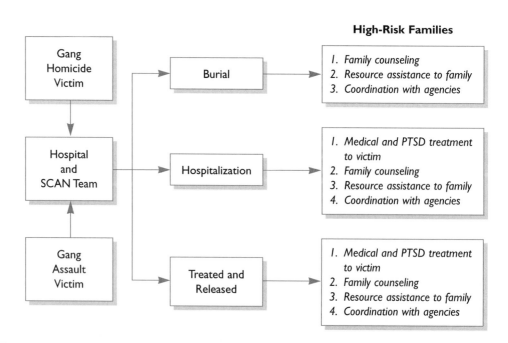

FIGURE 9-1 **Gang Homicide Psychosocial Prevention Model**

Within a three-mile radius of the agency are approximately 22,000 youths in a population of 379,000 persons, with 43 percent of the households headed by 15,000 single mothers over sixteen years of age with children up to eighteen years of age. This community has exceptionally high rates of school dropouts (56% of seventeen-year-old African American youths are functionally illiterate), AIDS, diseases of the heart, sexually communicated diseases, and homicide. Neighborhood homicide rates at 95 per 100,000 are almost twelve times the national rate, four times the Los Angeles rate, and at 600 per 100,000 in the neighborhood's gang population.

The agency, with 2,100 enrolled families, has an average daily attendance of 400 boys and girls (ages six to seventeen) during the summer months; 200 during the rest of the year. Program services, in addition to athletic and recreational services, include tutoring, classes in basic math, reading comprehension and computers, photography, woodshop, job application training, a new basic dental and health examination program, and mental health crisis intervention.[31]

In establishing a gang-homicide psychosocial prevention model, an assessment has to be made regarding the severity of the gang-related violence and homicide problem. Local law enforcement statistics are mandatory in this regard. Table 9-2 demonstrates the extent of the problem in the above targeted area.[32]

The target area is a very active, violent community, clearly contributing to making many young ethnic/racial youths an endangered species as they approach adolescence and young adulthood, being killed at the rate of 600 to 1,000 per 100,000 in the gang population, depending on the gang-related homicides for a given year.

The mental health crisis intervention program, staffed by the author as a mental health consultant, a full-time social worker, and a clinical social work trainee is available to those member families who experience a sudden, severe crisis such as the premature death of a family member brought on by an accident, suicide, or

TABLE 9-2   **Prevalence of Gangs and Gang-related Violent Crimes**

Total No. of Gang Members	24,200

Latino Gangs	204
African American *Crips*	109
African American *Bloods*	45
Types of Gangs: *Criminal* (making $); and *Conflict* (turf-oriented)	

No. of Gang-related Crimes (5/1992 to 5/1993)

Homicide	133
Attempted Homicide	247
Felony Assault	1259
Robbery	1034
Discharging Firearm into Inhabited Dwelling	61
Battery on Police Officer	19

Source: South Bureau, Los Angeles Police Department, 1993.

homicide. These tragic events are known to leave a spouse or parent emotionally immobilized for months and, at times, even for years. The death of a child results in a more severe grief reaction for a parent than that of any other family member.[33] The surviving siblings' loss may be more than that of the surviving parent because they have lost not only an immediate family member but also the grieving parent(s) who is temporarily emotionally unavailable to them. During this time, depending on their prior adjustment, age, and emotional strength, these children are at high risk for emotional, educational, and behavioral problems. Prompt intervention (assessment, counseling, and possible referral in acute cases) may lessen and *prevent* a child from having more serious difficulties and problems of adjustment. In specific cases where the sibling was a gang member and the victim of a gang homicide, younger adolescent or pre-adolescent siblings are at especially high risk for becoming either future victims or perpetrators of gang violence and homicide.

In this inner-city, agency-based, gang-homicide psychosocial prevention model, nearly 100 high-risk African American and Hispanic elementary school children (mostly males) were referred for treatment for assaultive, fighting behavior directed at peers either at school, at home, in the neighborhood, or at Challengers. Of these, ten cases were more directly impacted by violence. For the purposes of brevity, only two of these cases will be commented on.

In one case, a fourteen-year-old Challengers member was the victim of a "drive-by" shooting outside his home by a gang group. The youth was not a gang member, yet met the general, stereotypic profile of a gang member held by many police and gang members; that is, he was a minority male adolescent residing in the poor, inner-city neighborhood. A bullet to his brain resulted in four months' hospitalization and permanent neurological impairments, including dependence on a wheelchair. Ongoing supportive visits were made with the youngster at the hospital, along with conversations with medical and social service staff and his guardian aunt. (His mother had passed away three years previously due to illness, and his father was in a correctional facility.)

On release, efforts were made to reintegrate the youngster into the Challengers program components, with supportive counseling as needed and assistance in applying for victim's assistance and Social Security benefits. The victim did not have younger or adolescent siblings, hence other family members were not at risk for gang homicide as future victims or perpetrators.

The second case concerned a ten-year-old suicidal boy, whose father had been killed by a robber twelve months previously, and his paternal uncle three months before. The boy was experiencing school behavioral problems, sleep disturbance, and some somatic complaints, including vomiting. The mother had already taken the boy to a child guidance-counseling program and was now enrolling the youngster in the Challengers recreational program. The agency made available to the mother an adult supportive counseling group, led by the mental health consultant and social worker, for family members who have lost a loved one due to a sudden, premature death. The mother herself was seen individually, with plans to later involve her in a group with similarly affected families. Such groups are also needed for children and adolescents. Additionally, outreach efforts are made with law enforcement and other community agencies, hospitals, and churches to identify high-risk families who had a child who was a gang member and was killed as the result of gang violence. These families, in their psychological state of vulnerability, were extended an invitation to become part of the Challengers program. As they began to participate in the program, they received a host of social, recreational, educational, dental, health, and mental health services. It was anticipated that the cycle of gang violence and trauma, with its accompanying sequelae of psychosocial problems, was lessened.

Advocacy, Empowerment, and Prevention

Briar defines the social worker advocate as one who is:

> . . . his client's supporter, his advisor, his champion, and if need be, his representative in his dealings with the court, the police, the social agency, and other organizations that affect his well-being.[34]

On the other hand, Brager sees the social worker advocate as one who:

> . . . identifies with the plight of the disadvantaged. He sees as his primary responsibility the tough-minded and partisan representation of their interests, and this supersedes his fealty to others. This role inevitably requires that the practitioner function as a political tactician.[35]

Briar's concept represents advocacy on behalf of an *individual,* whereas Brager's concept represents advocacy on behalf of a group or *class* of people. The latter concept is similar to the role social workers would perform in *class action social work,* discussed later in this chapter.

Gilbert and Specht report that advocacy as a social work role (social change versus psychological change) has presented a dilemma for generations of social workers. Each generation redefines this issue in its own terms. For example, in 1909 Richmond defined the issue in terms of the "wholesale" versus the "retail" method of social reform. Lee approached it in 1929 as "cause" versus "function," and in 1949 Pray perceived it as "workmanship" versus "statesmanship." In 1962 Chambers conceptualized the matter in terms of "prophets" versus "priests," and in 1963 Schwartz analyzed this conflict in terms of providing a service as opposed to participating in a movement.[36] In 1977, in a special issue of the journal *Social Work* on conceptual frameworks for practice, Morales perceived the issue differently. He saw social workers as persons armed with appropriate knowledge and skills that enabled them to do clinical work in poor communities as well as to intervene via social action and advocacy in larger community systems.[37]

Social workers can help clients help themselves through the application of concepts such as *empowerment.* Solomon defines *empowerment* as:

> . . . a process whereby persons who belong to a stigmatized social category throughout their lives can be assisted to develop and increase skills in the exercise of interpersonal influence and the performance of valued roles. Power is an interpersonal phenomenon;

if it is not interpersonal it probably should be defined as "strength." However, the two concepts—power and strength—are so tightly interrelated that they are often used interchangeably.[38]

According to Solomon, empowerment, as a social work practice goal in working with African American clients or other persons living in oppressed communities, implies the client's perception of his or her intrinsic and extrinsic value and the client's motivation to use every personal resource and skill, as well as those of any other person that can be commanded, in the effort to achieve self-determined goals. Solomon attempts to develop a conviction in the client that there are many pathways to goal attainment and that failure is always possible, but the more effort one makes the more probable success must be.[39]

Solomon suggests three practitioner roles that hold promise for reducing a client's sense of powerlessness and leading to empowerment: the resource consultant role, the sensitizer role, and the teacher/trainer role. The resource consultant role finds the practitioner linking clients with resources in a manner that enhances the clients' self-esteem and problem-solving capacities. Minahan and Pincus identify five specific practitioner tasks for accomplishing this.[40] In the sensitizer role, the practitioner incorporates all the role behaviors that are designed to assist the client to gain the self-knowledge necessary for him or her to solve the presenting problem or problems. The teacher/trainer role, according to Solomon's conceptualization, finds the practitioner as manager of a learning process in which the principal aim is the completion of certain tasks or the resolution of problems related to social living.[41]

A *voluntary* relationship seems to be implied in Solomon's conceptualization when she speaks of the practitioner assisting the client to gain self-knowledge to solve problems. The practitioner does not appear to be working from a social control perspective in which the presenting problem is defined by someone other than the client. Such "helping" transactions might make *involuntary* clients feel powerless.

In prevention theory a social worker helping *clients* through advocacy and empowerment concepts would seem to be using a secondary prevention strategy, because the target population is already identified as persons with problems. The social worker has a significant role and performs specific key tasks in advocacy and empowerment efforts with the client. In applying advocacy and empowerment concepts toward primary prevention goals, however, the social worker's role is not central as it is in working with client populations. Rather, the role is multiple since the at-risk target population is comprised largely of nonclients or "unaffected" persons. The focus must be on strengths foremost in the target population, as opposed to problems, weaknesses, and inadequacies.[42]

One of the essential tasks of the social worker in working with an at-risk population toward primary prevention will be to network. Network may be defined as the process of developing multiple interconnections and chain reactions among support systems.[43] There are four levels of networking approaches: (1) personal networking; (2) networking for mutual aid and self-help; (3) human services organization networking; and (4) networking within communities for community empowerment.[44] The last approach will be highlighted as it has *primary* prevention goals.

The community empowerment model and process has several goals. The first is to create community awareness of neighborhood strengths and needs, with emphasis on strengths as perceived by the target population. The second goal is to strengthen neighborhood helping networks by developing linkages among natural helpers in the community, among helpers and neighborhood leaders, and among neighborhood residents themselves. A third goal is to strengthen the professional helping networks by organizing a professional advisory committee in the target population area to advise this community empowerment-directed process. Fourth, linkages are formed between the lay and professional helping networks. The fifth goal is to form linkages between the lay and professional helping networks and the macro system. In a mental health primary prevention context, mental health professionals would help the target population put together a database of information regarding federal, state, county, and local mental health and human services plans, or the macro system. The sixth and final goal would be to institutionalize the networking process, thereby creating a new mental health constituency, integrated into but not assimilated or taken over by the larger, bureaucratic human services system. Through such a networking process leading to community empowerment and an improvement in the quality of life, those problem areas that the professional system traditionally ends by treating (secondary and tertiary prevention) rather than preventing, the at-risk population may be spared unnecessary pain, stress, and anguish.[45]

Class Action Social Work and Prevention

The enormous mission of social work is to enhance the quality of life for all persons. Some of the injustices and obstacles that damage the quality of life are poverty, racism, sexism, and drug abuse; there are many more.[46] Social work's impact on these problems is sometimes limited by the clinical model, by inappropriate interventive strategies, and by the fact that it becomes too time-consuming and inefficient to try to help people on a case-by-case basis. On other occasions a referred client with a "problem" may not really have a problem. The problem may be in the referral system.

For example, a school may refer a problem student to a social worker to help him or her adjust to the requirements of the school system. The school system, however, may have serious defects that are the primary cause of the student's problem. The goal of the social worker should then be to help tailor the school system to meet the educational needs of the student. The student in this situation may represent a *class* of people, that is, a number of students in a similar predicament. Rather than the social worker working individually with each student to document the deficiencies in the school system, one student can represent all students in a *class action* suit to improve conditions in the school. Class action is a legal concept that has promising implications for social work. Closer working relationships will have to be cultivated with the legal profession to enable lawyers to conceptualize broad social work concerns and to translate these into legal class action suits. Such an approach can be called *class action social work*. Victories in the courts could provide relief for thousands of poor people.

There is precedent for having an organized body of social workers and lawyers, providing the potential for broader collaborative impact through class action suits on behalf of the poor. Recognition of matters of natural interconnection and mutual interest between lawyers and social workers led in 1962 to the creation of the National Conference of Lawyers and Social Workers, a joint committee composed of sixteen members, eight appointed from each parent organization. The Conference met twice a year.[47] In 1967 the Conference developed cooperative goals for the two professions to work toward in serving the needy. Some of these goals included:[48]

1. Identification of needs requiring their individual or joint professional competencies
2. Resolution of situations that involve both social and legal problems—including recognizing and reconciling respective professional orientations, especially with regard to the adversary role
3. The development of machinery and procedures for effective referral relationships

The nine papers in *Law and Social Work,* one of the Conference's publications, envisioned a rather narrow role for social workers working with lawyers, following the traditional clinical, case-by-case model. For example, social workers defined their function as providing "expertise in psychosocial diagnosis including evaluation of the *individual's* potential for social functioning."[49] The collaborative potential of class action suits to help the poor on a broad scale is not mentioned in this 1973 document. Let it again be emphasized that the central theme of the Conference— "lawyers and social workers, as close collaborators in situations involving both social and legal problems, should seek to utilize to the full the resources of each profession to help the poor"—provides the foundation for social work to have a greater impact on social reform.

In some states social workers have already made pioneering efforts to enter the legal arena. In California, for example, the Greater California Chapter of the NASW presented an award to John Serrano, a social worker, for his actions as a concerned citizen in the widely publicized *Serrano* v. *Priest* case, which argued that the quality of a child's education should not be dependent on the wealth of a school district.[50] The California Supreme Court, in this class action suit filed by the Western Center on Law and Poverty, Inc., ruled 6 to 1 that the California public educational finance scheme, which relies heavily on local property taxes, violated the equal protection clause of the Fourteenth Amendment to the U.S. Constitution. The court held that the financing system invidiously discriminated against the poor. The court also asserted that the right to a public education was a fundamental interest that could not be dependent on wealth, and it therefore applied the strict equal-protection standard. Finding no compelling state interest advanced by the discriminatory system, the court held it unconstitutional.[51]

The significance of the *Serrano* v. *Priest* decision transcends California boundaries because all states except Hawaii use similar educational finance systems. Wealthier districts are favored to the detriment of poorer school districts. A direct relationship exists between the number of dollars spent per child and the quality of education available to that child. In *Serrano* v. *Priest* it was discovered that poor communities were paying two to three times as much school tax per $100 of assessed valuation as were wealthy communities, yet wealthy communities received two to three times as many educational dollars per child from the state as did the poorer communities.[52]

In *Serrano* v. *Priest* the court's policy considerations focused on the pervasive influence of education on individual development and capacity within modern society and on education's essential role in the maintenance of free enterprise democracy. It was considered that the combination of these factors sufficiently distinguished education from other governmental services for it to merit recognition as a fundamental interest.[53] No court had previously placed education within the framework of interests meriting strict equal-protection scrutiny, and this decision represented the first time any type of governmental service had been held to involve fundamental interests.[54]

Considering the *Serrano* precedent, might not the areas of welfare, health, and mental health services also represent a set of circumstances as unique and compelling as education? A right to public education may not be maximally enjoyed if a child is poorly housed, impoverished, malnourished, or in need of physical or mental health care. *Serrano* v. *Priest,* as a social work class action concept, has the potential to be the cutting edge of social reform in a wide range of governmental services, including several in which social workers already have knowledge and experience. In view of the regressive social and economic policies of Reagan, Bush, and now Clinton with his harmful new welfare reform, the opportunity for class action collaboration between law and social work as a significant tool of intervention is possible. The class action social work concept and its application was tested by one of the authors in the courts as a mental health primary prevention activity.

Class action is a legal procedural device for resolving issues in court affecting many people. Those persons actually before the court represent the unnamed members of the class in a single proceeding in equity, thereby avoiding multiple case-by-case actions. *Class action social work,* developed by the authors, is a forensic social work/legal profession collaborative litigation activity involving social work concerns, with the goal of obtaining a favorable court ruling that will benefit the social welfare of a group of socioeconomically disadvantaged persons. Class action social work in a mental health primary prevention context finds social workers and attorneys pursuing a court ruling that will have a positive psychosocial impact on a disadvantaged class of people who, prior to the ruling, were at risk in developing psychological or psychiatric disorders or symptoms. Among the requirements needed to accomplish the primary prevention goals are—to borrow from public health terminology—a small sample of "infected" organisms, an identification of the suspected toxic agent, and a laboratory procedural test to show whether the toxic agent caused the infection in the organism. Translating this into class action mental health primary prevention terms using an actual case (*Nicacio* v. *United States INS*), the "infected organisms" were thirteen Hispanic plaintiffs (the injured, complaining parties) who were exhibiting psychiatric symptoms, allegedly caused by stressful interrogations conducted by patrol officers of the United States Immigration and Naturalization Service (INS). The courtroom became the laboratory in which the suspected toxic evidence (behavior of the INS officers) was analyzed as to potential harm. If found to be harmful, the court could issue an order terminating the toxic behavior of the INS, which thus prevented psychosocial harm (psychiatric symptoms) in a specific at-risk population (millions of Hispanics residing in the Southwestern states or the State of Washington area, depending on court boundary definitions).

In *Nicacio* v. *United States INS*, Hispanic plaintiffs brought suit contending that (1) the border patrol agents of the INS were conducting roving motor vehicle stops in search of "illegal aliens" on the roadways of the state of Washington that were in violation of Fourth Amendment rights to be free from unreasonable searches and seizures; (2) that the actions of INS officials were unlawful; and (3) that the plaintiffs were entitled to monetary damages for humiliation, embarrassment, and mental anguish suffered as a result of a violation of their Fourth Amendment rights.[55] The facts of the case were that (1) all plaintiffs were of Mexican descent and were either born in the United States, U.S. citizens, or permanent resident aliens who resided in the Yakima Valley area of the state of Washington; (2) the plaintiff class was defined by the court as "all persons of Mexican, Latin, or Hispanic appearance who have been, are, or will be traveling by motor vehicle on the highways of the state of Washington"; (3) at the time litigation was initiated, INS agents were regularly conducting roving patrol motor vehicle stops, detentions, and interrogations in the Yakima Valley area; (4) many of the stops were based solely on Hispanic appearance, the agents' subjective feelings or intuition, or the suspected "illegal aliens'" innocuous behavior, appearance, or traits; and (5) persons stopped were required, in most cases, to provide identification or documentation of legal presence in the United States.[56]

In attempting to document the amount of humiliation, embarrassment, and mental anguish suffered by the plaintiffs as a result of their contact with INS officers, plaintiffs' attorneys contacted one of the authors as an expert witness to conduct a mental health evaluation of all the plaintiffs. Having been sworn in by the court and qualified and accepted as an expert witness, the author rendered a DSM-III-R diagnosis of each plaintiff. The findings were that (1) not one of the thirteen plaintiffs had ever been hospitalized or treated on an outpatient basis for a mental health problem; (2) eleven of the plaintiffs suffered adjustment disorder symptoms, either with depressed mood, anxious mood, or mixed emotional features; (3) one plaintiff suffered acute posttraumatic stress disorder symptoms; and (4) one plaintiff was symptom-free.

The findings of the court were that (1) the INS border patrol practices were unlawful; (2) plaintiffs and class action members were entitled to a declaratory judgment covering future conduct of INS officers in stopping vehicles on public highways; and (3) plaintiffs were *not* entitled to recover monetary damages for their suffering, since plaintiffs were unable to specifically identify the officers.[57] The favorable court ruling affected *all* persons of Mexican, Latin, or Hispanic appearance residing only in the state of Washington, rather than in the Southwestern states, as had originally been requested by plaintiffs' attorneys. Even so, the court order stopped the noxious activities of the INS directed at Hispanics in the state of Washington. *All* Hispanics in the state of Washington, therefore, were spared INS-provoked psychiatric symptoms in future contacts with the INS. This case shows the growing potential of class action social work with a mental health primary prevention goal and outcome using social work psychosocial practice concepts.

Class action social work, as a macrolevel practice intervention prevention tool, can also be used to ensure that children at risk receive the welfare benefits and services to which they are entitled. Clinton's new welfare reform law could be a test case. As more children are growing up poor and without stable families, Harris impresses on social workers and the social work profession that they must renew their commitment to child welfare and continue to play an important role in the development and formulation of public policy and child welfare services to strengthen the ability of vulnerable families to raise healthy children.[58]

In many instances, it is not necessary to develop and formulate new public policy concerning child welfare; simply creating new laws will not solve the problems. There may be many national and local situations in which child welfare laws and policies already exist to benefit children, but are not—for any number of reasons—being implemented. It is in these cases that class action social work intervention can be applied to prevent children from experiencing harm when they are not receiving the services to which they have a right.

Stein suggests that child welfare agencies are vulnerable to class action suits, alleging that clients are being deprived of constitutional guarantees or entitlements specified in federal or state policy. In this recession era of reduced spending at the continued expense of domestic programs, reductions in personnel and social services increase welfare agency vulnerability to class action suits, as the lack of funds *is not* a defense for failing to provide federal and state legally mandated services.[59]

Class action suits on behalf of children have charged that state agencies have failed to develop case plans; made inappropriate placements of children, ignoring racial/ethnic factors; failed to pursue adoptive placements; and failed to provide preventive services. Currently, two class action suits are pending that allege state failure to provide preventive services, and one suit alleging maltreatment of children in foster care and failure to develop and implement permanent plans.[60] The specific role of social workers in these class action suits is not clear, that is, whether they are defendants, expert witnesses, or initiators and/or collaborators with the attorneys in the suits. It is when social workers are in the initiating, collaborating role with attorneys that it conforms to the earlier definition of class action social work.

Social workers need to pay careful attention to existing national and state benefits and welfare policies and to laws and regulations affecting vulnerable client groups, such as children, the homeless, welfare families, and institutionalized psychiatric and corrections populations, to ensure that they are receiving the services and benefits to which they are entitled. Continued denial of resources to clients by agencies, even after notification of mandated requirements, may have merits for attorney–social worker collaboration that eventually could result in a class action social work type of intervention. A favorable court remedy would prevent continued harm to the immediately affected client population (secondary prevention) and to future client populations (primary prevention).

Concluding Comment   Escalating costs, coupled with increasing need for human services and the fact that there will never be sufficient mental health practitioners to meet these needs, require the development and application of helping concepts, such as primary prevention, designed to benefit large numbers of persons *before* they are symptomatic. Because social work is one of the helping professions most involved in interacting with and helping communities, it is anticipated that the profession will play an increasingly vital role in applying primary prevention concepts in the twenty-first century.

Urban gang violence and homicide was highlighted in this chapter to indicate to the social work profession that, from a historical practice experience standpoint, it is best suited for the health and mental health professions to assume a leadership role in developing micro- to macro-intervention strategies to deal with a problem that is killing thousands of inner-city youths. Primary, secondary, and tertiary violence and homicide prevention programs were discussed and analyzed as to their impact on violence and gang homicide. A framework for identifying high-risk gang victims was developed to correspond to a suggested hospital-based prevention program. A bold, new approach based on prevention in dealing with violence is the "handwriting on the wall," with U.S. Attorney General Janet Reno being the writer and the nation's leading advocate. She is firmly supported by President Clinton. The social work profession and its schools need to "tool up" and meet this new challenge if they wish to become more relevant to the needs of society, especially those of the inner city.

More and more social workers are leaving the public welfare arena, going into private practice, and shifting their target population to the middle class. Lacking public agency bureaucratic constraints, they are potentially free to help the poor through social action activities such as writing proposals, conducting needs surveys, or building coalitions to apply pressure on government. Related strategies of advocacy and client empowerment may result in a transfer of power so that client groups in need of services gain and exercise their own economic and political might. A community empowerment model built with networking methods can, in the final result, produce a mental health primary prevention outcome.

Class action social work, which was first introduced into the literature in this text in 1977, continues to show promise as a macrolevel intervention strategy. *Serrano* v. *Priest,* a class action victory, established the precedent of the right to an equal education; it paved the road for the poor to fight for the right to health and welfare in order to maximize their new educational opportunity. Increasing an individual's opportunities through such assistance is in the best interests of the individual and society. The effectiveness of class action social work with a mental health primary prevention goal was demonstrated in *Nicacio* v. *United States INS,* in which a positive court ruling will have the effect of preventing literally thousands of at-risk Hispanics from developing psychiatric symptoms caused by discriminatory law enforcement practices. A rare opportunity for social work to help the poor on a broad scale seems very possible in light of *Serrano* and *Nicacio.* Examples were also provided to show how class action social work intervention can be applied on behalf of vulnerable client populations who are being denied legally mandated services. Collaboration with the legal profession should be vigorously pursued by social workers.

KEY WORDS AND CONCEPTS

Prevention

Primary prevention

Secondary prevention

At-risk population

Tertiary prevention

Class action social work

Gang homicide psychosocial prevention model

SUGGESTED READINGS

Johnson, Yvonne M. "Indirect Work: Social Work's Uncelebrated Strength," *Social Work* 44 (July 1999), No. 4.

Middleman, Ruth R., and Goldberg, Gale. "Social Work Practice with Groups," *Encyclopedia of Social Work,* 18th Edition, Vol. II. Silver Spring, MD: National Association of Social Workers, 1987, pp. 714–729.

Morales, Armando. "The Mexican American Gang Member: Evaluation and Treatment," in Rosina M. Becerra, Marvin Karno, and Javier Escobar, eds., *Mental Health and Hispanic Americans: Clinical Perspectives.* New York: Grune & Stratton, 1982.

Report of the Secretary's Task Force on Black and Minority Health, Vol. 5. U.S. Department of Health and Human Services, January 1986.

Roberts, Albert R., and Brownell, Patricia. "A Century of Forensic Social Work: Bridging the Past to the Present," *Social Work,* Vol. 44, No. 4, July 1999.

Solomon, Barbara Bryant. *Black Empowerment: Social Work in Oppressed Communities.* New York: Columbia University Press, 1976.

Soricelli, Barbara A., and Utech, Carolyn Lorenz. "Mourning the Death of a Child: The Family and Group Process," *Social Work* 30 (September–October 1985): 429–434.

Spergel, Irving A. "Violent Gangs in Chicago: In Search of Social Policy," *Social Service Review* 58 (June 1984): 199–226.

Stein, Theodore J. "The Vulnerability of Child Welfare Agencies to Class Action Suits," *Social Service Review* 61 (December 1987): 636–654.

ENDNOTES

1. H. John Staulcup, "Primary Prevention," in Aaron Rosenblatt and Diana Waldfogel, eds., *Handbook of Clinical Social Work* (San Francisco: Jossey-Bass, 1983), p. 1059.
2. Feldman et al., p. 6.
3. Stephen E. Goldston, "Defining Primary Prevention," in George W. Albee and Justice M. Joffe, eds., *Primary Prevention of Psychopathology* Vol. I: The Issues (Hanover, NH: University Press of New England, 1977), p. 20.
4. Ibid.
5. Ibid., p. 21.
6. Steven L. McMurtry, "Secondary Prevention of Child Maltreatment: A Review," *Social Work* 30 (January–February 1985): 43.
7. United States Senate Committee on the Judiciary, *Ford Administration Stifles Juvenile Justice Policy* (Washington, D.C.: U.S. Government Printing Office, 1975), p. 2.
8. Barry Krisberg and Ira Schwartz, "Rethinking Juvenile Justice," *Crime and Delinquency* (July 1983): 340.
9. Ibid., pp. 360–361.
10. Ron Schultz, "A New Prescription for Troubled Teens," *Los Angeles* 30 (January 1985): 159.
11. Ibid., p. 205.
12. *Los Angeles Times,* Part II, March 24, 1985, p. 2.
13. *Los Angeles Times,* Part I, Friday, October 22, 1993, p. 24.
14. "Truth, Justice, and the Reno Way," *Time,* Vol. 142, No. 2, p. 26.

15. "Teen Violence—Wild in the Streets," *Newsweek,* August 2, 1993, pp. 40–49.

16. Carolyn Rebecca Block, "Lethal Violence in Chicago over Seventeen Years: Homicides Known to the Police, 1965–1981," Illinois Criminal Justice Information Authority, p. 69.

17. Department of Justice, "Homicide in California, 1985" (Bureau of Criminal Statistics and Special State of California, 1985), p. 17; "Fiscal Year 1985–86 Statistical Summary," Los Angeles County Sheriffs Department; "Statistical Digest, 1986," Automated Information Division, Los Angeles Police Department.

18. Cited in N. Meredith, "The Murder Epidemic," *Science* 84 (December 1984): 42.

19. *Report of the Secretary's Task Force on Black and Minority Health,* Vol. 5, U.S. Department of Health and Human Services, January 1986, pp. 43–44.

20. Ibid., pp. 46–50.

21. Ibid., p. 50.

22. Police Foundation, *Domestic Violence and the Police: Studies in Detroit and Kansas City* (Washington, D.C.: The Foundation, 1976).

23. The Boston Youth Program, Boston City Hospital, 818 Harrison Ave., Boston, MA, cited in *Report of the Secretary's Task Force,* pp. 235–236.

24. C. Cooper, "Peer Dynamics, Final Evaluation Report, 1979–1980," Nebraska State Commission on Drugs (Lincoln: Nebraska State Department of Health).

25. "Early Gang Intervention," Transfer of Knowledge Workshop, Department of the California Youth Authority, Office of Criminal Justice Planning, 1985, pp. 11–12; also see Tony Ostos, "Alternatives to Gang Membership." (Unpublished paper, Paramount School District, Los Angeles County, California, October 1987.)

26. "Strike II," Hopkins Adolescent Program, Johns Hopkins Hospital, Park Building, Baltimore, MD, 1986.

27. Fattah Falaka, "Call and Catalytic Response: The House of Umoja," in R. A. Mathias, P. De Muro, and R. S. Allinson, eds., *Violent Juvenile Offenders: An Anthology* (San Francisco: National Council on Crime and Delinquency, 1984), pp. 231–237.

28. "Gang Violence Reduction Project, Second Evaluation Report: October 1977–May 1978," Department of the California Youth Authority, November 1978, pp. i, iii.

29. T. Tatara, H. Morgan, and H. Portner, "SCAN: Providing Preventive Services in an Urban Setting," *Children Today* (November–December 1986): 17–22.

30. Karil S. Klingbeil, "Interpersonal Violence: A Comprehensive Model in a Hospital Setting from Policy to Program," in *Report of the Secretary's Task Force,* p. 246.

31. Lou Dantzler, "Executive Summary, Challengers Boys and Girls Club" (Los Angeles, CA, 1990), brochure.

32. As reported to the author by the Los Angeles Police Department South Bureau, June 1993.

33. Barbara A. Soricelli and Carolyn Lorenz Utech, "Mourning the Death of a Child: The Family and Group Process," *Social Work* 30 (September–October 1985): 429–434.

34. Scott Briar, "The Current Crisis in Social Casework," *Social Work Practice, 1967* (New York: Columbia University Press, 1967), p. 28.

35. George A. Brager, "Advocacy and Political Behavior," *Social Work* 13 (April 1968): 6.

36. Neil Gilbert and Harry Specht, "Advocacy and Professional Ethics," *Social Work* 21 (July 1976): 288.

37. Armando Morales, "Beyond Traditional Conceptual Frameworks," *Social Work* 22 (September 1977): 393.

38. Barbara Bryant Solomon, *Black Empowerment: Social Work in Oppressed Communities* (New York: Columbia University Press, 1976), p. 6.
39. Ibid., p. 342.
40. Anne Minahan and Allen Pincus, "Conceptual Framework for Social Work Practice," *Social Work* 22 (September 1977): 348.
41. Solomon, p. 354.
42. Felix G. Rivera and John Erlich, "An Assessment Framework for Organizing in Emerging Minority Communities," F. M. Cox et al., eds., *Tactics and Techniques of Community Practice*, 2nd Edition (Itasca, IL: Peacock, 1984).
43. Lambert Maguire, "Networking for Self-Help: An Empirically Based Guideline," in *Tactics and Techniques of Community Practice*, p. 198.
44. Ibid., p. 199.
45. Ibid., pp. 206–207.
46. Scott Briar, "The Future of Social Work: An Introduction," *Social Work* 19 (September 1974): 518.
47. National Association of Social Workers, *Law and Social Work* (Washington, D.C.: The Association, 1973), p. vii.
48. Ibid., p. 15.
49. National Association of Social Workers, *Law and Social Work*, p. 25. [Emphasis ours.]
50. *NASW Newsletter*, Greater California Chapter, April 1975, p. 1.
51. Robert B. Keiter, "California Educational Financing System Violates Equal Protection," *Clearinghouse Review* 5 (October 1971): 287.
52. Ibid., p. 297.
53. Ibid., p. 298.
54. Ibid., p. 299.
55. *Nicacio* v. *United States INS*, 595 F. Supp. 19 (1984), p. 19.
56. Ibid., p. 21.
57. Ibid., pp. 19, 25.
58 Dorothy V. Harris, "Renewing Our Commitment to Child Welfare," *Social Work* 33 (November–December 1988): 483–484.
59. Theodore J. Stein, "The Vulnerability of Child Welfare Agencies to Class Action Suits," *Social Service Review* 61 (December 1987): 636–654.
60. Ibid., p. 640.

CHAPTER 10

Social Work Throughout the World

Prefatory Comment Throughout the world, people need assistance in addressing social issues that affect their lives and help in resolving or reducing the social issues that they confront. As the profession dedicated to both serving people and improving social conditions, the need for social work is global.

The prior sections of this book have focused on the ways in which social work has evolved in the United States. Lest the reader assume that the functioning of social workers in the United States is the only model for this profession, this chapter is concerned with similarities and differences in the expressions of social work throughout the world. In addition, it reflects the growing globalization of social work and the evolving efforts to address international social issues with a single voice.

World Population Changes: Creating a Global Demand for Social Work

In August 1999, the world population reached 6 billion people. This number had doubled in less than forty years and, prior to that, it had taken all of human history until 1804 for the world population to reach 1 billion persons. Given this rapid rate of growth in recent years, experts predict that the world population will increase another 3 billion by 2025, creating a severe drinking water shortage and limited food supply.

The world population continues to expand in spite of a reproductive revolution that has resulted in half of the world's married women using family planning interventions, compared to only 10 percent of fertile women thirty years ago. Even though up to 71 percent of women in the United States use some form of birth control, it has the highest fertility rate among wealthy industrialized countries. Projections are that the United States will double its current population of 270 million by the year 2060. In addition, it is projected that as early as 2025 there will be an explosion of retirees sixty and older in the United States, which will draw on savings and pension funds, causing a shortage for capital investment. Long-term population growth in the United States and other industrialized countries poses problems for the future. Yet these problems are relatively insignificant compared to the rest of the world. For example, 95 percent of the world's fertile young people live in developing countries, which are already characterized by lack of resources in education, housing, employment, and health care. Such global population stresses call for world communication, collaboration, and planning to address such impending problems.[1] Social work has an important role to perform in helping the world address these and related issues, but action is sometimes hampered by the difficulty of speaking with a single professional voice. There are several reasons for social work's slowness to develop into a global profession.

SOCIAL WELFARE: THE CONTEXT

Social work has developed differently in various countries because unique social, political, cultural, economic, and historical forces shape the manner in which human services are provided. Due to the fact that social work is highly interactive with a country's human services delivery system, this profession's evolution in any country is affected by the philosophy that underpins that country's social programs.

In Chapters 1 through 4 of this book, the manner in which social work evolved in the United States was described in tandem with the ebbs and flows of changing philosophies and support for the social welfare institution. Unlike medicine, nursing, and occupational therapy, which are tied mainly to the physical aspects of human functioning and display relatively little variation from one country to another, social work is based on the social structures that each society creates, making it inevitable that there will be substantial differences among countries. Indeed, no two countries have evolved identical human services (although they have borrowed ideas from each other), and thus the configuration of activities for social workers varies considerably.*

Several social welfare philosophies are helpful for characterizing the different approaches to human services throughout the world. For example, in preindustrial or agriculture-based societies, social needs are met primarily by families, churches,

---

*A particularly informative source when examining social work in several different countries is M. C. Hokenstad, S. K. Khinduka, and James Midgley, eds., *Profiles in International Social Work.* Washington, D.C.: NASW Press, 1992. London: Routledge, 1994. Included in this book are descriptions of social work in Chile; Great Britain; Hungary; India; Japan; Hong Kong, Singapore, South Korea, and Taiwan; South Africa; Sweden, Uganda, and the United States.

the few wealthy persons in the society, and various guilds (e.g., agricultural trade groups and civic organizations). This type of society is typically found among developing countries in Africa, Latin America, Asia, and elsewhere. In these societies, direct human services are most likely to be provided on a natural helping or volunteer basis, and social work practice tends to evolve as a macro social change profession. In these societies, social workers' efforts have been orientated toward *social development,* that is, social, economic, and political change to improve basic human conditions. Lusk and Horejsi, however, note a change now occurring in this approach, indicating that "social work in the developing world is setting aside its long standing preoccupation with political ideology and has shifted to a pragmatic effort to ameliorate poverty and social injustice."[2]

Another philosophy tends to emerge when industrialization begins to occur in a country. When this happens, individual and family mobility is required, urbanization increases, and people are viewed as commodities whose time and talent can be bought and sold. There is reliance on the market system to provide people with needed resources because the extended family may not be present or have the capacity to meet its members' social needs. Similarly, countries emerging from communist rule are typically in the process of creating or re-creating industrial economies and systems of delivering; human services that were abandoned under communism must be redeveloped. There must, therefore, be a backup to what can be done by a family or the market system, and a social welfare system is created. Thus a set of social programs and persons to deliver these programs evolves. It is in these postindustrial societies that professional levels of social work are most likely to develop.

Epsing-Anderson (1990) has developed a typology of three distinct social welfare systems that have emerged in postindustrial societies. Epsing-Anderson's typology is based on the analysis of the degree to which the social welfare system (1) treats people as having a right to services, and not just as commodities used in the production of goods and services; (2) redistributes money and other resources to achieve greater equality and reduce poverty; and (3) maintains a balance between the government and private sectors having responsibility for the well-being of people.[3] Examination of how countries differ on these three points (i.e., comparative social welfare) yields the following distinct variations in postindustrial welfare approaches—or social welfare states.

First, the *corporatist welfare state* is designed to maintain existing social class differences and the distribution of resources by the system. Services are distributed primarily by the private or corporate entities, and people are not viewed as having the right to services. This approach to social welfare is at the most conservative side of the continuum of approaches and attempts to maintain the status quo. Examples of countries where this approach is dominant include France, Italy, Spain, and Austria. In these countries, social workers' activities are primarily related to accommodating for material deficits (social provisions) and resolving marriage and family issues. Social work practice under this system is highly specialized, and most recognized social workers are required to hold a social work credential, usually with training at the vocational level.[4]

Second, the *liberal welfare state* is best represented by the United States, Canada, Great Britain, Australia, India, and Japan—although these countries differ in the degree to which each of the criteria for comparing welfare systems is embraced. These programs typically focus on redistributing income to the low-income population; are designed to reinforce the work ethic and view peoples' labor primarily as an economic commodity; maintain minimum standards of well-being through government programs, yet also subsidize the private for-profit and nonprofit welfare programs; tend to stigmatize people receiving services, thus maintaining social stratification; and only minimally treat people as having a right to services. In these countries social workers are expected to provide a range of services, from direct practice interventions to efforts to facilitate at least incremental change in social structures. Most professional social workers in these countries hold a professional social work credential at the undergraduate or graduate level.

Last, the *social democratic welfare state* provides universal services and contends that the peoples' work should not simply be treated as another commodity. Social programs in countries that have adopted this model (e.g., Norway, Sweden, the Netherlands) attempt to achieve maximum standards of human well-being through universal health insurance systems and are designed to socialize the costs of family living through governmental transfers such as children's allowances, sharing costs of caring for the aged and handicapped, and guaranteeing full employment to all who can work. In this type of welfare system, relatively few of the service providers hold a social work credential. Those who have credentials are prepared at the vocational or secondary levels, except when offering therapeutic services typically related to child behavior issues and parenting problems.[5]

In reality, no country exactly fits into any one of the welfare states in this typology and, indeed, social welfare systems are constantly changing. A country may move from one type to another, or closer to or more distant from any form of welfare state over time, yet understanding where this country stands at any one time is essential if there is to be a successful social technology transfer (e.g., adopting or adapting maternal leave programs or crisis intervention techniques).[6]

THE EMERGENCE OF SOCIAL WORK TRAINING AND EDUCATION

It is difficult to mark the beginning of a profession. In the United States, for example, the National Association of Social Workers designated 1998 as the centennial year for the profession, presumably because in 1898 the New York Charity Organization created a six-week training program known as the New York School of Philanthropy. If one holds social work up to all the criteria for professions proposed by Abraham Flexner and other experts on the sociology of professions (see Chapter 3), it is more likely that social work in the United States met the criteria to become a recognized profession somewhere around the late 1920s. Nevertheless, the initiation of education and training programs is usually well documented and thus is used to signal the advent of professions. It is informative, therefore, to note a few of the dates when significant training or education in social work was introduced in different countries throughout the world as a means of marking when social work began in each.*

1898	United States and Germany
1899	The Netherlands
1903	England
1920	Chile
1921	Sweden
1924	South Africa
1931	Ireland
1932	Spain
1936	India and Egypt
1963	Uganda
1989	Hungry
1992	Italy

Social work also varies in different countries in the educational levels recognized as preparation for practice. In some countries it is *training*, with no particular academic preparation (not even a high school diploma required). In others, high school or specific community college vocational training is the requisite preparation, while in many countries college-level professional education is the requirement to enter social work. In a few countries a professional master's degree is the terminal practice degree. Nowhere is a doctoral degree the expected preparation for social work practice.

A Global Approach to Social Work

The initial approach to developing a worldwide perspective on social work was termed *international social work* and was concerned with comparing social work as it exists in different cultures and countries. Increasingly, as social work has grown and matured worldwide, an effort has been made to address social work from a *global perspective,* that is, as one profession practicing in many different countries. A global approach requires the creation of international professional organizations to coordinate the formulation of a single concept of the profession, discover where

---

*The literature is somewhat inconsistent regarding the starting dates of educational programs and, therefore, the dates included in this list should be viewed as approximate.

common understanding exists, promote political positions regarding worldwide social problems, identify the common values of the profession and specify ethical guidelines for practice, clarify the roles and functions that are typical for all forms of social work practice, and develop professional education. What is the current status of global social work?

INTERNATIONAL PROFESSIONAL ORGANIZATIONS

Two international organizations provide the basic leadership for the globalization of social work. One, the International Federation of Social Workers (IFSW), is structured to work through various national professional membership organizations such as the National Association of Social Workers and the professional trade unions of social workers that exist in some countries. Begun in 1928 following the International Conference on Social Work held in Paris, today organizations from approximately 70 countries, representing 500,000 social workers, participate in the IFSW. The activities of IFSW include publication of a newsletter, maintaining a commission that advocates for the protection of human rights throughout the world, the development of a statement of ethical guidelines for social workers, and maintenance of updated policy positions on thirteen global social welfare issues.[7]

The second important international social work organization is the International Association of Schools of Social Work (IASSW), which was formed in 1948. This organization now includes more than 400 member social work education associations (e.g., Council on Social Work Education) and individual schools from seventy-seven countries. The IASSW is concerned with facilitating the inclusion of international content into social work education programs, providing consultation to the United Nations and the United Nations Children's Fund, and facilitating the transfer of academic credit among schools from different countries. With the IFSW, it publishes the journal *International Social Work*.[8]

DEFINING SOCIAL WORK GLOBALLY

Arriving at a generally accepted definition of social work in the United States proved difficult (see Chapter 2). Finding a definition that will encompass social work throughout the world is even more challenging. The International Federation of Social Workers (IFSW) established a Task Force for this purpose in 1996 and, a year later, the committee's deliberations resulted in agreement that, rather than being a collection of social professions, there was sufficient commonality to attempt to define social work as one profession, albeit at very different stages of development. The charge to the Task Force is to formulate a definition for consideration at the year 2000 meeting of the IFSW General Assembly,[9] although it may be much later before agreement on a definition is achieved. Until a definition of social work is adopted, a sanctioned "global" definition of social work will not exist.

VALUES AND ETHICS HELD BY SOCIAL WORKERS GLOBALLY

The underlying beliefs about the inherent value of people and the responsibility of societies to create conditions in which people can thrive are perhaps the glue that binds social workers together. These basic principles transcend the particular cultures and social welfare systems in various parts of the world and are the most universal expressions of the common beliefs that characterize social work globally.

The International Federation of Social Workers has given high priority to developing an international ethical code that includes twelve statements of the fundamental principles that underpin social work and provides a related set of guidelines for ethical practice. The following principles reflect social work's fundamental orientation to serving people.

1. Every human being has a unique value, which justifies moral considerations for that person.
2. Each individual has the right to self-fulfillment to the extent that it does not encroach upon the same right of others, and has an obligation to contribute to the well-being of society.
3. Each society, regardless of its form, should function to provide the maximum benefits for all of its members.
4. Social workers have a commitment to principles of social justice.
5. Social workers have the responsibility to devote objective and disciplined knowledge and skill to aid individuals, groups, communities, and societies in their development and resolution of personal–societal conflicts and their consequences.
6. Social workers are expected to provide the best possible assistance to anybody seeking their help and advice, without unfair discrimination on the basis of gender, age, disability, color, social class, race, religion, language, political beliefs, or sexual orientation.
7. Social workers respect the basic human rights of individuals and groups as expressed in the *United Nations Universal Declaration of Human Rights* and other international conventions derived from that Declaration.
8. Social workers pay regard to the principles of privacy, confidentiality, and responsible use of information in their professional work. Social workers respect justified confidentiality even when their country's legislation is in conflict with this demand.
9. Social workers are expected to work in full collaboration with their clients, working for the best interests of the clients but paying due regard to the interests of others involved. Clients are encouraged to participate as much as possible and should be informed of the risks and likely benefits of proposed courses of action.
10. Social workers generally expect clients to take responsibility, in collaboration with them, for determining courses of action affecting their lives. Compulsion, which might be necessary to solve one party's problems at the expense of the interests of others involved, should only take place after

careful explicit evaluation of the claims of the conflicting parties. Social workers should minimize the use of legal compulsion.

11. Social work is inconsistent with direct or indirect support of individuals, groups, political forces, or power structures suppressing their fellow human beings by employing terrorism, torture, or similar brutal means.

12. Social workers make ethically justified decisions, and stand by them, paying due regard to the *IFSW International Declaration of Ethical Principles,* and to the "International Ethical Standards for Social Workers" adopted by their national professional association.[10]

In addition to the basic values held by social workers, *the International Declaration of Ethical Principles of Social Work* provides guides to the ethical conduct of social work. Like the *NASW Code of Ethics* (see Chapter 7), this statement of ethical principles addresses the obligations of social workers to be fully prepared and to bring the most relevant knowledge and skill to the practice situation, to give priority to the interests of their clients, to be responsible to the agencies and organizations that employ them, to treat their colleagues with respect, and to contribute to the development of the social work profession.

GLOBAL VIEWS OF SOCIAL ISSUES

One direct result of the similar values held by social workers is that agreement has been reached regarding understanding and developing approaches to resolving social problems that are experienced throughout the world. Social workers can make comparative analyses of issues and adopt or adapt solutions that have been successful in other countries.

What are the social issues that are of primary concern to social workers on a worldwide basis? Clearly, social workers are in agreement that they want to make the world a better place for all people—and particularly for those who are most vulnerable to experiencing social problems. There is universal concern among social workers for improving the social, economic, and health conditions of the most vulnerable people throughout the world and in changing the political and social structures that have made these people likely to experience violations of basic human rights, hunger and other expressions of poverty (e.g., approximately one-fifth of the world's population lives in extreme poverty), disease, and/or various forms of abuse or oppression.

More specifically, social workers and organizations of social workers are concerned with such worldwide issues as achieving and preserving peace, preventing the use of landmines in wartime situations, distributing human and economic resources more equitably, protecting the rights and preventing the exploitation of children and youth, enhancing women's status and safety, minimizing substance abuse, facilitating appropriate international adoptions, and so on. Evidence of these concerns is found in the issues addressed in the IFSW policy statements that have been adopted to date.[11]

- Advancement of Women

- Child Welfare

- The Welfare of Elderly People

- Health

- HIV–AIDS

- Human Rights

- Migration

- Peace and Disarmament

- The Protection of Personal Information

- Refugees

- Conditions in Rural Communities

- Self-Help

- Youth*

The value of these position papers is not only to identify topics for which social workers are in general agreement throughout the world, but also to provide a more influential voice to international organizations such as the United Nations (UN). In that venue, social workers have been actively involved with a number of UN agencies including the United Nations Children's Fund (UNICEF), the UN Development Program, the Department of Policy Coordination and Sustainable Development, the UN High Commission for Refugees, and the World Health Organization.

Employment in International Social Work

Four forms of international practice are possible for a social worker. One form is to secure a position in an international organization that advances human services on a worldwide basis. The United Nations (UN) serves as the primary agency to coordinate the efforts of the various countries to overcome oppression, facilitate the delivery of health and welfare services that cross international boundaries, and promote social justice. Social work with UN agencies such as UNICEF, the Economic and Social Council, the World Health Organization, and the UN High Commission on Refugees are examples of such positions.

Second, the U.S. government, too, has positions concerned with international social welfare issues. The Department of Health and Human Services maintains an international affairs staff to give attention to worldwide human services issues, and its Office of Refugee Settlement is actively involved in promoting the safety, welfare, and rights of refugees. The International Development Cooperation Agency (USAID)

---

*All position papers are available from the IFSW Secretariat (P. O. Box 4649, Sofienberg, N-0506, Oslo, Norway) in English, French, and Spanish.

administers foreign aid programs in approximately 100 countries throughout the world, and the Peace Corps has provided developing countries with the human and technical resources to improve their physical infrastructure (e.g., water, sanitation, roads), health care, and human services.

Third, perhaps the most common form of international employment for social workers is to find a social work job in a government or voluntary agency in another country. These roles typically include service provision, consultation, and teaching or training activities. Particularly for countries that are in the process of developing services to individuals and families, the skills possessed by most U.S. social workers are highly valued. The reverse is true, too, for social workers from developing countries, who often have a strong social development background and bring a helpful expertise not typically found among U.S.-educated social workers.

Last, some international social work positions exist in multinational corporations that locate personnel in foreign countries. When families are relocated (or left behind), there are inevitable social adjustments to be made. As in other social work practice in business and industry, social workers provide direct services to help individuals and families to deal with their social problems, assist the company in sharpening its cultural sensitivity, and represent the company as a participant in the local community, making contributions to and interfacing with the human services delivery system.

How does one become prepared for international social work? Certainly, the demands on workers differ depending on the nature of a country's social welfare system and/or the type of position that the social worker holds. Specific preparation, then, cannot be identified that is essential for all positions. However, a few fundamental areas of preparation are somewhat universal.

First, become informed and stay current regarding international affairs, particularly issues of social and economic justice, human rights, and peace. Careful reading of both the social work literature on international issues and the general news sources is essential.

Second, develop competence in the use of one or more foreign languages. Although English is used for general communication in most parts of the world, it is respectful to others to attempt to speak their language (however faltering) and, particularly if providing direct services, much subtle meaning in communication is lost if one does not know the language.

Third, it is also essential to develop knowledge of the host county's culture. This is prerequisite to helping to avoid the tendency to believe that one's own culture is superior and, therefore, to force his or her way of doing things into the other culture. The concept of "the ugly American" reflects the reputation persons from the United States have developed by reflecting such cultural insensitivity. Just as in other forms of insensitivity (e.g., racism, sexism, ageism), the study of the other's culture and experience is a first step in increasing awareness and avoiding inadvertent acts of insensitivity.

Finally, the unique contribution that a professional social worker brings is his or her professional knowledge and skill. Experience in practicing social work after completing one's professional education is prerequisite for most international social work positions.

Although all the above competencies are necessary for successful international social work practice, one research project identified the basic social work principles of "individualizing the client," "maximizing client empowerment," "maximizing client participation," and "maximizing client self-determination"[12] as the factors most associated with successful Peace Corps and USAID projects. Ghavam's study of 74 projects throughout the world, found that "the greater the villagers' role and participation in start-up, assessment, and design phases of the projects resulted in more overall success of the development projects." This study also found that the project director's technical preparation for the position, experience in international work, and adequacy in the culture and language of the area were also associated with the overall success of the projects.[13] In short, good social work practice, plus orientation to the language and culture of the specific country, corresponds with successful international practice. The competent social worker already has a good start for international practice.

Concluding Comment

It can be argued that the Industrial Revolution created the need for the professional approach to helping represented by social work. As countries have become increasingly industrialized, traditional ways of meeting human needs have been supplemented by programs and personnel especially prepared to meet many human needs. It can be further argued that the Technological Revolution occurring today is moving social work from a profession oriented to its practice in a single country to one with an increasing global orientation.

As technology advances, the world shrinks. The presence of a worldwide economy makes countries increasingly interdependent. The ability of the media to immediately transmit information around the globe creates an unprecedented awareness of events as they occur in even remote areas of the world. And the availability of the World Wide Web and e-mail allows human services agencies and human services providers to exchange information through a virtually cost free and instantaneous process. Although some parts of the world have not yet fully experienced the Technological Revolution, in many ways international boundaries have become less significant.

Parallel to the diminishing isolation of individual countries, social work, too, is beginning to blur national distinctions and think of itself as a global profession. A challenge for the next generation of social workers will be to evolve a concept of social work that will bridge the differing philosophies of society's role in meeting human needs and yet maintain the social worker's unique function as the profession that addresses both individual and family needs and, simultaneously, is concerned with changing the society to reduce or eliminate factors that contribute to people's problems in social functioning.

KEY WORDS AND CONCEPTS

Social development

International social work

Global social work

International Federation of Social Workers

International Declaration of Ethical Principles for Social Work

Corporatist welfare state

Liberal welfare state

Social democratic welfare state

International Association of Schools of Social Work

Social technology transfer

SUGGESTED READINGS

Chatterjee, Pranab. *Repackaging the Welfare State.* Washington, D.C.: NASW Press, 1999.

Colton, Matthew, Casas, Ferran, Drakeford, Mark, Roberts, Susan, Scholte, Evert, and Williams, Margaret. *Stigma and Social Welfare: An International Comparative Study.* Brookfield, VT: Ashgate, 1997.

Healy, Lynne H. "International Social Welfare Organizations and Activities." In Richard I. Edwards, ed., *Encyclopedia of Social Work,* 19th Edition. Washington, D.C.: NASW Press, 1995, pp. 1499–1510.

Hokenstad, M. C., Khinduka, S. K., and Midgley, James, eds. *Profiles in International Social Work.* Washington, D.C.: NASW Press, 1992.

Lapidus, Gail W., and Swanson, Guy E., eds. *State and Welfare USA/USSR: Contemporary Policy and Practice.* Berkeley, CA: Institute of International Studies, 1988.

Lorenz, Walter. *Social Work in a Changing Europe.* London: Routledge, 1994.

Midgley, James. "International and Comparative Social Welfare." In Richard I. Edwards, ed., *Encyclopedia of Social Work,* 19th Edition. Washington, D.C.: NASW Press, 1995, pp. 1490–1498.

———. *Social Welfare in Global Context.* Thousand Oaks, CA: Sage, 1997.

Ramanathan, Chathapuram S., and Link, Rosemary J. *Principles and Resources for Social Work Practice in a Global Era.* Belmont, CA: Brooks/Cole–Wadsworth, 1999.

van Wormer, Katherine. *Social Welfare: A World View.* Chicago: Nelson-Hall, 1997.

ENDNOTES

1. Robin Wright, "World Population Reaches 6 Billion," *Los Angeles Times,* Part A, Saturday, July 17, 1999, p. A5.
2. Mark W. Lusk and Charles Horejsi, "Toward a Synthesis of International Social Development," *Indian Journal of Social Work* 60 (January 1999): p. 153.
3. Gøsta Epsing-Anderson, *The Three Worlds of Welfare Capitalism* (Princeton, NJ: Princeton University Press, 1990), pp. 21–29.
4. Matthew Colton, Ferran Casas, Mark Drakeford, Susan Roberts, Evert Scholte, and Margaret Williams, *Stigma and Social Welfare: An International Comparative Study* (Brookfield, VT: Ashgate, 1997), pp. 138–140.
5. Ibid.
6. Norma Berkowitz, Lowell Jenkins, and Eileen Kelly, "Reaching Beyond Your Borders: Social Technology Transfers." In Ka-Ching Yeung, chief editor, *Proceedings: Joint World Congress of the International Federation of Social Workers and International Association of Schools of Social Work, 1996,* p. 176 (publisher not identified, 1998).
7. International Federation of Social Workers, "General Information" [http://www.ifsw.org].

8. Lynne M. Healy, "International Social Welfare: Organizations and Activities," in Richard L. Edwards, ed., *Encyclopedia of Social Work,* 19th Edition (Washington, D.C.: NASW Press, 1995), pp. 1505–1506.

9. International Federation of Social Workers, "Activity Report: 1996–1998," [http://www.ifsw.org].

10. International Federation of Social Workers, "The Ethics of Social Work—Principles and Standards," [http://www.ifsw.org].

11. Ibid., "Activity Report."

12. Bradford W. Sheafor, Charles R. Horejsi, and Gloria A. Horejsi, *Techniques and Guidelines for Social Work Practice,* 5th ed. Boston: Allyn and Bacon, 2000, pp. 74–78.

13. Hamid Reza Ghavam, "Characteristics of External Activators in Third World Village Development." Unpublished Doctoral Dissertation, Colorado State University, Fort Collins, CO, pp. 148–149.

FOUR

Social Work Practice with Special Populations

Beginning with the first edition of this volume, the authors introduced the term *special populations*. In the definition of *special*, according to Webster's Third New International Dictionary, there is something "additional to the regular." In the context of human behavior, all humans have certain universal needs, but in addition to these needs some people have special needs beyond what might normally already be applicable or available to others. Within this conceptual definition, special populations such as children and youth, the elderly, the homeless, women, lesbians and gays, police brutality victims, AIDS patients, and minorities bring unique needs and circumstances that must be recognized when the social worker serves these persons. A year after the authors began using the term *special populations*, the President's Commission on Mental Health produced their definition, which was similar, defining special populations as:

> Americans who are characterized by (1) uniqueness and diversity in terms of race, ethnic origin, sex, and physical status and (2) by de facto second class status in American Society.[1]

The President's Commission added that special population groups are both at times overrepresented in the statistics on mental health and inappropriately served by the current mental health system in the United States. Women, for example, are overrepresented in the mental health system and suffer the stresses of second-class status. Children, youth, minorities, and the elderly are very underserved in human services systems, based on their needs, and also suffer the psychosocial consequences of second-class status. Citing what it referred to as a well-documented national scandal, the President's Commission reported that, whereas middle-class nonminority children with behavior problems receive appropriate mental health services in voluntary clinical settings, minority children are more likely to be processed by the police and juvenile courts for the same behavioral problems.[2] Those persons being tracked into the juvenile and adult criminal justice systems may also be included in the definition of a special population, in which there is a marked overrepresentation of minorities.

Societally Induced Stressors Affecting Special Populations

In attempting to help persons who are from special population groups, as previously defined, the social worker needs to understand what forces are at work to keep these groups in a disadvantaged, second-class position in society. The biopsychosocial experience of living as a second-class person is quite stressful, often resulting in nonhealth-related premature death (accidents, suicide, homicide), poor physical and mental health, chronic substance abuse, and repeated voluntary and involuntary institutionalization. The forces or stressors that keep many special population members from realizing their full potential to contribute to society include sexism, homophobia, ageism, racism, and class and people with disabilities discrimination. These factors are also directly correlated with and contribute to poverty.

Are women and racial minorities overrepresented among the poor because they are in some way inherently or biologically inferior to men and whites? Either women and minorities are inferior—women biologically and emotionally inferior to men, a sexist perspective; minorities biologically inferior to whites, a racist perspective—or sexism and racism have restricted women and minorities from functioning to their optimal capacity. The crippling effects of sexism and racism are being expressed through the structural fabric of U.S. society. Those who deny the existence of sexism and racism are, in effect, implying that women and minorities are biologically and inherently inferior. Beyond identifying sexism, racism, and ageism as factors that contribute to the poverty of special populations, one must also understand the *functions* these factors fulfill in U.S. society, hence their persistence. Sexism and ageism, like racism, provide definite benefits to those who dominate. These factors yield significant psychological, political, and economic advantages for the predominantly white middle and upper classes in U.S. society.[3] For example, men of all classes generally have a psychological need to feel superior to women. Whites representing all socioeconomic levels generally have a psychological need to feel superior to minorities. Younger persons of all ethnic-racial groups and classes generally are threatened by the aging process and have a need to feel superior to, and ignore and discriminate against, the elderly.

Those receiving the psychological and economic benefits and privileges will fight very hard to maintain their advantaged, superior position. This is the primary function of racism, sexism, ageism, and classism, even though the recipients of these privileges might not really believe or admit to anyone that they are superior to these subordinated groups of people. According to the Corporate Policy Institute, a nonprofit research and education center that focuses on the impact of law and public policy on business, out of 1,000 CEO and senior executives of the entertainment industry, which includes Columbia, Disney, Dream Works, and Universal and their counterparts at ABC, CBS, NBC, and Fox, barely a handful are of African American background, with no Asian Amer-

icans, American Indians, or Hispanics. This is virtually a homogeneous group of non-Hispanic white males who exert control over a more than $20 billion industry that influences commerce, culture, and values not only in the United States, but essentially in *every* nation in the world! Hoffman, the director of the Policy Institute, calls this apartheid in the entertainment industry, which is then the only industry in the United States permitted to perpetuate racism.[4]

Looking more specifically at the impact of apartheid in the cultural shaping of the TV entertainment industry in the United States, for example, which reaches tens of millions of Americans each day, the major networks (ABC, NBC, CBS, and Fox) decided not to feature a minority group person in a leading role when twenty-six new comedy and drama shows premiered in the fall of 1999. Minority writers are being dropped by their agents because they cannot get work, ethnic/racial actresses who previously had been praised for their beauty and talent are no longer in demand, and managers and agents are finding it difficult to justify to their minority clients why they are not being called in for casting sessions or readings. Those familiar with the entertainment industry say that the surest way to land an acting part is to fit the description "white, beautiful, male or female, can play 18 to 24."[5] Such deliberate discriminatory exclusion preserves, perpetuates, and exacerbates racism and ageism in America. This "whitewashing" of TV entertainment is being challenged by the NAACP, which plans to file a class action suit in the courts joined by Hispanics, Asians, and American Indians, claiming that the actions of these networks represents a violation of the 1934 Federal Communications Act, which provides that the airwaves belong to the public.[6] If successful, this will be another example of eradicating institutional racism through the use of a class action suit, as were the cases of social work class action suits entitled *Serrano* vs. *Priest* and *Nicacio* vs. *INS* detailed in Chapter 9.

The origin of these classist and racist discriminatory attitudes may be traced to England in the eighteenth century, as reflected in the political economy writings of Adam Smith and Thomas Malthus. England was in the midst of an industrial revolution that found the government catering to the interests of big business. The poor were economically exploited and further impoverished, but this did not seem to concern the middle class as they had developed the rationale of *laissez faire*—the doctrine of free enterprise unrestricted by government intervention. Out of unrestricted competition, in theory, the strong would survive and society would benefit—the "trickle down" theory of the eighteenth century. In *The Wealth of Nations*, Adam Smith argued that one of the roles of government was the defense of the rich against the poor. He saw public assistance for the poor as an artificial and "evil" arrangement in which they consumed money that could have been used for wages. "Unearned subsistence" (welfare), according to Smith, simply furthered human misery.[7]

Malthus, in his *Essay on Population*, believed populations would always outrun food supplies. War, pestilence, and famine were therefore seen by Malthus as positive checks on the growth of populations. These theories were absorbed into Social Darwinism as advocated by Englishman Herbert Spencer (1820–1903). Extending lower-life biological theories to humans, he originated the concept of "survival of the fittest." Spencer opposed all state welfare assistance to the poor because he felt they were unfit and should be eliminated. He stated:

> The whole effort of nature is to get rid of such, to clear the world of them, and make room for the better. If they are sufficiently complete to live, they do live. If they are not sufficiently complete to live, they die, and it is best they should die.[8]

Spencer's doctrines had significant impact on U.S. thought and many of his ideas were adopted.[9]

According to Powell and Powell, poverty was the most severely disabling condition in childhood, handicapping 9 million white children and 6 million minority children in the United States in 1983. The Powells pointed out that White House Conferences on Children, held each decade over the past seventy years, had been laudable in their ideals but short on action and accomplishment, particularly for minorities.[10] There was a significant drop in infant mortality in the United States during the twentieth century, but the mortality rate for minority infants was triple that for white infants. The maternal mortality rate was four times higher for minority mothers than for white mothers. Another disturbing fact is that the combined prenatal and maternal mortality rates have actually increased for minorities relative to whites. In considering the five leading causes of death at ages one to fourteen (accidents, congenital malformations, malignant diseases, influenza, and pneumonia), the rates for minority children have been consistently higher (often twice as high) than for white children over the past forty years.[11] Poverty is indeed a stressor that can and *does* kill. Poverty increased for four consecutive years from 1989 through 1993, with 39.3 million persons below the government poverty level of $14,763 for a family of four in 1993, according to census figures. Half of those in poverty were children (19.5 million) under eighteen years of age. In 1995, the federal government changed its definition of poverty to include a family of four who had an income below $15,569. Hispanic and African American families headed by a woman had the highest rates of poverty. For example, non-Hispanic white families headed by a woman with no husband present had a poverty rate of 26.6 percent. The corresponding rates for African American and Hispanic families were 45.1 percent and 49.4 percent, respectively. Half of the nation's poverty population consists of the elderly and children; 40.3 percent of the poor were under eighteen years of age, and 10.5 percent were 65 years of age or older.[12]

The institutionalized racism, classism, sexism, and ageism affecting the poor, minorities, gays and lesbians, women, children, and the elderly is very subtle, so it is difficult to hold anyone accountable; nevertheless, it is extremely effective and powerful.

Police brutality results in 10,000 to 15,000 assaults and the death of about 500 citizens each year. Because it is the clearest example of government oppression, neglect, and indifference, confirming a second-class citizenship on the special populations, this topic is briefly covered in the following section.

Police Brutality: The Ultimate Confirmation of Second-Class Citizen Status

Police brutality can be defined as the use of unnecessary force by one or more law enforcement officials toward a citizen or group of citizens, resulting in minor, moderate, or severe physical injury, up to and including death. *Psychological* police brutality can be defined as verbal insults, implied threats, apparent ability to inflict physical harm, and/or intimidation by police toward citizens, but with no actual physical harm. Other terms describing this behavior are police misconduct, police excessive force, police malpractice, and police abuse. Depending on the seriousness of the alleged misconduct, such acts may be prosecuted in local or state courts as misdemeanor or felony offenses, or in federal court as federal offenses. The principal federal criminal statutes with relevance to police misconduct are U.S. Code Section 1983 of Title 42 and U.S. Code Sections 241 and 242 of Title 18, the latter of which prohibits the deprivation of any rights, privileges, or immunities secured or protected by the Constitution or laws of the United States on account of an inhabitant being an alien or by reason of color or race.

Social work has a rich history of providing advocacy and other social services to victims of police brutality. Brutality was not an uncommon experience for recent immigrants settling in large cities in the 1910s, 1920s, and 1930s. Jane Addams, the founder of Hull House, fought against police malpractice and eventually became a founding member of the American Civil Liberties Union. The Abbott sisters, both respected social workers of that era, were part of Herbert Hoover's National Commission on Law Observance and Enforcement and its 1931 *Report on Crime and the Foreign Born*. This investigating commission uncovered numerous instances of injustice in the courts being visited on Mexicans in the United States. In addition, Mexican and Polish immigrants, in particular, often received brutal treatment at the hands of police.[13]

Since the days of Addams and the Abbotts, however, the social work profession has assumed a passive, dormant stance toward citizen abuse by law enforcement. In fact, with the increasing "clinicalization" of the profession, it has become the role of social workers to work with the police on a referral, diagnostic, and treatment services basis, rather than being advocates for clients who have been assaulted by the police. As stated by Morales in 1977, "This is not to say that poor people do not need social services when they are arrested, but rather that they have been denied assistance in an area of need (police–community conflict) that is far greater today than it was in the 1930s."[14] There is new evidence to indicate that the profession may be awakening from its nearly seventy-year state of dormancy. On April 5, 1992, following a policy statement submitted by the author, the NASW Board of Directors unanimously voted to make "police brutality" a social work practice priority.

About 75 to 80 percent of police brutality victims involve the poor and minorities. The special population groups mentioned in the following chapters are particularly vulnerable and not exempt from this harmful police practice. These groups are the homeless, women, gays, the elderly, the mentally ill, adolescents, and immigrants. Police brutality is briefly described next to give the student some understanding of this problem should clients complain about these experiences, which most people would find practically impossible to believe. Consider the following selected cases from at least 10,000 each year as examples of the problem.

Mentally Ill: In August 1994, two mentally ill women were shot and killed by Portland police in two incidents because they allegedly posed a threat to officers. One wielded a knife and the other pointed a fake handgun.[15] Jorge Guillen, a *Latino* with a history of mental illness, was verbally threatening his family on October 3, 1995, and Chicago police were called. He was handcuffed, hit with a flashlight, and choked. He immediately died.[16]

The Elderly: Sixty-five-year-old Mario Paz, a *Latino* grandfather of fourteen children, was shot to death in the back on August 9, 1999, by Sgt. Joe Hopkins, 43, of the El Monte Police Department (California) while he lay on his bed with his wife after the police had broken down his door looking for a drug dealer. The officer, who was a defendant in two prior excessive force lawsuits, stated that he shot Paz because he feared for his life. No drugs or drug dealer was found in the home.[17]

The Homeless: Joseph Carl Gould, a homeless man, was shot and killed on July 30, 1995, by a Chicago police officer after getting into an argument about payment for washing his car window.[18] Margaret Laverne Mitchell, a 5'0", 102-pound, fifty-five-year-old African American, a mentally ill homeless woman, was shot to death by two Los Angeles Police Department officers who feared for their lives when she brandished a screwdriver at them.[19]

Women: Chicago police detective John Summerville sexually assaulted three women over a two-month period while on duty by ordering them into his police car at gunpoint.[20] Tyisha Miller, a nineteen-year-old African American female, was shot at 24 times (12 bullets entered her body) in December in 1998 by four white Riverside Police Department officers in California as she lay sleeping in her car with a gun on her lap. Officers broke her car window to grab her gun, at which time she moved, causing officers to fear for their lives; they fired their guns, killing her instantly.[21]

Adolescents: Sixty-five suspects were tortured by Chicago police between 1972 and 1991, which included thirteen-year-old Marcus Wiggins, who was tortured by electric shock.[22] On October 12, 1996, nineteen-year-old Javier Francisco Ovando, an alleged *Latino* gang member with no arrests or convictions, was shot several times by two Los Angeles Police Department officers and permanently paralyzed because he pointed an assault rifle at them. When he was convicted and sentenced to twenty-three years in prison for this attempted assault on the police, the angry judge noted that he showed no remorse for what he had done. Three years later, in attempting to reduce his sentence for stealing narcotics from his police department, former LAPD officer Rafael A. Perez provided testimony in September 1999 that he and fellow LAPD officer Nino Durden shot unarmed Ovando, planted a rifle on him, and later provided false testimony in court. Ovando was released from prison after all charges were dropped by the prosecutors, but he is still being held by the LAPD for his own protection in spite of protests by his attorneys.[23]

Immigrants: On August 9, 1997, New York Police Department officers arrested Abner Louima, a Haitian immigrant, outside a Brooklyn nightclub following altercations between clubgoers and police. At the police station, Officer Justin Volpe shouted racial slurs at Louima and shoved a toilet plunger into his rectum and mouth. Louima was hospitalized for two months due to ruptured internal organs and broken front teeth.[24] On February 4, 1999, Amadou Diallo, a 22-year-old West African immigrant from Guinea, was shot at 41 times, with 19 bullets entering his body, by four white New York Police officers while he stood in his Bronx apartment building. Officers believed Diallo had a gun. His dead body revealed he did not have a weapon.[25] The four officers were acquitted by an Albany jury on February 25, 2000. On April 1, 1996, a news helicopter videotaped a high-speed freeway chase in Los Angeles county showing Riverside county sheriffs deputies following a pickup truck with suspected undocumented Mexican aliens. The truck finally stopped and all but two occupants fled. Two white deputies repeatedly struck unresisting Enrique Funes Flores, breaking his arm. They then grabbed Alicia Soltero Vasquez by her hair and struck her several times with a baton.[26]

It is extremely rare for a police officer to be convicted in court for assaulting a citizen. The International Association of Chiefs of Police states that over 10,000 civil rights violations charging brutality by police are being reported to the U.S. Department of Justice for prosecution every year, but that very few *convictions* occur. In 1977 for example, there were only sixteen convictions out of 12,000 reported cases.[27] In 1992, the Department of Justice admitted it had investigated 15,000 cases of police brutality, but their information was being kept "secret" on grounds that it was an internal report of sensitive information still being used in a "research process."[28] Whether 10,000, 12,000, or 15,000 cases per year, this might only be the "tip of the iceberg," and thousands of cases may not be reported for fear of further law enforcement retaliation. Police brutality is a human rights as well as a civil rights violation. These beatings stopping short of death may cause not only permanent physical impairment, but also permanent or chronic psychological pain known as post-traumatic stress disorder. Family members, particularly children, witnessing these brutal assaults on their loved ones, likewise may be permanently traumatized. Early, prompt intervention and treatment, both physical and psychological, are essential for reducing the course of decompensation. It can be assumed that each police brutality victim comes from a family of at least four to six persons; hence, those emotionally affected by this painful practice could reach anywhere from 60,000 to 90,000 persons—mostly poor and minority—each year.

The Relationship Between Police Brutality and Riots

In addition to family suffering, police abuse can even result in riots, with many lives lost and massive social and property destruction. The U.S. Riot Commission, more popularly known as the "Kerner Commission," found in its study of over 150 riots across the nation during the 1960s that many African Americans believed they were being politically and economically exploited by the white power structure and that they lacked channels of communication to that structure. Their feelings of powerlessness and frustration needed only a spark to ignite mass violence. The Kerner Commission reported that all the riots were precipitated by routine arrests of African Americans for minor offenses by white police. Because of numerous instances of police brutality, police symbolized white power, white racism, and white repression.[29] The connection between police brutality and rioting continues to be a timeless conclusion and was clearly evident in the Los Angeles-Rodney King police beating case.

The King *state* trial—that is, the officers had been charged with a state felony assault charge in violation of the California Penal Code—had been moved to Simi Valley in Ventura County, California, by the judge at the request of the attorneys representing the four LAPD defendants. Simi Valley is a predominantly white, conservative, middle-class community. The Simi Valley jury was comprised of one Asian Ameri-

can and eleven caucasians. At 3:10 PM on April 29, 1992, the "not guilty" verdicts were announced, which, within ten minutes, triggered this nation's most destructive and deadliest riot causing nearly a billion dollars of damage, sixty deaths, and nearly 3,000 injuries over a five-day period. Approximately 20,000 National Guard, local, county, state, and federal law enforcement personnel were required to stop the riot.[30] Riots on a much smaller scale in response to the King verdicts erupted throughout the nation in twenty-eight states and hundreds of cities, colleges, universities, and high schools. Rioters were represented by all ethnic and racial groups.[31]

Again demonstrating the clear relationship between police brutality and riots, on July 29, 1995, fourteen-year-old José Antonio Gutierrez, an Hispanic youngster with no juvenile arrest record, was shot and killed in East Los Angeles by LAPD officer Michael Falvo, age thirty-nine, one of the forty-four problem officers with six or more complaints of excessive force identified by the Christopher Commission that investigated the LA Riots of 1992. Immediately after the killing, the predominantly *Latino* community erupted into two days of rioting and a running battle between over one hundred helmeted baton-wielding police and enraged youths hurling bottles and setting fires in the streets.

Police called the shooting justified, contending that the youth had pointed a Tec-9 semi-automatic pistol at police, causing officer Falvo to fire six rounds at Gutierrez, with four striking him in the upper torso area.[32] The boy's mother, who witnessed the shooting thirty feet away, reported that the youth was not armed and that he was shot in the back. One to two hours later, a gun was found over a wall ten to fifteen feet from the dead adolescent, but it did not have his fingerprints. The coroner's autopsy revealed that three of the four bullets entered the 5'3", 110-pound teenager's back, and one bullet pierced his left armpit at an angle and exited through the upper right rib cage.[33] The family has filed a wrongful death suit against the Los Angeles Police Department and the City of Los Angeles. Neither the Attorney General, Los Angeles City Attorney, nor Los Angeles County District Attorney will criminally prosecute the officer.

The FBI was looking into the matter but, in four years' time they never conducted a formal investigation. On May 26, 1998, a Los Angeles civil court jury comprised predominantly of "whites" with no *Latinos,* found officer Falvo "not guilty" in a ten to two vote in violating the boys' civil rights. This verdict was given in spite of the fact that *two,* rather than one, Tec-9 semiautomatic pistols (neither with the boys' fingerprints) were introduced during the trial. Once again we learn that it is practically impossible to convict police officers in court for their unlawful behavior against citizens.

Working with Special Populations

In working with special population clients, a combination of a generalist practice approach and specialized clinical skills would seem preferable, considering the specialized issues, problems, and range of needs. The skilled practitioner would examine the situation needing intervention using an assessment scheme, such as the ecosystems framework developed and operationalized in what immediately follows in Section A, then apply the knowledge, values, and skills to initiate service and/or to obtain appropriate resources or specialized expertise. Generalist practice, therefore, involves both having the capacity to take a comprehensive view of a practice situation and also having the necessary knowledge and skills to intervene at multiple levels and in a broad range of client concerns. Numerous rich case examples employing the generalist practice model are given in the following thirteen chapters on special populations. Part Four, therefore, is organized as follows:

Section A: An Overview of Special Populations

Ecosystems Model

Section B: Selected Characteristics

This section identifies physical status issues such as gender, sexual preference lifestyle, child, youth and elderly populations, and physical disability as factors identified by many in society that subordinate, discriminate, and oppress these populations.

Chapter 11: Social Work Practice with Women.

Chapter 12: Social Work Practice with Lesbian, Gay, and Bisexual People.

Chapter 13: Social Work Practice with Children and Youth.

Chapter 14: Social Work Practice with the Elderly.

Chapter 15: Social Work Practice with People with Disabilities.

Section C: The Rural/Urban/ Suburban Context

This section places the social work practitioner in unique rural, urban, and suburban sites of practice which may feel to some as being in a "foreign land" or in a "war zone." The social worker learns about being effective in these areas as discussed in the following:

Chapter 16: Social Work Practice in Rural Areas: Appalachia as a Case Example.

Chapter 17: Urban and Suburban Gangs: The Psychosocial Crisis Spreads.

Section D: Race, Ethnicity, and Culture

Racial, ethnic, and cultural factors in other countries are seen as positive attributes of people, although there are exceptions, such as the ethnic or racial conflicts seen between Jews and Arabs in the Middle East, the Serbs and Albanians in Yugoslavia, and blacks and whites in South Africa. In the United States, the picture is mixed, usually with the darker skintone persons suffering the most discrimination.

Social work students need to be sensitive to these factors in their work with clients having these characteristics. Excellent in-depth micro and macro cases utilizing the ecosystems assessment framework are discussed in the following chapters.

Chapter 18: Social Work Practice with Asian Americans.

Chapter 19: Social Work Practice with American Indians and Alaskan Natives.

Chapter 20: Social Work Practice with Mexican Americans.

Chapter 21: Social Work Practice with African Americans.

Chapter 22: Social Work Practice with Puerto Ricans.

ENDNOTES

1. President's Commission on Mental Health, *Mental Health in America: 1978* Vol. III (Washington, D.C.: U.S. Government Printing Office, 1978), p. 731.
2. President's Commission on Mental Health, Vol. III, Appendix, p. 646.
3. The U.S. Commission on Civil Rights, *Racism in America and How to Combat It* (Washington, D.C.: U.S. Government Printing Office, 1970), p. 19.
4. Adonis Hoffman, "Through an Accurate Prism," *Los Angeles Times,* Opinion Section M, Sunday, August 8, 1999, pp. 1, 8.
5. Greg Braxton, "Faced with Reality of Exclusion," *Los Angeles Times,* Arts and Entertainment Calendar Section, Saturday, July 24, 1999, p. F16.
6. *Los Angeles Times,* Tuesday, July 14, 1999, p. A14.
7. Cited in Blanch D. Coll, *Perspectives in Public Welfare* (Washington, D.C.: U.S. Department of Health, Education, and Welfare, 1969), p. 9.
8. Cited in Richard Hofstadter, *Social Darwinism in American Thought* (Boston: Beacon Press, 1944), p. 41.
9. Ibid., p. 50.
10. Gloria Johnson Powell and Rodney N. Powell, "Epilogue: Poverty—The Greatest and Severest Handicapping Condition in Childhood," in Gloria Johnson Powell, Joe Yamamoto, Annelisa Romero, and Armando Morales, eds., *The Psychosocial Development of Minority Group Children* (New York: Brunner/Mazel, 1983), p. 579.
11. Ibid., p. 577.
12. U.S. Bureau of the Census, Current Population Reports, Series P23-194, *Population Profile of the United States: 1997.* U.S. Government Printing Office, Washington, D.C., 1998.
13. National Commission on Law Observance and Enforcement, *Report on Crime and the Foreign Born* (Washington, D.C.: U.S. Government Printing Office, 1931), p. 229.
14. Armando Morales, "Social Work with Third-World People," *Social Work* 26 (January 1981): p. 46.
15. Erin Hoover and Nena Baker, "Police and Deadly Force: Looking for Middle Ground," *Oregonian,* August 26, 1994.
16. Brian Jackson, "Fire Cops, Says Widow of Man Who Died in Police Struggle," *Chicago Sun-Times,* February 5, 1997.
17. Annie-Marie O'Connor, "Family of Police Shooting Victim Still out $11,000," *Los Angeles Times,* Thursday, September 23, 1999.
18. Don Terry, "Homeless Man's Life Gains Currency in Death," *The New York Times,* September 10, 1995.
19. Matt Lait, "L.A. Sued in Police Killing of Woman," *Los Angeles Times,* August 3, 1999.
20. "Ex-Cop Gets 4 Years in Sex Assault," *Chicago Sun-Times,* July 28, 1995.
21. Patrick J. McDonnell, "Plan to Fire 4 Riverside Officers Sparks Strong Opinions in Residents," *Los Angeles Times,* June 13, 1999.
22. Andrew Martin, "Badge Shields Cops Accused of Misconduct," *Chicago Tribune,* August 6, 1995.
23. Matt Lait and Scott Grover, "Ex Officer Says He Shot Unarmed Man," *Los Angeles Times,* September 16, 1999.
24. David Kocieniewski, "Man Says Officers Torture Him After Arrest," *The New York Times,* September 5, 1997.
25. *Los Angeles Times,* Thursday, September 30, 1999.
26. *Los Angeles Times,* Friday, June 14, 1996.
27. Kenneth J. Matulia, *A Balance of Forces,* a report of the International Association of Chiefs of Police, Gaithersburg, Maryland, 1982, p. 7.
28. *Los Angeles Times,* March 4, 1992, Metro News, p. B-8.
29. *Report of the National Advisory Commission on Civil Disorders* (New York: Bantam Books, 1968), p. 206.
30. See "The City in Crisis," *A Report by the Special Advisor to the Board of Police Commissioners on the Civil Disorder in Los Angeles,* William H. Webster, Los Angeles, California, October 21, 1992.
31. Michael Slate, "The Fire this Time: Anatomy of the 1992 Los Angeles Rebellion," RCP Publications, Chicago, Illinois, December 27, 1992.
32. *Los Angeles Times,* Monday, August 7, 1996, p. A-1.
33. *Los Angeles Times,* Wednesday, August 30, 1995, p. B-1.

An Overview
of Special Populations

Special population members, such as women, children and youth, the elderly, people with disabilities, and minorities, continue to share second-class status in the United States. Government oppression in various forms further reinforces their subordinate status and contributes to self-esteem issues.

In the past ten to twenty years, economic, social, and political forces fueled by increased discrimination against the poor and people with disabilities have created three new and growing special population groups that include the homeless, people with disabilities, and gay, lesbian, and bisexual persons. Society tends to ignore the homeless, believing that housing is readily available for anyone if they only worked to get a place to live. People with physical disabilities are seen as a bother and many in society would hope that disabled persons simply *adjust* to the environment (get a wheelchair that can climb curbs), rather than have to adjust the environment (ramps and driveways on corners) to facilitate the lives of persons with disabilities.

In addition to ageism, sexism, and racism, homophobia and biphobia continue to thrive in the late 1990s and into the twenty-first century. This is evident in the military's resistance to gay and lesbian members and in the national resistance (65% of voters) regarding gay and lesbian marriages. Excluding gays and lesbians, experts judge that about 15 percent of U.S. males and 10 percent of females are bisexual. This bisexual group of 25 million surpasses the gay and lesbian population. Social stigma keeps this group "in the closet" even more than gays and lesbians.[1]

All of these groups, therefore, suffer prejudice and discrimination that are often operationalized through the denial of economic resources, medical benefits, and the treatment and research they need to function in society in a humane, comfortable manner.

The practice skills of social workers are being challenged by these special population groups, and in beginning to meet this challenge, an evolving ecosystems model has been adapted by the authors to assist the social worker in obtaining a comprehensive analysis of a specific case for micro or macro intervention. The ecosystems intervention model has been found useful in social work practice with special populations and is described in detail with a case example in this section.

Ecosystems Model

The practice of social work involves a focus on the interaction between the person (or couple, family, group, organization, community, or larger societal structure) and the environment. The social work intervention focus might be directed at the person, the environment, or both. The goal of the social worker is to enhance and restore the psychosocial functioning of persons or to change noxious social conditions that impede the mutually beneficial interaction between persons and their environment.

The interaction between special population groups and their respective environments involves social, economic, and political factors, physical and mental health, and noxious forces such as ageism, homophobia, sexism, racism, and class discrimination, all exerting various effects on the lives of special population members. In identifying special population needs in order to provide services, the social worker should seek to understand both their feelings and attitudes about these factors and noxious forces, and the impact they exert. The social worker then attempts to meet social work goals to "enhance and restore social functioning and to improve social conditions."[2]

Meyer maintains that for many years social work has been offering its well-honed methods only to those who could use them instead of first finding out what was needed and then selecting a practice method from its interventive repertoire or inventing new methods. She believes the current social work methods framework maintains social work's denial of what had to be done with regard to broader social problems. She therefore suggests an ecosystems orientation to practice that involves the application of ecology (the study of the relationship between organisms and their environment) and general systems theory to professional tasks. This ecosystems perspective, according to Meyer, allows:

> . . . social workers to look at psychological phenomena, account for complex variables, assess the dynamic interplay of these variables, draw conceptual boundaries around the unit of attention or the case, and then generate ideas for interventions. At this point methodology enters in; for in any particular case—meaning a particular individual, family, group, institutional unit, or geographical area—any number of practice interventions might be needed.[3]

This ecosystems model of practice would help to promote social workers' understanding of the psychosocial problems experienced by special populations as well as the incidence, prevalence, intensity,

and harmfulness of sexism, ageism, racism, and class discrimination, and the social environments (enhancing as well as noxious) in which special populations struggle to survive.

Bronfenbrenner originally developed an ecological model in 1977 utilizing four factors—individual, family, social structural, and sociocultural—affecting human development.[4] Carlson in 1984 then adapted this model to the problem area of domestic violence. The model conceptualizes ecological space as comprised of four different levels or systems, each nested within the next.[5] This ecological framework, or ecosystems model, may be a helpful tool in analyzing from a micro to macro perspective the various factors impacting special population members. The author added a fifth-level factor for analysis, the historical.[6] Historical factors are particularly important for special populations as the historical origins of sexism, homophobia, ageism, and racism, for example, continue to function today to "lock in" these groups in U.S. society. In addition, minor modifications were made to two items—"sociocultural" is changed to culture and "social structural" to environmental-structural—as a means of more crisply delineating cultural from social or environmental–structural factors. The ecosystems model is presented in Figure A-1.

First, at the *individual level,* the focus is on the biopsychological endowment each person possesses, including personality strengths, level of psychosocial development, cognition, perception, problem-solving skills, emotional temperament, habit formation, and communication and language skills. Additionally, it is important to be knowledgeable about the person's attitudes, values, cultural beliefs, lifestyle, skills, and abilities; their view of the world; and how they respond to and cope with physical and psychological stress and problems. This only represents the highlights of factors at the individual level; the list is by no means exhaustive. The same brief format will be seen in the other levels of analysis.

Second, at the *family level,* the focus is on the nature of family lifestyle, culture, organization, family, division of labor, sex role structure, and interactional dynamics. Within a cultural context each family is unique. It is therefore important to know its values, beliefs, emotional support capacity, affective style,

Ecosystems Model for Analysis of Psychosocial Factors Impacting Special Populations

A special thanks to Professor Lois Miranda and social work faculty and students at the University of Wisconsin Oshkosh for assisting in the further refinement of the Ecosystems Model.

tradition, rituals, overall strengths and vulnerabilities, and how it manages internal or external stress. The nature and quality of the spousal relationship and the depth of connectedness to children and extended family are other areas requiring examination.

Third, in civilizations, cultures have evolved for survival purposes. Each culture develops behavioral responses influenced by the environment, historical and social processes incorporating specific structures such as language, food, kinship styles, religion, communications, norms, beliefs, and values. At the *cultural level* of the ecosystems model, therefore, the focus should be on understanding the cultural values, belief systems, and societal norms of the host culture and, in the case of minorities, their original culture. There may exist a conflict of cultures that, in advanced form, may result in mental-emotional impairment due to culture shock. The enhancing, nurturing aspects of the culture(s) should be noted as well as noxious elements such as sexism, ageism, and racism.

The fourth level of analysis involves *environmental-structural* factors and the positive or negative impact they have on special populations. Environmental-structural theories postulate that many of the problems of affected oppressed groups, such as special populations, are caused by the economic and social structure of U.S. society. Women, for example, are not poorer as a group than men because of biological or cultural inferiority. Rather, sexism is a U.S. male cultural value that is expressed and reinforced through the structure of economic, political, educational, and other social institutions. Ryan states that when U.S. white society looks at the poorly educated minority group child in the ghetto or *barrio* school, blame is placed on the parents (no books in the home), the child (impulse-ridden, nonverbal), minority culture (no value on education), or their socioeconomic status (i.e., they are socially and economically deprived and don't know any better). In pursuing this logic, Ryan adds, no one remembers to ask questions about the collapsing buildings, old, torn textbooks, insensitive teachers, relentless segregation, or callous administrators—in short, the environmental structure imposed upon the person with its accompanying negative consequences.[7]

The fifth and final level of the ecosystems model concerns positive and noxious factors in the *historical experience* of the special population member(s). The historical roots and experience of female subordination by males, for example, will affect the nature and quality of women's interaction with all agencies and their representatives. The male social worker may not be aware of his unconscious sexist behavior—the result of decades of conditioning—as he attempts to "help" female clients with their problems. Years of minority group oppression and exploitation, at times including genocide, lynching, and "police executions without trial," have left deep scars on minority group members and will affect the way they relate to human services agency representatives. Some elderly whites may recall very positive historical experiences remembering how supportive and encouraging U.S. social institutions had been, only to become depressed and discouraged when abandoned by the government when old. In addition to knowing about the U.S. historical experience, it is also of value to know the historical experience of immigrants and the countries they came from.

To illustrate how the ecosystems model might work, the following case example is presented:

CASE EXAMPLE

José is a small, frail-looking 14-year-old Spanish-speaking youngster brought into the community mental health center by his mother because he began to yell, cry, and scream and threw himself under a table at a public laundromat. The Anglo-American psychiatrist who saw José was able to speak some Spanish. José told the doctor that he was at the laundromat with his mother the day before and that he had seen a police car slowly pass by the laundromat. He insisted the police officer on the passenger side of the car pointed his machine gun at the laundromat. At that time, fearing for his life, he threw himself under one of the tables and began screaming.

The mother confirmed that a police car had passed the laundromat but stated that the officers merely passed and did not expose any firearms. Other symptoms José was exhibiting were fear of going to school (where he was failing), fear of leaving the house, nightmares (people trying to kill him), insomnia, fear of being arrested by immigration officials and deported, depression, agitation, increasing suspicion of people, and irritability, especially toward his mother, stepfather, and siblings. This progressively deteriorating behavior had been going on for about six months. The doctor concluded that José was, at times, incoherent, delusional, having visual hallucinations, and displaying disorganized behavior. This clinical picture was consistent with DSM-IV 298.8, Brief Psychotic Disorder. He was prescribed antipsychotic medication. He continued in treatment for two weeks but his symptoms did not subside. The medication was not having any effect.

An Hispanic bilingual–bicultural mental health consultant was asked to see José and his mother and make an assessment and treatment recommendation. José was born in "Muy Lejos," a rural, agricultural village in Guatemala. His parents were both farm laborers, as were his grandparents. He was raised in a very traditional, religious, rural culture where sex roles, division of labor, and respect for the elderly, extended family, and authority figures were valued. When José was six, his father was suspected of being a guerrilla and was killed by right-wing government forces. Sensing her life was also in danger, José's mother left him with his grandparents and came to the United States without documents in order to obtain employment and then send for José and other relatives. José felt abandoned and cried on the phone whenever his mother was able to call him, which was once every three or four months. Frequently, José would have to join other villagers and escape into the hills, sometimes for several months. José saw many killings, including decapitated bodies placed in the village by the right-wing forces to intimidate villagers.

In the meantime, the mother struggled for several years as a low-paid domestic and began to live with a documented Hispanic male. They had two children, two and four years younger than José. Finally, the mother was able to save enough money to send for José. He had been brought to the United States by a secret, underground system some six months previously. Initially he was happy to be reunited with his mother, but then the previously discussed symptoms began to surface.

José presents a difficult, complex case, although in no way is his situation unique. Rather than presenting one clearly identifiable problem for the mental health practitioner to treat, as is often the case with many middle-class clients, José brings at least five major problems that need to be prioritized in terms of severity and treated in a sequential manner. First, José is suffering acute *posttraumatic stress disorder* symptoms that have to be treated, including appropriately prescribed medication that will reduce his anxiety and fear, and permit him to sleep. Second, he is experiencing *culture shock,* having abruptly left an agrarian environment and come to the central cities area of Los Angeles. He doesn't understand the language or the requirements of school; he is being chased by urban gangs. Third, he is experiencing *separation anxiety* pain, having left his loving grandparents, who were really his substitute parents. It is also painful to be separated from relatives, friends, and one's country, never knowing if one will return. Fourth, he harbors a significant amount of unresolved anger toward his mother, who he believes *abandoned* him at a critical point in his life. These unresolved issues are intensified at his current psychosocial developmental level of adolescence. Finally, young José is confronted with a *reconstituted family.* He has to learn to deal with a stepfather who is taking the place of his beloved father. He also has to learn to live with a ten- and twelve-year-old stepsister and stepbrother. In short he is a complete outsider in all respects.

Following the treatment of the psychiatric symptoms, José then will have to work on cultural shock issues, separation anxiety, and unresolved matters related to his mother. At the appropriate time family therapy should also be initiated to help them function more positively as a family unit. The social worker may also have to help José resolve school and community-stress problems and link him up with community social-recreation programs.

In working with special population groups, once a sound knowledge base is established through the use of a conceptual tool such as the ecosystems model, the social worker has to intervene at both micro- and macro-intervention levels. In cases such as that of José, a detailed biological, psychological, sociological, cultural, and historical assessment has to be made in order to know what is needed and, more important, what has to be done. This case highlights more micro-intervention strategies than macro. Macro-intervention approaches would have utilized the helping concepts of client advocacy, empower- ment, social action, networking, and class action social work which involves collaboration with the legal profession on behalf of oppressed, disadvantaged special populations.

ENDNOTES

1. Jean S. Gochros, "Bisexuality," in Richard L. Edwards, ed., *Encyclopedia of Social Work*, 19th Edition (Washington, D.C.: NASW Press).

2. Armando Morales, "Social Work with Third-World People," *Social Work* 26 (January 1981): 45–51.

3. Carol H. Meyer, "What Directions for Direct Practice?" *Social Work* 24 (July 1979): 271.

4. Urie Bronfenbrenner, "Toward an Experimental Ecology of Human Development," *American Psychologist* 32 (1977): 513–551.

5. Bonnie E. Carlson, "Causes and Maintenance of Domestic Violence: An Ecological Analysis," *Social Service Review* 58 (December 1984): 569–587.

6. Nick Vaca, "The Mexican American in the Social Sciences," Part II, *El Grito IV* (Fall 1970): 17–51.

7. William Ryan, *Blaming the Victim* (New York: Pantheon Books, 1971), p. 4.

B

Selected Characteristics of Special Populations

This section, comprised of five chapters, will focus on selected characteristics of some special population groups pertaining to their gender (women), sexual orientation and lifestyle (gays, lesbians, and bisexuals), age (the elderly), and people with disabilities. Why these groups would require special attention in this text as oppressed persons is a sad commentary concerning the persistence of negative values acted out in public *behavior* (policy and practice) toward these persons.

The U.S. Senate Judiciary Committee's sexist handling of Anita Hill, an attorney who was alleging sexual harassment by Supreme Court Justice candidate Clarence Thomas, for example, and the homophobia expressed by Congress and the military regarding gays in the military, indicate the continued, powerful existence of an unsophisticated, sexist, homophobic, male-dominated American culture.

Chapter 11, "Social Work Practice with Women," an original work for this volume authored by Dr. Diane Kravetz, deals with the increasing health and mental health problems impacting women as a result of sexism, classism, and ethnic-racial discrimination—in effect, *multiple* stressors! Kravetz, a leading social work scholar on women, shows that women are impoverished in greater numbers than

men and are the fastest growing group of persons with AIDS.

Drs. George A. Appleby and Jeane W. Anastas wrote Chapter 12, "Social Work Practice with Lesbian, Gay, and Bisexual People." This is another original, brilliantly educational piece for this text, which painstakingly defines the complex and often misused term *homosexuality*. These authors also introduce readers to the new term *heterosexism,* which will not be defined now in order to not "steal the thunder" from these nationally known scholars concerning this topic.

The discrimination of the elderly by a "youth-oriented" Anglo-American culture that seeks to pressure fifty- and sixty-year-old persons into early retirement, thereafter isolating them from society by placing them in retirement facilities, is an example of *ageism.* Other cultures value the knowledge and life-long experiences of the "old and wise."

Chapter 13, "Social Work Practice with Children and Youth," is an original work by authors Armando T. Morales and Bradford W. Sheafor, making its first appearance in this volume. These authors examine the nation's ambivalence toward youth and children, and reinforce their perspectives with a solid micro and macro case.

Chapter 14, "Social Work Practice with the Elderly," by Drs. Manuel R. Miranda and Armando T. Morales, describes the elderly as one of the bio-psychosocial-neediest of all social work practice populations, as they constitute the fastest growing subgroup of the nation and will represent 25 percent of the total population by the year 2040.

This section ends with Chapter 15, "Social Work Practice with People with Disabilities," by Dr. Celia Williamson who was commissioned to write this piece. It concerns a group of 36 million persons who feel that they also have a right to an improved quality of life.

CHAPTER 11

Social Work Practice with Women

Diane Kravetz

Prefatory Comment

Dr. Diane Kravetz, Professor of Social Work, School of Social Work, University of Wisconsin, Madison, was commissioned to write this chapter pertaining to social work practice with women. Dr. Kravetz enjoys national respect for her scholarly work on women. She cautions that even though they live longer than men, women are the fastest growing group of persons with AIDS, representing 10 percent of all reported cases. As a special population group, large numbers of females of all ages suffer significant cases of physical, psychological, and sexual abuse, mostly by perpetrators known to them.

Dr. Kravetz calls for the elimination of sexism in the social work profession. One of the first steps in working toward this goal is to learn about the manifestations of this dynamic in the profession. This chapter will make a major contribution to that goal.

The special needs and concerns of women are relevant for every field of practice, social problem area, and level of intervention. Women's issues can be identified for female clients of every age, ethnic and racial group, and class. Correspondingly, for every women's issue, differences can be identified by age, class, ethnicity or race, and sexual orientation.

The first section of this chapter, current demographics, provides some basic facts about women's lives in the United States today. Then, using the Morales–Sheafor ecosystems model of practice as the framework for analysis, the chapter reviews the personal, social, and economic problems of women and presents the principles and methods of practice that provide the foundation for effective and ethical social work practice with women.

Current Demographics[1]

Over the past three decades, there have been dramatic changes in the composition of the family and women's participation in the work force. In 1992, 58 percent of women sixteen years old and over were in the civilian labor force, compared to 43 percent in 1970 and 38 percent in 1960.

In married-couple families, which represent 78 percent of all families, women's employment reflects not only changing social attitudes but also the economic necessity of two incomes. Over the past twenty years, family income has only substantially and consistently increased for married couples with the wife in the paid labor force. In 1991, the median income ($48,169) for a dual-earner family was significantly higher than the median income ($30,075) for married-couple families in which the wife was not in the paid labor force.

The major change in the composition of families has been the substantial increase in the number of families headed by women. In 1991, 17 percent of families were maintained by women, whereas in 1960, only 10 percent were. The proportion of families maintained by women differs greatly among African American (46%), Hispanic (24%), and white (14%) families.

The most significant factor for the increase in families maintained by women has been the increase in out-of-wedlock births. In 1950, 4 percent of all births involved single women. By 1989, the proportion of single women having children increased to 27 percent. Among African Americans, births to unmarried women represented 38 percent of births in 1970 and 65 percent in 1989. Among whites, the rates of births to unmarried women more than tripled between 1970 and 1989, increasing from 6 to 19 percent. Teenage mothers accounted for 13 percent of births to unmarried women.

The increase in female-headed families has been caused also by increasing rates of divorce. From 1970 to 1987, divorce rates more than doubled, and the proportion of one-parent families consisting of divorced women and children increased from 29 to 36 percent. With divorce, most women experience drastic declines in their standard of living and income, and their financial problems are compounded by inadequate or unpaid child support. In 1989, only 51 percent of women awarded child support received the full amount; almost 25 percent received no payments at all.

Predictably, female-headed families have the lowest median income of all family types. In 1991, female-headed families had a median income of $16,692, as compared to $28,351 for male-headed families.

Highly limited employment options and social norms that assign women primary responsibility for children are largely responsible for the so-called feminization of poverty. In 1990, 13 percent of adult women, as compared to 8 percent of adult men, were poor. The prevalence of poverty and gender differences are most evident among women of color. Nineteen percent of all African American men, as compared with 31 percent of African American women, live below the poverty level; as do 17 percent of Native American men and 29 percent of Native American women and 19 percent of Hispanic men as compared with 26 percent of Hispanic women. In contrast, 7 percent of white men and 11 percent of white women are poor.

Members of minority female-headed families are particularly at risk of poverty. In 1991, 47 percent of female-headed families with children under age eighteen were in poverty, as compared with 8 percent of married-couple families and 20 percent of male-headed families with children under age eighteen.

Women constitute the majority of older Americans. In 1992, women accounted for almost 60 percent of the population age sixty-five and over. Significantly more older women than men live alone due to women's greater longevity and the fact that widowed or divorced men are more likely to remarry.

Because of their relatively low incomes and greater likelihood of being widowed, older women have higher rates of poverty than do older men. By the age of sixty-five, a woman is almost twice as likely as a man of that age to be living in poverty. In 1991, more than two-thirds of older women living alone had incomes less than twice the poverty level ($13,064) and more than a quarter of all older women living alone were poor. Almost 90 percent of older African American women living alone had incomes below $13,064. Many older women lack adequate health care since Medicare provides little coverage for outpatient mental health services, long-term care, and nursing home care.[2]

HEALTH AND MENTAL HEALTH RISK FACTORS

Across the life span, women's health concerns differ from those of men. Women more than men experience infections and respiratory diseases and chronic conditions such as rheumatoid arthritis, systemic lupus erythematosus, fibromyalgia, osteoporosis, Alzheimer's disease, and diseases of the urinary system, as well as deaths due to childbearing, abortion, breast cancer, and stroke and related diseases.[3] The proportion of women who smoke (23%) is less than for men (28%). Although men are more likely than women to be heavy drinkers, women are more likely than men to use and abuse prescription drugs.[4]

There are significant differences in the health status of women of color and white women. Women of color have higher rates of obesity, tuberculosis, hepatitis B, and diabetes mellitus; and higher death rates from breast and cervical cancer, most likely because of their underutilization of Pap smears and mammography.

Women are the fastest growing group of people with AIDS, with the number of reported new AIDS cases from 1986 to 1990 increasing nearly twice as fast among women as among men. Of the total number of AIDS cases reported by 1991, slightly over 2 percent were Hispanic women, almost 3 percent were white women, and over 5 percent were African American women.[5] The Centers for Disease Control estimate that there are fifty to eighty times as many women infected with HIV as there are women with cases of AIDS. Many of these women have no symptoms and are unaware that they are capable of infecting others. The women at greatest risk are intravenous drug users, the sexual partners of male intravenous drug users and bisexual men, and prostitutes. Many are poorly educated and unemployed. Women of childbearing age (ages thirteen through thirty-nine) account for four out of five of all female AIDS cases, and it is estimated that half of the babies born to HIV-infected mothers may be infected with the AIDS virus.[6]

Finally, large numbers of women are victims of physical, psychological, and sexual abuse, often by members of their own families. Violence toward women is wide-ranging and includes child sexual assault, psychological and physical abuse, rape, and sexual harassment. Victims are subjected to physical injuries, unwanted pregnancies, and sexually transmitted diseases; victimization also has severe and prolonged negative effects on women's emotional health.[7]

According to a 1992 report of the American Medical Association, more than half of murdered women are killed by current or former male partners. About 4 million women are victims of domestic violence every year. In 1988, there were over 92,000 reported rapes. Reported rates of childhood sexual abuse in clinical populations are as high as 70 percent for women. In studies of nonclinical populations, approximately 20 to 30 percent of adult women report experiences of childhood sexual abuse.[8]

Ecosystems Perspective

The ecosystems model adopted by Morales and Sheafor for this volume provides a framework for understanding the beliefs, norms, institutional arrangements, and social roles that define and maintain women as a subordinate social group. Each of the five interconnected levels of the ecosystems model (historical factors, environmental-structural factors, culture, family, and individual) are discussed below in relation to the social and psychosocial problems of women.

The historical experience of women is best understood in terms of changing gender roles in the family and changes in women's social and economic circumstances. Therefore, historical factors are incorporated into the sections on the family and environmental–structural factors.

CULTURAL FACTORS

Cultural ideology about women shapes women's reality and maintains female subordination by men. Gender stereotyping, gender bias, and discrimination based on sex all reflect and promote negative cultural beliefs about women and their "appropriate" status in society. Women are defined as innately and inevitably different from and inferior to men. This androcentric view is supported by socially constructed definitions of woman as biologically destined to be dependent, nurturant, and domestic. The social, economic, and political arrangements that emerge from these cultural assumptions give males authority over females and formal power over public policies and practices.

Native American, Asian American, African American, Hispanic, and white women represent distinct cultural groups, each having specific and different problems, issues, and concerns. Within each of these groups, women's experience differs by class, and for some groups, by nationality or tribe. However, some generalizations can be made. Within every cultural group, female and male experience differs significantly, with women in each group having problems related to gender inequality within their own group and in society at large. For women of color, issues related to gender must be understood in terms of the overwhelming influence of racism and ethnic prejudice as well.

For lesbian women, oppression stems from sexism, homophobia, and heterosexism (heterosexism being a belief system that values heterosexuality as superior to and more natural than homosexuality). Misconceptions about and prejudice against lesbians are extensions of cultural myths and biases concerning traditional female roles and female sexuality. Lesbianism involves a life-style and subculture in which women function relatively independent of men. Thus, lesbianism challenges cultural mandates that women seek personal fulfillment and economic security through heterosexual bonding. Heterosexism is, then, a major aspect of male-dominated culture, for it functions to maintain traditional power relationships between women and men. Homophobia and fear of being labeled homosexual serve to keep both women and men within the confines of traditional gender roles.

ENVIRONMENTAL–STRUCTURAL FACTORS

Women's personal concerns, experiences, and problems are inextricably linked to the subordinate social, economic, and legal status of women as a group. Institutional sexism in education, law, and employment reinforces damaging views of women, creates role conflicts for women, and limits women's real and perceived options for personal growth and economic security. Although there is evidence of gender-role changes for women of every class and ethnic or racial group, all institutional arenas continue to be pervaded by male-centered values and discriminatory policies and practices.

WOMEN'S EDUCATION. The development of free, public elementary education by the mid-nineteenth century and public high schools by the end of the nineteenth century provided women with equal access to education. However, resistance to women in higher education remained firm. In 1920, a time when fewer than 8 percent of young people went to college, twice as many men as women received bachelor's or master's degrees and five times more earned doctorates.[9]

Due to social norms, structural barriers (including policies barring married women from employment and opposition from male professionals), and difficulties in combining family and career roles, many college-educated women chose to remain single in order to pursue their careers. These women provided leadership in the teaching profession, developed the professions of social work and home economics, established women's colleges and all-female medical schools, and became leaders in the first wave of the feminist movement.[10]

Currently, gender differences have largely disappeared at the high school and master's levels. The median number of school years completed by white women and men is almost thirteen years, as compared with about twelve years for Hispanic and African American women and men. In 1990, women received 53 percent of the bachelor and master's degrees awarded. However, women still received a smaller proportion (36%) of doctorate degrees, and they continued to be underrepresented in fields such as agriculture, computer science, dentistry, economics, engineering, law, medicine, and the physical sciences. Women earned the majority of the master's and doctoral degrees awarded in fields such as education, English, fine arts, foreign languages, home economics, library and archival science, and social work.[11]

WOMEN IN THE LABOR FORCE.   In pre-industrial American society, the workplace and the family were not separate entities. Although divisions of labor by gender were present, the basic economic roles of women and men were the same; that is, the production of goods and services to meet the needs of the family.

With industrialization, women and men's spheres became separate and differentially valued, especially in urban areas. During the nineteenth century, paid work outside of the home was viewed as masculine, was valued as contributing to the larger social good, and was predominantly performed by males. Work inside the home that produced goods and services for the benefit of the family was defined as a woman's responsibility. It was not viewed as contributing to the public good, and, as unpaid labor, was no longer considered productive work.

The ideology that defined women only in terms of their domestic role was reinforced by social norms defining paid work as deviant for married women of all classes. The pervasive power of this ideology ensured that most women in the paid labor force were single. Until the middle of the twentieth century, most female workers were young, single, and primarily from white working-class, immigrant, and African American families; they worked in factories, as servants and waitresses, as clerical workers and secretaries, and in retail sales. Women with postsecondary education became teachers, librarians, settlement house workers, and nurses. When economically feasible, married women of all racial and ethnic groups dropped out of the labor force.

However, some married women have always been part of the paid labor force. In the nineteenth and early twentieth centuries, employment was common for married African American women, most of whom still lived in the South. In 1890, for example, one-quarter of African American wives and two-thirds of the large number of African American widows worked, usually as field hands or domestic servants. Also at that time, paid work was common for married immigrant women in the textile-manufacturing towns of New England.[12] In 1920, 43 percent of African American females over the age of fifteen were employed, whether married or not, generally as domestic servants.[13] By World War II, although only 12 percent of white married women were paid workers, almost 25 percent of African American married women were.[14]

A series of changing social conditions made employment socially acceptable and necessary for women, including middle-class married white women. These include: (1) "labor saving" devices in the home; (2) recruitment of female labor during the World Wars and expanded employment opportunities post-World War II in "pink-collar" work (clerical work and sales); (3) increased economic need for two-income families; (4) increased educational opportunities for women; (5) a rising divorce rate and increasing numbers of female-headed households; (6) women's increased control of reproduction; (7) new anti-discrimination laws in education and employment; and (8) changing views of gender roles. These factors decreased barriers to female employment and increased women's opportunities and desire to enter the paid labor force.[15] The result has been a dramatic increase in the labor force participation of women, with rates for white women and women of color now similar (58% of African American and white women and 53% of Hispanic women).

Although single, divorced, and widowed women also increased their rates of participation, these figures are mostly due to increases in labor force participation among married women. In 1990, 58 percent of married women were paid workers, as compared with 31 percent in 1960.

In 1972, less than 30 percent of children under age six and less than 45 percent of children ages six to seventeen had working mothers. By 1992, over 50 percent of children under age six and over 65 percent of children ages six to seventeen had working mothers. Unlike women who were born prior to World War II, these women have tended to postpone marriage and children, have fewer children, have a longer prematernity history of employment, and remain in the work force after the births of their children.

Even with substantial gains in education and training, gender inequality still characterizes women's experiences in the labor force. The majority of employed women have jobs with low wages, low prestige, limited opportunities for advancement, lack of job security, and inadequate fringe benefits.

On average, women's full-time earnings in 1991 were $20,553; men's were $29,421. Women predominate in jobs at lower levels with less pay, even in so-called "women's" occupations. Regardless of race and level of education, women earn less than men in female-dominated jobs and when doing the same work as men.[16] Further, women's unpaid labor in their homes, on farms, and in their communities still is not included in cultural concepts of "work" and is not compensated by private pensions or social security.

WOMEN'S LEGAL RIGHTS.   Changes in women's roles and status are reflected in the legal system as well. Historically, women had few rights; they were viewed as the property of their fathers or husbands and in need of male protection. Unmarried women were viewed as deviants or exceptions and did not challenge legal definitions of women's rights and roles. The assumptions of the appropriateness and legitimacy of male control and dominance rendered invisible the needs of married women and their children to be protected from their "protectors."

The right to vote was extended to all women only in 1920 through ratification of the Nineteenth Amendment to the Constitution. Other major legal changes have occurred only within the past few decades. For example, Title VII of the 1964 Civil Rights Act bars sex discrimination in hiring, firing, promotions, and working conditions. Women now have the right to equal pay for equal work through the 1963 Equal Pay Act. Equal access and participation in education are covered by Title IX of the Educational Amendments of 1972. Abortions became legalized through the *Roe* v. *Wade* decision in 1973, though legal decisions since then have greatly restricted access to abortion for many women. Only in the past decade has there been some degree of reform in the laws and policies governing the treatment of rape victims, battered women, and victims of childhood sexual abuse.

THE FAMILY

Major shifts have occurred in women's marital and parental roles. Beginning with women born in the 1940s, there has been a significant shift toward marrying at a later age, delaying childbearing, and having fewer children. For example, women born in 1930 to 1934 had an average of 3.4 children; women born in 1950 to 1954 had an average of 2.2 children.[17]

Changing gender roles, increased education and labor force participation, and wider availability of contraception and abortion have contributed to women's delay of childbearing. In 1970, about 36 percent of women had their first child before they were twenty; another 46 percent had their first child when they were twenty to twenty-four years old. Only 4 percent of first births were among women over thirty. In 1987, at the birth of their first child, about 23 percent of women were under twenty, 33 percent were twenty to twenty-four, and 16 percent were thirty and older.[18]

Three percent of women of reproductive age terminate their pregnancies by abortion. Most women obtaining abortions (58%) are under age twenty-five; 20 percent are thirty or older. Fifty percent of all abortions take place at eight weeks or less from the time the woman had her last menstrual period; most (89%) take place in the first trimester.

By the 1980s, more heterosexual couples were choosing to remain unmarried and/or childless, and more women were part of nontraditional, "alternative" families (e.g., single parents, lesbian mothers, and lesbian couples with or without children). The traditional arrangement—married couple, wife not in the paid labor force—represented only 32 percent of families in 1991, down from almost 41 percent in 1980. Most common (46%) was the dual-earner family. Female-headed families accounted for over 17 percent of families, as compared with almost 11 percent in 1970.

Due to their increased participation in the labor force, higher levels of education, and changing social values, many women are more autonomous and have more egalitarian family structures. And, for most women, family responsibilities are willingly assumed and personally rewarding. However, traditional gender-role divisions in the family continue to have debilitating effects on women.

Despite women's expanded responsibilities as wage earners, they continue to have primary responsibility for household tasks and meeting the needs of husbands, children, and older relatives. Taking care of young children and providing long-term care for the elderly are stressful and time-consuming and have damaging consequences for women's paid work, social lives, personal relationships, and mental health. Women assume these family responsibilities with no financial compensation, little recognition, and few public supports. Moreover, leaving the labor force at various times in order to care for children and/or elderly family members places women at a disadvantage in competing for jobs and reduces their earnings and retirement benefits.[19]

Moreover, after divorce or the death of their husbands, women who have devoted themselves full time to their families often find that survivor benefits or alimony payments, if any, are inadequate; that they are living near or in poverty; and that they have inadequate medical care, housing, and health insurance.[20]

For every racial and ethnic group, women's roles in the family are shaped by the unique cultural values and traditions and the specific historical, social, and economic circumstances of each group. For women of color, family life has also been profoundly influenced by the effects of prejudice, discrimination, and poverty.[21] Racism has placed extraordinary burdens on African Americans, including poor housing, education, and health care; high rates of unemployment and limited job opportunities; and racial violence. Nonetheless, African American women have managed to create and maintain strong family and community networks. Because of their long-standing tradition of participation in the paid labor force, African American women are less tied to stereotypic female roles and behaviors and view paid work as compatible with family roles.[22]

In the lives of Hispanic women, patriarchal family, community, and religious systems have a pervasive effect. The *machismo* (male dominance) found in many traditional cultures, promotes female passivity and frequent childbearing, discouraging education and employment for women. Powerlessness is reinforced for those Hispanic women who do work, for they are often isolated by language barriers and in low status, low paying jobs as migrant farm laborers, factory workers, and clerical and service workers.[23]

Historically, Asian American women, having been raised in traditional cultures, have also held compliant and submissive roles within their families and communities. The experiences and goals of independent, career-oriented Asian American women are in conflict with traditional cultural expectations that women be unassuming, reserved, and highly family-oriented. Asian American women in the work force are concentrated in low-wage jobs, despite the fact that they tend to be relatively well educated.[24]

American Indians are the most economically depressed and least acculturated minority; and American Indian women earn less and are less acculturated than men. Although American Indian culture is not patriarchal, American Indian women's prestige and influence have decreased, due to federal policies and practices that gave decision-making power and other rights, minimal as they were, only to American Indian men. Being in the center of family life, American Indian women deal with all the stresses of their families, including poor living conditions, educational problems, and poor health, including high rates of infant mortality and alcoholism.[25]

Lesbian families have been stigmatized, marginalized, and pathologized. Social policy and practices actively punish or fail to acknowledge the growing and more visible presence of lesbian couples and families. In 1992, of the nearly 5 million households composed of two unrelated adults living as partners, both partners were female in over 13 percent. About one-sixth of households with two female partners included children under the age of fifteen. These families suffer the stresses of heterosexism and homophobia in their workplaces, schools, churches, hospitals, and community activities. While struggling with these pressures and with developing new models of family life, lesbian couples also have opportunities for escaping conventional notions of power and responsibility within the family and for developing new ways of parenting that are less likely to promote traditional gender role ideologies in children.[26]

THE INDIVIDUAL

Because gender is a central determinant of social status and socialization, it influences all of the individual's experiences, including those that contribute to the development of psychological disorders. The influence of gender can be seen especially clearly in disorders prevalent among women such as eating disorders, agoraphobia, and depressive disorders. Both the causes and the symptoms of these disorders have been linked to conventional gender roles and female socialization.[27]

Discrimination in the workplace exacerbates women's sense of powerlessness and personal devaluation. Sexual harassment reminds working women of their subordinate status. It causes considerable distress and disrupts job performance, leading some women to quit their jobs or seek transfers. For many women, paid work is a source of considerable stress rather than personal satisfaction and growth.[28]

There is a high rate of mental health problems among low-income women, with low-income single mothers particularly at risk. Social and economic stresses contribute to low-income women's heightened risk of distress and disorder. They are more likely to experience crime and violence, the illness or death of children, and the imprisonment of husbands; and to suffer from chronic life conditions such as inadequate housing, dangerous neighborhoods, and financial insecurities. Poverty subjects women to exploitation, physical danger, demoralization, maltreatment, and despair.[29]

For older women, the stresses of poverty, widowhood, retirement, and increased dependency on family members often result in loneliness, isolation, depression, alcoholism, and drug abuse. Also, women are at higher risk of elder abuse than men.[30]

Racism and ethnic prejudice exacerbate the mental health problems of women of color. They are subjected to stresses created by white ethnocentrism and discrimination based on race and sex, and often suffer the debilitating consequences of poverty as well. Also, many of these women experience psychological difficulties as they attempt to reconcile their cultural values and traditions with the demands of white society. In addition, some have problems related to the process of immigration.[31]

For lesbians, the pervasive homophobia and heterosexism of society can create psychological distress. Lesbians often experience rejection, ridicule, and actual or threatened physical violence. Other stresses include the risk of unwanted exposure and the ongoing process of coming out; discrimination in housing, employment, and child custody; and the lack of legal protection for and social recognition of their partnerships and parental status.[32]

Finally, victimization creates profound emotional difficulties for many women. Many victims of rape, childhood sexual abuse, and wife abuse experience high levels of depression, fear and anxiety, shame, social and sexual withdrawal, and low self-esteem. Sexual assault victims are at a higher risk for developing major psychiatric disorders, including affective disorders, substance abuse disorders, and anxiety disorders. Moreover, fear of victimization severely constrains the behavior of women as a group and undermines their psychological well-being.[33]

Intervention Strategies

For every level of intervention, social workers can use the ecosystems model to frame their understanding of how sexism affects the psychosocial problems experienced by women and the social conditions that enhance or restrict their lives. Social workers must analyze and evaluate the personal, social, and economic consequences of gender inequality in order to determine appropriate goals, targets of change, and interventions with women clients.[34]

Social workers continue to rely on theories and research that: (1) uncritically mirror social myths and stereotypes about women; (2) use the experiences of men as the standard against which the experiences of women are judged; (3) value "male" behaviors and roles over "female" ones; and (4) use female biology to explain women's feelings and behavior.

To counter the pervasive influence of incomplete, inaccurate, or biased information about women, it is essential that social workers be knowledgeable about current research on gender differences, gender roles, differences in the socialization and life experiences of women and men, and the nature of institutionalized inequality and female oppression. Social workers also need to understand the effects of sexism on their own beliefs, values, expectations, and behavior. They need to identify the range of ways gender bias can influence every phase of the planned change process.

Further, social workers must recognize that female experience differs by class, race, ethnicity, and sexual orientation, but that generalizations cannot be made for all women of color, all white women, all lesbians, or all poor women. Social workers need to understand the cultural heritages of minorities and the unique aspects of women's lives within their own cultural groups. Social workers need to understand the influence of homophobia and heterosexism on all women and become knowledgeable about the unique experiences of lesbians and the nature of the lesbian subculture.

In social work practice, issues related to female socialization, gender inequality, and sexism will be of varying significance, depending on the specific problem or issue. In every situation and for every client, the social worker needs to evaluate: (1) the relationships between traditional gender roles and gender inequality and the presenting problem; (2) the ways in which gender bias affects the established knowledge base about that problem and contaminates traditional services and treatments; (3) the new and corrective knowledge that has emerged; and (4) the range of methods and approaches that have been developed to deal with the gender-related aspects of the presenting problem. Ignoring the realities and complexities of women's lives, at best, fails to provide clients with the opportunity to reduce their social and economic powerlessness and vulnerability. At worst, social work practice that ignores the social circumstances of women may actually promote female subordination and victimization.

MICRO PRACTICE WITH WOMEN

To help women deal with problems in psychosocial functioning, social workers use a range of microlevel interventions. In the assessment phase, a social worker needs to evaluate women's functioning at home, at work, and in the community in terms of existing gender-role norms and discriminatory practices. Although the immediate target of change is the woman and/or her family, there must be ongoing recognition of the ways in which a woman's personal problems are shaped by her social, economic, and legal circumstances. Social workers must be realistic about the many ways in which discriminatory employment practices, sex-biased community attitudes, and restrictive family roles create barriers and place limits on women's options for change. The effects of racism, heterosexism, classism, and ageism must also be actively taken into account.

Understanding the full range of factors that shape women's lives, a social worker can extend the range of solutions and life changes to be considered and select interventive strategies that will help clients reach their goals. Social workers should incorporate knowledge concerning female oppression and gender-role socialization in the same manner that they incorporate knowledge concerning all other aspects of clients' problems and situations: selectively and sensitively, taking into account the values, needs, concerns, and goals of their clients.

With an awareness that women's lack of social power can generate passivity and dependence, workers should include female empowerment as a central goal. This can be accomplished by sharing resources, power, and responsibility with clients. Interventive strategies consistent with these principles include appropriate self-disclosure by the worker, having the client take an active part in goal-setting and outcome evaluation, making the worker's own values explicit, and emphasizing the client's strengths and assets. Such strategies minimize clients' dependency on the worker, increase the likelihood that clients feel free to reject the values and approaches of the worker, and concretely demonstrate the belief that women are capable of being autonomous and in control of their own lives.

As with all oppressed groups, it is empowering for women to understand the influence of social factors on their personal lives. Social workers can incorporate gender-role analyses into their work with women to encourage clients to evaluate the ways in which social roles, norms, and structural realities limit female autonomy and choice. Through this process, women can come to understand how, by internalizing cultural values about women, they sometimes act as coconspirators in their own oppression.

All-women groups can be used to deemphasize the authority of the social worker and help members share and understand the experiences that have influenced them as women. Such groups facilitate the respect and trust of women for one another and help them to develop a sense of solidarity with women as a group. Finally, workers can encourage their clients to participate in social action on their own behalf. It is growth-producing for women to engage in social actions designed to change those conditions at work and in their community that most directly have negative effects on their lives.

Being female increases the worker's ability to empathize with clients and to understand and share experiences related to being female in a male-dominated society. In their practice, male social workers must develop ways to ensure that traditional male–female power relationships and interactive strategies do not characterize their work with women clients. They need to recognize that there are limitations in their ability to empathize with women and serve as role models, and that the male worker–female client combination reinforces cultural views that women are dependent on male authority.

In working with groups, workers must be aware of the intersection of gender issues with group dynamics. This includes recognition of the differences between mixed groups and all-female groups in stages of group development, goals and structure, leadership, interpersonal relations, and communication patterns.[35] Workers should be aware of the ways in which groups have been especially useful in work with women with common issues; for example, with substance abusing women, women with eating disorders, lesbian mothers, unwed teenage mothers, women of color, and low-income women.[36]

Work with families must take into account the social, economic, and political realities that shape family roles and relationships, and conversely, how women's roles and responsibilities in their families support or constrain their participation in public life. In working with families, social workers can provide support and direction to help mothers and their female children become more assertive and self-directed. They can help clients challenge gender-role stereotypes in the family, examine more flexible and nontraditional roles, and equalize power.[37]

In establishing goals, in planning interventive strategies, and in evaluating outcomes, workers and clients must recognize that some changes *will* increase women's self-esteem, feelings of autonomy, and social functioning, but at the same time produce new stresses and conflicts. Presenting a self-image and behaviors that deviate from traditional roles and norms may incur difficulties for women. Some relationships may become more satisfying, but others are likely to become more stressful. Parents, spouse, children, friends, relatives, and coworkers may be ambivalent, if not hostile, toward a woman's desire to make nontraditional changes in her life. Also, because of sexism in education and employment as well as in other social institutions, women may not be able to fully or easily achieve the changes they desire. Assessment and evaluation must focus, therefore, on whether women are behaving in a self-directing, autonomous manner and whether their behavior is the result of a conscious understanding of available options and a deliberate weighing of costs and benefits.[38]

MACRO PRACTICE WITH WOMEN

The principles and methods that are incorporated into nonsexist micro practice are also used in nonsexist approaches to macro practice. Empowerment of women and the development of responsive policies and services require that workers emphasize client participation, egalitarian relationships, and collaborative decision making and that they reduce the power and status differences between themselves and their clients.

At the macro level, workers' tasks include assessing the impact of sexism, heterosexism, racism, and poverty on female clients; analyzing the unmet service needs of women and their children; evaluating the presence of bias in the design and delivery of existing services; and developing and/or modifying programs and services to meet the special needs of women. Neighborhood organizing, community development, and social action provide a range of methods that workers can apply to provide and/or improve local resources for women. Social planning, program development, and policy analysis engage higher level political processes and public education efforts on behalf of women.[39]

Empowering women includes helping them to gain the power to control their own lives. Community organization skills can be used to help women build and maintain their own groups, organizations, and agencies. Social workers can help women to translate their concerns into specific objectives and goals; to develop their organizational and leadership skills; to increase the resources available to the group; and to identify and evaluate strategies which will help them to reach their goals. Workers' knowledge of funding and resource development can be particularly valuable to such groups.[40]

In community and organizational practice, as in micro practice, there are some circumstances in which a female social worker is likely to be more effective than a male. For example, in the areas of physical abuse, child sexual abuse, and teen pregnancy, a female social worker is likely to be trusted more. Women workers' experience as women, and often as mothers, helps them identify women's needs and concerns and may enhance their credibility. Also, women community organizers, planners, and administrators can work with female client systems without the power–status differential that is inherent when men work with women.[41]

For female social workers, macro practice requires recognition that the workers themselves are likely to be influenced by the sexism pervading both the systems in which they work and those they want to influence. Administration and community organization are viewed as male domains and rely primarily on male models. Further, the policies, programs, and services that are targets of change are most likely controlled and administered by men. Women who enter these domains as workers or who attempt to change them on behalf of their clients often encounter gender-role stereotyping, devaluation, exclusion, suspicion, prejudice, sexual harassment, and discrimination.[42]

MICRO PRACTICE WITH A BATTERED WOMAN

The following case illustrates the ways in which women's problems involve social, economic, and legal factors; role socialization; and interpersonal and psychological distress and dysfunction. It demonstrates how micro practice can be used to improve the lives of battered women.

BACKGROUND

Tracy was brought to the shelter for battered women from the emergency room of the local hospital. She had been severely beaten by her husband, who had also threatened to kill her. She had two black eyes, two broken ribs, severely bruised legs and arms, and a broken finger on her left hand. According to Tracy, her husband pulled the phone from the wall when she tried to call the police; it was then that she sustained the black eyes. Fortunately, a cousin came by for an unexpected visit, at which time Tracy's husband fled the house. The cousin drove Tracy and her three-year-old daughter, Jane, to the hospital.

IMPACT ON THE FAMILY SYSTEM

Jane had witnessed her mother's physical and emotional abuse, on this occasion and on other occasions. The child was very upset and visibly terrorized that her father would come back, hurt her mother again, and take her away, as he had threatened to do.

When Tracy and her daughter came to the shelter, the taxi fare was paid by the shelter. Tracy's husband had taken her purse when he fled from the house. The only possessions

Tracy and her daughter had with them were the clothes that they had on. Tracy was still in serious pain from her injuries. Jane was crying off and on, asking, "Is Daddy going to come here and find us?" Despite her own pain and needs, Tracy attended to her daughter's fears. She held the child, which was painful due to her bruises and broken ribs, and comforted her.

INITIAL CLIENT CONTACT AND ENGAGEMENT
When she met with the social worker, Tracy expressed much concern about whether or not this was really the right thing to do. She was angry, confused, and very worried about how she would manage for herself and her child. The worker reassured Tracy that all her feelings were natural, and in fact, common to many of the women when they first came to the shelter. The worker emphasized that the shelter would provide Tracy with safety and security; no decisions about other services or goals would be made until Tracy was ready. The worker's goals were to communicate her caring and her willingness to help; to reduce the fears and anxiety associated with being in this new situation; and to assure Tracy of safety and confidentiality.

The worker explained that she would be meeting with Tracy and that Jane would have her own social worker and be part of the children's play group at the shelter.

IDENTIFYING NEEDS AND OBTAINING RESOURCES
At their second meeting later that same day, the worker began to collect information about Tracy's situation and needs for service. Tracy was severely depressed and on antidepressants. Following their session, the worker contacted Tracy's psychiatrist to coordinate services. She also began to work with the county social service department to obtain financial assistance for Tracy's medical and psychiatric care. The worker told Tracy about the range of resources and services available at the shelter and in the community.

PROVIDING SUPPORT
Throughout the first week, the worker assured Tracy that she would not be critical of her nor pressure her in any way. The worker looked for every opportunity to validate Tracy's feelings and to give her positive feedback. She let Tracy know that she understood and empathized with Tracy's many conflicting and confusing feelings about her husband and her current situation.

PROMOTING CLIENT SELF-DETERMINATION
The worker explained that her role was to help Tracy make decisions about her life, not to make decisions for her. Tracy would need to decide what she wanted to do and what would be in her best interests. The worker emphasized that she would support, encourage, and advocate for Tracy throughout, but that it was Tracy's right and responsibility to make her own decisions.

EMPATHY AND EMPOWERMENT
Tracy told the worker that she was very confused, that she trusted the worker, and that she would like the worker to develop a plan for her to leave her husband. The worker reassured Tracy that she appreciated her trust and that she understood her anxiety, but that Tracy would be able to determine her own needs and set her own goals, with the worker's help. Not taking over at this point, although this was the request of the client, began the process of empowering Tracy to take control of her own life.

WORKING THROUGH RESISTANCE EXPRESSED AS AMBIVALENCE

At their next few meetings, Tracy discussed her ambivalence about leaving her husband. The worker listened in a nondirective and supportive fashion. Also, she asked specific questions to collect information on the patterns of abuse; she helped Tracy begin to think about the various aspects of the problem and to identify her strengths and the ways in which she had coped and survived. A primary goal was to provide a supportive atmosphere in which Tracy could ventilate her anxieties, fears, shame, and anger, as well as sort out the love she felt for her husband.

IDENTIFYING AND BUILDING ON STRENGTHS

The worker was committed to helping Tracy explore her options without encouraging her to go in any one particular direction. The worker needed to support Tracy's discussion of the positive parts of her family life and her warm feelings for her husband without implying that she should stay with him. On the other hand, the worker needed to encourage Tracy to explore leaving her husband without implicitly suggesting that she should. She wanted Tracy to know that she would be there for her, regardless of the specific decisions she made.

RESISTANCE EXPRESSED AS FEAR OF CHANGING

Tracy had difficulty expressing any anger toward her husband. She blamed herself for provoking his anger. She was afraid of him but also felt he worked hard and deserved her sympathy and understanding. She said that sometimes he was very loving, that he often apologized for hitting her, begged for her forgiveness, and promised to change. He swore he loved her and could not live without her.

Tracy said that for years she believed he was trying to change and that she could find some way to prevent his attacks by keeping everything just the way he liked. Finally she realized she was unable to do this. No matter how hard she tried, he found things that bothered him about the house, about her, and about their child. Tracy was very upset that she had failed as a wife and mother. She could not imagine not being married, and she did not know how she could cope on her own, especially with a toddler.

COUNTERACTING LOW SELF-ESTEEM

The worker tried to refocus Tracy's feelings of self-blame and shame; instead of getting angry at herself, it was important that Tracy begin to focus on her anger toward her husband. She wanted Tracy to discover that she could deal with her anger, that she would not be rejected for her anger, and that anger can turn into positive energy for problem solving and self-protection. Also, she helped Tracy focus on her own needs and feelings. This was very difficult for Tracy, since she had only thought about predicting and meeting her husband's needs for many years.

FACILITATING EMPOWERMENT THROUGH GROUP SUPPORT

The worker also encouraged Tracy to join the shelter's counselor-facilitated support group. Here, Tracy was able to see that she was not alone. She saw the ways that other women were able to come to terms with their abuse; she heard from women who had begun to work with lawyers and to find housing; and she began to see some commonalities between her experiences and those of other battered women. The group helped her to feel more optimistic about her own ability to change and to become more assertive. She felt less isolated and received support for her attempts to help other women deal with their issues.

ENHANCING SELF-ESTEEM THROUGH VALIDATION

Tracy particularly liked group discussions about how they had been raised as females and brought up to expect that a happy marriage was a certainty and their most important goal. Sometimes they brought in magazines or discussed TV programs in terms of how women were portrayed. They described the pressures they felt from family to remain married no matter what. Tracy felt increasingly free to talk and express her own opinions, since she felt support and acceptance from the other members of the group. She became active in helping think through problems and possible alternatives for herself and other group members. The support group provided Tracy with opportunities to share experiences, overcome her social isolation and lack of female friendships, and find hope and strength by seeing the successes of others.

TRANSFORMING FEELINGS INTO ACTION

In their individual sessions, the worker progressed from encouraging Tracy to express her feelings and helping her to clarify emotions, to encouraging Tracy to take steps to improve her situation. The worker reassured Tracy that she was not to blame. She was neither the instigator of the abuse nor a willing participant; she was not responsible for her husband's violence. She helped Tracy believe she had the right to be safe and that no one had the right to abuse her.

DEVELOPING CLIENT INSIGHT

The worker also wanted Tracy to recognize that, with new information and options, she was responsible for protecting herself and her child. The worker helped Tracy to understand the dynamics of wife abuse and the ways in which social factors contributed to her abuse. In discussing social factors and common patterns of domestic violence, it was important that the worker not reinforce Tracy's feelings of helplessness. Instead, by understanding these social factors, Tracy was expected to take increased responsibility for the choices she made, thereby gaining a sense of personal power.

As part of their discussion, the worker presented factual information about the effects of violence on women and their children, Tracy's legal rights and options, and the difficulties in starting over. With Tracy, the worker explored intrapsychic factors *and* societal norms and roles, not to reinforce her view of herself as a victim but to help her understand that she had the power to change important aspects of her life.

PLANNING FOR CHANGE

In considering Tracy's leaving her husband, they discussed her needs for housing, employment, child care, and improved parenting skills, as well as financial aid to cover transportation, medical and psychiatric expenses, and legal assistance. Tracy did decide to leave her husband, although she was worried about her actual ability to do so. As Tracy set her goals, she and the worker outlined the steps that would be necessary, including Tracy's spending time with workers in other agencies.

The worker had a wide range of possible resources, but needed to tailor these to meet Tracy's specific needs. In many ways, Tracy was like many battered women and knowing these commonalities helped the worker predict what services would be necessary. However, Tracy was also a unique individual, and the worker wanted to make sure that she didn't stereotype Tracy as "a battered woman leaving her husband." The intervention had to be *individualized.*

MACRO PRACTICE ON BEHALF OF BATTERED WOMEN

Macro social work practice finds the social worker providing services on behalf of people, as opposed to micro practice in which the worker provides a direct service on a face-to-face basis with an identified client. In macro practice, the worker attempts to make social and legal institutions such as organizations, neighborhoods, and communities, responsive to the needs of clients. Macro practice may also involve developing or changing policies, regulations, and laws to help people. This can be seen in the following macro case.

DEFINING THE PROBLEM AND NEED

Shelter staff had already established community education programs with business leaders and church groups, and they had recruited volunteers to assist with the twenty-four-hour crisis line. However, several problems were constantly confronting the staff and their clients. All the workers at the shelter were frustrated with the ineffectiveness of restraining orders. Also, they increasingly saw ties between domestic violence and substance abuse, but their programs could not deal with the substance abuse, and the alcohol and drug programs did not address the battering. Finally, and most frustrating, they knew that therapists in their community continued to help battered women "resolve their conflicting feelings about their marriage and become more satisfied wives and mothers." These therapists, in assuming a traditional stance, were defining women's depression as the primary problem, seeing the depression as a symptom of the "neurotic conflicts that interfered with the woman's capacity to nurture and care for others" rather than seeing it evolving from the abuses they were suffering.

DEVELOPING STRATEGIES

The shelter workers decided to pursue a range of different strategies to address these specific problems. First, they wanted to gain more cooperation from the legal, law enforcement, social service, and medical systems in the community. Several workers began to meet with the police to explore their willingness to participate in a series of workshops on battered women. The goals of these workshops were to improve police officers' knowledge about and attitudes toward woman abuse and to try to improve the enforcement of restraining orders. The long-range goal was to involve other systems in such educational programs as well.

NETWORKING

Second, they decided to hold a meeting for alcohol and drug abuse counselors and social service providers to begin to assess the dual problems of substance abuse and battering in the community. They were particularly interested in improving cooperation between agencies that worked with battered women and those that worked with substance abuse.

COMMUNITY EDUCATION

Third, they decided to ask to speak at meetings of therapists and counselors in the community, to describe the shelter's services and provide information about the social and economic aspects of woman abuse. They would speak with some of the shelter residents to see if they were willing to come to these meetings to speak about their experiences with traditional therapists, counselors, and social workers.

NEEDS ASSESSMENT SURVEY

Finally, to gain a fuller perspective on service delivery problems, they decided to conduct a survey to assess the obstacles women encountered in receiving adequate services. The survey would be distributed to clients and former clients, shelter staff, and workers in other agencies encountering battered women. The survey would ask clients and workers to provide information about clients' interactions with medical, legal, and social service systems in the community. The workers would also be asked to assess agency policies and procedures in terms of whether they facilitated or impeded effective work with battered women.

GETTING RESULTS

Providing counseling and advocacy helped individual battered women to change their lives. Also, working with individual battered women helped the staff to identify inadequate or nonexistent services and the ways in which various helping systems were exacerbating or reducing the problems of battered women. The staff's work in community education and in changing the policies and procedures of other agencies helped the individual battered women who came to the shelter and ultimately would improve the circumstances of all women in their community.

Emerging Issues and Trends

Throughout the 1980s and 1990s, legislation and policies on affirmative action, abortion rights, discrimination in education and employment, and AFDC narrowed women's rights and options. We are still far from achieving equality for women. More than ever, women who are not attached to men are poorer than those who are, and women of color are poorer than white women. Health care is inaccessible to many families and elderly women due to their lack of health insurance, including Medicaid. Most employed women continue to be in sex-segregated, low-wage clerical, sales, and service jobs. Compared with men, women continue to have less independence and fewer resources.

Social workers should not minimize the significance of helping women to make changes in their own feelings, attitudes, everyday behaviors, and relationships. Women's oppression is supported by internalized cultural views that devalue them and legitimate their powerlessness and victimization. By helping women to alter these internalized views and change their behaviors in nontraditional ways, social workers can challenge one of the most basic ways that oppression is maintained. When the nature of personal change conflicts with the dominant values of society, personal change becomes political and holds broad social and political implications.

The profession of social work has a major role to play in the design and implementation of social policies, programs, and services. The feminization of poverty will continue to dominate the focus of social welfare policies and programs. Increases in the rates of divorce and out-of-wedlock pregnancies, sex segregation and discrimination in the labor force, and the lack of federal family-support policies will maintain women's disadvantaged status. Our challenge is to find ways to support the needs of employed women and at the same time create alternate approaches to support child-rearing and caregiving.

Social policies directed at reducing the feminization of poverty include: (1) promoting equality in the labor force; (2) providing additional economic supports for parents, especially single parents, including increasing the availability of low-priced housing and housing subsidies; and (3) disseminating information about sexuality and contraception to reduce the rates of teenage motherhood.[43] Welfare reform includes providing job training and education for women, but must also ensure services and supports for children so that women can attend school and enter the work force with the confidence that their children are safe and cared for.

Concluding Comment

For the benefit of all women, social workers should actively work for changes in social policies, including: (1) passage of the Equal Rights Amendment and other federal policies that will ensure equal opportunity and pay equity; (2) increasing the availability and affordability of child care, including employer-sponsored child care programs; (3) broadening employment options to include flextime, jobsharing, and parental leave to help families meet both family and work responsibilities; (4) enforcement of child support and alimony payments; and (5) improving women's health care, including working to maintain women's right to abortion, advocating for federal funding of family planning services and abortion, and preventing the further spread of AIDS to women and children.

Most important, social workers need to eliminate sexism within the profession as it impacts on the lives of female clients and workers. Services and programs need to be evaluated to eliminate the presence of sexism as well as racism, class bias, and heterosexism. Social workers must be knowledgeable about the relationships between female subordination, women's problems, and social work services. They must proactively work to eliminate gender inequality in schools of social work and in social work agencies and organizations. Until these conditions are met, we cannot presume that we have the theoretical, empirical, and ethical base for our practice with women. To develop meaningful and nonoppressive policies, services, programs, and interventions for women, social workers must work to eliminate stereotyping and discrimination for clients and women social workers as well.

KEY WORDS AND CONCEPTS

Women	Alternative families
Feminist	Women's Movement
Gender	Fourteenth Amendment
Sexism	Traditional culture

SUGGESTED READINGS

Bricker-Jenkins, Mary, and Lockett, Patricia W., "Women: Direct Practice," in Richard L. Edwards, ed., *Encyclopedia of Social Work,* 19th Edition. Washington, D.C.: NASW Press, 1995.

Bricker-Jenkins, M., Hooyman, N., and Gottlieb, N., eds. *Feminist Social Work Practice in Clinical Settings.* Newbury Park, CA: Sage, 1991.

Brown, L., and Root, M., eds. *Diversity and Complexity in Feminist Therapy.* New York: Harrington Park Press, 1990.

Burstow, B. *Radical Feminist Therapy: Working in the Context of Violence.* Newbury Park, CA: Sage, 1992.

Butler, S., and Wintram, C. *Feminist Groupwork.* London: Sage, 1991.

Comas-Diaz, L., and Greene, B., eds. *Women of Color: Integrating Ethnic and Gender Identities in Psychotherapy.* New York: The Guilford Press, 1994.

Hooyman, N., and Gonyea, J. *Feminist Perspectives on Family Care: Policies for Gender Justice.* Newbury Park, CA: Sage, 1995.

Pinderhuges, E. *Understanding Race, Ethnicity, and Power: The Key to Efficacy in Clinical Practice.* New York: Free Press, 1989.

Van Den Bergh, N., ed. *Feminist Practice in the 21st Century.* Washington, D.C.: NASW Press, 1995.

ENDNOTES

1. Unless stated otherwise, all figures presented in this chapter that refer to 1987 and earlier are taken from U.S. Bureau of the Census, *Statistical Abstract of the United States: 1989* (Washington, D.C.: U.S. Government Printing Office, 1989); data from 1989–1992 are taken from C. Costello and A. J. Stone, eds., *The American Woman 1994–95* (New York: W. W. Norton, 1994).

   In discussions of the racial and gender composition of the population of the United States, references to white women and men refer to persons who are white, non-Hispanic; statistical information about African American women and men refers to persons who are African American, non-Hispanic. The Census Bureau does not classify Hispanic as a racial category; therefore, persons of Hispanic origin may be of any race. Some statistical comparisons include only African Americans and whites because data from the 1970 census does not include a breakdown of persons of Hispanic origin by sex.

2. K. Davis, "Women and Health Care," in S. Rix, ed., *The American Woman 1988–89* (New York: W. W. Norton, 1988), pp. 162–204; L. Grau, "Mental Health and Older Women," in L. Grau and I. Susser, eds., *Women in the Later Years* (New York: Haworth Press, 1989), pp. 75–91.

3. P. Ries and A. J. Stone, eds., *The American Woman 1992–93* (New York: W. W. Norton, 1992).

4. L. Biener, "Gender Differences in the Use of Substances for Coping," in R. Barnett, L. Biener, and G. Baruch, eds., *Gender and Stress* (New York: The Free Press, 1987), pp. 330–349.

5. Ries and Stone, pp. 230–233.

6. D. Richardson, "AIDS Education and Women: Sexual and Reproductive Issues," in P. Aggleton, P. Davies, and G. Hart, eds., *AIDS: Individual, Cultural and Policy Dimensions* (New York: Falmer Press, 1990), pp. 169–179.

7. S. Martin, "Sexual Harassment: The Link between Gender Stratification, Sexuality, and Women's Economic Status," in J. Freeman, ed., *Women: A Feminist Perspective* (Palo

Alto, CA: Mayfield, 1984), pp. 54–69; S. Nolen-Hoeksema, *Sex Differences in Depression* (Stanford, CA: Stanford University Press, 1990), pp. 77–104.

8. J. Briere and L. Zaidi, "Sexual Abuse Histories and Sequelae in Female Psychiatric Emergency Room Patients," *American Journal of Psychiatry* 146 (December 1989): 1602–1606.

9. M. Ferree and B. Hess, *Controversy and Coalition: The New Feminist Movement* (Boston: Twayne Publishers, 1985), p. 6.

10. Hunter College Women's Studies Collective, *Women's Realities, Women's Choices* (New York: Oxford University Press, 1983), pp. 397–437; and V. Sapiro, *Women in American Society* (Mountain View, CA: Mayfield, 1990), pp. 95–120.

11. V. Sapiro, *Women in American Society* (Mountain View, CA: Mayfield, 1994), pp. 14–15.

12. F. Blau, "Women in the Labor Force: An Overview," in J. Freeman, ed., *Women: A Feminist Perspective* (Palo Alto, CA: Mayfield, 1984), p. 300.

13. Ferree and Hess, p. 2.

14. J. Lipman-Blumen, *Gender Roles and Power* (Englewood Cliffs, NJ: Prentice Hall, 1984), pp. 159–160.

15. For reviews of women's changing participation in the paid labor force, see Blau; Hunter College Women's Studies Collective, pp. 479–530; Lipman-Blumen, pp. 155–175; Sapiro, 1990, pp. 344–386.

16. Sapiro, 1994, p. 19.

17. U.S. Bureau of the Census, "Work and Family Patterns of American Women," *Current Population Reports,* P23-165 (Washington, D.C.: U.S. Government Printing Office, 1990).

18. Sapiro, 1990, pp. 308–343.

19. N. Chappell, "Aging and Social Care," in R. Binstock and L. George, eds., *Handbook of Aging and the Social Sciences* (San Diego, CA: Academic Press, 1990), pp. 438–454; A. Hochschild, *The Second Shift* (New York: Avon, 1989); N. Hooyman and J. Gonyea, *Feminist Perspectives on Family Care* (Thousand Oaks, CA: Sage, 1995); T. Sommers and L. Shields, *Women Take Care: The Consequences of Caregiving in Today's Society* (Gainesville, FL: Triad, 1987).

20. N. Hooyman and R. Ryan, "Women as Caregivers of the Elderly: Catch-22 Dilemmas," in J. Figueira-McDonough and R. Sarri, eds., *The Trapped Woman: Catch-22 in Deviance and Control* (Newbury Park, CA: Sage, 1987), pp. 143–171.

21. M. McGoldrick, N. Garcia-Preto, P. Hines, and E. Lee, "Ethnicity and Women," in M. McGoldrick, C. Anderson, and F. Walsh, eds., *Women in Families: A Framework for Family Therapy* (New York: W. W. Norton, 1989), pp. 169–199.

22. P. Collins, *Black Feminist Thought* (New York: Routledge, 1991); D. Wilkinson, "Afro-American Women and Their Families," *Marriage and Family Review* 7 (Fall/Winter 1984), pp. 125–142.

23. H. Amaro and N. Russo, eds., *Psychology of Women Quarterly: Special Issue on Hispanic Women and Mental Health* 11 (December 1987); M. Vasquez, "Power and Status of the Chicana: A Social-Psychological Perspective," in J. Martinez and R. Mendoza, eds., *Chicano Psychology* (New York: Academic Press, 1984), pp. 269–287.

24. A. Ryan, "Asian-American Women: A Historical and Cultural Perspective," in Weick and Vandiver, eds., *Women, Power, and Change* (Washington, D.C.: National Association of

Social Workers, 1981), pp. 78–88; J. Yung, ed., *Making Waves: An Anthology of Writings By and About Asian American Women* (Boston: Beacon, 1989).

25. E. Blanchard, "Observations on Social Work with American Indian Women," in Weick and Vandiver, pp. 96–103; T. LaFromboise, T. Heyle, and E. Ozer, "Changing and Diverse Roles of Women in American Indian Cultures," *Sex Roles* 22 (1990): 455–476.

26. E. Levy, "Lesbian Motherhood: Identity and Social Support," *Affilia*, 4 (1989): 40–53; F. Bozett, ed., *Gay and Lesbian Parents* (New York: Praeger, 1987); K. Weston, *Families We Choose* (New York: Columbia University Press, 1991).

27. R. Barnett and G. Baruch, "Social Roles, Gender, and Psychological Distress," in Barnett, Biener, and Baruch, pp. 122–143; J. Brumberg, *Fasting Girls: The Emergence of Anorexia as a Modern Disease* (Cambridge, MA: Harvard University Press, 1988); J. Marecek, "Engendering Disorder: The Social Context of Women's Mental Health," in M. Gibbs, J. Lachenmeyer, and J. Segal, eds., *Community Psychology and Mental Health* (New York: Gardner Press, 1992), pp. 277–294; Nolen-Hoeksema, pp. 77–104.

28. A. Conte, *Sexual Harassment in the Workplace: Law and Practice* (New York: John Wiley & Sons, 1990); B. Gutek, *Sex and the Workplace* (San Francisco, CA: Jossey-Bass, 1985).

29. D. Belle, "Inequality and Mental Health: Low Income and Minority Women," in L. Walker, ed., *Women and Mental Health Policy* (Beverly Hills, CA: Sage, 1984), pp. 135–150; P. Denny, "Women and Poverty: A Challenge to the Intellectual and Therapeutic Integrity of Feminist Therapy," *Women and Therapy* 5 (1986): 51–63; R. Lefkowitz and A. Withorn, eds., *For Crying Out Loud: Women and Poverty in the United States* (New York: Pilgrim Press, 1986).

30. C. Beck and B. Pearson, "Mental Health of Elderly Women," in J. Garner and S. Mercer, eds., *Women As They Age: Challenge, Opportunity, and Triumph* (New York: Haworth Press, 1989), pp. 175–193; D. Rodeheaver and N. Datan, "The Challenge of Double Jeopardy: Toward a Mental Health Agenda for Aging Women," *American Psychologist* 43 (1988): 648–654.

31. E. Almquist, "Race and Ethnicity in the Lives of Minority Women," in Freeman, pp. 423–453; O. Espin, "Psychological Impact of Migration on Latinas," *Psychology of Women Quarterly* 11 (December 1987): 489–503; C. Willie, P. Rieker, B. Kramer, and B. Brown, eds., *Mental Health, Racism, and Sexism* (Pittsburgh: University of Pittsburgh Press, 1995).

32. Boston Lesbian Psychologies Collective, eds., *Lesbian Psychologies* (Chicago: University of Illinois Press, 1987); D. Clunis and G. Green, *Lesbian Couples* (Seattle, WA: Seal Press, 1988); P. Falk, "Lesbian Mothers: Psychosocial Assumptions in Family Law," *American Psychologist* 44 (1989): 941–947.

33. M. Gordon and S. Riger, *The Female Fear* (New York: Free Press, 1989); R. Janoff-Bulman and I. Frieze, "The Role of Gender in Reactions to Criminal Victimization," in Barnett, Biener, and Baruch, pp. 159–184; R. Kluft, *Childhood Antecedents of Multiple Personality* (Washington, D.C.: American Psychiatric Press, 1985); C. Sheffield, "Sexual Terrorism: The Social Control of Women," in B. Hess and M. Ferree, eds., *Analyzing Gender: A Handbook of Social Science Research* (Newbury Park, CA: Sage, 1987), pp. 171–189.

34. For detailed discussions of social work practice with women, see M. Bricker-Jenkins, N. Hooyman, and N. Gottlieb, eds., *Feminist Social Work Practice in Clinical Settings* (Newbury Park, CA: Sage, 1991); D. Burden and N. Gottlieb, eds., *The Woman Client: Providing Human Services in a Changing World* (New York: Tavistock, 1987); L. Dominelli and E. McLeod, *Feminist Social Work* (New York: New York University Press, 1989); J. Hanmer and D. Statham, *Women and Social Work: Toward a Woman-Centered Practice* (Chicago, IL: Lyceum Books, 1989); N. Van Den Bergh, ed., Feminist Practice in the 21st Century (Washington, D.C.: NASW Press, 1995); N. Van Den Bergh and L. Cooper, eds., *Feminist Visions for Social Work* (Silver Spring, MD: National Association of Social Workers, 1986).

35. S. Butler and C. Wintram, *Feminist Groupwork* (London: Sage, 1991); L. Walker, "Women's Groups are Different," in C. Brody, ed., *Women's Therapy Groups* (New York: Springer, 1987), pp. 3–12.

36. C. Courtois, *Healing the Incest Wound* (New York: W. W. Norton, 1988); J. Lee, ed., *Group Work with the Poor and Oppressed* (New York: Haworth Press, 1989); G. Nicarthy, K. Merriam, and S. Coffman, *Talking It Out: A Guide to Groups for Abused Women* (Seattle, WA: Seal Press, 1984); B. Reed and C. Garvin, eds., *Social Work with Groups: Special Issue on Groupwork with Women/Groupwork with Men: An Overview of Gender Issues in Social Groupwork Practice* 6 (Fall/Winter 1983); J. Sprei, "Group Treatment of Adult Women Incest Survivors," in C. Brody, ed., *Women's Therapy Groups: Paradigms of Feminist Treatment* (New York: Springer, 1987), pp. 198–216.

37. M. Bograd, "A Feminist Examination of Family Therapy: What Is Women's Place?" in D. Howard, ed., *The Dynamics of Feminist Therapy* (New York: Haworth, 1986), pp. 95–106; L. Braverman, ed., *A Guide to Feminist Family Therapy* (New York: Harrington Park Press, 1988); R. Hare-Mustin, "A Feminist Approach to Family Therapy," in E. Howell and M. Bayes, eds., *Women and Mental Health* (New York: Basic Books, 1981), pp. 553–571.

38. M. Klein, "Feminist Concepts of Therapy Outcome," *Psychotherapy: Theory, Research and Practice* 13 (Spring 1976): 89–95.

39. R. Brandwein, "Toward Androgyny in Community and Organizational Practice," in Weick and Vandiver, pp. 158–170; C. Ellsworth, N. Hooyman, R. Ruff, S. Stam, and J. Tucker, "Toward a Feminist Model of Planning For and With Women," in Weick and Vandiver, pp. 146–157; M. Weil, "Women, Community, and Organizing," in Van Den Bergh and Cooper, pp. 187–210.

40. A. Bookman and S. Morgen, eds., *Women and the Politics of Empowerment* (Philadelphia: Temple University Press, 1988); S. Reinharz, "Women as Competent Community Builders: The Other Side of the Coin," in A. Rickel, M. Gerrard, and I. Iscoe, eds., *Social and Psychological Problems of Women: Prevention and Crisis Intervention* (New York: Hemisphere Publishing, 1984), pp. 19–43.

41. R. Brandwein, "Women and Community Organization," in Burden and Gottlieb, pp. 111–125.

42. R. Brandwein, "Women in Macro Practice," in A. Minahan, ed., *Encyclopedia of Social Work,* 18th Edition, Vol. 2 (Silver Spring, MD: National Association of Social Workers, 1987), pp. 881–892; N. Hooyman, "Supporting Practice in Large-Scale

Bureaucracies," in Bricker-Jenkins, Hooyman, and Gottlieb, pp. 251–270; M. Weil, "Women in Administration: Curriculum and Strategies," in Burden and Gottlieb, pp. 92–110.

43. G. Goldberg and E. Kremen, "The Feminization of Poverty: Only in America?" *Social Policy* (Spring 1987): 3–14.

CHAPTER 12

Social Work Practice with Lesbian, Gay, and Bisexual People

George A. Appleby and Jeane W. Anastas*

*Dr. George A. Appleby is Professor of Social Work, School of Social Work, Southern Connecticut State University, and Dr. Jeane W. Anastas is Associate Dean, School of Social Work, New York University.

Prefatory Comment

A social work intern came to realize that a significant number of her clients were lesbian or gay youth who had been kicked out of their homes or who had run away because of parental reactions to their gayness. As she got to know each individual, she was struck by the recurring themes of coming painfully to the recognition of their sexual orientation, family rejection, hostility of peers and friends, verbal and physical abuse, and the resulting confused, angry, and fearful feelings that increased their self-doubt. Homophobia and discrimination often give rise to "internalized oppression," which creates problems with self-esteem and self-image for lesbians, gays, and bisexuals.

Our intern, like all good social workers, attempted to formulate an assessment and intervention plan based on her knowledge of the clients' life situations. Unfortunately, she was unable to recall any required readings related to this topic, nor did she remember an in-depth discussion about lesbians or gays in her social work classes. She did recollect, however, that once someone in class said that "faggots and dykes" should not be allowed to work with children because what they did was sinful and would have a bad influence on the development of those in their care. The professor did not say much, and the subject was dropped. She thought this seemed consistent with a NASW workshop she had attended where the presenter confirmed the high level of homophobia among social work students and faculty.[1]

However, this intern knew that the NASW Code of Ethics encouraged her to further the cause of social justice by promoting and defending the rights of persons suffering injustice and oppression. Gays and lesbians certainly met this requirement. She recalled that the Code was translated into NASW policy statements that prescribed the practice behavior of members; thus social workers are enjoined to view discrimination and prejudice directed against any minority as adverse to the mental health of the affected minority as well as a detriment to society. Furthermore, social workers are urged to work to combat discriminatory employment practices and any other form of discrimination that imposes something less than equal status on bisexual, gay, or lesbian individuals. NASW, she recalled, affirmed the right of all persons to define and express their own sexuality. All persons are to be encouraged to develop their individual potential to the fullest extent possible.

Our budding Jane Addams, while highly motivated to act ethically and to give the most effective help, had no idea where to start. She, after some thought, decided to ask her supervisor for assistance. Her supervisor had received her MSW over a decade ago and knew little herself. She suggested that the intern do a literature review on this topic and that she start with reading this text.

Current Demographics

An understanding of the lesbian, gay, and bisexual population in the United States must begin with a presentation of the current demographic picture. There is a significant gap in our knowledge because scholars, like the general public, have been affected by the societal myths and taboos surrounding homosexuality. Thus, they have often avoided the objective analysis of this aspect of human functioning entirely. When the topic has been studied at all, its science has often been limited by moral and social doctrines, seldom debated, about the ways humans ought to behave.[2] Twenty years ago public discussion of homosexuality was minimal, very little research existed, and available studies were usually limited to the investigation of individuals who sought treatment or to change their sexual orientation; thus, they were not helpful in understanding the vast majority of homosexuals, who are not in treatment.[3] Even today, a process of selective attention in the study of gays, lesbians, and bisexuals continues to limit our knowledge.[4]

Because oppression has resulted in the invisibility of gays and lesbians as a whole until recently, and because it is hard to define and describe an invisible population, much of the data we have about the homosexual population today are inferred from small survey research and ethnographic studies. Developing representative samples of lesbian, gay, and bisexual populations for research is notoriously difficult.[5] The data we do have suggest, however, that there is greater similarity than difference between gay and straight people.

DEFINING HOMOSEXUALITY

Because of the myths and lack of knowledge that have surrounded this topic, it is especially important that we discuss who is and who is not lesbian, gay, or bisexual. A young Ph.D. candidate has a crush on her professor. She manufactures numerous ways to be near her. Is she a lesbian? An army captain is discharged from the service for having sexual relations with an enlisted man. Is he gay? Two adolescent boys masturbate one another to orgasm. Are they homosexual? While having sexual intercourse with her husband, a woman frequently fantasizes about having sexual relations with other women. She has never had actual sexual contact with another woman. What is her sexual orientation? Because human sexuality occurs on a spectrum of feelings, ideas, and behavior, the answers to these questions are not so easy.

Categorization can lead to understanding—or to stereotyping. For example, if a woman is labeled a lesbian, it may be assumed that she will date women, be involved in many tempestuous short-term relationships, wear pants, play sports, raise dogs, and drive a truck. Likewise, if a person is a gay male, then he may be assumed to be very promiscuous, be overly concerned about his body and youth, obsess about fashion and style, frequently flick his wrists, and become a hairdresser or nurse. These are common stereotypes, but in reality attributes such as these (even if true) are seldom so predictable or clear.

Despite these dangers, the task of understanding any phenomenon starts with naming and defining. Shively and DeCecco help to clarify the controversy over who is and who is not bisexual, gay, or lesbian. They warn that various behaviors and lifestyles have been confused with sexual orientation. They distinguish among social sex role (the way society expects you to act according to your sex), gender identity (whether you consider yourself female or male), and gender role (whether you act so as to be taken as a male or female).[6] Each of these often confuses the issue of being gay or lesbian.

Moses and Hawkins suggest we view sexual orientation as an individual's preference for partners of the same sex, opposite sex, or both sexes for sexual and affectional relations. The desire to share affection or become life partners plays a significant role, as does sexual attraction, in the determination of sexual orientation.[7] A lesbian or a gay male, then, is one who is attracted primarily to someone of the same sex to satisfy sexual, sexual fantasy, and affectional needs. Those oriented toward both sexes would be termed bisexual.

This, then, is our definition. Unlike the more traditional definitions, three aspects are included: (1) sexual behavior; (2) sexual fantasy; and (3) affectional preference. This definition is compatible with most contemporary thinkers.[8]

The term *lifestyle* has been confused with the definition of homosexuality. The term is used more appropriately to describe certain forms of lesbian, gay, and bisexual social and cultural expression, not fundamental sexual orientation. However, Friedman adds personal identity and social role to the dimensions of homosexuality discussed above, and notes that the various parts of the definition may be either congruent or incongruent in any one individual.[9]

Also problematic is the term *sexual preference,* widely used until recently. Research findings indicate that homosexual feelings are a basic part of the individual's psyche rather than something that is consciously chosen. Thus, the more appropriate term is *sexual orientation.*

Terminology has been changing along with definitions. The term *homosexual,* once the most common, is now sometimes rejected because it denotes a category first imposed from a medically oriented, heterosexual perspective. *Gay* is now the most common popular term for people who define themselves as homosexual, in contrast to the term *straight,* used to describe heterosexuals. While *gay* is used to describe both men and women, many homosexual women prefer to call themselves *lesbians.* Young people are increasingly using the term "queer." These newer terms reflect the stance that lesbians and gay men will no longer allow the heterosexual majority to name and define them.[10]

Given the complexities of terminology and definition just described, it is essential to be sensitive to language, culture, and geography. Ask clients or colleagues what they mean when you are uncertain of how homosexuality is being defined or of how they are defining themselves. Such a question will be interpreted more often as a demonstration of respect and concern for feelings than as ignorance.

POPULATION CHARACTERISTICS

Lesbians, gays, and bisexuals live in every area of the United States, but they appear to be found in larger numbers in urban areas where there are anonymity and relative tolerance for diversity. They are represented in all occupations and socioeconomic groups. They are white, African American, Hispanic, Asian, and American Indian. They probably reflect the same demographic proportions as found in the general population; impressionistic data, however, point to higher levels of education and disposable income than are found in the general population.

Although there are limits to our knowledge base, failure to acknowledge the variety of lesbians', gays', and bisexuals' social situations only adds to the marginalization of their lives. Gonsiorek and Weinrich reported that in 1991 homosexuals as a group are the first, second, or third most numerous minority in the United States—depending on which variation of the estimate is used.[11] The broad variation of affectional orientation and the prevalence of homosexual behaviors in the population have been well documented. It is estimated and widely believed that at least 10 percent of the U.S. population is lesbian or gay.[12]

In contrast, the National Opinion Research Center at the University of Chicago reported that approximately 5 percent of the male population and approximately 4 percent of the female population claimed to have had sex with a same-sex partner since the age of eighteen while almost 8 percent reported experiencing attraction to persons of their own sex. However, when respondents were asked to self-identify as either heterosexual, homosexual, or bisexual, only about 3 percent of the males and less than 2 percent of the females stated homosexual. The same study reported a homosexual or bisexual identity of 9.2 percent for men and 2.6 percent for women among residents of the twelve largest American cities.[13] Thus, prevalence estimates differ substantially depending on whether the questions are related to sexual conduct, sexual orientation, enduring attraction, or sexual identity. If we were to consider the typical size of an individual's network of family, friends, work colleagues, and others, these data suggest that most have a close relationship with someone who is lesbian, gay, or bisexual, whether or not they are aware of it.

Whatever the true numbers, it is important to recognize that there are a breadth of lifestyles and a number of subpopulations within the group, many of which overlap. Any community will have different social networks based on age, class, ethnicity, language, race, sex, and special interests. Hidalgo warns that class differences and racism do divide lesbian, gay, and bisexual communities.[14] Some observers suggest, however, that there is a greater commitment to democratic structures and an integration of subgroups than is commonly seen in heterosexual communities. This may be true because the need for affiliation is met in a group of similarly oriented people who share the common experience of oppression.

However, racial and ethnic factors do have an impact on associations. African American and Hispanic gays, for both economic and cultural reasons, often maintain residence with or near their families, unlike many white gays, who establish homes away from relatives, often in one of the larger urban areas. This has an impact on the amount and intensity of association with other gays. Smith suggests that is another factor in determining the level of association of African Americans with the gay community: "Gay whites are people who identify first as being gay and who usually live outside the closet in predominantly White gay communities. . . . Black gays, on the other hand, view our racial heritage as primary and frequently live 'bisexual front lives' within Black neighborhoods."[15] While there are no empirical data on the subject, the observation has been made that identification is equally important in other racial and ethnic groups.

Carballo-Dieguez notes that religion and folk beliefs strongly influence the Hispanic culture. Conservative and traditional values are barriers to an open gay lifestyle.[16] Of the various religions, fundamentalists and Baptists seem likely to condemn homosexuality, and African Americans, as Mays and Cochran point out, hold membership predominantly in these denominations.[17] Newby would concur with the importance of social structure, values, and religion on the public expression of sexual orientation in the African American community and proposes that this may explain the higher rate of bisexuality and lower percentage of gay exclusivity than is found among whites.[18] Thus, African American and Latino gays are a double minority, often stigmatized by being in both the minority of color and being gay, while lesbians of color are in "triple jeopardy."

Ecosystems Framework

Social work addresses the interaction between the person and the environment. The goal of practice is to enhance and restore the psychosocial functioning of persons, or to change the oppressive or destructive social conditions that negatively affect the interaction between persons and their environments. The ecosystems model of practice, the framework of this text, consists of five interconnected domains or levels: (1) historical; (2) environmental–structural; (3) cultural; (4) family; and (5) individual. The lives and social conditions of lesbians, gay men, and bisexuals are now assessed in relation to each of these domains.

HISTORICAL FACTORS

The ecosystems model is concerned with both positive and noxious factors in the historical experience of members of the population of interest. The history of minority group oppression and exploitation has already been noted. It has taken form in religion, culture, law, and social sanction. American society, strongly influenced by interpretations of Judaic and Christian moral codes, is one of the most homophobic. While change is in fact taking place in each of these areas, not one of these social structures could be characterized as nurturing. At best, they are benign.

The Stonewall "riot" in 1969, in which a group of gays resisted and protested against police harassment and brutality at a gay bar in New York, is usually regarded as the birth of the Gay Liberation Movement. Since that time, lesbian, gay, and bisexual individuals have become increasingly visible in our society. They are fighting for equal protection under our laws and for access to the same benefits afforded heterosexuals.

Religious groups have been in the forefront of opposition to homosexuality. However, not all religions oppose it. Biblical interpretations vary widely, with advocates of both sides quoting scriptures as their defense. Presently, each of the major Judaic and Christian denominations has begun to recognize the spiritual and civil rights needs of their lesbian, gay, and bisexual members. The Metropolitan Community Church, a nondenominational group founded to minister to homosexuals, has over one hundred member churches throughout the country.

While some members of the gay community choose to remain invisible in an attempt to isolate themselves from the effects of oppression, others have committed themselves to action and self-realization. Many lesbians and gays recognized the community's potential political clout in the 1960s, as they became aware of their size as a minority group and their significance as a voting bloc. This led to the enormous growth of gay political organizations on local and national levels in the 1970s and 1980s. Currently, lesbian, gay, and bisexual civil rights issues, including partnership rights, foster-parenting protections, custody rights, and access to all available health care and treatment options, especially in relation to the AIDS epidemic, are being addressed at both the state and local levels. For example, gay activists have helped to bring about a general reassessment of federal ethical guidelines in experimental medical treatment and research in order to bring potentially life-saving treatments to patients sooner than in the past. The visibility and influence of the lesbian, gay, and bisexual minority will continue to grow.

ENVIRONMENTAL–STRUCTURAL FACTORS

Heterosexism, homophobia, and "homohatred" are probably the most relevant environmental or structural issues affecting lesbian, gay, and bisexual persons, and this chapter has already described some of the ways in which homophobia has been institutionalized as a barrier in this society. *Heterosexism* is defined as *the belief that heterosexuality is or should be the only acceptable sexual orientation.* Blumenfeld suggests that it is heterosexism that results in prejudice, discrimination, harassment, and acts of violence and is encouraged by fear and hatred.[19] These three concepts help to understand the wide range impact of giving cultural precedence to heterosexuality. Compounded with sexism and racism, they have generated additional barriers to the healthy development and well-being of lesbian, gay, and bisexual persons.

The impact of environmental–structural factors gives a specific social form to this population. Paul and Weinrich identified three such factors: social invisibility, social diversity, and social and personal differentiation.[20] The great majority of homosexuals, including openly gay men and lesbians, are not easily identifiable. There are as many kinds of gays as there are kinds of straights.[21] Finally, the ways in which people adapt to having a gay or lesbian orientation vary according to the relative tolerance or hostility of the immediate social environment.

Social invisibility makes it possible for the general public to be ignorant of diversity as it really exists. One result has been widely held inaccurate stereotypes. An example would be the assumed connection between male heterosexuality and involvement in sports. Garner and Smith reported significantly higher rates of homosexual activity in several samples of athletes than had been previously found.[22] The current passion among some gay men for bodybuilding and athletic club membership also serves to challenge this stereotype.

Gays and lesbians have always been the victims of homicides, gay bashing, and extortion because of religious sanctions and legal discrimination. The social acceptance of homophobia, homohatred, racism, and sexism in our society serves only to exacerbate prejudice. And the incidence of hate, violence, and harassment have increased significantly as a result of the AIDS epidemic.[23] This oppression has had a significant impact on the health and mental health status of lesbians and gay men.[24] High rates of suicide, drug abuse, and alcoholism have been reported, as well as a range of psychosomatic illnesses.

The National Lesbian Health Care Survey,[25] polling almost 2,000 lesbians, reported that the most common health problem experienced was depression or sadness. Other stress-related illnesses (ulcers and weight problems) were reported by significant percentages. More than half the sample reported that they had been too nervous to cope with ordinary responsibilities sometime during the year. Twenty-one percent had suicidal thoughts, and 18 percent had actually made a suicide attempt. Three-fourths of those surveyed were in counseling. The mental health symptoms reported appear similar to those of other high-stress groups.

CULTURE

Popular images often suggest that gay and lesbian people are involved with a specific subculture or life-style. As a result, gays and lesbians may be thought to be readily identifiable by styles of dress or behavior, or to be invested only in activities or institutions designated as exclusively gay and/or lesbian. However, as a stigmatized group, lesbians and gays are in fact an invisible minority, only some of whom choose to make themselves and their interests visible individually and collectively in the gay and/or lesbian community and subculture.

Access to such gay- or lesbian-identified institutions and organizations is often very important for individuals who have affirmed, are exploring, or are consolidating a gay or lesbian identity. People who live in rural or small communities far removed from these centers of activity may sometimes be disadvantaged in making connections with others like themselves, in developing ways to receive affirmation for significant parts of their lives, or in finding help or support in coping with homophobia.

Contact with the gay/lesbian subculture, however, will quickly dispel any notion that gay and lesbian people are similar to each other in appearance or life-style beyond the sexual orientation that they share. Diversity within the identifiable lesbian, gay, and bisexual community is as great as among heterosexuals as a group. As in any other social group, these differences can be a source of tension, which may disappoint those looking to "the community" for an ideal way of life to emulate; or for a conflict-free environment as they work on developing their own identities or seek refuge from the discrimination from the community at large. The relationship between the individual and the community can thus be either a mutually enhancing or a conflicted one. Many lesbians and gays, however, draw essential support and affirmation from the subculture.

In addition, many gay and lesbian people do not participate in the identifiable gay and lesbian subculture even when it is available to them. Their political, social, and recreational pursuits may not be related to their sexual orientation at all, and their social and emotional supports may come exclusively from friends and/or family. Sometimes this choice may stem from a wish to remain private or "closeted" (or selectively "out") in their sexual orientation out of fear; at other times it may result from a choice to give other dimensions of their lives and identity priority. Thus, the degree of an individual's involvement with the gay or lesbian subculture is itself a dimension of diversity among lesbians and gays.

The concept of *biculturality* has recently been used to describe the socialization processes that lesbians and gays undergo.[26] Acceptance of a gay or lesbian identity means adopting new norms and values and being rejected by and/or rejecting old standards. Dating and coupling, definitions of family, celebrations and ritual participation, both secular and religious, and political and social interests are all affected by sexual orientation. For lesbians and gay men of ethnic- and racial-minority background, the cultural issues are even more complex.

This concept of a homosexual culture is viewed as controversial by some, because intergenerational transmission of this culture and socialization into it does not ordinarily take place in the family of origin, as it does in cultures as defined in other contexts. In fact, gay and lesbian individuals are usually first socialized into majority, heterosexual culture. However, applying the concept of culture to gay and lesbian ways of life highlights the inclusiveness of a lesbian or gay identity, the shared experiences of gay and lesbian people over time and across societies, and the diversity of gays and lesbians on other dimensions such as race, class, and gender. The related notion of biculturality points out that gays and lesbians live to differing degrees in multiple worlds, with the attendant opportunities and stresses of negotiation and boundary maintenance.[27]

FAMILY FACTORS

Lesbians and gay men have been categorized by society as people without families, uninterested in creating families, and threatening to family life. Despite this perception, the fact is that at least 2 million lesbians and gay men are parents of minor children.[28] Large numbers of the gay, lesbian, and bisexual population live in long-term, committed, coupled relationships.[29] Achtenberg notes that discriminatory treatment, misunderstanding, and prejudices often pose social and legal barriers to the recognition and protection of families created by lesbians and gay men.[30]

Many gays and lesbians credit their family of origin as the source of their emotional support and strength as well as their positive belief and value system. Yet for other gays and lesbians, the family is a source of interpersonal tension and conflict, hardly the basis for self-acceptance or a healthy adjustment to a hostile society. Many gays credit their "chosen family"—family of design consisting of lover and friends—as the buffer that has had the greatest impact on their adaptation.

The gay, lesbian, or bisexual person, his or her parents, and the spouse and their children are all confronted daily with stereotyping and social rejection. The images of homosexuality are all negative: the "sinner," the "drag queen," the "child molester," the "diesel dyke." By the time one reaches adulthood, the association (not necessarily conscious) between homosexuality and the stereotype is formed. These dehumanizing stereotypes are perpetuated by the peer group, the mass media, and cultural tradition. The individual may feel pressure to establish distance from homosexuality. Few people, then, are socially prepared to deal with this issue when it arises.

"Passing" is a second consequence of stigma. Anyone who does not fit the stereotype can "pass," while those who meet the stereotyped expectations become visible. An individual may come to recognize his or her special sexual orientation without realistic models of what this means. The reaction may be, "I'm the only person in the world like this"; or "I'm not like them, thank God." Parents, other family members, and friends are likely to avoid or deny disclosure when their loved one does not fit the stereotype. Gay, lesbian, and bisexual youths are reared in heterosexual families, peer groups, and educational institutions. Thus, these youths grow up learning the same stereotypes and negative judgments as their straight peers, threatening the sense of self. Because "passing" is so pervasive, they are deprived of positive role models of the preparation for dealing with their sexual orientation. Sustaining self-esteem and a sense of identity becomes problematic at best.

Rejection is the third consequence of stigma, which produces distancing between those with the stigma and those without. Disclosure can become a critical issue within the family. The gay or lesbian child may lose the sense of authenticity characteristic of family relationships if he or she keeps the secret, or face rejection if he or she seeks understanding and emotional support by disclosing his or her sexual orientation. This potential alienation from the family is one way in which the homosexual minority is different from other minority groups, who generally can count on support within the family in the face of stress from the outside world. This same dynamic will be true with friends and work colleagues. Bell, Weinberg, and Hammersmith note that secrecy brings about a different sort of distancing, offering the example of a gay person who appears outwardly popular and well liked by the group yet feels alienated and isolated.[31]

The development of a subculture, a separate space that allows a sense of community and naturalness, is the fourth consequence of stigma. The subculture may be an opportunity to develop a special kinship with fellow victims of stigma. The stronger the disapproval by the majority culture, the more attractive a subculture as a source of mutual support.

The final consequence is that of the self-fulfilling prophecy or secondary deviance. This means that features of the stereotype may be embraced in protest or defiance or for lack of support for more normative styles of life. "Camp" and "leather" are stereotypic styles reflecting theatrical and humorous responses to society's arbitrary distinctions between masculine and feminine cultures. This poking of fun at gender roles by flouting them is often seen by nongays as confirmation of their worst stereotypic fears.

FORMING FAMILIES: MYTHS AND REALITIES. Numerous studies have been made of children being reared by lesbians to determine what effects on development there may be. Because alternative insemination and access to adoption by gays are relatively new phenomena, the studies to date have generally compared children of divorced lesbian mothers to those of divorced women who are not lesbians. Taken together, the studies have consistently shown that gay men and lesbians who parent do not differ in child rearing practices or lifestyle from other parents and that the children of lesbian mothers and gay men have no more problems in adjustment or development than do others.[32] There is no evidence of gender-role confusion or higher rates of gay or lesbian orientation among them, as had initially been hypothesized. In fact, there is some evidence that children of lesbians have a greater appreciation for diversity of all kinds and value tolerance more highly than others, having seen first-hand the toll that prejudice like homophobia can take.

The concern that a child who grows up with a homosexual parent will develop a gay orientation appears to be a widely held myth. The assumption that children develop their sexual orientation by emulating their parents is false. Remember that the vast majority of lesbians, gays, and bisexuals were raised by heterosexual parents.[33]

Another myth is that children who grow up with a gay or lesbian parent are at risk of molestation or abuse by either the parent or the parent's friends. However, research on the sexual abuse of children shows that the offenders are, in disproportionate numbers, heterosexual men.[34] It is also a common assumption that children in the custody of a lesbian or gay parent will be harmed by social stigma, but there are no clinical reports or research of stigma or unusual emotional problems in these children.[35] The practitioner must also realize that the coping and adaptational qualities of gay people in families are also tempered by economics, ethnicity, race, and class identity.

INDIVIDUAL FACTORS

The study of why people become gay or lesbian usually starts with an exhaustive review of biological theories focusing on genetic and hormonal factors and on psychoanalytic and behavioral theories addressing pathology and dysfunction. The conclusions of these studies are seldom supported by the data presented. Thus, the attempt to identify etiological factors has a long history, but with close inspection one must conclude that no specific genetic, intrapsychic, or interpersonal causative factors can be generalized to the lesbian, gay, and bisexual population.[36] However, there is knowledge about individual development that has value for practice intervention.

One way to improve our understanding or our definitions of sexual orientation is to correct the myths and inaccuracies surrounding homosexuality. One myth, which represents the popular version of an outmoded psychoanalytic explanation of homosexuality, is that male homosexuality represents a fear or hatred of women. (The reverse is also sometimes said of lesbian women.) This myth has led to ineffective treatment based on the assumption that gay men can be converted to heterosexuality simply by having sexual experiences with women. This simplistic view is contradicted by the large proportion of gay men who have had or continue to have heterosexual experiences but retain a positive gay identity.

Another myth is that gay people are compulsively sexual. The Kinsey Institute's estimates of gay sexual activity are probably overstated. Like straights, most gays spend most of their time doing things other than looking for sex or having it. Since 1981, the AIDS epidemic has struck a large number of gay and bisexual men. The widespread awareness in the gay community that the virus believed to cause AIDS is transmitted through unprotected sex (i.e., without condoms) has led to significant changes in sexual practices and thus a dramatic reduction in sexually transmitted disease and the rate of AIDS infection among gay men.

Finally, while lesbians and gay men may often be accused of flaunting their sexuality, in fact, most conceal their sexual orientation at least part of the time. Stigma and the consequences of discrimination in many areas of daily living are convincing reasons for concealment.[37] Berger suggests that because lesbians and gay men are generally indistinguishable from other men and women, public attitudes are formed on the basis of those who are most open about their sexual orientation.[38] "Straight" heterosexuals apply a double standard to same-sex and opposite-sex behavior, in that public displays of affection between a man and a woman are taken for granted while even holding hands in public is considered "flaunting" when it occurs between two women or two men.

IDENTITY FORMATION. Sexual orientation may change over time. A woman who is primarily homosexual in early adulthood may become more heterosexual in later life or vice versa. In his study of older gay men, Berger found that it is not uncommon for a man with an essentially heterosexual orientation in early adulthood to develop predominantly homosexual interests in middle age.[39] These observations lead us to the view that homosexuality is an identity formation process occurring over time. This formulation has much promise for social work assessment and intervention.

Berger proposed a model wherein homosexual identity results when a person completes three tasks that are independent of one another. The first in this process is the sexual encounter; that is, physical contact of a sexual nature with someone of the same sex. Second is the social reaction; that is, the process of labeling the individual by others as homosexual. The last component in this model is the identity task; that is, the individual experiences identity confusion (the discomfort felt between a same-sex experience and a heterosexual self-image) and works to come to terms with this in some way.[40]

Viewing lesbian, gay, or bisexual orientation as the result of an identity-formation process has important implications for social work intervention. First of all, and most important, there is no empirical justification for the belief that homosexuality, in and of itself, is a psychiatric illness or a result of poor psychological adjustment. Practitioners who continue to advocate illness models based on "conversion therapies" are ignorant, irresponsible, or both.[41]

SOCIAL STRESS AND SOCIAL SUPPORTS.   Like Berger, other theorists have adopted an interactionist perspective to examine the intricate linkage between social life and personal experience. Human beings cannot escape the influence of social position and social expectation on their development and self-perception. Bradford and Ryan note that "those who are discriminated against or who expect to face discrimination if their 'condition' were to become known are different from those who do not occupy stigmatized or 'deviant' social positions. The connection between living on the margins of society and the impact of this upon daily life and an adequate sense of psychosocial security" is yet to be fully documented. However, we do know that lesbians and gay men always live with this tension.[42]

This stress and lack of support—rather than stresses related to sexual orientation—may result in higher rates of alcoholism among lesbians, gays, and bisexuals. Gay bars are one of the few public places where gay men and lesbians can meet to socialize. Drinking can also provide emotional insulation from homophobic or racist attitudes.[43] Anderson and Henderson estimate that one-third of lesbians are alcoholics. Legal, health, and social service agencies, often insensitive to lesbian, gay, and bisexual persons, have tended to focus on sexual orientation as the cause of this phenomenon, despite evidence that they do not differ in psychosocial functioning from heterosexuals. Lesbians of color, like their male counterparts, have a higher incidence of alcoholism than straights.[44]

Brooks emphasizes the importance of social support networks for lesbians and gay men. These are relationships with significant others, developed as a result of sharing a history of common experience through which people create environments of caring and support for each other.[45] While recognizing that the importance of supportive interactions among people is not new, Bradford notes that research evidence of social supports helping people in health crises is recent. Maintenance of good health is related to the number of people in a social network.[46] Alcalay adds that the number of contacts, the frequency and intensity of contacts, as well as the presence of family and friends within the network, are all related to health.[47] In other words, friends can be "good medicine."

Bradford and Ryan have synthesized the research related to social support and crisis in relation to lesbian health. They conclude that supports encourage preventive behavior, provide needed resources, increase a sense of personal control over one's environment, and reduce the social marginality of one's minority status. Supports are buffers against the distress of traumatic life events. Lesbians, gay men, and bisexuals without sufficient supports are especially vulnerable to commonplace stressors as well as the monumental stress related to minority status.[48] It is within the context of stress, social marginality, and minority status that the impact of a hostile, discriminatory environment should be understood. This approach to understanding developmental issues focuses our attention on life adaptations and thus is consistent with the ecosystems perspective.

Macro Practice with Lesbian, Gay, and Bisexual People

Germain and Gitterman, in their advancement of the ecological model, treated stress as a psychosocial condition "generated by discrepancies between needs and capacities, on the one hand, and environmental qualities on the other. It arises in three interrelated areas of living: life transitions, environmental pressures, and interpersonal processes."[49] The social work interventions related to support, empowerment, psychoeducation, consultation, case advocacy, and self-help seem appropriate for most clients while case management, individual, group, couple, and family therapy might be the preference of some gay, lesbian, and bisexual clients.

Oppression, power, heterosexism, and homophobia are the macro environmental context in which lesbians and gay men develop and function. These abstract social dynamics are experienced as nonnurturing social behaviors and as barriers to optimal social functioning, such as discrimination, prejudice, bias, and violence, and therefore are appropriate environmental or macro social change targets of social work intervention. Social workers should act to expand access, choices, and opportunities for all oppressed people. Community development, organizational change, staff training, coalition building, program and policy development, class advocacy, and social action are appropriate for change that will benefit lesbian, gay, and bisexual people as well.

Social workers should help gay and lesbian activists to organize their communities with the intent of developing educational and political strategies and of forming coalitions of advocacy groups, such as Human Rights Campaign, *class action social work* alliances with groups such as the American Civil Liberties Union, Lambda Legal Defense, and the National Gay and Lesbian Task Force. Goals are to advance civil rights legislation, to defeat efforts to limit civil rights, to advocate for programs to eliminate hate crimes and antigay violence, and to enhance education, treatment services, and research related to lesbians, gay men, and bisexuals. The intent is that homosexuals are entitled to Fourteenth Amendment equal rights, liberties, and privileges as are other citizens, such as housing, employment, public accommodation, inheritance and insurance, domestic partnership or marriage, child custody, adoption, foster care, and property rights.

The constitutional rights of privacy free from government regulation or intrusion and equal treatment before the law should be afforded to all lesbians, gay men, and bisexuals. This is basic to U.S. citizenship. Criminalization of homosexual acts is a violation of the right of individual privacy. Criminal statutes proscribing adult homosexual behavior create an environment of oppression arising from fear of prosecution and provide the means of blackmail. These statutes are most reprehensible when linked to enforcement by entrapment. Such laws perpetuate discrimination against homosexuals. Discrimination on the basis of homosexuality violates an individual's right of privacy and denies the person equal protection of the law.[50]

Achtenberg reminds us that to favor lesbian, gay, and bisexual rights or to support an end to discrimination must mean to deplore the ways in which society undermines the formation, preservation, and protection of the lesbian, gay, and bisexual family.[51] Gay rights must also include support for custody and visitation statutes that ensure strict neutrality with regard to the sexual orientation of the parent. Advocacy for adoption and foster parenting laws and administrative practices that are strictly neutral are needed. Joint adoptions by same-sex couples should be permitted when it is in a child's best interests and when the parent–child relationship has been cemented. Laws permitting delegation of personal and health care duties to nonrelatives should be created, as well as provision for fair determination of the guardian or conservator for an ill person. The same sentiment should inform the laws of interstate succession. Equity, not sexual orientation or marital status, should become the value undergirding the distribution of work-related and governmental benefits.

A nonjudgmental attitude toward sexual orientation allows social workers to offer optimal support and services, thus empowering lesbian, gay, and bisexual people through all phases of the coming out process and beyond. The outcome of interpersonal intervention, however, is also contingent on the agency's policies and procedures. Social workers must first focus on the level of staff knowledge and commitment before introducing gay-affirming programs. Agency policies and procedures should address the needs of lesbian, gay, and bisexual clients and staff.

Legislation embodying the above principles should be the goal of profession. Passage of such legislation on state or national levels requires building coalitions of like-minded civil rights advocacy groups and extensive public education. Social workers are skilled in problem identification and resolution through organization building and strategy development. These are the needed macro skills if environments are to be supportive of positive gay identity development and no longer barriers to healthful functioning and psychosocial adaptation.

Micro Practice with Lesbian, Gay, and Bisexual People

Failure to consider that a client may be lesbian, gay, or bisexual is the most common mistake made by workers in situations like the ones described above. Despite stereotypes, most lesbian, gay, and bisexual clients are not visually identifiable as such, and many may not identify themselves as lesbian, gay, or bisexual at first, especially when the problem for which they are seeking assistance may not have much to do with sexual orientation.[52] However, the social worker is unlikely to get a full enough picture of the client's situation in order to be helpful without keeping an open mind to the possibility of gender identity issues.

Effective work with lesbians and gay men requires what Hall has termed a dual focus: "The practitioner must be able to see the ways in which the client's presenting problem is both affected by and separate from her sexual orientation."[53] Damage to self-esteem resulting from oppression and stigmatization must always be considered, but at the same time the client probably occupies roles, works on developmental tasks, and experiences feelings in which being lesbian, gay, or bisexual is incidental. For example, the teenage prostitutes our intern met through her work at the AIDS service organization must deal with the rejection they experienced from families because they were gay or lesbian. At the same time, these teens have the same developmental needs for the support and approval of adults and peers that others do and would be seeking a way to separate and differentiate themselves from their families even if rejection based on their sexual orientation had not occurred. Thus, a worker counseling any of them might expect to hear both a longing for the love and approval of their parents, despite their rejecting behavior, and a simultaneous longing to be completely free of parental restraint or control.

Whether or not the client seeks help about an issue involving sexual orientation or during the "coming out" process, the worker's feelings, attitudes, and level of comfort with a lesbian, gay, or bisexual life-style or orientation must be examined; they require self-exploration over time.[54] It is the homophobia gay and lesbian individuals may encounter that is likely to be a problem, not the homosexuality itself. Rather than seeking causes or explanations for homosexuality, this perspective leads the social worker to explore and help the client to overcome the obstacles, internalized or external, that may stand in the way of healthy functioning as a lesbian, gay, or bisexual person.

Psychological and psychoanalytic theory have given more attention to male than female homosexuality over the years.[55] From a contemporary psychoanalytic standpoint, there are many varieties of both heterosexual and homosexual functioning, and homosexual or heterosexual object choices are not viewed in themselves as healthy or unhealthy. Nevertheless, studies suggest that negative attitudes toward homosexuality and homosexual clients persist among some social workers and social work students.[56] Such attitudes create barriers that keep lesbian, gay, and bisexual persons from seeking or receiving effective mental health services in times of need.

When homosexuality was viewed as pathological, it was assumed that some critical experiences early in life produced an outcome, same-gender object choice, which was thought to be immutable without psychological treatment. Not only has it proven very difficult to identify any experiential or developmental "causes" or antecedents of homosexuality with any confidence,[57] but the treatment of homosexuals in psychological distress was usually distorted to mean treatment of the homosexuality itself.[58]

On the one hand, adult developmental theory now tells us that the personality and life course is not "cast in stone" in childhood. Additionally, close study of the sexual practices of both heterosexual and homosexual people and attention to the life histories of lesbian, gay, and bisexual people suggest that sexual practices and self-identification may change over time. On the other hand, to self-identified lesbian, gay, or bisexual individuals the homosexual identity may feel immutable, essential, and core to their sense of themselves as persons. Psychological treatment is thus focused on addressing whatever distress a self-identified lesbian, gay, or bisexual person may be experiencing, rather than on the sexual orientation itself.[59]

Contemporary theory emerging from research and clinical work with lesbians, gays, and bisexuals, then, suggests that the developmental pathways to their sexual identity are numerous. This identity is no longer assumed to be pathological. The task of the worker is to understand and accept these varieties of sexual identity and experience that exist and to assist the lesbian, gay, or bisexual client to deal with any problems that may accompany or simply coexist with his or her particular sexual orientation.

COMMON PROBLEMS

As with other minority groups, oppression that may be visited on gay and lesbian people because of their sexual orientation can be destructive to individual self-esteem and well-being. At early stages of the coming-out process, many people actively resist acknowledging, even to themselves, that they are sexually attracted to or active with others of their own gender. This resistance is often the product of negative attitudes toward homosexuality they themselves have absorbed, as everyone does, from the society as a whole; or of negative reactions they fear from significant others such as parents, children, friends, associates, or authority figures such as teachers, coaches, or religious leaders. It is essential that the social work services lesbians, gays, and bisexuals receive be free of the homophobia and heterosexism that would add to or reinforce these fears and attitudes.

CASE EXAMPLE

Lynn, who was seventeen and a high school senior, was referred to a social worker for treatment following a brief psychiatric hospitalization. She had been admitted to the hospital after friends of hers, becoming alarmed, reported to her parents that she had ingested a number of pills and was "acting funny." This episode was viewed as a suicidal gesture by both the young woman and her parents. It followed a period of several months during which arguments between the girl and her parents had been growing in frequency and intensity. The arguments were over such issues as Lynn's style of dress, her social activities, her "lack of respect" for her parents, and the fact that she had stopped attending church with the family. Lynn was the youngest of three children and the only one still living at home. Her father owned his own small business and worked long hours; her mother worked as a nurse. Both parents were fundamentalist Christians, and their recreational activities, which were few, were centered on the church. The family lived in a suburban community on the outskirts of a large metropolitan area in the Northeast.

From the beginning of counseling, Lynn announced firmly that she was a lesbian, and she always appeared for her appointments dressed in tight blue jeans, studded leather jacket, and black boots. Her manner appeared angry and "tough," and the image she cultivated was that of the stereotype of the "dyke." Lynn had also told her parents she was a lesbian. Her father was extremely rejecting of homosexuality, which he regarded as sinful; her mother was slightly more sympathetic. Because she had also spoken openly about her sexual orientation in the hospital, Lynn had been referred to a worker who was also a lesbian, although Lynn was not aware of that fact.

Starting with what Lynn had said was important about herself, the worker began exploring Lynn's sexual orientation and what it meant to her. Lynn had begun heterosexual dating at fifteen and had enjoyed a relationship with a boy she liked very much. However, as time went on she realized she experienced her relationship with him as a "good friend" and not as a "boyfriend" like her friends did. About this time, she also became aware of her attraction to other young women. She had her first sexual experience with a woman at sixteen, which she described as her coming out. After this point, for her "there was no going back."

The worker began exploring what being gay meant to Lynn. It turned out that Lynn knew only two other lesbians, both "tough kids" from her home town. The worker then asked Lynn if she would be interested in making contact with an organization for lesbian and gay youth in the city. Lynn began to meet a much more varied and congenial group of peers with whom she could begin to talk about the pain of isolation and disapproval she was experiencing at school and at home. She also used the group to talk about her plans for college and her worries about what it would be like to be identified as a lesbian on campus.

As Lynn gained social support from the group and a sense of personal support and acceptance from her social worker in their meetings, her appearance and style of dress began to change somewhat. She also began tentatively to share with her worker some painful feelings she had about being gay, especially her parents' reactions to her and the religious beliefs she still heard from them that regarded her orientation as a sin. Lynn's presentation changed from angry and tough to depressed and vulnerable as she struggled to understand the painful feelings she was dealing with. During this stage, the worker was glad she had not shared information about her own sexual orientation with Lynn, who had never asked about it, thinking that doing so might have made it harder for Lynn to feel comfortable talking about the negative side of her feelings about her own homosexuality.

The more Lynn talked about her experiences in the family, however, the more it became clear that Lynn's parents had been distant from her in other ways for quite some time. It also became clear that her low self-esteem went back to early childhood. Lynn's father was quite rigid in his beliefs and standards and was rarely home because of his work; her mother was alcoholic and thus not reliably available to Lynn. Lynn increasingly expressed interest in understanding things in her family that had been going on long before her sexual orientation became an issue. In order to deal with these issues and to help prepare Lynn to leave home, Lynn and her parents were referred for family therapy as well.

Lynn continued in counseling until the time came for her to leave for college. Although she continued to suffer some periods of depression, no further suicidal gestures were made, and the conflict at home was somewhat reduced. When she left, Lynn was able to imagine herself meeting others at college who might share both her sexual orientation and some of her other interests as well.

This case illustrates the importance of attending to a range of issues in working with a lesbian, gay, or bisexual client. Clearly, comfort with the client's lesbian identity and understanding the homophobic reactions of others was essential to working with this case. This comfort must encompass both the positive and negative feelings a client will most likely experience in coming out. Second, the typical developmental issues and concerns of the age or stage of development must be considered as well. Here, the anxiety of an impending separation as Lynn "grew up" and went off to school was upsetting to parent and child alike. Third, it was important to be aware of the problems and vulnerabilities of both the individual and the family as they met the challenges of coming out and their life stage transitions. Finally, the role of social supports and ways to reduce isolation for lesbians and gays—lesbian and gay youth in particular—cannot be overestimated. Lynn's contact with peers provided validation for her sexual orientation and role models for the many ways in which people incorporate and express a gay or lesbian identity.

WORKING WITH COUPLES

Dating and coupling behavior is often what exposes gays and lesbians to their greatest risk from homophobia. It is not simply walking down the street alone but wanting to walk down the street holding a partner's hand that most often produces panic in the individual or fear of abuse from others. Going to a bar or expressing affection to a lover in public may, in fact, even precipitate a gay-bashing attack. With the incidence of such violence on the rise, gay and lesbian relationships are sometimes actually, as well as metaphorically, under assault.

The lack of formal and informal social sanction for the relationship is a source of strain for all gay and lesbian couples. Even if the relationship is one between partners whose lesbian or gay identity has long been established, the lack of validation of the relationship itself can produce a range of reactions, including sorrow and anger, at times that would otherwise be marked by joy. Holidays, for example, may find the partners separated as they fulfill commitments to families that may not welcome them together. Rituals of courtship and commitment may be lacking entirely or may be limited to the context of the gay community. Family and friends who are prepared to be generally supportive of the individual may react negatively to any steps taken by the couple to make the relationship public or legally sanctioned. Socializing in work or other contexts in which a husband or wife may be automatically included will leave gay and lesbian couples to decide whether to ask for the recognition and inclusion of a partner, or to give up validation of the relationship and the opportunity to be together in order to feel more private or more safe.

In the face of these strains, gay and lesbian couples have invented customs and rituals to sustain themselves and have adapted available supports to their own needs. Small groups of couples or friends may celebrate holidays together as faithfully as many families do. Some churches celebrate the vows of gay and lesbian couples, and some couples have chosen to invent their own spiritual or secular celebrations of commitment. Anniversaries are often carefully observed, although the date chosen is usually that of some significant event signifying involvement other than marriage.

Without the mechanisms of legal marriage, couples may register as domestic partners where permitted; may enter into joint financial ventures and arrangements, including home ownership; may write wills to benefit one another; and may seek devices such as a durable power of attorney or a living will to give to one another the right to make medical decisions and other legal arrangements on each other's behalf, as married couples can. In the absence of such an instrument as a will, next of kin, who may be estranged, can dispossess a lover of long standing in the event of a death, which can be a significant worry to one or both partners. Laws governing such arrangements and the limits on their use differ from state to state, and people may need assistance in finding information about resources for developing these supports in their own area.

Because these are same-sex couples, sex roles usually do not define the patterns within gay and lesbian couples to the extent they may among mixed-sex couples. In the absence of more common norms, patterns of work-sharing and relating may be more egalitarian, or they may follow some reciprocal pattern invented by the participants. As in all couples, rigid and inflexible roles may come to feel burdensome or stifling to one partner or the other, or both may be unaware of the habits that have developed. As with heterosexual couples, what couples do and what they say they do about roles and work-sharing may not be the same.[60] The role of the social worker, then, is to explore the wishes and feelings of both members of the couple and to help them design whatever arrangement for living seems most comfortable.

While sexuality does not define the lives or adjustment of gay and lesbian people any more than it does for heterosexuals, problems in sexual functioning can affect gay and lesbian relationships. Some of these may relate to social pressures, as partners who must suppress the expression of love and attachment outside the home may have difficulty in expressing tenderness and sexuality spontaneously and comfortably at home as well. Patterns of sexual behavior are often quite different in gay and lesbian couples. On average, lesbian couples often experience low levels of sexual activity after the first few years, and most are monogamous. Although ideologies about monogamy differ among lesbians, an affair often seems to precede the break up of a relationship. Gay couples, on average, enjoy higher levels of sexual activity for longer and have often been stably nonmonogamous. For gay couples, sexual behavior within and outside the couple relationship has been changing because of the AIDS epidemic, and the new patterns emerging may call for new adjustments. What is important, of course, is to assist each gay or lesbian couple in achieving open communication, mutually satisfying sexual expression, and acceptable negotiation of any differences that may exist between the partners in the context of their emotional relationship. It is common, however, for the break up of a couple relationship to precipitate a crisis, when a gay or lesbian person may seek professional help, and the experience of loss of a significant relationship is a piece of personal history for many, if not most, lesbians, gays, and bisexuals.

WORKING WITH LESBIAN, GAY, AND BISEXUAL PARENTS

There are some special issues lesbian, gay, and bisexual parents and their children must deal with that the practitioner must be prepared to respond to. Divorced parents and their children often worry that the other biological parent (or even a grandparent) may seek custody, claiming that the custodial parent is unfit simply because of sexual orientation. These fears can have profound effects on how the family represents and conducts itself, both outside and inside the home.

Each lesbian, gay, or bisexual parent must decide how to talk with the children about his or her identity. Children too young to understand much about sex understand clearly about love; a gay or lesbian identity may best be explained in terms of loving other men or women and by differentiating love between adults from the love of an adult for a child. Sex need not be the center of the discussion, any more than it would be if a heterosexual parent were talking about his or her relationship with another parent or lover. In addition, because children identify so strongly with parents, they do need to hear that they will not necessarily grow up to be gay or lesbian just because a parent is gay or lesbian. Most of all, the parent must try to help the child ask any questions or express any fears he or she may have. The meaning of the parent's lesbian, gay, or bisexual identity is not a topic that can be dealt with once and set aside; rather it must be revisited and reinterpreted as children grow older and their questions change.

In gay and lesbian families with children, the definition of the role of the parent who did not bear or legally adopt the child is usually an issue for the partners. What to call the "other mommy" or the "other daddy" may be a unique challenge, and the lack of language reflects the normlessness that gay and lesbian families face. In other ways, however, the issues of how child care, housework, and employment responsibilities will be managed and shared may differ little from what heterosexual couples who become parents go through. The issues for blended families in which each partner brings offspring into the relationship may be similar as well. Asking the family about the role of each parent and how each is named and defined will validate both partners and reveal much about how the family has organized and represented itself at home and in the wider world of the extended family, the school, the workplace, and the community at large.[61]

WORKING WITH OLDER LESBIANS, GAYS, AND BISEXUALS

Lesbians and gays are an invisible minority in general, and older bisexual, gay, and lesbian people may feel invisible both in the gay and lesbian community and among older people. Ageism keeps them marginal to the gay community; homophobia keeps them marginal to elder service agencies and programs. Research has shown that stereotypes of the older lesbian or gay man as isolated, depressed, and unfulfilled are untrue; health, access to needed material resources, and social contacts that reduce loneliness all contribute to life satisfaction among older gays and lesbians, just as they do among the nongay elderly.[62]

Today's older lesbians, gays, and bisexuals came of age in the pre–Stonewall era, and most had to come to terms with their sexual identity at a time when homophobia was even more widespread and overt than it is today. Professional mental health services were then more likely to be a source of stress than of support to lesbians and gays. Some elders may only have discovered or affirmed their gay or lesbian identity later in life, but they may still carry with them residues of the attitudes that were pervasive in their younger years.

Despite these obstacles, older lesbians and gays of today have much to offer the community. Their life stories are often tales of survival and affirmation that can instruct and inspire their younger counterparts.[63] Life review is often useful to the elderly, whose task is to consolidate a sense of the meaning of their individual lives and to understand them in the context of the historical events that have framed them. Because of the oppression they have confronted and survived, gay and lesbian elders may wish to share their stories with younger gays and lesbians as well as with family and nongay friends.

The common challenges of aging—retirement, ill health, the death of a lover or close friends—affects older gays and lesbians as well. Although many have strong social support systems, the majority will not have children to turn to when meeting these crises. Those who are sick, who care for a sick or disabled partner, or who are bereaved may find that access to the support services available to other older people in similar circumstances is not so easy for them. How can gay or lesbian partners provide for each other in retirement, illness, or after death? Will the hospital, nursing home, physician, or nurse give the gay or lesbian partner the same consideration and access to the patient a husband or wife would get? Will the widows' or widowers' group or the caregivers' support group accept a gay or lesbian member? Will the gay or lesbian elder feel comfortable in reaching out for the support that is needed?

Emerging Issues and Trends

The future of social work practice with lesbians, gays, and bisexuals will build on the advances in understanding gained in the recent past and highlighted in this chapter. There are some emerging issues and trends we know about today that will take the practice of social work in new directions in the years to come.

LESBIAN, GAY, AND BISEXUAL PROFESSIONALS

Many social workers are themselves lesbian, gay, or bisexual, some being openly identified to their colleagues as such, others not. Thus, the professional social worker must consider gender orientation issues in relation not only to clients and the community but also to professional relationships with students, supervisors, peers, and employers. As the Gay Liberation Movement and the professions come of age, the number of openly lesbian-, gay-, and bisexual-identified professionals is likely to grow.

Whether to "come out" when seeking employment or once on the job is a major dilemma that every lesbian, gay, and bisexual social worker must face. Fear of losing one's job is widespread and a major factor affecting their decisions to remain closeted on their own or a partner's behalf.[64] Although documented instances of such discrimination are scant, except in the military, few states have civil rights legislation explicitly protecting gays and lesbians from discrimination in hiring and other aspects of employment. Despite the provisions of the NASW Code of Ethics, few social work agencies and institutions have antidiscrimination policies of their own that explicitly mention sexual orientation, and most schools of social work also lack such protections. Workers who retain their jobs may experience social and/or professional isolation, mild harassment, or especially close scrutiny of their performance on the job.[65] For example, a recent survey of supervisors at one school of social work's field placement agencies suggested that the responses to a social work intern's "coming out" on placement might be quite variable.[66]

Providing training to all staff and support to those working with clients who are lesbian, gay, or bisexual or from families with lesbian, gay, or bisexual members, are ways both to legitimate the issues and to remove pressure from identified lesbian, gay, or bisexual staff to be the resident experts. Such practices are not just affirming for staff; they are therapeutic for clients as well, some of whom may be dealing with issues of sexual orientation themselves.

The profession, through its associations (e.g., NASW, Societies for Clinical Social Work, American Association of Black Social Workers, as well as other ethnic and specialty groups) has begun to respond to minority group pressure by increasing membership education, establishing state-level lesbian and gay caucuses, and supporting civil rights legislation. Many more social agencies, such as child and family services and mental health clinics, have broadened their mission to serve this population. The Council on Social Work Education has added lesbian and gay content to the required human diversity curriculum standards and sanction against those programs that continue to discriminate against lesbian, gay, and bisexual students, staff, and faculty. The profession has responded to similar changes in cultural ideology in the past and will continue to do so in the future.

IMPACT OF AIDS

Since the epidemic began, more than half a million Americans have developed AIDS; three out of five have died. The majority have been gay men. The psychological and social impact on gay men and the gay community has been deep and profound. Sixteen years into the HIV/AIDS pandemic, and the myth that lesbians are not living and dying with the disease persists. Unfortunately this perception is held by the general public, the lesbian, gay, and bisexual communities, many of the health care providers and researchers, and even educators and activists believe that lesbians are at the lowest or no risk. This false belief is fueled by a narrow focus upon woman-to-woman transmission, limitations of HIV/AIDS surveillance data, the notion that "real" lesbians don't get AIDS, and the failure to recognize differences between "identity" and "behavior."[67]

AIDS is now the leading cause of death of men and women between the ages of 25 and 44 years in our country. The number of cases is increasing most rapidly among women and among those infected through heterosexual contact. Some 40,000 to 50,000 Americans are infected with HIV yearly. Half are under the age of 25. Worldwide, 8,500 people are infected daily.[68]

Gay men and lesbians have experienced the death of lovers, friends, and associates in staggering numbers, and, given the numbers of those infected but not yet ill, this experience will no doubt continue until a cure is found. Many have not had the opportunity to process these multiple losses. In addition to the fear of AIDS, which may bring chronic anxiety akin to PTSD, there is a pervasive sense of mourning and depression in the homosexual community which affects many aspects of life, including sexuality, and a real risk exists of reverting to more negative attitudes about homosexuality, among lesbians, gays, and bisexuals themselves as well as among straights. This backlash has resulted in some bitterness and despair in the gay community, and fear that hard-earned gains and increased acceptance may slip away in the face of AIDS.

For many homosexuals, the stresses of being different in a nonaccepting, nonunderstanding society are intensified by the AIDS health crisis. The irrational fear of AIDS, exacerbated by contradictory information along with the actual threat, has resulted in a population of "worried well."[69] These are persons at risk of AIDS because of past or present sexual activity or intravenous (IV) drug use but without a known exposure to the virus, and those who have tested HIV positive but have not developed symptoms. Quadland and Shattls suggest that it is extremely important for mental health and other health professionals to clearly convey the message that homosexuality and sexual behavior did not cause AIDS and not allow society to blame the victims of this tragedy.[70] Without a significant effort to expand affirming mental health services, the emotional needs of lesbians, gays, and bisexuals will continue to be met primarily through organized self-help groups.

In response to the epidemic, lesbians, gays, and bisexuals combined their political energy and skill and assumed leadership of the nation's efforts by organizing local, state, and national self-help efforts, developing services, advocating for patients, lobbying for expanded research and treatment funds, and pressing for protective legislation. Most local AIDS service organizations were founded by gays and continue to be influenced by gays.[71] However, in recent years, there has been concerted effort to move AIDS planning, education, and service into the mainstream of health and welfare programs. This is happening as more health care providers accept their professional responsibility for the epidemic and as the profile of those infected changes from primarily white gay and bisexual men to African American and Latino IV drug users, their sexual partners, and their babies. Presently the fastest growing categories of victims are adolescents and minority women and their children. Because this process of mainstreaming services is quite slow and requires considerable experience, lesbians, gay men, and bisexuals will continue to provide leadership and financial support in this effort.

Concluding Comment	In the past decade, a revolution has taken place in gay people's perception of themselves. The notion of homosexuality as an individual illness has been discredited, replaced with a political and social definition which posits that to be gay is to be a member of an oppressed minority, similar in many ways to racial and ethnic minorities.[72] In response to oppression, lesbians, gays, and bisexuals have organized to reinforce this new self-view and to press for civil rights that are currently denied. The future political agenda of lesbian, gay, and bisexual communities will include macro-level state and national activity around each of the following issues: (1) civil rights (e.g., the repeal of state sodomy laws, passage of antidiscrimination statutes, and legal recognition of relationships); (2) violence/hate crimes (e.g., protection against gay-bashing, harassment, and abuse); (3) substance abuse (e.g., increased awareness of, access to, and the development of lesbian- and gay-sensitive drug and alcohol services); (4) health care (e.g., ensuring access to and the quality of gay-sensitive services, sexually transmitted disease and AIDS care, reproductive rights, new reproductive technologies such as alternative insemination, and women's health equity); (5) mental health service based on

lifestyle–affirming models; (6) community, family, and social life (e.g., custody, child, and foster care rights); (7) youth services (e.g., education, support services, and legal protections); (8) elder care (e.g., expansion of services to reflect the increase in numbers and the different life histories and expectations of the elders of the future); and (9) equal protection in the workplace, including the right to serve openly in the military without harassment and discrimination.

Same-sex marriage and equal treatment in the military will continue to be the battle ground for civil rights activism. While neither issue has captured widespread support of the lesbian, gay, and bisexual communities, both engage core social institutions where blatant discrimination and breach of a gay or lesbian citizen's privacy and equal protection rights persist. Recently, the State Supreme Court of Hawaii asked for compelling reasons why the state should not permit legal marriage between same-sex couples. Congress, in anticipation of an affirmative decision on behalf of the plaintiffs, passed a "Protection of (heterosexual) Marriage Act" intended to block the state's recognition of same-sex marriages. Many states have followed suit.

While "domestic partnership" recognition has been advanced in industry and in some municipalities, this new status as an option to marriage will only accord "second-class" rights and privileges in comparison to those awarded with marriage. The "Don't ask, don't tell" military policy is being challenged successfully in the federal courts because of its apparent violation of the Constitution's equal protection and privacy clauses. Legal process is slow and gains appear to be made at the margins, for example, more states promulgating administrative policy allowing for gay and lesbian foster parenting and adoptions. These advances are hardly secure in that the "Religious Right" and political conservatives are scapegoating gay men and lesbians as they targeted communists and Jews only a decade ago.

Social visibility of lesbian, gay, and bisexual people will become the norm. Social acceptance and integration will be illusory in some sectors of society while a reality in others. Social work professionals are in a position to have an influence on many of the issues facing lesbians, gays, and bisexuals today and in the future: civil rights, access to health and reproductive services, child custody, and adoption and foster care, to name but a few. We will all be challenged to use that influence for the good.

KEY WORDS AND CONCEPTS

Gays	Homophobia
Lesbians	Heterosexism
Bisexuals	Oppression
Homohatred	Conversion therapy

SUGGESTED READINGS

Appleby, G. A., and Anastas, J. W. *Not Just a Passing Phase: Social Work with Lesbian, Gay and Bisexual People.* New York: Columbia University Press, 1998.

Comstock, G. D. *Violence Against Lesbians and Gay Men.* New York: Columbia University Press, 1991.

D'Augelli, A. R., and Patterson, C. J., eds. *Lesbian, Gay, and Bisexual Identities over the Lifespan.* New York: Oxford University Press, 1995.

Edwards, R. L., ed. *Encyclopedia of Social Work,* 19th Edition. Washington, D.C.: NASW Press, 1995: following articles: Berger, R. M., and Kelly, J. "Gay Men: Overview," pp. 1064–1074; Hunter, J., and Schaecher, R. "Gay and Lesbian Adolescents," pp. 1055–1063; Gochros, J. S. "Bisexuality," pp. 299–304; Laird, J. "Lesbians: Parenting," pp. 1604–1615; Morales, J. "Gay Men: Parenting," pp. 1085–1094; Shernoff, M. "Gay Men: Direct Practice," pp. 1075–1084; Tully, C. T. "Lesbians: Overview," pp. 1591–1596; Woodman, N. J. "Lesbians: Direct Practice," pp. 1597–1603.

Garnets, L. D., and Kimmel, D. C., eds. *Psychological Perspectives on Lesbian and Gay Male Experiences.* New York: Columbia University Press, 1993.

Geller, T., ed. *Bisexuality: Theory and Research.* New York: Haworth Press, 1991.

Gonsiorek, J. C., and Weinrich, J. D., eds. *Homosexuality: Research Implications for Public Policy.* Newbury Park, CA: Sage, 1991.

Herek, G. M., and Berrill, K. T., eds. *Hate Crimes: Confronting Violence Against Lesbians and Gay Men.* Newbury Park, CA: Sage, 1992.

Hidalgo, H., Peterson, T. L., and Woodman, N. J., eds. *Lesbian and Gay Issues: A Resource Manual for Social Workers.* Silver Spring, MD: NASW Press, 1985.

McWhirter, D. P., and Mattison, A. M. *The Male Couple: How Relationships Develop.* New York: Prentice-Hall, 1984.

National Association of Social Workers. "Lesbian, Gay, and Bisexual Issues," *Social Work Speaks: NASW Policy Statements,* 4th Edition. Washington, D.C.: NASW Press, 1997.

Nava, M., and Dawidoff, R. *Created Equal: Why Gay Rights Matter to America.* New York: St. Martin's Press, 1994.

Slater, S. *The Lesbian Family Life Cycle.* New York: Free Press, 1995.

Sullivan, A. *Virtually Normal: An Argument About Homosexuality.* New York: Alfred A. Knopf, 1995.

Vaid, U. *Virtually Equal: The Mainstreaming of Gay and Lesbian Liberation.* New York: Anchor Books, 1995.

ENDNOTES

1. A. P. Weiner, "Racist, Sexist, and Homophobic Attitudes among Undergraduate Social Work Students and the Effects on Assessments of Client Vignettes," unpublished doctoral dissertation (New Brunswick, NJ: Rutgers University, 1989); also see G. Appleby, "Hearing: Gay Bashing and Harassment," unpublished conference proceedings (San Francisco: NASW Annual Program Meeting, 1989).

2. W. Paul and J. D. Weinrich, "Introduction," in W. Paul and J. D. Weinrich, eds., *Homosexuality: Social, Psychological, and Biological Issues* (Beverly Hills, CA: Sage, 1982).

3. I. Bieber, H. J. Dain, P. R. Dince, M. G. Drellich, H. Grand, R. H. Gundlach, M. W. Dremer, A. H. Rifkin, C. B. Wilbur, and T. B. Bieber, *Homosexuality: A Psychoanalytic Study* (New York: Basic Books, 1962).

4. J. C. Gonsiorek, "Psychological Adjustment and Homosexuality," in *Catalog of Selected Documents in Psychology* 7(2), 45, MS. 1478 (Arlington, VA: American Psychological Association, 1977).

5. A. P. Bell and M. S. Weinberg, *Homosexualities: A Study of Diversity among Men and Women* (New York: Simon & Schuster, 1978).

6. M. G. Shively and J. P. DeCecco, "Components of Sexual Identity," *Journal of Homosexuality* 3 (1977): 41–48.

7. A. E. Moses and R. O. Hawkins, *Counseling Lesbian Women and Gay Men: A Life-Issue Approach* (St. Louis, MO: C. V. Mosby, 1982), pp. 43–44.

8. J. C. Gonsiorek, ed., *Homosexuality and Psychotherapy: A Practitioners' Handbook of Affirmative Models* (New York: Haworth Press, 1982).

9. R. C. Friedman, *Male Homosexuality: A Contemporary Psychoanalytic Perspective* (New Haven, CT: Yale University Press, 1988).

10. S. F. Morin and E. M. Garkinkle, "Male Homophobia," *Journal of Social Issues* 34 (January 1978): 29–47.

11. J. C. Gonsiorek and J. D. Weinrich, eds., *Homosexuality: Research Implications for Public Policy* (Newbury Park, CA: Sage, 1991).

12. A. C. Kinsey, W. B. Pomeroy, and C. E. Martin, *Sexual Behavior in the Human Male* (Philadelphia: W. B. Saunders, 1948); also see A. C. Kinsey and P. H. Gebhard, *Sexual Behavior in the Human Female* (Philadelphia: W. B. Saunders, 1973); P. H. Gebhard, "Incidence of Overt Homosexuality in the United States and Western Europe," in J. M. Livingood, ed., NIMH Task Force on Homosexuality: Final Report and Background Papers, DHEW Publication No. (HSM) 72–9116 (Rockville, MD: National Institute of Mental Health, 1972); also see P. H. Gebhard and A. B. Johnson, "The Kinsey Data: Marginal Tabulations of the 1938–1963 Interviews Conducted by the Institute for Sex Research" (Philadelphia: W. B. Saunders, 1979).

13. E. O. Laumann, J. H. Gagnon, R. T. Michael, and S. Michaels, *The Social Organization of Sexuality: Sexual Practice in the United States* (Chicago: University of Chicago Press, 1994).

14. H. Hidalgo, "Third World," in H. Hidalgo, T. Peterson, and N. J. Woodman, eds., *Lesbian and Gay Issues: A Resource Manual for Social Workers* (Silver Spring, MD: National Association of Social Workers, 1985), pp. 14–16.

15. M. C. Smith, "By the Year 2000," in J. Beam, ed., *In the Life: A Black Gay Anthology* (Boston: Alyson Press, 1986), p. 226.

16. A. Carballo-Dieguez, "Hispanic Culture, Gay Male Culture, and AIDS: Counseling Implications," *Journal of Counseling and Development* 68 (September–October 1989): 26–30.

17. V. M. Mays and S. D. Cochran, "Black Gay and Bisexual Men Coping with More Than Just A Disease," *Focus* 4 (January 1988): 1–3.

18. J. H. Newby, "The Effects of Cultural Beliefs and Values on AIDS Prevention and Treatment in the Black Community," a paper presented at the Annual Program Meeting of the National Association of Social Workers, San Francisco, October, 1989.

19. W. J. Blumenfeld. *How We All Pay the Price* (Boston: Beacon Press, 1992).

20. W. Paul and J. D. Weinrich, "Whom and What We Study: Definition and Scope of Sexual Orientation," in *Homosexuality,* pp. 26–27.

21. A. P. Bell, M. S. Weinberg, and S. K Hammersmith, *Sexual Preference: Its Development in Men and Women* (Bloomington: Indiana University Press, 1981).

22. B. Garner and R. W. Smith, "Are There Really Any Gay Male Athletes? An Empirical Survey," *Journal of Sex Research* 13 (1977): 22–34.

23. National Association of Social Workers, National Committee on Lesbian and Gay Issues, unpublished Annual Report, August, 1990 (Silver Spring, MD: The Association, 1990).

24. J. Bradford and C. Ryan, *The National Lesbian Health Care Survey* (Washington, D.C.: National Lesbian and Gay Health Foundation, 1988); also see M. Shernoff and W. A. Scott, *The Sourcebook on Lesbian/Gay Health Care*, 2nd Edition (Washington, D.C.: National Lesbian and Gay Health Foundation, 1988).

25. Bradford and Ryan.

26. C. A. Lukes and H. Land, "Biculturality and Homosexuality," *Social Work* 35 (1990): 155–161.

27. Ibid.

28. N. Hunter and N. Polikoff, "Custody Rights of Lesbian Mothers: Legal Theory and Litigation Strategy," *Buffalo Law Review* 25 (1976): 691–733.

29. M. Mendola, *A New Look at Gay Couples* (New York: Crown, 1980); also see D. McWhirter and A. Mattison, *The Male Couple: How Relationships Develop* (Englewood Cliffs, NJ: Prentice Hall, 1984).

30. R. Achtenberg, "Preserving and Protecting the Families of Lesbians and Gay Men," in Shernoff and Scott, *The Sourcebook on Lesbian/Gay Health Care*; also see S. K. Hammersmith, "A Sociological Approach to Counseling Homosexual Clients and Their Families," in E. Coleman, ed., *Integrated Identity for Gay Men and Lesbians: Psychotherapeutic Approaches for Emotional Well-being* (New York: Harrington Park Press, 1988), pp. 174–179.

31. Bell, Weinberg, and Hammersmith.

32. M. Kirkpatrick, K. Smith, and R. Roy, "Lesbian Mothers and Their Children: A Comparative Study," *American Journal of Orthopsychiatry* 51 (1981): 545–551; also see B. Miller, "Gay Fathers and Their Children," *The Family Coordinator* 28 (1979): 544–552; F. Bozett, "Gay Fathers: Evaluation of the Gay Father Identity," *American Journal of Psychiatry* 51 (March 1978): 173–179; R. Green, "Thirty-five Children Raised by Homosexual or Transsexual Parents," *American Journal of Psychiatry* (1978): 135; B. Hoeffer, "Children's Acquisition of Sex-Role Behavior in Lesbian Mother Families," *American Journal of Orthopsychiatry* 51 (March 1981); S. Golombok, "Children in Lesbian and Single Parent Households: Psychosexual and Psychiatric Appraisal," *Journal of Child Psychology and Applied Discipline* 24 (1983); E. F. Levy, "Lesbian Mothers' Coping Characteristics: An Exploration of Social, Psychological, and Family Coping Resources," unpublished doctoral dissertation (Madison: University of Wisconsin, 1983).

33. Kirkpatrick, Smith, and Roy.

34. R. M. Berger, "Homosexuality: Gay Men," in *Encyclopedia of Social Work.*

35. S. Susoeff, "Assessing Children's Best Interests When a Parent Is Gay or Lesbian: Toward a Rational Custody Standard," *UCLA Law Review* 32 (April 1985); M. Kirkpatrick and D. Hitchens, "Lesbian Mothers/Gay Fathers," in *Emerging Issues in Child Psychiatry and the Law* (New York: Brunner & Mazel, 1985).

36. N. J. Woodman, "Homosexuality: Lesbian Women," in A. Minahan, ed., *Encyclopedia of Social Work,* 18th Edition (Silver Spring, MD: National Association of Social Workers, 1987).

37. M. S. Weinberg and C. J. Williams, *Male Homosexuals: Their Problems and Adaptations* (New York: Oxford University Press, 1974).

38. Berger.

39. Ibid.
40. R. M. Berger, "What Is a Homosexual?: A Definitional Model," *Social Work* 28 (February 1983): 132–135.
41. E. Coleman, ed., *Integrated Identity for Gay Men and Lesbians: Psychotherapeutic Approaches for Emotional Well-being* (New York: Harrington Park Press, 1988), p. 19.
42. Bradford and Ryan, p. 4.
43. L. Icard and D. M. Traunstein, "Black Gay Alcoholic Men: Their Culture and Treatment," *Social Casework* 68(5) (1987): 267–272.
44. S. C. Anderson and D. C. Henderson, "Working with Lesbian Alcoholics," *Social Work* 30 (June 1985): 518–525.
45. V. Brooks, *Minority Stress and Lesbian Women* (Lexington, MA: D.C. Heath, 1981).
46. J. B. Bradford, "Reactions of Gay Men to AIDS: A Survey of Self-Reported Change," unpublished doctoral dissertation (Virginia Commonwealth University, 1986).
47. R. Alcalay, "Health and Social Support Networks: A Case for Improving Communication," *Social Networks* 5 (1983): 71–88.
48. Bradford and Ryan, pp. 3–5.
49. C. B. Germain and A. Gitterman, *The Life Model of Social Work Practice* (New York: Columbia University Press, 1980).
50. M. Coles and W. Rubenstein, "Rights of Gays and Lesbians," paper presented at the Biennial Conference at the University of Wisconsin, Madison, June 15–18, 1987.
51. Achtenberg, p. 244.
52. M. Hall, "Lesbian Families: Cultural and Clinical Issues," *Social Work* 23 (1978): 380–385.
53. Hall, p. 380.
54. Ibid.
55. K. Lewes, *The Psychoanalytic Theory of Male Homosexuality* (New York: Simon & Schuster, 1988).
56. A. Rosenthal, "Heterosexism and Clinical Assessment," *Smith College Studies in Social Work* 52 (February 1982): 145–159.
57. A. P. Bell and M. S. Weinberg, *Homosexualities: A Study of Diversity among Men and Women* (New York: Simon & Schuster, 1978).
58. J. Krajeski, "Psychotherapy with Gay Men and Lesbians: A History of Controversy," in T. S. Stein and C. J. Cohen, eds., *Contemporary Perspectives on Psychotherapy with Lesbians and Gay Men* (New York: Plenum, 1986).
59. C. Golden, "Diversity and Variability in Women's Sexual Identities," Boston Lesbian Psychologies Collective, ed., in *Lesbian Psychologies: Explorations and Challenges* (Urbana: University of Illinois Press, 1986).
60. A. Hochschild, *The Second Shift* (New York: Viking Press, 1989).
61. S. Crawford, "Lesbian Families: Psychosocial Stress and the Family-Building Process," in *Lesbian Psychologies.*
62. R. M. Berger, "Realities of Gay and Lesbian Aging," *Social Work* 29 (January 1984): 57–62; also see M. Kehoe, "Lesbians over Sixty Speak for Themselves," *Journal of Homosexuality* 16 (March–April 1988): 1–78.
63. M. Adelman, ed., *Long Time Passing: Lives of Older Lesbians* (Boston: Alyson Publications, 1986).

64. M. P. Levine and R. Leonard, "Discrimination against Lesbians in the Work Force," *Signs: Journal of Women in Culture and Society* 9 (April 1984): 700–710.

65. J. Rabin, K. Keefe, and M. Burton, "Enhancing Services for Sexual-Minority Clients: A Community Mental Health Approach," *Social Work* 31 (April 1986): 292–298.

66. K. Lewes, *The Psychoanalytic Theory of Male Homosexuality* (New York: Simon & Schuster, 1988).

67. N. A. Humphreys and J. K. Quam, "Middle-Aged and Old Gay, Lesbian and Bisexual Adults," in G. A. Appleby and J. W. Anastas, eds., *Not Just A Passing Phase: Social Work with Gay, Lesbian and Bisexual People* (New York: Columbia University Press, 1998).

68. L. Daimant, ed., *Homosexual Issues in the Workplace* (Washington, D.C.: Taylor & Francis, 1993); C. Kitzinger, "Lesbians and Gay Men in the Workplace: Psychosocial Issues," in M. J. Davidson and J. Earnshaw, eds., *Vulnerable Workers: Psychosocial and Legal Issues* (New York: John Wiley & Sons, 1991), pp. 223–257.

69. K. J. Harowski, "The Worried Well: Maximizing Coping in the Face of AIDS," in Coleman.

70. M. C. Quadland and W. D. Sattls, "AIDS, Sexuality, and Sexual Control," in Coleman.

71. G. A. Appleby, "What Social Workers Can Do," in S. Alyson, ed., *You Can Do Something about AIDS* (Boston: The Stop AIDS Project, 1989).

72. W. Paul, "Social and Cultural Issues," in *Homosexuality: Social, Psychological, and Biological Issues* (Beverly Hills, CA: Sage, 1982).

CHAPTER 13

Social Work Practice with Children and Youth

Armando T. Morales and Bradford W. Sheafor

Prefatory Comment

This original chapter is making its first appearance in this textbook. It is a collaborative effort by Armando T. Morales, DSW, Professor of Psychiatry and Biobehavioral Sciences, Neuropsychiatric Institute and Hospital, School of Medicine, UCLA, and Bradford W. Sheafor, Ph.D., Professor, Department of Social Work and Co-Director of the Family and Youth Institute, Colorado State University. Children and youth in the United States may be seen as cherished beneficiaries of the past, symbols of the quality of society, and conveyors of the nation's hopes for the future. Like some societies, the United States attempts to place a priority on children's physical, psychological, and intellectual development. This is reflected in the substantial resources that are invested in social, recreational, and educational programs that benefit the youngest members of this very vulnerable special population. Philosophical differences may exist regarding how to best enhance the quality of life for children and youth, but there is little disagreement regarding the desirability of meeting their needs.

Such high value has not always been placed on children and youth. Children were once exploited as a source of labor in the sweatshops of urban America and on family farms in rural areas. At one time it was not uncommon for poor white families to abandon their children to the urban streets during hard economic times, for black slave children to be sold away from their parents for a profit, for children of Mexican migrant families to toil each day in the hot sun doing backbreaking farm labor, and so on. The condition of housing in which children lived was often crowded, unsanitary, and dangerous in urban tenements, Appalachian coal towns, and migrant camps, largely because wealthy owners were in complete control and their priority was to make a profit for themselves and their corporations. Children's education, too, was viewed as a luxury and was often made available to them only before they were old enough to provide productive labor in factories or, in rural areas, at the times of the year when crops were dormant and they were not needed in the fields.

In the early 1900s, concerns about the damaging conditions experienced by children became a national issue. Under the leadership of social workers such as Jane Addams, Florence Kelly, and Lillian Wald, the public was gradually made aware of the plight of children, and sentiment that this important resource should be protected and nourished began to evolve. Committees concerned about housing quality, child labor, the excessive placement of children in orphanages and other institutions, and basic child health issues contributed to President Theodore Roosevelt calling a White House Conference on the Care of Dependent Children in 1909. The subsequent formation of the U.S. Children's Bureau, which, under the direction of social worker Katherine Lenroot, initiated government oversight and advocacy in the interest of children and later youth, was a milestone in social welfare history.[1] As a result, child labor legislation was passed, mother's pensions (later public assistance) were provided, minimum housing quality was required, and public education mandated.

Current Demographics

Compared to the conditions prior to the twentieth century, the quality of life for many children and youth has improved considerably. Yet, nearly a century later, more is needed. The following brief examination of factors regarding children and youth today reveals two important conclusions. First, the fate of children is tightly bound to the family. For the most part, when a family's conditions are favorable, children thrive. When families are poor, dysfunctional, or experience discrimination and oppression, the likelihood of children and youth living up to their potential diminishes. Second, as in other aspects of life, the benefits of this civilization are not equally distributed. When a child or young person is also part of a population group that is vulnerable to social problems based on gender, ethnicity, a disabling condition, or the like, as described in other chapters in Part Four, the problems are compounded and the incidence of problem conditions increases.

It is difficult to appreciate the scope of the problems affecting this particularly vulnerable group because the size (69.4 million children and youth) is beyond the numbers with which people customarily deal. Therefore, in the following data boxes, which provide significant demographic characteristics for children and youth, the data are translated to a population base of 100,000 people. For example, in a city or county of 100,000 people there would be 26,160 persons under age 18. In a town of 50,000 there would be one-half that number, or 13,080 (0.50 × 26,200). For children and youth in a metropolitan area of 500,000, one would expect to find 130,800 (5.0 × 26,160) persons in this age group. Any individual community will vary from the national average, yet the data take on more meaning if they are translated to the size of community with which the reader is familiar.

PERSONAL CHARACTERISTICS

In 1996, more than 69 million persons were under age 18.* They were almost evenly divided among the 0 to 5, 6 to 11, and 12 to 17 age groups. More were males (51.2 percent) than females, almost two-thirds were classified as white (non-Hispanic), and 3.7 percent were born in a country other than the United States, with English usually not their first language.

Box 13-1 **Personal Characteristics of U.S. Children and Youth**
(per 100,000 population with 26,160 ages 0–17)

Gender (1998)
- Male, 51.3% = 13,389
- Female, 48.7% = 12,740

Age (1997)
- 0–5 years, 33.9% = 8,868
- 6–11 years, 33.4% = 8,734
- 12–17 years, 32.7% = 8,554

Race/Ethnicity (1997)
- White (non-Hispanic), 66% = 17,266
- African American, 16% = 4,186
- Hispanic, 14% = 3,662
- Asian American, 4% = 1,046
- Native American, 1% = 262

Foreign Born (1990)
- 3.7% = 968

Difficulty Speaking English (1995)
- Ages 5–17, 5.1% = 539

Born Out of Wedlock (1991)
- 29.5% = 7,712

Low Birth Weight (1996)
- Less than 5.5 pounds, 7.3% = 108

Victim of Child Maltreatment (1994)
- 1.3% = 338

---

*Data presented in this section are selected from the following sources: Federal Interagency Forum on Child and Family Statistics, *America's Children: Key National Indicators of Well-Being,* Washington, D.C., U.S. Government Printing Office, 1998; and U.S. Department of Health and Human Services, *Trends in the Well-Being of America's Children and Youth,* Washington, D.C., U.S. Government Printing Office, 1997. For additional data and policy positions on issues affecting children and youth, the web site of the Children's Defense Fund (http://www.childrensdefense.org) is recommended.

Various data corroborate the fact that young children are particularly vulnerable to health, safety, and caregiving problems within the home. Human services programs aimed at preventing these difficulties and enhancing the development of the more than one-third of the children in the youngest six-year increment (ages 0 to 5) are needed in every community. Furthermore, females are more likely to suffer from abusive situations within the family (see Chapter 12) and various forms of discrimination in the society, while nonwhite, Hispanic, and non-English-speaking children and youth are most often victims of societal discrimination (see Chapters 19 to 23).

Of particular note is the dramatic increase in the number of children born to unmarried parents. In 1960, 5.3 percent of all children were born out of wedlock. This percentage increased to 10.7 in 1970, 18.4 in 1980, and 28.0 in 1990 and was estimated to be 30 percent in 1995. As many as 75 percent of all births to young mothers ages 15 to 19 occur when the parents are not married. Much of the social problem data indicate that problems are substantially greater when children live with a single parent, particularly a single mother.

One predictor of subsequent health problems is the child's birth weight. An increasing percentage (from 6.8 percent in 1985 to 7.3 percent in 1995) of all children are born below the 5.5-pound low-birth-weight threshold and 1 percent below the 3.3-pound threshold for "very low birth weight." Of particular concern is the black population, in which low-birth-weight babies are double and very low birth-weight births triple that of any other population group. Once children survive the traumas of early life, many also face harmful experiences within their families. More than one child in every one hundred becomes a victim of physical, sexual, or emotional maltreatment that can create permanent damage. Preventive programs can be especially effective in addressing these conditions.

HOUSING AND RESIDENCE

The family with which children and youth reside affects their growth and development. In 1997, only slightly more than two-thirds of the young people in the United States lived with two parents, and 4 percent were living in foster homes or some other form of residential care—usually with the significant involvement of social workers in making those out-of-home placements. In addition, almost one-fourth of these young people lived with a single mother, a condition that is highly correlated with poverty and other social problems.

The physical condition of housing, too, affects the health and social development of children and youth. In 1995, as indicated in Box 13-2, more than one of every eight children and youth lived in rundown and dilapidated housing for example, with an absence of complete plumbing for the family, unvented room heaters as primary heating equipment, upkeep problems such as water leakage, open cracks or holes, broken plaster, and signs of rats. Often the space is crowded with an excessive number of people compared to the size of the housing unit. Twelve percent of children and youth reside in households that pay more than one-half of their income for this housing, and 5 percent are in neighborhoods where more than 40 percent of the people live in poverty. In short, for many children and youth, "home" is not

Box 13-2 **Household Composition and Housing of U.S. Children and Youth** (per 100,000 population with 26,160 ages 0–17)

> *Household Composition (1997)*
> - Living with married couple parents, 68% = 17,789
> - Living with single mother as head of household, 24% = 6,278
> - Living with single father as head of household, 4% = 1,046
> - Living with neither parent, 4% = 1,046 (including 680 in foster care)
>
> *Quality of Housing (1995)*
> - Live in housing with severe physical problems, 12% = 3,139
> - Live in crowded housing, 7% = 1,831
> - Live in household where rent/payments and utilities requires more than 50% of family income, 12% = 3,139
> - Live in neighborhood where 40+ percent families are below the poverty level (1990), 5% = 1,308

conducive to their well-being, but nevertheless is a substantial financial drain on family resources.

FAMILY INCOME AND EMPLOYMENT

A child's well-being is improved if the family income is adequate to support good quality housing, health care, food, clothing, education, and so on. However, nearly 20 percent of all children and youth live in families that are at or below the poverty line, and 8.4 percent live in extreme poverty, that is, less than one-half of the family income needed just to reach the poverty level. As Box 13-3 indicates, one's level of income is highly associated with marital status and race or ethnicity. Attaining sufficient income is also associated with having two breadwinners in a family. In 1995, nearly two-thirds of all mothers were employed on a full- or part-time basis, thus providing a major source of income for many families. In the mid-1990s, income transfers through financial assistance and food stamp programs helped bridge some of the financial problems of the one-fifth of the children and youth living below the poverty level. The full impact of the curtailment of these programs through "welfare reform" is yet to be realized. Plotnick[2] indicates that benefits are likely to be lower under Temporary Assistance for Needy Families (TANF) than they were under Aid to Families with Dependent Children (AFDC) because (1) the change to block grants to states provides a disincentive to states to maintain or increase benefits, (2) the federal funds available for block grants will likely grow more slowly than in the past, and (3) food stamp benefits have been reduced. The future continues to be uncertain for the lowest-income families.

POVERTY AND HUNGER

The single most clear predictor of social problems for children and youth is to live in poverty. When discussing the impact of poverty on children in a substantial study

Box 13-3 | **Income and Employment Status of Families of U.S. Children and Youth**
(per 100,000 population with 26,160 ages 0–17)

Family Income Level (1996)
- Very high income, 9.0% = 2,354
- High income, 14.5% = 3,793
- Medium income, 34.0% = 8,894
- Low income (above poverty level), 22.7% = 5,938
- Below poverty (but above extreme poverty), 11.4% = 2,982
- Extreme poverty, 8.4% = 1,197

Mean Family Income (1995)
- White married-couple family = $61,854
- Black married-couple family = $53,078
- Hispanic married-couple family = $38,145
- White single-mother family = $23,943
- Black single-mother family = $17,645
- Hispanic single-mother family = $15,956

Mother Employed (1995)
- Full-time, 46% = 12,034
- Part-time, 19% = 4,970

of child poverty funded by the independent David and Lucile Packard Foundation, Lewitt, Terman, and Behrman[3] conclude:

> Not only do poor children have access to fewer material goods than rich or middle-class children, but also they are more likely to experience poor health and to die during childhood. In school, they score lower on standardized tests and are more likely to be retained in grade and to drop out. Poor teens are more likely to have out-of-wedlock births and to experience violent crime. Finally, persistently poor children are more likely to end up as poor adults. (p. 8)

A 1994 study by Kearnsey, Grundmann, and Gallicchio[4] estimates that without the income supports of various social programs the child poverty level would increase from slightly more than 20 percent of the nation's children to 39.4%. Poverty, however, does not fall equally on children and youth (see Box 13-4). Unsatisfactory as it is that 16 percent of the white (non-Hispanic) children and youth live in poverty, this poverty rate compares very favorably to the unacceptable rates of 42 percent for Black children and 39 percent for those in Hispanic families. Furthermore, for children living with married parents, only 10 percent experience poverty, as compared to almost one-half of those living with a single mother.

One devastating impact of poverty on children and youth is the presence of hunger, because it represents a threat to one's very survival. Approximately 11.5 percent of all children and youth experience "food insecurity," a condition in which there is difficulty obtaining enough food, with reduced quality of diet and therefore improper nutrition, and anxiety about a continuing food supply. Three percent of

Box 13-4 **Poverty and Hunger Status of U.S. Children and Youth** (per 100,000 population with 26,160 ages 0–17)

Ethnicity of Family at or below Poverty Level (1995)

(*Note:* Annual income for a family of four at the poverty line was $16,588 in 1998.)
- White (non-Hispanic), 16% = 2,763
- Black (non-Hispanic), 42%= 1,758
- Hispanic, 39% = 1,428

Marital Status of Family at or below Poverty Level (1996)
- Living with married parents, 10% = 1,779
- Living with single mother, 49% = 3,076

Household Sometimes or Often Reporting "Not Enough to Eat" (1995)
- Food insecurity without hunger, 8.5% = 3,505
- Food insecurity with moderate hunger, 2.6% = 1,334
- Food insecurity with severe hunger, 0.4% = 262

the families of children and youth also report that there are significant periods when there is not enough food for the children and adults in the family.

LEARNING STIMULATION AND EDUCATIONAL STATUS

In many ways, hope for a nation's future in the twenty-first century depends on the education of its children and youth. In an increasingly high-tech universe, persons with limited education find it difficult to compete for jobs and earn the income necessary to support themselves and their families. From the basic learning provided in families or child-care facilities through formal education in elementary and secondary schools, the learning potential of children and youth is developed. Box 13-5 contains data indicating that the day-care arrangements for children of working mothers are about equally divided between a day-care center, someone caring for the child in his or her own home, or care in someone else's home. Income level and the family's educational background are highly correlated with the child's stimulation and learning opportunities. For example, 48 percent of the children from families above the poverty line are enrolled in formal education programs with curricula designed to prepare them for beginning kindergarten, as compared to only 34 percent of those from families who live below the poverty level. Furthermore, 37 percent of the 3- to 5-year-olds in homes where the mother's education is less than high school are read to on a daily basis, as compared to 77 percent of those whose mothers were college graduates.

Each year, 5 percent of the students in high schools drop out and, most likely, have difficulty succeeding in the employment market. Once again, educational level is highly associated with race and ethnicity. In 1996, for example, 92 percent of the white (non-Hispanic) youth completed high school, as compared to 83 percent of the black (non-Hispanic) and 63 percent of the Hispanic youth.

Box 13-5 **Educational Status of U.S. Children and Youth** (per 100,000 population with 26,160 ages 0–17)

> *Day-Care Arrangements for Child Under Age 5 with Employed Mother (1993)*
> - Day-care center, 30% = 2,128
> - Father, relative, or other in child's home, 31% = 2,199
> - Relative or other not in child's home, 32% = 2,270
> - Mother cares for child while working, 6% = 426
>
> *Early Childhood Education Program, Ages 3–4 (1996)*
> - 53% = 1,567
>
> *Daily Family Reading to Children, Ages 3–5 (1996)*
> - 57% = 2,527
>
> *High School Dropout, Ages 15–17 (1994)*
> - 5% = 214
>
> *High School Completions During Last Year (1996)*
> - White (non-Hispanic), 92% = 882
> - Black (non-Hispanic), 83% = 193
> - Hispanic, 63% = 126

HEALTH STATUS AND CHRONIC PHYSICAL CONDITIONS

A critical factor in the successful growth and development of children and youth that concerns social workers is their health. As Box 13-6 indicates, the health care system in the United States has failed many of the nation's children and youth, particularly those below the poverty line. More than one in every seven children are not covered by any health insurance, and almost 8 percent do not have regular access to any source of health care. Demonstrating that limited access to health insurance and care is largely a function of income, children below the poverty line are more than twice as likely to have poor health status (35 percent as opposed to 15 percent of those above the poverty level) and are almost twice as likely to experience a chronic health condition (9.2 percent compared to 5.4 percent).

Some chronic health conditions exist regardless of income or ability to secure health care. Social workers often work with children and youth experiencing these conditions as they affect their social, psychological, and educational functioning. Up to 3 percent of all children experience such conditions as a physical impairment or deformity; a speech, hearing, or visual impairment; heart disease; migraine headaches; and the like, that severely affect their lives and, as the mortality rates indicate, can result in death.

AT-RISK SOCIAL BEHAVIORS

Social behaviors, too, place children and youth at risk of harm. These are factors for which social workers can and should provide both preventive and treatment services. Youth are faced with many choices and are influenced by peer pressure to engage in activities that can at best damage the quality of their lives and, at worst, lead to their

Box 13-6 **Health Status of U.S. Children and Youth** (per 100,000 population with 26,160 ages 0–17)

Family Without Any Type of Health Insurance (1996)
- 15% = 3,924

Family Without Any Usual Source of Health Care (1995)
- 7.9% = 2,067

Health Status Less Than "Very Good" or "Excellent" (1995)
- Below poverty line, 35% = 1,831
- Above poverty line, 15% = 3,139

Activity Limited by Chronic Condition (1995)
- Below poverty line, 9.2% = 481
- Above poverty line, 5.4% = 1,130

Selected Chronic Condition (1994)
- Asthma, 6.1% = 1,805
- Physical deformity or orthopedic impairment, 2.8% = 733
- Speech impairment, 2.1% = 549
- Hearing impairment, 1.8% = 471
- Visual impairment, 0.9% = 235
- Heart disease, 1.8% = 471
- Migraine headaches, 1.6% = 419
- Epilepsy, 0.5% = 131
- Overweight, 85% above recommended body mass index (1991)
  - Ages 6–11, 22.3% = 1,965
  - Ages 12–17, 21.7% = 1,839

Mortality Rates per Year (1996)
- Infant deaths, 0.7% = 11
- Children ages 1–4 deaths, 0.04% = 3
- Children ages 5–14 deaths, 0.02% = 3
- Youth ages 15–17 deaths, 0.08% = 4

---

death. In Box 13-7, the data for rates for such teen-age social behaviors as sexual activity, contraceptive use, and pregnancy; smoking, drinking, and illicit drug use; involvement in crime; motor vehicle at-risk behavior; and potential suicide risk are presented.

Since the beginning of social work, members of this profession have been concerned about the plight of children and youth. The issues have changed over time, but the challenges today are perhaps as great as ever. Social workers, therefore, need tools to assist them in analyzing the available information in order to find ways to address these problems. One such tool is the *ecosystems model.*

THE ECOSYSTEMS MODEL

One way of attempting to organize an enormous amount of social, cultural, and physical and mental health data to develop points of intervention for the social worker is to apply the ecosystems model discussed in Part Four. For example, at the *historical level,* when one considers historical issues impacting children and youth

Box 13-7 **At-Risk Social Behavior of U.S. Children and Youth** (per 100,000 population with 26,160 ages 0–17)

Sexually Active (had intercourse) in Last Three Months (1995)
- 9th grader, 24% = 342
- 10th grader, 34% = 485
- 11th grader, 42% = 599
- 12th grader, 50% = 713

Sexually Experienced Females' Contraceptive Measures (1995)
- Condom use, 49%
- Birth control pill, 20%

Females Experiencing Pregnancy
- Pregnancies, ages 15–17 (1991)
- 7.5% = 156
- Abortions, ages 15–17 (1992)
- 2.3% = 48

Cigarette Smoker, smokes daily (1997)
- 8th grade, 9% = 128
- 10th grade, 18% = 257

Heavy Drinker, 5 or more drinks in a row in past 2 weeks (1997)
- 8th grade, 14.5% = 208
- 10th grade, 25.1% = 358

Illicit Drug Use, used in past 30 days (1997)
- 8th grade, 12.9% = 184
- 10th grade, 23.0% = 328

Involvement with Violent Crime (1996)
- Committed serious violent crime, 3.6% = 304
- Victim of serious violent crime, 3.3% = 289
- Firearms deaths, ages 15–17 (1995), 0.02% = 1

9–12 Graders Carried a Weapon, at least once in last 30 days (1995)
- Male, 31% = 907
- Female, 8% = 222

Motor Vehicle Use
- Seat-belt use, ages 15–17 (1990), 68% = 1,369 (not using belts)
- Crash deaths, ages 15–17 (1994), 0.03% = 2

Suicide, 9th to 12th graders
- Seriously considered suicide in last year (1995), 24% = 1,369
- Attempted suicide in last year (1995), 9% = 513
- Deaths, ages 10–14 (1994), 0.02% = 1
- Deaths, ages 15–17 (1994), 0.11% = 5

in the United States, it is clear that this country has come a long way from the days of exploiting children ten to fifteen hours a day in mines, agricultural fields, and factories during the Industrial Revolution and into the 1930s and even the 1940s. This practice is almost nonexistent today, except for migrant farmworker children who do not attend school in order to earn income to help their underpaid parents support the family. Authorities, business owners, and schools seem to look the other way when this is happening, since the children's work helps the economy significantly. Other examples reflect areas of progress, yet at the same time there are many examples of humanitarian violations and lack of compassion toward troubled youths. One such example concerns the capital punishment of juveniles. In the 1940s, the United States executed forty-nine youths ages 16 and 17 for homicides. Today, as a result of *Thompson* vs. *Oklahoma* in 1988, the Supreme Court ruled that no person under the age of 18 can be executed and no person can be executed for having committed a capital crime while under the age of 18.

Applying the ecosystems model at the *environmental/structural* level, it is evident that the environment has improved significantly for most children and youth in the nation. This, however, is directly related to affluence; that is, the higher the affluence, the better the environment. The structure of the environment is largely determined by policies, laws, rules, regulations, and allocation of resources by those in political power. Again, families with the most influence with the power structure receive the best treatment for their environment. For example, when the Los Angeles earthquake struck in January 1992, the areas that received the quickest relief; police and fire services; street, freeway, and building repairs; and food and water were the affluent areas of Los Angeles. American born children and youth of undocumented parents were denied assistance, even though the poorest families lived in the hardest hit areas of Los Angeles. Twenty and thirty years ago, such a dynamic would have been called either racism or institutional racism, terms that are considered obsolete and nonexistent today; however, these types of discriminatory behaviors and practices are very much alive. Social workers may apply whatever terms they wish to these environmental/structural issues, but they need to develop the critical and analytical skills to assess these issues, which cause children and youth harm.

At the *cultural level* in the ecosystems model, the focus is on the values, belief systems, and societal norms of American culture; but care must be given to not ignoring the cultural heritage of children and parents who were born and raised in other cultures. In most cases, children and youth possessing more than one culture are viewed as enriched, because they speak more than one language and have more than one culture to draw on as prescriptions for life and survival. In some states, however, this is viewed as anti-American, and informal to formal legislative efforts are made to discourage children and youth from using other languages in school or being taught in their own language as a transitional learning phase into English. In some states these programs are called "English as a second language" programs. Social workers, therefore, need to understand local and state policies that enhance educational development, as well as those that place additional burdens on children and youth, because poor academic performance is the highest predictor related to crime and delinquency.

Culture also determines the way in which families raise and discipline their children. For example, American culture highly values corporal punishment of children and youth by their parents. Some cultures outlaw this practice, yet some countries practice severe forms of corporal punishment that Americans would consider criminal. Social workers need to understand these differences and assess whether the practice is traumatic for the specific recipient of the punishment, as opposed to the rationale provided by the administrator of the discipline. A position paper developed by social workers on this subject is provided in the final chapter of this volume.

At the *family level* in the ecosystems model, emphasis is placed on the nature of the specific family life-style, culture, organization, division of labor, sex role structure, and interactional dynamics. Each family *is* unique. For children and youth raised in one intact, nuclear family, the task of incorporating all these potential benefits is far less difficult than it would be for children who are raised in foster or group homes, with relatives, or in separate two-parent families. Consider the often complex issues faced by minors in the *reconstituted* family, which finds two newly wed parents, each with his or her own children from a prior marriage (each child with its own sibling rivalry issues), moving into "one happy home." Each parent has his or her way of raising children, and the children in turn might resist the authority of the new parent, who might have different ideas of the role of children in the family and how they should be disciplined. Because of their complex developmental stage, adolescents sometimes are found to rebel in these types of families. It becomes even more complicated in reconstituted families when the new parents each come from a different culture. However, the majority of these families find ways of surviving in spite of all the obstacles, and only a few of these minors come to the attention of legal, health, and welfare agencies.

Finally, the ecosystems model calls for an analysis at the *individual level,* focusing on the biological and psychological endowment of each person. In the case of children and adolescents who are beginning to show symptoms of the risk behaviors mentioned earlier in the chapter, it is especially important to investigate the biological, genetic, and psychosocial factors in the family history, such as addictions, seizures, behavioral problems, hospitalizations (health and mental health), juvenile/adult corrections history, and psychiatric histories, such as depression, anxiety disorders, schizophrenia, and developmental disabilities. A thorough assessment will find the social worker asking questions about pertinent family history and obtaining this information from each parent, their parents, and, if possible, even their parents, which, in effect, would be the children's great-grandparents. Such family histories can offer extremely important clues to understanding the current problem behavior of a child or adolescent. Figure 13-1 highlights some of the factors discussed in this section.

A MICRO CASE ANALYSIS

The following represents a micro case composite to assist social workers in understanding what factors to look into as they attempt to understand the high-risk behavior of children and adolescents. The discussion will follow the ecosystems model format.

THE HIGH-RISK BEHAVIOR.   The high-risk behavioral problem in our micro case composite concerns a seventeen-year-old boy named "Joe," who is a biracial male who, upon being discovered in his girlfriend's apartment, hid in a closet while armed and shot through the door when called out by the police. He wounded one of the police officers. Upon the minor firing first, the officers (including the wounded

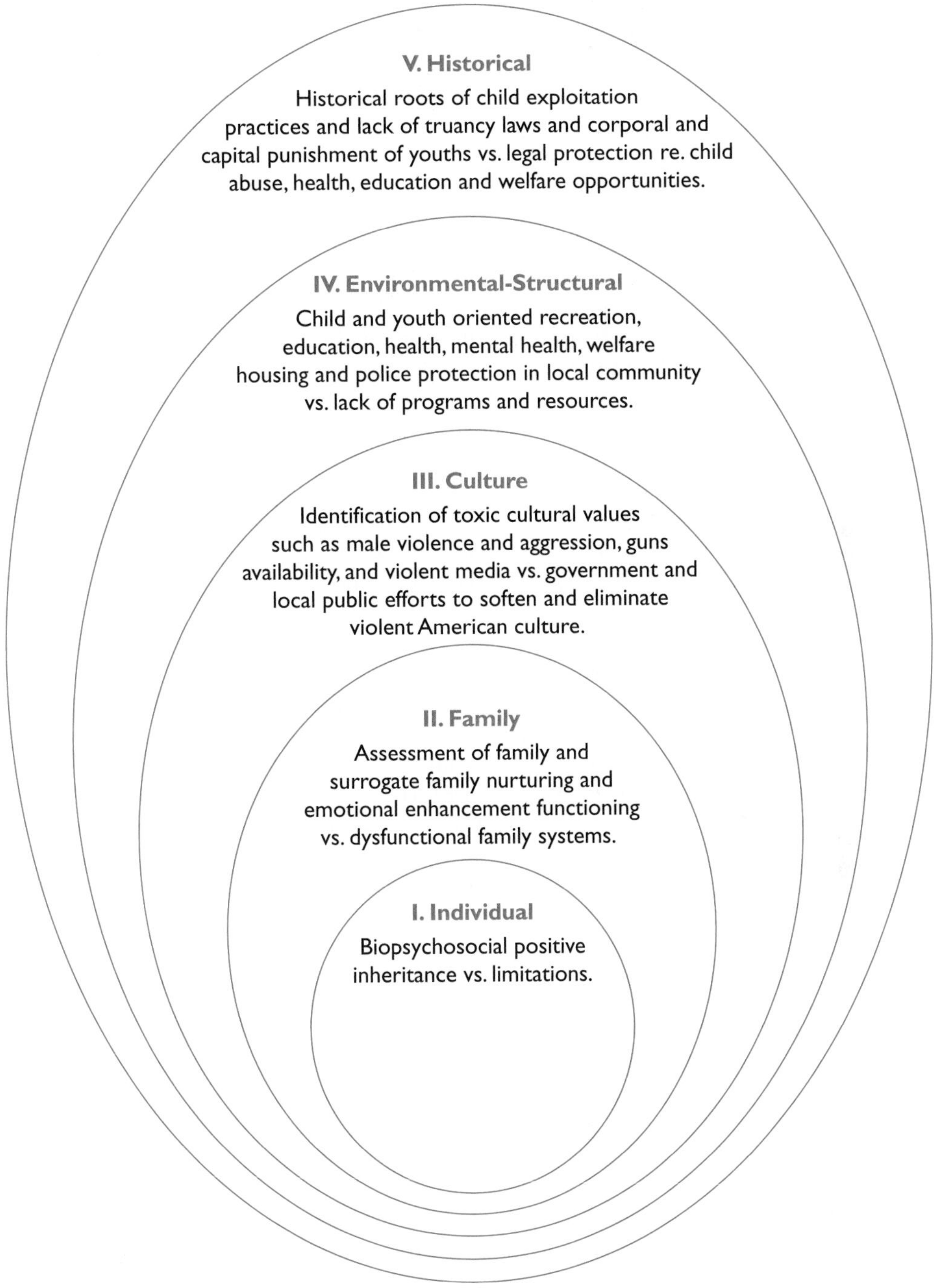

V. Historical

Historical roots of child exploitation
practices and lack of truancy laws and corporal and
capital punishment of youths vs. legal protection re. child
abuse, health, education and welfare opportunities.

IV. Environmental-Structural

Child and youth oriented recreation,
education, health, mental health, welfare
housing and police protection in local community
vs. lack of programs and resources.

III. Culture

Identification of toxic cultural values
such as male violence and aggression, guns
availability, and violent media vs. government and
local public efforts to soften and eliminate
violent American culture.

II. Family

Assessment of family and
surrogate family nurturing and
emotional enhancement functioning
vs. dysfunctional family systems.

I. Individual

Biopsychosocial positive
inheritance vs. limitations.

FIGURE 13-1 **Ecosystems Model for Analysis of Psychosocial Factors Impacting Children and Youth**

officer) retaliated in self-defense and fired 20 shots through the door, of which twelve bullets hit the minor. The minor's explanation was simply, "I wanted them to kill me. I shot at them so they would kill me." Is this normal behavior for adolescents? Is this a form of homicide, suicide, or both? Why did he do this? What factors led to this tragic confrontation, which resulted in the adolescent being tried and convicted as an adult for assault to commit murder upon police officers and sentenced to 25 years to life in state prison? He now joins nearly 2 million other troubled people in prison in the United States whose high-risk behavior began in childhood and adolescence. What can we learn? To assist the court and jury in understanding the reasons for this behavior, a social worker was appointed by the court to address these issues.

THE INDIVIDUAL.   Joe was interviewed in jail in English, which is his only language. He is of Anglo and African American descent, 6 feet 3 inches, very slim, about 143 pounds, and has light, olive-complexioned skin. He was dressed in the traditional bright orange jail clothing with one hand only showing out of his uniform. His right hand had been amputated as the result of wounds he received during his violent confrontation with the police. He exhibited excellent middle-class verbal skills and vocabulary and was above average intelligence with an IQ of 118, although he dropped out of school in the eleventh grade. He had fifteen prior contacts with police since age eleven, most of these for minor offenses such as trespassing, running away, vandalism, curfew, and theft from a neighbor. His most serious offense previously was for stealing a car and reckless driving in this stolen vehicle while being pursued by the police.

During the entire interview, he was attentive, socially comfortable, and friendly, made good eye contact, was cooperative, and answered all questions without hesitation, even elaborating in some of his responses. He was well-oriented to time, person, place, and surroundings. No distortions in perceptions were noted, nor was there evidence of psychosis, hallucinations, delusions, depersonalization, or other perceptual disturbances. His thought processes were clear and there was no evidence of a thought disorder. His thought content was not paranoid or delusional. He was not homicidal nor suicidal and, prior to the instant offense, he had never made homicidal attempts against anyone. He had never made any suicide attempts, but a year ago when his grandmother died he had suicidal thoughts, but with no specific plan. Now, while in jail, he has had occasional suicidal ideation, but with the absence of a specific plan. No brain disorder symptoms were present. He has always had sleeping problems, going to bed very late and getting up very late in the morning, almost at noon. In jail he is required to get up early and go to bed early, but he still suffers from insomnia. He has a poor appetite, and while in jail he has lost 30 pounds in one year. The weight loss and sleep disturbance could be related to depression and trauma, which then become an important area for further assessment as to etiology.

Depression can also be caused by alcohol and drugs. In Joe's case, it is seen that he began using alcohol at age 12 with regular use by age 13, usually two to three 40-ounce bottles of beer nightly until his arrest in the present matter. He smoked marijuana "like cigarettes." In his case, the marijuana lifted his depressed mood caused by the alcohol.

THE FAMILY.   Joe's parents were never married, although they always lived in the same city. They lived together for the first four or five years in a stormy relationship. The mother's parents never approved of her "being with a black man." The mother, age 34, a part-time waitress of Anglo American descent, had Joe when she was 16 years of age. She still lives with her parents. Teen-age motherhood can place a child at high risk for future psychosocial problems. The father, age 35, is of African American descent and is a periodically employed auto mechanic. The father reports that he is an alcoholic, as are his parents and three brothers and sisters. Joe's mother also admits to an occasional drinking problem and has used cocaine in the past. She reports that her only brother is dying of alcoholism. Addiction and depression genes run in families and can be inherited. Joe received a double genetic loading of addiction genes from both sides of the family, which certainly contributed to his alcoholism.

Joe did not have a stable childhood and really was never happy. He cried often as a child and was always angry as he got older. He was raised by at least three family groups: first by his mother and father; later by his mother and her parents; and thereafter by his mother, at times by his father when his mother could not tolerate him, and in later adolescent years by his maternal grandparents. After his maternal grandmother died, he lived with his maternal grandfather. Discipline was inconsistent and confusing for Joe as a child and later as an adolescent. For punishment, his mother would make him stand in a closet for hours as a "time-out"; his grandparents felt sorry for him and did not set any limits or form of discipline; and his father spanked him and on occasions hit him with his fists to counterbalance the grandparent's permissiveness.

CULTURE.   Joe is multicultural, having absorbed both the positive and negative elements of African and Anglo American culture. Although his parents did not complete high school, they valued education and tried to persuade Joe to do his homework, even to the point of severely punishing him, which made him resent school, education, and authority even more. A "drinking culture" and an acceptance of firearms were valued by all three family units, and each family had firearms in the home. At times Joe would go target shooting with his mother or rabbit hunting with his father. Only the maternal grandparents attended church regularly—Joe's parents had different religions and they fought about which religion Joe should incorporate into his moral value system. The problem was "solved" by Joe not being exposed to any religion. Corporal punishment is also determined by the cultural values of a society. Joe's three family units believed in corporal punishment, but only the father actually used it. Joe felt that both the father's corporal punishment and the mother's lengthy time-outs were equally stressing.

Being raised in the U.S. culture that has valued racism for centuries, it was especially painful for Joe as a child to hear his white grandparents' rejection of his father because he was "black." Some of the heated arguments between his parents involved the "race card," with the mother calling the father *nigger* and the father calling the mother "dirty white trash."

Such conflict in his early years contributed to an identity crisis in Joe; his mother recalls him frequently crying at home until nine or ten years of age, wishing he were "white." As he entered adolescence, he rejected the white in him, which he perceived as weakness, and instead accepted the "black" in him, which brought him power and respect. He began to dress in black-gang-oriented clothing, with *Raiders* logos. He founded a gang called the *HBRs* (Half-Breed Rainbows) comprised of biracial adolescent males (Japanese Anglos, Mexican Anglos, African American Anglos, Filipino Anglos, and American Indian-Anglos). Apparently, these biracial youths, or "half-breeds" as Joe preferred that they be called, were experiencing the same stresses and identity conflicts as Joe; together, they were a surrogate family.

ENVIRONMENTAL–STRUCTURAL ISSUES.   Joe's three family units resided in either white lower middle class or the poor African American community. Through elementary school, when living with his mother or grandparents, he was only one of just a handful of biracial children in a 95 percent plus white school. Almost on a daily basis, his mother reports that he would come home crying because the "white kids" called him *nigger*. It was not much better for him in the elementary school when he stayed with his father, because then he was rejected by the African American children because he was not "all black." When he formed his gang and dressed in black, he intimidated white high school students and earned some "respect." In the poor environment where juvenile gang culture was almost everywhere, it was not difficult to establish his gang. Frequent police harassment of gangs and Joe for being "black" only added to his defiance toward authority. Joe was never referred for counseling or mental health services in the middle-class community he was residing in, and these services did not exist in the African American section of town.

HISTORICAL ISSUES.   Joe received a sentence of 25 years to life in state prison for attempted murder of a police officer. Had he killed the officer, he would have automatically received the death penalty, because his state required this for the killing of a law enforcement official. Our penal code laws have evolved over a period of centuries for the protection of society and properly serve this function. Historically, Americans strongly believe in deterrence and the value of corporal punishment in meeting this end. It *might* work in at least 50 percent of the cases *with the appropriate person!* In other words, it is a practice that is risky, with no scientific proof that it does or does not work. Time-outs can also be harmful and psychologically torturing, as seen in Joe's case—again it depends on how it is perceived and felt by the recipient of the punishment.

Our historical values encourage firearms, drinking, and male assertiveness and masculinity. These factors were also very much present in this case. The centuries-old presence of white *and* black racism also played a significant role in this case. Joe was literally caught in the middle of this powerful, toxic, painful issue from birth up until the present. Historically, our nation finds it very difficult to have, as a budget priority, the provision of quality mental health services in poor communities, whether white or African American. The nation maintains a chronic indifference to the plight of the poor and prefers instead to spend billions of dollars on incarceration. In Joe's case, when he comes out of prison in 25 years, the government will have spent at least $1 million for his incarceration, and not one cent for prevention.

THE SOCIAL WORKER'S PSYCHOSOCIAL IMPRESSIONS.   The social worker diagnosed Joe as suffering from a conduct disorder, adolescent type, alcohol and cannabis dependence in full remission because of incarceration, and a recurring major depression, moderate type without psychotic features. Current stressors adding to his depression include incarceration and the loss of his hand. The initial depression, which might have had a biological origin, was present since childhood and could also have been caused by trauma (corporal punishment and time-outs in a closet).

Perhaps the stressor that exacerbated his depression was the painful loss of his grandmother, who he felt was really his mother. Following this loss, he was very depressed and talked with friends about being killed in a shoot-out with rival gangs (suicide by gang) or the police (suicide by cop). Persons who are suicidal are ambivalent about dying. Prior to being shot, he was attempting to avoid a confrontation with police by hiding in the closet, which unconsciously also represented his old familiar chamber for punishment. However, the confrontation escalated, and he forced the police to shoot him (suicide by cop). Psychoanalytically, he was expressing his rage at his own parents (police) for all the punishment they had administered to him. Now he was seeking the ultimate punishment from these parent figures, death! The social worker recommended treatment for him, but neither the jail nor prison had these mental health resources available, because the primary goal of such facilities is detention and punishment.

A MACRO CASE EXAMPLE

Although Joe clearly made decisions that negatively affected his life, he was also a victim of his genetic makeup, his family and environment, and the culture of U.S. society that tolerates racism and fails to actively prevent human problems. Like Joe, many children are highly vulnerable to social problems. Social workers are often involved in programs that provide treatment or rehabilitation for such children and youth.

Some children and youth, however, attempt to become part of the solution to human problems. It is not uncommon, for example, for a child to befriend an elderly neighbor, to develop a special caring relationship with a person experiencing a handicapping condition, or to become an active volunteer providing services in hospitals, schools, churches, or synagogues and in other forms of human services organizations.

Youth sometimes also become involved in the macro side of human services. Although human services agencies do not uniformly engage young people in making policy and program decisions, those that do—and particularly those programs that provide services to youth—find that the engagement of representatives of their consumers can lead to programs that are more relevant to today's youth. Just as effective school principals and teachers actively involve students and student organizations in important decisions about their schools, so too should social workers and human services agencies.

One macro function that supports human services that is frequently performed by children and youth has been fund raising to support an agency cause. Children selling cookies, candy, and magazines to support schools and human services agencies have become an accepted part of U.S. society. Similarly, people are asked to pledge contributions for agencies based on a child's distance in running, skating, swimming, or biking. A good example of youth raising funds to support a worthy cause occurred following the traumatic and seemingly senseless massacre at Columbine High School (Littleton, Colorado) in 1999, in which twelve students and a teacher were killed and many other students were injured and maimed. The two gang members who perpetrated this crime then killed themselves, adding further to the tragedy and the world's confusion about the moral, spiritual, and social values of today's youth. A few months after the shooting, an African American youth in San Francisco, Rashad Williams, decided to raise funds to help pay for medical expenses for a white student from Columbine High School, Lance Kirklin, who had part of his face blown away in the shooting. Although he had not met Kirklin, Williams devoted much of his time and energy to obtaining pledges for individuals and businesses based on the miles he would run in the Bay to Breakers race to support this cause. Williams' mother reported him saying, "You know what, Mom, that could have been me. . . . He could be in a wheelchair the rest of his life. All I have to give him are my two legs."[5] This one effort helped the Kirklin family pay $18,000 of the medical expenses incurred from this tragedy.

Certainly, children and youth have a great deal to contribute to society, particularly to the human services. Social workers and other human services providers too often overlook this important resource that cannot only enhance the services and also help tomorrow's adults prepare for their role as citizens.

Concluding Comment

Growing up in America as an infant, child, and adolescent can be stressful for many and deadly for a small number of young people, with traffic accidents, suicide, and homicide being the major causes for premature death. Poverty, ill health, lack of stimulation, inadequate housing, and other social problems can diminish the quality of life for many others. However, in spite of the many problems and barriers outlined in this chapter, almost 95 percent of our young people survive and become productive citizens.

For the social worker to be effective in his or her intervention with young clients and their families, in-depth knowledge about the issues they face is necessary. The ecosystems model can guide the worker in organizing the direction of the case inquiry so that the information is organized in a form relevant to an accurate assessment and helpful to the client. A detailed micro (or direct service) case was presented to help the reader to understand the many bio- psychosocial issues that may appear in one case and to identify the dynamic interplay of these factors. Effective macro interventions to address the lack of social and mental health services in poor communities, the absence of youth delinquency services, and the lack of attention paid by elementary, middle, and high schools to the prejudice, discrimination, and racism directed at very vulnerable children and adolescents, such as Joe, might have helped to prevent his situation.

In a very different form of macro intervention, social workers can play a vital role by involving young people in establishing and critiquing existing programs and policies, raising funds for social programs (as reflected in Rashad Williams's actions following the Columbine High School shooting), and preparing for responsible citizenship. Perhaps social workers and others have done too little to engage youth in community activities, allowing the 5 percent who are troubled, destructive, or harmful to others to become inaccurately viewed as representative of the young people in the United States today.

KEY WORDS AND CONCEPTS

U.S. Children's Bureau

Child maltreatment

Child poverty and hunger

Child learning and education

Child health conditions

At-risk social behavior

Biracial children and adolescents

Biracial families

Reconstituted families

Corporal punishment

White and black racism

Suicide by cop

Surrogate family

SUGGESTED READINGS

Behrman, Richard E. (ed.). *The Future of Children: Children and Poverty.* Los Altos, CA: Center for the Future of Children, 1997.

Bilchik, Shay. "A Juvenile Justice System for the 21st Century," *Journal of Research on Crime and Delinquency,* 44 (January 1998).

Bremner, Robert H. *From the Depths: The Discovery of Poverty in the United States.* New York: New York University Press, 1969.

Child Trends, Inc. *Trends in the Well-Being of America's Children and Youth: 1997.* Washington, D.C.: U.S. Department of Health and Human Services, 1997.

Federal Interagency Forum on Child and Family Statistics. *America's Children: Key National Indicators of Well-Being, 1998.* Washington, D.C.: U.S. Department of Education, 1998.

Lubove, Roy. *The Professional Altruist: The Emergence of Social Work as a Career, 1880–1930.* Cambridge, MA: Harvard University Press, 1965.

Reno, Janet. "Taking America Back for Our children." *Journal of Research on Crime and Delinquency,* 44 (January 1998).

Wallace, Harvey. *Family Violence: Legal, Medical, and Social Perspectives.* Boston: Allyn and Bacon, 1996.

ENDNOTES

1. Robert H. Bremner. *From the Depths: The Discovery of Poverty in the United States.* New York: New York University Press, 1969, pp. 204–229.
2. Robert D. Plotnick. "Child Poverty Can Be Reduced." In Richard E. Behrman (ed.), *The Future of Children: Children and Poverty.* Los Altos, CA: Center for the Future of Children, 1997, p. 79.
3. Eugene M. Lewit, Donna L. Terman, and Richard E. Behrman. "Children and Poverty: Analysis and Recommendations." In Richard E. Behrman (ed.), *The Future of Children: Children and Poverty.* Los Altos, CA: Center for the Future of Children, 1997, p. 8.
4. John R. Kearnsey, Herman F. Grundmann, and Salvatore J. Gallicchio. "The Influence of Social Security Benefits and SSI Payments on the Poverty of Children." *Social Security Bulletin* 57 (Summer 1994): 27–38.
5. Rob Morse. "Breakers to Littleton: S. F. Teen Runs Race to Aid Shooting Victim." *San Francisco Examiner,* May 11, 1999, p. A-1.

CHAPTER 14

Social Work Practice with the Elderly

Manuel R. Miranda and Armando T. Morales

Prefatory Comment

This is the most recent, "state-of-the-art" scholarly essay in the field on social work practice with the elderly. It was developed by Dr. Manuel R. Miranda, Edward R. Roybal Endowed Chair in Applied Gerontology, California State University, Los Angeles, and Dr. Armando T. Morales, Director of the Clinical Social Work Department of the Neuropsychiatric Institute, School of Medicine, UCLA. They report dramatic demographic changes in the U.S. population, with projections that by the year 2030 the proportion of young persons and elderly will be equal.

Unless a cure is found for Alzheimer's disease by the year 2050, 14 million people will be affected, resulting in $88 billion per year in health care costs. This figure does not measure the emotional costs that will be borne by their families. Social work can play a significant psychosocial role in assisting this major population group. A case example involving an elderly couple demonstrates how micro- and macro-level practice can benefit elderly clients.

One of the most needy populations within the social work practice spectrum is that of the elderly. The fact that they represent the most rapidly increasing subgroup in the United States demands attention to present as well as future policy developments in relation to the social service delivery system.

The elderly population increased eleven-fold from 1900 to 1994, compared with only a three-fold increase for those under age sixty-five. In addition, from 1960 to 1994, the oldest old population (persons aged eighty-five and over) increased by 274 percent, compared with 100 percent for the sixty-five and over and 45 percent for the total population.[1] It is predicted that elderly population growth rates for the 1990–2010 period will be modest, but during the 2010–2030 period, elderly growth rates will increase significantly as Baby Boomers turn sixty-five and over.

The implications of these projected growth rates will have an enormous impact on the field of social work. Issues of health care, housing, social security, and older-worker programs will generate a rapid expansion of programs and services specifically developed for the elderly.

General Population Figures

The rapid increase in the number and proportion of older persons is reflected in the population estimates prepared by the U.S. Census Bureau.[2] As of 1994, there were 33.2 million Americans who were at least sixty-five years old. This figure represents 12 percent of the population. In reference to growth rate, it should be noted that at the beginning of the twentieth century fewer than 4 percent of Americans were age sixty-five and above.

From 1900 to 1991, life expectancy at birth increased from forty-six years for men to seventy-two years; for women, the increase was from forty-eight years to nearly seventy-nine years. In the past few decades, the most dramatic mortality reductions among the elderly have occurred among women and among the oldest old. It is predicted that by the year 2020, the average life expectancy will be 82.0 for women and 74.2 for men. By the year 2040, it is predicted that the average life expectancy will rise to 83.1 for women and 75.0 for men. This projected increase in life expectancy will raise the median age of the U.S. population from thirty-three in 1990, to thirty-six by the year 2000 and to forty-two by the year 2040. Between 1985 and 2050, the total U.S. population is projected to increase by one-third, while the age fifty-five plus population is expected to more than double. This shift in the proportion of elderly to young represents one of the most dramatic incidences of changing age distribution in the United States. In 1900, 4 percent of the population was age sixty-five and over, while young persons birth to seventeen years of age made up 40 percent of the population. By 1994 the proportion of age sixty-five plus had increased to 12 percent, whereas those birth to seventeen had decreased to 30 percent.

U.S. Census Bureau projections suggest that by the year 2030 the proportion of young persons and elderly will be approximately equal, those falling within the first seventeen years of life representing 22 percent and the elderly equaling 21 percent of the population.

The older population is growing older. In part, because of gains in life expectancy at advanced ages, the population age eighty-five and older makes up the fastest growing age group in the U.S. population. The number of American centenarians, which more than tripled to 52,000 between 1980 and 1995, may reach 1 million by the middle of the twenty-first century. Because advanced old age is associated with chronic illness and functional impairments, the aging of the older population portends a substantial increase in the need for health care and supportive social services.

The "young-old" (age sixty-five to seventy-four) will continue to make up the majority of older Americans until about 2030. After that time, people age seventy-five or older will account for more than half of all elderly. By the middle of the twenty-first century, most of the projected growth of older Americans will occur because of increases in the population age eighty-five and older. (See Figure 14-1.) This surge in the number of oldest old can be explained both by the aging of the baby-boom generation into very old age and by the continuing mortality declines at the advanced ages that many expect.

SEX RATIOS

Among Americans age sixty-five and older in 1995, there were sixty men for every one hundred women. The disparity becomes even more marked for those age eighty-five and older—thirty-nine men per one hundred women. This shortfall of men reflects higher male mortality at all ages. Male babies have higher infant mortality rates; men have higher death rates in the teen and young adult years (accidental injuries and AIDS); and middle-age and older men have higher death rates from heart disease and other chronic illnesses. Although about 105 boys are born for every one hundred girls, women outnumber men by age thirty because of the higher male mortality rates. At age sixty-four, the sex ratio, or the number of men per one hundred women is eighty-eight.

Women benefited more than men from improvements in life expectancy in the twentieth century. Consequently, the gender differentials in mortality widened and the sex ratio of men to women decreased. Because women are more likely than men to survive to the oldest ages, the health, social, and economic problems of the oldest old are primarily the problems of women. This fact requires a significant shift in an existing social service system if the growing needs of these elderly women are to be met.

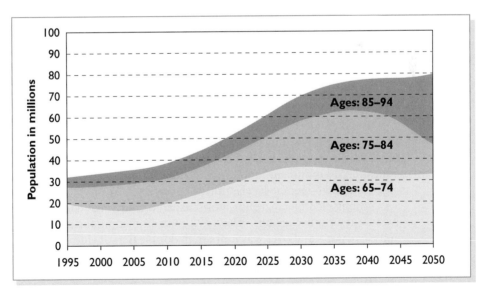

FIGURE 14-1 **Projection of the U.S. Elderly Population, by Age: 1995–2050**

Source: U.S. Bureau of the Census, *Current Population Reports,* P25-1104 (Washington, D.C.: U.S. Government Printing Office, 1993), Table 2.

RACIAL AND ETHNIC DIVERSITY

The older population is becoming more ethnically and racially diverse. Because of higher birth rates and immigration rates of ethnic and racial minority groups, African American, Hispanic, and Asian populations are increasing more rapidly than is the non-Hispanic white population.[3] Non-Hispanic whites made up about 80 percent of the U.S. population in 1980, but this share slipped to 74 percent by 1995. Similarly, the ranks of the minority elderly are growing more rapidly than those of the non-Hispanic whites. The non-Hispanic white share of the elderly population declined from 88 percent in 1980 to 85 percent in 1995. This trend will accelerate in coming decades. By 2050, the non-Hispanic white share of the elderly population is projected to fall to 67 percent.

The ethnic composition of the elderly minority population will change dramatically in coming decades. Although African Americans and Native Americans will slowly gain population share, the most remarkable growth is projected for Hispanics and for Asians and Pacific Islanders. African Americans were the largest minority in 1995, with 8 percent of the sixty-five-and-older population, but they may be surpassed in number by Hispanic elderly before 2020. By the middle of the twenty-first century, one in six Americans age sixty-five and older is expected to be Hispanic. Asians and Pacific Islanders are expected to grow from 2 percent of older Americans in 1995 to 7 percent in 2050.

INCOME AND ASSETS

In general, the income level of older Americans is significantly lower than for younger adults. For the most part, this is due to retirement from the work force, with limited replacement of lost wages though Social Security and pension benefits. Many elderly individuals are unable to find employment due to age discrimination in the workplace, or they are encumbered with physical disabilities preventing them from working. As a consequence, many older individuals are placed in a position of economic vulnerability frequently heightened by inflation, loss of a spouse, and increasing frailty.

While the overall economic picture for the elderly is, in general, less than satisfactory, it would be a mistake to perceive them as a homogenous group. Income differs greatly as a result of such variables as age, sex, race, living arrangements, educational attainment, and work history. Some of the elderly have considerable assets and high income levels; others have very little.

Among elderly subgroups, non-Hispanic white men had a much higher median income than other groups. The 1992 median income for non-Hispanic white men sixty-five years and over was more than double that of elderly African American and Hispanic women. (See Figure 14-2. The differences in median income were not statistically significant between African American and Hispanic women and between non-Hispanic white women and Hispanic men.) Data from the 1980 and 1990 censuses showed a similar pattern.

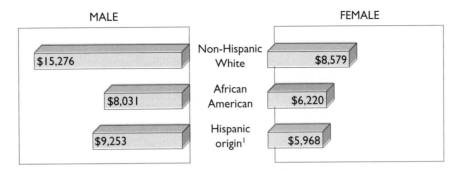

FIGURE 14-2 **Median Income of Persons 65 Years and Over, by Sex and Race: 1992**

¹Hispanic origin may be of any race.

Source: U.S. Bureau of the Census, "Money Income of Households, Families, and Persons in the United States: 1992," *Current Population Reports*, P60-184 (Washington, D.C.: U. S. Government Printing Office, 1993), Table 26.

EDUCATIONAL BACKGROUND

Those Americans sixty-five years and over are less likely than those aged twenty-five to sixty-four to have completed high school. In 1993, only 60 percent of noninstitutionalized elderly persons had at least a high school education compared with 85 percent of persons aged twenty-five to sixty-four.[4] While there are no significant sex differences in educational level within the elderly population, there are considerable differences among non-Hispanic whites, African Americans, and Hispanics. Fewer than 33 percent of older African Americans and 26 percent of Hispanics had completed high school in 1994, with the median level of education equivalent to an eighth-grade education. Approximately 21 percent of older non-Hispanic whites had completed at least one year of college, relative to 8 percent of the elderly African Americans and 7 percent of elderly Hispanics.

While the elderly are reflecting higher educational levels as new cohorts enter the sixty-five-and-above bracket, the present situation seriously limits their ability to compete for employment in the modern technological world. Alternate educational opportunities, such as extension programs at local educational institutions as well as government-sponsored vocational rehabilitation programs, are greatly needed. The role of social work in assisting the elderly to re-enter employment or remain productively employed is a challenge to the profession.

HEALTH STATUS AND NEEDS

Advancing medical interventions and preventive programs have markedly improved the health status of our elderly population. The average individual sixty-five and older generally perceives him- or herself to be in good health. In fact, 70 percent of individuals included in the 1993 Health Interview Survey conducted by the National

Center for Health Statistics rated their health excellent, very good, or good relative to others their age.[5] However, given that the most chronic diseases and disabilities occur in the later decades of life, the increasing aging of our population is likely to have a substantial impact on the need for medical services, long-term care, and social services. Of the percentage of the gross national product spent on health care in 1994, one-third of the expenditures for personal health care were for older individuals.[6] The significant increase in the number of elderly individuals in the population, presently as well as into the distant future, will require a substantial allotment of medical, economic, and social and mental health resources to meet their needs.[7]

Maintenance of the quality of life for our older citizens will become an increasingly vital issue for the health and social welfare professions. Existing governmental programs such as Medicare and Medicaid are presently experiencing difficulties in covering outpatient as well as inpatient expenses. There is currently no long-term care provision in Medicare for either nursing home care or in-home assistance. Only those elderly individuals "spending down" to poverty are eligible for long-term nursing home care supported by Medicaid—a frightening prospect for the vast majority of our elderly.

As for the major health problems afflicting the elderly, heart disease leads all other conditions in both cause of death and utilization of health care services.[8] Heart disease, cancer, and stroke taken together are responsible for more than 75 percent of all deaths among the elderly. All three of these physical problems frequently lead to chronic conditions requiring long-term care.

Alzheimer's disease and other forms of dementia are major and rapidly growing public health problems in the United States. Based on findings in a recent study, it is estimated that as many as 4 million people in the United States are suffering from Alzheimer's disease, with half of those aged eighty-five and older thought to be afflicted.[9] Unless a prevention or cure is discovered, as many as 14 million individuals in the United States may suffer from Alzheimer's disease by the year 2050. In 1990 the cost of caring for victims of Alzheimer's disease was thought to exceed $88 billion per year. The economic and emotional impact on the family and care providers of Alzheimer's patients are devastating.

The elderly are more likely than younger groups to be afflicted with multiple health problems, thus creating a synergistic effect in increasing their degree of emotional despair. This problem is particularly acute in nursing home settings, which have increasingly become the dumping ground for our mentally ill elderly.[10] The degree of mental illness coupled with the virtual absence of significant mental health treatment in nursing homes represents one of the most neglected problems in the field of mental health services in this country.

Ecosystems Model Analysis

A reasonable understanding of the aging process may be obtained through an interactional process providing multivariate input into the analysis of the phenomenon. The ecosystems model developed for this volume by its authors provides such an analytical scheme and will thus serve as the outline for this section.

HISTORICAL FACTORS

The diseases of the aged, the quality of their lives, their ability and willingness to care for themselves, their capacity to cope with stress—all these are shaped not only by individual histories, such as hereditary and early family life, but also by the society in which the aged lived as they were growing up. What were work conditions like? What was family life like? What social services were provided? Were there economic calamities, such as a severe depression?

Certainly, the milieu of today's aged is very different from that of the aged in 1900. There were fewer aged then, both in absolute numbers and as a percentage of the total population: 4 percent in 1900 (3 million) versus 12 percent in 1994 (33 million). Work was usually a lifetime affair in 1900, with formal retirement and a pension an oddity. Today, work is more a stage of life, one that is increasingly entered at an older age and left at a younger one. One pension (Social Security) is now usual, with two pensions per retiree becoming more frequent. The aged today also are better educated.

Less quantifiable changes have also occurred. The belief that the aged are the fittest survivors and the mystiques of old age as a time when cares are gone were shattered early in the twentieth century as the realities of the lives of many of the aged became more widely known. Desperate poverty was often the reward of a lifetime of labor, since there were no pensions and no room for elderly workers in an increasingly efficiency-conscious industrial society. Illnesses often went untreated, either because the aged could not afford to pay, because illness was considered inevitable in old age, or because the medical profession preferred to treat the problems of younger people.

In the early twentieth century, with public support perceived as charity, with poorhouses and homes for the aged usually perceived as nothing more than warehouses for the unfit and the dying, with steady employment uncertain, and often with parents and older children all working, the family was essential for survival. Grandparents, parents, and children assumed various roles in ensuring the integrity and well-being of the family. The elderly maintained their property rights, in part as insurance that they would always be cared for. There was no clear distinction between family life and work; no formal retirement age.

The elderly today reflect different experiences. Various centrifugal forces on the family—social legislation giving individuals more independence and greater mobility, more emphasis within the family on raising children, and more mothers working outside the home—have distorted the traditional interdependencies between the elderly and their children and grandchildren. The Great Depression left its economic and psychological scars. A lifetime of relatively low earning now shows up as relatively low pensions for many of the elderly. And life expectancies for men and women have changed; today most elderly women are likely to be widows.

Any effort to understand and deal with the problems of the aged must include these and other elements of their background. Similarly, social work interventions intended to help shape future policies and strengthen current ones must consider changes now occurring in U.S. society. The family today is radically different from what it was thirty-five years ago, and there is evidence of further forces for change.

For example, single-parent families have become a significant phenomenon. The number of adults per household (including those with no children) dropped in 1994 to an average of two. The proportion of families living with a relative such as a grandparent (extended families) has dropped appreciably in the past forty years, and the majority of mothers now work or seek work outside the home when their children reach school age.

These facts are being interpreted by some students of family life as symptomatic of a long-term decline in relationships between parents and children—parents more involved in work or community activities, and children placed in group settings, formal or informal. Whatever the interpretation, what will be the effects of these changes on people, both parents and children, as they age? How will they as elderly adults cope with stresses, with chronic illness? What problems will they have that are not evident now among the elderly?

The needs and demands of the future aged will be different from those of today, but we are uncertain of what those differences will be. Many of the future aged will be better educated. Their Social Security pensions, increasingly supplemented by a second pension, should enable them to sustain a tolerable standard of living, although paradoxically the gap between their employment earnings and their pensions may be greater than it is for many of today's aged.

All in all, an understanding of the terrain in which the aged have lived and are living is needed if the field of social work is to perform its task of providing the information and insight needed by society to optimally serve its current and future aged.

ENVIRONMENTAL–STRUCTURAL FACTORS

How do the elderly maintain themselves? Elderly widows and couples? Urban and rural elderly? Well-to-do, suburban white and poor, inner-city African American elderly? What perceptions do different groups of the elderly have of their lives—of health, of their status in society, of their regard to younger people? How are these perceptions formed, and what do they imply about the services needed by the aged? How do these perceptions square with their needs as seen by others? How does this pattern of life prepare the individual for retirement, for the change in income and often in status that may accompany it? How does the individual who has worked for thirty or forty years find new values to replace economic ones?

Infusing these and other questions pertaining to the aged in society are attitudes toward the aged and aging—attitudes held by the aged themselves and by the younger population. Prejudice against the aged—ageism—is displayed in several ways: (1) in our obsession with youth (although that may wane as the average age continues to rise); (2) in the emphasis by the media on extraordinary achievements of the aged, rather than on their ordinary, often satisfying lives; and (3) in the poor general understanding of the values of old age.

Anthropologists have found that the aged are regarded differently in different cultures. Gerontocracies seem to be the norm in traditional, preliterate folk societies. Urbanization, industrialization, and increased mobility may have been among the elements reducing the significance of gerontocracies and lowering the regard for old age. Continued cross-cultural research should further illuminate these elements, which are disputed. The point is that views of the aged widely held in Western societies, including the notion that the old are useless, are not shared by other societies. Bias against the old is not inevitable; rather, it is shaped by various, only partly known forces.

One important element affecting the Western attitude toward the elderly and becoming old is the materialistic economic valuation of human worth—how much money a person makes, how big his or her house is, how much money his or her material possessions cost. In retirement, income drops markedly for most Americans, and there may be the false perception that with retirement one's income is no longer determined by work, but by pension policies. Such changes in level and source of income may result in a loss of esteem among the elderly.

In addition to ageism and the potential loss of status as a result of reduced income with retirement, the elderly generally face a number of additional stresses during the later years of life. As stated by Butler and Lewis, "The elderly are confronted by multiple losses, which may occur simultaneously: death of a partner, older friends, colleagues, relatives; decline of physical health and coming to personal terms with death; loss of status, prestige, and participation in society; and for large numbers of the older population, additional burdens of marginal living standards."[11]

The process of aging, even in the absence of health problems or loss, can be acutely distressing. Confusion and uncertainty confront the elderly as they attempt to deal with the variety of changes accompanying the aging process. Some of these changes occur slowly, such as physical appearance and social status, whereas others occur much more dramatically, such as catastrophic health problems or forced retirement. The process of aging should be visualized as a continuous stream of changes occurring within an environmental–structural setting that more or less dictates how the changes will affect the elderly. The increasing unpredictability and loss of physical and/or mental control accompanying aging, plus the inevitability of death, contribute to making this life stage one of considerable difficulty.

The sensitivity of one's environment in responding to the multitude of physical, economic, and social needs accompanying old age symbolizes its valuation of its elderly population. The disease of the aged, the quality of their lives, their ability and willingness to care for themselves, their capacity to cope with stress—all these are shaped not only by individual histories, such as heredity and early family life, but also by the environmental–structural setting in which the elderly live. This setting must provide the acceptance needed in structuring effective policies, planning effectively for the future, enabling both society and the elderly to make optimum use of available resources and, above all, enriching the lives of the elderly.

CULTURE

The question as to whether an elderly culture exists remains unclear in the social science literature. Comparability to other minorities, such as ethnic or racial subgroups, as well as other age groups (e.g., teenagers), are seen by some researchers as inappropriate and lacking in clarity as to the special role of the aged in our society. This can be noted in the following excerpt:

> The aged do not share a distinct and separated culture; membership in the group defined as "aged" is not exclusive and permanent, but awaits all members of our society who live long enough. As a result, age is a less distinguishable group characteristic than others such as sex, occupation, social class, and the like. True, many aged persons possess distinctive physical characteristics. But even here there is a broad spectrum, and these "stigmata" do not normally justify differential and discriminatory treatment by others.[12]

With the rapid increase in the number of individuals sixty-five years of age and older, as well as the dramatic rise in their percentage of the general population, the social and political visibility of the elderly has never been higher. A multitude of professional, political, economic, and social organizations representing the elderly have developed over the past twenty years, forcing an increased focus on both social service and political action. However, evidence as to whether the elderly can be thought of as a separate and distinct culture remains equivocal at best. The tremendous heterogeneity among our elderly (e.g., race, ethnicity, economic status, health, sex, education level, and geographic location) makes it quite difficult to think of them as an age-segregated subculture. But they do reside within the context of an American culture that values and practices ageism, with its accompanying social, economic, and psychological consequences.

It would seem more appropriate to think of the elderly as a group with many common concerns related to their physical, social, and economic status; and that our social service delivery systems should become more cognizant of these needs in developing effective intervention modalities. The fact that the elderly are often economically vulnerable and beset with health and social problems are factors associated with the aging process, as opposed to cultural organization or process. The concept of a distinct subpopulation, however, does assist in the reorganization and development of social policy, planning, and service delivery. Perhaps the only "cultural" factor related to the elderly in the United States is the fact that they are not as valued as people in more traditional cultures value their elderly.

FAMILY ISSUES

With the increase in aging of our society, separate generations of children, parents, and grandparents will share such experiences of adulthood as work, parenthood, and even retirement. Altered mortality and fertility patterns have resulted in the development of a new atmosphere for the building and maintenance of family relations. The fact that contemporary parents and children will spend a greater proportion of their lives together as adults than ever before in history speaks directly to the opportunity to form deep bonds of rapport and empathy. In addition, with reduced fertility rates, there are fewer individuals within the family network, thus affording the opportunity for not only a more extensive intergenerational network but a more intensive one as well.

As a result of the reduction in fertility and mortality, our society is currently confronted with a situation in which, for the first time in history, the average married couple has more parents than children.[13] With a significant reduction in the number of childbearing years, as well as a reduction in the number of years between the first- and last-born child, generation demarcations have become clearer. For most women, the active years of child raising are over by the time they become grandmothers. And with the extension of life, grandparents are now living independently of their children for twenty-five years or more. The implications of this are not totally clear, but serving as some familial stabilizing force due to their experience, wisdom, and economic resources is a distinct possibility.

The elderly are frequently portrayed as a frail and dependent group who create a drain on our national resources and are a strain on family caregiving. There is no doubt that the oldest-old, those eighty-five and above, are in greater need of medical assistance and long-term care. Meeting the physical and social needs of our rapidly growing oldest-old represents one of the major social welfare concerns of the future. However, there are a vast number of our elderly who are healthy, independent, and willing to contribute to the enhancement of their families' well-being. In fact, available research indicates that the elderly in industrialized societies tend to give more economic assistance than they receive.[14]

The ability of the elderly to serve as a "safety valve" within the family network can express itself in a variety of ways. They could serve as arbitrators between their children and grandchildren, specifically assisting grandchildren in understanding parental responsibilities, as well as give economic backup during the usual family problems of home ownership, educational expenses for children and grandchildren, and unexpected financial burdens. With the increasing number of separations, divorces, and single-parent households, grandparents are frequently called on to serve as stress buffers for their children, as well as serving as substitute parents for their grandchildren.

Clearly, the changing roles of the elderly in family life include an increasing degree of multigenerational networking, with more distinct lines between the generations due to decreased mortality and fertility. The opportunities for more extensive and intensive bonding within families in an aging population could provide the basis for the strengthened interdependency necessary for meeting an individual's needs in the eighth and ninth decades of the life cycle.

INDIVIDUAL ISSUES

Self-concept among the aged has shown some interesting changes throughout history. In preindustrial eras, the elderly generally enjoyed revered status, although their numbers were much smaller than is the case today. With the advent of the industrial and post-industrial eras, however, the value placed on accumulated historical knowledge and experience has given way to innovation, creativity, and productivity. At this point, the elderly were increasingly perceived as outdated, a burden on society's overall economic development. Over time, more and more employers developed strategies to remove older individuals from the workforce with early retirement incentives or outright dismissal. As a consequence, the perception of growing old frequently implied being unproductive, not retainable, and physically incapable. Many of the elderly accepted these negative stereotypes, thus creating a diminished sense of self-worth and low motivation to continue to engage society in a meaningful manner.

With the aging of our population, these negative stereotypes are beginning to change. What it means to be sixty-five and older in today's aging society differs significantly from what it meant in earlier periods. The majority of those over sixty-five today are healthy, youthful in outlook, and willing to remain actively involved in the world of work, family, and community affairs. Clearly, the elderly in contemporary society are redefining the concept of being old, particularly as it applies to societal norms of age-appropriate behavior. Old age in an aging society should be seen as a fluid concept, defined by the traits and abilities of each generation as it becomes older, not determined by past expectations and norms. Perhaps for the specific *individual,* being "old" is more related to "life-style" rather than chronological age. For example, a forty-year-old television "couch potato" might be older *mentally* than a sixty-five-year-old who jogs, roller skates, plays the guitar and keyboard, and is raising a two-year-old daughter.

With better health and independence in the later stages of life, becoming sixty-five does not have to begin a period of withdrawal and decline. On the contrary, this period of the life cycle should represent the opportunity for renewal, with the development of new skills and goals for leading a productive life. Being productive does not necessarily imply working full time. Many of today's elderly seek part-time employment and/or full- or part-time volunteer work. With the aging of our society, never before has there been such a need to keep our older individuals actively involved in our general welfare. Likewise, with the lengthening of their lives, the elderly in turn need more than ever to remain meaningfully engaged in productive activity. The development of such opportunities in our society will greatly contribute to a continuing sense of self-worth and overall good health among our elderly citizens.

Intervention Strategies with the Elderly

The ecosystems model provides an excellent framework for the development of both macro and micro practice with the elderly. The inclusion of a multivariate set of factors representing the internal as well as external influences on the elderly client provides the necessary guide in structuring an effective intervention strategy. In addition, the profession of social work, with its values and interactional approach, is ideally suited to effectively serve our elderly population. With the variety of changes and needs confronting the elderly client (e.g., financial stability, acute and long-term health care needs, adequate housing, loss of a spouse and other family members, etc.), a profession such as social work, with its focus on making changes in the sociostructural environment as well as within the individual, provides the necessary practice base for effectively developing intervention strategies.

As a field of practice, the profession of social work has enjoyed a longer period of involvement with the elderly than other practice professions.[15] However, social work, as is the case with other practice professions, is frequently guilty of ageism. Butler has defined ageism as a "process of systematic stereotyping of and discrimination against people because they are old, just as racism and sexism accomplish this with skin color and gender. Old people are categorized as senile, rigid in thought and manner, old-fashioned in morality and skills."[16] The categorization of all elderly by a simple set of stereotypes leads to their exclusion from the more advanced techniques of social, mental, and physical health interventions. The perception of their lack of psychological abilities and skills has generally left them excluded from both public and private mental health settings.[17] The great diversity among our elderly in terms of health, income, and educational, occupational, and familial status should immediately disallow any simplistic perception of who they are and what we can do for them. Although their health status may be more vulnerable, the elderly are more often than not very much as they were during earlier periods of their life cycle. To think of them as diminished representations of their former selves results in two failures: one's ineffectiveness as a social work practitioner; and one's inability to meet the needs of a worthy elderly client.

In general, the development of any intervention strategy for the elderly, whether macro or micro, should have as its basic objectives: (1) the promotion of independence to the maximum degree possible; (2) the assistance in obtaining the necessary resources for the maintenance of a good quality of life; (3) the facilitation of effective interaction between the elderly and others in their environment; and (4) the influencing of the development of social policy enhancing the elderly's lives. As noted by Cantor, "Basic to the concept of social care is the notion that assistance is provided as means of augmenting individual competency and mastery of the environment, rather than increasing dependency."[18] With these premises in mind, mental health services for the elderly will be discussed, accompanied by an example of a macro and micro intervention.

Mental Health and the Elderly

While the problem of mental illness occurs in all age groups, the elderly in the United States represent one of our more seriously afflicted populations. Recent studies suggest that between 15 and 25 percent of the 28 million Americans over the age of sixty-five suffer from some form of mental illness.[19] As many as 7 million elderly Americans may be in need of mental health services, a figure that would be considered epidemic in any other health context. The factors responsible for the high degree of emotional disruption among the elderly are multiple, but the increasing degree of alienation from significant societal responsibility, fragmented family support system due to loss of spouse and mobility of children, and declining physical health and/or the demands of caring for a chronically ill spouse contribute to increased feelings of alienation and hopelessness. Depression, for instance, is a major problem whose seriousness cannot be overestimated, especially in light of the fact that elderly men over the age of seventy-five display one of the highest suicide rates of all age categories. Alcohol abuse is increasing in its degree of severity among the elderly, as is the misuse of prescription drugs. All of these represent reactions to feelings of severe stress and alienation. The elderly are also more likely than younger age groups to be afflicted with multiple health problems, thus creating a synergistic effect in increasing their degree of emotional despair. This problem is particularly acute in nursing home settings, which have increasingly become the dumping ground for many of our mentally ill elderly, as an alternative to state institutionalization.[20] The degree of mental illness, coupled with the virtual absence of significant mental health treatment in nursing homes, represents one of the most neglected problems in the field of mental health services in this country.

Unfortunately, the lack of mental health services to the elderly is not limited to nursing home settings. The elderly, while comprising 12 percent of the American population, represent only 6 percent of all persons served by community mental health centers, and only 2 percent of those served by private therapists.[21] The under-representation of the elderly among recipients of mental health services, in both the public and private sectors, directly reflects the lack of sensitivity within the mental health system to the mental health problems and needs of our elderly population.

Existing mental health service delivery systems have generally failed to recognize the diverse nature of our elderly population. The depressed elderly female living alone, the severely stressed and overwhelmed elderly male attempting to care for his Alzheimer's-afflicted wife, and the economically deprived elderly couple forced to live with their children represent just a few examples of the multitude of life-stress situations the elderly confront. This increased vulnerability in the health, economic, and social areas of life would seem to justify the expectation that the elderly would be among the most active utilizers of existing mental health services. The fact that they do not use these services speaks directly to the various impediments preventing effective access.

Traditionally, ageism has prevented many mental health professionals from servicing the elderly, in the belief that therapeutic efforts with older people are likely to be difficult or unproductive. The focus on younger clients, both at the professional practice level and in the training setting, has prevented an understanding of and sensitivity to the special needs of the elderly client. Unfortunately, reversal of this trend is frequently confounded by the elderly themselves. Long-standing negative stereotypes of the mentally ill and "snakepit" institutions frequently prevent the current cohort of elderly from seeking needed services. The end result is that many of them are reluctant to admit to emotional problems and tend to recategorize the situation as either a moral problem, thus seeking assistance from the church, or as a physical problem, resulting in visits to a physician.

A number of practical barriers contribute to the limited access of the elderly to receiving mental health services. Misinformation, coupled with the lack of even the most basic knowledge about the availability of mental health services, contribute to the underutilization problem. Even the healthy, more mobile elderly are frequently discouraged from seeking mental health services due to poor service locations and/or settings lacking environmental sensitivity (e.g., not employing "seniors" in key staff positions) in helping the elderly to seek assistance. In addition, many of the elderly are intimidated by the often-confusing regulations and paperwork imposed by federal and state programs. The fragmentation of the service delivery system, encompassing the processing of each case only as part of a treatment plan and its accompanying red tape, provides a strong disincentive to continue treatment.

The lack of mental health services specifically for the elderly is particularly problematic, especially for ethnic/racial elderly. Recent research demonstrates that participation by the elderly in community mental health center programs could more than double if there were services specially designed for the elderly and staffed with trained mental health professionals.[22] Unfortunately, the consolidation of federal support of mental health services into a block grant, as mandated by the Omnibus Budget Reconciliation Act of 1981, has resulted in a dramatic decrease in funding.

The health care system in this country must be strengthened and restructured so as to encourage the improved delivery of desperately needed mental health services to our nation's elderly. These services should include a variety of support systems for both the elderly and their families and caregivers. Mechanisms are needed to ensure not only that elderly persons and their families have access to the full range of needed services, but that these services be appropriately modified to meet the special needs of the various elderly populations. While admittedly a difficult task, current research demonstrates that increased cooperation between federally funded area agencies on aging and community-based mental health centers has dramatically improved service utilization rates, even among our most difficult-to-reach elderly.[23] Coordination and cooperation among agencies whose responsibilities involve successful aging, health, and mental health services must be ensured if the elderly with mental health needs are to be served adequately.

MICRO PRACTICE WITH THE ELDERLY

What follows is a case example of social work practice with the elderly clients. It highlights the special nature of the elderly's problems, which at times require a different intervention response from social workers than would be so with younger clients.

BACKGROUND
Mr. and Mrs. Soto, age seventy-five and seventy-three, respectively, are an elderly Mexican American couple living in a lower-income Hispanic section of El Paso, Texas. Mr. Soto, who had six years of formal education, came to the United States as an immigrant laborer in his early twenties. He eventually settled in El Paso as a laborer with the Southern Pacific Railroad. Mrs. Soto, who also had six years of formal education, was raised as an orphan in Northern Mexico and immigrated to Los Angeles with an older sister in her late teens. The couple met in El Paso, married, and raised two sons and a daughter. The eldest son was killed in Vietnam, leaving the second-born daughter and the younger son.

STRAINED FAMILY RELATIONSHIPS
While the Sotos had a close and caring relationship, their children experienced severe difficulties with the acculturation process. Their daughter became pregnant in her middle teens, dropped out of high school, and eventually married.

Their son was heavily involved in gang activities as a youth and was in and out of the penal system. The son "grew out" of gang activities and now is supporting a wife and three children as a mechanic in a local El Paso auto shop. As a result of the children's problems during their earlier years, the relationship between Mr. Soto and his children is seriously strained. The son feels particularly rejected by his father, believing that he always favored the eldest son who was killed in Vietnam. In the early years, Mrs. Soto frequently attempted to intervene on behalf of her adolescent children, but was generally forced to accept Mr. Soto's negative perception of his children's behavior and life-style. Mr. Soto has not spoken with his daughter in over five years, and only rarely visits his son on holidays or special occasions. Mrs. Soto has maintained telephone contact with both of her children.

CULTURAL FACTORS

Although Mr. and Mrs. Soto are bilingual, they have always felt more comfortable speaking Spanish. Since Mr. Soto's retirement seven years ago, the couple has spoken Spanish almost exclusively. Neither has been actively involved in the political or social life of the community. They have been content during their married life to regularly attend the local Catholic church, as well as annual cultural events marking significant Mexican holidays. Both have always been actively involved in their garden on weekends, being proud of their skills. On retirement, Mr. Soto also began spending a couple of afternoons during the week at a social club developed for retirees (mostly Hispanic) by the Southern Pacific Railroad.

HEALTH CRISIS CHANGING TRADITIONAL ROLES

Mrs. Soto's activities mainly consisted of taking care of her husband, talking to her children and grandchildren on the telephone, maintaining her garden, and attending church on the weekends. Over a five-year period, Mrs. Soto's visits to the local comprehension health clinic became more frequent, because she suffered from osteoporosis and had fractured her hip in a fall six months before. Following two months of hospitalization, she was released to be cared for at home by her husband.

After fifty-one years of marriage, Mr. Soto was now placed in the position of being the caregiver instead of the care receiver. While at first assuring his wife and hospital staff that he could manage her care on his own, Mrs. Soto's minimal hearing and limited mobility began to overwhelm him. He began to feel guilty about his anger at her dependency and too proud to accept his estranged daughter's request that she be allowed to help out. Mr. Soto's son was having severe difficulties meeting his own family's needs and wasn't sure how to approach his father to offer whatever help he could give. Mr. Soto also was not particularly good in providing clarity to his son as to how he could assist.

PHYSICAL AND EMOTIONAL DECOMPENSATION

As the months passed and his wife's condition did not improve, Mr. Soto became withdrawn and depressed. Mrs. Soto had regressed to the point of requiring her husband's assistance in bathing and toilet needs. He found these activities particularly distasteful and became increasingly impatient with his wife's requests. Sensing her husband's discomfort and feeling increasingly guilty about her dependency, Mrs. Soto attempted to take care of her own toilet needs and fell, fracturing her hip. She was immediately rehospitalized, with a prognosis of long-term nursing home care. She went home temporarily, awaiting Mr. Soto's decision.

LIMITED RESOURCES

The hospital social worker informed Mr. Soto that nursing home care would cost approximately $32,000 per year. Considering that Mr. Soto's total yearly income from his railroad pension and Social Security came to approximately $28,000 per year, placing his wife in a private nursing home was out of the question. Because Mr. Soto, a homeowner, was not sufficiently impoverished to qualify for Medicaid, his only alternatives were to attempt to care for his wife in their home again, or spend down to the poverty level required to qualify for Medicaid. Neither of Mr. Soto's children was in a position to help financially. With their Medicare eligibility quickly reaching its limits, Mr. Soto became increasingly despondent. He stopped answering his telephone. Following a telephone call from the hospital social worker, Mr. Soto's son went to his father's home to find him in a deeply depressed state and cognitively disoriented. He kept mentioning that there was no hope and that both he and his wife would be better off dead, as they were now useless and of no benefit to society. "Ni para que vivir," Mr. Soto remarked.* Hearing this frightened the son, who the following day called his old parole officer asking for advice. The parole officer referred the son to the local community mental health program.

THE INITIAL PLEA FOR HELP

The son phoned the El Paso Community Mental Health Center (EPCMHC) and spoke to the intake worker, who in turn referred him to Ms. Lewis, a twenty-seven-year-old Anglo social worker. The son explained his father's situation and the fact that he wanted to die. Ms. Lewis explained that she did not speak Spanish and asked if the father spoke English. She was assured that the father spoke English but was more fluent in Spanish. Because the only Spanish-speaking therapist at the EPCMHC was already overextended with Spanish-speaking clients, and, because of the urgency of the case, Ms. Lewis decided to accept the case herself. Ms. Lewis asked the son to have his father call for an appointment.

CLIENT, WORKER, INTERVENTION MODEL, AND AGENCY RESISTANCE

The following day the son reported to Ms. Lewis that he had talked to his father but that his father did not want to see Ms. Lewis because he was not crazy. Ms. Lewis did not want to see the father unless he was motivated to ask for help. The son was very worried about his parents and pleaded with Ms. Lewis to visit his father at home. Ms. Lewis thought to herself that this would be counterproductive, might stimulate transference, and might be considered overidentifying with the client. Furthermore, the agency frowned on home visits. The son by now was near tears and was pleading for Ms. Lewis's help. Finally Ms. Lewis stated that she would make an exception to visit the father at home, if he agreed to join her for the visit. Sighing with relief, the son agreed.

VISITING THE INVOLUNTARY CLIENT

The son and Ms. Lewis arrived at the home unannounced, and the father seemed annoyed and made a comment in Spanish to the son. The son appeared to be pleading with the father. The mother's voice from the bedroom inquired as to what was going on. The son replied that he had asked Ms. Lewis to come over to see if she could be of some help. Mrs. Soto invited Ms. Lewis to the bedroom, and at this point the father criticized the son's bad manners and asked him to prepare coffee and Mexican bread for their guest. Mr. Soto observed how well Mrs. Soto and Ms. Lewis were interacting and began to smile, seeing how responsive his wife was. Ms. Lewis then involved the husband in the conversation and remarked in a supportive, concerned way that their life had certainly changed since Mr. Soto's retirement and Mrs. Soto's physical injuries. The son was standing at the door listening, prompting the father to reestablish his position of authority by asking his adult son not to listen in on "grown-up conversations." The son smiled and thanked Ms. Lewis for visiting the parents, adding that he had to return to work.

---

*In Spanish, "Ni para que vivir" means: There is no reason to live.

TRANSFORMING THE INVOLUNTARY CLIENT INTO A VOLUNTARY CLIENT

Ms. Lewis did not want to stay long, as she did not want to impose on the Sotos. She excused herself, stating she had to return to the office. Mr. Soto offered to walk Ms. Lewis to her car, commenting on how much she had helped his wife and made her smile again. Ms. Lewis said she noticed that he also had been smiling at times and wondered whether he sometimes felt lonely, isolated, unsupported, and overwhelmed with all of his responsibilities. He nodded in agreement. Ms. Lewis, handing her card to Mr. Soto, stated that if he wanted to talk more about these matters, he could phone her. He looked at the card, replied that he was not crazy, and said he had heard they saw "locos" at her clinic. Ms. Lewis stated that they did see a few people who needed medication to help them think more clearly, but that the majority of people were just like him and every-body else—struggling with problems of daily living.

ENGAGEMENT PHASE

A few days later Mr. Soto phoned for an appointment to see Ms. Lewis. Although he kept his first appointment, he was a little nervous and mostly spoke about his wife and her problems. He did not want his wife to know he was visiting Ms. Lewis. In the initial interviews Ms. Lewis assumed a tactful, supportive approach, not wanting to frighten or embarrass Mr. Soto. She observed him to be depressed and asked whether there were times when he just wanted to give up and run away. He became serious as his eyes red-dened, stating firmly that he never would run away from anything, as a man always faces his responsibilities. The following week Mr. Soto stated that he wondered if not wanting to live, or wanting to die, was a form of running away. Ms. Lewis explored this further and made a determination that Mr. Soto had suicidal thoughts, but was not suicidal, as he did not have a specific suicide plan or give indications of a major depression. Ms. Lewis assured Mr. Soto that his depression was in response to his wife's physical condi-tion. He denied this, stating that it was due "to other things," but would not elaborate, adding that she just would not understand.

TRANSFERENCE AND COUNTERTRANSFERENCE

The following week Ms. Lewis explored what Mr. Soto had meant about "other things." He became annoyed (transference), stating that she was too young to know, probably not married, and that this was something related to men and she could not help. Ms. Lewis became defensive (countertransference), stating that she was not too young, was married, had children, and knew something about male impotence. Mr. Soto was not familiar with the word impotence. Ms. Lewis, red-faced and in a clumsy manner, tried to explain what impotence was, using her index finger to demonstrate. Mr. Soto burst out laughing, stating that it had never happened to him, and that young Ms. Lewis looked funny explaining this to a man with sixty-three years of sexual experience. Ms. Lewis became aware of her embarrassment, anger, and anxiety, and recalled how once her own father had tried to speak with her about sex when she was a young adolescent. She also became aware of the fact that she was perhaps stereotyping Mr. Soto as an old man who had lost his sexual ability and desire.

CULTURE VERSUS SITUATION

This brief emotional confrontation "broke the ice," as Ms. Lewis by now was also laugh-ing, pointing to her finger. She then said, "Really, tell me what is happening." Mr. Soto stated that he had always had a big sexual appetite but that since the injuries of his wife, she was not able to meet his sexual needs. He stated that he had taken younger women that he was meeting at the retirement club out for sex. Initially he enjoyed this, but then he began feeling guilty because it was against his religious and cultural beliefs. He was feeling unfaithful to his ill wife. The more he did this, the worse he felt, and he was unable to face her. Ms. Lewis had initially thought that Mr. Soto's "fooling around" was simply a Latin cultural requirement for males, but now realized that Mr. Soto was an honorable, religious man who was ashamed of his unfaithfulness. Ms. Lewis reminded him about how she had once raised the concept of "running away" from problems and asked if this wasn't an example of that. He seemed puzzled and replied that it could be seen that way. She also asked if whether, being overwhelmed with financial and caring responsibilities for his wife, "a person might not want to live?" He acknowledged that possibility but argued that taking one's life was more of a solution to a problem than running away. Ms. Lewis did not want to argue the point; she left him with his dignity and a sense of control over his life.

CLIENT INVOLVEMENT IN PLANNING

At the sixth session Ms. Lewis inquired about Mr. Soto's response to their meetings, and he commented that he found them helpful and that even though she was young and inexperienced in life, she had made him think about things in a different manner. He hadn't been "fooling around," but his desire for sex was building, he remarked with the wink of an eye. Prior to her medical condition, Mrs. Soto had been fulfilling his sexual desires. Ms. Lewis commented that with his and his wife's permission, she could speak to her physician about any possible limitations she might have. Mr. Soto thanked her for this, stating that he would just feel too uncomfortable discussing this with his wife, because he did not want to hurt her. Furthermore, he did not think he could talk to the physician because "they all use such big words." Ms. Lewis inquired if Mr. Soto wanted to continue with their weekly problem-solving meetings. He stated that they had been helpful for him but wondered how they could be more helpful for his wife, especially not knowing what to do if he couldn't take care of her at home. "I just don't understand it all. All these people and agencies talk so much about what they're going to do for my wife, but nothing gets done. That's when I feel down and useless." Ms. Lewis agreed that at times it became very complicated, but at the next meeting, together they would try and figure what had to be done.

MACRO PRACTICE WITH THE ELDERLY

IDENTIFYING RESOURCES

Prior to her next meeting with Mr. Soto, Ms. Lewis set up a consultation with an EPCMHC social work colleague who was in charge of a senior citizens' day care program. On hearing of Mr. Soto's situation, the colleague informed Ms. Lewis of the services provided by the El Paso Area Agency on Aging (AAA), as mandated by the National Older Americans Act. Ms. Lewis was pleasantly surprised to learn that in addition to a neighborhood senior citizen center providing midday meals, AAA was capable of arranging homemaker support programs at the neighborhood Senior Citizen's Center. In addition, Ms. Lewis was informed that a national senior citizens' organization had recently set up a demonstration project in El Paso to provide special health services for the elderly Hispanic population.

SHARING INFORMATION WITH THE CLIENT

Following further information gathering on available support programs for the elderly population, Ms. Lewis scheduled her next meeting with Mr. Soto. The meeting proved to be a real "eye-opener" for Mr. Soto. He was delighted to learn that he could receive assistance, in the home, in meeting his wife's daily living activities as well as special transportation to ensure that she was able to keep her medical appointments. Of particular interest to Mr. Soto was Ms. Lewis's description of the special health demonstration projects being set up for the Hispanic elderly. These projects contained a physical rehabilitation program directed at reducing frailty among the elderly as well as increasing their independence. Mr. Soto inquired as to his wife's ability to benefit from such a service and was informed that she was a prime candidate, because one of the major goals of the rehabilitation program was building muscle mass and bone density. The prospect of reversing his wife's current state of dependency to that of increased mobility, physical strength, and independence brought a smile to Mr. Soto's face. Perhaps he really could have his wife back to the way she was prior to her hip fractures.

TOWARD CULTURALLY SENSITIVE PRACTICE

Ms. Lewis informed Mr. Soto that the rehabilitative process would take some time, but with the assistance of the in-home support services, daily meal, and transportation provided by the El Paso AAA, Mrs. Soto had a good chance of resuming her normal activities. Mr. Soto acknowledged his gratitude for such assistance but pondered his existing sexual needs and lack of social outlets, because he refused to return to the Southern Pacific social club due to his sense of guilt. Ms. Lewis mentioned that her agency sponsored a senior citizen day-care program that included a weekly support group for senior citizens undergoing emotional stress. Mr. Soto inquired as to the composition of the group and was informed that it consisted of mostly white, elderly females, with an occasional Hispanic person. This disturbed him, and he relayed his disappointment to Ms. Lewis as to her agency's lack of cultural sensitivity in not sponsoring a support group for elderly Hispanics with problems similar to his. Ms. Lewis gave careful consideration to Mr. Soto's concerns and then asked what they should do about the problem.

BUILDING ON FAMILY STRENGTHS

Following several more individual sessions between Mr. Soto and Ms. Lewis, it was decided that Ms. Lewis would contact the national senior citizens' organization sponsoring the rehabilitation program in which Mrs. Soto was participating, to inquire about helping with the problem. It was quickly discovered that although the rehabilitation project had been developed as a basic medical intervention strategy, they had received numerous requests for greater involvement of the healthy spouse in his or her mate's rehabilitation. A quick survey noted that approximately 70 percent of the patients were female, thus providing a cadre of Hispanic men who could be recruited to participate in a support group. The sponsoring organization quickly agreed to participate in organizing a support group and asked Ms. Lewis to assist them.

CLIENT INVOLVEMENT IN TREATMENT PLANNING

In further conversations with Mr. Soto, Ms. Lewis inquired as to whether he felt the support group should be all male or a mix of males and females. Ms. Lewis argued that a mixture of males and females would help the two sexes appreciate the differences and similarities in their problems as well as help them to resolve these problems. Mr. Soto argued that it would be culturally inappropriate to have Hispanic men and women openly discussing their sexual problems and opted for an all-male group.

GROUP SUPPORT

Mr. Soto entered an all male, English-speaking seniors' support group comprised of non-Hispanic whites and a few Hispanics. He was relatively quiet during the first few sessions, but at the third session he announced that he thought he had entered a sex therapy group but they had not been discussing sex. Mr. Green, the social worker who led the group, asked if he felt he had a sexual problem.

Mr. Soto replied that he had, in that he had "desires" and his ill wife was unable to fulfill his needs. One of the "old-timers," Mr. Gonzales, who had been in the group about a year, commented to Mr. Soto that a few members in the group had had a similar problem and solved it by having visits as needed with "Manuela." "Where do I find Manuela?" Mr. Soto innocently asked. "In either your right or left hand," whispered a laughing Mr. Gonzales. As the group laughed, Mr. Soto joined in, adding "Oh, *that* Manuela. I had forgotten about her!"

A DIFFERENT ENDING

In the following months, Mr. Soto felt increasingly supported and enjoyed "his group." He had now terminated his meetings with Ms. Lewis. Contributing to his improved morale was also the gradual but steady improvement of Mrs. Soto's health. It was hard for Mr. Soto to believe that just four months previously he had been thinking of taking his *and* his wife's lives!

Emerging Issues and Trends

With the aging of our population, increasing concern for the maintenance of the quality of life among our elderly will continue to be one of our major societal goals. The extension of life and the compression of the morbidity period serve as ideal objectives in ensuring that our elderly citizens lead full, productive, and satisfying lives, with minimal dependency and physical and mental deterioration prior to death.

There are those who believe that with emerging patterns of physical and psychological health behavior and more widespread preventive medicine, the total proportion of elderly living in states of dependency will significantly decrease, thus lessening the need for both informal and formal care.[24] Others paint a much more negative picture, with widespread assumptions of a serious shortage in our ability to meet the health care needs of our elderly in the near and distant future.[25] While the truth may lie somewhere in between, we can be assured that our present as well as our future elderly citizens will be major utilizers of our public and private health, economic, and social welfare resources.

Solutions to the problems that will confront our service delivery system must represent a combination of economic and social change, from both the public and private sectors. The following macro-level recommendations represent those issues most pertinent to the field of social work and should be evaluated in the context.

ECONOMIC IMPROVEMENTS

The problem of economic deprivation among our elderly can generally be traced back to their employment histories prior to age sixty-five. Income inequality during their working life translates into income inequity in retirement. The vast majority of those elderly who have labored in low-income occupations with minimal or no benefits will end up with inadequate retirement benefits and savings. Efforts to change this situation must be directed at existing federal programs. The Social Security program must be modified to provide increased benefits for those elderly individuals having worked many years at minimum wage levels or experienced extended periods of unemployment. As the Social Security Trust Fund becomes increasingly solvent, this should become possible. Infusion of additional general revenues into Social Security would provide the rest of the resources for the implementation of such a program.

The Supplemental Security Income (SSI) program represents the federal government's intention to provide a safety net of income support for the poorest and most vulnerable of our older, blind, and disabled citizens. However, this program only brings needy individuals up to 75 percent of the poverty level and currently reaches only one-half of those who are eligible. Many potentially eligible recipients of SSI fail to apply for the benefits due to the complexity of the forms and lack of publicity of its existence. In addition, SSI has an asset eligibility test, the cutoff for which has been cut in half by inflation since 1974. And there is an additional problem for those minority elderly unable to read, write, or speak English because they must provide their own interpreter at the local SSI office.

Clearly, SSI revision is a must if we are to reduce the increasing percentage of our elderly living in poverty. The fact that minority elderly are six times more likely to be on SSI than white elderly provides a solid rationale for improving the benefits.

As a third recommendation, legislative action to increase the minimum wage level would significantly assist those individuals currently working in these types of positions, as are many within our minority populations. The current minimum wage provides only 73.6 percent of the projected poverty level for a family of three; a disproportionate percentage of these are minorities. Improved income levels for individuals in these positions will have a direct impact on their future Social Security benefits.

HOUSING IMPROVEMENTS

The family and all its associated responsibilities are among the most treasured experience for the elderly. Proximity to family members is significant in urban as well as rural settings. Proximity is particularly sought out by the elderly as they strive to maintain intergenerational continuity with their children and grandchildren. Thus, housing is of critical importance in affording the elderly the opportunity to remain in the community, near their families.

Existing federal housing programs have created barriers to the maintenance of extended family relationships. Low-income housing projects are generally located away from minority communities, with occupancy limited to an elderly couple or single person. Housing assistance in the form of vouchers requires searching for apartment units that are difficult to find, frequently unaffordable, and again located outside the community.

Clearly, significant modification of our national housing policies must be undertaken if we are to meet the needs of those elderly most in need of this form of assistance. The first general goal on an improved national housing policy for the elderly is freedom of choice. They must have the opportunity to choose the type of housing and living environment that best reflects their preferences and needs.

Thus, some elderly may prefer to stay in their own homes as long as possible, while others may prefer some type of group quarters. Likewise, some elderly prefer living in neighborhoods relatively balanced in age composition, while others prefer age-segregated retirement communities. The goal of freedom of choice means that a one-dimensional housing policy emphasizing only a few choices is unacceptable.

A second general goal, clearly related to freedom of choice, is that housing policy should be designed to preserve or sustain independent living situations as long as possible. There is considerable agreement that those elderly who prefer to remain in their own homes should be allowed to do so, and that public programs sustaining independent or noninstitutional living should be made available. This particular recommendation has great relevance for our minority elderly because it provides the opportunity to maintain intergenerational relationships and cultural continuity. This suggests that more attention be paid to services and support facilitating independent-living status.

A third goal provides for adequate housing assistance and services. These could take the form of direct financial or income support through housing allowances, or income supplements that enable the elderly to secure the type of housing that best meets their needs, while staying within their limited financial resources. Housing counseling programs for the elderly enable them to select the most appropriate living arrangements to maintain intergenerational continuity. In addition, service programs providing homemaker services, home repairs, home-delivered meals, and special transportation increase the ability of the elderly to maintain independent or semi-independent existences within their communities.

Effective housing assistance for the minority elderly must incorporate a multi-faceted and flexible set of policies and programs. Freedom of choice, coupled with effective support services, will greatly prolong the ability of minority elderly to remain in their communities, continuing the intergenerational dialogue so critically important to their cultural identity. Current housing policies limiting choices will only continue to fragment minority families. Future legislation must appropriate resources for the development of creative alternatives for and maintenance of aging "in place."

ENHANCING HEALTH: THE NEED FOR CONTINUING CARE

The elderly's ability to obtain adequate health care services is frequently reduced by their low-income levels and lack of health insurance. The relationship between income, the cost of care, and access/utilization of services is complex and not well understood. As the cost of health-related services continues to rise, people of limited financial means will obviously be at a disadvantage. Among the elderly, women, minorities, and those living alone are particularly vulnerable; their limited social support systems are unable to compensate for inadequate economic resources. Providers of continuing care services favoring self-paying clients find the elderly among the least attractive potential clients. Medicare and Medicaid are limited in the extent to which they cover continuing care services—particularly those delivered outside nursing homes, where the vast majority of the elderly reside.

The elderly are bounced from one provider system to another, each with its own (often conflicting) eligibility criteria. Recently there has been a significant promotion of case management to reduce the existing barriers and fragmentation in elderly health care services. Case management can be of help to the elderly, but only to the extent that they can access the services. The elderly need to be educated in case management as an effective tool in receiving services; and such services need to be developed in communities where the elderly reside. For case managers, a full understanding of the resources of continuing care, both formal and informal, within the community is a must. Case managers also need to fully understand those cultural factors influencing preferences for care arrangements within elderly minority populations.

Lack of cultural sensitivity in the design and delivery of services has a negative impact on the retention of minority elderly clients after they enter the service system. Use of appropriate language, traditional leisure activities, ethnically familiar foods, and acknowledgment and celebration of cultural holidays are examples of enhancements of the quality of life in continuing-care facilities for ethnic-minority elderly. Attention to these factors in the delivery of services to the home, adult day-care center, and nursing home would significantly improve the participation of the ethnic-minority elderly in these programs.

Concluding Comment

While improvements in the development and delivery of continuing-care service to the elderly are greatly needed, in reality the vast majority of continuing care in the community will be provided by the informal support system. More information is needed on the care-giving capacity and resources within the extended family. This will obviously vary with economic status and family size, but we need a comprehensive picture of these informal systems and their major contributors.

Caregivers in particular, need information, referral, economic assistance, and respite. The middle-aged woman, most likely the primary caregiver for her elderly parents or in-laws, struggles to meet the needs of her own children, and sometimes those of her grandchildren as well. Her lack of economic resources to independently handle all these caregiving responsibilities forces her to use an already overutilized, informal support system. The development of an effective home care system providing nursing care assistance and home helper activities holds the greatest promise for assisting the dependent elderly.

Legislative efforts to renew the long-term care home services bill must begin immediately. We must continue pushing for better Medicare coverage of continuing care services offered outside the institutional setting. In addition, there should be a sliding scale applied to Medicare deductibles and copayments, reducing current negative effects on service utilization by the low-income elderly.

Intermediate-care facilities, skilled nursing homes, and home care services are absent or significantly underdeveloped in ethnic minority communities. Needs assessments and feasibility studies should be initiated at local levels to plan service development. Technical assistance should be granted to business and professional and social organizations wishing to fill service voids. Contributions from public and private sources should fund such enterprises.

The development of effective health and welfare policies enhancing the quality of life among our elderly citizens must focus on economic stability, housing, and health care. Universal access to health resources is a goal not only for the elderly, but for the population as a whole. As this country moves to assist the most dependent segment of our society (e.g., the elderly, children, and disabled), all citizens in turn benefit. This country cannot afford to think of fragmented subpopulations as separate from each other but must conceive of an intergenerational partnership providing the resources, time, and caring to ensure that those most in need receive the appropriate assistance.

KEY WORDS AND CONCEPTS

Elderly

Aging

Gerontology

Young Old

Ageism

Geriatric

Oldest Old

SUGGESTED READINGS

Crimmins, E. M., and Saito, Y. "Getting Better and Getting Worse: Transitions in Functional Status Among Older Americans," *Journal of Aging and Health*, 5(1), 1993, pp. 3–36.

Department of Health and Human Services. *Aging America: Trends and Projections*. Washington, D.C.: U.S. Government Printing Office, No. FCOA 91–28001, 1991.

Dunkle, R. E., and Norgard, T. "Aging Overview," in R. L. Edwards, ed. *Encyclopedia of Social Work*, 19th Edition. Washington, D.C.: NASW Press, 1995, pp. 142–152.

Fogel, B., Furino, A., and Gottlieb, G. *Mental Health Policy for Older Americans: Protecting Minds at Risk*. Washington, D.C.: American Psychiatric Press, 1990, pp. 1–22.

Gitterman, A., ed. *Handbook of Social Work Practice with Vulnerable Populations*. New York: Columbia University Press, 1991.

Kane, R., and Kane, R. L. *Long-term Care: Principles, Programs, and Policies*. New York: Springer, 1987.

Leutz, W. N., Capitman, J. A., MacAdam, M., and Abrahams, R. *Care for Frail Elders: Developing Community Solutions*. Westport, CT: Auburn House, 1992.

Markides, K. S., ed. *Aging and Health: Perspectives on Gender, Race and Ethnicity, and Class*. London: Sage, 1989, pp. 111–176.

Markides, K. S., and Miranda, M. R. *Minorities, Aging, and Health*. Newbury Park, CA: Sage, 1997.

Special Committee on Aging. *Developments in Aging: 1989*, Vol. 11, Report 101-249. Washington, D.C.: U.S. Government Printing Office, 1990.

Torres-Gil, F. *The New Aging: Politics and Change in America.* Westport, CT: Auburn House, 1992.

Zuniga, Maria A. "Aging: Social Work Practice," in R. L. Edwards, ed., *Encyclopedia of Social Work,* 19th Edition, Washington, D.C.: NASW Press, 1995, pp. 173–183.

ENDNOTES

1. U.S. Bureau of the Census, "65th in the United States," *Current Population Reports,* Special Studies P23-190. (Washington, D.C.: U.S. Government Printing Office, 1996).
2. Ibid.
3. J. Treas, "Older Americans in the 1990s and Beyond," *Population Bulletin,* Vol. 50, No. 2, May 1995.
4. U.S. Bureau of the Census, "Education Attainment in the United States: March 1993 and 1992," *Current Population Reports* P20-476 (Washington, D.C.: U.S. Government Printing Office, 1994).
5. National Center for Health Statistics, "Current Estimates from the National Health Interview Survey, United States, 1986," *Vital and Health Statistics Series* 10, No. 164 (October 1987).
6. K. Davis, "Aging and the Health Care System: Economic and Structural Issues," *Daedalus* 11 (May 1986): 217–246.
7. A. S. Flemming, L. D. Rickards, J. F. Santos, and P. R. West, "Report on a Survey of Community Mental Health Centers," Vol. 3 (Washington, D.C.: Action Committee to Implement the Mental Health Recommendations of the 1981 White House Conference on Aging, 1986).
8. Committee of National Statistics, "Trends in Disability at Older Ages: Summary of a Workshop," Vicki A. Freedman and Beth J. Soldo, eds., National Academy Press, 1994.
9. D. A. Evan, H. H. Funkenstein, M. S. Albert, et al., "Prevalence of Alzheimer's Disease in a Community Population of Older Persons: Higher than Previously Reported," *Journal of the American Medical Association* 261 (1989): 2552–2556.
10. M. Harper and B. Lebowitz, eds., *Mental Illness in Nursing Homes: Agenda for Research* No. ADM 86–1459 (Washington, D.C.: U.S. Government Printing Office, 1986).
11. R. N. Butler and M. I. Lewis, *Aging and Mental Health,* 2nd Edition (St. Louis, MO: C. V. Mosby, 1977), p. 34.
12. G. F. Streib, "Are the Aged a Minority Group?" in B. L. Newgarten, ed., *Middle Age and Aging* (Chicago: University of Chicago Press, 1968), pp. 46–47.
13. S. H. Preston, "Children and the Elderly in the U.S.," *Scientific American* (December 1984): 44–49.
14. R. Hill and N. Foote, *Family Development in Three Generations* (Cambridge, MA: Scheukman, 1970).
15. L. Lowy, *Social Work with the Aging,* 2nd Edition (New York: Longman, 1985).
16. R. N. Butler, *Why Survive? Being Old in America* (New York: Harper & Row, 1975), p. 12.
17. D. I. MacDonald, ADAMHA Testimony before the U.S. House of Representatives Committee on Appropriations, Subcommittee on Labor-Health and Human Services Education (Washington, D.C.: Congressional Record, 1987).
18. M. H. Cantor, "Social Care: Family and Community Support Systems," *The Annals* 503 (May 1989): 100.

19. Flemming et al.
20. Harper and Lebowitz.
21. Flemming et al.
22. MacDonald.
23. E. Light, B. D. Lebowitz, and F. Bailey, "CMHCs and Elderly Services: An Analysis of Direct and Indirect Services and Service Delivery Sites," *Community Mental Health Journal* 22 (1986): 294–302.
24. MacDonald.
25. Flemming et al.

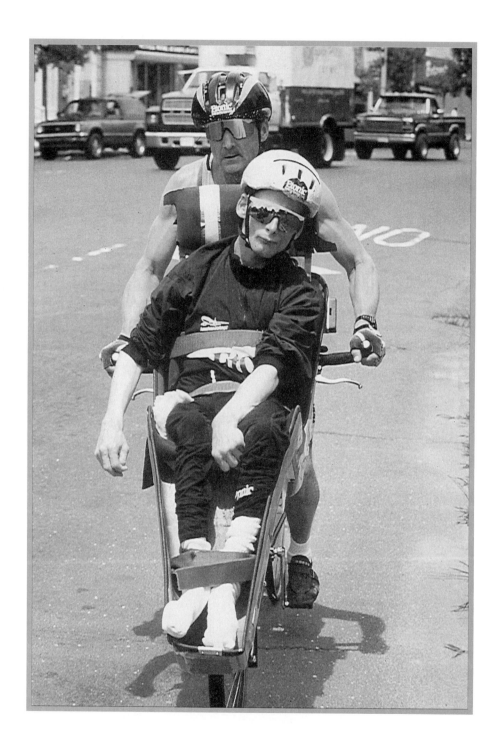

CHAPTER 15

Social Work Practice with People with Disabilities

*Celia Williamson**

*Dr. Celia Williamson, a social worker, is Associate Professor and Director of the Department of Rehabilitation, Social Work, and Addiction, University of North Texas, Fort Worth, Texas.

Prefatory Comment

Social work students trickled into the classroom on the first day of class to take the required course called "Social Work Practice with People with Disabilities." Among the last to arrive was the professor, Dr. Soo Gary, who used a joystick to guide her electric wheelchair deftly around the trash can and podium to settle in at the desk.

"I am Professor Gary," she said, "and on this first day of class I would like for you to tear out a sheet of notebook paper and write your name and today's date." She continued, "When you have done that, write 'First Exam,' at the top of your paper in block letters." After the groans subsided she read out a short series of true/false questions. Below are the actual questions. See how you would do:

1. True or False: A person can have a disability and not be handicapped.
2. True or False: There are many more people with mental retardation than there are with mental illness.
3. True or False: People with disabilities demonstrate unusual courage and determination as they work within the limitations of their disabilities.
4. True or False: People with disabilities are appropriately described as a minority group.
5. True or False: The medical condition is the foremost factor in determining how well a person with a disability will carry out the activities and responsibilities of life.
6. True or False: The majority of people 65 to 74 years old have a disability.
7. True or False: The United States has never had a president with an obvious physical disability.

Social Work Practice with People with Disabilities

The phrase, "people with disabilities" is now familiar to many in the United States. During the 1980s, the debate surrounding the Americans with Disabilities Act (ADA) and its final passage in 1990 have helped to cultivate a growing awareness of disability. During this time, social work literature increased its focus on disability issues. Many introductory and human behavior textbooks now make reference to disability issues and social work journals have engaged in discussions of this emerging area.

But why would this be considered a *new* area for social work practice? Disability is certainly not new. Since the beginning of time, individuals and families have encountered illness and injury and, as a result, have had to adjust their lives. Social work, from its inception, has been involved in helping people to deal with a wide variety of life's problems, including those which come from disability. In fact, a close look at early social work history shows a clear involvement with people impacted by disability. The settlement house movement grew up around immigrants who were drawn to cities during the industrial revolution and was vitally involved in issues surrounding occupational injuries, workers' compensation, and public health. Social workers have long played prominent roles in advocacy and service delivery for people with mental and physical disability.[1]

The phrase "people with disabilities" is relatively new, though. It first began appearing in literature in the 1980s.[2] Its appearance is more than just a matter of semantics, more than simply a new term to address old problems. It represents a significant change in the understanding of how disability impacts individuals and society—one that conceptualizes people with disabilities as a minority group, instead of as isolated individuals with specific disorders.

Before this change occurred, discussions about disability emphasized *medical* conditions. The "problem" was the disorder itself, and interventions were directed at the micro level, at helping individuals to correct, compensate, or cope with their own specific medical conditions. In the wake of the civil rights movement, however, people with disabilities began to gain an awareness of how the environment played a role in their disability. They began to address their situations in light of what they had learned from civil rights advocates and racial minority groups. They took a more "macro" look at the situation and it changed the whole approach. Suddenly solutions could be found by changing the environment as well as by changing the individual.

This is a clear application of the Morales-Sheafor ecosystems approach,[3] because it allows for a comprehensive examination of the problems and resources that impact minority groups by directing attention to each of five different levels of systems, nested one inside the other. These include the individual level, the family level, the level of culture, the level of environmental and structural influences, and the historical level. Each of these levels impacts the development and the resolution of human problems.

Consider this example. As you walk across town, you happen to pass a man without legs who is sitting in a wheelchair outside a restaurant. There are five steps up to the front door of the restaurant and no ramp. How would you describe this problem?

The medical model would focus on the fact that the man cannot walk. It would seek to fix his condition or find him prosthetic legs. The ecosystems model, on the other hand, might just as easily see the lack of a ramp as the problem. The environment could be adjusted so that the man could use his wheelchair to get into the restaurant, as could other wheelchair users and mothers with strollers. In fact, today this would be a legal problem, as well, because public access to restaurants is covered by the ADA.

The primary point is that, when the ecosystems viewpoint is used, the problem no longer resides solely with the individual. The focus moves to a much broader issue: the right of all citizens to access the benefits of society and the obligation of society to remove barriers to that access. There is a distinct civil rights ring to it, eloquently voiced by twelve-year-old Jade Calegory in his 1988 testimony before Congress in support of the ADA:

> I guess my teacher was right about history repeating itself. I learned in school that black people had problems with buses, too. They had to sit in the back of the bus, but some of us with disabilities cannot even get on the bus at all. Black people had to use separate drinking fountains and those of us using wheelchairs cannot even reach some drinking fountains. We get thirsty, too. Black people had to go to separate theaters, schools, restaurants, and some of us have to, also. That is not because we want to, but because we cannot get in.[4]

Defining Disability

Language is a powerful vehicle for the expression of our cultural understanding. The words we speak convey both overt and covert meanings and subtly impact the way we think. Thus, it is not surprising to see that the reconceptualization of disability from a medical condition to a civil rights issue is reflected in the words we use in discussing it.

In everyday discussions, the terms "impairment," "disability," and "handicap" are often used interchangeably, a reflection of the earlier medically based emphasis, where the impairment and the handicap were one and the same. A broader understanding of disability requires a careful delineation of these terms, and an understanding of how they differ.[5]

The term *impairment* refers to loss or abnormality at the level of body system or organ. Examples might include a distortion in vision caused by a weakening of blood vessels in the retina or the loss of a limb by amputation. A medical diagnosis is often used in describing an individual's impairment and the focus is not on the whole person, but on the specific part of the anatomy that is impacted.

A *disability* results when an impairment causes a restriction in the ability to carry out normal life activities. For example, the loss of a leg, the impairment, results in limitations to mobility. The weakening of the blood vessels in the retina results in an inability to read standard size print. The focus here is on the *functional* results of the impairment for the individual. Because short-term medical problems have a more limited impact on individuals, the term disability is usually reserved for discussions related to functional limitations which are long-term or result from chronic conditions.

The term *handicap* takes an even broader perspective and looks at the barriers that are created by an interaction between the disability and the environment. If a restaurant does not have large-print menus and if the waiters have not been trained to assist patrons by reading the menu to them, individuals with visual disabilities might be handicapped in regard to eating out. The combination of poor vision and lack of accommodation results in a loss of public access for the individual and a loss of revenue for the restaurant.

It is very possible for a person to have a disability but not to be handicapped. In fact, this is the focus of the new approach—to remove barriers so that people with disabilities are not handicapped in regard to their life activities.

It should be noted that, in addition to clearly delineating the meaning of words, it is also important to understand the emotional impact words can carry. The word "handicap" is a good example of this. In the 1970s "handicap" was the politically correct term. It was seen as a term that helped to normalize the experience of disability. After all, golfers were given a handicap to compensate for differences in ability levels so that all could compete from an equal starting point. When the historical roots of the word were discovered, however, it lost its political correctness. Historically, it referred to beggars, seeking handouts with "cap-in-hand." This was certainly not the image that people with disabilities wished to reinforce. Although the term handicap can still be appropriately used to denote the interplay between environment and disability, the term "barrier" is more often used today. In fact, "barrier" places the problem even more squarely in the environmental context.

Other changes in our language have also occurred in this process of reconceptualizing disability. One of the most important is the delineation of the principle of "people first language." The underlying concept is that the structure of verbal expression itself can reinforce either the predominance of the disability as the defining characteristic of an individual (retarded child) or relegate the disability to only one element among many that define that person (child with mental retardation). By putting the disability in the secondary position, the preeminence of personhood is emphasized: people with disabilities are always *people* first.

In choosing words that honor personhood, derogatory terms, such as imbecile or cripple or deformed, should be avoided altogether, as should the implication that people with disabilities are inevitably victims. For example, people are not "confined" to wheelchairs, they use them. In fact, wheelchairs are liberating devices. To refer to people with disabilities as afflicted, unfortunate, or stricken places them in a disempowered position. Even suggesting that they are unusually courageous because they live with a disability sets them apart. It broadens the impact of the disability from its specific functional implications and places an aura over the whole character and life circumstance of the individual. When people with disabilities are assumed to be essentially *un*able, the societal stigma turns out to be much more of a barrier to effective functioning than the specific limitations of the disability itself.[6]

DEMOGRAPHIC CONSIDERATIONS

Despite the work that has been done to clarify terminology, different government agencies and programs work from slightly different definitions of disability, based on the focus of the program. This means that different surveys report somewhat different numbers in terms of the prevalence of disability in the United States. According to 1991–1992 information from the Survey of Income and Program Participation (SIPP),[7] which uses a broad definition of disability, 19.4 percent or 48.9 million people experience a limitation in a functional activity or a socially defined role or task due to an impairment or chronic health condition. Of these, almost half experience severe disability or an inability to perform a major function or social role. Generally, a severe disability involves a *lack* of function in a particular area, while a nonsevere disability involves *limitations* in function.

The 1990 Census looks at disability in relation to three specific functional areas: work, mobility, and self-care.[8] By focusing the questions on these areas, more specific service needs can be identified. It is important to remember that a person might be limited in self-care but not be limited in relation to work. For example, a college professor with paralysis in all four limbs might need assistance getting dressed in the morning but be very capable conducting class, advising students, and carrying out research activities. The Census data indicates that 8.2 percent of the "working-age" population experiences a work disability. This includes 4.2 percent who have a severe work disability and 4 percent with a non-severe disability. Mobility-related disabilities affect 4.3 percent of the population over age sixteen and 4.8 percent experience limitations in self-care. Of course, a single individual might be counted in all of these areas, if he or she experiences limitations in all three.

Employment rates among people with disabilities have been a subject of much concern. According to 1991–1992 SIPP data, 80.5 percent of nondisabled people between twenty-one and sixty-four years old are employed. For people with a non-severe disability, the rate drops some, to 76.0 percent. However, for those with a severe disability, the rate plummets to 23.2 percent.[9] While males have a higher employment rate than females, the same patterns of employment are evident for both genders. Severe disability severely limits employment.

The National Health Interview Survey (NHIS) provides information about the prevalence of various impairments that cause disability. Orthopedic impairments, arthritis, and heart disease account for nearly 40 percent of activity limitations.[10] Mental illness and mental retardation, together, were identified as causing 7.7 percent of the activity limitations (see Table 15-1). However, LaPlante notes that the NHIS includes only the noninstitutionalized population of the United States. People with mental disabilities account for a large portion of the institutionalized population. Two-thirds of the individuals in nursing homes have a mental disability, as do most people in state hospitals and state schools.

Figures 15-1 through 15-5 examine the relationship between disability and age, gender, race or ethnic origin, income, and education. It is clear from Figure 15-1 that age and disability are interrelated. Older individuals are much more likely to experience disability than younger ones.[11] It makes sense that the longer one lives, the more chances one has of encountering illness or injury. Lifelong choices about smoking, drug use, diet, and exercise have a cumulative effect, impacting function more in later years. Notice, though, that even in the highest age group, not all individuals experience disability. It is important not to assume that aging and disability are inevitably related.

TABLE 15-1 Prevalence of Impairments Causing Activity Limitation in the United States: 1990

Main Cause	Number of People in 1000's	Percent of People Limited in Activity
Orthopedic impairments	5,873	17.4
Arthritis	4,010	11.9
Heart disease	3,430	10.2
Intervertebral disc disorders	1,762	5.2
Asthma	1,710	5.1
Nervous disorders	1,560	4.6
Mental disorders	1,525	4.5
Visual impairments	1,347	4.0
Mental retardation	1,069	3.2
Diabetes	1,032	3.1
Hypertension	837	2.5
Cerebrovascular disease	679	2.0
Hearing impairments	649	1.9
Emphysema	560	1.7
Osteoporosis/bone disorders	322	1.0
All impairments	33,753	100.0

Source: National Health Interview Survey, 1990, as presented in M. LaPlante, "How Many Americans Have a Disability?" *Disability Statistics Abstract* No. 5 (U.S. Department of Education [NIDRR], 1992).

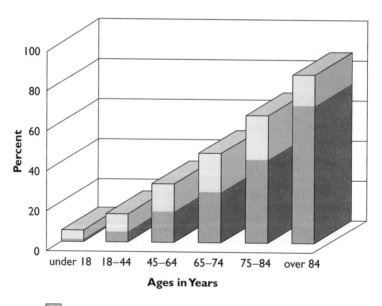

Percent with a non-severe disability

Percent with a severe disability

FIGURE 15-1 Percent of Persons with a Disability, by Age: 1991–1992

Source: J. McNeil, *Americans with Disabilities: 1991–92: Data from the Survey of Income and Program Participation* (Washington, D.C.: U.S. Government Printing Office, P70-33, 1993), p. 10.

There is some relationship between disability and gender as well (Figure 15-2), particularly noticeable when age and gender are considered together. Younger males experience more disability than females, in the middle years the distribution is fairly even, and in later years females show the highest rates.[12] The impact of gender is not nearly as strong as the impact of age, however.

Race and Hispanic origin are considered in the SIPP data as well, reflecting lower rates of disability among Asian and Pacific Islanders and whites and higher rates among Native Americans and African Americans (Figure 15-3). African Americans have the highest rate of severe disabilities, while Native Americans experience more nonsevere disabilities. Although the overall disability rate for people of Hispanic origin is lower than that of whites, those of Hispanic origin experience higher rates of severe disabilities when compared to whites.[13] Other studies indicate that a full understanding of the variation between racial and ethnic groups may be facilitated by examining specific impairments,[14] though space does not permit such an examination here.

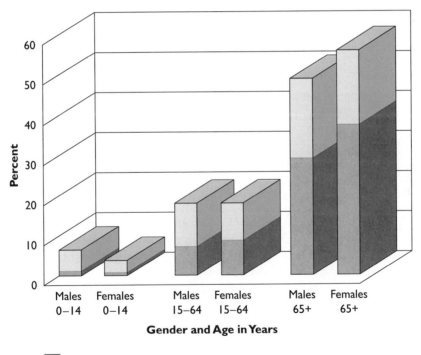

Percent with a non-severe disability

Percent with a severe disability

FIGURE 15-2 **Percent of Persons with a Disability, by Age and Gender: 1991–1992**

Source: J. McNeil, *Americans with Disabilities: 1991–92: Data from the Survey of Income and Program Participation* (Washington, D.C.: U.S. Government Printing Office, P70-33, 1993), p. 5.

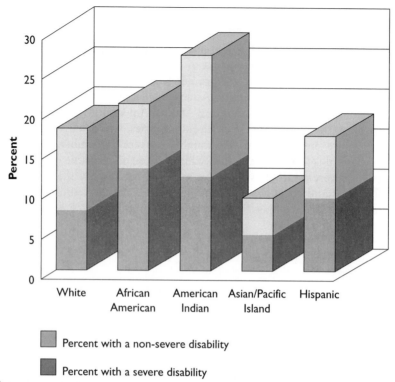

FIGURE 15-3 **Percent of Persons 15 to 64 Years Old with a Disability, by Race and Hispanic Origin: 1991–1992**

Source: J. McNeil, *Americans with Disabilities: 1991–92: Data from the Survey of Income and Program Participation* (Washington, D.C.: U.S. Government Printing Office, P70-33, 1993), p. 11.

A clear relationship can also be seen between income status and disability.[15] Figure 15-4 groups individuals based on the ratio of their income to the government poverty guidelines. Lower income is associated with a higher rate of disability. One should be careful, however, not to assume that low income causes disability. It is more likely that the interaction goes both ways. Poorer individuals are less likely to have access to good preventive health services and may be more likely to be employed in high-risk jobs and thus they may be more subject to incurring a disability. On the other hand, once a person has a disability his or her income may be significantly reduced, often as a result of job loss. So it is not clear from the data that poverty causes disability or that disability causes poverty. What is clear is that the two are related.

Education and disability are also related (Figure 15-5).[16] Higher education is associated with a lower incidence of disability. Again, one should not imply a causal relationship. Significant disabilities during childhood, adolescence, or early adulthood may limit the amount of education received. On the other hand, the jobs available to people with lower levels of education more often involve physical labor and/or risk of injury.

It is clear from the demographic data that age, education, and income are closely related to disability rates. We can also see a differential impact in relation to race and ethnic origin, and to gender. Using the medically-based concept of disability, researchers might look at the prevalence rates of particular disabilities among these population groups to explain the differences. For example, they might point to a higher incidence of high blood pressure among African Americans as part of the explanation for differences in racial and ethnic groups.[17] Sex-linked genetic disorders may play a role in gender differences. The prevalence rates of many disorders increase with age.

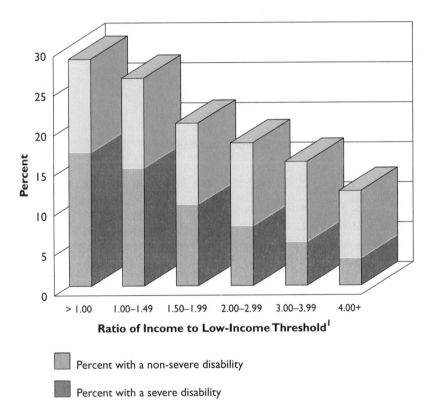

Ratio of Income to Low-Income Threshold[1]

☐ Percent with a non-severe disability

■ Percent with a severe disability

FIGURE 15-4 **Percent of Persons 15 to 64 Years Old with a Disability, by Income Group: 1991–1992**

[1]A ratio of 1.00 means the individual is just at the low-income threshold, while a ratio of 2.00 means that the individual has two times the income of the threshold, etc.

Source: J. McNeil, *Americans with Disabilities: 1991–92: Data from the Survey of Income and Program Participation* (Washington, D.C.: U.S. Government Printing Office, P70-33, 1993), p. 38.

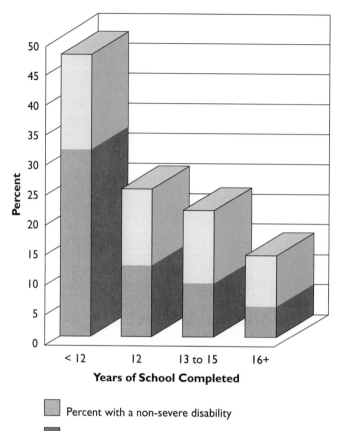

Percent with a non-severe disability

Percent with a severe disability

FIGURE 15-5   **Percent of Persons 25 to 64 Years Old with a Disability, by Education: 1991–1992**

Source: J. McNeil, *Americans with Disabilities: 1991–92: Data from the Survey of Income and Program Participation* (Washington, D.C.: U.S. Government Printing Office, P70-33, 1993), p. 36.

These are the explanations of the medical model. They seem to work fairly well with biologically based groups—gender, race, and age. Even income and education might be partially explained by the different levels of risk between high-pay, high-education jobs and low-pay, low-education jobs. Indeed, these explorations do have some validity. It would be a mistake to discount the importance of the medical viewpoint in discussions of disability.

It does not show the whole picture, however. The ecosystems model would point to other factors that also impact these differences in disability rates, factors that are present in the social environment and social systems in which people with disabilities find themselves. This model would suggest that discriminatory practices that limit minority access to health care and education may help to account for some of the differences between groups. It would suggest that historic patterns of lower levels of rehabilitation service delivery to minority group members[18] impact the level of disability and level of function achieved by these groups.

Even age, which seems so firmly rooted in the biological perspective, is subject to the impact of societal perceptions. Several researchers have suggested that older people are less likely to receive rehabilitation services than younger ones.[19,20] Ageism seems to suggest that resignation to dysfunction is part and parcel of the aging process. So, instead of treating urinary incontinence, a major problem among the very old, we sigh and talk of getting older and just change the sheets. In fact, incontinence is often reversible. Often it is not the medical problem, but the *attitude* that stands in the way of recovery.

OTHER RISKS ASSOCIATED WITH DISABILITY

It is important to briefly mention some additional risks that are associated with disability. Some studies have suggested that children and adults with disabilities are more often the targets of physical and sexual abuse than people without disabilities, though other studies have failed to support this finding.[21] It is clear that injuries resulting from abuse, including child abuse, and other forms of family and societal violence can cause disability.

While chemical dependency is, itself, a disability, studies indicate increased rates of substance abuse and chemical dependency among people with other disabilities. Again, reciprocal causality makes it difficult to fully interpret these figures. Although that it is true that many traumatic head injuries occur as a result of intoxication and as many as 62 percent of injuries resulting in mobility impairments are substance abuse related, there are also indications that substance abuse rates are higher among people with congenital disabilities,[22] indicating that disability may also precede chemical dependency.

Disability and each of these other variables—education, income, abuse, and addiction—are interrelated in a complicated fashion. There is no straight-line cause and effect pattern which can be established. Instead, there is a circular interaction pattern, where each variable impacts all other variables. This pattern of interaction requires an ecosystems approach because that model provides a framework in which to examine these complicated interrelationships.

Disability and the Minority Model

It is clear from the demographic information presented above that people with disabilities comprise a large subgroup of the American population, larger than any single racial or ethnic minority group. But is it really appropriate for people with disabilities to think of themselves as a minority? Dworkin and Dworkin describe four essential criteria for a group to be accorded minority status.[23] A minority group:

1. Is *identifiable*, either in terms of appearance or behavior;
2. experiences *less access to power* so that fewer resources, influence, and control are afforded to it;

3. experiences *discriminatory treatment,* often evidenced by segregation and stereotyping; and
4. *sees itself as a separate group.*

Many people with disabilities are readily identifiable in terms of appearance. A difference in physical appearance itself, such as the body posture of a person with cerebral palsy, or the visibility of the accommodations, such as braces or a white cane, announce the presence of a disability. Behaviors, such as the use of sign language or the onset of a seizure, also serve to identify the person as someone with a disability.

Some individuals may choose not to disclose or to hide their disability, and thus avoid probing questions, stereotypes, and other issues of discrimination. During the 1930s President Roosevelt was rarely photographed in his wheelchair or using his crutches. Today, Senator Robert Dole has incorporated his disability into his public image, neither hiding nor emphasizing its presence. The very fact that one would have to choose whether to talk about a facet of themselves because of possible discrimination reinforces the group's separate identity.

If one considers income and education as indices of power,[24] then people with disabilities clearly fit the second criteria for minority group status. Figures 15-4 and 15-5 clearly illustrate that lower levels of income and education are highly associated with disability.

The discriminatory treatment of people with disabilities is also easy to establish. When diagnostic terms can be hurled as insults, as "retarded" and "spastic" often are, the presence of stereotyping becomes very apparent. Federal law recognizes that "individuals with disabilities continually encounter various forms of discrimination in such critical areas as employment, housing, public accommodations, education, transportation, communication, recreation, institutionalization, health services, voting and public services."[25] Attitude surveys of human service providers, employment rates, and research in basic patterns of social interaction suggest that American society harbors significant prejudice against people with disabilities.[26] Physical barriers result in de-facto segregation. People with disabilities clearly meet the third criteria for designation as a minority group.

It is the fourth criteria that has only recently been met. Until the late 1960s, the medical model dominated the conceptualization of disability and separate diagnostic groups often found themselves competing with each other for limited federal funds. People may have labeled themselves with a particular diagnosis and joined in advocacy activities to support services for that group, but they did not necessarily see themselves as objects of discrimination. "Object" is the correct term here—discrimination denies personhood.

The 1960s, however, focused public attention on civil rights, feminism, deinstitutionalization, and consumerism. It was in the context of these social movements that the conceptualization of disability began to change.[27] In 1972, in Berkeley, California, a group of students with disabilities banded together to demand access to classes on the University of California campus and to pool their resources for transportation and attendant care. They developed the first Center for Independent Living, building it on the principles of consumer sovereignty, self-reliance, and political and economic rights.

As people with disabilities began to recognize that they were being treated differently based on the stigma associated with being disabled, rather than merely in regard to differences in functional abilities, they began to see similarities that spanned across disability areas. This cross-disability awareness led to coalitions between groups that previously saw each other as competing for the same funds. This alliance of various disability-specific advocacy groups provided the political muscle which helped to bring about the passage of the ADA.

Thus, the minority perspective holds some distinct advantages for people with disabilities. It allows the cultivation of cross-disability alliances that results in increased political power. It provides a vehicle for identification with a group that looks at itself with pride, as self-reliant survivors, and it expands the pool of potential solutions, because environmental change as well as personal change is now an option.

Societal Responses to Disability

In addition to broader sociocultural influences, the way a society responds to disability is influenced by its perceptions about the *causes* of disability, the *threats* that it perceives to be related to the disability, and the amount and kinds of *resources* that are available to deal with the disability.[28]

The perceived causes of disabilities have shifted dramatically over the course of history. Early explanations often centered on spiritual dimensions. Mental and physical disorders alike were often viewed as punishment from the gods and those with disabilities were often shunned or even tortured. In the latter half of the eighteenth century, when genetics was seen as the cause of mental deficiency, laws prohibiting marriage or providing for sterilization of people with mental or emotional disorders were passed in half of the states.[29] Later, the perception that disability was essentially a medical condition came to prominence and medical interventions were the preferred course of action.

When society was seen as the cause, there was increased pressure for the society to provide solutions. Historically, services for people with disabilities have been afforded first to soldiers injured in war because societal responsibility was clear. Indeed the first federal-level public aid program in the United States established pensions for soldiers who were disabled during the War for Independence.[30]

Society also responds differently to specific impairments based on perceived cause. People with mental retardation or congenital disorders are not often seen as responsible for their disorder, and public willingness to provide services is relatively high. Visible volunteer efforts and fund-raising keep these disabilities before the public eye and encourage increased private and public support. Mental illness or chemical dependency, which are still perceived by many as resulting from character flaws, receive less public attention and support, although the prevalence of either mental illness or chemical dependency far exceeds that of mental retardation.[31]

The potential threat of a disability can also greatly influence societal response. The polio scare of the late 1940s and early 1950s brought significant governmental and volunteer response. The March of Dimes was born out of the impetus to stop this public threat and government as well as private research efforts helped to eradicate the virus. Once the vaccine was developed, the presence of a clear and decisive medical intervention helped to mobilize the community response to the disease. Here, a "guilt-free" cause, a substantial threat, and an effective technology combine to shape society's response in a positive way. It should be noted that the disease itself and the disability resulting from it are different. Society mobilized primarily against the disease, but the wave of public sentiment carried over into the provision of services for those who became disabled because of the virus.

The Acquired Immune Deficiency Syndrome (AIDS) epidemic reveals an interesting, though distressing, interplay between perceived cause and perceived threat and resources. It stands in contrast to the polio epidemic. Early on, those who were identified as "responsible for" the spread of the Human Immunodeficiency Virus (HIV) that causes AIDS were seen as the only ones threatened. The general public response was low. Later, when the extent of the threat was realized, efforts at prevention and intervention were intensified. Now, ironically, the potential threat is an economic one as well as a medical one and the level of economic resources that might be required to provide services for individuals with AIDS makes the public somewhat uneasy about committing itself to a specific level of care. The fact that no clear medical response is yet available also complicates efforts to gain public and governmental support in combatting the disorder.

SOCIAL WORKERS AND PEOPLE WITH DISABILITIES

Social workers will encounter people with disabilities in all aspects of their lives—as friends, colleagues, clients, and even in the mirror. All service settings should provide access to people with disabilities, and social workers should not assume that a client with a disability is seeking services in relation to the disability. Some service systems, however, are designed to address issues specific to disability. Social workers can find active roles within these systems of services. Their practice roles, however, are directly related to public policy and the government programs in which they are employed.

Five major areas of legislation address disability issues specifically. These include workers' compensation, rehabilitation, social security, education, and civil rights. In addition, a distinct service system exists to serve veterans with disabilities. Each of these legislative areas addresses different issues and addresses them from a unique viewpoint that grew out of the historical context in which they were formulated. They do not always complement one another.

Workers' compensation laws were passed on a state-by-state basis during the early 1900s. This means that many different workers' compensation laws exist, and a disability incurred in California may be addressed very differently from one incurred in Mississippi. Most of these laws address disability from within the medical model, with specific impairments resulting in specific reparations. In some states, each part of the anatomy is assigned a percentage, so that, for example, the loss of the index finger on the dominant hand results in a particular percentage of disability for the individual.[32] Other states allocate a lump sum payment of a specified amount for each body part lost. Social workers, along with nurses and rehabilitation professionals, often fill roles in medical case management as a part of the workers' compensation service system.

On the heels of World War I, the federal government enacted the 1918 Soldier's Rehabilitation Act. It authorized vocational rehabilitation services for veterans whose disabilities were a result of military service. The first civilian rehabilitation services followed two years later, in 1920, under the Smith-Fess Act. This separation of veterans' and civilian services continues to this day. Although veterans are not excluded from the civilian system, veterans' services often provide for more extensive benefits. Social workers fill positions in Veterans' Administration hospitals and may work extensively with veterans with disabilities and their families in the process of adjustment to disability and in finding the resources to support employment and independent living.

The overriding purpose of the civilian act, which has since been designated as the Rehabilitation Act, is to help people with disabilities become employed. Each state provides vocational rehabilitation services under the auspices of this act. Vocational rehabilitation counselors purchase a range of services for people with disabilities in order to help them to secure employment. These may include medical services, vocational assessments, training or education, counseling services, adaptive equipment, supported employment, and job placement services. Social workers may be employed as vocational rehabilitation counselors or may contract to provide services directly to the consumers of the vocational rehabilitation program.

The act also has provisions for funding independent living centers, which are charged with promoting consumer control, self-help, and self-advocacy and with assisting communities to meet the needs of people with disabilities. Services provided by independent living centers include peer counseling and individual and community advocacy. Typically the staff of independent living centers are, themselves, individuals with disabilities. Social workers with disabilities can play a vital role in bringing both professional training and personal experience to bear in these service settings.

The Social Security Act provides important income and medical insurance supports for people with disabilities through the Supplemental Security Income (SSI) and the Social Security Disability Insurance (SSDI) programs. Special work incentive programs are available through SSI and SSDI to help individuals with disabilities make the transition from Social Security income supports to employment. Social workers are often employed by SSI/SSDI programs to assist people in accessing these services.

The Individuals with Disabilities Education Act mandates that all children with disabilities have access to a free, appropriate public education designed to meet their unique needs. These educational services are provided through the local school district and school social workers often assist in the process of determining just what services are needed and then help families and schools to access those services. Efforts are made to keep children involved with their non-disabled peers, avoiding isolated, "special" settings.

Although there are provisions in other laws to help secure the civil rights of people with disabilities, the ADA is the seminal piece of legislation in this area. There are no services provided under this bill, but social workers need to be aware of its provisions in order to help people with disabilities to maintain their full rights as citizens of this country. Social workers can also take an active role in ensuring that the services they provide are available to all people, regardless of disability.

In addition to these government programs, social workers may provide disability-specific services in private for-profit and private not-for-profit service systems. Today many companies are taking a proactive stance toward work-related injuries, establishing their own disability management programs that are focused on making accommodations that allow workers to quickly return to work after an injury. Social workers find active roles in this arena, both through positions in disability management programs themselves and through involvement of employee assistance programs.

Social workers can also be found in private not-for-profit organizations that often contract with government agencies to provide services in relation to disability. Disability-specific organizations and foundations, such as United Cerebral Palsy or the Arthritis Foundation, employ social workers. In addition to direct services that may be provided by these organizations, social workers are involved in extensive public education and advocacy campaigns. It is clear that there are many roles that social workers can fill in providing services to people with disabilities, their families, and the communities in which they live.

The Ecosystems Model and People with Disabilities

The ecosystems framework[33] provides the opportunity for a broader conceptualization of disability, recognizing that the history of discrimination against people with disabilities, the structural impact of governmental policies, the cultural assumptions about what people with disabilities can and cannot do, and the impact of disability on the family, as well as the individual psychological and biological specifics of the disorder all play a part in determining both problems and solutions. Figure 15-6 frames some of the issues specific to disability that must be considered within each level of the concentric spheres of the ecosystems model.

Social workers may focus the intervention at any one of these levels or at several levels at the same time. Wherever the intervention is focused, its success will be dependent on the social worker's understanding of the impact at all levels. This is clearly illustrated in the case example below.

THE INDIVIDUAL

Jerry Desoto is almost ready to be discharged from a rehabilitation hospital where he spent the past two months. He was injured three days after his eighteenth birthday when he crashed his motorcycle, a birthday gift from his parents, into a telephone pole. He was intoxicated at the time of the crash. His spinal cord injury resulted in paralysis from the waist down.

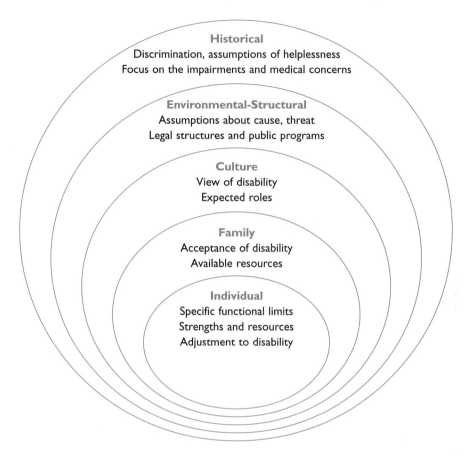

Historical
Discrimination, assumptions of helplessness
Focus on the impairments and medical concerns

Environmental-Structural
Assumptions about cause, threat
Legal structures and public programs

Culture
View of disability
Expected roles

Family
Acceptance of disability
Available resources

Individual
Specific functional limits
Strengths and resources
Adjustment to disability

FIGURE 15-6 **Example of Ecosystems Model for People with Disabilities**

Jerry had been a starter on the high school basketball team. School began three weeks ago. Jerry has been working with a tutor and will be able to return to school on a part-time basis. Between attending classes and continued tutoring he should be able to finish his senior year with his class. His superb physical condition before the injury has greatly helped his recovery.

Jerry is counting the days until discharge. For him, it represents a milestone in his recovery, a move back into the "real world" and a chance to reestablish his friendships. For Jerry's social worker, Chris, the process of discharge began as soon as Jerry was admitted to the rehabilitation hospital.

At the micro level, the biopsychosocial factors that impact Jerry are many and varied. Jerry has lost all sensation and all voluntary use of all his muscles below the waist. His friends are aware that he can no longer walk and that he would need a specially equipped car in order to drive. Only his family and closest friends are aware that he has also had to learn new ways to control bowel and bladder elimination. He has learned to handle the catheter well, but still has occasional difficulties with bowel control. That is one of his major concerns about returning to school. Jerry has also lost sexual function, though he has not yet allowed himself to admit it. He is having enough trouble adjusting to the fact that he will not be the school's top basketball player, and is not ready to address the way his sexual function will impact his self-image.

Jerry had been looking forward to leaving home at the end of the year. This accident has placed him back in a more dependent mode, at least temporarily, and it irritates, even angers, him that he will have to look to his mother for assistance. He cannot even go to town without getting someone to take him. His mother is too eager to help. She wasn't really ready for her youngest to leave home, anyway.

THE FAMILY

Jerry's father is a line worker in an automobile assembly plant and his mother teaches fifth grade. He has an older brother, Jake, who works in an autobody repair shop and has just moved out into an apartment. Even with good medical insurance coverage, the costs of this accident have been substantial and Jerry's father takes every opportunity to work overtime. His mother has been primarily responsible for working with the hospital in regard to Jerry's rehabilitation.

Jerry is acutely aware of the additional financial burden that the accident has placed on the family. He blames himself because he had been drinking. His parents could not afford to give him a car, so they had compromised when his father found the used bike. Now they blame themselves for being stingy with his safety. In addition to medical expenses, there were renovation expenses. Jerry's home had to be modified so that he could live there. The strain over finances has surfaced some old issues in the marriage.

CULTURAL ISSUES

Jerry's buddies have been attentive but Jerry is a bit wary of the town's response. It's not that he is afraid that they will not welcome him, it's just that he is afraid of their expectations. They raised money for renovations to his home by putting a change jar in the local hamburger joint. They want to see him happy, but he is often angry, depressed, and discouraged. The church youth group has asked him to speak about his "courageous recovery" and how his faith has helped him through. He hasn't been to church in two years.

Jerry's status in his community to this point has been built on American youth cultural issues such as his athletic abilities, his ability to drink and go out with his buddies, and his ability to charm the girls in his class. While there are accommodations that can help him to overcome the biological limitations of his condition, he must also come to terms with how his status as a person with a disability has impacted the way people expect him to act. Society has proscribed certain "sick roles" that require that he play the part of an always optimistic, grateful recipient of the kindness of others. In his community, it would be selfish for him to expect accommodations to be made on his behalf and it would be presumptive of him to think that any girl's parents would be willing to have their daughter date someone who is "damaged."

ENVIRONMENTAL–STRUCTURAL ISSUES

Jerry is fortunate that his injury occurred after the passages of the Individuals with Disabilities Education Act and the Americans with Disabilities Act. These important pieces of legislation provide a legal framework to ensure his access to education, transportation, and governmental and public services. His legal rights and the physical realities of his community environment do not always match, however, and there is pressure on him not to pursue the issue. "Surely," his old girlfriend's mother confides in a friend, "he does not expect the school to spend all that money putting in a lift so he can get into the weight room in the school basement when that means they will have to delay buying new band equipment another year. After all, it's so much money to spend on only one person."

HISTORICAL ISSUES

Historical patterns of discrimination have left a deep mark on the lives of people with disabilities, particularly in the area of employment and economic self-sufficiency. Even with the non-discrimination assurances in the ADA, Jerry will have to counterbalance years of Labor Day telethons and pity-based pleas with a strong message of his own competence if he is to convince employers to truly consider his job application. The history of discrimination is ensconced not only in employer attitudes but in legislation, such as the Social Security Act, that defines disability as an *in*ability to work; and in the very brick and mortar of our cities, in stairs and curbs without cuts. Changes are not realized with the stroke of a legislative pen. History is impacted only by living life differently day to day, building tomorrow's history with today's actions.

MULTILEVEL INTERVENTIONS

Chris, Jerry's social worker, has begun to work with Jerry's mother, both to ensure that she knows how to assist Jerry, and also to help her see how important it is for Jerry to take charge of his life, to make his own decisions. Chris was also able to involve Jerry's father in renovating the house. She arranged for a staff member from an independent living center to visit the home and work with the father to develop a common-sense and cost-effective plan for renovation that the family can afford. The independent living center also offered the services of a peer counselor to help Jerry learn how to negotiate his town in a wheelchair and do minor wheelchair repairs. The peer counselor can also talk to Jerry on a personal and practical level about using catheters and facing stereotypes, including Jerry's own stereotypes, about what life is like from a wheelchair.

At the time of discharge, several issues hang in the balance. Jerry has learned to handle the biological demands of his condition within the context of the hospital, but the community brings new challenges. He must also find a new place for himself socially, within his high school and community, and come to terms with the impact of his injury upon his sense of who he is. Despite the fact that this accident had been related to alcohol use, Jerry has been looking forward to drinking with his buddies once he gets out. He figures, if nothing else, he can still drink with the best of them. In addition, both Jerry and his mother have important lifecycle steps to accomplish, which his accident has complicated. Family finances may also require changes in his plans for college.

When Chris attended Jerry's high school graduation several months later, she could point to several specific interventions that helped to tip the balance in Jerry's favor. With Chris's encouragement, Jerry's mother turned her attention from its intense focus on Jerry to a broader look at the community's, and particularly the school's, accessibility issues. Mrs. Desoto enlisted the help of a sixth-grade student who had spina bifida and had used a wheelchair all his life. Together, they made a survey of all the local schools and delivered a list of needed accommodations to the school board. Mrs. Desoto was encouraged by this student's easy acceptance of his disability and his clear enjoyment of life.

Chris used a macro perspective to work with Mrs. Desoto to understand the provisions of the ADA and the best tactics to take in advocating change. The top priority was to make the high school weight room accessible. When Jerry began using the weight room, he was able to reduce his outpatient trips for physical therapy to once a month. It gave Jerry an opportunity to work out with his friends and reestablish the easy camaraderie he had with them in the context of sports. The coach asked him to help manage the basketball team.

Chris had also referred Jerry to vocational rehabilitation to assist him in finding employment. A combination of student loans, grants, and assistance from vocational rehabilitation will make it possible for Jerry to attend a community college next year and receive training specifically targeted to his vocational goals. His brother will move to an accessible unit in his apartment complex and they will share expenses.

As is true in any situation, each level of analysis in the ecosystems framework impacted Jerry's recovery and adaptation process, from individual factors of biology to the presence of federal laws that ensure the availability of accessible educational opportunities and housing options. For Chris, once again micro and macro practice dovetail. In her experience, it is often the energy and insight gained from personal experience that give direction and focus to larger advocacy efforts.

Emerging Issues for Social Work Practice with People with Disabilities

Health care has been an important political issue for the nation as a whole and is a predominate concern for people with disabilities. Although many individuals with disabilities are quite healthy and one should be careful not to confuse illness with disability, portability of health insurance and coverage of pre-existing conditions has a particular impact on many people with disabilities. Often insurance packages only cover acute care, leaving the continuing costs associated with a chronic condition uncovered. Specific disorders, such as mental illness, may be poorly covered, or not covered at all. In addition, because work is the primary vehicle in the United States for access to health insurance and many people with disabilities are unemployed, a large percentage of individuals with disabilities do not have health care coverage at all.[34]

Employment itself is a major concern. Employment rates for people with severe disabilities are the lowest of any minority group, making full participation in society more difficult. Work provides not only the financial means for participation, but it also accords adult status and establishes networks for building friendships and community connections. Not only is employment important for people with disabilities, it is vitally important for the economic health of the nation as well. When individuals with disabilities move from Social Security rolls to active roles in the workforce, the economy profits from their productivity and avoids the cost of the income support.

Unfortunately, disincentives exist within the Social Security legislation, often making it difficult for people with disabilities to move from SSI and SSDI rolls into the workforce. Insurance availability is one such issue. People who move from SSI or SSDI to a job will eventually lose access to Medicare or Medicaid, though current provisions allow for a transition period. Still, exclusions related to pre-existing conditions can mean that an individual would lose ground financially by taking a job that did not adequately cover health care costs. Health care reform legislation passed in August of 1996 may begin to address these concerns by requiring insurance companies to provide for coverage of preexisting conditions after a waiting period of twelve months. Individuals must have an assurance of other sources of health care coverage before they can risk moving off Social Security rolls.

The Americans with Disabilities Act was signed into law in 1990, but people with disabilities continue to face issues of access and equality. Inaccessible work, education, and recreational environments continue to present barriers to full participation in society, and those who push for changes may be seen as "ungrateful" or "selfish" because they have moved outside of the expected "sick role" of passive acceptance. Other attitudinal barriers also persist. Old stereotypes of helplessness and incapacity continue to limit the opportunities open to people with disabilities and reduce their contributions to their communities and to the nation. Many people incur a disability later in life and may, themselves, hold some of these assumptions about incapacity. Discrimination, therefore, must be fought at all levels—from self-image to societal image.

Concluding Comment

While medical advances hold great promise for the treatment of many disabling conditions, the impact of disability on American society is likely to increase greatly over the next five to ten years. At this time, medicine has advanced further in the area of emergency services than it has in rehabilitative care. More people are surviving head injuries and other traumas, but often with multiple disabilities. In addition, the American population is becoming older—and age increases the risk of disability. Add to this the number of infants affected by fetal alcohol syndrome and the ingestion of other chemicals of abuse during pregnancy. Add, again, the number of individuals who may be impacted by AIDS. It is clear that, in the near term, the number of people with disabilities in the United States is likely to increase substantially.

The need for services will also increase dramatically. Medical professionals will continue to address the biological issues, and vocational rehabilitation counselors will focus on issues of employment, but social workers will bring a unique focus that includes interventions at all system levels. Social workers must join hands with the disability rights movement in recognizing that disability issues should not focus exclusively on the medical problem or the individual's skills for a particular job. Disability issues are civil rights issues. Social workers must work to ensure that public policies and service programs are made more responsive. They must help individuals, families, and their communities to find room within their own cultural frameworks to value the lives and contributions of people with disabilities. In this way, social workers can truly work *with* people with disabilities, enhancing their lives and enriching society.

KEY WORDS AND CONCEPTS

ADA

People with disabilities

Medical model

Reciprocal causality

People first language

Impairment vs. disability

SUGGESTED READINGS

Asch, A., and Mudrick, N. R. "Disability," in Richard L. Edwards, ed., *Encyclopedia of Social Work,* 19th Edition. Washington, D.C.: NASW, 1995.

Blaska, J. "The Power of Language: Speak and Write Using 'Person First,'" in M. Nagler, ed., *Perspectives on Disability: Text and Readings,* 2nd Edition. Palo Alto, CA: Health Markets Research, 1993.

Ferguson, P., Ferguson, D., and Taylor, S., eds. *Interpreting Disability: A Qualitative Reader.* New York: Teachers College Press, 1992.

Nagler, M., ed. *Perspectives on Disability: Text and Readings,* 2nd Edition. Palo Alto, CA: Health Markets Research, 1993.

ENDNOTES

1. N. Groce, *The U.S. Role in International Disability Activities: A History and a Look Towards the Future* (New York: Rehabilitation International, 1992).
2. J. Blaska, "The Power of Language: Speak and Write Using 'Person First,'" in M. Nagler, ed., *Perspectives on Disability,* 2nd Edition (Palo Alto, CA: Health Markets Research, 1993), pp. 25–32.
3. A. Morales, "Social Work Practice with Special Populations," in A. Morales and B. Sheafor, eds., *Social Work: A Profession of Many Faces,* 7th Edition (Boston: Allyn & Bacon, 1995), pp. 287–293.
4. United States Congress, Senate Committee on Labor and Human Resources, Subcommittee on the Handicapped, *Americans with Disabilities Act of 1988: Joint hearing before the Subcommittee on the Handicapped of the Committee on Labor and Human Resources, United States Senate, and the Subcommittee on Select Education of the Committee on Education and Labor, House of Representatives,* One Hundredth Congress, second session on S.2345, September 27, 1988 (Washington, D.C.: USGPO, 1989).
5. World Health Organization, *International Classification of Impairments, Disabilities and Handicaps* (Geneva: World Health Organization, 1980).
6. Blaska, pp. 25–32.
7. J. McNeil, *Americans with Disabilities: 1991–1992: Data from the Survey of Income and Program Participation,* U.S. Bureau of the Census, Current Population Reports P70-33 (Washington, D.C.: U.S. Government Printing Office, 1993).
8. M. LaPlante and J. Cyril, "Disability in the United States," *Disability Statistics Abstract* #6 (Washington, D.C.: National Institute of Disability, Rehabilitation and Research, 1993).
9. McNeil, p. 10.
10. M. LaPlante, "How Many Americans Have a Disability?" *Disability Abstracts* #5 (Washington, D.C.: National Institute of Disability, Rehabilitation and Research, 1992).

11. McNeil, p. 10.
12. McNeil, p. 5.
13. McNeil, p. 11.
14. S. Walker, C. Asbury, V. Malhomes, and R. Rackley, "Prevalence, Distribution and Impact of Disability Among Ethnic Minorities," in S. Walker, F. Belgrave, R. Nicholls, and K. Turner, eds., Proceedings of the 1990 National Conference, *Future Frontiers in the Employment of Minority Persons with Disabilities* (Washington, D.C.: Howard University Research and Training Center for Access the Rehabilitation and Economic Opportunity, March 28–30, 1990), pp. 10–24.
15. McNeil, p. 11.
16. McNeil, p. 11.
17. F. Belgrave and S. Walker, "Differences in Rehabilitation Service Utilization Patterns of African Americans and White Americans with Disabilities," in S. Walker, F. Belgrave, R. Nicholls, and K. Turner, eds., Proceedings of the 1990 National Conference, *Future Frontiers in the Employment of Minority Persons with Disabilities* (Washington, D.C.: Howard University Research and Training Center for Access the Rehabilitation and Economic Opportunity, March 28–30, 1990), pp. 25–36.
18. Belgrave and Walker, pp. 25–36.
19. G. Becker and S. Kaufman, "Old Age, Rehabilitation and Research: A Review of the Issues," *Gerontologist* 28 (August 1988): 459–468.
20. B. Holland and D. Falvo, "Forgotten: Elderly Persons with Disability—A Consequence of Policy," *Journal of Rehabilitation* 56 (April, May, June, 1990): 32–35.
21. J. Garbarino, "The Abuse and Neglect of Special Children: An Introduction to the Issues," in J. Garbarino, P. Brookhouser, K. Authier, eds., *Special Children–Special Risks: The Maltreatment of Children with Disabilities* (New York: Aldine DeGruyter, 1987), pp. 3–14.
22. D. Corthell and J. Brown, "Introduction," in *Substance Abuse as a Coexisting Disability*, Eighteenth Institute on Rehabilitation Issues (Menomonie, WI: Research and Training Center, Stout Vocational Rehabilitation Institute, 1991), pp. 1–25.
23. D. Stroman, *The Awakening Minorities: The Physically Handicapped* (Lanham, MD: University Press of America, 1982), pp. 6–8.
24. D. Stroman, p. 7.
25. Americans with Disabilities Act of 1990 (Preamble) 42 U.S.C.A. Section 12101 *et seq.* (Washington, D.C.: West, 1993).
26. United States Congress, House of Representatives, Committee on Small Business, *Americans with Disabilities Act of 1989,* One Hundred First Congress, Serial No. 101–45, February 22, 1990 (Washington, D.C.: USGPO 1990).
27. G. DeJong, *The Movement for Independent Living: Origins, Ideology, and Implications for Disability Research* (East Lansing: University Centers for International Rehabilitation, Michigan State University, 1979).
28. S. Rubin and R. Roessler, "Historical Roots of Modern Rehabilitation Practices," in *Foundations of the Vocational Rehabilitation Process,* 4th Edition (Austin, TX: Proed, 1995), pp. 1–40.
29. Rubin and Roessler, pp. 15–16.
30. President's Committee on Employment of the Handicapped, "Disabled Americans: A History," *Performance* 27 (November–December, 1976, January 1977): 8.

31. LaPlante, p. 2.
32. Rubin and Roessler, pp. 23–24.
33. Morales, pp. 287–293.
34. A. Asch and N. Mudrick, "Disability," *Encyclopedia of Social Work,* 19th Edition (New York: NASW), pp. 752–761.

The Rural, Urban, and Suburban Context of Social Work Practice

The rural poor have been ignored for many years in the delivery of social, health, and mental health services. They often have the same needs and problems as urban clients, but, because they are so isolated, rural residents encounter numerous barriers in the delivery of services. Chapter 16, "Social Work Practice in Rural Areas: Appalachia as a Case Example," by Bradford W. Sheafor and Robert G. Lewis, is an original, scholarly response to practitioners in the field who want more exposure to the literature on an incredibly large, neglected special population in the United States numbering 9.9 million persons below the poverty line, over 90 percent white. Being white has not been an advantage for this population. Is their poverty due to their culture, being physically isolated in rural areas? Or simply policy neglect by politicians who do not view them as a strong voting group?

Chapter 17, "Urban and Suburban Gangs: The Psychosocial Crisis Spreads" by Armando T. Morales,

is a very timely, major renovation and updating of "Urban Gang Violence: A Psychosocial Crisis," which appeared in earlier editions. This major change was stimulated by the Trench Coat Mafia gang members in Littleton, Colorado, who killed 13 students and one teacher and who then committed suicide at Columbine High. Dr. Morales, a former "street gang" group worker, senior deputy probation officer, and for the last twenty-four years a state parole mental health consultant and gang member therapist, sees these white middle-class gang homicide perpetrators as having very similar psychiatric, biological and gang culture characteristics as poor, inner-city gang homicide perpetrators. The key common denominator is male adolescent *major depression* expressed through the fabric of gang culture. Dr. Morales highlights an understanding of the "gang homicide–suicide continuum" and helps readers to assess these fine distinctions.

CHAPTER 16

Social Work Practice in Rural Areas: Appalachia as a Case Example

Bradford W. Sheafor and Robert G. Lewis

Prefatory Comment

One of the many faces of social work finds social workers serving the residents of the rural areas of the United States. The U.S. Bureau of the Census estimates that in 1996 there were more than 53.5 million people, or slightly more than 20 percent of the population, living in nonmetropolitan areas. Approximately 16 percent of these people live below the poverty line, and many more experience serious social problems. Rural people, however, often find it difficult to obtain professional help to deal with these problems due to limited availability of services in rural areas. Sheafor and Lewis illustrate aspects of the uniqueness of rural social work using Appalachia as a case example.

If social workers are to respond to the special needs prevalent among the rural U.S. population, appropriate knowledge and practice competencies will be required. Social workers in rural areas should be aware that rural people have several experiences in common: they usually share a dependence on the land; they tend to be more religious than urban dwellers; and they are reluctant to make use of professional helpers and human services programs.[1] They also tend to be more independent and conservative in their attitudes about social problems and resist governmental interventions to resolve them. In addition, in most rural communities the people have the experience of living in an environment undergoing such rapid social change that existing social institutions cannot adequately adapt. The ensuing social problems require human services programs and human services professionals who are aware of these special needs.

The initial part of this chapter presents an overview of significant changes in rural United States and the special problems in service delivery experienced by social workers who serve rural people. Rural areas, however, are not all alike. Martinez-Brawley has clearly shown that social problems experienced in rural areas and the intensity with which they are felt by the population vary from region to region.[2] The final part of the chapter examines the unique dimensions of rural social work practice in one geographic area of the United States, Appalachia. Appalachia includes all of the state of West Virginia and parts of twelve other states, extending 1,300 miles from New York to Mississippi. Although this region includes several large urban centers, nearly one-half of the Appalachian population is considered rural, and a unique culture has developed among the residents of this region.

Characteristics of the Rural United States

The ability to describe rural life is partially hampered by the difficulty in finding agreement on a definition of rural. In the early periods of U.S. history, the isolation rural people experienced made it sufficient to define rural areas in terms of the number of people who lived in a given geographic area where they bought and sold goods, attended churches and schools, and experienced most of their social interaction. The population-based definition of the U.S. Bureau of the Census, which defined those sparsely populated areas with 2,500 people or less as rural, then was sufficient. However, as timber was cleared, mines closed, farms mechanized, and employment for more and more rural people was available only in urban centers; as urbanites moved to rural areas in search of the good life; and as cities annexed large amounts of rural land without subsequent housing or industrial development, the line between urban and rural became blurred. The Census Bureau refined its definition of rural areas by considering rural as those areas that are smaller than or outside of the metropolitan areas, that is, central cities and their surrounding territory (suburbs) that together have a minimum of 50,000 persons. Rural areas, then, include the nonmetropolitan population who live a distance from the urban centers either in small towns or in unincorporated areas.[3]

Most experts on rural United States consider the Census Bureau definition a valid measure for developing approximations of the number of people in rural and urban areas, but some contend that there are other factors that should be considered when identifying a rural population. Waltman, for example, notes that the word rural means "more than a numerical population limit. It connotes a way of and an outlook on life characterized by a closeness to nature, slower pace of living and a somewhat conservative life-style that values tradition, independence and self-reliance, and privacy."[4] DuBord further suggests that an additional characteristic of rural communities is that they are primarily dependent on occupations tied to the land.[5]

THE LAND

Rural life is directly linked to the land and to nature. The primary land uses in rural areas have been for agriculture, mining and energy development, timber, fishing, recreation, and absorbing urban sprawl. The urban population has depended on farmers and ranchers to provide their food supplies. They have also expected rural communities to incorporate the often dramatically different population groups that may suddenly arrive to set up oil rigs, extract minerals, or fish or ski during relatively short periods of the year. Similarly, rural people are expected to give up farmland to housing developments and to integrate new residents into their social structures.

One by-product of the dependence on the land and nature for earning a living is always living with a degree of risk. A wet planting or harvest season, an early frost, a hail-storm, a forest fire, the presence of pollutants in a lake, a mine shaft cave-in, or even the price of a barrel of oil in the Middle East can dramatically affect life for the rural population. For these reasons, religion and fatalism are inherent parts of rural culture, and a certain amount of emotional stress is ever-present in rural life.

THE ECONOMY

The rural economy is intertwined with the land. Changing employment patterns in agriculture and the extractive occupations (e.g., timber, mining) affect the rural economy, as do changes in land use patterns. For example, the primary rural occupations—agriculture and the retail trades that support it—are currently experiencing rapid change due to mechanization and the large capital investments required for farming, as well as the increased amount of land required to maintain a profitable farm or ranch. Between 1930 and 1990 the number of farms in the United States declined from 6.5 million to 2.1 million, and the number of farmers dropped from 30.5 million to 4.6 million.[6] Similarly, reports of boom-and-bust conditions in the Rocky Mountain West and virtually every other rural area of the United States document dramatic changes in ownership, management, and demand for differing occupational skills. Inevitably, these changes impact the employment patterns, the economy, and the quality of life of rural communities.

THE PEOPLE

People typically select rural life because their livelihood is bound to the land, they prefer what they consider the qualitative aspects of rural life over urban life, or they are trapped there by lack of resources and skills or by family situations requiring their presence. For whatever reasons, a substantial number of people have elected to reside in rural areas. Compared to their urban counterparts, rural families include more older people, have a higher ratio of males to females, and experience higher rates of poverty (i.e., 16.0 percent compared to 14.2 percent in metropolitan areas).[7] They are also more likely to be a traditional two-parent family with only one bread-winner (usually a male) in the household. They also tend to have higher rates of unemployment, more disabled persons, lower educational levels, and lower annual income than urban families. Whereas urban communities have considerable ethnic diversity (the white population in the United States was 76.9 percent in 1990), the population of rural United States was mostly white (90.6%).[8] The only racial minority group that had a substantial portion of its population residing in rural areas was the Native Americans.

Historically, rural people have been exceptionally family oriented. The demands of farm life required that all able family members help with preparing and tilling the land, planting and harvesting the crops, and maintaining the equipment and farm. The extended family, therefore, was an important part of rural life, and there was usually some meaningful work that could be done by people of all ages—even those with physical and intellectual handicaps. Rural culture was family centered.

The reality of rural family life today is that economic conditions have forced millions of families to leave agriculture, and the characteristics of rural families are now much more similar to urban families. Rural families now include their share of single-parent families, dual-employment families, and families living in poverty. They, too, experience rising rates of substance abuse, divorce, family violence, and adolescent pregnancies. Despite these similarities to urban families, the culture of rural life continues to maintain the family as a central social institution, and many social activities and social programs are designed around the family.

Religion plays a particularly important role in the lives of rural people. Studies of rural and urban populations indicate that rural people are more religiously oriented than are their urban counterparts. Meystedt summarizes the findings of several such studies:

> In comparison to urban populations, rural people are more likely to rate themselves as "very" or "fairly" religious and to a greater extent feel that religion can answer "all or most of today's problems." In other dimensions, such as Bible reading, they also exceed urbanites; rural people are resisting the nationwide downward trend in church attendance. Nearly 75 percent of persons in rural areas profess "a great deal" or "quite a lot" of respect for and confidence in the church and organized religion.[9]

In addition to worship, instruction, and other activities of religious expression, churches have a central place in rural life because of the various social functions such as dinners, group meetings, and youth activities they sponsor.

The more conservative political positions held by the people of rural United States are documented by Glenn and Hill in their analysis of a series of Gallup polls conducted in the mid-1970s. These data indicate that people living in communities of less than 50,000 population differed from people living in larger communities on many political and social issues. For example, they tended to be more opposed to abortion, premarital sex, the Equal Rights Amendment, female presidential candidates, amnesty for draft evaders, the registration of firearms, and re-establishing diplomatic ties with Cuba than persons living in urban areas.[10]

People of rural areas, then, differ from the urban population in the central role played by the family and religion in their lives. Further, they tend to be more conservative politically than their urban counterparts and often elect to suffer from social problems rather than to seek help from human services agencies or professional caregivers. The rural population has an especially strong dedication to the earth and the land, making foreclosure or the necessity for an elderly person to sell the farm and move to a town or nursing home, for example, an event that has significant emotional as well as economic implications.

Finally, rural culture places great value on friendships, interpersonal communication, and helping acquaintances in need. The pace of life tends to be slower than in urban areas, there is time for more leisurely interpersonal interactions, and perhaps the strongest natural helping networks in the United States exist in rural communities. At the same time, sparse population creates high visibility, making it difficult for a person or family to maintain the level of privacy that urban people expect. Family history colors the perception of the individual, few matters remain secret for any length of time, and gossip serves as an effective social control mechanism. Rural people, then, reflect a mix of attitudes that can best be characterized as "conservative, provincial, traditional, primary relationships, informal decision-making process, sense of independence and self-reliance, wholesome, simple, natural, and folksy."[11]

THE COMMUNITIES

Rural United States cannot be fully appreciated without recognizing the importance of communities in enhancing the quality of life for the people. Rural towns serve as important centers of business, trade, education, religion, and interpersonal interaction. The relative isolation experienced by many rural people makes community activities especially important. These activities tend to center around schools (especially school sports), churches, retail stores, and outlets where necessary equipment or products grown and produced are bought and sold (e.g., the local co-op grain elevator or farm implement store).

Several types of rural communities can be identified—including the farm/ranch trade center, the mining/energy/timber company town, the tourist center, and the bedroom community for a metropolitan area. Each type of community faces unique problems, but all are undergoing rapid transition and experience difficulty in maintaining appropriate decision-making structures that can address these problems. Rural towns have traditionally exercised a considerable degree of internal control and have been tenacious in maintaining the power to decide community issues. That power was usually located in a few influential, but accessible, members of the community. Increasingly, community issues have been decided by the often "invisible" representatives of corporations that control the economy of rural towns and by state and national governmental bodies that construct guidelines or make decisions that affect the schools, roads, and other public programs. Local control in rural communities has clearly diminished.

Social Welfare in Rural Areas

The major programs developed to respond to the social welfare needs of the U.S. population have characteristically been designed in an urban mode, where it is assumed that people can readily visit helping professionals. For persons residing in rural areas, where the population is insufficient to support even a limited number of highly specialized, full-time human services providers, the ability of rural people to obtain professional help is severely restricted.

Two factors work against rural inhabitants gaining access to professional services. First, rural people are reluctant to seek professional help for personal problems. In a study conducted in Iowa and Pennsylvania by Martinez-Brawley and Blundall, farm families identified the following obstacles they perceived in using social services, in descending rank order: concerns about families' reputations in the community; lack of understanding about what services do and how they work; grew up with the idea of not reaching for help from social agencies; lack of money; feeling that one must bear one's problems; fear of being perceived as lazy or incapable of taking care of oneself; feeling that no one has real answers to life's problems; fear of being perceived as mentally ill; distrust of workers who get paid to do the job; fear of social workers; and pride.[12] Second, the human services delivery system often makes services inaccessible to rural people. The financial burden and time required to simply reach a social agency is too often placed on the person needing the service. It is simply too costly and time consuming for many potential recipients of services to travel great distances to reach the providers; thus many do not receive needed services. Their health and social problems go unattended—or family and friends are left to address the matter as best they can.

Human services in rural areas are typically provided through governmental agencies, on a county or regional basis, by public welfare departments, community mental health centers, the criminal justice system, nursing homes, hospitals and public health care agencies, and schools. Private or voluntary services are not plentiful in rural areas and, when they are offered, they are typically provided through churches and youth-oriented programs such as 4-H and scouting. Although serious social problems pervade much of rural America, communities that experience rapid growth and the infusion of a new population group into an established area often experience a dramatic increase in problems requiring professional services. Bachrach cites the following example:

> In one Colorado boom town the population increased by 43 percent. Over the same time period there were parallel—but strikingly disproportionate—increases in selected reported social problems for that community: respectively, a 130 percent increase in reported child neglect and abuse, a 222 percent increase in crimes against property, a 352 percent increase in family disturbances, a 623 percent increase in substance abuse, and a dramatic 900 percent increase in crimes against persons.[13]

Another common source of rapid change for rural areas is rural towns becoming bedroom communities for urban areas. Often an idealized view of rural life attracts the urban family, who hopes the wholesome rural environment will solve their problems; they commute many miles each day in order to raise their children in a rural environment. One rural school superintendent reported that when a large, ten-acre-per-home-site land development was created in his school district, he found that children from this area represented 5 percent of the school population, required 15 percent of busing funds, involved 85 percent of the school-attendance problems, and used more than half of the pupil personnel resources.[14]

Research into the provision of human services in rural areas suggests that there are no significant differences in the social problems addressed or the manner in which practice is conducted. The most substantial difference is in the delivery of services. The solution to this problem appears to lie in taking programs to the people and adopting practice approaches incorporating as fully as possible the rural orientation toward self-help and mutual aid.

Implications for Social Work Practice in Rural Areas

Given the uniqueness of rural life and the particular problems experienced in delivering human services, the social worker in a rural area must have special competencies. Often he or she is the only (or one of a very few) professional in a community, and this requires the worker to possess wide-ranging knowledge and skill to improve conditions for both individuals and communities. Specialization is a luxury that sparsely populated rural areas simply cannot support. The "all-purpose" rural social worker must be innovative, resourceful, self-motivating, and able to function with minimal supervision.

Employing agencies must also recognize that rural practice requires more than just transporting urban social workers to rural areas. Needed practice skills will most likely focus on the middle range of social work activities, such as generalized counseling with individuals and families, building support networks and accessing natural helpers, and facilitating the efforts of communities to engage in self-help to prevent or resolve their problems. Agencies must select and/or prepare their staff members for the breadth of rural practice. The fact that substantial differences in the tasks performed by urban and rural social workers do not appear to exist may suggest an unresponsiveness by social work education and agency staff development programs to the unique requirements for social work practice in rural areas.

The practice model most generally accepted as appropriate for rural practice is labeled *generalist*. The generalist perspective requires that the social worker approach practice without a bias as to which intervention approach(es) would be most appropriate until the situation is carefully examined. As reported by Sheafor and Landon in the *Encyclopedia of Social Work*, "Generalist practice requires that the social worker examine the various facets of a situation that need intervention and apply the knowledge, values, and skills either to initiate service or to secure appropriate specialized expertise. Thus generalist practice involves both the capacity to take a wide view of the practice situation and the necessary abilities to intervene at multiple levels and in a range of situations."[15]

In social work education, preparation for generalist social work practice is required by the Council on Social Work Education for all accredited social work education programs. Advanced generalist preparation is also available in a growing number of MSW programs, which view the generalist approach as desirable for both rural and urban social work practitioners. A national study of BSW social workers suggests that the generalist preparation of graduates has been well received by rural social agencies. Whereas approximately 23 percent of the U.S. population resides in communities of 40,000 or fewer people, 43.9 percent of BSW graduates reported they were employed in human services agencies serving communities of 40,000 or fewer, and 16.7 percent served communities of 10,000 or fewer.[16]

MICRO PRACTICE IN RURAL AREAS

At the micro, or direct, practice level, rural social workers provide face-to-face services to clients, as would any other social worker. However, the social worker must be especially alert to the fact that because of the strong value placed on self-reliance, rural clients may be resistant to counseling services and reluctant to accept tangible assistance, that is, social provisions. When combined with the traditional dependence on friends, family, or other natural helpers, the professional helper is truly a "resource of last resort," and the problems presented tend to be severe. Due to the high visibility of people and the likelihood of interaction between worker and client in other activities in small communities, it is essential that the client understand the special nature of professional relationships and that the social worker provide protections to maximize confidentiality regarding the practice activity.

The generalist worker must be prepared to offer a wide range of services but must also be cautious not to slip into the trap of believing he or she has the tools to solve all problems. There are times when specialized service is in the best interest of the client and referral to existing services within the community or in urban areas is essential. The task of becoming knowledgeable about the available resources in the region for the many problems the rural social worker confronts is an onerous, but essential, activity. Once appropriate resources are identified, considerable care and skill are required to complete a successful referral. While many people view referral as a relatively simple task, it is actually a very complex procedure and many attempted referrals end in failure.

Another direct practice activity that is compatible with the orientation of rural people involves engaging clients in self-help groups and supporting the use of natural helping networks to meet their less complicated needs. This activity is especially important, both because the culture supports caregiving by friends and families and because professional service providers have limited time to devote to any single practice situation. The challenge for the social worker is to determine which situations are appropriate for this type of intervention and to mobilize the appropriate natural helpers to perform this service.

MACRO PRACTICE IN RURAL AREAS

While all social workers are expected to engage in both direct and indirect service activity, the rural worker should be prepared to devote a substantial part of his or her time to macro, or indirect, practice activity. The central place of community life in rural areas suggests the importance of providing community-centered, rather than problem- or case-centered, services.

Existing social organizations such as churches, schools, and local government agencies are important resources for collaboration by the rural social worker. To effectively use these resources to solve or prevent social problems in the community, the worker must be skilled at needs assessment, social policy analysis, and small-town politics, and be able to work intimately with community leadership. It is important for the worker to be able to accurately assess the local decision-making structure and effectively interpret the needs of the residents to these people. The opportunity for face-to-face contact to influence these decision makers, or even become one of the key decision makers, is especially possible once the social worker is well established in a rural community.

Efforts to advocate for client services need not stop with the local community. The rural social worker has a particularly good opportunity to interpret the community's needs and to lobby directly with county and state legislators who represent that district. To work at these levels, the social worker needs to be competent in program and practice research, social policy development, community planning activities, and influencing the legislative process.

Social work practice in rural areas, then, requires knowledge of the special issues that face rural people, a generalist perspective for practice, and skills for working with people at both the micro and macro levels. Regional differences, too, affect practice in various parts of the United States. The Appalachian region illustrates a rural area with some unique characteristics and needs.

Rural Social Work Practice in Appalachia

The remainder of this chapter examines some of the unique factors that would affect a social worker practicing in Appalachia, a large and primarily rural region of the United States. The following case illustrates a social worker's need to understand Appalachia as a context for social work practice with a young woman from that region:

> Mary, a twenty-two-year-old, unmarried community college student, grew up in a coal-field county in central Appalachia. She became pregnant while attending college, and a college counselor urged her to visit with the caseworker who staffs the county welfare department's satellite center three days each week. The social worker interviewed Mary when she first requested care and recorded the following information.
>
> Mary, the oldest of four siblings, is a bright young woman who is committed to completing her college degree. She is a first-generation college student who feels that she will let herself down if she does not move ahead with her education at this time. Mary's mother has no marketable employment skills, her father is disabled because he contracted Black Lung Disease from his years in the coal mines, and her youngest sister has a chronic health problem that constantly drains the family's financial resources. For generations the family lived below the poverty level, and Mary sees college as her way out of poverty. Mary's family belongs to a fundamentalist church in their community, and Mary fears her out-of-wedlock pregnancy has caused her family disappointment and embarrassment.

To adequately understand Mary's situation, the social worker needed to be familiar with several unique characteristics of Appalachia, the context in which service was to be provided to Mary. Some of the general knowledge the social worker should have about this region of the United States is included in the following paragraphs.

CHARACTERISTICS OF APPALACHIA

Appalachia is a term that has become widely used since the mid-1960s to identify residents of a large, primarily rural region of the United States. Prior to that time, terms frequently used to describe the rural Appalachian people were *mountaineers, Southern mountain people, highlanders,* and *hillbillies.* Although those terms are sometimes used today, the common identification of the people is with the Appalachian Mountain chain that extends from Maine to Georgia. There is no doubt the lives of people who live in or near the Appalachian Mountains are shaped by the climate, topography, and minerals contained in those mountains.

Stereotyping by the mass media has contributed significantly to the region's negative image. At the same time, media attention has made the U.S. public aware of the problems experienced by the rural Appalachian people, which contributed to the creation of massive economic development projects in the region. In the 1960s publicity surrounding Lyndon Johnson's War on Poverty again focused attention on Appalachia. Extreme poverty in the region, along with the associated problems of poor health, illiteracy, substandard housing, and so forth, were depicted in the media as the plight of most Appalachians. Public knowledge of the conditions in this region helped to generate support for passage of the Economic Opportunity Act in 1964.

The Appalachian Regional Redevelopment Act, passed in 1965, focused entirely on the needs of the region, and the Appalachian Regional Commission (ARC) was created immediately to implement the provisions of the act. Hundreds of federal programs resulting from the federal legislation inundated the region for the next two decades. Although duplication, lack of coordination, mismanagement, and questionable priorities hampered the effectiveness of these efforts, much was accomplished. More than $7 billion has been spent by the ARC since its inception, with most aimed at improving the infrastructure. For example, the construction of over 2,100 miles of new highways, vocational-technical schools, hospitals, clinics, airports, and public service systems has placed many sections of the region in an improved competitive position in the national marketplace.

Some sections of the region, especially those that are dependent on coal mining and associated industries, continue to experience extremely high rates of unemployment, poverty, poor health, illiteracy, and other social problems. Although Appalachia is now closer to the national average in terms of education, health care, income, and the like, than before these federal programs were initiated, the region is still somewhat below the rest of the country on most important indicators of social well-being. Also, the ARC has experienced severe reductions in funding during the past two decades, and continuing economic development efforts do not appear likely to be underwritten or heavily subsidized by the federal government.

THE LAND.   A map of the eastern United States (Figure 16-1) shows the enormous land area of the Appalachian region. Although its boundaries have been redefined several times during this century, the current boundaries contain 200,000 square miles—an area comparable in size to Central America, and 75.4 percent of the 399 Appalachian counties are nonmetropolitan.[17] The ARC has defined three subregions: the Northern, Central, and Southern. The Northern subregion is the most populous and urbanized. The Central subregion is the smallest, most rural, and experiences the highest degree of poverty and isolation. The Southern subregion is developing a modern infrastructure and experiencing the highest level of industrial diversification and expansion.[18]

In contemporary rural Appalachia, the uses of the land and the close relationship between the people and the land are similar to other parts of rural United States. Yet notable differences exist. Although the steep mountain slopes and narrow valleys, which are prone to flooding, have prohibited extensive commercial agricultural development, the land is central to the way of life for the Appalachian people. Family farms continue to shrink as each generation has fewer acres to subdivide among heirs, and many small farmers have to seek outside employment. The extractive industries (especially coal mining and gas production), timber harvesting, and tourism and recreation dominate the rural economy. Each depends on the land and is subject to the risks of depleted resources, changing demand, and fluctuating price structures throughout the world. Few of the local people, however, own mineral rights or mineral land, which are possessed by absentee corporate owners, resulting in little return to the local economy.

THE ECONOMY.   The economic history of Appalachia is intertwined with the land and its outside ownership. First came the timber barons, who purchased hundreds of thousands of acres of prime virgin timber at only a fraction of their true value. Next came the large corporations, who bought mineral rights and land at prices substantially below their real value. Then the railroads were built, using government subsidies in order to have a means to transport timber, coal, and other extracted natural resources to national markets, as well as to distribution points for international markets. Finally, the tourism and recreation industry emerged as another central feature of the economy. However, problems associated with tourism, such as seasonal employment, low wages, and high property taxes, undermined a stable economic base for many local residents.

The fact is that economic prosperity has been achieved by many non-Appalachian corporations through exploitation of the landowners. Caudill effectively drew public attention to this in his popular book, *Night Comes to the Cumberlands*, as he writes:

> We have seen that the mountaineer sold his great trees for a consideration little more than nominal, but if his timber brought him a small financial reward, his minerals were virtually given away. The going price in the early years was fifty cents an acre . . . and a seam of coal five feet thick produced a minimum of five thousand tons per acre! Where more than one seam was mined, a single acre sometimes yielded fifteen or twenty

FIGURE 16-1 The Appalachian Region as Defined by the Appalachian Regional Commission: 1965

Source: ©1996, The Center for Appalachian Studies and Services.

thousand tons! . . . For this vast mineral wealth the mountaineer in most instances received a single half-dollar.[19]

Chronic economic problems have persisted due to the lack of a diversified industrial economy. Although improvements have been realized in many areas, the region has suffered historically from boom and bust periods associated with the extractive industries. As the price of oil changes on the international market, or as modernized mining methods reduce the labor force, poverty increases because viable alternative sources of employment are limited or nonexistent in parts of the region. For many, the only alternative is long-term unemployment—or migration to urban areas, without the assurance of employment there. The skills required for the mining, steel, and textile industries do not readily transfer to other jobs, except in manufacturing. Attracting large manufacturers to an area, however, requires modern highways and other transportation systems that are not currently present in the mountainous areas of Appalachia. Much of the central subregion and some counties in other subregions are even more economically distressed than they were in earlier decades. Unemployment and poverty rates in rural Appalachia continue to range above national averages and, as a result, the ACR identified 115 counties in nine states as "distressed" counties in the fiscal year 1995. These counties fell into the lowest quartile for all three economic indicators of poverty, unemployment, and income (excluding transfer payments).[20]

All rural Appalachia should not be viewed as economically depressed or under the control of multinational conglomerates. Although the economic situation in the coal, steel, and textile industries is dismal, many other areas are economically healthy and closely resemble affluent areas elsewhere in the United States.

THE PEOPLE.   The estimated 20.7 million people who reside in Appalachia constitute over 8 percent of the population of the United States. Although hundreds of small towns and cities and some larger cities (e.g., Pittsburgh, Pennsylvania; Roanoke, Virginia; Knoxville, Tennessee; and Birmingham, Alabama) dot the landscape, 45.5 percent of the region's population is rural—nearly double the national percentage.[21]

Many academics, authors, and others believe that Appalachians are a distinct ethnic minority group and should be recognized officially as such. However, this designation has been rejected by most Appalachian scholars as well as a large majority of the Appalachian people. Miller sums up the prevailing viewpoint noting that:

> while Appalachians are in no legitimate sense an ethnic group, they are classified by other Americans as something quite similar to an ethnic group; and have many of the same problems—economic, social, and psychological—as members of various ethnic groups. But there is an important difference. Appalachians have none of the obvious distinguishing features of most ethnic groups—no distinguishing racial or physical features, no different language or religion. Because of this, Appalachians bear a special stigma. They have none of the marks of an "ethnic"—which serves as an explanation of different attitudes and values emphases—and yet they are so different.[22]

Although the majority of the people are of Anglo-Saxon extraction and descendants of several generations of Appalachians, diversity does exist. The region has a negligible foreign-born population, and Native Americans, concentrated primarily in western North Carolina, make up less than one percent of the residents. African Americans, who account for a large segment of the Appalachians in Alabama, Mississippi, and South Carolina, constitute only 7.3 percent of the region's total population.[23] Indeed, there is enormous social, economic, and cultural diversity in Appalachia and a social worker should be aware that numerous subcultures exist. Even the most rural families today are becoming increasingly less isolated and insulated from the outside world. They are made aware of mainstream culture through regular exposure to the mass media, especially television. Also, today's money-oriented society, unlike the former trade-oriented economy, makes it necessary for people to interface with social systems and institutions in mainstream America. It is perhaps most accurate to characterize rural Appalachian people as being bicultural, because most learn and practice mainstream and mountain culture simultaneously.

The mass media have regularly provided the people of the United States with distorted images of the region and its people. Most stereotypes are centered on a few perceived character or behavioral traits such as laziness, ignorance, uncleanliness, immorality, violence, and passivity. Television programs that have been the most stereotypical include "The Beverly Hillbillies," "Dukes of Hazzard," "Green Acres," "Gomer Pyle," and "Hee Haw." Comic strips like "Snuffy Smith" and "L'il Abner" have also contributed their share of mythical descriptions of Appalachian life. Among the many movies that have stereotyped the Appalachian people, few can surpass "Deliverance." Stereotypes usually have some basis in fact, but accuracy is soon lost through distortion and exaggeration, which is then generalized to include a whole region, race, or class of people.

The prevalent cultural values ascribed to Appalachians had their origins in the early frontier-agrarian society. These values include strong family ties, individualism and self-reliance, traditionalism, fatalism, and religious fundamentalism. They are an outgrowth of the harsh realities of survival in the rugged mountains and hollows during the eighteenth, nineteenth, and early part of the twentieth centuries. Historically, families were self-contained social units, with each household living its own life independent of other families in the hollow. Family members were dependent on one another for survival, and opportunities for activities outside the nuclear or extended family were severely restricted. Naturally, family relationships have changed as Appalachia has changed, but there is strong evidence that rural Appalachian families continue to be among the most closely knit families in the United States.

Another characteristic of the people in the rural areas of Appalachia is the importance of the family surname. Individuals are evaluated, and even judged, to a large extent, on the reputation of their family, which may be considered more important than one's accomplishments or lack thereof. Also, individualism and self-reliance were traits necessary for survival on the frontier, but the ability to exercise these traits is increasingly restricted in today's expanding industrial economy. With the change to an industrial economy the Appalachian lost autonomy, but the belief in independence and self-reliance is still there.

Traditionalism, too, has characterized the Appalachians for generations. It was easier and safer to hold on to the "old ways" than to adapt to a changing society. That characteristic may be passing as many Appalachians have demonstrated their desire and capacity to be progressive and participate in the emerging industrial economy.

Another characteristic of Appalachia is that fatalism is intertwined with religion and internalized primarily by the poor and oppressed. It is viewed as an adjustive or survival technique of the powerless. For those who endure deprivation and hardship on a daily basis, it is comforting to have something to sustain them. The black Delta sharecropper, the white mountain tenant farmer, and the chronically unemployed and dispossessed believe, with good reason, that their living conditions will never improve and thus are comforted by religious fatalism. One hears statements in rural Appalachia such as "This is God's will," "God will not put more on you than you can take," and "Blessed are the poor. . . ." Present life is devalued, and there is an expectation of receiving rewards in heaven. Not surprisingly, most rural Appalachians adhere to fundamentalism, which includes a belief in the literal interpretation of the Bible and results in selection of churches that reflect this view. One cannot understand the Appalachian without first understanding his or her religion. Religious beliefs and practices permeate every facet of life.

Finally, additional strong values among Appalachians are neighborliness and hospitality, personalism, love of place, modesty and being oneself, sense of beauty, sense of humor, and patriotism. Jones interprets the values held by the Appalachian people as primarily positive, but also recognizes that some of them are counterproductive:

> Our fatalistic religious attitudes often cause us to adopt a "What will be, will be" approach to social problems. Our "Original Sin" orientation inhibits us from trying to change the nature or practices of people. Our individualism keeps us from getting involved, from creating a sense of community and cooperation and causes us to shy away from those who want to involve us in social causes. Our love of place, sometimes, keeps us in places where there is no hope of creating decent lives.[24]

THE COMMUNITIES.   The social worker employed in rural Appalachia must recognize that the typical communities in that region are small towns and even smaller villages and hamlets. The changing economy has created distressed conditions for many towns that traditionally were dependent on agriculture and coal mining. Many once-vibrant towns have become little more than ghost towns. The few business establishments left in the small "crossroads" communities are primarily self-service establishments serving a motoring public. The discontinuation of many post offices in very small localities has also affected the role of the community as a gathering place for residents of the area. The social activities of "loafing" and visiting with neighbors in the stores and post offices have practically ceased, and the important role of communities as social centers has diminished.

School consolidation has also affected community life. Many rural parents feel intimidated by contact with larger, consolidated schools and find that they do not represent a meaningful place for social interaction because of the many people they do not know face-to-face. Many rural children, too, do not adjust to large, consolidated schools because of their perceived social and cultural inferiorities, as measured against more affluent "town kids." Consequently, neither parents nor children involve themselves in school-related activities, and the school dropout rate, already high, increases as schools perform a less important role in rural Appalachian life. However, churches and church-centered social events continue to be important in these communities. Churches have been the most stable institutions in rural Appalachia and continue to perform a central social function as well as religious ones.

In sum, in the past the daily activities of rural families took place in the community of their residence. With few exceptions, people worked, shopped, worshipped, and attended school within walking distance or a short commuting distance from home. This changed with the abandonment of family farms, the disappearance of coal camps, school consolidation, and greater mobility. Now many workers commute many miles each day to reach their jobs, shop outside their local community, and send their children by school bus or other means to a consolidated school. These societal changes have lessened the Appalachian's sense of community identity and cohesiveness. The decreasing isolation and increasing interaction with mainstream society are causing many rural communities to lose their central role in the lives of their people.

Social Welfare in Rural Appalachia

To illustrate the functioning of the human services delivery system in Appalachia, we return to the case of Mary as she deals with her out-of-wedlock pregnancy:

> It was evident that Mary was going to need a variety of services. In addition to prenatal care, she would require financial assistance if she were to remain in school and complete her degree. She also would need help as she made her decision about whether to place the baby for adoption when it was born. Finally, she would need support as she interacted with her parents and community when the out-of-wedlock pregnancy became known.

For the social worker, knowledge of the human services delivery system in rural Appalachia and of the resources available to help Mary was essential to helping her through this difficult period in her life.

Social welfare in rural Appalachia includes restrictive service delivery modes and other barriers to effective human service provision. The major differences in the utilization of human services in Appalachia, compared to other parts of the United States, lie in the severity of the communities' inability to finance adequate services and outreach efforts, as well as the reluctance of many potential recipients to seek out and utilize the services that are available. Although this characterization of rural problems and services does not apply universally, it does accurately reflect the difficulty a social worker in rural Appalachia often experiences in locating services for clients. Not only do localities typically have a tax base insufficient to support even a limited number of highly specialized full-time human services providers, but they are often unable to either recruit or support an adequate number of service providers with desired qualifications. For example, positions designed for social workers are often held by persons whose educational backgrounds are not in social work; their clients too often do not receive service of adequate quality. This is not unique to Appalachia, but in vast areas of the region it is virtually impossible to recruit professionals who are not native to the localities—and few qualified natives are available.

Cultural emphasis on independence and self-reliance are thought to influence Appalachians more than any other group of people. The kinship group generally does what it can to take care of its own, and outside help is usually sought only as a last resort. Therefore, social agencies are constantly dealing with crisis situations. In addition, the topography of the region causes enormous transportation problems for consumers of services. Although this is generally the situation throughout rural America, much of Appalachia is especially hampered if travel is required. Many recipients must depend on neighbors or other individuals for transportation, and even the cost of gasoline places an additional burden on extremely limited budgets. Also, out-migration consists mostly of the young and healthy and has left many areas with a disproportionate share of elderly for whom travel to receive services may be a virtual impossibility. One alternative is to take the services to the clients. Service delivery in some agencies is primarily through home visits, but the travel time required for service creates a costly and inefficient system for the agencies and workers. Travel time often exceeds the time available for professional contacts with recipients of service.

The public welfare department is the major service agency and generally the only source of financial assistance, except for those eligible for Supplemental Security Income (SSI). Mental health centers have been slow in locating in the more rural areas, and many have only satellite centers staffed part-time as extensions of urban mental health agencies. Also, the staff of the rural centers too often simply transfer their urban approaches to practice to the rural areas.

Nursing homes and hospitals are often overburdened with indigent patients, and the support services that would enable many of these patients to remain in their own homes or with relatives seldom exist. The problems of the aged are magnified in Appalachia because of the presence of a large, aged population.

Limited private or voluntary services are provided by churches and other benevolent groups on a selective basis. One frequently hears the statement "God helps those who help themselves," so those organizations working through churches tend to provide assistance only to those considered "deserving." This problem is compounded by the fact that rural Appalachians are reluctant to contribute to "worthy causes" that have unknown beneficiaries. Thus few private human services agencies exist in rural Appalachia. However, on a personal level individuals and small groups are characteristically generous in sharing their limited resources with others.

The attitudes of Appalachians toward social welfare are heavily influenced by cultural beliefs in the importance of independence, self-reliance, and religious fatalism. However, these views have been modified during major economic downturns that resulted in massive unemployment. In the eastern Kentucky coalfields in the 1950s and early 1960s, for example, the rapid decline in the coal industry created special hardships for the unemployed middle-aged miner, who was less likely to find employment outside the industry and less able and willing to leave the area.

Therefore, the only way for the family to survive was to qualify for public assistance based on disability of the wage earner. Caudill reports that many became "symptom hunters" in order to convince physicians they were "sick enough to draw." They complained of a wide range of ailments, and many could point to scars on arms, legs, and chest—mementos of old mining accidents—to support their claims. Above all, they complained of having "bad nerves."[25] Nooe discovered similar behavior among mental patients in rural Appalachia, noting that often among unemployed coal miners, being judged mentally ill was preferable to being labeled lazy, enabling them to maintain some dignity and justify receiving financial assistance to support their families.[26]

The solutions to service delivery problems in Appalachia approximate those considered desirable for other rural areas. Circuit riding has been the mainstay of public welfare departments. Circuit riders conduct initial as well as follow-up services in locations other than the main offices. Due to funding limitations and the occasional need for technical diagnostic equipment, it is not feasible for all human services providers to make home visits, and serious attention should be given to the establishment of mobile units as well as permanent substations of social agencies. Some agencies have been innovative in scheduling nontraditional office hours, but there is an increasing need for more flexibility in this regard. The problems of transportation cannot be seriously reduced without changes in agency policies, and proposals for such changes have been rejected because funding for these programs would create additional tax burdens for the towns and counties.

MICRO PRACTICE IN APPALACHIA

The rural social worker must be prepared to address both individual troubles and social problems existing within a community or region. At the individual, couple, or family (micro) level, the social worker must provide services to directly benefit the client and/or help the client gain access to helping services that might be available. This can be noted in the case example of Mary:

> The caseworker from the county welfare department soon found that Mary was eligible for food stamps and helped to arrange for this financial aid, which would assist her in maintaining a diet sufficiently nutritious for the baby.

> In the course of her interviews with the social worker, Mary revealed that when she first discovered she was pregnant, she considered suicide. Rejecting that option, she went to her counselor at the college to explore the possibility of obtaining an abortion. It was that counselor who referred Mary to the agency. As they worked together, the social worker helped Mary to carefully examine her beliefs related to abortion, and Mary decided to carry the baby to term. Mary and the caseworker then initiated a contract to explore her decision about keeping the child or placing it for adoption after birth.

> The social worker also arranged for Mary to have an appointment every Wednesday morning, when the mobile clinic from the county health department was in town. Mary was told that the clinic opened at 8 AM and that she could appear when it was convenient,

as the clinic's policy was to take patients on a first-come first-served basis. Mary indicated she would be there promptly at 8 AM because she had a 10 AM class and was determined to not let this pregnancy interfere with her college education. Her family had put their faith in her, and she did not want to let them down any more than she already had.

Like Mary's social worker, most professional service providers in rural Appalachia serve lower-class or working-class clients, whose cultural values may be different from their own. It is imperative that the professional helpers understand and appreciate the clients' culture as being different—not deficient—and develop innovative service approaches and tools appropriate for this population. Although his remarks were not directed specifically toward practice with Appalachians, Kadushin accurately captured this perspective:

> Good interviewing in a contact with a client who differs from the interviewer in some significant characteristics requires more than a knowledge of the culture and life-style of the interviewee. It also requires an adaptation of interview techniques—pace of interview, activity level, choice of appropriate vocabulary, modification of nonverbal approaches—to be in tune with the needs of the interviewee.[27]

The rural Appalachian places great value on personal relationships and is dismayed by persons perceived as cold, methodical, or indifferent. During the first contact with a human services agency, the Appalachian can be expected to be cautious, suspicious, and highly anxious. It is essential that the worker demonstrate empathy, unconditional acceptance, and warm personal regard for the client. Otherwise, the person is likely to withdraw from the situation, regardless of the severity of need. Although the professional relationship is essential in social work practice regardless of the clientele served, it takes more effort and time to develop this with the Appalachian client, especially if the worker is viewed as an outsider. The Appalachian client is not impressed by professional qualifications and credentials. However, "who" the helping person is likely is to be of great concern. For example, one's belief in God, friendliness, and a familiar name or location will expedite the client–worker relationship.

Use of language and communication skills are also important considerations for the social worker. The uneducated, rural Appalachian has a very limited vocabulary and usually a slow pattern of speech. Communication may be deliberate, passive, and unexpressive, and there may be difficulty in responding to open-ended questions until the client feels comfortable with the social worker. Particular localisms, colloquialisms, and maxims may be unique to this subculture, and the social worker should be prepared to seek clarification when necessary.

It is very difficult for the rural Appalachian to understand the need for the extensive documentation often required when receiving services. Appalachians, too, typically expect immediate results when they do request service; thus, long-term intervention strategies are often inappropriate when working with Appalachians.

The generalist perspective to social work practice is critical to the social worker serving rural Appalachian people. In addition to providing services that meet client needs, the social worker often serves as a broker in assisting with arrangements and advocating on behalf of clients. The client is usually fearful about entering another unknown situation when a referral has been made, and the social worker should be especially careful to "pave the way" by helping with logistical factors such as transportation and appointment scheduling. The worker also needs to prepare the client very carefully to actually utilize the services, providing as much information as possible in order to reduce the client's anxiety. Whenever possible the social worker should try to make use of the natural helping networks in the community. These resources are especially important because of the underdevelopment of human services and the individual's preference for being in an environment with family and friends.

The essence of micro practice with rural Appalachians was succinctly summarized by Humphrey:

> If agency workers are to help mountain people they must understand what their clients' words and actions are actually trying to convey to them. It is then that services may be offered in ways people can accept. Their place, their families and their religion all are parts of a very intricate culture which must be respected and taken seriously. The social worker must first come to know the person before he or she can help him.[28]

MACRO PRACTICE IN APPALACHIA

When referrals are made, it is important for the social worker to follow up, to be sure that the services are actually received by clients. When clients experience problems obtaining needed services, the generalist social worker, who is equally prepared to intervene with both the person and the environment, may need to help the client find ways to change the human services delivery system. We return again to the case of Mary:

> During one interview, the social worker at the county welfare department's satellite center asked Mary about the prenatal care she was receiving from the health department's mobile clinic. Mary reported that she arrived each week before 8 AM, hoping her checkup would be completed in time to attend her first class of the day at 10 AM. However, Mary so far was not able to be finished in time to attend that class. She saw her options as foregoing prenatal care or possibly failing her class.
>
> The social worker, sensitive to Mary's goal not to let the pregnancy keep her from progressing with her college education, suggested that she and Mary might discuss this matter with the director of the health department. Mary was reluctant to get involved, but later indicated she knew two other young women who were having the same problem and wondered if it would be okay if they, too, went to the county seat to discuss this problem. The meeting was set for the following week.
>
> The director of the health department declared that he did not have the authority to change any policies established by the state health department for the operation of mobile clinics. Unwilling to accept this defeat, the social worker and three young women decided to seek help from area legislators and ultimately succeeded in getting a resolution passed by the state legislature calling for greater flexibility in the manner in which services were made available. By then, however, the process could not be concluded in time to resolve

Mary's dilemma. She continued her weekly check-ups but failed her 10 AM science class. Nevertheless, she was hopeful she had helped others to avoid such situations in the future.

Much of the social life of the rural Appalachian centers around reference groups (e.g., family, a close circle of friends, church groups, and neighbors) that provide comfort and security but also discourage them from engaging in change efforts unless the rest of the reference group is involved. Weller suggests that "everyone who works in the Appalachian South take cognizance of the power of these reference groups, which stand at the very center of the mountaineer's life. To step out of the group would mean loss of identity. To stand out in the group or to try to change the group from within is practically impossible, for one would quickly be ostracized. Any outsider who tries to change the reference group is very likely to find himself rejected by it."[29] Although many changes have been realized through group efforts, the impetus and leadership have generally been provided by persons not strongly entrenched in the reference groups. The social worker must find ways to creatively engage reference group support for social change efforts.

In order to facilitate change at the community level, the social worker must become an accepted member of the community to some degree. The circuit rider, who lives elsewhere and comes into the community only periodically to fulfill his or her professional role, is unlikely to be successful in stimulating community change. The same holds true for the outsider, who comes into the community for a temporary period in an effort to effect change. This was forcefully demonstrated by President Johnson's War on Poverty programs, which brought thousands of "saviors" from outside the region. They were community action program workers, VISTA volunteers, Appalachian volunteers, and others whose motives were benevolent but whose actions reflected considerable naiveté. The local power structure and established social agencies were often ignored, thus ostracizing potentially strong allies.

To be successful at community change, social structures and organizations that are indigenous to the people must be utilized to the fullest extent, and the social worker must have a thorough knowledge of the power structures and invisible influences that affect decision making. Local governing bodies are powerful, and many have real or implied obligations to outside corporate owners. Therefore, the social worker must constantly walk the thin line of garnering political support for needed changes while maintaining a productive relationship with the power structure. Some very sensitive areas relate to health and environmental concerns, where this balance is particularly difficult to maintain. For example, occupational hazards and industrial pollution generally cannot be dealt with effectively at the local level because of the locality's overdependence on a particular industry. However, changes that take place at the state and national levels relieve the localities of possible blame and retribution. It is essential for the social worker, then, to develop and maintain close relationships with area legislators at all levels, with the goal and ability to influence legislative processes for community improvements.

Concluding Comment

Changes in rural areas have placed nearly one-fifth of the population of the United States into a category of special population that requires some adaptations to social work practice. A new practice specialization based on the generalist perspective is emerging, which is helping to address the uniqueness of practice in rural America. The definition of *rural social work* included in the *Social Work Dictionary* captures the essential elements that make this specialization unique:

> Social work practice oriented to helping people who have unique problems and needs arising out of living in agricultural or sparsely populated areas or small towns. These people face most of the same problems and needs as do urban clients; in addition, however, they often encounter difficulties because of limited services and "resource systems," less acceptance of any variations from the social norms prevalent in the area, and fewer educational and economic opportunities.[30]

It is important for social workers who intend to practice in rural areas to recognize that it is not sufficient to simply transfer an urban perspective to a rural environment. Effective rural social work requires understanding the specific culture (e.g., Appalachian culture), rural people, and the unique role rural communities play in the lives of the people. It involves working with both clients and communities that are, perhaps, best served by the generalist practice perspective. And it involves tolerance for professional isolation, a more conservative political climate, resistance to professional services, and greater dependence on natural helping systems.

Due to the isolation professionals experience in rural practice, employing agencies must make special efforts to help social workers regularly experience professional stimulation and development through conference and workshop attendance. In addition, innovative approaches, such as televised staff development programming and teleconference consultation services, are needed to support rural practice.

The uniquenesses discussed in this chapter in the description of social work practice with rural Appalachians can help one to appreciate the importance of adapting to the special characteristics of any client(s) being served. Not all Appalachians are alike, and not all rural people are alike. Yet, there are many similar issues that rural social workers need to address. The National Association of Social Workers' public policy statement, "Social Work in Rural Areas," points out some actions that would address these issues. Social work plays an important role by (1) advocating for the empowerment of people in rural areas; (2) influencing public policies at all levels of government and the reorientation of the service delivery systems in rural areas; (3) supporting rural social work educators in their attempts to incorporate rural content into curricula of schools of social work; (4) continuing to work for broadly based legislation or health care, transportation, employment, and housing for rural America; (5) developing further expertise and becoming more involved in issues related to the ownership and retention of land; and (6) refining social work's position regarding rural development.[31]

KEY WORDS AND CONCEPTS

Rural definition

Characteristics of rural people

Characteristics of rural communities

Characteristics of rural human services

Micro practice in rural areas

Macro practice in rural areas

Appalachia

SUGGESTED READINGS

Boyle, David P. "The Influence of Appalachian Culture on the Delivery of Social Services," *Human Services in the Rural Environment* 17 (Winter/Spring 1994): 15–20.

Davenport, Judith A., and Davenport, Joseph III. "Rural Social Work Overview," in Richard L. Edwards, ed., *Encyclopedia of Social Work,* 19th Edition. Washington, D.C.: NASW Press, 1995, CD-ROM.

Ginsberg, Leon H., ed. *Social Work in Rural Communities,* 2nd Edition. Alexandria, VA: Council on Social Work Education, 1993.

Lusk, Mark W., and Mason, Derek T. "Development Theory for Rural Practice," *Human Services in the Rural Environment* 16 (Summer 1992): 5–10.

Martinez-Brawley, Emilia E. *Perspectives on the Rural Community: Humanistic Views for Practitioners.* Silver Spring, MD: National Association of Social Workers, 1990.

Martinez-Brawley, Emilia E. *Seven Decades of Rural Social Work.* New York: Praeger, 1980.

Watkins, Julie M., and Watkins, Dennis A. *Social Policy and the Rural Setting.* New York: Springer, 1984.

Wilkinson, Kenneth P. *The Community in Rural America.* New York: Greenwood Press, 1991.

ENDNOTES

1. Emilia E. Martinez-Brawley and Joan Blundall, "Farm Families' Preferences Toward the Personal Services," *Social Work* 34 (November 1989): 513.

2. Emilia E. Martinez-Brawley, "Social Work and the Rural Crisis: Is Education Responding?" *Journal of Social Work Education* 24 (Fall 1988): 255–257.

3. U.S. Bureau of the Census, "Metropolitan Area Definitions" (http://www.census.gov/population/www/metroarea/html).

4. Gretchen H. Waltman, "Main Street Revisited: Social Work Practice in Rural Areas," *Social Casework* 66 (October 1986): 467.

5. Richard A. DuBord, "The Rural Minority in an Urban Society: Content for Social Work Education," unpublished paper (Salt Lake City: University of Utah, 1979), p. 9, cited in O. William Farley, Kenneth A. Griffiths, Rex A. Skidmore, and Milton G. Thackeray, *Rural Social Work Practice* (New York: Free Press, 1982), pp. 6–7.

6. U.S. Bureau of the Census, "Income and Poverty: 1994, Table 8." (http://www.census.gov/hhes/poverty/histov/histov8/prn)

7. U.S. Bureau of the Census, *Statistical Abstracts of the U.S., 1992,* 112th Edition (Washington, D.C.: The Bureau, 1992), Tables 1075 and 1077.

8. U.S. Bureau of the Census, *1990 Census of the Population* (Washington, D.C.: U.S. Government Printing Office, 1991), Table 3.

9. Diana M. Meysted, "Religion and the Rural Population: Implications for Social Work," *Social Casework* 64 (April 1984): 219–220.

10. Norval D. Glenn and Lester Hill, Jr., "Rural–Urban Differences in Attitudes and Behavior in the United States," in Richard D. Rodefield, Jan Flora, Donald Voth, Isao Fujimoto,

and Jim Converse, eds., *Change in Rural America: Causes, Consequences, and Alternatives* (St. Louis, MO: C. V. Mosby, 1978), p. 356.

11. DuBord, p. 9.

12. Martinez-Brawley and Blundall, p. 519.

13. Leona L. Bachrach, "A Sociological Perspective," in L. Ralph Jones and Richard R. Parlour, eds., *Psychiatric Services for Underserved Rural Populations* (New York: Brunner/Mazet, 1985), p. 6.

14. Farley et al., p. 231.

15. Bradford W. Sheafor and Pamela S. Landon, "Generalist Perspective," in Anne Minahan, ed., *Encyclopedia of Social Work*, 18th Edition, Vol. I (Silver Spring, MD: National Association of Social Workers, 1987), p. 664.

16. Robert J. Teare and Bradford W. Sheafor, *Practice-Sensitive Social Work Education: An Empirical Analysis of Social Work Practice and Practitioners* (Alexandria, VA: Council on Social Work Education, 1995), p. 35.

17. *Appalachian Regional Commission: 1994 Annual Report* (Washington, D.C.: The Commission, 1995), p. 2; Thomas Plaut, *People, Politics and Economic Life: An Interactive Exploration of the Appalachian Region* (Dubuque, IA: Kendall/Hunt, 1996), p. 21.

18. Appalachian Land-Ownership Task Force, "Alliance Releases Land Ownership Study Findings: Land Task Force Urges Community Response," in Bruce Ergood and Bruce E. Kuhre, eds., *Appalachia's Social Context Past and Present,* 2nd Edition (Dubuque, IA: Kendall/Hunt, 1983), p. 173.

19. Harry M. Caudill, *Night Comes to the Cumberlands: A Biography of a Depressed Area* (Boston: Little, Brown, 1963), p. 75.

20. Fred D. Baldwin, "Appalachia's Distressed Counties: Catching Up and Ready to Grow," *Appalachia, Journal of the Appalachian Regional Commission* 29 (January–April 1996): 14–15.

21. *Appalachian Regional Commission: 1991 Annual Report* (Washington, D.C.: The Commission, 1992), pp. 25–49.

22. Jim Wayne Miller and Phillip J. Abermiller, "The Question of Appalachian Ethnicity," in William W. Philiber and Clyde B. McCoy, eds., *The Invisible Minority: Urban Appalachians* (Lexington: The University Press of Kentucky, 1981), p. 10.

23. Richard A. Couto, "Appalachia," in Richard A. Couto, Nancy K. Simpson, and Gale Harris, eds., *Sowing Seeds in the Mountains: Community Based Coalitions for Cancer Prevention and Control* (Bethesda, MD: The National Cancer Institute, 1994), pp. 17–18.

24. Loyal Jones, "Appalachian Values," *Twigs Magazine* 10 (Fall 1973): 93.

25. Caudill, pp. 279–281.

26. Roger M. Nooe, "A Clinical Model for Rural Practice," in Ronald K. Green and Stephen A. Webster, eds., *Social Work in Rural Areas: Preparation and Practice* (Knoxville: University of Tennessee School of Social Work, 1977), p. 355.

27. Alfred Kadushin, *The Social Work Interview* (New York: Columbia University Press, 1983), pp. 303–304.

28. Richard A. Humphrey, "Religion in Appalachia: Implications for Social Work Practice," *Journal of Humanics* 8 (December 1980): 17.

29. Jack E. Weller, *Yesterday's People* (Lexington: University Press of Kentucky, 1965), p. 59.

30. Robert L. Barker, *The Social Work Dictionary,* 3rd Edition (Washington, D.C.: NASW Press, 1995), pp. 330–331.

31. National Association of Social Workers, *Social Work Speaks: NASW Policy Statements,* 3rd Edition (Washington, D.C.: NASW Press, 1994), pp. 244–248.

CHAPTER 17

Urban and Suburban Gangs: The Psychosocial Crisis Spreads

Armando T. Morales

Prefatory Comment

This new chapter replaces "Urban Gang Violence: A Psychosocial Crisis," which made its initial appearance in 1989 in the fifth edition of this book. A few faculty and student reactions were mixed, because gang violence was not seen as something relevant to the profession of social work as many students were planning to work in either private practice or in agencies in affluent communities. Some social workers feel uncomfortable and unsafe working in the inner city—that is, until the Trench Coat Mafia adolescent gang exploded with rage on April 20, 1999, killing thirteen students and one teacher, wounding an additional twenty-three students, and then committing suicide. They broke the all-time record for the most gang-related homicides at one time (seven), which previously had been held by Al Capone's Saint Valentine's Day Massacre in Chicago in 1929! The 1999 gang-related mass killing happened at Columbine High School while students were attending class in beautiful, peaceful, affluent, white, suburban Littleton, Colorado. "The chickens have come home to roost," reported the June 1999 issue of *NASW News* in response to Littleton: that is, the profession can no longer ignore this problem—it has followed them into white, affluent suburbia.

Whether in the inner city or in white suburbia, violent gangs are in social work's practice arena contributing to social disorganization, trauma, grief, and family dysfunction. Youth gangs and their violent behavior are a symptom of the community telling the world that their needs are not being met by the family, school, neighborhood, social institutions, and the social work profession. These young people have the same rights to services as other clients.

Many social workers deal daily with people suffering the effects of social, psychological, economic, and political oppression and dehumanization, some of whom eventually become either victims or perpetrators of violence and homicide. June Hopps argues that social workers are in the best position to articulate the relationship of micro to macro psychosocial forces to violence and to contribute recommendations for positive change. Offering a challenge to social work, Hopps asks, "If we in the social work profession don't, who will?"[1] Actually, Hopps was right on target in 1987 as well as in 2000; there are now more clinically trained social workers than members of other core mental health professions combined (192,814 clinical social workers, 73,018 psychologists, 33,486 psychiatrists, 17,318 psychiatric nurses).[2] The most violent gang members have always had their share of psychological and psychiatric problems, but, historically, the mental health professions have been resistant for the most part in applying their skills to this population. The California Youth Authority, with approximately 17,000 criminal wards (8,000 in institutions) of which 75 percent are gang members, reports that about 42 percent have psychological–psychiatric problems.[3]

Understanding Gangs

Gangs represent a subject area of immense proportions, and social workers, as in any practice area, need to develop a knowledge base of the problem in order to be prepared with appropriate strategies for micro and macro psychosocial intervention. What follows, therefore, will be a definition of a gang; theories of gangs; their prevalence in society; the types of gangs, including gender, race and ethnicity; and age levels of gang members.

DEFINITION OF A GANG

There does not exist one accepted standard definition of a gang. Over 90 percent of juvenile crime is committed in groups, but not all these groups can be considered gangs. Defining a gang, therefore, largely depends on the criteria being used. For example, a 1996 National Youth Gang Survey of 1,880 city and suburban police departments defined a gang as a group of youths that the departments were willing to identify and classify as a gang.[4] In other words, if the police say you are a gang member, even if you are not, you *are* a gang member. A popular criteria is "If it looks like a duck, walks like a duck, and quacks like a duck, it is a duck." But not all ducks are the same, and even among ducks, some are more passive and some are more aggressive than others. Even with many years of experience in working with gang members, your author cannot tell if an eight- to twenty-five-year old person ten feet in front of him is in fact a gang member with a violent criminal past or simply one who has knowingly or unknowingly adopted some of the gang culture (e.g., clothing, hairstyle, or speech). To complicate matters further, law enforcement agencies in different cities and states develop their own definitions of a gang. Gang researchers frequently use five criteria: (1) formal organization structure, (2) identifiable leadership, (3) identified with a territory, (4) recurrent interaction, and (5) engaging in serious or violent behavior.[5] Within this definition, a group could qualify for a gang definition but not engage in serious or violent behavior, which then would make it a nonviolent gang. Prosecutors in some states rely on penal code definitions and criteria as to what groups are defined as gangs, because confirmation of gang membership can *enhance* the penalty significantly for a gang-related crime. For example, in California's Penal Code Section 186.22 (Street Terrorism Act) a gang is:[6]

A. Any ongoing organization, association, or group of three or more, having as one of its primary activities commission of one or more of the following crimes:

   1. Assault with a deadly weapon
   2. Robbery
   3. Homicide or attempted homicide
   4. Sale or possession of narcotics
   5. Shooting at a house or vehicle
   6. Arson
   7. Vehicle grand theft

B. Has a common name, sign, or symbol; whose members individually or collectively engage in a pattern of criminal gang activity.

These legally defined criteria are biased toward lower-class, inner-city *street* gangs, because that is usually where they associate. However, the Trench Coat Mafia gang, which killed 13 persons, might not have met these criteria. The author, therefore, offers a more general definition that is not biased against any ethnic racial group or social economic class, as follows:

A *gang* is a peer group of persons in a lower-, middle-, or upper-class community who participate in activities that are either harmful to themselves and/or others in society.[7]

This definition is general enough to capture the criminal group behavior of former President Nixon's Watergate gang, the Trench Coat Mafia, Lakewood's white suburbia Spur Posse (a group of white adolescent males who kept score of all the girls they raped at a California high school), as well as "garden-variety" street gangs.

Given the fact that many young people, because of their psychosocial stage of development, need to be in groups, conform to youth culture, and at times dress in provocative clothing and sport distinctive hairstyles, they often draw attention to themselves from adults and especially police officers. Whether in the inner city, city, or suburbia, it is difficult to determine who is actually a violent threat to the community. Middle-class youth, particularly white youths, are given the benefit of the doubt by police and not apprehended. Inner-city, city, and suburban lower- or middle-class African American, Asian, and Hispanic youth, however, are overly suspected of being gang members and a genuine threat to society and hence often arrested as a *preventive* tactic. This controversial practice is known as *profiling,* that is, "criminal suspects" meet the arrest profile of certain offenders, for example, DWB (African American and Hispanic motorists stopped by police for "driving while black or brown"). This subjective profiling practice makes as much sense as would the police in Europe frequently stopping American tourists to look for murderers, because the United States has a homicide rate nine times the rate in Europe.

To assist the social worker to distinguish which "ducks" are actually the dangerous ones, since they all "look, walk, and talk alike," the *gang behavior career continuum* in Figure 17-1 provides criteria to help to differentiate the degree of violent commitment to the gang.

Non-Gang

Exhibits some gang culture traits, few contacts with police, no arrests or *convictions*.

Pre-Gang

Some gang culture and contacts with police.

Wannabe

Unpredictable, few police contacts to major *convictions*.

Soft Core

Few contacts, arrests, and *convictions* for minor gang crimes, on probation, in school.

Moderate Core

Arrests and *convictions* for violent gang crime, institutionalized at local and state level, on probation or parole, rarely in school, unemployed.

Hard Core

Arrests and *convictions* for attempted and/or homicide, long-term placement in juvenile or adult state prison, no school or job.

Super Hard Core

Adult court *convictions* for one or more homicides, long-term prison or death row, poor school and work history.

 Gang Behavior Career Continuum*

*This *Gang Behavior Career Continuum* was developed by Armando T. Morales, UCLA Neuropsychiatric Institute and Hospital, School of Medicine, Los Angeles, California.

There are seven career levels of involvement in some aspect of gang behavior and participation. In the least involved level, referred to as *nongang,* are found large numbers of youth, up to 70 to 80 percent in some inner-city areas, who have consciously or unconsciously, knowingly or unknowingly, as impressionable preadolescent and adolescents, incorporated the gang culture prevalent in their community. Understandably, they have accepted some of the gang music (e.g., gangsta rap), gang clothing, the walk, talk, hairstyle, tattoos, and even knowledge and skills in writing and understanding graffiti; but they have no arrests or juvenile court convictions for offenses related to gang involvement.

At the *pregang* level, the youths have also absorbed some of the gang culture previously mentioned, but now they are beginning to have some contact (field interrogation cards) with police and a few arrests and have been taken to the police station for being with more sophisticated gang members. But no petitions are filed in juvenile court.

The *wannabes* (want to be) are in the next level on the gang career continuum. These youths are often quite disturbed, unpredictable, and very much want to be in the gang. But they are not respected by legitimate gang members nor do they want them in the gang because they lack the consistency, dedication, and loyalty expected of "good" gang members. Wannabes have been known to abandon their pursuit of the gang when they experience their first incarceration or first real fight with rival gang members. Some are manipulated by the gang to "prove themselves" by, for example, asking them to carry out an assigned gang homicide.

The *soft-core* level finds the young gang member with his or her first minor gang-related arrests for group drinking or drugs, or perhaps a gang-related "joy ride" (auto theft), or a misdemeanor gang assault requiring an arrest, probation investigation, juvenile court appearance, and a sustained petition (conviction). The soft-core gang member is now placed on probation and continues going to school.

The *moderate-core* gang member is much more experienced, a little older, and rarely attends school. By now the youth has had two or three convictions in juvenile court for gang-related violent offenses and has experienced incarceration at least two or three times in local or state youth correctional facilities. Multiple tattoos not only advertise the local gang, but also an affiliation with state-wide northern, southern, or east–west gangs.

The *hard-core* gang member is similar to the moderate core, except that the hard-core gang member has higher status and respect in the gang. Not only has he or she been incarcerated in local and state juvenile facilities, but now has convictions in adult court for gang-related offenses, including attempted homicide and homicide. Some have had their first experience of being sentenced to state prison as adults, even though they might have been only sixteen or seventeen when they committed a serious crime. Usually, the hard core are a little older and are among the local leaders of the gang, have impressive respect and "juice" (power) in the gang, and often are "shot callers" (give orders). This gang member not only has injured others in battle, but also wears his "war medals" (knife and/or bullet wound scars) proudly. This ritual is significantly less for females.

Finally, at the most violent level of the gang career continuum are the *super-hardcore* gang members. They have adult court convictions for gang-related violent offenses, at times for one or more homicides, "three strikes," or witness–victim intimidation. They continue to have close ties with the local gang and are well established in the prison gang, and they may attempt to serve a liaison function under orders from the state prison gang to conduct "business" (e.g., drugs, extortion, executions) in the community of the local gang. They are not only respected by the local gang, but also feared, because they might be in a position to carry out contracted "hits" (executions) locally or even order "hits" on gang members not complying with their wishes. Some of the super hardcore are serving sentences of ten to twenty years or life without the possibility of parole, and a few are on death row for multiple gang-related homicides.

THEORIES OF GANGS

Five theoretical perspectives explaining the causes of gangs will be examined. The first theory is similar to Thrasher's classic description of gangs in the 1920s, in which gangs are seen as a natural progression from, and the consequence of, a youth's search for excitement in a frustrating and limiting environment. They are usually a result of a general breakdown of social controls and are characterized by persons with few social ties, such as immigrants, the mentally ill, the destitute, and by a corresponding lack of parental control over the young.[8]

A second causal factor has been proposed by anthropologist Miller, who studied lower-class gangs in Boston. He describes gang members as males who usually were reared in a female-dominated household and, consequently, in adolescence the gang, he says, "provided the first real opportunity to learn essential aspects of the male role in the context of peers facing similar problems of sex role identification."[9] This theory does not account for the fact that even though 68 percent of African American and 67 percent of Hispanic poor families were headed by a woman, according to a 1983 U.S. Commission on Civil Rights report, approximately 95 percent of the youths were *not* gang members or delinquents.[10]

A third perspective is suggested by social scientists such as Cohen, and Cloward and Ohlin. They maintain that the gang is the collective solution of young, lower-class males to a situation of stress wherein opportunities for the attainment of wealth and/or status through legitimate channels are blocked. In response, the gang develops a subculture or *contra-culture*. The gang, therefore, must be explained in terms of social conditions in which lower-class youths are placed by the dominant society.[11] This would account for the continued existence of minority group gangs in Chicago since 1918 and the general absence of white ethnic gangs. In other words, minority youth are far more likely to be blocked from having equal access to resources in society. However, this theory does not explain the growing number of white, middle-class gangs in some parts of the country, such as Stoners and Skinheads, and other neo-Nazi gangs, which will be addressed in the micro analysis of the Trench Coat Mafia.

A fourth perspective is advanced by Matza, who challenges the "blocked-out" subculture theory, stating that it explains too much delinquency. He believes that gangs exist because adolescents are in a state of suspension between childhood and adulthood; hence, they spend most of their time with peers and are anxious about both their identity as males and their acceptance by the peer group (gang). They conform to the norms of the gang because not to do so would threaten their status.[12] This theory is limited in explaining the continued involvement of adult and middle-aged *veterano* (veteran) gang members found in some Hispanic *barrios,* who are responsible family providers yet occasionally participate in some gang activities. All the above theories have merit and are applicable in many instances, as gangs are very complex and cannot be explained by any *one* theory.

The author proposes a fifth theoretical perspective. In a study of East Los Angeles Hispanic gang and nongang probation juvenile camp graduates, gang members, significantly more than nongang members, came from families exhibiting more family breakdown, greater poverty, poorer housing, more alcoholism, drug addiction, and major chronic illness, and more family members involved with law enforcement and correctional agencies.[13] In the face of these overwhelming problems, the youngster turns to the gang as a *surrogate family.* Here, the gang member receives affection, understanding, recognition, loyalty, and emotional and physical protection. In this respect the gang is psychologically adaptive rather than maladaptive. It would not appear to be a coincidence that one of the largest Hispanic gangs in California is called *Nuestra Familia* (Our Family). Hispanic gang members call themselves *homeboys* or *homegirls,* labels consistent with a family and home orientation. Likewise, African American gang members often refer to themselves as *brothers* or *sisters.* Close friends *can* be good medicine. But many gang members will often die or kill rival gang members for their gang or turf in the neighborhood. When this occurs, membership then becomes maladaptive. Adding to the powerful group cohesion of Hispanic gangs, which have existed in Chicago, El Paso, and East Los Angeles *barrios* for over seventy years—as have the socioeconomic conditions that produced them—is the reinforcement of the gang culture and tradition by older brothers, uncles, fathers, and even grandfathers.[14]

One also finds increasing evidence of Hispanic female gangs, estimated at 10 percent (about twenty to thirty gangs) in Los Angeles. This is significantly more than the five female gangs Thrasher found among his 1,313 gangs. White middle-class family breakdown or emotional neglect may also be one of the factors accounting for an increase in non-Hispanic white adolescent gangs in urban and suburban areas throughout the country.

THE PREVALENCE OF GANGS

The most comprehensive study of gangs was undertaken by Thrasher in Chicago between 1919 and 1927. In his book *The Gang: A Study of 1313 Gangs in Chicago,* he found that the gangs comprised various ethnic and racial groups, which included Polish, Italian, Irish, Anglo-American, Jewish, Slavic, Bohemian, German, Swedish, Lithuanian, Chinese, African American, and Mexican youths. Three hundred and fifty-one of these gangs contained "mixed nationalities"; the other 962 gangs comprised a single ethnic or racial group. The Polish, numbering 16.4 percent of the population, had the most gangs, 148, followed by the Italian, 99, Irish, 75, and African

American, 63. Membership in gangs and conflict between gangs were related more to turf than to racial or nationality factors. A "fair-minded" thirteen-year-old Lithuanian gang leader once remarked, "I never ask what nationality he is. A Jew or nigger can be a pal of mine if he's a good fellow."[15] It is interesting to note that, by and large, the *white* ethnics described above have faced fewer barriers in the road to assimilation than have the Asians, African Americans, and Hispanics, who still have gangs in Chicago seventy-nine years later.

As far as can be determined, to date there has not been a solid, data-based gathering of information comparable to Thrasher's classic work as to the numbers of gangs currently in cities or suburban areas. This is largely due to there not being a national reporting system with precise information. A major problem is attempting to find agreement as to who really are gang members and, if they are, whether they are still active or in *remission* (no longer participating in gang violence). Without a precise definition, the data are difficult to interpret. The best *national* effort is found in the 1996 National Youth Gang Survey of 2,629 responding agencies, with 53 percent reporting that gangs were active in their jurisdiction. Respondents in large cities claimed the highest level of gang activities, 74 percent, followed by suburban areas (57%), small cities (34%), and rural counties (25%). Based on this response, the researchers concluded that up to 4,824 U.S. cities were experiencing gang problems and that there may be as many as 31,000 gangs, with a total membership of 846,000.[16]

It is generally agreed that the County of Los Angeles has the most youth gangs in the nation, with 1995 estimates at 1,142 gangs and 150,000 members.[17] Even the larger figure falls significantly short of Chicago's 1,313 gangs in the 1920s. In that period Chicago had approximately 65 gangs per 100,000 population, compared to 12.7 gangs per 100,000 for Los Angeles in 1995. In other words, Chicago had a ratio of gangs per population five times greater than Los Angeles! In Los Angeles, where "non-whites" represent 64 percent of the population, Hispanics being the largest minority group at 3.7 million, two-thirds of all gangs were composed of Hispanics, followed by African Americans, non-Hispanic whites, and Asians.

Ewing reports that in 1988 Chicago had 12,000 youths belonging to approximately 125 gangs, significantly fewer than Thrasher's 1,313 gangs in the 1920s in the same city.[18] Los Angeles, on the other hand, apparently has not peaked in the prevalence of gangs.

TYPES OF GANGS

Youth gangs can be analyzed from the standpoint of their primary function, orientation or activity, organizational structure, age, ethnicity, race, and sex. Most social scientists investigating gangs today would agree that there are at least three types of gangs: the *criminal,* the *conflict,* and the *retreatist.* The author suggests that a fourth type of gang is emerging in recent years, which could be called the *cult/occult gang.*

The *criminal gang* has as its primary goal material gain through criminal activities. Success is obtained through the theft of property from premises or persons, extortion, fencing, and obtaining and selling illegal substances such as drugs. In the 1920s Thrasher discovered that some of the wealthiest youth gangs—which he called *beer gangs*—were involved in the liquor business during Prohibition.[19] Today, some former gang members are making their money in drugs in criminal racketeering organizations.

Asian gangs are similar to other racial/ethnic gangs, as they grew out of a need to protect their communities. However, according to authorities, contemporary Asian gangs are more likely to be the criminal type, as they are more concerned with generating profits from illegal activities (extortion, gambling, prostitution) within their communities rather than protecting their turf. The newest Asian gangs are composed of Cambodian, Korean, and Vietnamese youth.[20]

Breaking with the traditional Asian gang speciality of making money illegally as their primary gang activity (e.g., *criminal gang*), the *Asian Boyz* of Los Angeles took on a *conflict gang* role and in a matter of weeks killed six rival Asian gang members, including Hispanic gang members who traditionally are not in conflict with Asian gangs. The seven *Asian Boyz* perpetrators, ranging in age from 15 to 22, were all outstanding students either in high school or college. During the seven-month trial, *Asian Boyz* members also killed the state's key witness, Dong Dinh, in his home in San Jose. Six of the seven gang members received life in prison sentences, and the leader, Son Than Bui, 18 at the time of the killings in 1995, received six life terms in prison in June 1999. A psychologist and psychiatrist testified that Bui was suffering from posttraumatic stress disorder as the result of his childhood experiences in work camps during the bloody Khmer Rouge communist regime.[21]

The *conflict gang* is very turf oriented and will engage in violent battle with individuals or rival groups that invade their neighborhood or commit acts they consider insulting or degrading. Respect is highly valued and defended. Hispanic gangs, in most cities, are highly represented among conflict gangs. Their mores, values, rituals, and codes are highly consistent in various neighborhoods and cities throughout the nation and have existed in some areas for almost seventy years. As Sweeney learned in his work with conflict gangs:

> The Code of the *Barrio* means watching out for your neighborhood. This entails protecting your homeboys (and family) and the area designated as your "neighborhood." The Code demands absolute loyalty; every gang member must be willing to die for his *neighborhood* (homeboys and turf).[22]

Of the 1,142 gangs in Los Angeles, approximately two-thirds are Hispanic, and most of these are conflict gangs. Currently in Chicago, where Spergel identified fifty-five conflict gangs, thirty-three were Hispanic, fifteen were African American, and seven were non-Hispanic white.[23]

The predominant feature of the *retreatist gang* is the pursuit of getting "loaded" or "high" on alcohol, marijuana, heroin, acid, cocaine, or other drugs. Retreatism is seen by Cloward and Ohlin as an isolated adaptation, characterized by a breakdown in relationships with other persons. The drug user has a need to become affiliated with other retreatist users to secure access to a steady supply of drugs.[24] What distinguishes the criminal gang involved in drugs from the retreatist gang is that the former is primarily involved for financial profit. The retreatist gang's involvement with drugs is primarily for consumption.

The fourth type of adolescent delinquent group is the *cult/occult gang*.[25] The word *cult,* as used here, pertains to a system of worshiping the devil or evil. *Occult* means something hidden or secret, or a belief in mysterious or supernatural powers. Not all cult/occult devil or evil worship groups are involved in criminal activity or ritualistic crime. The Ku Klux Klan, for example, may be seen as a cult group, and some chapters, in spite of their hate rhetoric, are law abiding, whereas other chapters have committed criminal acts. The Charles Manson Family is perhaps one of the better known cult/occult criminal groups. Some occult groups place a great deal of emphasis on sexuality and violence, believing that by sexually violating a virgin or innocent child, they defile Christianity. One occult group, called *OTO* (Ordo Templi Orientis), had eleven members convicted of felony child abuse in Riverside County, California.[26]

The majority of occult groups, whether criminal or law abiding, are composed of adults. However, some juvenile groups are becoming interested in satanic and black magic practices and are using them for their own gratification of sadistic, sexual, and antisocial impulses. Their knowledge and application of rigid, ritualistic occult practices, however, is often haphazard. Los Angeles has perhaps the largest number of these adolescent cult/occult gangs, numbering about thirty-two.[27] These gangs are composed predominantly of white, non-Hispanic middle-class youths and a few middle-class Hispanics. They are not turf-oriented like conflict gangs, but are found in several middle-class locations. These gangs call themselves *Stoners,* such as the *Alhambra Stoners* or the *Whittier Stoners.* Stoners from one location are allied with Stoners of other locations. They originally named themselves after the Rolling Stones and valued getting "stoned."

Their philosophy is based on "Do what you will. The end is soon; live for today." Heavy and Death Metal music is very popular with Stoners, and among their heroes are Charles Manson, Adolf Hitler, and Aleister Crowley, leading occultist in the United States in the early 1900s, who advocated violation of every moral law from sexual perversion to homicide. Some of the self-destructive activities in which Stoners participate, in addition to substance abuse, include sadism, masochism, and suicide. Their antisocial crimes are violence for violence's sake, ritual rape, ritual child abuse, and ritual homicide. Some examples of the graffiti of these groups are 666 (Biblical sign of the beast), KKK, FTW (Fuck the World), and SWP (Supreme White People). Law enforcement officials are becoming more concerned about the growth of white, middle-class Stoner-type gangs. The author suggests that these cult/occult gangs are a symptom of psychologically deteriorating middle-class white families. Economic pressures brought on by Reaganomics, continued by Presidents Bush and Clinton, often force both parents to spend many hours working, keeping them away from their children. In treating Stoners and Skinheads coming out of juvenile correctional institutions, the author has observed some of them to be quite emotionally disturbed, having been raised in families that physically abused them as children or having had a parent or sibling with severe mental illness.

Another neo-Nazi subtype of white cult/occult gang groups are the Skinheads, whose racist, anti-Semitic, homophobic "gay bashing," and other violent behavior has appeared in the South, Midwest, and West Coast. According to Spergel, their group structure and behavior comply with the gang pattern, including use of colors, tattoos, common dress and hairstyle, name, drug use, and criminal behavior (usually "hate" crimes). The majority of Skinheads come from middle-class and/or working-class white families.[28] The gothic-cultural Trench Coat Mafia could have fitted in with the Stoner and Skinhead neo-Nazi cult gang.

AGE LEVELS AND GENDER

The age levels of male gang members are fairly consistent among the four types of gangs and seem to be related to maturational and natural developmental stages of growth. Thrasher in the 1920s described four general gang-age types, as follows:[29]

	Psychosocial Developmental Stage
Gang child:	6–12 years (child)
Gang boy:	11–17 (early adolescent)
Gang boy:	15–25 (later adolescent)
Gang man:	21–50 (adult)

Thrasher only found five female gangs in the 1,313 gangs he studied in Chicago in the 1920s. In contemporary conflict and criminal gangs, a similar natural, developmental stage, age-group phenomenon may be observed, however, with more specific age categories required by the gang. Small gangs may range in size from ten to twenty members, but in larger gangs with 200 to 300 members, age categories are more obvious, as follows:[30]

	Psychosocial Developmental Stage
Pee Wees:	8–12 years (latency)
Tinys:	12–14 years (early adolescent)
Dukes:	14–16 years (mid adolescent)
Cutdowns:	16–18 years (or major name of the gang) (late adolescent)
Veteranos:	19–45 years (young adult, adult)
Locos:	mixed ages (the "crazies")

Girls' gangs adopt similar age categories and gang names. For example, the Cloverettes will be from "Clover," where the Clover Street gang is found. Female adolescent gangs either assume a subordinate, supportive role to male gangs or are completely independent from the male gangs and, for defensive purposes, even engage in violent confrontations with male gang members from their own neighborhood. Female gang members have been known to murder both male gang members and rival female gang members.

The age levels of retreatist and cult/occult gangs are less formal, and female participation is minimal. Age categories for the cult/occult gang are more consistent with school grade levels, such as fifth and sixth grade, junior high, and high school. Older adolescent and young adult members, predominantly male, are often found in juvenile and adult correctional facilities.

Female youth gangs (ages eleven to eighteen) are beginning to increase and make their presence felt. For example, in Los Angeles County, law enforcement gang experts estimate that female gangs number 10 to 15 percent of all gangs (1,142 gangs), and their number is increasing. Female gang-related crimes rarely involve major violence, but rather incorrigible behavior, truancy, and theft-related crime. In 1991 in Los Angeles County, of 207 gang-related homicides, only 13 involved female gang members.[31]

The Ecosystems Model

The ecosystems model highlighted in Section A of this book is particularly helpful in examining the gang problem in more depth, as gangs involve all the main points and five levels of the model: historical, environmental–structural, culture, the family, and the individual. More specifically, what might be the *historical* issues related to gangs and why have they been with us so long? Part of the reason might be seen in the impact of *environmental–structural* issues on gangs and how these issues might alleviate or aggravate the problem even more. The gang exists and perhaps thrives in American *culture,* and what is it about our culture that may be contributing to gangs in America?

What about the role of the *family*? Is it in any way contributing to the gang problem. And why are parents having more difficulty in raising sons than daughters? What went wrong in Littleton, Colorado, with the families of the Trench Coat Mafia gang members in white, affluent suburbia? The final level of the ecosystems model pertains to the *individual.* Here we try to understand why a person does what he does. Why does the preadolescent or adolescent join the gang, and what distinguishes the violent, homicidal, and at times suicidal gang member from others who are not so violent?

Figure 17-2 demonstrates these areas of inquiry. Following a discussion of the five levels, a *micro* psychosociocultural case analysis of the Trench Coat Mafia gang massacre will be made, comparing this suburban gang with inner-city gangs.

HISTORY OF GANGS

There is no doubt that gangs have been with us since the beginning of civilization, but the concept of gangs was first reported in the literature by a former gang member, St. Augustine (A.D. 354–430), nearly 1,600 years ago. His father was described as a pagan who lived a "loose life," and his mother, whom he loved greatly, was a pious Christian who had difficulty controlling St. Augustine during his adolescent years. In his book *Confessions,* he demonstrates astute understanding of the psychology of adolescent gangs with his discovery that committing a crime in the company of others enhances the gratifications derived from it. Through his autobiographical psychoanalytical method, he discovered that actions are determined by more than a single motive, stating:

> I loved then in it also the company of the accomplices with whom I did it . . . for had I then loved the pears I stole and wished to enjoy them I might have done it alone, had the bare commission of the theft sufficed to attain my pleasure; nor needed I have

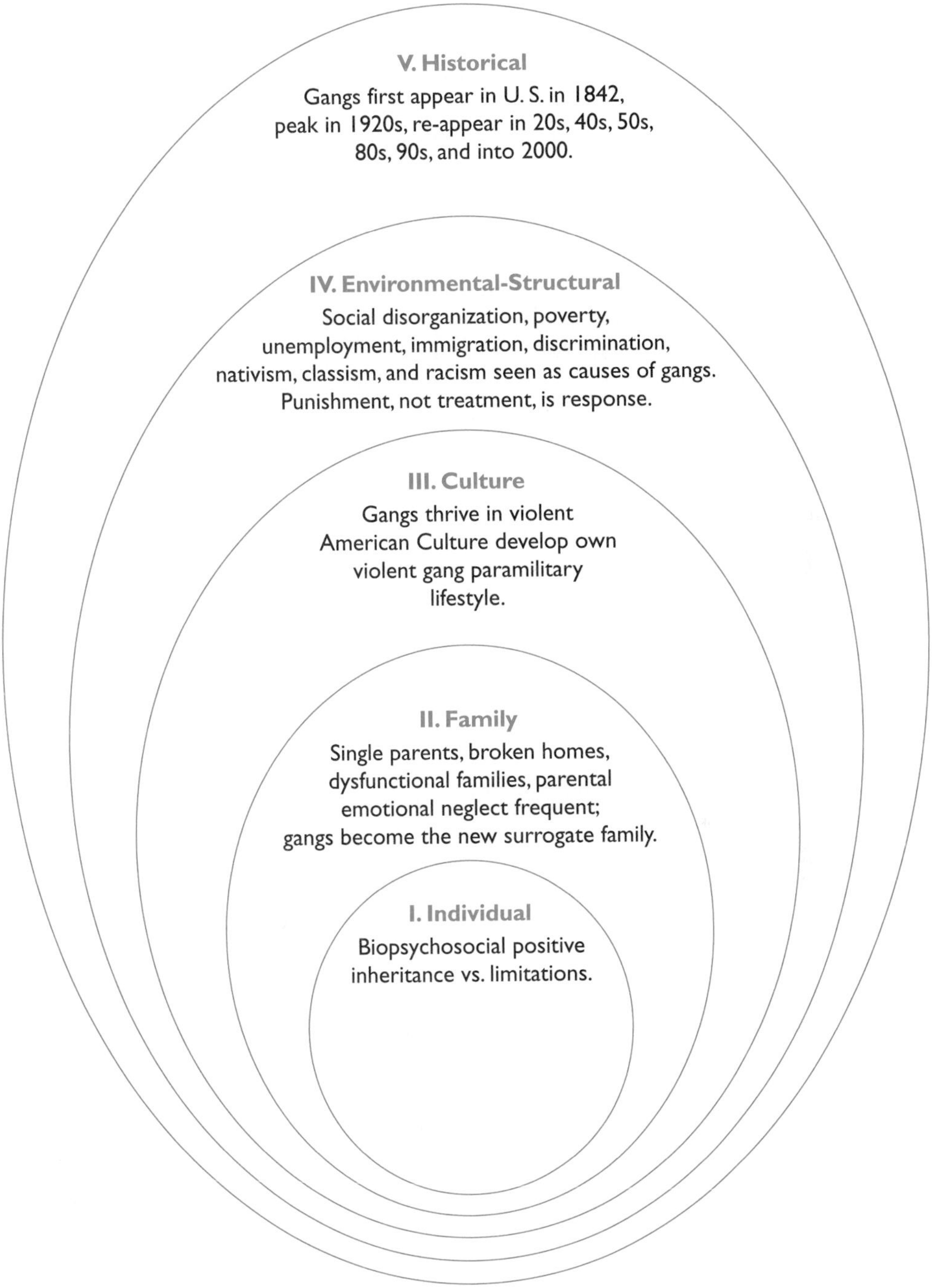

FIGURE 17-2 Ecosystems Model for Psychosocial Analysis of Factors Impacting Gangs

inflamed the itching of my desires by the excitement of accomplices. But since my pleasure was not in those pears, it was in the offense itself, which the company of fellow-sinners occasioned.[32]

The first youth gangs in the United States made their appearance in the national turf-oriented atmosphere of "manifest destiny"—the rationale for the forceful takeover of the Mexican-owned Southwest—in the mid-1800s. These gangs did much more than steal pears from neighbors and were first seen in Philadelphia in the 1840s. They evolved from volunteer fire companies. Volunteer fire companies provided status and recognition to young, white, lower-class adult males, who were competitive with other companies in trying to be first in extinguishing a fire. The intense competition at times developed into physical conflict and even killing when a company extinguished a fire on a rival company's "turf." The tough firemen—the Super Bowl heroes of the era—were the idols of neighborhood adolescents, who looked upon them with awe. These "groupies," who likewise identified with the company's turf, also engaged in physical fights with rival fire company youth groups. These early gangs had names such as the *Rats,* the *Bouncers,* and the *Skinners.* With graffiti they defaced walls, fences, and buildings, similar to what gangs do today in urban areas. The *Philadelphia Public Ledger,* on August 13, 1846, described them as being "armed to the teeth with slug shots, pistols, and knives." The biggest provocation to violence was the intrusion of rival gangs into their turf.[33]

During this pre–Civil War period, intense conflict was also seen in New York among white adolescent and young adult gangs forcibly attempting to establish dominance over a particular neighborhood. Asbury writes in *The Gangs of New York:*

> The greatest gang conflicts of the early nineteenth century were fought by these groups (the Bowery Boys and the Dead Rabbits). . . . Sometimes the battles raged for two or three days without cessation, while the streets of the gang area were barricaded with carts and paving stones, and the gangsters blazed away at each other with musket and pistol, or engaged in close work with knives, brickbats, bludgeons, teeth, and fists.[34]

Police were reluctant to and did not intervene in this gang conflict, which at times lasted two or three days. Gangs comprised of latency-age children eight to twelve years of age, such as the Little Plug Uglies or the Little Daybreak Boys, were almost as ferocious as the older gang members whose names they adopted and crimes they tried hard to imitate.

Such intense, prolonged conflict is not seen today among gangs. Rather, one of the most frequent violent gang crimes committed today is the "drive-by" shooting, made possible by automobiles. A gang will seek out a home, vehicle, or "hangout" of a rival gang and, using an assortment of weapons including automatics, drive by and shoot randomly. As in the nineteenth century, there are instances in which innocent people are accidentally wounded and/or killed. Now the "Littleton syndrome" finds violent youth killing their peers inside schools.

It would be difficult to document whether the nineteenth-century gangs were more lethal than contemporary urban gangs, as homicide statistics were not uniformly recorded at that time. However, the Littleton Trench Coat Mafia ranks among the most violent, since only four instances of six or more homicide victims inside a school have taken place in the world since 1966.

ENVIRONMENTAL–STRUCTURAL FACTORS

Periodic national government reports responding to social crises are useful in highlighting the environmental–structural factors impacting gangs in the United States. For example, after studying the causes of hundreds of riots in 150 cities across the United States in the mid-1960s, the U.S. Riot Commission issued its findings, known as the Kerner Report, stating:

> White racism is essentially responsible for the explosive mixture which has been accumulating in our cities since the end of World War II. . . . The ghettos too often mean men and women without jobs, families without men, and schools where children are processed instead of educated, until they return to the street—to crime, narcotics, to dependency on welfare, and to bitterness and resentment against society in general and White society in particular.[35]

Similar findings were reached in a report by the Congress of Mexican American Unity and Chicano Moratorium Committee as the causes of the Hispanic community riots in 1970–1971 in East Los Angeles.[36]

Thrasher did not attribute the existence of 1,313 gangs in Chicago in the 1920s to white racism—because the great majority of those gangs *were* "white" (not Hispanic). However, he cited similar underlying causes as the Kerner, and Webster Commission (L.A. Riots of 1992) reports, that is, failure of social institutions to function efficiently in a youngster's experience, as indicated by disintegration of the family, "inefficiency of schools," political indifference, low wages, unemployment, and lack of recreational opportunities. Thrasher added:

> The gang functions with reference to these conditions in two ways: It offers a substitute for what society fails to give; and it provides a relief from suppression and distasteful behavior. It fills a gap and affords an escape. . . . Thus the gang, itself a natural and spontaneous type of organization arising through conflict, is a symptom of disorganization in the larger framework. These conclusions, suggested by the present study, seem amply verified by data from other cities in the United States and in other countries.[37]

Thrasher, therefore, taught us over seventy years ago that the gang was a function of specific conditions, and does not tend to appear in the absence of these conditions. Perhaps the core problem is societal discrimination against the *poor* (*classism*), which in turn is compounded by ethnic and racial prejudice and *racism*. The "conditions" nevertheless continue to exist, as do gangs in these communities, *that* being the bottom line.

But how does the Trench Coat Mafia gang massacre fit into this traditional gang explanation and equation? They were not being impacted by the discriminatory social conditions mentioned above as they came from intact, affluent families. A contributing factor may be seen in the antifamily government economic policies implemented over the last twenty-five years by both Republican and Democratic administrations who expounded "family values." These policies made it more stressing and difficult for parents to have more options available for them to spend more time with their children. See Figure 17-3 which shows how the number of working mothers increased from 40 percent in 1976 to 65 percent in 1997. In other words, increased taxes, mortgages, and other expenses passed on to families by government

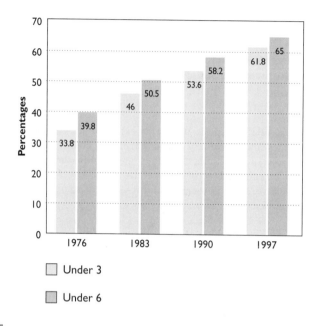

FIGURE 17-3 **Working Mothers with Children under 3 and under 6**

Source: U.S. Bureau of the Census, Current Population Survey, Special Studies P23-194, 1997.

forced parents to spend less time at home nurturing and supervising their children. Their children, therefore, experience the same emotional neglect and rejection felt by poor inner-city youths and then join or create gangs to fulfill their psychosocial needs. This neglect may really be the *bottom line*—emotional neglect and lack of supervision whether in poor *or* affluent families.

CULTURAL FACTORS

Compared to other nations around the world, the United States is perceived as a violent nation with an ultra-violent culture. A nation founded on violence, preoccupied with power and oppression of Native Americans and other minorities, women, and the poor, occurring within the powerfully violent modeling context of wars, the advocacy and practice of capital punishment, and an obsession with the possession and use of firearms, all contribute to the creation of a violent citizenry.

There is evidence of an association between war and individual violence, as a society at war is teaching its members that such behavior is acceptable under certain circumstances. Warring nations are more likely to experience increases in homicide rates than nations not involved in war. The nation's homicide rate more than doubled (4.5 per 100,000 in 1963, to 9.3 in 1973) during the Vietnam War years. Researchers found the fact of war to be the most plausible explanation and the most influential variable in the causal equation.[38] Vietnam veterans, especially combat veterans, are more likely than nonveterans to be violence-prone and evidence more social, psychological, and substance abuse problems than nonveterans.[39] Although the Persian Gulf War had about 200 casualties, scores more were wounded and/or witnessed violence. The traumatic psychological consequences of combat for U.S. male *and* female military personnel may visit violence upon their families, neighbors, and communities for many years to come.

Although humanitarian violations are occurring in different parts of the world, such as China, South America, and Africa, in 1999 President Clinton chose to intervene in a small European country whose violations were not on the scale of the previously mentioned areas. Under the rationale of humanitarian violations against some of its own citizens in Yugoslavia and using NATO as a puppet front, President Clinton's seventy-nine day bomb and missile war ended in June 1999. This brief war, which escalated humanitarian violations by Serbs against Albanians, additionally resulted in thousands of Serbian and Albanian deaths and trauma casualties caused by the U.S.-led intervention. Traumatized Yugoslavian families, therefore, will be paying the same price of increased perpetrator violence in their country for decades as has been the U.S. experience.

This may not be the case for the United States because, unlike in other U.S. wars, there were fewer than a dozen American casualties. It is not expected therefore, to see war traumatized combat veterans venting their violent pathology upon U.S. citizens as has been the case following previous wars. But the cultural *modeling* effect, especially on impressionable youth, may cause more psychological harm than is currently realized. For example, as Clinton was responding to the Trench Coat Mafia gang massacre in Colorado and advising America's youth to talk out their problems rather than resort to violence as a solution, American planes were bombing Iraq and Yugoslavia. Youths seem to follow more what adults *do,* rather than what they preach.

The easy access to firearms, including assault rifles, in the United States was seen by the public as a major cause of school killings over the last few years, with Columbine High being "the last straw." There appeared to be a cultural shift in America's love affair with firearms, which resulted in overwhelming public support for new restrictions on firearms. However, the wealthy, potent National Rifle Association with its lobbyists fought strongly against any gun control reforms. *Both* Democrats and Republicans in the House of Representatives rejected these reforms by a large margin, 280 to 147 votes. This bill would have required gun safety lock requirements and a ban on juvenile possession of assault rifles.[40] Furthermore, the House, in a vote of 248 to 180, failed to endorse a Senate-approved bill requiring a three-day background check for gun show purchases, rather than the current twenty-four hour check. Instead, the House voted to improve the environmental safety of the nation by permitting states to post the Ten Commandments in schools as a deterrent to violence. Ironically, was the president of the NRA, Charlton Heston, who played Moses in the movie *Ten Commandments* and the NRA being paid homage to by Congress?[41]

These votes clearly demonstrate the resistance of policy makers, who in effect are the "environmental–structural engineers" of U.S. society, to make changes in laws demanded by the voters representing a cultural softening concerning the access to firearms. Tragic as it may be, there are probably no amount of gun control laws that will keep firearms out of the hands of city and suburban youths intent on killing others. At least fifteen laws "in the books," for example, did not deter the Trench Coat Mafia gang from carrying out its mission to kill students.

Like war, capital punishment may have a negative effect on the public. One study concluded that publicized executions by the state, instead of deterring further violence, may incite imitative executionlike behavior in society.[42] With nearly 600 executions since 1977, the United States leads the world in executing its citizens, about seventy to one hundred per year, which former Supreme Court Justice Blackmun called a failed experiment in deterrence fraught with arbitrariness, discrimination, caprice, and mistake.[43] Not only does Texas lead the nation in executions, but it may also provide the United States with a presidential candidate for the 2000 campaign, George W. Bush. If he wins the presidency, the model of killing of people to solve problems will continue and quite probably escalate under Bush.

The U.S. media also play a significant role in modeling and influencing young minds. Children spend more time watching television than in any other single activity, and by the age of eighteen the average person has witnessed over 18,000 homicides on television. Sixty percent of prime-time TV programs contain violent solutions to conflict situations, with cartoons being among the most violent. Research findings do not support the notion that television violence has a cathartic effect on the viewer. In fact, children who watch TV violence are much less likely to stop other children from hurting one another than those who do not.[44]

In response to the Columbine High School killings, Washington, D.C., unleashed a set of proposals designed to prevent youths from watching movies with violent imagery. According to a *Time/CNN* poll in May, 1999, 64 percent of respondents stated that they favored legislation to restrict teen-agers access to violent and sexually explicit material. Hollywood seems very skeptical.[45]

FAMILY FACTORS

While on the one hand in response to the Columbine High gang massacre, Congress refused to do very little if anything at the national environmental–structural level to curb youth firearm violence, especially access to military-type assault rifles, some local state governments are "passing the buck" to parents and requiring them to get tough with their children. Hundreds of cities, for example, have now passed curfew laws for adolescents, and Tennessee and Indiana now require parental permission for their children to have their ears pierced. Oklahoma passed the harshest law, which permits parents to deliver a "spanking, paddling, or switching" to their children who are under eighteen years of age without fear of state intrusion.[46] Perhaps these legislators did not know that over half of incarcerated juvenile and adult violent offenders had been subjected to physical punishment and that at least 50 percent of adolescents living at home were still being hit by their parents (see "America's Dependence on Corporal Punishment" in the final chapter).[47]

It was seen in Figure 17-3 that the percent of working mothers with children under six increased from 40 percent in 1976 to 65 percent in 1997, thereby making it more difficult for mothers to be home nurturing and supervising their young children. The situation appears to be worse for fathers. Prompted by the Trench Coat Mafia gang killings, a June 1999 national poll of children ages twelve to fourteen living in twenty-five cities revealed that 60 percent of these sampled respondents reported that they wanted to spend more time with their parents. Two-wage earner households and those headed by a single parent obviously make the child's wishes difficult to fulfill. Forty-one percent of the respondents stated they spent an equal amount of time with both parents; 47 percent spent more time with mother, and 11 percent spent more time with father. However, 76 percent of African American youths spent significantly more time with their mothers than with their fathers.[48] It appears that African American and Hispanic youths coming from poorer families have less contact with fathers due to many factors, such as single-parent households, separations, divorce, premature death, desertion, and long working hours by fathers who still reside at home.

According to child psychologist Judith Rich Harris, "Parenting matters zilch." In looking at behavioral genetics and socialization data, she does not find that a parent's behavior toward her or his children has any important long-term effect. She believes that the world of a child's friends and schoolmates exerts a potent and even more decisive influence on them than do their parents.[49]

There might be an inherent major error in looking at data from a macro perspective, such as conducting national youth and family surveys, like those described in attempting to find *the* answer as to why some youths join gangs and then begin to kill others. A similar error might be present in attempting to generalize from micro specific genetic twin studies raised in separate households by different parental figures to determine the actual influence that parents have on their children. The latter was the method employed by Harris, who believes that parents matter "zilch." Perhaps the biggest error in both of these approaches is in not looking specifically at families who *have* children who *have* been convicted of violent juvenile crimes. Such a study, but still very relevant today, was conducted by the author in 1962. It involved a random sample of Hispanic nongang families (28%) and gang families (72%) taken from a universe of eighty-five adolescents committed to and successfully graduated from Los Angeles County probation camps over a three-year period.

In this study, all families were low income and residing in the same poor, high-delinquency environments. In looking at marital and family factors in both the nongang and gang-member families, both were marked by divorce, separations, common-law relationships, instability, and temporary relationships. However, there was significantly far more marital instability in the gang families than in the nongang families. For example, in the gang families, five mothers had a total of fifteen spouse-type relationships resulting in forty children. Sixty percent of nongang families had another sibling convicted of either a juvenile or adult crime, compared to 90 percent in the gang families. In *all* cases, the criminal sibling was a male. With regard to recidivism (being convicted of a new crime following graduation from probation camp), 90 percent of gang members became recidivists within four months following graduation from camp, whereas 50 percent of nongang members became recidivists after six-and-a-half months following camp graduation.[50] Given the seriousness of severe multiple problems in the gang group families, the author concluded that these youths, deprived of parental affection, nurturing, and validation, joined gangs in search of these primary needs; the gang, therefore, became their *surrogate family*.

Healthy, positive parental supervision and nurturing *do* make a difference. What NIMH Director and psychiatrist John E. Bell told over 400 psychiatrists, social workers, and psychologists thirty-seven years ago was true then and is perhaps even more so today:[51]

> When you see a person with his family, you also see those who contribute to making the person what he is. We are the products of our social relationships—in other words, family relationships.

THE INDIVIDUAL

Here the ecosystems model focuses on the individual level, examining the biological and psychological factors of each person, with specific attention to what makes certain persons vulnerable to not only joining gangs, but also to becoming violent members of the gang. The violent behavior does not appear in a vacuum and is in many ways related to the previously discussed historical context in the person's background, the environmental–structural conditions in which the violence occurs, the violent cultural conditioning of society, marital and family vulnerabilities exacerbating the individual's psychosocial condition, and finally the individual's biological and psychological endowment interacting with the former factors. Few would disagree that the United States has the highest youth suicide and homicide rates in the world. Both are violent acts involving murder either of the self or others and, on occasion, both. There are penal code sanctions for people who commit murder, but they are absent for those who commit suicide as they in effect have exercised upon themselves the ultimate penalty—death!

Persons in the fifteen to twenty-four years of age category are by far at highest risk for death related to *behavior*, as opposed to disease, such as cancer and heart disease. In other words, had it not been for certain behaviors leading to premature death, these young people would be alive today. In this age category, death by motor vehicles ranks number 1, killing about 13,872 persons per year (83.3 deaths per 100,000), with homicide number 2, causing 6,548 deaths (18.1 deaths per 100,000), and suicide number 3, with 4,369 deaths (12.1 deaths per 100,000).[52] Age and gender are powerful factors, as about 80 to 90 percent of these victims are males. For non-Hispanic white males, suicide is the second leading cause of death following vehicle accidents. For Native Americans, African Americans, and Hispanics, homicide is the number 1 cause of death.[53] Table 17-1 highlights the U.S. states and cities with the highest homicide rates per 100,000 population and compares this with gang homicide rates, which are seventy times higher than the national rate in one specific urban area.

As can be seen in Table 17-1, in one year in Los Angeles, there were 779 gang-related homicides that did not in any way whatsoever alarm the country, as was the case for a handful of school homicides over the last few years. In fact, there were so few public school homicides and suicides among 80,000 elementary, middle, and high schools (less than a dozen) that they do not appear statistically. See Table 17-2.

Since the vast majority of these victims and perpetrators are males, some may conclude that the culprit obviously must be the principal male hormone *testosterone*.

TABLE 17-1 **U.S. Homicide Rates per 100,000 Population, 1996ᵃ**

Area	Rate
United States	7.4
States with Highest Rates	
Nevada	13.7
Maryland	11.6
New Mexico	11.5
Mississippi	11.1
Illinois	10.0
California	9.2
New York	7.4
Cities with Highest Rates	
Washington, D.C.	73.1
New Orleans, Louisiana	31.9
Jackson, Mississippi	20.0
Birmingham, Alabama	18.1
Gary, Indiana	18.1
Shreveport, Louisiana	18.1
Baton Rouge, Louisiana	17.9
Richmond, Virginia	16.0
Baltimore, Maryland	15.8
Los Angeles, California	15.1
Los Angeles Areasᵇ	
East Los Angeles *Barrio*	25.4
77th Street Precinct (African American)	46.0
L.A. Gangs (1,141 gangs, 150,000 members committing 779 homicides)	519/100,000

aCrime in the United States 1996, Uniform Crime Reports, U.S. Department of Justice, table created by A. Morales, UCLA-NPI, 1999.
ᵇA. Morales and B. Sheafor, *Social Work: A Profession of Many Faces*, 8th ed. (Boston: Allyn and Bacon, 1998).

If this were so, then American males must have more of it than European males, since Americans commit eight times more homicides than Europeans, and in the United States *Latinos*, African American, and American Indian males must have more of it than non-Hispanic whites since they commit more homicides. Applying this theoretical explanation to U.S. women, non-Hispanic white women must have more of this hormone than African American, Hispanic, and Asian American women since they commit significantly more homicides than these ethnic/racial groups, up to three times more than Hispanic women and four times more than Asian women.[54] Certainly, gender, life-style, socioeconomic status, and culture are variables that have to be factored in when we consider the causes of violence.

A significant amount of controversy exists in attempting to link biological factors to violence. At best it can be said that *some* biological factors, such as genetic conditions, hormonal imbalances, brain diseases, and brain chemistry dysfunctions,

| TABLE 17-2 | **U.S. Rates of Crime per 100,000 Public School Students, 1996–1997, Sample of 1,234 Schools** |

Crime	All Public Schools	Elementary	Middle	High School
Homicide	0	0	0	0
Suicide	0	0	0	0
Fight with Weapon	26	7	49	46
Rape or Sex Battery	10	3	17	18
Fight, No Weapon	444	96	872	808
Robbery	17	2	28	38
Vandalism	234	157	283	347

Violent Crime: *<5% minority, 19/100,000;*   *>20–49% = 51/100,000;*   *>50% = 96/100,000*

U.S. Department of Education, National Center for Education Statistics. *Violence and Discipline Problems in U.S. Public Schools: 1996–97,* Washington, D.C., March, 1998, table created by A. Morales, UCLA-NPI, 1999.

may predispose *some* individuals toward violence, under certain circumstances. One cannot predict who will be violent with any high degree of accuracy, only that given certain biological predisposition factors, the *potential* for violence exists.[55]

A growing body of brain chemistry research with animals and humans has demonstrated that pharmacologic modulation of neurotransmitter systems and electrical stimulation of certain regions of the brain can produce marked alterations in aggressive and violent behavior. Such treatment has been found to be successful in some institutionalized psychiatric patients and forensic prisoners.[56] However, even the most adamant proponents of the biological perspective maintain that social factors are by far the most significant determinants of violent behavior.[57]

Chemicals such as food additives, environmental pollutants, toxic metals, and vitamin deficiencies or imbalances have been known to trigger violent behavior or aggravate pre-existing tendencies toward violence in *some* people. Poor nutrition and/or substance abuse by a mother during pregnancy can negatively affect the fetus, causing low birth weight, premature birth, mental retardation, or abnormal brain development, conditions that are related to increased probability of violent behavior by the parent or child. Depressant drugs, such as barbiturates and alcohol, are highly conducive to violence. Alcohol use is associated with up to two-thirds of all violent situations. Drugs and violence often depend on the interaction of factors such as the type of drug substance and dosage, the personality of the user, user expectations of the drug experience, and the environmental situational context.[58]

The major physiological factors related to homicide concern age and gender. Almost 90 percent of homicide victims are males, mostly killed by other males. The majority of homicide victims and perpetrators are older juveniles, young adults, and adults up to thirty-five years of age.[59]

Juvenile homicide continues to shock and befuddle the mental health professions and the nation, especially when "normal" youths commit heinous homicides or suicides. The usual response is "But he(she) was such a nice child and teen-ager, and always a good student; this was a complete surprise." Almost like a religion, we have very strong "faith" in the belief that a positive psychological development experience for a child will produce a nonviolent person. This may not be necessarily so. In theory, a positive birth experience, characterized by a gentle, loving, and nontraumatic experience in every respect, increases the likelihood of healthy emotional, cognitive, and behavioral child development, and hence a nonviolent person. However, there is no *direct* link known to exist between the birth experience and violent behavior.[60] Quality of parenting, early childhood development, and experience may be more important in determining the nature of subsequent social relations. Many juvenile and adult violent criminal offenders had a history of childhood physical abuse (including corporal punishment) and neglect by their parents. These factors can lead to poor self-esteem, a negative or criminal self-image, and feelings of distrust, frustration, and powerlessness—feelings not uncommon among violent offenders.[61]

Unlike other health problems, homicide is the outcome of psychological thinking processes that result in conscious efforts to cause harm to another person. Although there are many psychological and psychiatric theories to explain violence and homicide, there is broad agreement, according to the Secretary's Task Force on Black and Minority Health, that persons who commit homicide and other violent crimes fall into a number of modal groups, as follows:[62]

1. Normal, socialized persons exposed to extremely provocative or frustrating situations or circumstances, at times coupled with inhibition-lowering drugs or alcohol.
2. Persons committed to a violent lifestyle with supporting attitudes and values.
3. Persons whose inhibitions against violence are impaired by functional (e.g., paranoia) or organic pathology (e.g., abnormal brain chemistry).
4. Overcontrolled persons, whose violence stems from excessive, inflexible inhibitions against the expression of normal aggressive behavior.
5. Persons who are highly prone toward aggression or anger resulting from frustration, revenge, jealousy, and oppression.
6. Persons who engage in violence as a means to achieve goals other than injuring the victim, such as robbers.

Considering these homicide modal groups, the suburban Trench Coat Mafia gang would have fallen into the first five categories. Individual or group urban gang homicide perpetrators would qualify for all six types of modal groups.

Urban and Suburban Gang Homicidal–Suicidal Behavior

On April 27, 1999, in Los Angeles, fifteen-year-old Renzo Alvarado killed his father, mother, a four-year-old brother, and then himself with a 22-caliber handgun found in his hand. Prior to killing himself, he had turned on the gas stove and lit a candle next to himself. His intent was to blow up their home following this multiple homicide and then kill himself.[63] This tragic incident provides clear insights into why adolescents individually or in gangs, as in Littleton, Colorado, commit homicide and then suicide. Littleton's Trench Coat Mafia *was* a gang—specifically, a neo-Nazi white middle-class gang with some gothic characteristics and attracted to Marilyn Manson's industrial gothic, death metal music. Prior to the Columbine High massacre, the Trench Coat Mafia gang was like most gangs in the country, neither homicidal nor suicidal. Furthermore, it is extremely uncommon for a gang to commit a homicide on school grounds. Table 17-3 highlights all homicides (only a few were gang-related homicides) and suicides in the United States occurring on school grounds over a three-year period from February 1996 through May 1999. All these sixteen homicide and suicide perpetrators, with one exception, were adolescent white males who shot and wounded fifty-five persons and killed thirty-seven; in turn, three of them committed suicide. The one exception was a black male who asked his female friend to carry his gun in her backpack. While reaching for a pencil, the gun accidently went off in the classroom, wounding her in the leg. The thirty-seven deaths burst into a national psychosocial outcry and a demand for immediate answers for this problem.

On the other hand, to date, there has not been even a whimper concerning the thousands of inner-city youths being killed each year by gangs in the nation. Consider the nearly 1,800 youths killed by gangs in a comparable three-year period (1995, 1996, 1997) in just *one* U.S. urban area, Los Angeles, as demonstrated in Figure 17-4.

It was seen earlier in this chapter that there are at least four major types of gangs: conflict gangs (inner-city gangs fighting over turf), criminal gangs (crimes for profit, drug sales, robberies), retreatist gangs (retreating into alcohol and drugs as

TABLE 17-3 **U.S. School Homicides and Suicides, 1996–1999**

Date	Location	School	Offender[a]	No. Killed	No. Wounded	Suicide
5-20-99	Conyers, GA	Heritage High	WM, 15	0	6	No
4-20-99	Littleton, CO	Columbine	2 WM, 17, 18	13	20	2
6-15-98	Richmond, VA	High school	WM Adolescent	0	2	No
5-21-98	Springfield, OR	High school	WM, 15	4[b]	0	No
5-21-98	Onalaska, WA	High school	WM, 15	0	0	1
5-21-98	Houston, TX	High school	BM, 17	0	1	No
5-19-98	Fayetteville, TN	High school	WM, 18	1	0	No
4-28-98	Pomona, CA	Elementary	WM, 14	2	1	No
4-24-98	Edinboro, PA	Mid-school	WM, 14	1 (Teacher)	0	No
3-24-98	Jonesboro, AR	Mid-school	2 WM, 11, 13	5	10	No
12-1-97	W. Paducah, KY	High school	WM, 14	3	5	No
10-1-97	Pearl, MS	High school	WM, 16	3[c]	9	No
2-16-97	Bethel, AK	High school	WM, 16	2	2	No
2-2-96	Moses Lake, WA	Mid-School	WM, 14	3	1	No
TOTAL:				37	55	3

[a]WM = white male, BM = black male.
[b]Two of the four killed were the perpetrator's parents.
[c]One of the three killed was the perpetrator's mother.
"Violence in U.S. Schools," List of School Shootings, ABC News Internet Ventures, *www.abcnews.com,* May 20, 1999, table created by A. Morales, UCLA-NPI, 1999.

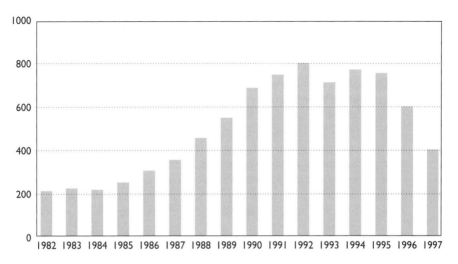

FIGURE 17-4 **Los Angeles City and County Gang-Related Homicides, 1982–1997**

Source: L.A. Co. Sheriff's Dept.; District Attorney; LAT 1-19-93; LAT 9-18-96; McBride, 5-1-98; A. Morales, UCLA-NPI.

consumers), and cult/occult gangs (Satan or evil worship or exaltation of persons such as Hitler by Skinheads, neo-Nazis, White Supremacists, Ku Klux Klan, and Aryan Brotherhood gangs). Los Angeles, with a population of 9 million people, has 150,000 to 200,000 gang members in approximately 1,000 to 1,500 gangs, and has the four types of gangs, with the majority being *Latino* and African American conflict and criminal gangs. Figure 17-4 shows that they commit about 400 to 500 gang-related homicides per year, but only a small percent of these involve homicide and suicide, but they are not detected or reported as such. It is not suggested that the vast majority of gang members suffer from serious mental illness—it is mainly those who actually commit the 400 to 500 homicides, which represents less than half of one percent of the 150,000 to 200,000 gang members. Those who commit homicide and then suicide, as was the case with the Trench Coat Mafia, are the most emotionally disturbed.

Americans who kill themselves (approximately 30,000 suicides per year) are very emotionally disturbed, with most suffering from major depression. The majority of people who murder others in the United States (approximately 23,000 homicides per year) are also emotionally disturbed and suffering from a mental disorder. Ninety-five percent of suicides are individual acts, with only 4 to 5 percent involving persons killing another and then themselves. Most of these homicides–suicides involve marital couples and families as was the case with Renzo Alvarado. Adolescent gang members killing others and then themselves represent an even smaller population, perhaps one-half of one percent, or about 50 to 150 cases per year nationally. Multiple homicides of ten or more victims followed by suicide inside a school are extremely rare, with only four having taken place in the world since 1966, with Littleton having been the fourth. Nevertheless, Littleton frightened the nation immensely, and people tend to view each youth wearing a black trench coat as a potential mass murderer. This is how Hispanic and African American youth wearing "gang clothing fashions" have historically been perceived and treated.

In homicide–suicides as observed in the case of Renzo Alvarado, the Trench Coat Mafia gang, and a few Los Angeles gang members, studies show that depression is found in up to 90 percent of these cases, alcohol and/or drugs in 60 percent of the cases, and schizophrenia in about 2 to 14 percent.[64] Alvarado would have been a prime candidate to join a gang, because he was experiencing conflict in his family. Joining a gang, which in fact is a surrogate family, is a symptom that a youngster's emotional needs are not being met by the family, whether poor or affluent. Gang members who experience parental, police, church, recreational agency, peer and school rejection find other adolescents similarly situated. This common experience begins to bond them, and they adopt a provocative fashion of clothing that identifies and unites them even further, while simultaneously intimidating and alienating non-members. Gang "uniforms," whether suburban black gothic trench coat or inner-city dark, baggy, hooded sweatshirts and pants, *are* a red flag that the adolescent is calling attention to himself, even if it is negative attention. Many schools prohibit these outfits and have been known to suspend students for not complying with dress codes.

There is, however, far greater tolerance in affluent suburban schools as parents, police, "good students," and teachers enter a state of denial and view these "gang uniforms" and possibly unique hairdos (often bald heads), tattoos, and gothic makeup as simply harmless adolescent rebellion, a stage they will soon outgrow. This is true for at least 95 percent of the students, as only 5 to 7 percent actually end up in state prison; and even fewer, except for the most disturbed suffering from male adolescent major depression, are involved in homicide–suicides. It is impossible to predict which gang member or members will actually commit a homicide–suicide. This was very much the case as it pertained to the ten to fifteen Littleton Trench Coat Mafia gang members.

The new group bond builds the individual's esteem, which really is not permanently internalized—it is a pseudo confidence. Most feel empowered mainly in the presence of their gang or when carrying a weapon. When alone without the backing of the gang and not carrying a weapon for protection, their self-esteem and confidence disappear, causing them to feel inadequate and insecure. The more firepower they carry, the more it tells us how insecure they are. The NRA wants more civilians to carry firearms for protection. This is something that some gang members have been doing for years, and it has not protected them or deterred rivals from attacking and killing them; but they do "feel" more confident when carrying a concealed weapon.

Homicide–suicides are expressed through the cultural fabric of the society, the community, the group, and the individual. In the case of Renzo Alvarado, for example, as a Hispanic the home and the family were very important to him and, paradoxically, also the most painful place for him. The Trench Coat Mafia gang perpetrators carried out their pathological act in the school that had been the most painful place for them, where they had experienced ridicule by "jocks." Homicidal–suicidal Los Angeles gang members act out their deadly impulses in their or rival neighborhoods, sites of great physical and psychological trauma, where they have encountered assaults, beatings, and grief caused by loved "homeboys" dying in their arms.

Gang culture requires its members to place their primary loyalty and allegiance to the gang and/or their "cause," rather than to their family. A few very disturbed gang members, therefore, will actually kill and/or die for their gang, turf, cause, or respect. The importance of *respect* is also related to how secure they feel about themselves. The more vulnerable and inadequate they feel, often exacerbated by depression, the more drastic actions they believe are required to reestablish that respect. Major depression can distort the clarity of one's thinking, at times causing an obsessed tunnel vision that blinds the impaired youngster's ability to consider alternative solutions. Gang members do not want to "punk out" (not be a man); hence they will fight and kill or die to gain respect. In the case of the Littleton gang members, they felt "put down" and disrespected by many students, particularly the physically strong athletes. The gang and military weapons culture served not only to psychologically empower them, but to give them an unfair advantage to carry out their "payback." Some gang members seeking more psychological strength, abandon the gang and join forces with a greater power and become "born again Christians." The Trench Coat Mafia found that ultimate power in Hitler, who killed 6 million Jews and later committed suicide. As a neo-Nazi gang and in recognition of Hitler's birthday, the Trench Coat Mafia gang carried out their massacre and, like their leader, committed suicide.

Within the framework of psychoanalytic theories, Freud once stated in the early 1900s that suicide was anger turned toward oneself; that is, the person hates and murders himself. Menninger in the 1950s conceived of suicide as "inverted homicide," as the result of the person's anger toward another; but for fear of further rejection by the loved one, the anger and murderous impulses are turned toward oneself. The author's experience with homicidal–suicidal gang members suggests that they participate in an *inverted suicide,* with anger, rage, and frustration with oneself projected onto one's identical image; *they are killing themselves by killing their image!* This represents both an inverted homicide and suicide when both the homicides and suicides are carried out. In the Littleton case, with the exception of one African American athlete and an adult teacher, the perpetrators killed their own images—white adolescent male and female students who had special athletic or artistic talents that they obviously envied. They killed their enemies where they congregate, inside the school! *Latino* and African American gang members kill their images where they congregate, out in the streets in rival neighborhoods. Homicidal–suicidal middle-class gang members, therefore, are more likely to kill their images in school and homicidal–suicidal inner-city youth, to kill their images out in the streets.

A suicide note left by one of the Littleton gang youths indicated that they did exactly what they had planned to do. Some street gang members leave "notes" of their deadly accomplishments in graffiti at or near the crime scene. Some will actually call out the name of their gang as they are killing or being killed by their rivals. Lower-class homicidal–suicidal street gang members believe it is "stupid to blow your brains out." Instead, those who are homicidal–suicidal will consciously or unconsciously, while alone and unarmed, challenge a group of armed rival gang members or the police and cause these potentially deadly opponents to kill them. This represents "suicide by gang or cop." They believe in "going out with a bang!" Some fantasize about wanting to witness their own funerals after death and seeing how many people cry for them as they pass their caskets, how many cars will be in their funeral procession, and how many people will actually be at their burial.

The two Trench Coat Mafia perpetrators literally planned to go out with a bang, as evidenced by many of their planted bombs—some of which did go off. They indeed grabbed the nation's attention. They had and continue to have their moment of glory in the spotlight. They made the front cover of the May 3, 1999, issue of *Time* in large, colored photographs, framed by the small black and white pictures of their thirteen dead victims, who were given second billing.[65] The main cover photo could have been of the heroic teacher who sacrificed his life to save his students—*that* would have been a role model for all to follow. As far as can be determined, there has never been a *Time* magazine cover of two teen-age gang homicide perpetrators. For these troubled gang members who kill and then kill themselves or cause others to kill them, death with its morbid "glory" was preferable to living a life in the psychological pain caused by depression. *Time's* distinguishing these gang members reinforces and confirms the glory fantasy of highly vulnerable homicidal–suicidal youth. As one gang member told the author, "If I had known then the way I was thinking, it would have been worth killing others and then myself in order to get *my* picture on the front cover of a magazine!"

Micro Intervention with Homicidal–Suicidal Gang Members

Social workers attempting to help gang members who have either committed homicides, attempted homicides, or aggravated assaults *and* who have also been harmed by gang rivals or police, or who are showing homicidal–suicidal tendencies and symptoms need to have a good knowledge of the various manifestations of depression, since this is often at the core of these violent, deadly behaviors. Depression may have different causes, such as (1) a biological and genetic origin; (2) a psychological reaction to a major loss, such as the death of a loved one; (3) trauma as found in PTSD caused by injury, physical or sexual abuse; (4) alcohol and drug abuse and dependence; or (5) a combinations of these factors. In treating several thousand or more violent *Latino,* non-Hispanic white, Asian, and African American gang members, the author has found these factors to be present in practically all homicidal–suicidal violent (gang and nongang) youth.

In males, the expression of depression may manifest itself in irritability, impatience, and anger, rather than the more common symptoms of crying, sadness, loss of appetite, low energy, insomnia or frequently staying in bed, as seen more often in females. See Table 17-4 for a comparison of DSM-IV major depression symptoms with symptoms expressed by gang members.

TABLE 17-4	**DSM-IV Criteria for Depression versus Gang Member Depression**

DSM-IV 296, Major Depression	Gang Member Depression
1. Depressed mood almost daily.	1. Often angry, irritable, negative, frequent fights, antiauthority.
2. Loss of interest and pleasure nearly every day.	2. Passive, reactive behavior, gang determines activities.
3. Weight gain or loss, increase or decrease in appetite.	3. Lacks energy, in poor physical condition; weight gain or loss.
4. Insomnia or hypersomnia nearly every day.	4. Goes to bed late, gets up late, needs alcohol or drugs to sleep.
5. Psychomotor agitation or retardation.	5. Restless, uncomfortable with strangers.
6. Fatigue or loss of energy almost every day.	6. Frequently complains of boredom, "kicking back" (doing nothing) with gang is primary activity; poor employment history.
7. Feels worthless and guilty often.	7. Masks feelings of inadequacy by feeling empowered by gang.
8. Diminished ability to think or concentrate, indecisive.	8. School failure, cannot concentrate, lets gang make his or her decisions.
9. Recurrent thoughts of death, suicidal ideation without plan, or with a specific plan, prior suicide attempt.	9. Thoughts of premature death, funeral fantasies, thoughts of being killed by rival gang or police. Prior injuries due to police or gang physical, knife, or firearm assaults.

Diagnostic and Statistical Manual of Mental Disorders, 4th ed., DSM-IV (Washington, D.C.: American Psychiatric Association, 1994), p. 327; gang depression criteria and table created by A. Morales, UCLA-NPI, 1999.

DSM-IV criteria for a diagnosis of major depression require that at least five of the symptoms listed in Table 17-4 be present. Depression criteria for gang members was developed by the author based on clinical experience. At least five or more of the gang criteria could indicate a major depression, with particular attention to the actual experience of having seriously injured or killed others and having been injured by others. Posttraumatic stress disorder (PTSD) should be ruled out or might be an accompanying diagnosis.

A dysthymic or a dependent personality disorder may mirror some of the depressed gang member criteria, but there will be an absence of aggressive proactive violence, practically no risk-taking behavior, and an absence of premature death ideation. Substance abuse and/or dependence may exacerbate a preexisting depression or actually cause the depression. If the depression does not dissipate after at least a two-week abstention from drugs and alcohol, then the depression was present *prior* to the use of drugs and alcohol and may indicate a biological or endogenous depression. There might be a few cases in which depression with psychotic features or schizophrenia is present.

Depressed female gang members more likely will meet the DSM-IV criteria for depression, rather than the gang member criteria. To date, female gang members have not been known to commit a gang-related homicidal act, later followed by suicide, but they have committed gang homicide. Rather, they have been known to attempt suicide following the killing of one of their own children (maternal filicide–suicide). Depressed female gang members are more likely to carry out their violence through suicidal acts such as slashing their wrists, a drug overdose, or shooting themselves with a gun. In addition to meeting the traditional criteria for depression found in DSM-IV, female gang members, however, commonly exhibit a significant amount of irritability and anger. This may also indicate a second DSM-IV diagnostic category of borderline personality disorder and conduct disorder. Boys, in addition to depression, may also qualify not only for a borderline personality disorder, but also a conduct disorder, paranoid personality disorder, or a bipolar depressive disorder, or combinations of these diagnostic categories. Older hard core and super-hard core depressed gang members who have done "adult time" may, in addition to the diagnostic categories mentioned, meet the criteria for the diagnosis of antisocial personality disorder.

At times some gang members are given "anger management" counseling, as was the case of Trench Coat Mafia gang member Eric Harris. Renzo Alvarado might also have been prescribed the popular "anger management" treatment. However, overt anger often masks a major underlying depression. Anger management counseling may be very appropriate in those cases of adolescents who do not have an underlying clinical depression. Depression when diagnosed appropriately can be treated with medication *and* psychotherapy. Untreated depression can result in death to oneself and/or others. For some male adolescents who are diagnosed with depression and prescribed antidepressant medication, defiance, at times paranoia, and the reality that something is "wrong" with them, hence making them different, can result in failure to take the medication; this happened with Eric Harris.

White, middle-class violent gang members are far more likely to be diagnosed and treated for their depression than African American and *Latino* violent offenders, whose behavior is seen more as emanating from a lower-class criminal and gang culture. When treating gang members with a major depression, it is paramount that they be evaluated by a licensed psychiatrist so that they can be prescribed the appropriate medication. These potentially homicidal–suicidal cases cannot be taken lightly, and there must be a collaborative professional working relationship with the youngster, his parents, the probation or parole officer, and the psychiatrist. This is required even when the gang member is over eighteen years of age. Involving the family provides the social worker an opportunity to not only understand the gang member's behavioral functioning at home and compliance with the medication program, but also to educate the family in understanding the specific mental disorder and dealing with and providing emotional support to their son or daughter. Through this team work approach, some of these gang members have been able to qualify for and receive Social Security disability benefits of $500 to $700 per month. It provides them with a new status as financial contributors to the family, rather than continuing to function under a criminal label. Without such psychosocial intervention, they may possibly become homicide–suicide perpetrators at some point in the future.

Macro Intervention with Gangs

It would be difficult to specifically target and influence homicidal–suicidal gang members through a macro intervention approach because they use the gang and its culture (often "packing" a firearm and being hypersensitive to being disrespected) to vent and express their violent pathology. Their homicidal–suicidal violent behavior can, however, serve as an indicator for individual special attention as described in the preceding section. If they have already committed and been convicted in court of serious gang-related violence against others, such as homicide, attempted homicide, and aggravated assault, incarceration will protect the community and make their gang less violent. Mental health resources should be available in the institution to provide them with the necessary treatment. An absence of these programs and a failure to identify these disturbed youths in the institution places them at suicide risk and other inmates at great risk for violence, victimization, and even death. Rather, macro preventive intervention for this population would involve the creation and provision of community mental health programs for children to assist in the early elementary school detection of problem behavior symptoms, such as attention deficit disorder (ADD), attention deficit hyperactivity disorder (ADHD), fetal alcohol syndrome (FAS), crack cocaine babies, and childhood conduct disorder and depression.

For the majority of healthier, higher-functioning gang members with greater ego strength who are not in the older hard core or super-hard core categories previously described in Figure 17-1, and who are involved with gangs as a temporary, acting out developmental phase, community-based macro-type programs can be successfully designed and implemented. Such a program, called The Little Village Project, was developed by social workers Spergel and Grossman in Chicago, Illinois. This community approach to the prevention and control of gang violence was based on the following six key interrelated intervention strategies:[66]

1. *Community mobilization*—This strategy calls for involving local citizens and organizations, including local residents and groups, youth agencies, police and probation officers, and former gang youths, in a common goal and enterprise.
2. *Opportunities provision*—Here the intervention strategy is based on the premise that relevant opportunities, such as more and better jobs, special education, and training programs, are foremost in meeting the needs of low-income youths relevant to their psychosocial developmental cycles.
3. *Social intervention*—This intervention calls for assertive outreach to gang youths in the streets or in problematic social contexts and is based on the assumption that many youths are not able to use available opportunities to become part of legitimate social institutions. The modalities of crisis counseling, individual and family counseling, and referrals for drug treatment, job training, recreation, and educational programs by case managers, who also serve as advocates and service coordinators, are key components of social intervention.
4. *Suppression*—Controlling the gang in order to suppress its criminal behavior calls for the application of informal and formal controls on the behavior

of individual youths and the structure and process of gangs by social control agencies, such as police and probation, to provide surveillance, arrest, supervision, and imprisonment.

5. *Organizational change and development*—This calls for agency collaboration through a closely knit structure that develops a common objective for preventing and reducing gang crime, with an overall goal of mainstreaming at-risk and gang youths.

6. *Targeting*—This strategy involves a multidiscipline team who targets specific youths, gangs, and social contexts that might induce or result in new crime situations. This intervention has a preventive goal that attempts to define who is a gang youth, what is a gang, and what constitutes a gang incident or crime.

The results of this macro, social work, community organization, gang intervention program was positive. An analysis of 125 targeted youth over a three-year-period indicates that 98 percent had contact with community youth workers and 95 percent received some kind of informal counseling or support from project staff. Family contacts were made with 64 percent of the cases, and 66 percent of youths were involved in athletic programs. Sixty-four percent were referred to jobs and 53 percent received assistance or referrals for school-related problems. Police and probation officers reported that they engaged in suppression activities for 31 percent of the targeted youths. Finally, there was a relative reduction in gang crime, especially gang violence, as a result of this macro intervention.[67]

Concluding Comment

Violent, delinquent gangs have been part of the United States scene since at least 1842. It may very well be that gangs have never been more violent than they are today, with homicides at an unbelievable rate of 400 to 500 per 100,000 in some cities, compared to the national rate of 9 per 100,000. Gangs have always been primarily a law enforcement problem area. The 1920s to 1960s attracted some group work and community organization practice interest in gangs from the social work profession. However, beginning in the 1970s and into the late 1990s, the profession has steadily been moving away from juvenile and adult criminal justice populations, gangs, and the urban problems of poor ethnic–racial groups, with only 1 percent of MSWs in the justice field. Accounting for this exodus has been the attraction for social workers of private practice in affluent communities. Might this be social works' version of classism? One of the very few exceptions to this trend is the outstanding pioneering community organization macro gang intervention work of Spergel and associates in Chicago reported previously.

Today, 94 percent of U.S. urban and suburban areas with 100,000 people or more (177 out of 189 areas) report that they have youth gangs.[68] For the last twenty to thirty years, Americans have shown a callousness and indifference to the thousands of predominantly African American, Hispanic, and Asian American inner-city gang killings occurring each year nationally, but we received a shocking "wake-up call" when the white neo-Nazi Trench Coat Mafia gang massacred thirteen people (twelve students and one teacher) at Columbine High in affluent white suburbia. The suicide of these two perpetrators, who were also its leaders, "cooled off" the violence potential of the remaining twelve to fifteen Trench Coat Mafia gang members. This phenomenon is also seen in inner-city gangs. The homicide–suicide psychiatric pathology uncovered in the Trench Coat Mafia gang perpetrators should have some carry-over implications, leading to an understanding of inner-city gang homicide and "suicide by gang and cop" behavior.

The values, knowledge, and skills base of the social work profession place it in a unique position, compared to other helping professions, to seriously address the growing urban and suburban gang psychosocial crisis. For example, the profession has a historical knowledge base concerning group work with gangs and an impressive theory and practice foundation relating to community organization. These practice modes have been successfully updated and implemented with the gang problem, as was seen in Spergel's macro intervention model. Additionally, the profession's clinical skills and modern scientific discoveries of the biology–brain chemistry etiologies contributing to depression and violent behavior have advanced significantly since the 1940s, 1950s, and even 1980s, to improve significantly the prognosis of what were once considered hopeless cases. Gang violence, therefore, can be significantly reduced by helping the few "worst of the worst" in gangs. Such a micro intervention in collaboration with the macro intervention highlighted above, provides a practice intervention framework that could be effective in working with gangs in both urban and suburban areas of the nation.

The environmental–structural, cultural, familial and psychological–physiological causes of urban and suburban gang members and gangs are still very much "alive and thriving" and will not go away; actually, they appear to be spreading in the nation and increasingly involving young females. This is a challenge to the profession and an opportunity to demonstrate that social work is a unique micro- to macro-level practice discipline that can do some things that other helping professions cannot. Social works' values make it imperative that the profession has no choice but to help those most in need. Gang members have a right to social services as they struggle in their attempts to free themselves from this 1,650-year-old world deadly resolvable adversity first reported in the literature by St. Augustine in 390 A.D. This problem has been in the United States since 1842, in all of the twentieth century, and now is following us into the twenty-first century.

KEY WORDS AND CONCEPTS

Conflict gangs	Suicide by cop
Retreatist gangs	Suicide by gang
Criminal gangs	Gang homicide–suicide
Cult/occult gangs	PTSD
Neo-Nazi gangs	Anger management counseling
Wannabe	Super-hard core gang member
Micro gang intervention	Macro gang intervention
Maternal filicide	Beer gangs

SUGGESTED READINGS

Ewing, Charles Patrick. *Kids Who Kill.* Lexington, MA: D.C. Heath, 1990.
Fox, Jerry R. "Mission Impossible? Social Work Practice with Black Urban Youth Gangs," *Social Work* 30 (January–February 1985): 25–31.

Goldstein, A. P., and Huff, C. R., eds. *The Gang Intervention Handbook*. Champaign, IL: Research Press, 1993.

Hopps, June Gary. "Violence—A Personal and Societal Challenge," *Social Work* 32 (November–December 1987): 467–468.

Huff, C. Ronald. *Gangs in America*. Newbury Park, CA: Sage, 1990.

Klein, Malcolm W. *The American Street Gang*. New York: Oxford University Press, 1995.

Monti, D. J. "Gangs in More- and Less-Settled Communities," in S. Cummings and D. J. Monti, eds., *Gangs: The Origins and Impact of Contemporary Youth Gangs in the United States*. Albany: State University of New York Press, 1993.

Morales, Armando. "Homicide," in Richard L. Edwards, ed., *Encyclopedia of Social Work* 19th Edition. Washington, D.C.: NASW Press, 1995.

Morales, Armando. "The Mexican American Gang Member: Evaluation and Treatment," in Rosina M. Becerra, Marvin Karno, and Javier Escobar, eds., *Mental Health and Hispanic Americans: Clinical Perspectives*. New York: Grune & Stratton, 1982.

Morales, Armando. "Therapy with Latino Gang Members," in L. A. Vargas and J. Koss-Chioino, eds., *Working with Culture*. San Francisco: Jossey-Bass Publishers, 1992.

Morales, Armando T. "Urban Gang Violence: A Psychosocial Crisis," in Armando T. Morales and Bradford W. Sheafor, *Social Work: A Profession of Many Faces,* 8th Edition. Boston: Allyn and Bacon, 1998.

Regulus, T. A. "Gang Violence," in Richard L. Edwards, ed., *Encyclopedia of Social Work,* 19th Edition. Washington, D.C.: NASW Press, 1995.

Report of the Secretary's Task Force on Black and Minority Health, Vol. 5. U.S. Department of Health and Human Services, January 1986.

Schopler, J. H., and Galinski, M. J. "Group Practice Overview," in Richard L. Edwards, ed., *Encyclopedia of Social Work,* 19th Edition. Washington, D.C.: NASW Press, 1995.

Spergel, Irving A. *Street Gang Work: Theory and Practice*. Reading, MA: Addison-Wesley, 1996.

Spergel, Irving A. "Violent Gangs in Chicago: In Search of Social Policy," *Social Service Review* 58 (June 1984): 199–226.

Spergel, Irving A., and Grossman, Susan F. "The Little Village Project: A Community Approach to the Gang Problem," *Social Work,* September, 1997, Vol. 42, No. 5.

Thrasher, Frederick M. *The Gang: A Study of 1313 Gangs in Chicago*. Chicago: University of Chicago Press, 1963.

ENDNOTES

1. June Gary Hopps, "Violence—A Personal and Societal Challenge," *Social Work 32* (November–December 1987): 467–468.
2. Kelley O. Beaucar, "The Violence Has Come Home to Roost," *NASW News*, Vol. 44, No. 6, June 1999, p. 3.
3. As reported by Ruben Lopez, Director, East Los Angeles Area Parole Office, California Youth Authority, during a workshop on "Depression in Gang Members," June 1, 1999.
4. James C. Howell (1997, December) Youth Gangs, *Fact Sheet #12*. Washington, D.C.: U.S. Department of Justice, Office of Juvenile Justice and Delinquency Prevention.
5. Ibid.
6. Penal Code Section 186.22, Participation in a criminal street gang, *West's California Juvenile and Court Rules 1993* (St. Paul, Minn.: West Publishing Co., 1993).

7. Armando Morales, "The Need for Nontraditional Mental Health Programs in the Barrio," in J. Manuel Casas and Susan E. Keefe, eds., *Family and Mental Health in the Mexican American Community,* Monograph No. 7 (Los Angeles: UCLA Spanish Speaking Mental Health Research Center, 1978).

8. Frederick M. Thrasher, *The Gang: A Study of 1313 Gangs in Chicago* (Chicago: University of Chicago Press, 1963), pp. 31–35.

9. W. B. Miller, "Lower Class Culture as a Generating Milieu of Gang Delinquency," *Journal of Social Issues* 14 (1958): 5–19.

10. *Los Angeles Times,* Part I, April 12, 1983, p. 6.

11. See A. K. Cohen, *Delinquent Boys: The Culture of The Gang* (Glencoe, IL: Free Press, 1955); and R. A. Cloward and L. E. Ohlin, *Delinquency and Opportunity* (New York: Free Press, 1960).

12. D. Matza, *Delinquency and Drift* (New York: Wiley, 1964).

13. Armando Morales, "A Study of Recidivism of Mexican American Junior Forestry Camp Graduates," unpublished Master's thesis (School of Social Work, University of Southern California, 1963).

14. A. Morales, "The Mexican American Gang Member: Evaluation and Treatment," in R. Becerra, M. Karno, and J. Escobar, eds., *Mental Health and Hispanic Americans: Clinical Perspectives* (New York: Grune & Stratton, 1982), p. 153.

15. Thrasher, p. 151.

16. John P. Moore and Craig P. Terret (1998, November), Highlights of the 1996 National Youth Gang Survey, *Fact Sheet #86.* Washington, D.C.: U.S. Department of Justice, Office of Juvenile Justice and Delinquency Prevention.

17. *Los Angeles Times,* Wednesday, October 5, 1995, p. B-9.

18. Charles Patrick Ewing, *Kids Who Kill* (Lexington, MA: D.C. Heath, 1990), pp. 102–103.

19. Thrasher, p. 117.

20. *Report on Youth Gang Violence in California,* The Attorney General's Youth Gang Task Force, June 1981, pp. 16–20.

21. *Los Angeles Times,* Section B-5, Wednesday, June 16, 1999, p. 1.

22. T. A. Sweeny, *Streets of Anger: Streets of Hope* (Glendale, CA: Great Western Publishing, 1980), p. 86.

23. I. A. Spergel, "Violent Gangs in Chicago: In Search of Social Policy," *Social Service Review* 58 (June 1984), p. 206.

24. Cloward and Ohlin, p. 178.

25. *State Task Force,* p. 8.

26. T. Kerfoot, "Crime and the Occult," *Peace Officers Association of Los Angeles County* (October 1985): 23.

27. M. Poirier, "Street Gangs of Los Angeles County," unpublished pamphlet, 1982.

28. Irving A. Spergel, "Youth Gangs: Continuity and Change," in *Crime and Justice* (Chicago: University of Chicago Press, 1990), p. 613.

29. Thrasher, p. 60.

30. Morales, "The Mexican American Gang Member," p. 156.

31. Operation Safe Streets Gang Detail, L.A. Style: A Street Gang Manual of the Los Angeles County Sheriff's Department, March 1994.

32. Saint Augustine, *Confessions* (New York: The Modern Library, 1949), p. 34.

33. A. Davis and M. Haller, eds., *The People of Philadelphia* (Philadelphia: Temple University Press, 1973), p. 78.

34. H. Asbury, *The Gangs of New York: An Informal History of the Underworld* (New York: Alfred A. Knopf, 1972), p. 29.

35. Report of the National Advisory Commission on Civil Disorders (New York: Bantam Books, 1968), p. 206.

36. Armando Morales, *Ando Sangrando: I Am Bleeding: A Study of Mexican American–Police Conflict* (La Puente, CA: Perspectiva Publications, 1972), pp. 91–122.

37. Thrasher, *The Gang*, p. 33.

38. Irwin L. Kutash, Samuel B. Kutash, and Louis B. Schlesinger, eds., *Violence: Perspectives on Murder and Aggression* (San Francisco: Jossey-Bass, 1978), pp. 219–232.

39. "Ounces of Prevention: Toward an Understanding of the Causes of Violence," *1982 Final Report to the People of California,* Commission on Crime Control and Violence Prevention, State of California, p. 137.

40. *Los Angeles Times,* Part A, Saturday, June 9, 1999, p. 1.

41. *Los Angeles Times,* Part B, Tuesday, June 22, 1999, p. 15.

42. *1982 Final Report,* p. 138.

43. *Callins* vs. *Collins,* No. 93-7054 (1994) Justice Harry Blackmun dissenting opinion, p. 1.

44. Ronald S. Brabman and Margaret H. Thomas, "Children's Imitation of Aggressive and Pro-Social Behavior When Viewing Alone and in Pairs," *Journal of Communication* 27 (1977): 199–205.

45. John Cloud, "Taking Aim at Show Biz," *Time,* June 21, 1999, pp. 42–43.

46. *Los Angeles Times,* Part A, Saturday, July 3, 1999, p. 1.

47. Murray A. Straus and Richard J. Gelles, "Societal Change and Change in Family Violence from 1975 to 1985 as Revealed by Two National Samples," *Journal of Marriage and the Family* 48 (August 1986), p. 469.

48. Claudia Wallis, "The Kids Are Alright," *Time,* July 5, 1999, pp. 56–58.

49. Melissa Healy, "Debate Rises on Parents' Influence over Children," *Los Angeles Times,* Part A, Sunday, July 4, 1999, p. 3.

50. Armando Morales, "A Study of Recidivism of Mexican American Junior Forestry Graduates," unpublished Masters Thesis, School of Social Work, University of Southern California, June 1963.

51. *Los Angeles Herald Examiner,* Part B-1, March 17, 1963, p. 1.

52. National Vital Statistics Reports, *Centers for Disease Control and Prevention,* National Center for Health Statistics, Vol. 47, No. 9, November 10, 1998.

53. Armando Morales, "Homicide," in Richard L. Edwards, ed., *Encyclopedia of Social Work,* 19th Edition (Washington, D.C.: NASW Press, 1995).

54. Ibid.

55. *Final Report,* pp. 81–82.

56. Burr Elchelman, "Toward a Rational Pharmacotherapy for Aggressive and Violent Behavior," *Hospital and Community Psychiatry* 39 (January 1988): 31.

57. *Final Report,* p. 82.

58. Ibid., p. 11.

59. *Report of the Secretary's Task Force on Black and Minority Health,* Vol. 5, U.S. Department of Health and Human Services, January 1986, p. 32.

60. *1982 Final Report,* p. 13.

61. Ibid., p. 6.

62. *Report of the Secretary,* pp. 29, 31.

63. *Los Angeles Times,* Part B, Wednesday, April 28, 1999, p. B7.

64. Peter M. Marzuk, Kenneth Tardiff, and Charles S. Hirsch, "The Epidemiology of Murder–Suicide," *JAMA,* June 17, 1992, Vol. 267, No. 23, p. 3179.

65. Nancy Gibbs, "The Littleton Massacre," *Time,* May 3, 1999, Vol. 153, No. 17, pp. 24–36.

66. Irving A. Spergel and Susan F. Grossman, "The Little Village Project: A Community Approach to the Gang Problem," *Social Work,* September 1997, Vol. 42, No. 5, pp. 456–470.

67. Ibid., p. 464.

68. Malcolm W. Klein, "The Gang's All Here, There, and Everywhere," *USC Trojan Family Magazine,* 26 (1), p. 14.

Race, Ethnicity, and Culture in Special Populations

Ethnic and racial minorities have been and continue to be overrepresented among the underclass. A racist might state, for example, that African Americans are overrepresented among the poor because they are somehow inherently or biologically inferior to whites, who generally continue to have a higher standard of living. Either minorities are inferior (a racist perspective), or white racism has prevented their natural equality with whites from asserting itself during their more than 100 to 300 years in the United States. Those who deny that overt racism and institutional subordination are essentially responsible for the current lower status of minorities are implying that minorities are biologically or inherently inferior.

Following the unexpected death of social work Asian scholar Dr. Man Keung Ho in 1993, several years were consumed in searching for a comparable replacement. Such an outstanding published scholar is Dr. Doman Lum. He was commissioned to write Chapter 18, "Social Work Practice with Asian Americans," an original state-of-the-art dissertation. Dr. Lum clearly defines the various subgroups of the Asian population and highlights the traumas some Asian subgroups experience prior to arriving in the United States. He also describes the new stressors that Asians experience as they attempt to adjust and acculturate to the United States.

Drs. E. Daniel Edwards and Margie Egbert Edwards were commissioned by the authors of this text, to write a major work, "Social Work Practice with American Indians and Alaskan Natives," which appears as Chapter 19. It is an outstanding contribution and the most current work on American Indians and Alaskan Natives in social work. It is filled with rich demographic and cultural information combining excellent suggestions for micro and macro social work practice intervention. The Edwards advise that the concepts of "balance" and "harmony" are important concepts based on the Native American value of showing respect for all living things. Incorporating these concepts into social work practice with Native Americans and Alaskan Natives will foster respect, collaboration, and growth.

Chapter 20, "Social Work Practice with Mexican Americans," by Drs. Armando T. Morales and Ramon Salcido, has undergone major revisions and has been significantly strengthened with current demographic data which indicate that there are 23 million Hispanics in the nation, with persons of Mexican descent being the largest Latino subgroup representing 60 percent (14 million). It is a very heterogeneous population, exhibiting much diversity. Like Native Americans, it is one of the oldest groups in the United States, since the Great Southwest was a part of Mexico until 1846, but because of continuing migration it is also one of the newest. The chapter is further enriched with a detailed, in-depth clinical case of a police brutality victim that demonstrates the multiple stressors accompanying these oppressive acts. The reader is also exposed to community organization and related macrolevel intervention opportunities related to police brutality.

Chapter 21, "Social Work Practice with African Americans," by Dr. Barbara Bryant Solomon, helps social workers understand the nation's largest minority of 31 million persons. African Americans also are a very heterogeneous group, with more than half residing in central cities throughout the United States. This popular author maintains that racism and discrimination, rather than the process of urbanization, contribute to the creation of an underclass among some African Americans. Dr. Solomon encourages social workers to learn to know them better by becoming actively involved in the sociopolitical lives of African Americans. In helping this population, Solomon suggests the intervention strategy of empowerment, which encourages the social worker to engage in activities with clients that will help reduce the psychosocial powerlessness caused by society.

Section D ends with a commissioned Chapter 22 entitled "Social Work Practice with Puerto Ricans," by Gloria Bonilla-Santiago. Dr. Bonilla-Santiago points out that among Latino groups, Puerto Ricans are the only "colonized" group that has migrated and settled in the United States in massive numbers with currently over 2 million persons on the "mainland." With 3 million persons on the Island of Puerto Rico, Puerto Ricans number 5 million persons. Puerto Ricans are an impoverished group with approximately 42 percent of its families living below the poverty line. Seventy-four percent of these families are headed by women. Colonialism, racism, classism, sexism, and political oppression are all forces and stressors contributing to many of their struggles in life. Excellent suggestions for clinical intervention within the context of Puerto Rican cultural values are offered to the reader.

CHAPTER 18

Social Work Practice with Asian Americans

Doman Lum

Prefatory Comment

Dr. Man Keung Ho initially made his appearance in this volume writing about social work with Asian Americans in the second edition in 1980 and stayed with us for several published editions until his untimely death due to cancer in 1993. After a few years of searching for another outstanding social work scholar to continue this important contribution to the field, Dr. Doman Lum, Professor of Social Work at California State University at Sacramento, was commissioned to write this original chapter.

Dr. Lum describes the heterogeneity of Asian Americans, which includes Chinese, Filipino, Japanese, Asian Indians, Koreans, Vietnamese, Hawaiian, Laotian, Cambodians, Thais, Hmong, Pakistani, Samoan, and Guamanians. Asian Americans totaled nearly 8 million people in the 1990 U.S. census. It is expected that they will number over 12 million in 2000. He provides keen insights about the unique socioeconomic and acculturation stresses that Asians endure in the United States and offers micro and macro treatment suggestions. Although some Asian subgroups are outperforming all American students, overall they still fare poorly in the professions, political representation, and distribution of resources.

The term Asian American may be seen as a geographical and political designation that covers a wide and diverse group of people whose country and culture of origin are from the continent of Asia and islands of the Pacific. The proper designation for this group is *Asian American/Pacific Islander.*

From a geographical perspective, there are thirty-eight Asian nations, which can be grouped into the five following entities: (1) China and India dominate the Asian population and land mass; (2) Japan is an island group; (3) Korea is positioned between China and Japan; (4) the Southeast Asian satellite primary countries are Vietnam, Thailand, Cambodia, Laos, and Malaysia; and (5) the island nations of Indonesia and Philippines, which are closer to Asia than the island regions of Micronesia, Melanesia, and Polynesia.

These Asian nations have historically often been in conflict with each other and have differing and blended cultures, religions, and customs. Yet they have been arbitrarily grouped as Asian Americans by the U.S. Census so that they can be a political entity in the United States. Russell points out that the *Current Population Survey* classifies as Asian and Pacific Islander anyone who identifies him- or herself as Asian or Pacific Islander; the Census Bureau designates as Asian or Pacific Islander anyone who names a Far Eastern or Pacific island nation as their origin; and the Immigration and Naturalization Service includes people from the Middle East (e.g., Israel, Lebanon, and Iran) as Asian immigrants.[1]

Demographics

The Asian population in the United States was 7.5 million in 1990 and is projected to grow from 10.5 million (4% of the population) in 1998 to nearly 20 million (6% of the population) by 2020. Driving this population growth is primarily Asian immigration. For example, in 1990, 63 percent of Asian Americans were foreign born, emigrating particularly from Vietnam, India, and Korea, whereas in 1996, 34 percent of all immigrants were from Asia, with large numbers from the Philippines, India, Vietnam, and China. Most speak English very well, with only 38 percent (ages 5 or older) and 37 percent (ages 65 or older) unable to speak English fluently or very well.[2]

In 1990 the 7.5 million Asian American/Pacific Islander populations consisted of Chinese (1.6 million), Filipino (1.4 million), Japanese (848,000), Asian Indian (815,000), Korean (799,000), Vietnamese (615,000), Hawaiian (211,000), Laotian (149,000), Cambodian (147,000), Thai (91,000), Hmong (90,000), Pakistani (81,000), Samoan (63,000), Guamanian (49,000), and others (263,000).[3] In the year 2000 the projected regional distribution of 11.2 million Asians will be 2.1 million (18.7%) in the Northeast, 1.2 million (10.8%) in the Midwest, 1.9 million (16.9%) in the South, and 6.02 million (53.5%) in the West. This projected pattern remains the same in 2010, with 15.3 million Asian Americans consisting of 2.9 million (19%) in the Northeast, 1.6 million (10.6%) in the Midwest, 2.6 million (16.7%) in the South, and 8.2 million (53.7%) in the West.[4]

GENDER

More attention has been devoted to Asian American women due to a lack of information about their gender status and condition.[5, 6] There is a high rate of interracial marriage among Asian American women, with Japanese American women outmarrying the most in the continental United States and Chinese Americans in

Hawaii (more than 75% combining men and women). Domestic violence against Asian battered women is often hidden due to family and marriage images portrayed to the Asian community. Asian women spousal abuse reveals factors such as extreme isolation, immigration dependency, reinforced powerlessness from society, traditional views of family and community, which place family before oneself, and a lack of economic and cultural resources to leave a violent situation.[7]

SOCIOECONOMIC ISSUES

Education is an important priority for this group. Asians are better educated than the U.S. population as a whole. In 1996, 83 percent of Asians were high school graduates, compared with 82 percent of the total population. Moreover, 6 percent of college students and 10 percent of first-professional-degree program students were Asian, while 42 percent of Asians were college graduates, in contrast to 24 percent of the total population, with bachelor degrees. These trends are due to the value of educational achievement and success placed by parents on their children and the hard work by Asian American students who spend much time studying. Asian parents are willing to sacrifice economic comforts to see that their children are educated in undergraduate and graduate education. Higher education is the gateway to professional jobs in such fields as science, medicine, engineering, law, and business.

In 1990, labor force rates were highest for Asian Indian men (84%) and Filipino women (72%). Fifty-three percent of Asian Americans have two-earner households (the highest proportion among all racial groups), compared with 45% of total households. In 1996, more than 4.6 million Asians (66% of Asians ages 16 or older; 74% males, 59% females) were in the civilian labor force, with 50 percent full-time workers in managerial or professional specialty occupations. Between 1996 and 2006, the Asian work force will grow 41 percent and will become 5.4 percent of the total work force.

The median household income of Asians (20% with incomes of $75,000 or more, 1995) was significantly higher than the average household due to two or more earners per household (Asian couples with a median income of over $50,000; one in four Asian couples with $75,000 or more incomes). Full-time working Asian males earned a median income of $35,788 (1996), while Asian women earned a median of $26,313 due to their education. Asian groups reflecting these income trends are upper-middle-class professionals who have lived in the United States over several generations and include Chinese, Japanese, East Indians, Koreans, Filipinos, and more recently Vietnamese. At the same time, wealthy Chinese families from Taiwan and Hong Kong have moved to the United States with business and investment holdings.

However, poverty (12.4%) was more common (1995) among Asians, particularly recent immigrants from Southeast Asian countries who lack education, are unable to speak English, and have no marketable skills, than among the population as a whole.[8] Asian refugees end up in dead-end jobs, such as restaurant and garment factory workers, and lack occupational mobility due to an inability to understand and communicate in English, their occupational background in their home countries, and lack of education.[9] At the same time, many Southeast Asian refugee children have graduated from universities and are mainstreamed into American society, thus helping with the socioeconomic needs of their parents.

HOUSING AND HEALTH STATUS

In 1990, 35 percent of Asian households were concentrated in Los Angeles–Long Beach metropolitan areas, followed by New York City, Honolulu, and San Francisco. In 1995, Asians (53%) were less likely to own a home, compared with a national average (65%). However, Asians, many living in California and Hawaii, own homes with a median value of $178,300 (1990), compared with a median value of $78,300 for the average American home. In 1996, Asian householders were younger than average due to the young adult ages of many Asian immigrants. There were 61 percent Asian married-couple householders, compared with 54 percent nationally, and 83 percent of Asian children living with both parents, compared to 72 percent in the average household. Asians were more likely to be married: 60 percent of Asian men and women (ages 15 and older), particularly Asian Indian men (65%) and Asian Indian women (70%).

Regarding health status, Asians have lower rates of infant mortality (5.8 deaths before age 1 per 1,000 live births in 1993, compared with a total population indicator of 8.4) and death rates for accidents, heart disease, and cancer than for the population as a whole (295.9 compared with a total population indicator of 513.3 per 100,000 population in 1993). However, there is an above-average incidence of tuberculosis (45.3 compared with a total population indicator of 9.4 per 100,000 population in 1994) due to Asian immigrant living conditions in cramped metropolitan counties with poor air quality. However, life expectancy in 1996 for Asians as a group was above average, with males expected to live to age 80 (seven years longer than average) and females to age 85 (five years longer than average).[10]

Health and Mental Health Risk Factors

Among the health and mental health problems of Asian Americans are depression, somatic complaints, anxiety disorders, adjustment disorders, and suicide.[11] Lee reports: "Work-related stress among the Asian American working class and underclass has exacerbated domestic tensions. Adjustment difficulties and challenges to traditional relations have troubled many marriages. Indeed, domestic violence afflicts all classes of Asian American families."[12] Hate crimes due to racism (e.g., the murder of Vincent Chin in Detroit in 1982, the discharge and racial harassment of Bruce Yamashita at the Marine Office Candidate School in 1989, the 1989 Cleveland Elementary School murders of five Southeast Asian refugee children in Stockton, California) have compounded the environmental stress experienced by the Asian American community. Posttraumatic stress disorder is common among Southeast Asian refugees (particularly Vietnamese, Cambodian, Hmong, and Mien), who fled their homelands and experienced atrocities (e.g., rape, murder, and robbery) in the process of leaving their countries, in refugee camps, and on entering the United States.

Ethnic Group Stressors

Loo has documented sustained racism against Asian Americans in the United States during the last two decades.[13] She declares: "In the 1980s, Asian Americans became scapegoats for Americas economic woes. Americans of Asian ancestry wore the mantle of foreignness, falsely blamed for the economic recession of the U.S. automobile industry. The 1982 race-hate murder of Vincent Chin in Detroit and rising incidents of anti-Asian violence in the 1980s were cases in point."[14] Later Loo observes: "The focus on suspected illegality of Asian donations to the Democratic Party campaign funds in 1997 ha[s] reactivated racial stereotypes of the Chinese. Racist cartoons of President Clinton, Hillary Clinton, and Al Gore with slant eyes and clothed in Mandarin coats, appeared in the *National Review.* The cartoon was a startling throwback to anti-Asian cartoons of the 1800s."[15] Minority group racism against Asian Americans remains a national reality. Among older Americans, there are traces of racism against Japanese Americans, who were scapegoats during World War II. In many parts of the country where there are few Asian Americans, an individual experiences being an isolated and lonely minority person surrounded by invisible barriers of exclusion.

Intergenerational Asian American group stressors include the "parachute kid" phenomena of teen-age children from upper middle class and wealthy Asians from Hong Kong, Taiwan, and other Asian areas who are dropped off in large metropolitan areas populated by Asian Americans, housed in exclusive-area homes, and left to attend American high schools on their own. Parents visit periodically from abroad or ask relatives in the United States to look after them. An alternative is to ask a sister or a brother in the United States to be a surrogate parent and to raise a teen-age nephew or niece so that an Asian-born child can graduate from an American high school and enter an American university. Family development and raising a child are sacrificed for an American education. Parental responsibilities are abdicated by parents in their own country for a relative to assume teen-age rearing in the United States.

Asian husband "astronauts" are depicted as business men who must travel abroad between their homes and family in the United States and various parts of Asia to maintain their business contacts and enterprises in, say, Hong Kong. Being left alone for months, Asian American families are stressed by the absence of the father, by the role of the mother as interim head of the household, and by the acting out of the children. Such families must constantly adjust and readjust to the husband and father who is coming and going.

The frail, elderly, single male in Chinatown who never married due to miscegenation laws lives alone in a small and dingy room. Early state laws prohibited the marriage of white women and nonwhite men. At the same time, immigration laws excluded admitting Chinese into the United States during the first half of the twentieth century. With no family to care and little government assistance, this elderly person struggles from day to day on small means, is isolated, and dies alone and forgotten.

Asian youth gangs in large cities with overseas-born members who are marginal students or school dropouts have been responsible for intimidating Asian businesses, such as restaurants and grocery stores, for protection money or have committed home invasion robberies, which target Asian families who keep large sums of money, jewelry, and other valuables in their homes. Some Asian families avoid putting assets in the bank for safe keeping and have them available at home for ready access. Brutal force (beatings or murder) is used to obtain "easy money."

Asian American gays and lesbians have experienced stress in coming out to their families. The homosexual life-style is against Asian cultural mores and the importance of perpetuating the next generation of the family and is still a source of shame for many traditional Asian Americans. Sexuality is a private matter. Social-support networks are needed to work with gay and lesbian persons, their families, and the attitude of the Asian American community.

Service Systems

SERVICE DELIVERY

Service delivery involves the detailed arrangements of programs, staffing, facilities, funding, and administrative management that take into account the unique features of the Asian community. Five principles are related to service delivery: (1) location and pragmatic services, (2) staffing, (3) community outreach programs, (4) agency setting, and (5) service linkage.[16] The following discussion explains the meaning of these service delivery areas.

It is important for the *location* of services to be within walking distance of the designated Asian American target group that the agency wishes to serve as a provider. Many Asian service centers are located in areas heavily populated by Asian Americans and are housed in storefronts, churches, ethnic associations, and agencies. Chinatown, Japantown or Little Tokyo, Koreatown, Little Saigon, and other designated areas reach Asian clients who live in the area, depend on public transportation, and are without private cars. Asian clients tend to avoid services labeled mental health center (mental illness is a social stigma) and are drawn toward services that have a *pragmatic* value (child and family education). An agency should select a location and a name that reflect these principles.

Bilingual and bicultural *staffing* should reflect the Asian American client population. In Asian American agencies, there are ethnic and linguistic skilled workers who are Chinese, Filipino, Japanese, Korean, Vietnamese, Hmong, and related groups and who have access to bilingual workers matching other clients. At the same time, a nonminority social worker who is both bilingual and bicultural can be an integral and effective part of the staff. He or she is able to speak the language and is familiar with the culture.

Community outreach programs afford an agency staff exposure and credibility to the key institutions in the Asian American community. It is crucial to conduct educational workshops and set up information booths at ethnic festivals, language schools, ethnic churches, family associations, and related community groups. Planting the seeds of knowledge and service provision reap referrals and follow-up opportunities with community leaders.

The *agency setting* should reflect art and cultural items that communicate a message of sensitivity to the Asian community. A friendly bilingual receptionist, a welcome and relaxed atmosphere, and a plan to respond to walk-in clients creates a conducive environment that sends a positive message to client and community.

Service linkage establishes a working relationship between existing agencies in the Asian community and institutions in the wider social service network. It is important to establish professional ties to key workers in grass-root ethnic organizations, churches, and service professional groups so that Asian clients are able to move easily through the service systems.

ROLE OF THE SOCIAL WORKER

The role of the social worker in the service delivery system to Asian Americans involves the development of culturally specific services to meet the needs of specific Asian American client groups. There has been a debate between culture-common (etic) and culture-specific (emic) service delivery that can be framed around Asian American service agencies.[17] That is, should there be culturally common services that meet the needs of all clients or should there be culturally specific services to address the particular needs of Asian American people? Or, in a narrower perspective, should there be culturally common services for all Asian Americans or should there be single-ethnic agencies to meet the unique problems of a specific Asian American group? The social worker could advocate for a service agency to meet all types of Asian Americans, because it is cost effective and integrates the diversity of the Asian American community. At the same time, the worker might see the need for a service agency that addresses a particular group (e.g., Chinese, Japanese, Korean, or Vietnamese) due to the heavy community demands and ethnic leader support.

Sue, Mak, and Sue point out that the diversity in the Asian American community is becoming even more heterogeneous. There are Asians who have resided in the United States for many generations and those who immigrated here recently and cannot speak English, and their socioeconomic status is quite diverse, from those considered affluent to those far below the poverty line. They conclude: "Coupling these factors with the varying ethnicities (e.g., Asian Indian, Cambodian, Chinese, Filipino, Hmong, Japanese, Korean, Laotian, Samoan, Thai, Tongan, Vietnamese) it does not take much to conclude that any single theory of Asian American identity development would be an oversimplification and inadequate."[18] Discussion around focusing services on all Asian American groups housed under one roof or fostering single Asian group services is an interesting point of communication among social workers who are concerned with service delivery arrangements.

SERVICE GAPS AND NEEDS

Asian American communities in large metropolitan areas, such as Los Angeles, New York City, San Francisco, Seattle, and Sacramento, have nurtured clusters of Asian American social service networks that meet a variety of needs in their locales. Service delivery cooperation and coordination among Asian American service providers are crucial as funding diminishes or shifts toward specialized needs or new immigrant influx, and federal or state programs come on line to meet other needs.

Iglehart and Becerra offer a number of interesting agency linkage principles that are applicable to Asian American service delivery. They point out that ethnic agencies often receive funding for specialized services to ethnic groups from mainstream social services on the county or state levels. This means that Asian American agencies must conduct program evaluations to justify their existence and be accountable to government entities. Moreover, they must be cost effective and target funding wisely. In an interorganizational relationship, they observe that the ethnic agency has access to a particular ethnic population because of its presence in the ethnic community and its relationship with specific target populations.[19] In other words, Asian American agencies must cultivate good lines of communication, cooperation, and collaboration with the local Asian community, in general, and with particular groups if they want to continue serving them. Moreover, changing federal funding requirements develop partnerships between mainstream agencies and ethnic agencies, demand reduction in service duplication, and define special populations in need. Asian American agencies should cultivate working relationships with county, state, and federal officials who have special knowledge about service program trends affecting Asian American populations. There is a nucleus of important Asian Americans in the House of Representatives and the U.S. Senate who are willing to brief Asian service providers about legislative program development and funding that is anticipated or available. These are some of the ways that social workers in the Asian American community can proceed to close gaps and meet needs.

Micro Practice Perspectives

THE PROBLEM-SOLVING APPROACH

Chin reports that Asians who seek assistance expect a generalist helper or advice giver, an authority figure who takes a directive approach and provides concrete social services.[20] Lee asserts: "*A problem-focused, goal-oriented, and symptom-relieving approach* is highly recommended in the beginning phases of treatment. Rather than defining goals in abstract, emotional terms, goals may be best stated in terms of external resolution or symptom reduction."[21] Lee recommends the following treatment strategies with Asian American families:

1. Form a social and cultural connection with the family during the first session.
2. Acknowledge the family's sense of shame.
3. Establish expertise, power, credibility, and authority.
4. Define the problem.
5. Apply a family psycho-educational approach.
6. Build alliance with members with power.
7. Employ reframing techniques.

8. Assume multiple helping roles.
9. Restructure the social support system.
10. Integrate Eastern–Western health approaches.
11. Mobilize the family's cultural strength.
12. Employ the concept of empowerment as a treatment goal.
13. Understand the family's communication style.
14. Acknowledge countertransference and racial stereotypes.[22]*

The problem-solving, task-centered intervention is familiar to social work practitioners. Uba observes that Asian Americans expect the worker to give advice, recommend courses of action, and tell them how to resolve their problems. In a way, the social worker is asked to behave like a physician: to conduct an examination, make a diagnosis, and write out a prescription. This intervention strategy emphasizes a clear, detailed plan and straightforward solutions to concrete and immediate problems.

Problem solving is a rational, step-by-step procedure that requires cognitive mental comprehension and behavioral action. It involves six steps:

1. *Problem identification.* It is important for the Asian client to acknowledge and define the problem he or she is facing. It may be done in an indirect way ("I have a friend who has this problem . . ." or the worker may have to piece together the problem and define the problem cluster or the interrelated set of problems for the client who may be too ashamed to articulate the problem directly.

2. *Problem analysis.* Analyzing a problem involves uncovering its history, placing the events and persons in chronological order, and assessing the needs of the person involved. It is important to find out what has happened in the last four to six weeks (acute crisis) and within the last six months to one year (important past history). Socioenvironmental stressors affecting the Asian client are an integral part of problem analysis.

3. *Solution alternatives.* Based on the identified problem, problem solving moves to examining a range of alternative solutions. The worker should ask the Asian client about possible solutions to the problem, several of which may be realistic and possible. The worker and the client should work on feasible solutions together, although the worker may have to generate some alternatives to initiate discussion. A potential solution is clear, realistic, specific, and attainable in a short period.

4. *Solution prioritization.* Each viable solution should be reviewed in order to find the most effective and realistic way to solve the problem. It is important to engage the client in a discussion of the pros and cons of each potential solution so that the client may ultimately "own" the solution for him- or herself.

---

*The reader is encouraged to read Evelyn Lee's Chapter 1, "Overview: The Assessment and Treatment of Asian American Families," in Evelyn Lee, editor, *Working with Asian Americans: A Guide for Clinicians* (New York: Guilford Publications, 1998).

5. *Solution implementation.* After the client selects a solution, the next step is to implement the solution by constructing a number of task assignments that leads the client from the present situation to the changes needed. A task is a constructive action taken in response to a problem.

6. *Problem-solving evaluation.* It is important to observe and monitor behavioral and situational changes that have occurred in the process of implementing a problem solution. Keeping a diary or journal and logging who was involved, where and when the changes occurred, and what actually happened provide an opportunity for the worker and client to review progress at the next session.[23]

Ecosystems Model Framework

With the problem-solving, task-centered approach as a micro practice intervention for Asian Americans in mind, we turn to the ecosystems model framework, which involves gathering information and exploring and weighing dynamics in problem-solving processing. There are five dimensions of ecosystems problem solving: historical factors, environmental–structural factors, culture, the family, and the individual. Figure 18-1 illustrates the various levels.

HISTORICAL FACTORS

Asian Americans may incorporate a psychohistorical reaction response. That is, the history of oppression impacting this group may cause a psychological survival response from an Asian American client. Uba summarizes research on Asian American personality patterns regarding abasement, affiliation, anxiety, assertiveness, autonomy, conformity, expressiveness, extroversion, formality, locus of control, self-concept, and sex roles, with allowances for intraethnic variation in personality. The social worker should take a brief ethnic history of the client.[24]

During the mid-1800s and early 1900s, Asians of many nationalities came to the United States to pursue economic opportunities, to escape political oppression, and to migrate permanently to the West. Many Chinese and Japanese entered as laborers who expected to return to their homeland and retire in comfort after making their fortune in this country. As the Chinese succeeded in agricultural and mining endeavors, growing anti-Chinese sentiment spread among white gold miners and farmers. Riots, hangings, and evictions of Chinese spread throughout the West Coast. The Chinese were barred from entering the country through the Chinese Exclusion Act of 1882, denied American citizenship and the right to intermarriage, and contained in Chinatowns of major American cities. Similarly, the Japanese suffered limited immigration in the 1907 Gentlemen's Agreement and were denied ownership of land in the 1913 Alien Land Bill. The Immigration Act of 1924 closed the door to Asian immigrants and favored those from European countries. At the early stages of World War II, President Roosevelt issued Executive Order 9066 on February 12, 1942, removing Japanese Americans along the West Coast from their homes and businesses to rural internment camps for the duration of the war. This had a

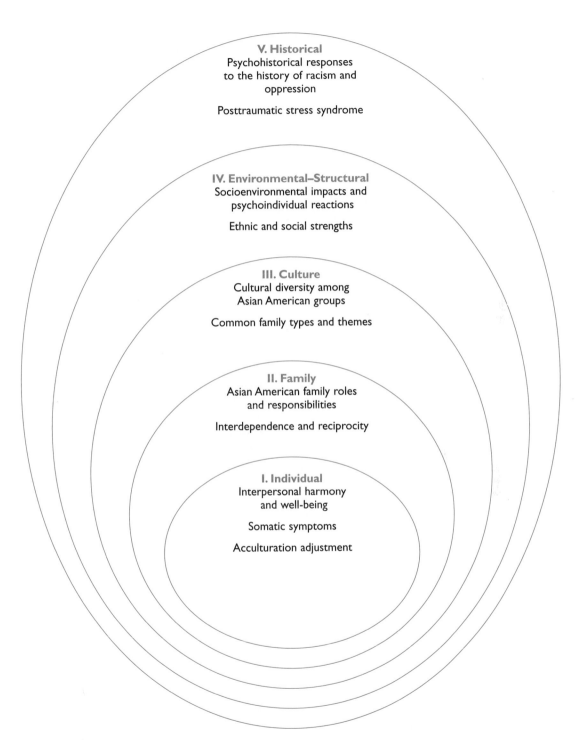

V. Historical
Psychohistorical responses
to the history of racism and
oppression

Posttraumatic stress syndrome

IV. Environmental–Structural
Socioenvironmental impacts and
psychoindividual reactions

Ethnic and social strengths

III. Culture
Cultural diversity among
Asian American groups

Common family types and themes

II. Family
Asian American family roles
and responsibilities

Interdependence and reciprocity

I. Individual
Interpersonal harmony
and well-being

Somatic symptoms

Acculturation adjustment

FIGURE 18-1   **Ecosystems Model for Analysis of Factors Impacting Asian Americans**

major psychohistorical impact on all Japanese Americans, which is still felt today. However, since China was an ally during the war, war refugees from China were allowed into the United States for relief purposes.

The 1965 Immigration Act opened the United States to all countries. Asian immigrants from Hong Kong, Korea, the Philippines, and later from Southeast Asia after the Vietnam War (Vietnamese, Hmong, Mien, Laotians, and Cambodians) streamed into the United States.

Ho reports that the Filipino immigration population in the 1960s consisted of young professional males and females, many of whom experienced difficulties with obtaining U.S. professional licensure for foreign graduates. Moreover, many elderly Filipinos who came as unskilled laborers in the early 1920s are alone and isolated, with health care problems and living in cheap substandard housing. Korean immigration since 1965 has mushroomed due to political problems and the influx of Koreans who have been educated in the United States. The Korean American community is represented in the major West and East Coast metropolitan areas with small businesses (e.g., dry cleaning shops, convenience stores) and Christian churches. Pacific Islanders, particularly residents of American Samoa and Guam, have arrived in the United States because of their U.S. citizenship. Pacific Islanders from Tonga, Fiji, and Hawaii have been influenced by the Church of Jesus Christ of Latter-Day Saints, who believe that these regional groups are part of the lost tribe of Israel. Vietnamese, Cambodians, Hmong, and Mien entered this country as a result of the Vietnam War. Many Southeast Asian refugees have suffered posttraumatic stress in their flight from their homelands through holding camps in Thailand to their entrance into the United States. The first wave of refugees, mainly from Vietnam, consisted of highly professional and educated Vietnamese who integrated into this country, while succeeding waves were unskilled and minimally educated and became welfare dependent. Second-generation American-born Vietnamese have graduated from American universities and adjusted and acculturated in their communities.[25]

Part of taking an ethnic history incorporating psychohistorical factors is becoming aware of acculturative stress (e.g., loss of family members, role reversal, language handicaps) and related mental health needs. The social worker should look for the following signs of posttraumatic stress, even among Asian immigrants who have been in this country for several years, but who may have residual elements. The chief symptoms are the following:

1. Recurrent or intrusive recollections of past traumas
2. Recurrent dreams and nightmares
3. Sad feelings, as if the traumatic events are recurring
4. Social numbness and withdrawal
5. Restricted affect
6. Hyperalertness, hyperactive startled reaction
7. Sleep disorders
8. Guilt
9. Memory impairment
10. Avoidance of activities that might trigger recollection of events
11. Reactivation of symptoms caused by exposure to events similar to the original trauma

The psychohistorical dimension of ecological problem solving is a beginning point of reference for social work practice with Asian Americans, particularly immigrants and refugees.

ENVIRONMENTAL–STRUCTURAL FACTORS

Lum holds that there are external socioenvironmental impacts that cause a psycho-individual reaction of the client. Among these are basic survival needs (language barrier, reasonable housing, adequate employment, transportation, school for children), which trigger such psycho-individual reactions as culture shock (stressful adjustment to unfamiliar culture) and cultural conflict (e.g., loss of face, self-hatred, negative identity, and marginality).[26]

The task is to assess the environmental and social strengths of the client and the environment and to mobilize these potentials. Positive coping skills (e.g., the ability to restore cognitive commonsense problem solving in the client), cultural strengths (e.g., the mobilization of the extended family and ethnic community agencies, such as family associations and the local church), and other positive assessment areas are ways that the social worker can move rapidly to utilize environmental–structural support systems for the Asian American client.

Tran and Wright conducted a study of social support and well-being among Vietnamese refugees, underscoring the need for environmental and structural supports. According to their findings, a contented Vietnamese refugee seems to have stronger social supports, is not afraid to interact with Americans, has a relatively high family income, and is married. "To be happy in America," state Tran and Wright, "a Vietnamese person also needs good English communication ability, a high level of formal education, and a relatively long time of living in this country, and that person also needs to be in the younger age cohort."[27] The social worker should strive toward opening such environmental–structural doors as family and community groups, job training and employment opportunities, English as a second language classes, high school and technical school or college education, and a stable residence in a community.

CULTURE

Culture is the sum total of life patterns passed on from generation to generation within a group of people and includes institutions, language, religious ideals, habits of thinking, artistic expressions, and patterns of social and interpersonal relationships.[28] Asian/Pacific Islander cultures are varied and different from each other. On the Asian continent, the history of China as the Middle Kingdom and the dominant culture of Asia has influenced Japanese, Korean, and Southeast Asian cultural expressions (e.g., art, food, religion, and language), although each group has evolved its own variations. While it is important to acknowledge the uniqueness and difference of each Asian/Pacific Island group, there are common cultural themes that cut across the spectrum of Asian Americans.

Asian American parents who were born in an Asian country and their first-generation, American-born children have gone or are going through culture shock and bicultural conflict. Coming from an Asia country to the United States poses particular challenges to acculturate from a culture of origin to the dominant American society. Asian American families are in the process of integrating a meaningful life by selecting values and traditions from both societies. Often social workers help Asian American families resolve cultural tension and conflict and achieve bicultural integration.

Social workers must also learn cultural boundaries and protocols when working with Asian Americans. Cultural boundaries are lines of demarcations that separate an Asian American individual and/or family unit from the larger society. There may be personal matters that are kept within the family. Mental health problems, socioeconomic issues, and related family areas are withheld from the public. Cultural protocols are exercised in terms of formality, proper subject areas for discussion, and respect. To go beyond these spheres and to reveal personal problems affecting family well-being may require more time and patience on the part of the social worker, who must gain the trust and confidence of the Asian American person or family.

Asian Americans often operate in a cultural duality. They appear assertive, competent, and influential in their business dealings or on the job in the workplace, but they may exercise restraint, respect, and deference to their parents and elderly in the home situation. This is a cultural-integration example of how Asian Americans survive and cope with two related cultures that may require differing sets of expectations.

Maintenance of culture is important for many Asian Americans, who hold that the use of cultural beliefs, customs, celebrations, and rituals are a source of strength, renewal, and identity. Cultural values and practices are a means to cope with present and future life problems.

THE FAMILY

The family is the central value of the Asian American. Traditional Asian American families have specific roles and relationships. The family is patriarchal, with father as the leader of the family, mother as the nurturing caretaker, and sons with more value and status than daughters. The child is expected to obey parents and elders, while the parents are responsible to raise, educate, and support their children. The family's reverence for their ancestors is important for traditional families. Family members are interrelated with each other. The emphasis is on interdependence (caring for one's family and integration into the extended family). The family fosters positive life events and avoids negative shame. Modesty and reciprocity are important family characteristics to the extent of understating and minimizing individual achievement.

Children, particularly sons, are expected to bring honor to the family. The son carries on the family name. Family strengths include valuing respect, interacting with the extended family, and offering support for each other.

Lee identifies five types of Asian American families as follows:

TYPE I: THE TRADITIONAL FAMILY.   All family members are born and raised in Asian countries and have limited contact with the mainstream of American society. Family members hold traditional values, speak their native language, and belong to family associations and other social clubs of people with similar cultural orientations.

TYPE 2: THE CULTURAL CONFLICT FAMILY.　The family consists of parents and grandparents with traditional beliefs and values and children with more western acculturated perspectives, which are in conflict with each other. Issues are related to independence versus interdependence, obedience versus freedom, respect versus self-assertiveness. Arguments occur over dating, marriage, educational goals, and career choice. There is role reversal when the children speak better English and can broker problems for parents who have minimal English skills.

TYPE 3: THE BICULTURAL FAMILY.　Bicultural families consist of acculturated parents who are born in Asia or in America and are acculturated to the industrial western society. Parents are usually well educated and hold professional jobs, are bilingual, and have an egalitarian family structure in which problems are resolved through negotiation between family members. These families live in integrated middle-class neighborhoods and visit and care for grandparents on weekends.

TYPE 4: THE AMERICANIZED FAMILY.　Parents and children are born and raised in the United States, have a reduced understanding and practice of Asian culture, speak primarily English, and operate as individuals in an egalitarian relationship. Friends of the family may include Asians and non-Asians, and the mentality and attitude are more Americanized than Asian.

TYPE 5: THE INTERRACIAL FAMILY.　An Asian American has intermarried with another Asian American (e.g., Chinese with Japanese or Korean with Vietnamese) or has chosen a spouse outside the Asian American groups. There is a wide variety of family responses, from acceptance, resignation, indifference, to rejection, depending on the traditional and nontraditional spectrum of cultural values. Children of interracial families must shape their ethnic identity, ethnic group affiliation, and socialization.[29]

Cultural family types may be a useful vehicle for understanding the common dynamics of varying Asian American families, which transcend viewing separate but differing groups.

Yee, Huang, and Lew have also identified a number of common Asian American family concepts and themes, such as the following:

1. Strong family and social ties that buffer families from the consequences of life crises.
2. Family problem-solving skills, culturally shaped emotional responses and communication patterns.
3. Healthy identities with life and social skills to deal with life-span development challenges.
4. Interdependence, reciprocity, and collectivism in family patterns.
5. Cultural traditions that offer a prescription for living and a code of behavior.

6. A sense of autonomy and competence within close family relationships.
7. The importance of repaying parents for their sacrifices through high educational achievement and occupational aspirations.
8. A system of hierarchical roles based on age, birth position, and gender.
9. Marriage as the continuation of the husband's family line.
10. Reciprocity between generations based on emotional, financial, and child-care support exchanges.
11. Caring for elderly relatives as the family's responsibility.[30]

THE INDIVIDUAL

The biopsychosocial dimensions of the Asian American client involve an examination of biological, psychological, and social aspects. From a biological health perspective, the Asian American concept of interpersonal harmony advocates minimizing conflict and maximizing getting along with each other. Health and healthy relationships in balance are interrelated to each other. Thinking "good thoughts" is more important than dwelling on sickness, mental illness, or death. The latter is a self-fulfilling prophecy for misfortune, whereas the former leads to good fortune. Somatic symptoms or the psychophysiological interaction between mind and body are important to uncover if an Asian American client has internalized stress and manifests physical problems. Often Asian Americans are taught to suppress negative feelings and reactions, rather than openly ventilate them. Mental health problems tend to be expressed as psychosomatic complaints (e.g., headaches, backaches, digestive troubles, and peptic ulcers). This goes back to maintaining harmony and cultivating a pleasant disposition. Physical problems are culturally acceptable expressions, but mental health problems are taboo areas that evoke a social stigma for the family in the eyes of the local Asian community. If there are biological health problems, the social worker should work with the client's physician to clear up somatic symptoms.

From a psychological perspective, it is important to assess the relation between the person's mental state and his or her behavioral interaction with significant others in the cultural community and the society as a whole. The level of motivation for change, as well as the resistance or unwillingness to cooperate or participate in the process of growth, are crucial to uncover from a psychological assessment. Stressing positive change and acknowledging feelings of anger and disgrace change the psychological atmosphere. Prolonged silence may be part of the psychological mix. Asian Americans may remain silent as a sign of respect to the authority of the worker or as a culturally distinct way of relating and responding in an indirect manner. Significant others investigate the relationship of self and others, particularly family, peers, and other persons who are meaningfully related. The social worker needs to know the following:

1. Does the Asian client come from a nuclear, single-parent, blended, or extended family?
2. Are the parents foreign-born or American-born?

3. Does the family have a clear sense of parental authority and interdependence, a sense of democratic autonomy, or a mix of both?
4. Are the parents recent immigrants or refugees who are acculturating well or poorly to a new environment?
5. Are there differing value systems between the parents from their country of origin and their Americanized children?
6. Does the mother function as a go-between for an authoritative distant father and their children?

The answers to these questions may affect the psychological state of the Asian American client.

The social assessment of the Asian individual focuses on how the person interacts with group and community living. Lum identifies four aspects of social assessment:[31] (1) immigration history or the family's transition from the culture of origin to American society; (2) acculturation or the adjustment, change, and maintenance of culture in the family; (3) school adjustment or the academic and social experiences of children in their primary institution; and (4) employment or the primary work setting critical for adult self-esteem and respect in the ethnic community.

MICRO CASE EXAMPLE

Annie, a 15-year-old teenager from Hong Kong, was sent to relatives in Monterey Park, California, by her parents who have an import–export business and travel throughout Asia and the United States. Annie is the oldest of four siblings and has misgivings about leaving her friends in school behind. Her parents want her to graduate from an American high school and establish citizenship and residency so that she can be admitted to a University of California school. Her relatives in California consist of an uncle and his wife who are in their early thirties, without children, and married for five years.

Annie has had difficulties for several months adjusting to her new environment (living situation, school, peer relations) after arriving and entering school. She has cut classes, been in arguments with her uncle and his wife, and has made friends with some overseas-born Asians at school. She is a *parachute kid* (literally dropped into an American community from an Asian country of origin) who is separated from her primary nuclear family and is going through her teen-age identity crisis with her surrogate parents, an uncle and aunt.

After repeated attempts by Uncle Chuck and Auntie Phyllis to resolve Annie's problems, they turn to the Asian American/Pacific Islander Counseling Center in Los Angeles for help. The social worker, David Lee of Chinese descent and Cantonese/English speaking, is assigned the case and has worked at the Asian Youth Center.

After becoming acquainted with the background and home situation of Annie and her uncle and aunt, the social worker obtains the following ecosystems dimensional information:

HISTORICAL FACTORS   Annie is reacting to her particular psychohistorical situation. It is common among upper-middle-class and wealthy families in Hong Kong and other parts of metropolitan Asian countries to send their children abroad for schooling. While Annie's friends remain in Hong Kong, the social worker finds out from Annie and her relatives that teen-age children have been sent to various large American cities, Canada, and England where there are relatives and friends of families. At the same time, Annie reveals that many of the American-born Asians have made fun of her since she is a FOB (fresh off the boat) or foreign-born Asian. This type of intragroup racism has isolated Annie from her school peer group and has caused her to gravitate toward some Asians who are marginal students. She also feels rejected by her parents and has flashbacks of being sent away by her parents, who have no time for her because of their business and social commitments.

ENVIRONMENTAL/STRUCTURAL FACTORS Annie's present environment involves an uncle and an auntie who are trying to help her make a transitional adjustment to a new environment (Monterey Park, a predominately Asian American affluent suburb near east Los Angeles); a new school, which is academically demanding with few friends; and a new set of surrogate parents, who have tried to be flexible but firm with her. Her immediate reactions have been mixed: cutting classes and hanging out with other Asian high schoolers who are not interested in learning; testing her limits with her uncle and auntie, who previously allowed her freedom and space, but have misgivings about how to deal with Annie; and expressing her unhappiness about being away from her family and friends in Hong Kong, whom she dearly misses.

Yet Annie has some ethnic and social strengths. In Hong Kong she was a happy, serious, and bright student in her grade school. She was friendly and able to garner a variety of neighborhood and school mates. Yet in Monterey Park the opposite is true, because many of the Asian students are American born, speak English without an accent, and are Americanized in their behavior.

CULTURE Annie is the product of a traditional Asian family who is a part of the Hong Kong business and social circles. Her parents could be termed "Asian jet setters"; they travel to nearby countries on business, pleasure, and shopping trips and leave their children in the care of nannies and relatives. Annie's Asian peers in California are either bicultural Asians who came from Hong Kong, Taiwan, and Malaysia many years ago or are American-born and Americanized to the point of speaking English without a trace of an Asian foreign accent and/or being unable to speak a Chinese dialect. Often these students are student body government leaders and model minorities, who academically compete well with their white counterparts and have Asian and non-Asian friends. Annie is painfully aware of the contrast and how she does not fit in with Asian American teen-agers in terms of dress, makeup, language, conversational topics, and circle of friends.

FAMILY FACTORS Annie's parents in Hong Kong have a role responsibility to be fulfilled on behalf of their daughter. Her father and mother need to come for a visit and to be aware of Annie's feelings and situation. Annie's mother could ease the transition by staying with her for an indefinite period until an adjustment has been made. A sense of interdependence and reciprocity should be established between parents and daughter. That is, Annie will try to make an adjustment to her new situation, and Annie's father and mother will each take turns staying with her in Monterey Park until everyone involved feels that there is progress in this transition. Otherwise, the family should agree that Annie may be happier and can thrive if she returns to her home, school, and friends in Hong Kong.

INDIVIDUAL FACTORS Annie is painfully aware that she is unhappy, lonely, and somewhat depressed and that her sense of interpersonal harmony and well-being has been impaired by this move to California. Rather than dealing with her stress, she internalizes her feelings and keeps her personal thoughts to herself. At times the stress has been exhibited with such somatic symptoms as periodic outbreaks of acne, stomach-aches, and headaches. When she is anxious or worried, Annie catches herself picking her lips, a nervous gesture. There are hole marks and raw patches in her lower lip as a result. Annie is an example of the acculturation adjustment for a growing number of teen-age Asians from various countries of Asia who have been called parachute kids because they are dropped off the plane by their parents. As they parachute to various parts of the United States, their landing is at times rough and unwelcomed. They must fend for themselves alone or with the help of relatives and friends of their families of origin who are forced to become surrogate parents. One wonders whether the family disruption and resulting instability and crisis are worth the effort of fulfilling the American dream, without the necessary parental support that is necessary for growing up from childhood through adolescence to young adulthood.

As you review the ecological problem-solving approach, the ecological systems model, and the unique case study of Annie, brainstorm the various intervention strategies that you would employ as the social worker in this situation.

Macro Practice Perspectives

Macro practice with Asian Americans involves large regional and institutional change that results in social justice, new institutional structures, and the distribution of wealth and resources to meet the problems of this particular target group. Social policy, planning, and administration are macro intervention tools to affect social change in problem areas.

Of all the various Asian American groups in need, Asian refugees and immigrants have the greatest acculturation adjustment and socioeconomic survival needs. High-risk refugees face problems of underemployment, breakdowns in the family network, and changing family roles. Moreover, with the implementation of welfare reform (the 1996 Personal Responsibility and Work Opportunity Reconciliation Act), legal immigrants have partially lost medical and food stamp benefits. The Clinton administration proposes a $1.3 billion five-year restoration program that will benefit 132,000 people, particularly Latino and Asian immigrants. So far, the Balanced Budget Act of 1997 restored Supplemental Security Income for disabled persons and Medicaid benefits to 420,000 legal immigrants who were in the country before welfare legislation was enacted on August 22, 1996. The Agricultural Research Act of 1998 provided food stamps for 225,000 legal immigrant children, senior citizens, and the disabled who came to the United States before the new welfare law.[32] Asian American refugees and immigrants in the welfare system need to be trained in such jobs as gardeners, restaurant cooks, bakers, child-care workers, and other hands-on positions. These Asians are hard working and dependable if they are given the opportunities of employment.

On the local level, social policy, planning, and administration are tools to organize the indigenous Asian American community to meet the specific needs of Asian elderly, unemployed, new arrivals, and other target groups in need. Rather than waiting for federal and state assistance, it is more effective to identify Asian American leaders who have the social awareness and financial knowledge and skills to plan and implement local projects that benefit the Asian American community. An example of this was accomplished in Northern California.

In twenty-five years as an Asian American faculty member of California State University, Sacramento Division of Social Work, the author has witnessed a remarkable alliance between Asian American social work students, working professionals, and county officials. During the early 1970s, a nucleus of graduate Asian American social work students and faculty developed a National Institute of Mental Health (NIMH) training grant that offered field stipends and placed students in various Asian American field settings among the Japanese and Filipino elderly, downtown refugees and immigrants, and Asian residents of low-income public housing. As a result of these field placements and Asian American social work courses, MSW (Master of Social Work) Asian American graduates founded a variety of Asian American social service centers as follows:

HEALTH FOR ALL   June Otow of Japanese descent researched the needs of Asian and other ethnic groups for adult day health care and started a downtown center that included nursing services, rehabilitation, and day-care programs for the disabled and a health screening program for preschool children.

ASIAN LIAISON WORKER   Hach Yasumura of Japanese descent became the Asian liaison worker for Sacramento County Department of Social Services upon his graduation. His task was to establish a planning and program exchange network among the various Asian groups and grass-roots agencies in the county and to coordinate existing and future services to the local Asian community.

ASIAN RESOURCE CENTER   May Lee of Chinese descent began a job training and employment service for Asian Americans and focused on the growing Asian immigrant and refugee populations who need English as a second language training, job testing and training, and employment placement in the greater Sacramento area. Periodic job fairs for adults and career planning workshops for Asian high school youth have resulted in strengthening the economic stability of the Asian American community.

ASIAN/PACIFIC COUNSELING CENTER   Harriet Taniguchi of Japanese descent was instrumental in founding, with a group of Asian mental health and health care professionals, an Asian multilingual counseling program with staff representing major Asian ethnic groups. Funding came from the United Way, the minority mental health advisory board that oversees Sacramento County mental health funding, and various short-term state and federal grants, which have been shaped to meet the medical problems of Asians.

SOUTHEAST ASIAN ASSISTANCE CENTER   Ninh Van Nguyen, a social work graduate and ordained Presbyterian minister of Vietnamese descent, started the Southeast Asian Assistance Center, which focused exclusively on the employment and family needs of Vietnamese, Hmong, Cambodian, Mien, and Thai refugees. The emphasis is on responding to the practical, everyday living needs of these populations.

ASIAN AMERICAN NURSING HOME   Under the leadership of the Asian Community Center, led particularly by Japanese and Chinese prominent professionals in Sacramento, funds were raised through community campaign drives, large-scale bingo, and federal grants for the construction and operation of a ninety-bed Asian nursing home that serves Asian food and promotes Asian family care involvement for bed-ridden elderly clients. A former social work graduate student, Calvin Hara of Japanese descent, recently became the administrator of the nursing home. Graduate Asian American social work students participated in a county-wide research assessment project to pinpoint the needs of the Asian elderly.

The Sacramento model for Asian American community planning brings together social work students who conduct research, participate in Asian field placements, and later assume agency roles in the Asian social service community; Asian American social work faculty, who foster an interest in academic and research projects that benefit the local Asian needs; and Asian community leaders, who are responsive to the changing social trends of the Asian groups in need. There is a unique town and gown arrangement that has borne the fruit of Asian American social service agencies that are affecting the lives and well-being of Asian clients today. On the drawing boards for the Sacramento Vietnamese community are two research proposals for a Vietnamese elderly adult day health care center, written by Vanessa Nguyen, and a Vietnamese senior center patterned after the On Lok program in San Francisco, by Lena Chon.

Asian American social workers in heavy populated Asian metropolitan areas of the United States may wish to adopt this cooperative macro practice model, which involves social work students, faculty, and community leaders in a creative partnership.

Emerging Issues

Asian Americans are an 11 million member minority group in the United States. There are heavily populations in the western United States in Los Angeles–Long Beach, San Francisco, Honolulu, and Seattle; on the East Coast, there are moderate populations in New York City, Boston, and Washington, D.C.; and they are modestly represented in the American heartland (Chicago and Houston). As indicated in this chapter, Asian Americans have been the subject of racism and racial stereotypes and acts of racial violence and hate crimes, and they continue to cope with this stress.

At the beginning of the twenty-first century, Asian Americans are still aware of their weak influence on the political scene in the United States. With few Asian American politicians on the state and national levels, there is no political or legislative force to advocate for the rights of this group. There have been no cabinet-level appointments of Asian Americans at the presidential level in the history of the

United States. Asian Americans were the focus of investigation in the 1997 Senate and House investigation on presidential campaign reform and abuse as a result of the 1996 Clinton versus Dole election. The selection of a Chinese American, Bill Lee, as the civil rights head of the Department of Justice in 1998 was heavily contested by the Republican Congress and sent a message about conservative politics and Asian Americans. Chinese dissenters who were expelled from the People's Republic of China and came to the United States for political refuge were ignored in 1998 and 1999 by the Clinton administration and U.S. State Department officials for fear that their counsel may offend U.S. and China relations.

Asian Americans need to organize themselves in an effective way on a par with the Japanese American Citizenship League, which has chapters in major cities where there is a Japanese American constituency and is a lobbying force at the national level in Washington, D.C. As the population of Asian Americans exceed the 11 million mark, Asian Americans will be heard as a formative political, financial, technological, and scientific force to shape and influence the American political, medical, and engineering scene. An Asian American governor, Gary Locke, was elected in the state of Washington in 1998, which is a major breakthrough. However, this offers a small glimmer of hope in a realm of dominant forces that intentionally exclude the presence of Asian Americans as full partners in promise of the American dream.

Concluding Comment

Asian Americans/Pacific Islanders are diverse groups of ethnic persons who were born in or whose parents came from the continent of Asia and the Pacific areas. Lee offers a sensible appraisal of Asian Americans in the United States when he reports that, with the dawn of the twenty-first century, Asian Americans undoubtedly will play an increasingly important and complex role in American society. With the growth and expansion of Asia's economy, some Asian Americans are intermediaries between the two continents, whereas others are continuing the fight for freedom and democracy in their homelands. Lee observes:

> Some are achieving high office as governors of states or managers in corporations, whereas others are barely surviving on poverty wages or hiding from the Immigration and Naturalization Service. All are grappling with the age-old issues of place and identity that inhabit the boundaries between disparate cultures. Coming to understand the forces and conditions that have created such diversity requires far-reaching and diligent efforts. The task will continue to challenge scholars in the years ahead.[33]

The paradoxes of economic influence versus political underrepresentation, political dissent versus democratic exile, and places of leadership versus illegal immigration fuel the fires of trying to figure out the place of Asian Americans in the United States. With such a disparity of diversity among Asians and such nonrecognition by the dominant political forces of America, it will be interesting to see how Asian Americans steer their course in human history.

In the year 2000, Asian Americans/Pacific Islanders are still aware of their weak influence on the political scene in the United States. However, as their population exceeds 11 million by the year 2000, this group will be heard as a formative political and financial force in shaping and influencing the American political scene. At the same time, hard work, education, the drive for achievement, thriftiness, and helping each other have been ethnic-group qualities that have caused this group to cope with racism, prejudice, and discrimination in spite of societal barriers.

KEY WORDS AND CONCEPTS

Asian American/Pacific Islander	Parachute kid
Asian husband astronaut	Posttraumatic stress syndrome
Chinese Exclusion Act of 1882	Psychohistorical responses

SUGGESTED READINGS

Ho, Man Keung. *Family Therapy with Ethnic Minorities*. Newbury Park, CA: Sage Publications, 1987.

Lee, Evelyn, ed. *Working with Asian Americans: A Guide for Clinicians*. New York: Guilford Press, 1997.

Lee, Lee C., and Zane, Nolan W. S., eds. *Handbook of Asian American Psychology*. Thousand Oaks, CA: Sage Publications, 1998.

Lum, Doman. *Culturally Competent Practice: A Framework for Growth and Action*. Pacific Grove, CA: Brooks/Cole Publishing Company, 1999.

Lum, Doman. *Social Work Practice & People of Color*. Belmont, CA: Brooks/Cole Wadsworth/Thomson Learning, 2000.

Sue, Derald W., and Sue, David. *Counseling the Culturally Different: Theory and Practice*. New York: John Wiley & Sons, 1999.

Uba, Laura. *Asian Americans: Personality Patterns, Identity, and Mental Health*. New York: Guilford Press, 1994.

ENDNOTES

1. C. Russell, *Racial and Ethnic Diversity: Asians, Blacks, Hispanic, Native Americans, and Whites* (Ithaca, NY: New Strategist Publications, 1998).
2. Russell, p. 7.
3. Bureau of the Census, *Statistical Abstract of the United States 1998: The National Data Book*. No. 30 Resident Population by Region, Race, and Hispanic Origin: 1990 (Washington, DC: U.S. Department of Commerce, Economics and Statistics Administration, 1998), p. 31.
4. Russell, p. 65.
5. R. Homma-True, "Asian American Women," in E. Lee, ed., *Working with Asian Americans: A Guide for Clinicians* (New York: Guilford Press, 1997), pp. 420–427.
6. M. P. P. Root, "Women," in L. C. Lee and N. W. S. Zane, eds., *Handbook of Asian American Psychology* (Thousand Oaks, CA: Sage Publications, 1998), pp. 211–231.

7. B. Masaki and L. Wong, "Domestic Violence in the Asian Community," in E. Lee, ed., *Working with Asian Americans: A Guide for Clinicians* (New York: Guilford Press, 1997), pp. 439–451.

8. Russell, p. 37.

9. F. T. L. Leong, "Career Development and Vocational Behaviors," in L. C. Lee and N. W. S. Zane, eds., *Handbook of Asian American Psychology* (Thousand Oaks, CA: Sage Publications, 1998), pp. 359–398.

10. Russell, pp. 16, 27, 34.

11. E. Lee, "Overview: The Assessment and Treatment of Asian American Families," in E. Lee, ed., *Working with Asian Americans: A Guide for Clinicians* (New York: Guilford Press, 1997), pp. 3–36.

12. L. C. Lee, "An Overview," in L. C. Lee and N. W. S. Zane, eds., *Handbook of Asian American Psychology* (Thousand Oaks, CA: Sage Publications, 1998), p. 16.

13. C. M. Loo, *Chinese America: Mental Health and Quality of Life in the Inner City* (Thousand Oaks, CA: Sage Publications, 1998).

14. Loo, xxii.

15. Loo, xxviii.

16. D. Lum, *Social Work Practice & People of Color: A Process Stage Approach* (Belmont, CA: Wadsworth Publishing Company, 2000).

17. D. Lum and C. Guzzetta, "Should Programs and Service Delivery Systems be Culture-Specific in their Design?," in D. de Anda, ed., *Controversial Issues in Multiculturalism* (Boston: Allyn and Bacon, 1997), pp. 54–70.

18. D. Sue, W. S. Mak, and D. W. Sue, "Ethnic Identity," in L. C. Lee and N. W. S. Zane, eds., *Handbook of Asian American Psychology* (Thousand Oaks, CA: Sage Publications, 1998), p. 312.

19. A. P. Iglehart and R. M. Becerra, *Social Services and the Ethnic Community* (Boston: Allyn and Bacon, 1995).

20. J. L. Chin, "Toward a Psychology of Difference: Psychotherapy for a Culturally Diverse Population," in J. L. Chin, V. De La Cancela, and Y. M. Jenkins, eds., *Diversity in Psychotherapy: The Politics of Race, Ethnicity, and Gender* (Westport, CT: Praeger, 1993), pp. 69–91.

21. E. Lee, pp. 26–27.

22. E. Lee, pp. 28–33.

23. L. Uba, *Asian Americans: Personality Patterns, Identity, and Mental Health* (New York: Guilford Press, 1994).

24. Uba, pp. 61–87.

25. M. K. Ho, "Social Work Practice with Asian Americans," in A. Morales and B. W. Sheafor, eds., *Social Work: A Profession of Many Faces,* 8th ed. (Boston: Allyn and Bacon, 1998), pp. 465–483.

26. Lum, Chapter 8.

27. T. V. Tran and R. Wright, Jr., "Social Support and Subjective Well-Being among Vietnamese Refugees," *Social Service Review* 60 (1986): 449–459.

28. J. L. Hodge, D. K. Struckmann, and L. D. Trost, *Cultural Bases of Racism and Group Oppression* (Berkeley, CA: Two Riders Press, 1975).

29. E. Lee, pp. 11–13.

30. B. W. K. Yee, L. N. Huang, and A. Lew, "Families: Life-Span Socialization in a Cultural Context," in L. C. Lee and N. W. S. Zane, eds., *Handbook of Asian American Psychology* (Thousand Oaks, CA: Sage Publications, 1998), pp. 83–135.

31. Lum, Chapter 8.

32. M. Janofsky, "Some Legal Immigrant Benefits May Return," *Sacramento Bee,* January 25, 1999, A4.

33. L. C. Lee, pp. 18, 19.

CHAPTER 19

Social Work Practice with American Indians and Alaskan Natives

E. Daniel Edwards and Margie Egbert Edwards

Prefatory Comment

Drs. E. Daniel Edwards, Professor of Social Work and Director of American Indian Studies, University of Utah, and Margie Egbert Edwards, Professor Emeritus, School of Social Work, University of Utah, present a very thoughtful, sensitive, and careful analysis of the current status of the human condition of American Indians and Alaskan Natives in the United States. This timely, original scholarly work written specifically for this volume, represents the end of a lengthy search of many years attempting to identify American Indian and Alaskan Native social work scholars. These authors' academic efforts are seasoned with practice experience as they recommend that intervention strategies need to be operationalized within the context of numerous cultural beliefs, customs, and values among American Indians and Alaskan Natives. They caution that these techniques may differ depending on the specific tribal group being worked with and the location of that intervention, whether an urban or a rural reservation. Each Native American is unique, as is each of the 542 tribal groups.

Across the United States, Native American Indians* are reclaiming their heritage. Indian tribes are re-instructing youth and adults in their native languages. Spiritual ceremonies are held to attain and retain a *balance* with nature that is so important to spiritual and temporal well-being. Cultural activities are promoted in social gatherings. Powwows are opportunities to enjoy music, dance, and social traditions, while sobriety powwows celebrate and reinforce the sobriety of Native Americans. Education is available in tribal-owned and operated schools, as is instruction in tribal arts, their history, and cultural significance. Emphasis on tribal self-determination

---

*The terms "Native American" and "American Indian/Alaska Native" are used interchangeably to refer to the first native people of this country and their descendants.

and self-governance is furthering the unique development of communities and tribal groups. Increased mobility is resulting in larger populations of Native Americans in urban areas. Spiritual ceremonies most often held in reservation settings are becoming more available in urban settings, such as "rites of passage," "sweats," and healing ceremonies. In creative and respectful ways, Native Americans are reinforcing their traditional teachings and positively enhancing their identification with tribal and Native American values, beliefs, and traditions.

Current Demographics

According to the 1990 United States Census, the Native American population now numbers approximately 2 million people—less than 1 percent of the total United States population. These figures represent a 38 percent increase from the 1,400,000 population reported in 1980. Historically, the 1890 Census reported an American Indian population of 148,000. By 1950, Census figures were 357,000. Within the past forty years the population of American Indians, Eskimos, and Aleuts has increased more than five times.[1]

Of these 2 million people, approximately two-thirds (1,220,126) reside in off-reservation areas throughout the United States. Only 739,108 Native Americans (38%) reside in tribally-governed areas, including 314 reservations, trust lands, tribal jurisdiction, and tribal-designated statistical areas, and Alaskan Native villages.[2]

The 1990 U.S. Census included tribal population figures for 542 tribes throughout the United States, its regions, divisions, and states. Two-thirds (366) of these tribes reported populations of less than 1,000 persons. The five largest tribes with their population figures include the following: (1) Cherokee, 308,132; (2) Navajo, 219,198; (3) Chippewa, 103,826; (4) Sioux, 103,255; and (5) Choctaw, 82,199.[3] Four states have American Indian populations over 100,000. These include: (1) Oklahoma, 252,000; (2) California, 243,000; (3) Arizona, 204,000; and (4) New Mexico, 134,000.[4] The Navajo Reservation has, by far, the largest American Indian population with 143,405 people residing within their reservation and trust lands in Arizona, New Mexico, and Utah.[5]

The impressive increase in population among Native Americans has been influenced by several factors. Significant strides have been made in provision of prenatal and maternal health care to American Indian people. Infant mortality rates have dropped from twice the nonwhite rates in 1955 to slightly less than the white rate in 1985.[6] In addition, there are larger numbers of people who are "part" American Indian reporting this information on Census surveys. Improved Census procedures on reservations have resulted in more accurate population figures. Even with improved reporting procedures, there continue to be concerns that the Native American population is underrepresented in Census surveys.

SOCIOECONOMIC ISSUES

Family is an important unifying concept for American Indian people. "Nuclear" and "extended family" figure prominently in the well-being of Native American people, as do "clan" and "tribal" families. When all these "families" are intact, Native

American people maintain a connectedness, individually and collectively, to their tribal heritage and identity. When there are problems within these systems, individuals and subgroups are adversely affected.

American Indian families tend to be larger than all other American families.[7] Hodgkinson reported that the birth rate per 1,000 population in 1986 was highest among American Indians (27.5), as compared with the total nonwhite population (21.4) and the total United States (15.7).[8]

Almost one-third (31%) of all Native Americans had incomes below the poverty level, according to 1990 Census data,[9] as compared with a national poverty rate of 13 percent.[10] In 1990 the median family income of American Indians was $21,750 compared with $35,225 for the total population.[11] In 1989, 31 percent of American Indians were living below the poverty level, compared with a national poverty level of 13 percent. Approximately 27 percent of American Indian families were maintained by single females sixteen years of age and over, compared with 17 percent of the national population.[12]

EDUCATION

Native Americans have well-defined cultural values that encourage attainment of knowledge and wisdom. The judicious use of knowledge has sustained American Indian people in their quest to live harmoniously with nature. Strong cultural values support attainment of education within both non-Indian and Native settings. There is, however, considerable need for exerted efforts to improve American Indian graduation rates from both high school and higher education settings. According to the 1990 U.S. Census, only 65 percent of American Indians, Eskimos, and Aleuts, twenty-five years of age and older have attained high school graduation or higher in our educational systems. Again, for this group, only 9 percent have attained a bachelor's degree or higher.[13] The American Indian dropout rate is the highest of any minority group. In 1988 the American Indian dropout rate was 35.5 percent, compared with a 1988 United States dropout rate of 28.8 percent.[14] While American Indian SAT scores increased steadily during the 1980s to 828; they dropped to 812 in 1989. Factors that tend to interfere with educational attainment of American Indian students include: (1) inadequate budgets for Bureau of Indian Affairs (BIA) and tribal-contracted schools; (2) large numbers of young people who repeat at least one grade; (3) low test scores in history, math, reading, and science; (4) inconsistent attendance; (5) higher student expectations that they will not finish high school; (6) lower student expectations that they will attend college; (7) language problems; (8) low income; and (9) siblings who have dropped out of school.[15]

HEALTH AND MENTAL HEALTH ISSUES

Family issues impact the health and mental health status of Native American people. Culturally, when Indians, individually and collectively, adhere to traditional cultural beliefs, they maintain a "balance" with nature, and achieve wellness—mentally, physically, and spiritually. These beliefs and behaviors promote positive interrelatedness with people, the environment, and all living things. When individuals or systems are "out of balance," ceremonies and "family" actions are necessary to restore this "balance."

Indian Health Service (IHS) is responsible for providing federal health services to American Indians and Alaskan Natives. IHS provides a broad range of preventive, corrective, rehabilitative, and environmental services.[16]

Some areas in which significant progress has been made on behalf of the health status of American Indian people include the following: (1) the infant mortality rate decreased 85 percent from 1954 to 1988; (2) the maternal death rate decreased 91 percent from 1957 to 1988; and (3) Native American life expectancy rates have improved considerably and now are quite comparable to those of the Anglo-American population.

According to IHS publications, the leading causes of death for American Indian men include diseases of the heart, followed by accidents. The two leading causes of death for women are diseases of the heart and malignant neoplasms. Leading causes of death for infants are Sudden Infant Death Syndrome (SIDS) and congenital anomalies; for children one to fourteen years of age, accidents; for young people ages fifteen to twenty-four, accidents, followed by suicide and homicide; and for adults ages twenty-five to forty-four, accidents, followed by chronic liver disease and cirrhosis, homicide, suicide, diseases of the heart, and malignant neoplasms.

In 1988 IHS reported significantly higher mortality rates for Native Americans than the U.S. population related to alcoholism, tuberculosis, diabetes mellitus, accidents, homicide, pneumonia/influenza, and suicide.[17]

Alcoholism among American Indians has been observed to have reached epidemic proportions and has been described as the number one health problem in these cultural groups.[18] According to IHS, the 1988 age-adjusted alcoholism death rate for American Indians and Alaska Natives was at its highest level since 1981, with 33.9 deaths per 100,000 population or 5.4 times the U.S. "all races" rate of 6.3.[19] Recent data indicate that alcohol abuse is a contributing factor in four of the ten leading causes of death for Native Americans including accidents, chronic liver disease and cirrhosis, homicide, and suicide.[20] An estimated 75 percent of all traumatic deaths and suicides among Native Americans are alcohol-related.[21] Other statistics from the National Clearinghouse on Alcoholism Information indicate that "almost 100 percent of all crimes for which an Indian is incarcerated were committed under the influence of alcohol, while 90 percent of homicides and 80 percent of suicides were alcohol-related, as were 75 percent of all fatal accidents. Seventy percent of all treatment services from the IHS are alcohol-related."[22]

Another area of concern to Native American people is Fetal Alcohol Syndrome, the number one preventable birth defect in our country. This problem is adversely affecting many American Indian children and their families. Aggressive education, outreach, and community prevention programs are recommended to help eradicate the disastrous effects of this crippling birth defect.

NATIVE AMERICAN YOUTH

The health of Native American youth has been a cause of concern to American Indian people over the past several years. A recent study of 14,000 American Indian and Alaskan Native adolescents revealed important data.[23] Of concern to Native American people are the following research findings: (1) less than half of these young people lived with two parents; (2) less than half of the youth received preventive health services in the past two years; (3) 65 percent reported being bored; (4) approximately two-thirds of high school seniors reported they have had sexual intercourse; and (5) 29 percent of males and 44 percent of females use no contraceptive devices. Other findings of concern to the researchers included the early experimentation and extent to which youth use alcohol; the extent to which youth worry about economics and domestic abuse; and the extent to which heavy use of substances is linked to every risk behavior described in the report.

Positive findings, however, are also reported from these youth. Approximately 80 percent of the youth reported being happy, not depressed, in good health, and believe that "family" care about them "a great deal."

Several recommendations were offered by the researchers. These included (1) recruiting teenagers and adults to play active roles as peer leaders and supportive role models; (2) strengthening Native American families; and (3) developing community-wide, culturally-grounded prevention and intervention programs.[24]

Ecosystems Framework

Social work practice requires assessment of the interaction between clients and their environments. The social worker will often look to peer and family relationships as important components in an individual's sphere of functioning. Particularly important to Native Americans are the cultural variables that embody all aspects of living. The broader environment also contributes to the individual's adjustment and availability of resources important to personal well-being. Neighborhoods, educational systems, social and health services, employment opportunities, recreational and leisure resources—all may be viewed differently and approached selectively depending on individual preferences, previous experience, and availability of choices. The environmental–structural factors that influence well-being may be quite different for Native Americans living in reservation/rural areas as compared with those in urban/metropolitan areas. Individual personality characteristics such as assertiveness and language skills may positively or negatively impact a person's access to these resources, as might material factors such as availability of reliable transportation, appropriate wearing apparel, and task-related skills. The historical experiences of Native Americans are also varied and complex. Many older Native Americans have survived a disparaging and contradictory set of social policies implemented to govern their welfare—with little opportunity for input from American Indian people themselves.

HISTORICAL INFLUENCES

Columbus's "discovery" of the Americas subjected American Indians to the control of the dominant groups that settled within their homelands. European settlers enacted governmental systems based on those of their own homelands. Policies were often established for the benefit of their "mother" countries. The emancipation of the Colonies from England began a series of federal legislative actions that have continued today. Initially American Indians were governed by the War Department. Later, the responsibilities were transferred to the Bureau of Indian Affairs (BIA) within the Department of the Interior.

Historically, numerous federal policies have influenced the population, lifestyles, geographical locations, language usage, education, and general well-being of American Indians. Detailed descriptions of American Indian and non-Indian relations in this country are covered in considerable detail in Berry's book, *Race and Ethnic Relations.*[25] Five major governmental policies have been identified by Berry as being most influential. They are (1) extermination; (2) expulsion; (3) exclusion (reservations); (4) assimilation; and (5) self-determination.

EXTERMINATION.   Historically, extermination was used as a method of handling conflicts between races. Disease, war, alcohol, and slavery are examples of extermination methods practiced against American Indians. Disease was one of the most effective extermination practices as American Indians were particularly vulnerable to smallpox, measles, and chicken pox. The most prevalent reason for the extermination of American Indians was the unrelenting desire for Indian land and its resources. Because American Indians did not utilize deeds and written agreements, there were no records of ownership, and the land was easily usurped by non-Indians.

EXPULSION.   As the nation's westward movements expanded, American Indians were forced to leave their homelands for more remote western areas. Many non-Indians viewed expulsion as a more humane way of resolving the "American Indian problem" and advocated expulsion in lieu of extermination.

EXCLUSION (RESERVATIONS).   Under this policy, American Indians were removed from their larger geographical homelands to smaller, well-defined "reservation" lands. Though reservations were strongly resisted by most American Indian tribes, the Native inhabitants were unable to withstand the military strength of the government. The final removal of Indians onto reservations was completed with the massacre of the Sioux at Wounded Knee in South Dakota in 1890.[26]

Many negative sanctions and restrictions were imposed on American Indians living on reservations. They were often denied use of their language and participation in religious ceremonies. The reservation system, however, did acknowledge the American Indians' right to live and retain land, and maintain their identity and many components of their culture.

ASSIMILATION.   Assimilation policies were enacted to promote the integration of American Indians within the "American" mainstream. Several laws promoted termination of federal programs and trust relations with American Indian tribal groups. The Dawes Act, or Land Allotment Act of 1887, provided for the allotment of plots of Indian lands to individual American Indians. In many cases, Indians sold their lands to non-Indians. Before the Dawes Act, American Indians owned 188 million acres of land. After the Dawes Act, American Indians were left with 47 million acres. *Relocation* (later Employment Assistance) was another assimilation policy enacted in 1952 by the Bureau of Indian Affairs. Under this program American Indians were recruited for off-reservation employment. Training and financial support for living expenses were made available to American Indians who participated in this program. Estimates indicate that approximately one-half of the American Indian trainees under this program returned to their reservations. In 1953 Congress passed another resolution declaring termination of Indian reservations to be the official federal policy. In the next five years, the trust status and federal programs of sixty Indian tribes and groups were terminated. This policy was reversed in the early 1960s because of the detrimental consequences that resulted from the termination policy. Many of these "terminated" tribes have once again been restored to trust status and qualify for federal programs available to other American Indian tribes.

SELF-DETERMINATION AND SELF-GOVERNANCE. Present federal policies are promoting self-determination and self-governance of Native American affairs by the Native peoples themselves. These policies are the result of organization and mobilization of American Indian professional groups on behalf of their own causes. The National Congress of American Indians (NCAI) brings together Indian leaders from rural, reservations, and urban areas for problem solving and lobbying efforts on behalf of Native American people. American Indian professional organizations are working in collaborative efforts on behalf of many American Indian needs and causes.

ENVIRONMENTAL–STRUCTURAL FACTORS

Many environmental–structural factors have adversely influenced the lives of Native Americans. Reservation systems were confining for people who had experienced considerable freedom in moving about their vast ancestral lands. Several reservations now accommodate more than one tribe. Some of these "combinations" include tribes that historically were enemies. American Indian and Alaskan Native children were forced to attend boarding schools located some distance from their families. Many children remained in the boarding school environment throughout the entire year, attending school in the fall, winter, and spring and working on local and school-owned farms during the summer.

Many Native Americans were recruited and enlisted in the Armed Services for World War II, and the Korean and Vietnam Conflicts. These experiences and subsequent urban employment training and relocation programs led to the migration of many Native American adults and families to urban areas.

Reclamation projects have claimed Indian lands for dams and water projects. Water resources used for irrigation of Indian farm lands have been usurped "up river" by non-Indian people, forcing Indian tribes to relinquish traditional farming activities. Contracts have been signed allowing non-Indian organizations access to oil, mineral, and timber resources for long periods of time. "Termination" of Indian tribes had negative repercussions on Native people individually and collectively. Repatriation and reinstatement of Indian tribes have begun to address these wrongs. Currently,

American Indian people are achieving considerable success through self-governance initiatives. They are addressing "reburial" issues through legal procedures. Decisions regarding the storage of toxic waste on Indian lands are being debated in Tribal Councils with considerable community input. Tribal economic development projects are actively pursued. Gambling industries continue to be operated on and debated on many Indian lands. Subsistence life-styles are promoted where important to the survival and economic security of American Indian tribes and Alaskan Native villages. Fishing, hunting, and trapping continue to be debated as they relate to subsistence and treaty rights. The return of Indian land is being pursued through legal avenues and through economic ventures—the revenue from which is being used to purchase Indian land previously sold or awarded to non-Indian people.

NATIVE AMERICAN CULTURAL CONSIDERATIONS

The study of Native American culture is a complicated and fascinating educational experience. Each of the 542 Native American tribal groups is unique. Each language is tribal-specific. Customs and beliefs are representative of distinct cultures and daily living practices.

There is considerable interest in and fascination with Native American culture today from non-Indians; people claiming Indian ancestry; Indian people who were adopted as infants and are researching their natural lineage; urban Indians with few ties to their tribal lands; and Native Americans who are strongly identified with their tribes, culture, and heritage.[27]

There is also considerable interest in rediscovering and preserving the cultural teachings of specific tribes. Native American tribal and spiritual leaders are advocating the return to cultural and spiritual teachings. Concepts such as the medicine wheel, the circle, spirituality, sweats, rites of passage, and vision quests are being taught as important to the maintenance of "balance" and "harmony" in individual and group living. One professional American Indian, Larry Brendtro, has conceptualized the "medicine wheel" as a symbol of wellness, with four dimensions: belonging, independence, mastery, and generosity.[28] *Belonging* reinforces the importance of the group. *Independence* recognizes the importance of each individual. *Mastery* denotes respect for the skills and talents of each member. *Generosity* is reflected in the ways in which members share their talents, themselves, and their material goods with others. These four concepts promote "wellness" for the individual and collective good.

While each tribal group maintains considerable uniqueness as demonstrated through their cultural customs, beliefs, and traditions, there are several values that are evidenced in varying degrees among most Native American tribal groups. Some of these values include:

1. Belief in a Supreme Being and the continuity of life.
2. Belief in the importance of achieving balance and living in harmony with nature—showing respect for all living things.
3. Belief in the importance of acquiring and using knowledge judiciously—transforming knowledge into wisdom.

4. Respect for the individuality of all people.
5. Respect for the value of the group and solidarity.
6. Importance of behaving honorably—to avoid shaming one's self, family, clan, or tribe.
7. Belief in honoring and respecting elders as cultural guardians and educators.

FAMILY CONSIDERATIONS

Nuclear, extended, clan, and tribal families play dominant roles in the lives of traditional American Indian people. Historically, the rearing of children was a tribal and clan responsibility. It is not unusual, therefore, for families to gather as a group to help resolve problems which, at first glance, appear to be specific to an individual. On occasion, family members may speak "for" the "identified" client. Matriarchal and patriarchal systems continue to rely heavily on the "wisdom" of the designated family matriarch or patriarch. It is not unusual for large numbers of extended family members to participate in healing ceremonies for cousins, aunts, uncles, parents, and grandparents. It is sometimes confusing to accurately identify family members, as cousins may be affectionately referred to as brothers and sisters, and respected aunts and uncles (sometimes several times removed) may be addressed as mothers, fathers, and grandparents are. Elders are often referred to as "Grandmother" or "Grandfather" when there are no kinship ties to these people.

Traditional American Indian families that have relocated in urban areas may often be frustrated by demands of non-Indian systems that require regular school attendance, daily employment performance, and maintenance of strict daily living schedules. When traditional roles are required on behalf of their families on reservations and Indian lands, it is often difficult to meet the demands of both the non-Indian and Indian responsibilities to which Indian people are committed. It is also difficult for some Indian people to explain the conflicts they are experiencing because they have little confidence that either the non-Indian systems or the traditional systems will understand or appreciate the dilemmas they face in fulfilling their traditional and modern-day roles and responsibilities.

INDIVIDUAL CONSIDERATIONS

Just as each of the 542 Native American tribal groups is unique, so, too, is each individual. Some American Indians are traditional people who have learned their Native language as their first language. Others have deep respect for their Native culture and understand their language, but are not fluent in oral Native language expression. Some have been reared in homes with parents from different tribal groups and have experiences with several Native American cultures. Many Indian parents today spent their younger years in boarding schools or foster homes and have had limited year-round exposure to their Indian cultural heritage. Some Indian people were born off-reservation and have returned to their tribal lands for vacations and purposeful visits. All of these factors, and many more, complicate considerably identification and self-esteem issues with which many American Indian people must deal. They also challenge professional social workers who engage with American Indian clients in assessing, understanding, and resolving the psychosocial problems and growth opportunities for which American Indian clientele seek the services of a social worker.

Micro Social Work Practice with American Indians

Given the diversity of American Indian and Alaskan Native tribal groups and individual members, it is important to reinforce the necessity of individualization. The following information may be helpful in guiding sensitive social work intervention when considered thoughtfully with each client and assignment.

Casework, group work, marriage/couples counseling, and family therapy are all important social work interventions with Native American people. The treatment of choice is often determined by the presenting problem(s), intervention goals, willingness of the participants, client's previous experiences with professional helping people, and social work practitioner skills.

RELATIONSHIP STRATEGIES

The development of professional helping relationships requires considerable time with many Native American people. Relationships are complicated by such factors as the therapist's age, sex, race, and professional experience. Native American social workers will be "tested" by clients regarding their knowledge and understanding of Native American culture; their respect for their "brothers and sisters"; their identification with their own tribe and Native Americans generally; their knowledge and experience; and their professional and cultural commitment to Native Americans generally, and their professional roles specifically. In many respects, American Indian social workers are expected to thoroughly know and understand Native American culture.

Non-Indian social workers are often tested for longer periods of time than Native American social workers. As a rule, Native people will not expect the same level of cultural understanding from non-Indian social workers as they will from Native professionals, but they will expect that all social workers make efforts to understand and respond in culturally sensitive ways in the provision of their services.

Another area in which professional social workers will be tested relates to professional competency. Clients expect competent services. They expect social workers to follow through on their commitments. Clients often assess professional competence by the extent to which social workers keep their commitments.

Native Americans often approach a beginning relationship with a professional person in a calm, unhurried manner. They observe the friendliness of the professional and assess the atmosphere in the setting. Some clients may greet a professional with a brief handshake (more touching than shaking); while others may acknowledge the person with a nod of the head. It is important to greet traditional Indian people respectfully. Staring and excess eye contact constitute a major breach of etiquette, as does any other action that may be taken as overfamiliar.[29]

In many Native languages, there is no single word to describe systems, programs, or processes important to social work intervention. Many "professional" terms are not easily translated into Native languages. It is often important to explain the details and services of a program, rather than its name.

Each tribal group will have different customs that facilitate relationship building. Newly employed social workers should seek information from more experienced social workers regarding establishing beginning and working relationships, customs and traditions important to the development of professional relationships, and effective termination skills.

INTERVENTION STRATEGIES

Intervention strategies will also be influenced by numerous cultural beliefs, customs, and values. These may differ somewhat depending on the tribal group with which you are working, the client's identification with their culture, and the location of the service delivery system—reservation/rural or urban.

Interventions in reservation/rural areas may be complicated by the fact that tribal members are "related" to large numbers of people and know each other's present and past histories. Group work contracts must be well defined, especially as they relate to issues of confidentiality. Breeches of confidentiality must be addressed quickly and openly to resolve issues and further the attainment of group and individual goals.

Confidentiality in all aspects of the social worker's interventions is extremely important. *Moccasin telegraphs* are active. However, much misinformation circulates freely. Professional people must maintain well-defined boundaries in terms of sharing information.

Indian time is a concept that acknowledges and excuses behavior that results in Indian people being late for appointments. There is considerable difference of opinion regarding the cultural significance of Indian time. Some people maintain that Indian people "live in the present" without much cultural importance attached to promptness in meeting demands for closely monitored schedules. Others insist that Indian people have substantial recent experience with scheduling their time and meeting appointments, and that lateness should not be excused because of past cultural values. Social workers often find that up-front confrontations of lateness reveal a multitude of reasons that resulted in clients' being late, including (1) last-minute interruptions; (2) unreliable transportation; (3) transportation was provided by someone who had other complications; (4) unreliable clocks; (5) visits from others to whom it would appear rude to leave; (6) misunderstandings about the appointment time; and (7) apprehensions about the visit. The authors' experience has been that, generally, most Native Americans make the same efforts to be on time as the general population. The following interventions have been helpful in encouraging maintenance of appointments: (1) clarifying appointment times; (2) reviewing the schedules and work assignments of the social workers; (3) clarifying procedures to cancel or postpone an appointment; and (4) summarizing the content of the interview, future goals, and the next appointment.

In reservation/rural settings, many social workers find it advantageous to schedule several home visits in the same area on the same day. Many elders and others have limited transportation resources. If family members can provide transportation to a trading post or shopping center, elders will take advantage of that offer, even when they know a social work home visit has been set for that day. Other family, social, and spiritual activities also may take precedence over an appointment with the social worker, and many of these occur spontaneously. If a social worker fails to find one client at home, there are several others with whom appointments have been made to justify the often extensive travel time required on some reservations.

It is important to remember that although clients may miss appointments because of unforeseen difficulties or opportunities, social workers are expected to keep their appointments with clients. When court sessions or crises interfere with a social worker keeping a client appointment, contacts should be made prior to the scheduled appointment to arrange for a later meeting.

Native American clients will likely benefit from services of both professional social workers and Native medicine people. Many tribes use a variety of traditional medical diagnosticians and healers including medicine men, hand tremblers, and Indian doctors.[30] Knowing the different Native medicine specialists in specific tribes, and speaking respectfully about their potential use, will often earn the respect of American Indian clients. While traditional medicine practices are important to many Native American people today, it is often not appropriate to talk in depth about these spiritual beliefs and practices with non-Indians or non-tribal members. Many symbols, totems, and objects have spiritual and healing significance. These may be acknowledged as helpful to a client's recovery, but are seldom discussed with others at any length.

Compiling social histories and assessments requires ongoing discussions (usually of a brief nature at each session) and considerable observation. Traditional Native Americans are often more present-oriented than past- or future-oriented. They believe that living in harmony with nature and all living things protects their physical and mental well-being. There is little need to discuss the past or make elaborate plans for the future.

Those Indian people who have a strong belief in the continuity of life view death as a part of nature's plan. This is particularly true with the death of an elder. One Yurok family gathered for the funeral of their patriarch who had lived an active, productive life well into his eighties. At the feast following the funeral, family members recounted stories of their positive experiences with their grandfather, grandmother (also deceased), and extended family members. Many of these stories were humorous in nature. The laughter prompted tears of emotional release, comradery, and closeness as family members validated and celebrated the positive experiences they had enjoyed with their grandparents and other friends and relatives. Deaths of elders are how nature intended life to be. Deaths of children, youth, and young adults, however, are occasions of much sadness and remorse. Given the extent of accidents within American Indian communities, considerable attention should be given to the accumulated losses experienced in many Indian families. Grief groups are being viewed as therapeutic resources for Indian people who are finding support and understanding in releasing accumulated pain and sorrow that has so profoundly impacted their emotional and physical well-being.

Indian people believe that health is nurtured through balance and living in harmony with nature. Professional social workers who understand these concepts can help Indian people restore the spiritual balance that may be affected by personal, family, or extended family problems. All cultural teachings reinforce this principle. Clients can be encouraged to achieve balance in work, leisure, recreation, family, and cultural and spiritual activities. Identifying and developing resources within the Native American community can be especially helpful as these opportunities promote therapeutic cultural relationships and positive identification with "Indianness."

CASEWORK INTERVENTION

Individual interventions require thoughtful attention to the clients' agenda. Clients may request help with specific problems. They often do not wish to explore emotional feelings in depth, particularly in initial interviews. Social workers who facilitate problem resolution in initial interventions encourage future use of professional services. Some clients will seek help with a tangible problem. When that problem is resolved, they may be willing to discuss problems of an emotional nature. Some clients are confused about the roles of social workers. They have known social workers who have been involved in the removal of children for placement in foster homes, boarding schools, or correctional facilities. They have also worked with social workers who were responsible for overseeing the disbursement of their financial resources and those of their children—often for school clothes, holiday gifts, summer clothing, and personal expenses. Developing trusting therapeutic relationships from this memory base is often difficult for clients to achieve and will take time.

A variety of services are now available to American Indians in both reservation/rural and urban settings. Children and youth are receiving casework prevention and treatment services to address issues related to (1) school adjustment and achievement; (2) abuse and neglect; (3) drug and alcohol use/abuse; (4) development of coping and communication skills; (5) behavioral management skills; (6) teen pregnancy and parenting; (7) emotional crises; (8) suicide prevention; (9) relationship and assertion skills; (10) peer counseling and leadership skills; (11) personal growth development; and (12) future planning.

Adults and elders are utilizing casework prevention and treatment services to address (1) emotional crises, including depression and anxiety; (2) health and wellness concerns; (3) adult and elder protective services; (4) family issues, including violence; (5) employment; (6) alcohol and drugs; (7) AIDS; (8) fetal alcohol syndrome/fetal alcohol effects (FAS/FAE); (9) sexual and physical abuse; (10) poverty and economics; (11) concerns regarding care of children and elders; and (12) development and use of community resources.

Wherever possible, both reservation/rural and urban social workers should assess these issues within the cultural context of the person's American Indian heritage.

Regardless of a person's current residence, it is likely that Native American values and beliefs will be important in both the assessment and treatment processes. Resources from within the Native American community can be helpful in understanding and resolving personal, social, and behavioral problems.

The two case examples below describe social work intervention on behalf of children and their families—one in a reservation/rural setting and the other in an urban setting.

CASE EXAMPLES

Arthur is a bright, active eight-year-old, full-blooded American Indian residing on a reservation with his ten-year-old brother under the care of his maternal grandfather. The social worker was asked to contact the grandfather regarding Arthur's problematic school attendance. The social worker talked with Arthur's school teacher and learned that Arthur's attendance had been irregular throughout the year. He had not attended school during the past two weeks. When Arthur was in school, he was pleasant, completed the assigned work at high levels of competency, and related well with the other children. The grandfather lived alone in a comfortable home near the elementary school. The social worker met with the grandfather and Arthur's aunt who was visiting her father. The grandfather indicated that Arthur left for school each day with his brother, George. The social worker asked if the grandfather and aunt would help her locate Arthur and bring him back to the grandfather's home. Arthur's aunt found Arthur playing nearby at the local park. Arthur willingly went with the social worker to the school where the following plan was developed and agreed to by Arthur, the school teacher, and the social worker: (1) Arthur would attend school each day; (2) the social worker would meet with Arthur sometime during the morning of each day at the school; and (3) Arthur would complete all his school work and bring examples of what he was learning to the social work sessions.

The social worker visited with the grandfather at his home that afternoon. She learned that Arthur and George had lived with the grandfather since their early years, and permanently for the past three years. Their mother and father were divorced, and their natural father was deceased. Their mother had remarried and lived in a neighboring community off-reservation. The mother visited her children regularly, but they had not discussed issues regarding the care of Arthur and George. The social worker asked how the grandfather would feel about the social worker's meeting with the boys' mother to discuss Arthur's current behavior. The grandfather agreed and provided the mother's address and telephone number.

Arthur's mother, Shirley, had remarried and was living with her husband and a new baby in a small community a short distance from the reservation. Her husband was employed full-time, and Shirley was employed, during the school year, as a cook at the local elementary school. Shirley was concerned about her two sons and the burden of care assumed by her father. Shirley was embarrassed by her irresponsible care of Arthur and George. Both she and her husband would like to have Arthur and George live with them, but she was reluctant to discuss this with her father. She didn't know what her father's feelings were regarding his continuing to care for the children. The social worker asked for Shirley's permission to discuss these matters with the grandfather, and Shirley agreed. The grandfather was willing to return the children to their mother. He said he was "too old to take care of such active boys." With his permission, these messages were shared with Shirley, and within two months the children were returned to the care of the mother and their stepfather. To accomplish this goal, the social worker: (1) met daily with Arthur at the school for the first two weeks, then three times a week for two weeks, twice a week for two weeks, and then weekly until the boys were returned to their mother; (2) met with George to discuss his feelings regarding living with his mother and stepfather; (3) set up meetings with the grandfather and Shirley and her husband to discuss the return of the children to their mother and regular visiting schedules with the grandfather; and (4) informed school officials of the social work intervention and reinforced their positive work with Arthur and George.

CULTURAL CONSIDERATIONS IMPORTANT TO THESE INTERVENTIONS.   Many cultural factors were considered in planning social work intervention with this family. Among these were the following:

1. Contacts had to be initiated quickly with nuclear and extended family members in decisions and plans related to their children.
2. The social worker had to act as an intermediary, especially because a family member was ashamed of past behaviors. It is culturally appropriate to have someone speak for you in these situations. Shirley was uncomfortable about asking for the return of her children, especially now that they were getting old enough to be of more help to the grandfather. Traditionally, these roles were strongly reinforced—grandparents cared for grandchildren; and grandchildren, in turn, cared for grandparents in their elder years.
3. A regular visiting schedule was important to support the adjustment and relationships of the children, parents, and grandfather. It was also important to see that the grandfather's needs are met.
4. It was particularly important to keep commitments to the children who were feeling "abandoned" by significant adults in their family systems.
5. It was also important to "check back" with all parties to facilitate any additional adjustment issues and to celebrate goals that have been accomplished. Native Americans appreciate and enjoy opportunities to celebrate.

The following case example details the work that was accomplished with a fourteen-year-old American Indian boy who was residing in an urban area.

Robert is a full-blooded American Indian who has lived most of his life in a larger metropolitan area. He was hospitalized in a residential treatment facility for depression, anxiety, weight loss, verbal and social regression, agitated moods, hysterical behaviors, and night terrors. During his hospitalization, his behavior worsened. He would not participate in group therapy and responded poorly to individual casework. Robert lived with his mother and two half-siblings. Robert's mother was recently divorced from his stepfather. Robert's father died six years earlier.

An urban American Indian social worker from Robert's tribe was asked to consult with the hospital staff regarding Robert's deteriorating mental and physical health. The social worker met with the staff and then with Robert. In the initial meeting, Robert and the social worker conversed in their Native language regarding their parents, siblings, clans, home reservation areas, and cultural activities in which they had participated. They then talked about Robert's current situation, the hospitalization, his separation from his family, and his fears. Robert believed that his father had been hexed and died as a result of evil forces associated with this hex. Robert also believed that these evil forces could be unleashed on him, and that he, too, might die. The social worker talked with Robert about spiritual ceremonies that could be made available to him on his reservation to restore balance and harmony in his life. Robert knew and understood the significance of these healing ceremonies and was willing to participate with the social worker in arranging for a ceremony for him. The social worker also talked with Robert about positive forces from his Native American culture that could provide protection and balance in his life. They discussed the power of the eagle and the protective nature of an eagle feather. The social worker volunteered to give Robert an eagle feather. A healing ceremony was arranged for Robert on his reservation. The Indian medicine people were able to provide information and healing forces to return Robert to a state of balance and wellness. Robert placed the eagle feather under his mattress and from that time on, did not experience any night terrors. Upon Robert's return from the reservation, he was able to participate in group and individual therapy at the residential treatment center and address issues that were interfering with his home and school adjustments in the urban setting.

Culturally significant social work interventions included the following:

1. The Native social worker was able to discuss Robert's situation in his Native language with an understanding of the cultural significance of the problems Robert was experiencing.
2. The Native social worker was able to explain to the non-Indian hospital staff and Robert's mother, Robert's perceptions of his problems and desire to participate in an American Indian healing ceremony.
3. The Native social worker had access to an eagle feather (which is unlawful for non-Indians to possess) and was willing to give the feather to Robert.
4. The gift of an eagle feather demands considerable generosity from the giver and utmost respect for the person to whom the gift is given.
5. It is important to remember that regardless of the current residence or length of time Native people have lived off-reservation, there is substantial likelihood that cultural identification and spiritual connectedness remain strong and highly important to the Native person's health and well-being.
6. Combinations of western and Indian medicine are effective in the treatment of Native peoples and the facilitation of recovery and health promotion.

SOCIAL GROUP WORK AND FAMILY INTERVENTIONS

Social group work is often the treatment of choice for interventions with American Indians and Alaskan Natives. Culturally, groups are traditional avenues for recreational, social, community, and planning activities. Feasts, ceremonies, celebrations, and decision making are promoted in Native American group gatherings.

Social workers have organized prevention and treatment groups to provide services for children, youth, adults, and elders. Among the prevention and education groups of importance to children and youth are the following: (1) self-esteem enhancement; (2) cultural skills; (3) drug and alcohol education and prevention;

(4) gang prevention; (5) community-sponsored groups (4-H, Scouting); (6) peer-support groups; (7) peer-leadership groups; (8) youth/elders mentoring; (9) subsistence and survival skills; (10) service-oriented groups; and (11) future planning and goal setting.

Among the treatment groups that have proven helpful for American Indian children and youth are those addressing (1) behavioral and anger management; (2) sexual abuse issues; (3) residential treatment; (4) learning and physical disabilities (FAS/FAE); (5) school refusal; (6) school achievement and in-school suspension problems; (7) alternative education—stay-in-school programs; (8) alcohol and drug treatment; and (9) life-skills training.

Groups are also effective prevention and treatment resources for adults and elders. Among the prevention groups in which adults and elders have participated are those that focus on (1) relationship and communication enhancement; (2) parent education, with a cultural focus; (3) cultural education (history and heritage); (4) life and coping skills; (5) foster-, adoptive-, and single-parent training and support; (6) addiction and co-dependency groups (tobacco, drugs, alcohol, gambling, FAS/FAE); (7) AIDS prevention; (8) diet, nutrition, and weight loss; (9) cultural skills; (10) subsistence, survival; (11) Native language skill development; (12) cultural oral history and poetry groups (myths, stories, legends); (13) grandparents as foster grandparents and guardians of their grandchildren; (14) Elder/youth mentoring; (15) leadership enhancement; and (16) "medicine men" career training.

The treatment groups that are proving effective for Native American adults and elders address the following: (1) adults who have been abused as children in families, boarding schools, or communities; (2) alcohol, drug, and gambling treatment, after care, and relapse prevention; (3) emotional problems such as depression, anxiety; (4) victims of domestic abuse; (5) perpetrators of abuse; (6) post-traumatic stress syndrome; (7) grief, loss, separation; (8) stress identification and management; and (9) discrimination and prejudice awareness, education, and resolution.

Family interventions are also being used successfully in many Native American communities to address needs of individual families and clusters of family groups. Some examples include (1) crisis intervention—parent–child relationship or child behavior focused; (2) family separation, loss, grief, and healing; (3) family preservation; (4) family reconciliation; and (5) family enhancement through drug-free activities.

Task groups are proving to be effective in community interventions. Examples of task groups that are being used positively within Native American communities are addressing the following: (1) community partnership development (Healthy Communities, Year 2000); (2) child protection teams; (3) tribal action plans for addressing alcohol problems; (4) tribal histories; (5) cultural advisory committees; (6) language instruction and revitalization; and (7) community service. Two social group work experiences with Native American clientele are described below.

GROUP WORK EXAMPLES

The University of Utah's Graduate School of Social Work continues to recruit and graduate a significant number of Native Americans with master's degrees in social work. The majority of these students are traditional American Indian people, strongly identified with their cultural heritage, and interested in encouraging positive cultural identification of their children with their native heritage. At the request of American Indian graduate social work students, the authors organized a group experience for the daughters of these graduate students—nine girls, seven to eleven years of age. The purposes of the group were to: (1) increase members' knowledge of Native American culture, generally, and their own tribal groups, specifically; (2) enhance positive identification with Native American culture; and (3) enhance positive feelings of self, talents, and abilities to function within Indian and non-Indian cultures. All of the programming was related to Native American culture. Group sessions were organized according to units related to history, values, beliefs, art, music, dance, games, foods, stories, legends, discrimination, and current events.

During the unit related to music and dance, group members sang songs in the native languages of the group's members, played Native American musical instruments, made their own "shawls" for dancing, and learned a variety of Indian dances. Although interest verbally was high, the responses of the group members to the initial dancing activity were surprising. Only one group member had danced at powwows. She was a talented and accomplished dancer. The taped music was playing as group members entered the meeting room. When members were invited to join the leaders in learning specific dance steps, eight of the nine group members literally dove for cover—under the tables and into the open closetlike shelves. Leaders danced along with the one group member, with no effect on the other group members, who remained hidden. With considerable encouragement, one by one the group members were enticed from their hiding places by opportunities to take turns beating the Indian drums and wearing the "bells" from the group facilitator's fancy dance outfit. *Slowly,* over several weeks' time, the girls became more comfortable in dancing—always with opportunities to take turns drumming and wearing the bells. In the meantime, group members attended monthly powwows, at the Indian Walk-In Center, to observe the dancing of other community members. When the girls had completed their shawls, all of the group members and leaders attended a community powwow, and, finally, group members and leaders made their entrance onto the dance floor. Group members were obviously self-conscious, but with the support of the entire group and the leaders, members circled the dance floor and then broke off from the security of the group, in subgroups of two's and three's and then individually to spend the rest of the evening dancing with other community members.

CULTURAL CONSIDERATIONS IMPORTANT TO THIS GROUP EXPERIENCE. Among the cultural considerations important to this dance activity and group experience are the following:

1. It is important to understand that all Native Americans will not have similar interests in or talents for every component of their culture.
2. Native Americans may be reluctant to participate in cultural activities, even in supportive group environments, if they are unsure of their abilities to perform.
3. Embarrassment is to be avoided. Performing poorly not only reflects upon self, but also upon family, clan, and tribe.
4. Removing the focus from an individual to a group may be helpful in encouraging more risk-taking behaviors.

5. If one (or more) group members can perform a cultural skill capably, their expertise may contribute to less willingness on the part of other group members to try to develop these skills.

6. Group leaders must model appropriate risk-taking behaviors for group members.

7. One positive experience may "break the ice," but groups must provide ongoing cultural activity experiences to promote integration of this learning and willingness to take risks in other activities.

8. Support of parents, siblings, and extended family members is crucial to the risk-taking behavior of children in activities in which they perform in front of others.

9. It is important that parents encourage participation of their children in cultural activities in their early developmental years, when embarrassment may not be such a prohibiting factor.

The second example comes from a group experience with recovering Native American adults enrolled in an American Indian alcoholism counselor training program. One component of each of the one-month, on-campus training sessions required counselors-in-training to participate in group-work laboratories where they processed what they were learning and how it could be applied to their alcoholism-counseling assignments.

> In one group session, the members were concerned that one of the recovering alcoholism counselors had left the program—the result of his return to active drinking behaviors. The group members were hurt, disappointed, and saddened. They discussed their friendships with this counselor; their regret that they had not been aware of his struggles; their inability to be of help to him at this time; and their fears that they, too, might "slip" and return to their previous drinking behaviors. After considerable discussion, thoughtful contemplation, and some personal sharing, the session was summarized. At this point, a group member who had been unusually quiet for the entire session asked if the group could help him. He then described a terrifying emotional experience during that day's early morning hours. He had experienced every emotional and physical response he could remember from his prior drinking experiences—but he was certain he had not been drinking—at least he could not remember drinking. The social workers asked if other group members could be of help to him. Almost one-third of the group members admitted to having had a previous "dry drunk" experience, where they, too, suffered similar emotional and physical responses—much like those of their active drinking days. These group members verbalized their experiences while others acknowledged their understanding by quietly nodding their heads. The members shared that dry drunks had happened to them during times of recovery; that the episodes became less frequent and emotionally painful with the passage of time; that members should reassure themselves that they have not been drinking; and that it is often helpful to talk to someone at the time of these reactions, or the next day, as appropriate. At the conclusion of this discussion, the social workers again thanked group members for their sensitive sharing and their help to this group member. The group member also quietly expressed his appreciation to the group and said, "Thank you for helping me. I thought I was going crazy." As group members left, several members shook hands with the group member and the group leaders without any additional verbal expression.

CULTURAL CONSIDERATIONS IMPORTANT IN THIS GROUP EXPERIENCE   It is important to understand the cultural significance of many of the interactions in this group session. For example:

1. At times of stress, American Indian group members will often respond with nonverbal expressions that may escape the notice of a nonattentive group worker, such as brief nods of the head, short-term eye contact, and active listening behaviors.

2. American Indian people do not often feel a need to express opinions or restate information that has been adequately conveyed by another group member. (An exception is when elders are asked to advise. Elders often repeat advice or counsel that has already been given by another elder.)

3. The shaking of hands at the end of the group session is an example of sincere respect and appreciation. No verbalization was necessary.

4. It is impolite to interrupt a discussion of significance with an unrelated personal experience. It is not unusual for an American Indian person to wait until a current discussion topic is concluded before beginning a new, different discussion topic of a personal concern. This is not an example of avoidance, or control, or postponing group session termination. It is an example of respect for the discussion and concerns of others.

5. When American Indian people risk sharing an emotional, personal experience, they may be concerned that their respect is diminished in the eyes of other group members. American Indian people are often taught to handle their problems independently. The handshakes and "nods" convey understanding, appreciation, and respect.

6. After sharing an emotional experience of this magnitude, it is likely that the next session may be one of less involvement. It is important to acknowledge the difficult work that was accomplished in the previous session and to allow group member self-determination regarding the depth to which they will discuss problems in the next session.

7. Group workers, too, can discriminately use handshaking after a group session to acknowledge the work and progress of group members.

Macro Social Work Practice with Native Americans

Community is an important concept for American Indian people. The most universal symbol in Indian art, the circle, symbolizes cycles of life and tradition. The circle is a metaphor for living in harmony with one another, with the environment, and with the spiritual forces of the Indian universe.[31]

Community organization principles have much to offer in furthering the community concept that is so important to Native American people. Many American Indian communities are implementing programs through activation of all potential resources. An important first step, according to Beauvais and LaBoueff, is to create an awareness that a community problem or need exists.[32] After a thorough assessment of the facts, steps must be taken to actively involve all community members in the planning, implementation, and ongoing evaluation process.[33]

Many reservation and urban communities have implemented these principles in organizing and motivating their communities to achieve problem resolution. In so doing, they have also expanded and strengthened their community circle through increased awareness and responsiveness in enhancing individual and community pride in positive identification with Indianness. Edwards and Egbert-Edwards describe several successful community efforts, including (1) planning and implementation of Tribal Action Plans to combat community alcohol and drug problems; (2) children and youth cultural awareness and cultural arts enhancement programs; (3) establishment of community group homes and residential treatment centers; (4) development of youth community service groups; (5) educational support and achievement programs; and (6) urban and reservation recovery and healing programs.[34]

Examples of Native American community development programs in urban areas include (1) community development/partnership programs to address concerns of urban communities; (2) establishment of American Indian schools for those students who do not adjust to public schools; (3) programs that provide services for children, adults, and elders—at the same time—in consideration of transportation and time issues and developing feelings of community; and (4) task groups that plan and organize pow-wows, feast days, peer-support groups, holiday celebrations, elders' appreciation days, youth appreciation days, and other cultural and community support activities.

Examples of reservation community development programs include (1) community sobriety activities such as camp-outs, powwows, bowling leagues, traditional dances, rodeos, and holiday celebrations; (2) designation of areas of tribal lands as drug-free "healing" centers to promote recovery, cultural activities, growth activities, and celebrations; and (3) "Healthy People 2000" campaigns to encourage sobriety and positive use of personal and community resources.[35]

Successful Native American community development programs require strong leadership from community leaders who have long-term, realistic commitments to their programs, goals, and communities. These leaders understand the strengths and developmental needs of their communities. They respond to criticism openly. They welcome suggestions for improving their programs and creatively modify and expand their service delivery systems. They give credit to all factions of the community who are contributing to community development. They support the programs of other agencies. Cultural principles are incorporated into all aspects of their programs. Positive identification with tribal and Indian heritage is enhanced through celebrations that promote and reinforce success.

NATIVE AMERICAN URBAN COMMUNITY CASE STUDY

In several urban areas, Native American communities have recognized the need to support their youth in positive growth experiences that strengthen their identification with their Native culture while promoting nonsubstance use and abuse. One particularly successful youth group has achieved considerable success through the combined efforts of urban community agencies, community adults and elders, and the youth themselves. A Native American Coalition Task Force was formed in connection with a Community Partnership grant awarded to the Salt Lake County Alcohol and Drug Division through the Center for Substance

Abuse Prevention (CSAP). This Task Force includes membership of community agency representatives and local Native American leaders, community elders, parents, and youths. The Task Force established a Youth Leadership Development Program with four major goals: (1) to prevent use of drugs and alcohol; (2) to enhance the leadership potential of each participant; (3) to educate all youth in Native American culture generally and in tribal-specific culture; and (4) to promote active participation in educational and recreational activities with a nonusing peer support group.

All Native American community teenagers were invited to participate in this group experience. Parents and community leaders provided transportation to the group meetings and were invited to attend the meetings as observers. On occasion, parents and other adults participated in the discussion, when invited to do so. This structure was necessitated by the distance participants traveled to attend these activities. The arrangement strengthened ties to the program by youth and adults, and contributed to feelings of community.

Cultural enhancement/identification programs discussed (1) self-identity; (2) American Indian values and culture; (3) self-esteem and Indian identity; (4) alcohol, drugs, AIDS awareness and prevention—from the perspectives of Native Americans; (5) Native American dance, music, art, beadwork, moccasins, story telling, and games; and (6) Native American pride.

Educational and recreational activities included local and out-of-state excursions and participation in (1) camp-outs, hikes, and picnics; (2) water park activities; (3) local recreational centers; (4) movies and theater; (5) winter activities including skating, sledding, and skiing; (6) holiday activities throughout the community; (7) university and professional sporting events; (8) discussions and excursions to local universities and colleges for information regarding courses of study and careers; and (9) Native American cultural activities.

Leadership was enhanced through opportunities to understand and exercise leadership principles. All youth had leadership assignments and opportunities. They attended local, state, and national youth leadership conferences. In addition to these opportunities, youth (1) organized booths for local community and Native American fairs; (2) planned and managed their youth group logo design contest; (3) organized and rotated their own youth group leadership officers; (4) participated in youth panel discussions at community events; (5) learned public speaking skills through practice and presentations at several youth group meetings and community programs; (6) fulfilled public speaking assignments on behalf of their own group; and (7) planned and developed their own youth leadership retreat.

All of these experiences have proven beneficial to the youth, their families, and the community. After participating in a National Youth Leadership Conference in Minnesota, these young people organized and directed a community effort that resulted in their own Native American Youth Motivational Conference in 1993 in Park City, Utah. Youth leaders directed the planning efforts for this conference in cooperation with local and state Native American and non-Indian organizations. The Conference was attended by youth and adults from three western states. The programs were directed by youth leaders with considerable success.

The Future

As indicated throughout this chapter, there continues to be considerable energy and commitment directed by Native American people toward the enhancement of their communities—reservation/rural and urban. Individual and community pride are reinforced through positive program planning and goal achievement. Problems are viewed as challenges to restore balance and promote harmony within individuals and communities. Creativity has been and will continue to be fostered as renewed efforts are directed toward meeting the needs of Native American people.

There is continuing determination to address problems that interfere with the achievement of the potential of individuals and communities. Native Americans are determined to more positively enhance the image of their leaders and expand their leadership base. Leaders are committed to portraying positive leadership roles as culturally appropriate. Backbiting is being addressed and replaced by individual and community partnerships, open communication, and furthered collaboration. Constructive criticism is being directed toward problem resolution and collective development.

Creativity of Indian people is being acknowledged and encouraged in program development and problem resolution. It is likely that the coming years will be eventful and profitable for American Indians and Alaskan Natives and will lead to considerable growth in many areas, including the following:

1. Further attention must be directed toward active participation in political processes. While some reinstatement of 1996 budget cuts to the Bureau of Indian Affairs funding has been accomplished, significant cuts to education funding must be addressed to meet critical education needs.

2. The Indian Child Welfare Act (ICWA) of 1978 was enacted to halt the excessive removal of Indian children from their natural parents and to reestablish tribal rights and responsibilities over the care of their children. Recent research indicates that while progress has been made, compliance under the Act has been uneven.[36] Increased resources and professional staff were recommended to ensure that the intent of the Act was achieved. In 1995–1996, the ICWA was challenged by a Congressional Committee attempting to amend the Act in ways that would diminish tribal responsibility over voluntary adoptions. Subsequent negotiations appear to protect the original intent of the ICWA while promoting more expeditious handling of cases involving American Indian children. Continued vigilance is necessary to ensure that the best interests of Indian children and tribal groups are maintained.

3. Wellness programs must emphasize the "whole" being, including the physical, mental, social, emotional, spiritual, and cultural.

4. Healthy People 2000 campaigns must continue to promote sobriety, leadership development, cultural skills development, and collaboration among Indian people, tribes, and communities and non-Indian communities.

5. Cultural programs could benefit from collaborative efforts of tribal leaders, elders, and Native archaeologists and anthropologists who will instruct all tribal members in the historical and cultural heritage of tribal groups.[37]

6. Culturally oriented therapy groups can continue to expand through use of Native concepts such as *talking circles*.

7. Continuity of care services must be emphasized in planning group homes for children and youth in need of residential treatment for emotional or drug and alcohol problems; halfway houses for those released from residential settings such as correctional facilities, and emotionally disturbed or alcohol and drug treatment programs; and young adult group living homes or apartments for emancipated teenagers and young adults.

8. Family therapy residential homes could be helpful for families who need counseling, parent education, and relationship skill development. Families could maintain residence in a supportive, therapeutic environment, with after care provided when families return to their own homes.

9. Creative, comprehensive drug and alcohol programs must be planned to address individual, family, and community needs, including those related to FAS/FAE and AIDS.

10. Economic development is crucial to the further success of Native American people.

11. Throughout the United States, there is an interest in history and the accurate portrayal of history. Native Americans are championing their cause for the inclusion of historical content into public and higher education systems that more accurately portray the American Indian and Alaskan Native experience. This is not only just, but will result in greater understanding and appreciation of Native Americans, and increased positive identification of Native peoples with their heritage.[38]

| Concluding Comment | Social work with American Indians is a challenging and rewarding experience. Native Americans have much to contribute to society—their own tribes, other American Indian and Alaskan Native groups, and the non-Indian world. "Balance" and "harmony" are important concepts, as is the Native American belief in showing respect for all living things. Incorporating these concepts into professional social work practice with Native American people will foster respect, collaboration, and growth. According to Hill, "In the Indian world, culture is not a commodity or a performance, it is the act of living as an Indian. How you live is an art."[39] Professional social work has been defined as an "art." We have much to learn in sharing our art with one another in professional relationships. |

KEY WORDS AND CONCEPTS

American Indians	Traditional native medicine
Alaskan Natives	Balance
Indian Child Welfare Act	Talking circles

SUGGESTED READINGS

Dykeman, C., Nelson, J. R., and Appleton, V. "Building Strong Working Alliances with American Indian Families," *Social Work in Education* 17, No. 3 (July 1995): 148–158.

Edwards, E. D., and Edwards, M. E. "Native American Community Development," in F. G. Rivera and J. L. Erlich, eds., *Community Organizing in a Diverse Society.* Boston: Allyn and Bacon, 1992.

Franklin, C. "Culturally Relevant School Programs for American Indian Children and Families," *Social Work in Education* 17, No. 3 (July 1995): 183–193.

Hodgkinson, H. L., Outtz, J. H., and Obarakpor, A. M. *The Demographics of American Indians: One Percent of the People; Fifty Percent of the Diversity.* Washington, D.C.: Institute for Educational Leadership, November 1990.

Indian Health Service: Trends in Indian Health—1991, U.S. Department of Health and Human Services; Public Health Service; Indian Health Service; Office of Planning, Evaluation, and Legislation, Division of Program Statistics.

Minority Aging: Essential Curricula Content for Selected Health and Allied Health Professions, American Indian and Alaska Native Elderly Section. DHHS Publication No. HRS-P-DV 90-4, 1990.

Nichols, R. L. *The American Indian: Past and Present.* New York: Alfred A. Knopf, 1986.

The State of Native American Youth Health. Minneapolis, MN: University of Minnesota, February 1992.

U.S. Senate Holds Hearings on ICWA Amendments, *NICWA News,* National Indian Child Welfare Association's Quarterly Newsletter, Summer 1996.

ENDNOTES

1. U.S. Bureau of the Census, "Census Bureau Completes Distribution of 1990 Redistricting Tabulations to States, CB91–100, *United States Department of Commerce News* (Washington, D.C.: U.S. Department of Commerce, March 11, 1991); U.S. Bureau of the Census, "We, The First Americans," (Washington D.C.: U.S. Department of Commerce, September 1993).

2. U.S. Bureau of the Census, "Census Bureau Releases 1990 Census Counts on Specific Racial Groups" CB91–215, *United States Department of Commerce News* (Washington, D.C.: U.S. Department of Commerce, June 12, 1991); U.S. Bureau of the Census, "Do You Know Which 1990 Products Contain Data on the American Indian, Eskimo, and Aleut Population?" CPG-I-11 (Washington, D.C.: U.S. Department of Commerce, 1990); U.S. Bureau of the Census, "We Asked . . . You Told Us" CQC-4 (Washington, D.C.: U.S. Department of Commerce, July 1992).

3. U.S. Bureau of the Census, "Cherokee, Navajo, Chippewa, Sioux Top Census Bureau's 1990 Tribe List" CB92–244, *United States Department of Commerce News* (Washington, D.C.: U.S. Department of Commerce, November 18, 1992).

4. U.S. Bureau of the Census, "Race and Hispanic Origin, 1990 Census Profile" No. 2, (Washington, D.C.: U.S. Department of Commerce, June 1991); Bureau of the Census, "Major Findings on American Indian and Alaska Native Populations from the 1990 Census" (Washington, D.C.: U.S. Department of Commerce, n.d.).

5. U.S. Bureau of the Census, "Major Findings on American Indian and Alaska Native Populations from the 1990 Census"; U.S. Bureau of the Census, "1990 Census Counts of American Indians, Eskimos, or Aleuts and American Indian and Alaska Native Areas," (Washington, D.C.: U.S. Department of Commerce, n.d.).

6. H. L. Hodgkinson, J. H. Outtz, and A. M. Obarakpor, *The Demographics of American Indians: One Percent of the People; Fifty Percent of the Diversity* (Washington, D.C.:

Institute for Educational Leadership, November 1990); U.S. Bureau of the Census, "We Asked . . . You Told Us."

7. U.S. Bureau of the Census, "We, The First Americans."

8. Hodgkinson, Outtz, and Obarakpor.

9. U.S. Bureau of the Census, "Percent of American Indian, Eskimo, and Aleut Persons Below Poverty Level by Age: 1990" CPH-L95 (Washington, D.C.: U.S. Department of Commerce, n.d.).

10. U.S. Bureau of the Census, "We, The First Americans."

11. U.S. Bureau of the Census, "Selected Social and Economic Characteristics by Race and Hispanic Origin," 1990 Census Profile, No. 2 (Washington, D.C.: U.S. Department of Commerce, June 1991); U.S. Bureau of the Census, "We, The First Americans."

12. U.S. Bureau of the Census, "Employment Status of American Indian, Eskimo, and Aleut Males and Females, 16 Years and Over: 1990" CPH-L-95 (Washington, D.C.: U.S. Department of Commerce, n.d.); U.S. Bureau of the Census, "We, The First Americans."

13. U.S. Bureau of the Census, "Educational Attainment of American Indian, Eskimo, and Aleut Males and Females, 25 Years and Over: 1990" CPH-L-95 (Washington, D.C.: U.S. Department of Commerce, n.d.).

14. Hodgkinson, Outtz, Obarakpor.

15. Ibid.

16. Public Health Service, Indian Health Service, *Indian Health Service: Trends in Indian Health—1991* (Washington, D.C.: U.S. Department of Health and Human Services, Office of Planning, Evaluation, and Legislation, Division of Program Statistics, n.d.).

17. Public Health Service, Indian Health Service, *Prevention Resource Guide: American Indians and Native Alaskans* (Washington, D.C.: U.S. Department of Health and Human Services, Office for Substance Abuse Prevention, June 1991), p. 1.

18. Public Health Service, Indian Health Service, *Indian Health Service: Trends in Indian Health—1991,* p. 49.

19. Ibid.

20. R. Blum et al., "American Indian–Alaskan Native Youth Health," *JAMA,* 267 (December 1992).

21. E. R. Rhoades et al., "The Indian Burden of Illness and Future Health Interventions," *Public Health Report,* 102 (April 1987).

22. Hodgkinson, Outtz, Obarakpor.

23. *The State of Native American Youth Health* (Minneapolis, MN: University of Minnesota, February 1992).

24. Ibid., pp. 54–55.

25. B. Berry, *Race and Ethnic Relations* (Boston: Houghton Mifflin, 1965).

26. W. L. Wax, *Indian Americans* (Englewood Cliffs, NJ: Prentice Hall, 1971), pp. 65–78.

27. D. Johnson, "Census Finds Many Claiming New Identity: Indian," *New York Times NATIONAL,* March 5, 1991.

28. L. K. Brendtro, "Dancing with Wolves: A New Paradigm for Reclaiming Youth at Risk," The Sixth Annual Robert J. O'Leary Memorial Lecture, Ohio State University College of Social Work, February 26, 1991.

29. E. R. Rhoades, "Profile of American Indians and Alaska Natives," in M. Harper, ed., *Minority Aging: Essential Curricula Content for Selected Health and Allied Health Professions* (Washington, D.C.: U.S. Department of Health and Human Services, 1990), p. 59.

30. Ibid.

31. R. Hill, "Indian Insights into Indian Worlds," *Native Peoples Magazines* 6, 1 (Fall 1992): 14.

32. F. Beauvais and S. LaBoueff, "Drug and Alcohol Abuse Intervention in American Indian Communities," *International Journal of the Addictions* 20 (January 1985): 139–171.

33. E. D. Edwards and M. Egbert-Edwards, "Native American Community Development," in F. G. Rivera and J. L. Erlich, eds., *Community Organizing in a Diverse Society* (Boston: Allyn and Bacon, 1992).

34. Ibid.

35. S. Scott, *Promoting Healthy Traditions Workbook: A Guide to the Healthy People 2000 Campaign* (St. Paul, MN: American Indian Health Care Association, 1990).

36. M. C. Plantz, "Indian Child Welfare: A Status Report," *Children Today* 18 (January/February 1989).

37. K. Dongoske et al., "Understanding the Past Through Hopi Oral Tradition," *Native Peoples Magazine* 6, 2 (Winter 1993).

38. I. Thunderhorse, "Democracy: An Indian Legacy," *The Witness* (April 1993).

39. R. Hill, "Indian Insights into Indian Worlds," *Native Peoples Magazine* 6, 1 (Fall 1992): 13–14.

CHAPTER 20

Social Work Practice with Mexican Americans

Armando T. Morales and Ramon Salcido

Prefatory Comment

This chapter was written specifically for this book. Mexican Americans are conspicuously absent from social work literature; only thirty-four articles concerning this distinct ethnic group appeared in the literature over the last thirty-five years—about one per year!

The authors, Dr. Armando T. Morales, Professor of Psychiatry and Biobehavioral Science, Department of Psychiatry, UCLA School of Medicine, and Dr. Ramon Salcido, Associate Professor and Chairman of the Community Organization Planning Concentration, School of Social Work, University of Southern California, maintain that Mexican Americans do have mental health needs and do avail themselves of direct services when they are provided at minimum cost, in their primary language (Spanish), and near their homes. They offer practice suggestions that have implications for macro social work in the barrio, mobilizing various indigenous social support systems such as churches, neighbors, and the family. They also recommend the intervention strategy of advocacy to reduce institutional barriers to services for Mexican Americans. A police brutality case serves to highlight the micro and macro skills required in these delicate cases that are common in the Latino community.

Meeting the ever-increasing social service needs of disadvantaged groups, which are often isolated by class and cultural differences, is a continuing challenge to social work. If the social work profession hopes to be more viable among disadvantaged groups, especially among the Mexican American population, human services institutions must modify their service delivery systems. Moreover, social workers must understand the dynamics of both individual and institutional racism, which have discouraged or prevented Mexican Americans from availing themselves of existing services. At times those services have appeared impersonal, and even nonsupportive.

Despite the recent attention focused on the special needs of Mexican Americans, any explanation of their situation is complicated by the difficulty of defining this population as to size and demographic characteristics. More has to be learned about the variations within this group and its immigration pattern.

Mexican Americans: A Heterogeneous Population

Mexican Americans are one of the most diverse ethnic groups in the United States in comparison to white ethnic groups and minority groups of color. On the one hand, like American Indians, Mexican Americans were an indigenous people who resided in the Southwest, were overpowered by Anglo settlers, and are therefore one of the *oldest* minorities. On the other hand, their continuing immigration from Mexico to the United States also makes them one of the *newest* and *largest* immigrant groups. Some are fully assimilated into Anglo society, and some reside almost exclusively in *barrios*.[1] Some retain strong ties to Mexico and return there frequently, while others prefer to remain in the United States. There are also those who partially integrate without assimilating but do not center their interactions exclusively within the *barrio*.[2]

With the Treaty of Guadalupe–Hidalgo in 1848, most of the Southwest, including California, became the possession of the United States. The actual number of Mexicans in the new Territory of the Southwest was relatively small. Harry Kitano reports that all laborers who were Mexican, whether they were "pure" Spanish or not, were perceived as "half-breeds" and inferior by Anglos.[3] By 1900 these people were already a subordinated population; they lived in segregated enclaves and were controlled by the Anglos. From 1848 to 1910 very few Mexicans migrated to the United States. The relative ease of entry across a long, 3000-mile border; the difficulty in distinguishing between Spanish-speaking, U.S.-born people and Spanish-speaking immigrants from Mexico, both legal and illegal; and dubious official data make precise quantification impossible. However, the following official census figures on early immigration of Mexicans to the United States are of some use.

To 1900	28,000
1901–1910	50,000
1911–1920	219,000
1921–1930	460,000
1931–1940	22,000
1941–1950	59,000
1951–1960	319,000
1961–1970	453,000

Significant migration of Mexicans to the United States did not take place until after 1910. It is estimated that fully 10 percent of the Mexican people immigrated to the United States early in the twentieth century, and the vast majority of them assumed agricultural work in the Southwest. This migration peaked in the 1920s but was curtailed during the years of the Great Depression when large numbers of Mexicans, including those born in the United States, were repatriated (deported) by social services and immigration agencies. Many of those deported were U.S.-born children of the Mexican immigrants—U.S. citizens!

Moreover, as the Mexican American population of the United States grew, it remained highly localized, with almost 90 percent of the people located in the five Southwestern states. California's share of this population steadily increased, as Table 20-1 shows.

The next large influx of migrants arrived in the post–World War II period. The need for agricultural laborers and unskilled workers to keep pace with economic expansion of the post-war years made Mexican immigration attractive to businesses and small industries. Business was the only contact between the two cultures; U.S. society was not concerned with housing conditions, lack of schooling, or availability of social services for Mexican Americans. This neglect, coupled with racism, caused Mexicans as well as Mexican Americans to maintain a distance from institutions and governmental agencies.

Certain social demographic characteristics have made the Mexican American experience unique in comparison to those of Europeans and Asians. This population is the second largest minority of color that is both indigenous and immigrant in character. Because of geographical proximity to Mexico, Mexican-born persons have followed a wide variety of migration patterns to the United States since the early part of the century. Generally, immigration to the United States has been greater from Mexico than from any other country in recent years. For example, Mexico has been the primary source of both legal and illegal immigration to the United States since the 1950s.

The Mexican American population comprises at least three major subgroups: those who are born in the United States; those who are born in and emigrate legally

TABLE 20-1 **Mexican Population in the United States: 1910–1990**

Year	U.S. Bureau of the Census Definition	Total United States	Total California	Percent in California
1910	Mexicans of foreign-born and mixed parentage	382,002	51,037	13.4
1920	Mexicans of foreign-born and mixed parentage	731,559	86,610	17.4
1930	Mexicans	1,282,883	368,013	29.3
1940	Spanish mother tongue	1,570,740	416,140	32.9
1950	Spanish surname	2,281,710	591,540	35.8
1960	Spanish surname	3,464,999	1,141,207	40.1
1970	Spanish surname	9,600,000	2,222,185	23.1
1980	Spanish origin	14,605,883	4,543,770	31.1
1990	Hispanic persons	22,354,059	7,687,938	25.8

from Mexico; and those who are born in and emigrate illegally from Mexico. The term *Mexican American* will be used to designate anyone having a Mexican heritage, regardless of time or place of arrival in the United States. During the highly political period of the 1960s and early 1970s, many persons of Mexican descent preferred the term *Chicano* rather than Mexican American. Some still prefer this designation today.

Demographic Profile

The 1970 census showed that 9.6 million persons of Spanish origin lived in the United States.[4] The 1988 census report showed an increase to 19.4 million, and, by March 1991, population reports showed a jump to 21.4 million, or about 8.6 percent of the total population.[5,6] The 1991 population reports showed that, of the 21.4 million Mexican Americans, 62.6 percent were of Mexican origin, 11.1 percent Puerto Rican, 4.9 percent Cuban, 13.8 percent Central and South American, and 7.6 percent other Hispanic origin.[7] Not included in these figures are an estimated 6 million undocumented aliens, predominantly from Mexico.[8] Although statistics vary widely on the basis of base lines and possible growth rates, demographers predicted (1) that Hispanics would be this country's largest minority by 1990; (2) that half the population in California and a third in Texas would be Spanish-speaking by the same date; and (3) that Hispanics could be the majority population group in three states by the year 2000.[9] However, the first two projected estimates did not occur by 1990.

Nevertheless, the Mexican American population is much larger than most figures indicate, primarily because of census undercount and continued immigration, both legal and illegal, to the United States from Mexico. Mexican Americans make up about 60 percent of the Hispanic population in the United States, and their numbers grew by 75 percent in the past decade. A recent government census found that Mexican Americans make up 19 percent of California's population and 28 percent of Los Angeles County, making Los Angeles the largest urban concentration of Mexicans outside Mexico City.[10]

The majority of Mexican Americans live in the states of California, Texas, and New Mexico. However, there are significant numbers in other states of the Southwest as well as in the Northwest and Midwest. Illinois, with its availability of manufacturing and agricultural jobs, has become home to many Mexican American migrants. Furthermore, contrary to stereotypes, the vast majority (90.5%) live in urban areas, with the remaining 9.5 percent residing in rural areas.[11,12]

Compared to Anglos, Mexican Americans are a relatively young population. The median age of Mexican Americans is 24.3 years, compared to 33.8 years for the population overall.[13] Moreover, the 1990 census showed that the proportion of Mexican Americans over age sixty-five was only 4.4 percent, compared to 12.1 percent for the general population. The fact that there are few elderly Mexican Americans is a startling statistic.[14]

There is clear evidence that Mexican Americans have large families, a characteristic of lower socioeconomic status. A recent population report showed that among the Hispanic subgroups, Mexican American families had the highest proportion of families with five or more members (34%), and were larger than non-Hispanic families which had an average of 3.13 members.[15] About one of every six Mexican American families had six or more members.

The income level reported for 1970 shows that 13.8 percent of Mexican Americans had incomes of less than $3,000, while only 5.7 percent of Anglos reported such low incomes.[16] The median family income for families identifying themselves as "of Mexican origin" in the 1975 population survey was $9,559, compared to $12,836 for all U.S. families.[17] The gap widened further: the 1980 median income for Hispanics was $12,952 compared to $19,116 for the entire population of the United States.[18] The trend continues in the 1990s, as population reports show the median income of Mexican families to be $23,200 and Hispanics, $23,400, compared to $36,300 for non-Hispanic families.[19] The median income for Hispanic men in 1990 was $14,100, whereas the median income for non-Hispanic men was $22,200. On the other hand, the median income for Hispanic women ($10,100) was half that of Hispanic men, and less than non-Hispanic women ($12,400).[20]

Again based on 1990 census data, the trend continues. Income figures show 28.1 percent of Hispanic persons were living in poverty compared to 12.1 percent of non-Hispanics. Similarly, the gap also widened for Hispanic families. Based on 1990 estimates, 25 percent of Hispanic families fell below the poverty level, compared to 9.5 percent of non-Hispanic families.[21] The increased percentage of Hispanics below the poverty level was due to Reaganomics-type policies (favoring the rich) pursued by the two previous Republican administrations. The poverty hits Hispanics harder, because they have larger families than Anglos.

Most Mexican Americans have occupations of low prestige. The 1976 population study conducted by the U.S. Bureau of the Census found that more than 60 percent of the occupations held by men of Mexican origin sixteen years of age and older were classified as blue-collar workers.[22] According to the 1991 *Current Population Report,* there were fewer than one-third as many managerial and professional specialty-type occupations among employed Mexican American males (8.9%) as among non-Hispanic males (27.6%). On the other hand, there were more Mexican American males (32.1%) in occupations such as operators, fabricators, and laborers than non-Hispanic males (19.1%).[23]

Among employed women, 14.1 percent of Mexican American women were employed in managerial and professional specialty occupations (higher than Mexican American males), compared to 28 percent of non-Hispanic women. In service-type occupations the same pattern holds as for men. About 26.9 percent of Mexican American women were employed in service-type occupations compared to 17 percent of non-Hispanic women.[24]

Mexican American unemployment was 12.9 percent, compared to 8 percent for the white work force; and in 1990, Hispanic unemployment rate was 10 percent versus 6.9 percent for non-Hispanics.[25] The disparities are even greater for youth. For instance, in 1974 30 percent of Hispanic youth sixteen to nineteen years of age were unemployed, compared to 18.4 percent of white youth.[26] In addition, according to the National Urban League, in the first quarter of 1978 teenage unemployment by race and ethnicity showed that 22.1 percent of Hispanic youth were unemployed, compared to 15.7 percent of Anglo youth.[27] Some reasons for the above-average unemployment among most groups of Hispanics, especially Mexican Americans, include educational disadvantages, language barriers, and discrimination. Furthermore, a significant number of Mexican American youth are employed as migratory farm workers, a sector of the economy that has high seasonal unemployment.

Despite the relative youth of the Mexican American population, school enrollment data indicate low educational attainment. Although 67 percent of non-Mexican American or non-Hispanic adults completed high school, only 34.3 percent of Mexican American adults completed high school.[28] Data concerning adults with less than five years of schooling again show this group trailing other minorities and Anglos. *U.S. News and World Report* stated that "a drop-out rate as high as 85 percent in some cities, to achievement scores that are two grade levels or more below national averages" are found in this population.[29]

The Spanish language is another important characteristic of the Mexican American population. According to information obtained from the 1976 *Survey of Income and Education Data,* 80 percent of Hispanic Americans lived in households where Spanish was spoken.[30] While there are few studies on Spanish-language usage, the small amount of data that do exist clearly illustrate the importance of language use by this group. The report of the National Center for Education Statistics, entitled *The Condition of Education for Hispanic Americans,* states, "The language one speaks is related to one's place of birth."[31] Among Mexican Americans born in Mexico, about two-thirds spoke Spanish as their primary language. Among those of corresponding heritage who were born in the United States, fewer than 20 percent usually spoke Spanish. The rest of the population of corresponding heritage was either monolingual or bilingual.

Mexican Americans (Latinos) *in Social Work Literature*

A survey of social work literature covering Mexican Americans between 1964 and 1999 and Latinos (a more generic term, which also includes Mexican Americans) from 1992 to 1999 serves to exemplify the trends and volume available to the social work profession concerning this group. Much that has been written on Mexican American and Latinos focuses on racism, cultural differences between this group and the majority, and the family. To be consistent with the previous survey, the articles surveyed were obtained again from the *Journal of Education for Social Work, Families in Society,* and *Social Work;* articles appearing in books or nonsocial work journals were not included.[32] In this survey, the selection of articles was based on titles from abstracts specifically stating Mexican American/*Chicano* and Hispanic or *Latino* content. Using this criteria may have excluded other social work articles used in practice. Although this survey does not encompass all social work articles on *Latinos* and Mexican Americans, it does allow some inferences to be drawn about the literature concerning the group.

Concerning Mexican Americans, of the thirty-four articles published between 1964 and 1999, 86 percent were written between 1968 and 1995 (see Table 20-2). The remaining 14 percent appeared over the last three years from 1996 to 1999,

TABLE 20-2	**Number of Articles on Mexican Americans/Chicanos (by years)**									
Articles	1964–67	1968–71	1972–75	1976–79	1980–83	1984–87	1988–91	1992–95	1996–99	Total
Mexican Americans/ Chicanos	0	9 (26%)	7 (21%)	5 (15%)	1 (3%)	2 (6%)	2 (6%)	3 (9%)	5 (15%)	34

indicating an upward trend from 1980 numbers. No articles were published about Mexican Americans during the mid-1960s. In general, the greater number of articles was written during the last years of the 1960s, fewer articles were written during the 1980s decade, with a slight upward trend during the 1990s. The last two intervals, 1992 to 1999, show a slight upward trend starting with 9 percent and moving upward to 15 percent, similar to 1976–1979 numbers. Regarding *Latinos* (not reported on the table), of the sixteen articles published between 1992 and 1999, six were written from 1992 and 1995. The remaining ten were written between 1996 and 1999.

The articles appearing between 1972 and 1976 were conceptual articles concerned with social justice for Mexican Americans. These articles emphasized the bilingualism and biculturalism of Mexican Americans, almost to the exclusion of other topics of interest to the profession. In contrast, the articles appearing between 1992 and 1999 were mostly research articles focusing on social conditions, various other topics, and the importance of culturally relevant services. No articles were written during the 1990s about police brutality, undocumented aliens, and racism. Articles on *Latinos* were mostly research focusing on social conditions, immigration issues, culture, and community services. In general, the change toward a research approach does not include research on practice interventions or action research to address social justice concerns. This pattern suggests that some topic may have been overlooked because of the values and research interests of the authors.

Table 20-3 clearly shows that, in the total thirty-five years, cultural differences, experiences of racism, and the family appeared more frequently than any other topics in the literature. These topics were for the most part not related to a discussion of how the social worker can use his or her knowledge in seeking to help Mexican Americans. One article in the 1970s discussed the application of knowledge in reporting a study of clients' perceptions of helping relationships formed with social workers of different ethnic backgrounds from their own. The study revealed that Anglo clients and Mexican American clients reacted positively to initial helping relationships with workers of different cultural backgrounds from their own. Although not reported in Table 20-3, our survey also showed that no *Latino* articles focused on knowledge that the social worker can use in seeking to help *Latinos*.

Similar conspicuous absences appeared in articles about social work practices for both Mexican Americans and *Latinos*. Only three articles gave suggestions for working with Spanish-speaking Mexican Americans, but offered no practice framework. Only one article describes the use of folk sayings (metaphors) as a culturally appropriate practice tool for treating Mexican American clients. Only one article

TABLE 20-3	Major Themes of Literature on Mexican Americans	
	Themes	No. of Articles
	Cultural differences	6
	Experience of racism	6
	The family	5
	Elderly	2
	Field education	2
	Psychosocial casework	1
	Language	2
	Empathy, warmth, genuiness	1
	Social system theory	1
	Community practice	2
	Work environment	2
	Outreach	1
	Immigrants	1
	Adoptions	1
	Caregivers	1

presented a training model describing how knowledge could be applied to mental health training and incorporated in schools of social work. In the *Latino* articles, one article emphasized understanding social characteristics in practice, such as national origin, language, religion, immigration, and citizen status. Another article focused on the practitioner becoming aware of clinician bias when diagnosing *Latino* clients. Finally, one article focused on cultural competency training for mental health counselors serving *Latino* families. Overall, one shortcoming of the available literature is a dearth of articles prescribing methods of practice and intervention research.

Although the literature is limited in usable practice frameworks, it is rich in identifying those areas of knowledge the authors deemed to be most significant for social work intervention. In earlier years, the authors were profoundly concerned with the effects of racism and cultural differnces; this was not the main focus of later work. More research is still needed in these areas. Still, the limited literature provides the profession with practice knowledge regarding both Mexican American and *Latino* issues that can be incorporated by social workers into their work with this population.

Ecosystems Model

The five-level ecosystems model detailed in Section A will be adopted as an assessment tool to analyze the Mexican American. The five levels of analysis include historical, environmental-structural, cultural, family, and individual factors impacting Mexican Americans. The emphasis will be on mental health and psychosocial issues, as social work practice focuses on the interaction between the person and the environment. The term *person* may refer to an individual, a community, or even a larger social structure of society. Social work intervention might be directed at the person, the environment, or both. In each case, the social worker seeks to enhance and restore the social functioning of people and/or to change social conditions that impede the mutually beneficial interaction between people and their environment. This will be seen later in a police brutality case highlighting micro and macro intervention.

The ecosystems orientation involves the application of ecology and general systems theory to professional tasks. It permits social workers to look at psychosocial phenomena, account for complex variables, assess the dynamic interplay of these variables, draw conceptual boundaries around the unit of attention or the specific case, and then generate ideas for intervention. At this point methodology enters in, because in any particular case—meaning a particular individual, couple, family, group, institutional unit, or geographical area—any number of practice interventions might be needed. The ecosystems model can promote social workers' understanding of (1) the psychosocial problems experienced by Mexican Americans; (2) the crippling effects of institutional racism, such as the police brutality detailed in the Part Four introduction; and (3) the oppressive environments in which these people struggle to survive. For the purposes of this chapter, the five levels of analysis will be further subdivided as follows:

1. Historical
   a. History of treating mental illness (international)
   b. Mexico's approach to treating mental illness
2. Environmental–structural
   a. Mental health treatment for Mexican Americans in the United States
   b. The ethnosystem as an adjunctive helping service
3. Cultural
   a. *Barrio* service systems as adjunctive and alternative helping systems
4. The family
   a. Extended family, surrogate family, and support networks
5. The individual
   a. Assessment and treatment of a police brutality victim

Normally, for a deeper and more comprehensive understanding of a client's situation, the ecosystems five levels of assessment should be tied to and relevant to the specific case being assessed as was shown in the case example in Section A. With the exception of the *individual level,* this was not done in this chapter to allow for greater generalization to other Mexican Americans.

HISTORICAL FACTORS

HISTORY OF TREATING MENTAL ILLNESS.   Societies throughout the world have developed various approaches for treating persons suffering from psychological problems. Three basic explanations and corresponding intervention strategies pertaining to psychological problems can be traced back to the earliest times: (1) the attempt to explain diseases of the mind in physical terms; that is, the organic approach ("It's in your blood/chemistry"); (2) the attempt to deal with inexplicable events through spiritual or magical approaches ("The devil/spirits made you do it"); and (3) the attempt to find a psychological explanation for psychological problems ("It's all in your mind"). Hippocrates (460–377 B.C.), the father of medicine, pioneered the organic approach, believing that black bile caused depression. Several centuries later, Cicero (106–43 B.C.), the Roman statesman and attorney, objected to the black bile theory, maintaining that depression was the result of psychological difficulties. He proclaimed that people were responsible for their emotional and psychological difficulties—in a psychological sense, *they* could do something about them. Cicero laid down the theoretical foundations for psychotherapy. The magical/spiritual approach found people treating the afflicted person through appeasement, confession, incantations, magical rituals, or exorcism.[33]

The effectiveness of any treatment approach often depends on the suggestibility of the person on whom the approach is worked, the suggestive power of the influencing practitioner, and the sympathetic connection (relationship) between the practitioner and the person seeking assistance. If a person strongly believes, for example, his or her headache, stomachache, or depression has as its basis a physical or chemical factor and that only a medical person can help, a physician or psychiatrist who prescribes medication may have the greatest likelihood of relieving that person's symptom. If, on the other hand, the person believes he or she is suffering certain symptoms because he or she has sinned and that only a minister or priest can help, the church's representatives may indeed have the greatest impact. And if the person believes his or her symptom has a psychogenic basis and can only be alleviated by talking to someone who can be "objective" in understanding the symptom or problem, the psychiatrist or social worker may offer the best help.

MEXICO'S HISTORICAL APPROACH TO TREATING MENTAL ILLNESS.   Mexican society, like other societies, also developed approaches to help people with psychological problems. The ancestors of Mexican Americans, the Aztecs, numbering 20 million persons in Central Mexico in the fifteenth century, created a wealthy, powerful, and progressive empire. Their culture was highly developed, and in that intellectual atmosphere flourished highly advanced forms of psychiatry and psychotherapy. Translations of Aztec literature reveal that Aztec therapy was provided by competent personnel in institutions of high repute. They had an amazing grasp of psychology and developed concepts about ego formation similar to those advanced by Freud almost 500 years later. Those concepts appear in an Aztec document about dream interpretation. The Aztec psychiatrists knew how to recognize persons who were manic, schizoid, hysterical, depressive, and psychopathic—major mental disorder classifications not unlike the ones used today. Aztec patients were treated by a variety of methods, including an early form of brain surgery, hypnosis, "talking out" bad things in one's mind, and specific herbal potions for specific disorders.[34]

With the colonization of Mexico by Spain in the early sixteenth century came Spanish medicine based on European concepts. Spanish colonial physicians still held primitive ideas about the causes of disease, believing it was a punishment for sins caused by devils who had taken possession of the patient's body and spirit. Because military might was associated with racial superiority, Spanish medicine was also believed by Spaniards to be superior to that of the Aztecs. Had Spanish oppression not occurred, Aztec psychiatry might have made a very significant contribution to the mental health practices of the Western world. In spite of this overt conflict and clash over psychiatric approaches, however, the first hospital for the mentally ill founded in North America was in Mexico City in 1567.[35] The first hospital for the mentally ill in the United States was founded 185 years later, in 1752, in Philadelphia, Pennsylvania.[36] The United States established two additional hospitals for the mentally ill during this period, one in Williamsburg, Virginia, in 1773, and the Bloomingdale Asylum in New York in 1821. In a comparable period, Mexico also established a hospital in Yucatán in 1625, the Manicomio de lä Canoa in Mexico City in 1687, the Hospital Civil in Guadalajara in 1739, a hospital in Belém in 1794, and the Divino Salvado in Mexico City in 1796.

Other mental health milestones found Mexico establishing its first department of psychiatry in 1860 in Jalisco; the United States began its first program in 1906. Mexico began the systematic training of physicians in psychiatry in 1910; the United States initiated its training program in 1937. Mexico launched its community mental health movement in 1951 by establishing mental health programs in health centers; the United States initiated community programs in 1964 with the passage of the Federal Community Mental Health Act.[37] Today in Mexico the major mental health trends and various theoretical orientations are similar to those in other Western countries. No single therapy orientation prevails, and, as in the United States, psychiatrists are by and large in control of mental health programs, with psychologists, social workers, and psychiatric nurses having lesser roles. From the standpoint of mental health resources, the United States, being a much wealthier country, far overshadows Mexico in terms of mental health resources and manpower. The United States, for example, has 12.4 psychiatrists per 100,000, versus less than one psychiatrist per 100,000 in Mexico.[38]

ENVIRONMENTAL–STRUCTURAL FACTORS

MENTAL HEALTH TREATMENT FOR MEXICAN AMERICANS. In the United States, persons of Mexican descent have found it very difficult to obtain mental health services. The nation's first community mental health program specifically for persons of Mexican descent was established in East Los Angeles in 1967. The staffing pattern included four psychiatrists, four psychiatric social workers, three nurses, a clinical psychologist, a rehabilitation counselor, a community services coordinator, a community worker, and six secretaries. All but one of the staff were bilingual. In applying one measure of utilization (the percentage of Spanish surname population in the area, 76 percent), the program was successful in that 90 percent of the clients seen had a Spanish surname. Clearly here there was maximum utilization of services by Hispanics. The program offered traditional mental health services provided in the clients' primary language and at a fee ranging from 50 cents to $15.[39] There are a few other, rare examples of overutilization of mental health services by Hispanics,[40] but overall the utilization rate by this population rarely exceeds 50 percent. In other words, Hispanic receipt of services is usually one-half or less of their representation in the population.[41]

There are a number of reasons proposed to explain this underutilization. The literature is now making it increasingly clear that the major factors involved are structural in nature and pertain to the availability, accessibility, and acceptability of services to the very heterogeneous bilingual, bicultural characteristics of Hispanics.[42] When Hispanics finally do receive services, they are often of inferior quality, with diagnoses often based on assessment procedures developed for the middle-class Anglo population that have no validity or applicability to these people. Furthermore, Hispanics are more likely to receive somatic and medication treatment and less individual or group therapy. These experiences can and do result in premature treatment termination.[43] Another important factor, accounting for premature termination or resistance to treatment, is whether the Hispanic is a *voluntary* client seeking help for a problem *he* or *she* defines, or an *involuntary* client being referred for treatment regarding a problem of concern to the referring agency.[44] Racist and political policies and economic decisions (raising fees) by mental health agencies to deny services to "undocumented" or poor persons are other growing contributing factors related to the underutilization of services by Hispanics.

THE ETHNOSYSTEM: AN ADJUNCTIVE HELPING SYSTEM.   Assuming that social work abandons its constricted methods framework and adopts the ecosystems perspective, then this question must be asked: What other knowledge is needed to understand the psychosocial problems of Mexican Americans that is specific to their ethnic background? Solomon's framework provides one option for integrating Mexican American concerns into a practice framework.[45] She utilizes the ethnosystem and empowerment concepts as major integrative concepts. The *ethnosystem* is defined as a society comprising groups that vary in modes of communication, in degree of control over material resources, and in the structure of their internal relationships or social organization.[46] Moreover, these groups must be in a more or less stable pattern of relationships that have characteristics transcending any single group's field of integration; for example, the ethnosystem's political, educational, or economic subsystems. Solomon defines *empowerment* as a process whereby persons who belong to a stigmatized social category throughout their lives can be assisted to develop and increase skills in the exercise of interpersonal influence and the performance of valued social roles.[47]

Ethnosystems are the natural networks, the primary patterns of interaction, survival, and adjustment indigenous to societies. As used here, the concept of *natural networks* has its origins in several disciplines: social work, sociology, social psychology, and anthropology, as well as in the mental health "community support—significant others" literature.[48] Social workers need to be aware that these natural networks and primary systems exist apart from the usual modes of secondary interactions that Mexican Americans have developed for survival within Anglo-urbanized systems, including those with the social establishment. There is a basic similarity between the ethnosystem with secondary interaction for coping with the Anglo society and the concept of two environments, the immediate or nurturing environment and the wider environment. When, as Norton notes, the larger societal system rejects the minority group's immediate environment or ethnosystem, there is incongruence between the two (Solomon refers to this as negative valuation of a stigmatized collective), and power blocks are directed toward the minority individuals, groups, and communities.[49]

CULTURAL FACTORS: BARRIO SERVICE SYSTEMS

Mexican Americans have been immigrating to *barrios* (Mexican neighborhoods) in U.S. urban areas in large and small waves. The *barrio* is a microcosm of the dominant society as well as an ethnosystem. Although the communities interrelate with external institutional structures such as law enforcement, schools, and the public welfare system, *barrios* also have indigenous service systems that provide mutual aid and psychological support in time of need. Indigenous support systems include churches, neighbors, friends, the family, and alternate services.[50]

Many Mexican Americans, especially the elderly and immigrant groups, have strong religious ties and attend church on a regular basis. The church, whether Roman Catholic or Protestant, is an important spiritual support for many Mexican Americans and, in addition, is a vehicle for disseminating information about *barrio* activities and services, reaching individuals who would be largely inaccessible to public agencies. There is trust in the church. For example, the parish priest or minister often knows of potential adoptive parents who would provide an excellent home for an unwed mother's child.

Concerned neighbors and friends also provide aid and act as a resource. Perceived as confidential sources of advice, these significant persons act as referral agents. Lee's study on the use of the services of a model neighborhood health center by Mexican Americans observed that some groups sought primary groups such as friends and neighbors as their major source of information about health care services.[51]

FAMILY FACTORS

The family unit clearly plays an important role in providing economic, social, and psychological supports. Families also serve as adoptive parents for family members who are no longer able to care for their children. Especially in the case of older children, grandparents may care for and eventually adopt them. Other relatives, or the child's godparents or *compadres,* may also accept the responsibility of raising the child or children. Infants, of course, may also be adopted in the same manner. However, no matter how effective this network may be, it is the welfare agency, rather than the network itself, that has access at all times to the greatest amount of provision and greatest number of providers in the greatest geographical area; it is the agency that has legal responsibility for bringing services to the community.

As a result of the Chicano movement in the 1960s and 1970s, alternate service systems are being developed within the *barrio* to deal with the special needs of the Mexican American community. Although there are variations in the services offered in each *barrio,* common patterns in both structure and function are observable. Self-help groups, social action organizations, and specialized service agencies staffed exclusively by bicultural and bilingual personnel are considered the most essential aspects of the alternate service system.

Siporin writes that the ecological perspective is an "effort to improve the functioning and competence of the welfare service system of natural self-help mutual aid networks, and to improve the social functioning and coping competence of individuals and their collectivities."[52] This approach calls for the practitioner to broaden his or her view of the client. Intervention involves assessment of the total social, physical, and psychological needs of the client and his or her network system. Intervention also calls for advocacy in the amelioration of identified problems related to barriers created by social welfare systems. Intervention strategies are initiated in anticipation of resolving psychosocial problems. Two examples of such macrolevel strategies include networking and advocacy.

EXTENDED FAMILY, SURROGATE FAMILY, AND SUPPORT NETWORKS. Collins and Pancoast refer to *networks* as consisting of both people and relationships.[53] The social network is relatively invisible, though it is a real structure in which an individual, nuclear family, or group is embedded. The term *support systems,* as used here, parallels Caplan's conceptualization. He states, "Support systems may be of a continuing nature, intermittent or short-term in the event of an acute need or crisis."[54] Both enduring and short-term supports are likely to consist of three elements:[55]

1. The significant others help the individual mobilize his psychological resources and master his emotional burdens;
2. they share his tasks; and
3. they provide him with extra supplies of money, materials, tools, skills, and cognitive guidance to improve the handling of his situation.

Individuals usually belong to several networks at the same time. Networks can be based on kinship, friendship, employment, recreation, education, politics, ethnicity, religion, or whatever interests or elements individuals find in common.

The content of exchanges can also be varied.[56] Although the informal network is important, it cannot provide for all needs. Formal resources (social services agencies, medical services, and other service providers) are likely to be utilized. Social network intervention, therefore, is an approach to service delivery that involves significant individuals in the amelioration of identified psychosocial problems.

Social network intervention takes into consideration both formal and informal systems. Also of significance to Mexican Americans is that this approach incorporates the sociocultural components of the family. The utilization of support systems can be conceptualized into two main divisions: (1) to engage existing networks and enhance their functioning; and (2) to create new networks or "attach" a formerly isolated person or family to a network.[57]

The approach considers both psychological and environmental stresses and incorporates them into the total reality of a family. It focuses on rallying the life-sustaining forces of the individual and family. This viable system of self-help continues to function after the professional helper has been disengaged.

In social network intervention, the goal is to deal with the entire structure by rendering the network visible and viable and by attempting to restore its function. The social network for Mexican American families may include extended kin, *compadres* (co-parents), friends, *curanderos* (folk healers), and other concerned individuals. These subsystems are identified because of their potential to provide emotional strength, support, and other types of assistance to the family. Social network intervention, therefore, emphasizes engagement of the family's network of support systems.

INDIVIDUAL FACTORS

At the individual level of the ecosystems assessment model, attention is given by the social worker to the biopsychological endowment of the person, which includes personality strengths, level of psychosocial development, mental status, attitudes, values, cultural beliefs, lifestyle, educational attainment, and coping strengths when faced with physical and psychological stresses and problems. In turn, these factors are analyzed, not only within the ecosystems framework, but also in relationship to growth and development life-cycle theories such as those developed by Freud, Erikson, and Bowlby, to name a few.

Armed with the knowledge gained from the ecosystems assessment tool, the social worker is in a better position to plan his or her intervention. The central task for the social worker is to help clients resolve existing or potential problems in psychosocial functioning. This process may involve helping the client resolve problems within themselves or with other people such as a spouse, parent, children, friends, or coworkers. This focus is called direct service, or microlevel social work practice. Intervening on behalf of clients with larger social structures such as neighborhoods, organizations, or the community—in effect all those social work activities that fall outside of the domain of *micro* social work practice—is referred to as indirect service, or macrolevel social work practice. In working with poor people, especially documented or undocumented Mexican immigrants who are often at the mercy of various social, economic, and political forces in society, both levels of intervention, micro and macro, are necessary for optimal helping effectiveness. What follows is a detailed case concerning *micro* intervention by a social worker with a documented Mexican immigrant adult male who was assaulted by the police. Following the *micro* intervention, a discussion will focus on what interventions were made at the *macro* level.

Micro Social Work Practice

CASE EXAMPLE

Mr. Sanchez, a Spanish-speaking, married, thirty-five-year-old male of Mexican descent and father of three children, was referred for treatment to the *barrio* community mental health center by his attorney. He came to the center with his wife. He refused to tell the intake worker what his personal problems were that brought him to the center. He was unemployed and did not have money to pay for his treatment. The case was assigned to one of the licensed clinical social workers, Mr. Rubio.

The agency had a policy that in special circumstances when a potential client did not wish to discuss the reason for seeking services, the social worker assigned to the case would discuss this matter with the client. The agency, in addition to having a sliding scale for payment, had a special fund raised through community donations to sponsor clients who did not have the means to pay for services. Mr. Sanchez primarily spoke Spanish, hence a Spanish-speaking worker was assigned to him. In those instances when a bilingual social worker is not available, a trained *translator,* rather than an interpreter, would be used. An interpreter "interprets" (provides his or her interpretation of what is being discussed), but a translator provides a literal word-for-word translation of the communication. To avoid emotional involvement in the translation, it is preferable not to use a family member or friend of the client.

Mr. Sanchez sat down and sighed, looking at Mr. Rubio with one eye as he had a fresh, medical eyepatch bandage over the other.

"Are you in pain?" asked Mr. Rubio.

"Not very much now, but I was in more pain a month ago when this happened," replied Mr. Sanchez.

"Please tell me what happened to you. Take your time, and if there is something I ask that you don't want to answer or find it too difficult to answer, please tell me," instructed Mr. Rubio.

Rather than going through a rigid interview format in this initial meeting in order to obtain a social, family, educational, financial, employment, and health and mental health history, Mr. Rubio decided to begin "where the client is," that is, with what appeared to be an emotional and physical state of discomfort indicated by the sigh, and possibly pain related to an eye injury. By permitting Mr. Sanchez to tell his story at his own pace and allowing him to determine what questions he would answer, the worker was, in effect, "empowering" the client to participate in the interview by having control of the content of the discussion. His wife was quiet and did not say anything. She had a worried, concerned look.

Mr. Sanchez stated that three weeks previously on a Sunday afternoon, he had been playing basketball at the park with a group of friends. The losers of the game purchased the beer. Mr. Sanchez smiled when he said he had been on the winning team and didn't have to pay for the beer. He drank three small cans of beer and was driving home with his brother-in-law seated in the passenger's side of the car. He passed a police car which was going to make a right turn at an intersection. He continued traveling toward his home and noticed the police vehicle in his rearview mirror. Mr. Sanchez then turned right into his neighborhood street and parked his car in his driveway. Then he and his brother-in-law entered Mr. Sanchez's home where their wives were preparing dinner.

Mr. Sanchez entered his bedroom to change out of his gym clothes, which were wet with perspiration. As he was changing his clothes with his back to the bedroom door, the door opened swiftly, and he thought it was his children. He yelled out to close the door as he was changing. He then felt a powerful blow to his eye and did not remember anything after that. Mr. Sanchez bowed his head in silence, nodding "no" in a slow manner. Mr. Rubio joined him in this moment of silence, as if he were resting between rounds in a fight for his life. Mr. Sanchez looked at his wife as if he wanted her to continue with the story. Trying to hold back tears, Mrs. Sanchez stated, "It was the police. They hit him with a "billy club" on his right eye. After they hit him there was complete silence. I was able to peer through the door which was open about three inches, and my husband was lying on the floor, completely unconscious. I saw a lot of blood coming from the area around his eye, and I became very frightened and began screaming. I thought they had killed him." At this point, Mrs. Sanchez became very emotional and sobbed deeply. Mr. Rubio attempted to provide support to Mr. and Mrs. Sanchez by stating, "Few things in life cause so much pain and hardship." Both nodded in agreement. Mrs. Sanchez then continued, "I tried to push the door open but the officers slammed it shut. My children started becoming hysterical and began crying, too. My sister and brother-in-law took my children with them, as they didn't want them to continue seeing their father in his unconscious state. After three or four minutes, the police officers picked up my husband, who was staggering and bleeding even more from his eye, and placed him in the police vehicle. One of the officers stated that they were taking my husband to jail for resisting arrest, assaulting police officers, and drunk driving. I asked the officers *where* they were taking him, and one officer yelled back, "To the station." I asked "*Which* station?" and the officer smiled and said, "Just the station."

At this point in the interview, Mr. Rubio could have stated something like "You must have felt helpless," or "You probably thought you would never again see your husband." But these comments would have elicited even more affect or surfaced fears which might have still have been unconscious, thereby changing the focus and purpose of the interview away from Mr. Sanchez. By coming to the interview and participating, Mrs. Sanchez was in a supportive role to her husband and Mr. Rubio's intent was to help her in that role.

Mr. Rubio stated, "It must have been very difficult for you. You have been very helpful to your husband."

Mrs. Sanchez nodded "yes," as Mr. Sanchez tenderly hugged her. There was a brief silence as both looked at Mr. Rubio to continue the interview. Mr. Rubio then asked, "What was the extent of your eye injury?"

"The doctor said my eye was totally destroyed and it's dying. I can't see anything out of it. In two weeks he'll remove it and then give me a brown leather patch because I can't afford to buy a glass eye." His remaining eye became red and teary as he stared at Mr. Rubio, searching for a solution to his problem.

Resisting the impulse to have a ready, quick answer such as "Everything will turn out all right, you'll see," instead Mr. Rubio went with the feelings Mr. Sanchez's tragic story had invoked in him. Mr. Rubio stated, "I feel stunned and speechless. No one can really know what it is to lose your sight in one eye, other than a person who has experienced it. It must be both physically and psychologically painful."

Mr. Sanchez nodded in agreement, but added; "It is painful, especially at night. I can't sleep well because of the pain. I think I can stand it, and I'll eventually adjust to having only one eye. Maybe that is why God gave us two, in case we lose one." He smiled and then remarked, "But what I find most painful is that I cannot work and support my family and pay the rent. I don't know what I'm going to do. I don't feel like a man anymore."

Now Mr. Rubio had three major interrelated issues to consider in this first interview: (1) to increasingly focus on post-traumatic stress disorder (PTSD) questions to "rule out" PTSD; (2) to shift the focus of questions to determine the existence of and the gravity of depression Mr. Sanchez was experiencing or to rule out major depression; or (3) to focus on the issue of perceived loss of self and role as a man, husband, father, and only "breadwinner" in the family. This is especially catastrophic for those Hispanic males who have internalized a traditional cultural role wherein each family member has a clear, prescribed role. Losing the capacity to fulfill that role expectation for some traditional Latinos is like losing the meaning and purpose in life. For some wives a comparable loss would be never being able to have a child. Cultural expectations are not set in "concrete," hence, people can be helped to modify their position and adapt to a new situation. Mr. Rubio decided to deal with the "I don't feel like a man anymore" response which, if not addressed, would have resulted in increasing depression, perhaps even leading to suicide since Mr. Sanchez was in a very high-risk age level and profile for *Latino* male suicide (75% of *Latinos* who commit suicide in the United States are married and between twenty to thirty-five years of age). In Mr. Rubio's clinical judgment, this currently was the most powerful stressor Mr. Sanchez was experiencing. Mr. Rubio had to help Mr. Sanchez view the situation in a less stressful way (cognitive restructuring, reframing).

"You certainly feel like a different person and in some ways you are. I agree with you that eventually you will learn to adapt to using only one eye. You are in a psychological and economic crisis which, in fact, will be only temporary. Once your eye pain lessens, you will be able to resume some type of work and once again support your family." His wife was nodding in agreement and smiling. "I never thought of it that way. I guess you are correct," stated Mr. Sanchez. "But what am I going to do for money now? We need food, and I have to pay the rent."

"I can go to work and you can stay home and take care of the children and send them off to school," commented Mrs. Sanchez enthusiastically. "No, no. That is not right. A man's wife should never have to work. That is an insult," responded Mr. Sanchez, shaking his head from side to side. Mr. Rubio did not comment, creating an atmosphere for dialogue between a man and his wife during a period of crisis. "Why should we have to lose our home and return to Mexico to live with and depend on relatives when we can survive here if I go to work temporarily?" Mrs. Sanchez asked. "I know I can find work as a domestic or in a sewing factory. Besides, the children would really enjoy spending more time with you. They worry about you all of the time."

"*They* worry about me?" responded Mr. Sanchez in a surprised tone. "They really should not! I will be fine!" Mr. Sanchez responded in a firm, confident tone. This gave Mr. Rubio an opportunity to uncover Mr. Sanchez's inner strength and competitive spirit within a *Latino* cultural context.

"You *are* a proud man, good father, and husband. You are loved by your wife and children. You are a real *macho*, a man who provides for and protects his family in the most positive ways. A 'crisis' in Chinese philosophy means 'an opportunity to change.' This crisis has presented you an opportunity to become even more of a man, by providing your children and wife emotional support rather than primarily economic help as the sole breadwinner. You are being challenged to temporarily change in order to continue to help your family."

Mr. Sanchez sat up straighter and smiled again as his wife was nodding affirmatively and holding her husband's hand. "We *can* do it," she said. "I guess we can," replied Mr. Sanchez in a soft tone.

"And I will be here to continue to help you," added Mr. Rubio. "We're just about out of time. Do you want me to schedule an appointment for you three days from now?"

"Is this therapy? Is this all that is going to happen?" inquired Mr. Sanchez.

"This was our first visit, and in this hour we covered many important things," stated Mr. Rubio. "This is just the beginning of therapy, to get information in order to know what to do. Normally, we see people once a week to help them with their concerns. In your case, I want to see you in three days to see how this trauma has affected you. Do you think you feel well enough now so that I can see you in a few days?" Mr. Rubio asked. "Yes, that would be fine," replied Mr. Sanchez.

Mr. Rubio was attempting to assess whether Mr. Sanchez felt sufficiently emotionally and physically capable to return in a few days. It was a subtle way of empowering him to be involved in making important decisions about his welfare. Had he been in significant physical pain, he would have been referred to the center's staff psychiatrist for a medical opinion and treatment referral. Psychologically, Mr. Sanchez seemed intact, possessed good ego strength, and did not appear suicidal. Had Mr. Sanchez replied, "I don't even know where I'll be tomorrow, or if I'll even be alive" or verbal comments to that effect indicating possible suicidal ideation, Mr. Rubio would have extended the interview to assess his suicidality, and, if indicated, treated it by evaluating the need for medication and/or hospitalization with the center's psychiatrist.

Mr. Sanchez returned for his appointment. He appeared less depressed, and his depression was "reactive" in nature; that is, it was in response to his two major losses—loss of an eye and loss of employment. In addition, Mr. Rubio confirmed his clinical opinion that Mr. Sanchez qualified for a diagnosis of PTSD, and he was placed on the appropriate antianxiety medication by the center psychiatrist. Subsequent treatment sessions involved conjoint sessions with Mr. Sanchez and his wife, who was now working, to help *them* adapt to their changing roles in the family, and evaluation sessions with the three children. They had all observed their bleeding father taken away in the police car. One of the children was found to also be suffering from PTSD, and the other two children had adjustment disorder symptoms. The children were treated by another social worker. After ten visits, Mr. Sanchez's symptoms diminished significantly with the exception of being very fearful of uniformed police and "black and white" police vehicles. After three months of treatment, Mrs. Sanchez phoned to state that her husband had been convicted of misdemeanor drunk driving and had been sentenced to ninety days of jail. She added that her husband wanted her to communicate his appreciation for the help extended to him and his family and that he felt stronger and confident that he could handle this new crisis. Mrs. Sanchez stated that Mr. Sanchez's mother was coming up from Mexico to take care of the children to give her the opportunity to keep working.

Macro Social Work Practice

Mr. Rubio knew quite well that excessive force from police was not an uncommon experience in the *barrio*, occurring on the average of three to four times per day, and usually the victims were African Americans or *Latinos*. Mr. Rubio was also aware of volunteer "alternative community resources" in the *barrio* such as the "Police Misconduct Lawyer Referral Service." This service has a board of directors comprised of community people, attorneys, and social workers and has a panel of private attorneys for representation in those cases where the conduct of the police was improper and caused injury or damages. Prior to his assault, Mr. Sanchez was working as a plumber's assistant earning $9 per hour. He did not have medical or unemployment insurance, as he was working for a relative who was a licensed, freelance plumber.

Mr. Sanchez was also going to night school to learn English and more about plumbing to prepare for his plumbing certificate. Mr. Rubio referred Mr. Sanchez to the police misconduct referral service.

This service was codirected by Cindy Torres, a licensed master's level social worker, and Roland Goya, an attorney. Both volunteered a few evenings per week to the program. They were assisted by a few social work and law students who handled most of the incoming calls and initial in-person interviews. Based on the legal merits of the cases, some were referred to the panel of volunteer attorneys who did "pro bono" (free service) work for the *barrio*. A panel of licensed and prelicense clinical MSWs belonging to *Trabajadores de La Raza*, a *Latino* social work organization, likewise provided free clinical services for victims of police misconduct who could not afford to pay a modest fee for services.

In addition to clinical and administrative skills, Cindy Torres also had macro community organization skills and was attempting to mobilize several "key" community players, both elected and appointed leaders, and "grass-roots" *barrio* residents, to help reduce police malpractice and improve *barrio*–police relations. Law enforcement representatives were also invited to meetings, including the Chief of Police. Rather than emphasizing the negative by simply organizing groups to protest and be critical of the police, hence alienating them even further, Ms. Torres appealed instead to the positive forces, both in the police department and the *barrio,* who wanted to work on the problem of *barrio*–police conflict.

Ms. Torres prepared for the first meeting and had a good response from various members of the community, including the Chief of Police who was going to send his Deputy Chief and local Precinct Captain as his representatives to the first meeting. At the meeting, which was the first of several meetings, Ms. Torres used a "force-field analysis" procedure developed for use with community groups in problem identification and problem solving. The basic concept in force-field analysis is to identify forces that are potential supports for, or barriers to, the achievement of a specific goal.[58] A group must already have a clear idea of the problem and have a desired goal. *Barrio* residents wanted the police to stop beating them and treat them with more respect. The police wanted more respect and cooperation from the community in reducing crime.

Figure 20-1 illustrates the force-field chart written on the blackboard by Ms. Torres during the meeting as she obtained the input from the thirty-two participants. The typed information was printed by Ms. Torres, and the information written in italics represents the input from the group during the discussion facilitated by Ms. Torres.

As can be seen in Figure 20-1, after the major goal had been established, and the competing forces (driving vs. restraining forces) list was created to show the status quo, Ms. Torres guided the group in determining how powerful each force was and then drew an arrow (thin, medium, or thick depending on the estimated power of the force) in the direction of the force (toward or away from the goal). For example, the thicker the arrow, the stronger the driving or restraining force. This would indicate that more effort would be required to improve the situation in the identified problem area, especially when a thick arrow indicating a driving force encountered a thick arrow representing a *restraining force*. Such was the case in

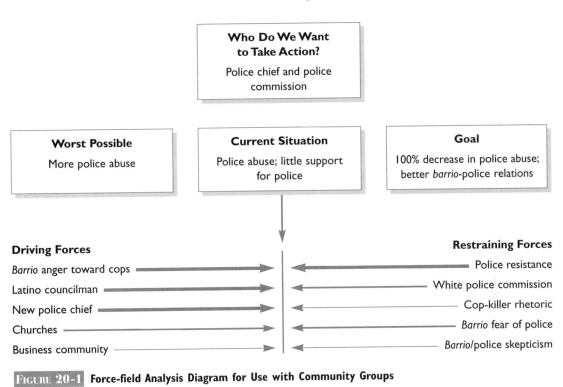

FIGURE 20-1 **Force-field Analysis Diagram for Use with Community Groups**

barrio anger toward the police (driving forces) being met with police resistance to change (restraining forces).

Thereafter, Ms. Torres helped the group establish small committees to mobilize the driving forces to work on the problem and other small committees to reduce the impact of the restraining forces. Applying her knowledge of group dynamics, she asked the group to establish mixed, balanced committees reflecting persons with law enforcement, *barrio,* political leader, church, "militant," and business community perspectives. Through such group composition, the committees were able to work out their differences in the small groups and develop cohesion before they approached other groups and bodies of resistance, such as the police commission.

The large group continued to meet on a monthly basis over a period of fifteen months, with the small committees meeting more regularly. An unexpected outcome was that the group, in working toward its goals, also planned and conducted a *Barrio–Police Relations Conference* a year later, which featured as speakers the District Attorney, the *Latino* Councilman, the Chief of Police, and a police brutality victim. The latter was Mr. Sanchez!

Following Mr. Sanchez's three months in jail for his drunk driving conviction, his attorney filed a civil suit in his behalf against the police department and the city for pain, injury, permanent blindness in one eye, and suffering. The jury ruled that the police did not have a right to enter his home without a bench warrant because Mr. Sanchez had not committed a felony offense, only a misdemeanor drunk-driving violation. Mr. Sanchez was awarded $250,000. He donated $5,000 to the Police Misconduct Referral Service and $5,000 to the *barrio* mental health center where he had been treated by Mr. Rubio. He told Mr. Rubio that he would prefer to have his eye back rather than the money he had received. Mr. Sanchez planned to return to Guadalajara, Mexico, because he found Southern California to be too violent.

Concluding Comment   Mexican Americans are one of this country's most diverse ethnic groups. Because they were an indigenous population, in their own land, prior to the Anglo-American conquest of Mexico in 1848, they, like Native Americans, are one of the oldest minorities. On the other hand, continuing immigration from Mexico also makes them one of the newest and largest immigrant groups. They are a very heterogeneous Hispanic group, responding to all categories of any language and cultural scale. Mexican Americans primarily reside in urban areas in the Southwest, generally occupy a low socioeconomic status, and have large families, a high unemployment rate, and low educational attainments—all symptoms of working class exploitation, sexism, and racism. Mexican Americans have a small elderly population (4%), almost one-third the proportion of elderly whites, and a very large youth population. Because their age profile is the opposite that of whites, their human services needs are different from those of whites, who are currently preoccupied with the needs of the elderly. As is the case with African Americans, Hispanics are increasingly being caught up in the juvenile justice system, a field of practice in which social work has not expressed much interest.

The authors' survey of the social work literature pertaining to Mexican Americans revealed that much of it is of a descriptive nature, highlighting racism and value and cultural differences between Mexican Americans and whites. Only two articles focused on the elderly Mexican American. With only an exception or two, there were no articles written specifically about juvenile and adult offenders, gangs, police–community conflict, stress caused by fear of deportation, divorce and separation, child abuse, family therapy, marital therapy, or mental health needs.

Mexican Americans *do* have mental health needs, and many do avail themselves of direct services when they are provided at modest cost, in their primary language, and near their homes. A rich psychiatric history, originating almost 700 years ago with the Aztecs, provides Mexican Americans with a foundation to build on, as both consumers and providers of mental health services. However, the current regressive trend in the United States, with its accompanying stresses, is creating new racism and poverty casualties among the poor and minorities. As needs for services increase, there is a corresponding increased effort to "economize" by "phasing out" or denying services to the poor. Mexican Americans are particularly affected by these trends, especially new Mexican immigrants and the "undocumented."

Practice suggestions were offered that may have implications for macro social work in the *barrio*. The *barrio* as an ethnosystem is comprised of indigenous social support systems such as churches, neighbors, friends, alternative services (self-help groups), and the family. Applying the concept of social network intervention to Mexican Americans signifies the inclusion of extended family members, *compadres* (co-parents), friends, coworkers, and other concerned persons in their support systems. These subsystems have the potential to provide emotional strength, support, and other types of assistance to the family.

This chapter highlighted micro and macro social work practice intervention in a police brutality case. Police brutality has now become a NASW practice priority since April 1992.

These tragic incidents committed by a few irresponsible law enforcement officials under the "color of law" (in uniform, on official duty) number some 10,000 to 15,000 episodes per year. Police brutality impacts 60,000 to 90,000 persons—mostly poor and racial/ethnic minorities—when emotionally affected family members are included. This is definitely a human rights and quality-of-life issue for the profession. The values and ethics of the profession demand social work practice involvement and inclusion in the curriculum of schools of social work.

KEY WORDS AND CONCEPTS

Mexican Americans	*Barrio*
Curanderismo	*Compadres*
Chicano	Treaty of Guadalupe–Hidalgo
Mexicans	*Barrio* service system
Aztec psychiatry	Positive *machismo*

SUGGESTED READINGS

Burnette, Denise, "Custodial Grandparents in Latino Families: Patterns of Service Use and Predictors of Unmet Needs," *Social Work* (January 1999): 22–34.

Casas, J. M., and Vasquez, M. J. T. "Counseling the Hispanic Client: A guiding framework for a diverse population," in P. Pedersen, J. Draguns, W. Lonner, and J. Trimble (Eds.), *Counseling Across Cultures,* 4th ed. Honolulu: University of Hawaii Press, 1996, pp. 146–176.

Curiel, Herman, "Hispanics: Mexican Americans," in R. L. Edwards, ed. *Encyclopedia of Social Work,* 19th edition (Washington, D.C.: NASW Press, 1995), pp. 1233–1244.

Hurtado, Aida, 1995 "Variations, Combinations, and Evolutions: Latino Families in the United States," in *Understanding Latino Families: Scholarship, Policy and Practice,* ed. Ruth E. Zambrana. Thousand Oaks, Calif.: Sage Publications, 1995, pp. 40–61.

Padilla, Yolanda, "Immigrant Policy: Issues for Social Work Practice," *Social Work* 42 (March 1997): 595–606.

Ruiz, Pedro, "Challenges in Providing Psychiatric Services to Hispanic Americans," *Psychline,* Vol. 2, No. 4, 1998, pp. 6–10.

Simoni, J. M., and Perez, L. (1995). "Latinos and Mutual Support Groups: A Case for Considering Culture," *American Journal of Orthopsychiatry* 65 (1995): 440–445.

Skolnick, Jerome H., and Fyfe, James J. *Above the Law: Police and the Excessive Use of Force.* New York: The Free Press, 1993).

Vargas, Luis A., and Koss-Chioino, Joan D., eds. *Working with Culture: Psychotherapeutic Interventions with Ethnic Minority Children and Adolescents.* San Francisco: Jossey-Bass Publishers, 1992.

Vega, William A., Kolody, Bohdan, Aguilar-Gaxiola, Sergio, Catalano, Ralph, "Gaps in Service Utilization by Mexican Americans with Mental Health Problems," *American Journal of Psychiatry* 156 (June 1999): 928–934.

Vega, William A., Kolody, Bohdan, Aguilar-Gaxiola, Sergio, Alderete, Ethel, Catalano, Ralph, Caraveo-Anduaga, Jorge, "Lifetime Prevalence of DSM III-R Psychiatric Disorders among Urban and Rural Mexican Americans in California," *Archives of General Psychiatry* 55 (September 1998): 771–781.

Zayas, Louis H., Evans, Mary E., Mejia, Luis, and Rodriguez, Orlando, "Cultural Competency Training for Staff Serving Hispanic Families with a Child in Psychiatric Crisis," *Families in Society* (July/August 1997): pp. 405–412.

ENDNOTES

1. For the purposes of this chapter, a *barrio* is defined as a neighborhood or community area of a town or city occupied predominantly by persons of Mexican descent.
2. Harry H. L. Kitano, *Race Relations* (Englewood Cliffs, NJ: Prentice Hall, 1976), p. 242.
3. Ibid.
4. U.S. Bureau of the Census, "Persons of Spanish Origin in the United States: March 1976," *Current Population Reports* P20-310 (Washington, D.C.: U.S. Department of Commerce, March 1977).
5. "The Hispanic Population in the United States: March 1986 and 1987" (Advance Report).
6. "The Hispanic Population in the United States: March 1991," *Current Population Reports,* Population Characteristics Series P20-455, U.S. Department of Commerce, Economics and Statistics Administration, Bureau of the Census, 1991, p. 2.
7. Ibid.
8. Wayne A. Cornelius, *Illegal Mexican Migration to the United States* (Cambridge, MA: MIT Press, 1977).
9. *Business Week,* June 23, 1980, p. 86.
10. *Los Angeles Times,* August 4, 1981, Part II, p. 1.
11. U.S. General Accounting Office, *Hispanic Access to Health Care: Significant Gaps Exist,* GAO/PEMD-92-6, Washington, D.C., January, 1992.
12. "The Hispanic Population in the United States: March 1991," p. 16.
13. Ibid., p. 2.
14. Ibid., p. 2.
15. Ibid., p. 5.
16. U.S. Bureau of the Census, *Current Population Reports,* 1977.
17. Ibid.
18. U.S. Bureau of the Census, "Household and Family Characteristics: March 1979," *Current Population Reports* P20-352 (Washington, D.C.: U.S. Department of Commerce, July 1980), p. 1.
19. "The Hispanic Population in the United States: March 1991," p. 8.
20. Ibid., p. 12.
21. Ibid., p. 8.
22. U.S. Bureau of the Census, "Persons of Spanish Origin in the United States: March 1976," *Current Population Reports* P20-310 (Washington, D.C.: U.S. Department of Commerce, July 1977).
23. "The Hispanic Population in the United States: March 1991," p. 12.
24. Ibid.
25. Ibid., p. 3.

26. Ibid.

27. National Urban League, *Quarterly Economic Report of the Black Worker,* No. 11, First Quarter (June 1978).

28. U.S. Bureau of the Census, *Current Population Reports,* 1977.

29. *U.S. News and World Report,* 1993.

30. U.S. Department of Health, Education, and Welfare, National Center for Education Statistics, "Place of Birth and Language Characteristics of Persons of Hispanic Origin in the United States," *Survey of Income and Education Data,* No. 78-135 (Spring 1976).

31. National Center for Education Statistics, *The Condition of Education for Hispanic Americans* (Washington, D.C.: U.S. Department of Education, July 1980).

32. Publications 1964 to 1991: Lydia R. Aguirre, "The Meaning of the Chicano Movement"; Tomas C. Antencio, "The Survival of La Raza Despite Social Services"; John Florez, "Chicanos and Coalition as a Force for Social Change"; Alejandro Garcia, "The Chicano and Social Work"; Faustina Ramirez Knoll, "Casework Services for Mexican Americans"; Armando Morales, "The Collective Preconscious and Racism"; Phillip D. Ortego, "The Chicano Renaissance"; Faustina Solis, "Socioeconomic and Cultural Conditions of Migrant Workers"; and Marta Sotomayor, "Mexican American Interaction with Social System," all found in *Social Casework* 52, No. 5 (May 1971). See also Ignacio Aguilar, "Initial Contacts with Mexican American Families," *Social Casework* 17 (May 1972): 66–70; Miguel Montiel, "The Chicano Family: A Review of Research," *Social Work* 18 (March 1973): 21–23; R. J. Maduro and C. F. Martinez, "Latino Dream Analysis: Opportunity for Confrontation," *Social Casework* 55 (October 1974): 461–469; F. Souflee and G. Schmitt, "Education for Practice in the Chicano Community," *Journal of Education for Social Work* 10 (Fall 1974): 75–84; L. A. Santa Cruz and D. H. Hepworth, "News and Views: Effect of Cultural Orientation on Casework," *Social Casework* 56 (January 1975): 52–57; Teresa Ramirez Boulette, "Group Therapy with Low Income Mexican Americans," *Social Work* 20 (September 1975); David Maldonado, "The Chicano Aged," *Social Work* 20 (March 1975): 213–216; I. Aguilar and V. N. Wood, "Therapy through a Death Ritual," *Social Work* 21 (January 1976): 49; C. Medina and M. R. Neyes, "Dilemmas of Chicano Counselors," *Social Work* 21 (November 1976): 515–517; Armando Morales, "Institutional Racism in Mental Health and Criminal Justice," *Social Casework* 59 (July 1978): 387–396; Henry Ebihara, "A Training Program for Bilingual Paraprofessionals," *Social Casework* 60 (May 1970): 274–281; Ramon M. Salcido, "Undocumented Aliens: A Study of Mexican Families," *Social Work* 24 (July 1979); Ramon M. Salcido, "Problems of the Mexican American Elderly in an Urban Setting," *Social Casework* 10 (December 1979); 609–615; Ted R. Watkins and Richard Gonzales, "Outreach to Mexican Americans," *Social Work* 27 (January 1982): 68–73; Ernesto Gomez, Louis A. Zurcher, Buford E. Farris, and Roy E. Becker, "A Study of Psychosocial Casework with Chicanos," *Social Work* 30 (November–December 1985): 477–483; Maria E. Zuniga, "Mexican-American Clinical Training: A Pilot Project," *Journal of Social Work Education* Vol 23, No. 3 (Fall 1987); Christine Marlow, "Management of Family and Employment Responsibilities by Mexican American and Anglo Women," *Social Work* 35 (May 1990): 259–265; Peter Manoleas and Ernestina Carillo, "A Culturally Syntonic Approach to the Field Education of Latino Students," *Journal of Social Work Education* Vol 27, No. 2 (Spring/Summer 1991): 135–140; Publications 1992–1999: M. Hines, Nydia Garcia-Prieto, Monica McGoldrick, Rhea Almeida, and

Susan Weltman, "Intergenerational Relationships Across Cultures," *Families in Society* (June 1992): 323–338; Deborah J. Monahan, Vernon L. Greene, and Patricia D. Coleman, "Caregiver Support Groups: Factors affecting use of services," *Social Work* (May 1992): 254–260; Alison Solomon, "Clinical Diagnosis among Diverse Populations: A Multicultural Perspective," *Families in Society* (June 1992): 371–377; Luis H. Zayas, Nancy A. Busch-Rossnagel, "Pregnant Hispanic Women: A Mental Health Study, *Families in Society* (November 1992): 515–521; Robert Aponte, "Hispanic Families in Poverty: Diversity, Context, and Interpretation," *Families in Society* (November 1993): 527–537; Graciela M. Castex, "Providing Services to Hispanic/Latino Populations: Profiles in Diversity," *Social Work* 39 (May 1994): 288-296; Andre G. Jacob, "Social Integrations of Salvadorian Refugees," *Social Work* 39 (May 1994): 307–312; Helen Land, "Aids and Women of Color," *Families in Society* (June 1994): 355–361; Diane Drachman, Young-Hee Kwon-Ahn, and Ana Paulino, "Migration and Resettlement Experiences of Dominican and Korean Families," *Families in Society* (December 1996): 626–638; Larry M. Gant, "Effects of Culturally Sophisticated Agencies on Latino Social Workers," *Social Work* 41 (November 1996): 624–631; Christian E. Molidor "Female Gang Members: A Profile of Aggression and Victimization," *Social Work* 41 (May 1996): 252–257; Marceline M. Lazzari, Holly Ford, and Kelly J. Haughey, "Making a Difference: Women of Action in the Community," *Social Work* 41 (March 1996): 197–205; Robert S. Baush and Richard T. Serpe, "Negative Outcomes of Interethnic Adoption of Mexican American Children," *Social Work* 42 (March 1997): 136–144; Melvin Delgado, "Puerto Rican Sons as Primary Caregivers of Elderly Parents," *Social Work* 42 (March 1997): 121–216; Melvin Delgado, "Role of Latina-owned Beauty Parlors in a Latino Community," *Social Work* 42 (March 1997): 346–356; Yolanda Padilla, "Immigrant Policy: Issues for Social Work Practice," *Social Work* 42 (March 1997): 595–606; Ruth Planos, Luis H. Zayas, and Nancy A. Busch-Rossnagel, "Mental Health Factors and Teaching Behaviors among Low-income Hispanic Mothers," *Families in Society* (January/February, 1997): 4–12; Luis H. Zayas, Mary E. Evans, Luis Mejia, and Orlando Rodriguez, "Cultural Competency Training for Staff Serving Hispanic Families with a Child in Psychiatric Crisis," *Families in Society* (July/August, 1997): 405–412; Melvin Delgado and Jorge Santiago, "HIV/AIDS in a Puerto Rican/Dominican Community: A Collaborative Project with a Botanical Shop," *Social Work* 43 (March 1998): 184–186; Melvin Delgado and Keva Barton, "Murals in Latino Communities: Social Indicators of Community Strengths," *Social Work* 43 (July 1998): 346–356; Judith Baer, "Family Relationships, Parenting Behavior, and Adolescents Deviance in Three Ethnic Groups," *Families in Society* (May/June 1999): 279–284; Denise Burnette, "Custodial Grandparents in Latino Families: Patterns of Service Use and Predictors of Unmet Needs," *Social Work* (January 1999): 22–34.

33. Franz G. Alexander and Sheldon V. Selesnick, *The History of Psychiatry* (New York: Harper & Row, 1966), pp. 7–14.

34. Guido Belsasso, "The History of Psychiatry in Mexico," *Hospital and Community Psychiatry* 20 (November 1969): 342–344.

35. Ibid.

36. Alexander and Selesnick, p. 120.

37. Belsasso.

38. Ramon Parres, "Mexico," *World Studies in Psychiatry* 2, No. 3 (Medical Communications, Inc., 1979).

39. Marvin Karno and Armando Morales, "A Community Mental Health Service for Mexican Americans in a Metropolis," *Comprehensive Psychiatry* 12 (March 1971): 116–121.
40. Morales, "Institutional Racism in Mental Health and Criminal Justice," pp. 394, 395.
41. *Report to the President's Commission on Mental Health,* "Special Populations Sub-Task Task Panel on Mental Health of Hispanic Americans" (Washington, D.C.: U.S. Government Printing Office, 1978), p. 3.
42. Ibid.
43. Joe Yamamoto, Quinston James, and Norman Palley, "Cultural Problems in Psychiatric Therapy," *Archives of General Psychiatry* 19 (1968): 45–49.
44. Armando Morales, "Social Work with Third-World People," *Social Work* 26 (January 1981): 49.
45. Barbara Bryant Solomon, *Black Empowerment: Social Work in Oppressed Communities* (New York: Columbia University Press, 1976), p. 6.
46. Dolores G. Norton, *The Dual Perspective: Inclusion of Ethnic Minority Content on the Social Work Curriculum* (New York: Council of Social Work Education, 1978).
47. Solomon.
48. Ramon Valle, "Ethnic Minority Curriculum in Mental Health: Latino/Hispano Perspectives" (Paper presented at Mental Health Curriculum Development Conference sponsored by Howard University School of Social Work, November 16–18, 1979, Chicago.)
49. Norton.
50. Valle, p. 7.
51. E. P. Tsiaiah Lee, "The Pattern of Medical Care Use: Mexican American Patients at a Model Neighborhood Health Center in Los Angeles" (Doctoral thesis, University of California at Los Angeles, 1975).
52. Max Siporin, *Introduction to Social Work Practice* (New York: Macmillan, 1975).
53. Alice H. Collins and Diane L. Pancoast, *Natural Helping Networks: A Strategy for Intervention* (Washington, D.C.: National Association of Social Workers, 1976).
54. Gerald Caplan, *Support Systems and Community Mental Health* (New York: Behavioral Publications, 1974).
55. Ibid.
56. Collins and Pancoast.
57. Carol Swenson, "Social Networks, Mutual Aid, and the Life Model of Practice," in Carel B. Germain, ed., *Social Work Practice: People and Environment and Ecological Perspective* (New York: Columbia University Press, 1979), pp. 213–238.
58. Mark A. Mattaini, *More Than a Thousand Words: Graphics for Clinical Practice* (Washington, D.C.: National Association of Social Workers, 1993), pp. 135–37.

CHAPTER 21

Social Work Practice with African Americans

Barbara Bryant Solomon

Prefatory
Comment

This chapter was commissioned for this book. The author states that people have a stereo-typic view of the 31 million African Americans residing in the United States; that is, that they are all criminally oriented. Like other minority group members, African Americans are a very heterogeneous population, with more than half residing in central cities. The process of racism and discrimination, rather than urbanization, according to Solomon, contributed to the creation of a permanent underclass.

Solomon suggests social workers can increase their effectiveness in working with African Americans by becoming actively involved in their educational, political, and cultural lives. In discussing African American family structures and dynamics, Solomon points out that African American families share mainstream cultural values and in many cases do not differ from those of other U.S. families. She adds, however, that African Americans must deal with experiences that many other families do not confront, such as police brutality, employment and educational discrimination, and helping their children to understand and learn to cope with racism and the negative self-images it generates. For those who suffer from powerlessness in their social environment, Solomon recommends the intervention strategy of empowerment, whereby the social worker engages in a set of activities with the client to reduce the powerlessness created by negative valuations based on membership in a group oppressed by discrimination.

Solomon is critical of social work's preoccupation with person variables, rather than system variables, and believes this factor has been an obstacle in developing effective intervention strategies with African American clients. It would appear, therefore, that poor third-world communities need a social worker who has the knowledge and skills to obtain needed direct services and is also able to intervene in larger social and community systems.

Responding to African American Needs

Social work is a profession that by definition must be responsive to changing social realities. In the case of African American communities, the changing reality has been as rapid as the rise of the middle class and as creepingly slow as the progress of the working poor. The reality cannot be characterized by a single direction or trend line as it includes both the ascent of Clarence Thomas to the U.S. Supreme Court and the resignation under pressure of U.S. Surgeon General Joycelyn Elders; both the jury verdict in the Rodney King beating trial, which enraged almost every black citizen, and the jury verdict in the O. J. Simpson trial, which enraged almost every white citizen; both the proliferation of African American mayors, city council members, school board members, and state legislators and the elimination of thousands of well-paying jobs held by significant numbers of African Americans in factories throughout the nation. Moreover, changing demographics has meant that problematic cross-cultural relations are no longer mostly African American and white. The flow of immigrants from Vietnam and Mexico, Korea and El Salvador, and the rising consciousness of indigenous American Indian and Mexican American populations have led to the kind of complex cross-cultural relationships that are inevitable in an open, multiethnic society. As a consequence, African Americans have made it clear that social workers' old preoccupations both with finding the source of problems *in* the individual psyche and in helping clients handle oppressive, white social institutions are inadequate. At the same time social workers are questioning whether models of service delivery embraced by African Americans in the immediate past, such as ethnic-specific agencies or agency programs, are adequate to help empower African American clients who must now negotiate multicultural environments.

Who Are the African Americans?

Police officers have often observed the predominantly African American faces among the petty thieves, pimps, violence-prone families, and hardened felons with whom they are in constant contact, and they have made a quantum leap to the erroneous conclusion that these few are representative of all African Americans in general.[1] Social workers are frequently guilty of a similar error. Because the probability is higher that clients who are on welfare, on probation or parole, in poor housing, and in chaotic family situations are African American, the generalization is made that most African Americans share these problems. The reality is that social workers, like police officers, lawyers, or psychiatrists, are most likely to encounter *biased* samples of the African American population in their clientele. Knowledge of "other" African Americans, that is, those for whom the client sample is not representative, is necessary if African American persons are not to be perceived as acting out a predestined scenario.

Who, then, are these African Americans who constitute 12 percent of the population of the United States—some 31,025,000 individuals?[2] They are, first of all, descendents of slaves brought to the United States during the period before and after the Declaration of Independence. They are also descendents of African Americans who immigrated later to the United States from the Caribbean, Central and South America, and, to a lesser extent, Africa. Early in the nation's history, African Americans were found in every state, although they were primarily a rural population located in the South. World War I, however, marked the beginning of a great migration as large, segregated communities of African Americans developed within many U.S. cities. The trend has continued into the 1990s; most African Americans reside in central cities. Gilder has even suggested that the large proportion of poor African Americans who receive welfare, in comparison to poor whites, is a result of their concentration in urban areas where they are accessible to the pressures of social service bureaucracies that encourage their dependence.[3] Other authors have attributed this overrepresentation of African Americans in welfare caseloads to the creation of a more or less permanent underclass through the processes of institutional racism and discrimination rather than urbanization.[4] Nevertheless, African American urbanization has created a number of cultural, social, and political changes that have implications for social work practice.

Historically, the Urban League has been the social agency most clearly directed toward alleviating the negative conditions encountered by African Americans in cities. The strong social work emphasis in the League and its local affiliates stimulated the development of a school of social work in the predominantly black Atlanta University in 1921, as well as the provision of fellowships to African American students for professional social work training in predominantly white universities.[5] Ironically, the League was strongly denounced by more radical groups during the 1960s and 1970s for its conservative approach to the problems of racism and discrimination. For example, the League was more likely to use the strategies of negotiation and coalition-building than confrontation and boycotts. Yet it can be argued that it was the League's support of social work education for African Americans that provided the "critical mass" of social work professionals who moved into previously "lily white" social welfare settings and who finally answered the demands for more relevant services and more sensitive service providers among African Americans.

Though migration patterns have been relatively easy to interpret, socioeconomic changes in the African American population have been more difficult to characterize. For example, in the early 1970s, Wattenberg and Scammon contended that on the whole African Americans had made considerable progress in the preceding decade and that, in fact, a majority could be considered "middle class."[6] This contention was based on 1970 census data and other statistics which demonstrated that during the preceding decade African American family incomes had increased by nearly 100 percent, in contrast to 69 percent for white family incomes.

Similarly, Gilder supported the idea of a closing income gap between whites and African Americans. In his opinion, differences could be a consequence of factors other than discrimination, despite the myths disseminated by the "politics of persecution."[7] On the other hand, Hill described these same data as the "illusion of black progress."[8] His analysis indicated that during the 1970s the number of poor blacks increased, whereas the number of poor whites declined. More recently, Darity and Myers identified a marked discrepancy between the earnings of African American and white individuals and significant income differences between African American and white families.[9] These economists contend that despite the convergence of earnings among African American and white individuals, earning differentials among *families* are widening. This is occurring as labor force participation rates of African American family heads are declining and as female-headed African American families are on the rise. Swinton reveals that at the time the 1990 census data were collected, fewer African Americans (67.1%) worked than whites (73.1%); African American family incomes ranged from 54.9 percent of white family income in the Midwest to 60.8 percent in the South; 31.9 percent of African Americans and only 10.7 percent of whites were in poverty; 13 percent of the African American population and 3.33 percent of the white population received public assistance or supplemental security income.[10]

These data demonstrate the difficulties experienced by the social work practitioner who seeks to use social science information as the basis for developing intervention strategies. Social scientists disagree on the extent to which African Americans experience discrimination as well as on the extent to which dramatic changes have occurred in the relative incomes of African American and white individuals and families. The disagreements are not only in the size of differences in income but in the meaning of the differences to individuals and families in the respective groups. For example, Kaus contends that material equality or "money inequality" is less important than social inequality. However, social inequality, according to Kaus, is a consequence of the decline of class-mixing opportunities in both public and private spheres. "Much of today's social inequality . . . derives from neither money differences nor 'merit' differences, but from the breakdown of public sphere institutions (like the draft and schools) that once discouraged the translation of these differences into inegalitarian attitudes. This is the most solid ground for optimism. It suggests that restoring these institutions, or inventing their modern equivalents, will restore social equality even in the face of rising money inequality."[11]

This social inequality is not race-based but class-based: "Is the underclass African American?" Certainly most African Americans are *not* in it. Two-thirds of African Americans currently live above the poverty line. And it has become fashionable among some conservatives to downplay the significance of race in the poverty culture. But it's simply stupid to pretend that the underclass is not mainly African American. A large ongoing survey at the University of Michigan shows that although African Americans compose only 12 percent of the population they make up 55 percent of those who stay poor for a long time, and over 60 percent of those who remain on welfare for a long time. In 1990, of the 1.8 million poor people in "extreme poverty" neighborhoods in America's one hundred largest cities, African Americans constituted 58 percent, of those living in neighborhoods with extreme social problems (high dropout rates, female-headed families, etc.), while whites made up 21 percent, and Hispanics 19 percent.[12]

In July 1996, President Clinton signed a welfare reform bill that drastically reduced the time a family could receive public assistance. Without dramatic increases in employment assistance programs, problems are certain to escalate for families in which the parent, usually a single female, is unable to find a job but has reached the limit for public assistance. However, disagreements about the relative significance of discrimination against members of the group versus individual differences in capacity to utilize opportunities will necessarily create differences in intervention strategies aimed at increasing the effectiveness of social functioning among African American families. A belief in the severe impact of *institutionalized* discrimination results in more advocacy and social action; a belief in the *individual's* lack of capacity to utilize opportunities provided leads to more intrapsychic, person-centered strategies.

Perhaps the most important characterization of African Americans is their heterogeneity. The *majority* are employed and do not present major problems in social functioning. On the other hand, their overrepresentation among the poor implies that a disproportionate number are consumers of social services; that is, those programs made available by other than market criteria to ensure a basic level of health and welfare. Therefore, social workers who are the primary professionals in the social welfare field must be familiar with African American culture, lifestyles, and help-seeking behavior if they are to be effective practitioners.

African American Culture and Life-style

Landrine and Klonoff have developed a measure of African American acculturation based on the concept of acculturation as "the extent to which ethnic-cultural minorities participate in the cultural traditions, values, and beliefs of their own culture versus those of the dominant white society."[13] From their perspective African Americans are most appropriately treated as an ethnic or cultural group rather than as a race. This is consistent with the concept of the United States as an ethnosystem; that is, a composite of interdependent ethnic groups, each in turn defined by some unique historical and/or cultural ties and bound together by a single political system. The largest ethnic group, Anglos, has successfully assimilated some groups who were ethnically distinct at the time of their extensive immigration to this country— the Dutch, German, Scandinavian, and Irish, for example. On the other hand, African Americans for a variety of reasons have not been assimilated; the result has been the maintenance of a distinctive culture that possesses elements of the dominant culture, elements of other subcultural groups who have been oppressed, and elements that are a consequence of the unique African American experience. This cultural distinctiveness may be observed in language and communication, in family structures, in religion, and in relationships with major social institutions. Knowledge of these distinctive cultural patterns should not encourage stereotyping but rather should sensitize practitioners to a wide range of behavioral possibilities.

LANGUAGE AND COMMUNICATION

There are different and sometimes conflicting ideas about how important it is to understand the vocabularies and communication styles of the various subcultures from which African American clients come. For example, since most African Americans are at least bicultural, some assume that, although the non-African American social worker may not understand the subtle nuances of language and communication styles current in African American communities, the African American client will understand the mainstream language of the social worker. Thus, the mainstream language must be the medium of communication in problem-solving activity. This attitude, however, ignores some dynamics of communication that transcend the simple issue of a common vocabulary. For example, a social worker is more likely to communicate feelings of warmth, understanding, and acceptance when clients view him or her as similar to themselves and as having problems, goals, and coping styles with which they can identify.[14] At the same time clients who view their counselors as similar to themselves tend to be more willing to freely disclose their thoughts, self-doubts, and concerns than they are with social workers whom they view as different from themselves.[15]

Block has found that African Americans may have a tendency to communicate ideas and feelings by analogy rather than analysis.[16] Feelings of depression may be described as, "I feel like I do not have a real friend in the world," rather than, "I have feelings of intense loneliness." The client's tendency to give examples of his or her experience of a problem rather than to isolate and analyze specific factors is often considered reflective of the lack of insight or ability to abstract, rather than a style of communication. Furthermore, the kind of response the social worker makes to the client may cause additional problems. There is evidence that African Americans who come for help expect the social worker to offer certain values and opinions on the issues they present. Though these opinions may differ from their own, clients expect that communication about differences will be a major aspect of the counseling process. The neutral counselor appears to be someone who has nothing to offer!

Lerner offers an example of the kind of consequences that can result when the helping person does not understand the language of the client served.[17] A white psychologist was required to make an evaluation of African American school children. The evaluation procedures called for each child to be given one-half hour of unstructured play with blocks, Tinker Toys, and beads, followed by a brief discussion between the child and psychologist about what the child had made. However, because the psychologist was unfamiliar with African American dialect, he could not understand the child's answer to the question of what she had made. Thus, he repeated the question several times, thereby increasing the child's anxiety. When the child finally was able to make the psychologist understand the word "sticks," she was so relieved that she responded "sticks" whenever the question was asked, regardless of what she had actually made. After all, isn't it better not to frustrate the poor psychologist with words he cannot understand? Yet the child is likely to be assessed as having limited capacity to verbalize or limited ability to conceptualize on the basis of the psychologist's inability to communicate.

Banks has recommended that helping persons who work with African American clients should recognize the heterogeneity of African American culture and should become actively involved in the educational, political, and cultural life of different kinds of African Americans.[18] Doing this would enhance the worker's ability to understand distinctive language patterns and communication styles, particularly if he or she spends some time in barbershops, churches, bars, and other places where people congregate within African American communities. Social workers should familiarize themselves with these African American communities and experience the texture of life so that they will be able to project a shared life space in verbal and nonverbal communication, regardless of how words may be accented.

FAMILY STRUCTURES AND DYNAMICS

Perhaps more has been written about African American families than any other aspect of African American life in the United States. Since the late nineteenth century influence of the psychoanalytic movement on social work and other helping professions, there has been an emphasis on the significance of the family in the etiology of problem behavior. For example, African American families have been subject to sweeping generalizations about the effects of their behavior on problems experienced by family members. Much of the social science literature attempts to account for the overrepresentation of African American families in certain problem categories—among the poor, the unskilled, the uneducated, and the poorly housed, for example. One view is that African American and white families share the same cultural values and norms but differ because of socioeconomic class.[19] Another view is that lower socioeconomic class status is an outcome of culture, rather than its determinant.[20] Therefore, African American families have different values and norms based on the harsh and oppressive experience of slavery, which developed behavior patterns that have persisted into the present and that have impaired the family's ability for social functioning. However, the most likely view is that African American culture contains elements of "mainstream" white culture, elements from traditional African culture, and elements from slavery, reconstruction, and subsequent exposure to racism and discrimination.[21] Biculturalism serves to explain both similarities and differences in comparing African American families with non-African American families.

Billingsley has pointed out that African American families must teach their young members not only how to be human but also how to be black in a white society.[22] Pinderhughes has expanded on this idea by identifying what African American families need in order to cope effectively with the "victim system" of racism, poverty, and oppression:

> What these families need are (1) flexible boundaries to deal with the outside systems, and (2) a family structure and process that reinforce a high degree of differentiation; effective leadership; and the ability to communicate and negotiate, tolerate differences in values and perceptions among members, function biculturally and build and use strong support systems such as the extended family.[23]

The concept of an ethnosystem also incorporates the idea of biculturalism as the primary force in the dynamics of African American family behavior. African American families share mainstream cultural values to the extent that in many cases their family structures and process are no different from those of other U.S. families. At the same time, however, they are required to deal with experiences with which many other families do not have to deal, such as discrimination in access to educational and employment opportunities or helping their children understand how to deal with racism and the negative self-images it generates.

Certain aspects of family functioning are more characteristically encountered in African American families and should be mentioned here. For example, the extended family is a common family pattern in which "base households" and "affiliate households" are interconnected in an extensive mutual-aid family network.[24] Although this structure and its various components vary from place to place and with the circumstances of individual families, it can serve to help identify possible sources of family support beyond the nuclear family, which is the essential functional family unit in middle-class, white culture. Studies of working-class and middle-class African American families show that nurturing and provider roles in the family are frequently shared equally by husband and wife.[25] African American child-rearing patterns often emphasize individual uniqueness, assertiveness, early independence, and avoidance of early gender identity, all of which may create problems for the child in encounters with the white middle-class-dominated school.[26] Finally, in families that have become unstable because of excessive exposure to negative valuation from the oppressive social institutions a variety of dysfunctional behaviors may be observed—extreme lack of motivation to achieve, apathy, negativism, irresponsibility, and violence.[27] Although most middle-class African American families are able to cope with oppression better and have more resources to cope with oppressive social institutions than do poor African American families, they do not escape entirely; thus, recognition of the vulnerability of their status has meant that middle-class African American families do not function *exactly* as do middle-class white families.

RELIGION

No African religious cults were established in the United States during slavery. However, with the coming of Baptist and Methodist missionaries, the slaves found an avenue for the expression of emotion as well as bonds of kinship with their fellow slaves. After emancipation, the enlarged church organizations played an even more important role in the organization of the African American communities. They promoted economic cooperation for the purpose of erecting and buying churches, establishing mutual assistance and insurance companies, and building educational institutions.[28] As the main form or focus of organized social life, the church has been both a secular and a religious institution, a fact that may well account for its playing a broader role in African American communities than in white communities.

The role of the church in community life far beyond its strictly spiritual mission is exemplified by the campaign of four hundred African American ministers in Philadelphia in 1958 to end rigid patterns of job discrimination against African Americans. This alliance of ministers brought an end to the more blatant forms of job discrimination by simply having members of their congregation boycott companies that practiced it. Because segregation had ensured that managers of the offending businesses were not members of the churches or their boards of trustees or even acquaintances, the ministers did not have to worry about pressure from these individuals. The strategy was effective, and the ministers, led by Reverend Leon Sullivan, went one step further and established Opportunities Industrialization Centers to provide African American people with the skills and training needed to fill the jobs selective patronage would open. Reverend Sullivan has attributed the success of this movement to prayer, moral initiative, black unity, and the appreciation of money as a prime determinant in human behavior.[29]

The spiritual side of the African American church is far more personal than that of the traditional white church: God is never an abstraction apart from the here and now. He is personalized and included in daily life situations. It is not uncommon to hear African Americans relate a conversation they have had with God or with His son, Jesus Christ. Prayer is a frequent response to everyday crisis, even by those who do not profess to any deep religious convictions. Comments like "I prayed that my husband would find a job," or "I prayed that my child would get well," may be heard. The church provides significant services in African American communities that can be utilized by creative social work practitioners seeking to enhance social functioning in those communities. For example, Leigh and Green point out that churches have served to develop leadership skills and mutual aid activities, as well as emotional catharsis for those in need of some release of emotional tensions.[30] If social workers routinely assess the significance of the church in the lives of African American clients, they may find avenues for enhancing their service effectiveness through collaborative activity.

Areas of scholarly research that may aid assessment include (1) the influence of religious orientation on individual and group identity; (2) the effects of religion on perceptions of personal control and competence; (3) the relationship between religion, emotional well-being, and mental health; (4) the involvement of African American churches in the provision of social and emotional support; and (5) the status of African American religious institutions within the African American community.[31]

RELATIONSHIPS WITH SOCIAL INSTITUTIONS

Although the family, neighborhood groups, and the church represent the primary institutions influencing the behavior of African Americans, schools, social welfare agencies, health care institutions, and the justice system also influence their behavior. In contrast, however, these institutions are usually controlled by those committed to the dominant culture. Because African Americans have had the historical experience of being subjected to negative valuations by these institutions, they are likely to view them defensively. For example, the schools have frequently perceived African Americans as less capable of developing cognitive skills than whites; yet research has indicated that school failure is often a self-fulfilling prophecy reinforced by students' acceptance of that judgment. Students fail to expend the effort required to succeed, even in those instances in which that effort could certainly lead to success. The consequence is a high dropout rate among African Americans and the accusation that "they lack interest in or appreciation for education." Yet failure in school is not a culture-based phenomenon.

Because health care institutions have long discriminated against African Americans, blacks exhibit considerable distrust of health care practitioners. Jacquelyne Jackson has suggested that mainstream medical practitioners are most effective in treating urban African Americans in emergency or critical situations and least effective in treating them in situations where much of the management of the illness is really the responsibility of the patient or his or her guardian.[32] The influence of the physician in those instances is somewhat small.

Particular targets of distrust are social welfare agencies, which have been given primary responsibility to help poor and disadvantaged persons. The policies of these agencies have contributed to their negative valuation by African Americans; for example, the welfare departments of Southern states have employed differential payment schedules for white and African American clients in the belief that "blacks do not need as much as whites who have been accustomed to a higher standard of living." In addition to distrust, African Americans exhibit feelings of anger, hostility, passiveness, and dependency in their dealings with welfare agencies. These constitute responses to the frustration and powerlessness that are experienced when opportunities are denied because of membership in a stigmatized collective. They do not reflect individual deficiency.

Social Work Intervention

Prior to the 1960s, *culture* as viewed in social work education and practice was primarily concerned with the esoteric groups and variables encountered in the works of Margaret Mead and Clyde Kluckhohn. Only token attention was given to the special problems or techniques of service delivery to African Americans. When these concerns were discussed, the focus was more often on the effects of discrimination or the role of culture in general. Acts of discrimination were perceived as generating cultural attitudes and behaviors such as concern for immediate gratification, lack of interest in personal achievement, and lack of commitment to marriage and family. Moreover these supposed characteristics were viewed as deterrents to the involvement of African Americans in problem-solving relationships with social work practitioners.

The Civil Rights Movement and subsequent Black Power Movement raised issues of self-determination and institutional racism that precipitated the development of more responsive social services and a more responsive social work profession. The literature of that era, which dealt with psychosocial services to African Americans, focused primarily on consciousness raising. However, the history of limited access to services and the ineffectiveness of traditional problem-solving processes received relatively little attention from the social work profession.

The rhetoric of the 1960s gave way during the 1970s to greater concern for the development of more appropriate theories of behavior and theories of practice for guiding social work intervention with African American clients. Leigh and Green have identified three major criticisms of the existing theoretical frameworks:[33]

1. Intervention based on psychodynamic theories is, at best, palliative and at worst counterproductive. Since the problems presented by African American clients are most often not ones of personal deficiency but of personal reactions to oppressive social institutions, an exclusive focus on the mental state

of the African American client or on the worker's own intellectual and emotional problems in relating to social issues diverts attention from system as source of the client's problem and from the possible reasons that the client came to the attention of the social worker in the first place.

2. The role of the black family as a source of strength rather than as a source of dysfunctional behavior patterns has been virtually ignored.

3. Indigenous social institutions, such as the African American church, have also been overlooked as a natural support system for troubled black individuals and families. More effective strategies for social work intervention with black families would seek to remove the basis for these criticisms.

THEORETICAL FRAMEWORKS

Recent social work literature has included several attempts to infuse an African American perspective into existing theoretical frameworks so that they serve to explain behavior of African Americans more accurately, especially in terms of how these people are influenced by the larger social environment. For example, in addition to viewing the social system in the United States as an ethnosystem, the literature now cites *power* as the primary force governing the interrelationship between the dominant Anglo group and negatively valued ethnic groups. Therefore, power is as significant a concept in understanding the individual's or family's experience of problems in psychosocial functioning as are anxiety, guilt, or some other psychodynamic concept. The interrelationship of power, powerlessness, and human growth and development can be discerned most clearly through the basic process whereby individuals develop skills in social functioning:

> The individual experiences a complex series of events monitored by the family or surrogate family which involves the self, significant others, and the environment. These experiences result in the acquisition of personal resources such as positive self-concept, cognitive skills, health, and physical competence. These personal resources lead to the development of certain interpersonal and technical skills such as sensitivity to the feelings and needs of others, organizational skills and leadership ability. The personal resources as well as the interpersonal and technical skills can then be used to perform effectively in valued social roles such as employee, parent, or community leader.[34]

Racism, discrimination, and the general negative valuation of African Americans may act directly or indirectly to decrease the individual's power to deal effectively with psychosocial problems. For example, the negative evaluations from more powerful white persons in their environment are reflected in the family processes of many rural and low-income urban African Americans. Because these families accept society's label of inferiority, they are prevented from developing such optimal personal resources as a positive self-concept or certain cognitive skills. In other instances, powerlessness may be expressed as an inability to develop interpersonal or technical skills because of low self-esteem or underdeveloped cognitive skills, which in turn are a direct consequence of interaction in an oppressive society. The final step in this vicious circle would be a reduction of the African American's effectiveness in performing valued social roles because of his or her lack of interpersonal and technical skills. Finally, the inability to perform valued social roles confirms and reinforces feelings of inferiority and of negative values, and the vicious circle begins again.

Some negative valuations do not result in powerlessness because strong family relationships or strong group relationships provide a cushion or protective barrier against them. Despite the experience of discrimination or disadvantages simply because they are black, some individuals are able to obtain and utilize a broad range of personal, interpersonal, and technical resources to achieve goals effectively. Not all African Americans can be considered powerless or unable to function effectively in the wider social system. On the other hand, for those who do suffer that powerlessness, which has at least some of its source in the relationship between the individual and oppressive social institutions, empowerment is an important goal and process for social work with these clients, as noted:

> *Empowerment* is defined here as a process whereby the social worker engages in a set of activities with the client system that aim to reduce the powerlessness that has been created by negative valuations based on membership in a stigmatized group. It involves identification of the power blocks that contribute to the problem as well as the development and implementation of specific strategies aimed at either the reduction of the effects from indirect power blocks or the reduction of the operation of direct power blocks.[35]

This theoretical perspective on the relationship between African Americans in the ethnosystem and its oppressive social institutions provides a basis for the generation of practice principles that are consistent with the definition of empowerment. These principles serve to specify the goals of social work intervention; that is, intervention should be directed toward:[36]

1. Helping the client to perceive himself or herself as causal agent in achieving a solution to his or her problem or problems.
2. Helping the client to perceive the social worker as having knowledge and skills which he or she can use.
3. Helping the client to perceive the social worker as peer collaborator or partner in the problem-solving effort.
4. Helping the social worker to perceive the oppressive social institution (schools, welfare department, courts, and so forth) as open to influence to reduce negative impact.

These objectives are not substitutes for other objectives that may be derived from other theoretical perspectives; for example, helping clients to gain insight into their emotional reactions to significant others in their social environment, or helping them to extinguish some problem behavior. However, the objectives related to empowerment take into account the fact that the problem may be created or exacerbated by the actions of external social institutions.

PRESENTING PROBLEMS

The criticism that traditional theoretical frameworks were not relevant to problem solving with African American clients suggests that there is some inherent difference in the nature of the problems brought by these clients to social work agencies or settings. Social work has identified a broad range of problems in social functioning as amenable to change if subjected to application of social work skills. These problems are encountered not only in primary social work agencies (such as family agencies and adoption agencies) but also in host settings in health, education, law and justice, and income maintenance. Regardless of the setting, however, most African American clients come to these agencies because they perceive them as a means for obtaining some needed material assistance or because they have been sent by agents of social control—judge, doctor, or educator—who have defined a problem for the client. Because most practice theories assume that the client will express a "felt difficulty," they are not very useful when the client expresses no felt difficulty or a very concrete one that, if accepted, requires only the connection of the client to the resource. In such cases, traditional practice theories indicate few options for intervention because they assume that the client is not motivated to help him- or herself. However, given the African American experience in the ethnosystem, which generates little trust for social institutions, including those considered to be helping agencies, it should be expected that the majority of African American clients will fall into the following two categories: (1) those who have a mild to severe emotional and or social dysfunction but who perceive the social work practitioner as having no expertise for real assistance; or (2) those who perceive the "system" as a major contributor to the problem and believe it is not amenable to change or behavior modification. The incorporation of an empowerment goal in social work means that the social worker must intervene to change these attitudes of the client.

The distinctiveness of the presenting problems of African American clients is not merely in their resistance to presenting the problems at all. In addition, even when the problems are clearly articulated by the client and not very different from problems presented by non-African American clients (parent–child conflict, adolescent school difficulties, inability to function effectively in the workplace, teenage pregnancy, gang violence, marital conflict, schizophrenia, or depressive reactions), the chances are good that the experience of the client or family with oppressive social institutions will have created either direct or indirect power blocks to satisfactory functioning. Thus, the parent–child problem is exacerbated by the child's membership in a peer group that is spawned because of its negative valuation in the inner-city environment. Similarly, employment problems or adolescent school difficulties may be to some extent a consequence of low expectations and self-fulfilling prophecy. Depressive reactions may be a consequence to some extent of the cumulative frustration encountered in efforts to deal with school, employers, and social agencies. Eventually anger is turned inward, and the depreciated self is created. The presenting problems of these African American clients all involve stress from external systems. If the theoretical frameworks that serve to guide social workers all relate primarily to intrapsychic functioning as the determinant of ability to cope with one's environment, and not to institutional factors that might need to be changed instead or as well, the profession will have limited effectiveness in helping African Americans.

ASSESSING THE PROBLEM

The social worker's initial problem-solving task is to assess (1) those factors that have contributed to the development and maintenance of the problem situation; and (2) the client's particular personal and social assets and liabilities that influence the problem-solving process. African American individuals and families are often perceived in biased ways that lead to erroneous conclusions about the source of the problem (for example, personal deficiency rather than environmental stress) and the degree to which they have the ego strengths (cognitive skills, language skills, and ability to relate to others) necessary to engage in effective problem-solving work. The social worker should operate from an empowerment perspective and attempt to discern and overcome the powerlessness felt by the client as a member of an oppressed minority group. However, the social worker must also assess the extent to which intrapsychic and/or intrafamilial forces also contribute to feelings of powerlessness and impaired social functioning. This assessment must be a two-pronged one: that of the client's unique personal problems, and of the effect on him or her of negative valuation as a consequence of being African American in a white-dominated society.

Certain elements of personality in African American individuals have been directly connected with growing up black in a white-dominated ethnosystem. For example, Grier and Cobb have suggested several defensive postures that often characterize black–white relationships:[37]

1. Cultural paranoia that assumes that anyone white or any social institution dominated by whites will potentially act against a black's best interests.
2. Cultural depression that is a consequence of life experiences and serves to define a black as less capable, less worthy than whites.
3. Cultural antisocialism that develops from a black's experience with laws, policies, and institutional procedures, which have no respect for him or her as an individual or blacks as a group; the black, in turn, has no respect for, or obligation to conform to, these laws, policies, or procedures.

Each of these defensive postures can be represented on a continuum: at one end there is just enough defensive posture to reduce the person's vulnerability to a potentially hostile social environment; at the other end there is so much defensive posture that the person is prohibited from functioning effectively.

The idea that personality development in African Americans involves the task of achieving a balanced response to the experience of racism and discrimination is also found in Chestang's contention that African Americans have dual personality components. One is a "depreciated" component that recognizes the low status society has ascribed to him or her and responds with feelings of worthlessness and hopelessness. The other is a "transcendent" component that seeks to overcome this low status and actualize the potential for successful psychosocial functioning. If either the depreciated or the transcendent component of the personality becomes too dominant, problems in social functioning are likely to arise. The overly depreciated personality projects the image of the deserving victim, whereas the overly transcendent personality projects a false power that has no basis in reality.[38]

The attitudes and behaviors exhibited by many African Americans who come for help to social agencies are often labeled as *resistance;* instead, these behaviors really reflect attempts at coping with discrimination and powerlessness. For example, because African Americans often perceive delays in provision of service when requested from a counseling agency as indicative of indifference and/or low priority, they may not approach the agency again. Similarly, they may "drop out" because they view lengthy gathering of background information and nondirective, neutral counseling styles as signifying the social worker's disinterest in them or inability to deal with their problems. It is a mistake to label this dropping-out behavior as lack of motivation or resistance to dealing with the problem, since this behavior could just as easily signify resistance to the experience of negative valuation or being "put down" by those representing white-dominated social institutions or practice disciplines. Moreover, dropping out is not always the same as failure to cope with the problem. The client may have opted for a solution that may or may not be less functional; for example, attempting a self-help strategy or attempting to find help in the informal support network of family and friends.

In order to determine the *extent* to which the powerlessness expressed in an African American individual's or family's request for help stems from membership in the stigmatized collective, certain questions should be explored:

1. How has the client's family perceived the fact of being black in its life experiences (for example, quality of education, job opportunities, and marital relationships)?
2. What has been the interaction of social class and race in the formation of attitudes, beliefs, values, and behavior patterns?
3. How have formal and informal support systems within the African American community been utilized by the individual and/or family?
4. To what extent does the individual consider it possible to change the outcome of his or her interactions with white-dominated social institutions?

In those instances where answers to these questions indicate that much of the powerlessness being experienced by the individual or family stems from negative encounters with social institutions, the social worker's role necessarily involves at least strengthening the client's ability to deal with these institutions and at most modifying the functioning of the institution.

ESTABLISHING A WORKING RELATIONSHIP

Most African American clients who come to social agencies for assistance have been sent by others who have defined their problem as requiring some type of social work intervention. For the most part, a social worker is viewed as synonymous with a welfare worker so that he or she is considered the one who is in a position to determine whether the client can receive or continue to receive concrete benefits such as financial assistance, food stamps, housing subsidies, and emergency shelter or referrals for employment, medical care, or educational programs. The social worker is not perceived as a therapist, nor is therapy often considered a solution to emotional problems. If the social worker insists on defining the problem only in psychological terms (the need for changes in the individual's emotional functioning), the client is likely to reject this definition. On the other hand, if the social worker focuses only on deficiencies in basic social supplies (such as food, clothing, and shelter), then any provision of help is unlikely to break the cycle of dependency created by dysfunctional attitudes, impaired intrafamilial and interpersonal relationships, and intrapsychic conflicts. A satisfactory working relationship can only be established for African American clients when there is an expressed willingness on the part of the social worker to consider the multiple problems of clients as an interrelated whole.

Another aspect of establishing a satisfactory working relationship with African American clients is to recognize the basis on which they will permit the social worker to influence their life situation. Two major orientations to interpersonal relationships have been identified in sociological literature. One is the *gesellschaft* orientation, which is most characteristic of white, urban, middle-class individuals and identifies appropriate behavior according to the social status of the individuals involved. Therefore, these individuals would examine the social worker's educational attainment, credentials, and license in order to assess his or her competence to perform a helping role. Framed degrees or certificates, titles such as "doctor," and the location and decor of the offices would all have some bearing on the client's judgment of the practitioner. The other is the *gemeinschaft* orientation, which is more characteristic of rural, low-income, minority individuals for whom relationships are based on personal attributes of the individuals involved. For example, for these individuals, the social worker's answers to personal questions about marital status, number of children, religious beliefs, or time spent in the community may determine whether or not he or she is perceived as competent.

Establishing rapport between client and social worker is particularly difficult when ethnic boundaries are involved. Draper has suggested the following ways in which developing such rapport with low-income African American clients may be more readily achieved:

> The white worker must try to enter the life space of the black client. He/she must listen to the expression of black language, its sounds and meaning. Read black literature and newspapers. Listen to black radio stations to get with the tempo and temper of blacks' feelings. Leave the office and walk around in black neighborhoods—look at the parts that are slums, but also acknowledge the blocks that are kept with pride. . . . Look at the addict and the pimp but also see those who carry themselves with dignity. Look at the hustler but also see the shopkeeper, the dentist, the doctor. Go with the black client to the hospital and the social service agency. Notice the very real differences in the way services are often given to black and white clients. . . . There is an infinite variety among blacks whether in the metropolis or the small town.[39]

A personalized approach to establishing relationships with African American clients and a keen sensitivity to in-group diversity may overcome apparent obstacles. Attempts to encourage discussion of thought, feelings, and problems in an open manner by a white person may fail because of the African American client's lifetime of conditioning in an opposite direction. The characteristic black–white relationship was based on white superiority and was not a peer relationship; that is, the African American was expected to defer to the white and to provide the white person with any information demanded, but at the same time was constrained from expecting similar deference or any information from the white person in return. This kind of relationship must be rejected totally; instead a peer–collaborator relationship, in which there is mutual respect and mutual sharing of information, must be established.

The Problem-Solving Process

Social workers who are committed to an empowerment perspective in their practice constantly apply specific strategies aimed at helping clients to achieve a sense of control over their lives. They are particularly concerned with developing clients' abilities to influence the decisions of social institutions when such decisions will affect their lives.

The sense of control is often impaired by specific agency procedures. For example, clients of most social agencies are invariably required to answer myriad questions, often to satisfy the needs of the agency (e.g., to identify client population). These questions have little relevance to the problem-solving process. Therefore, a client who comes to an agency to present a problem of parent–child conflict may in the initial session be required to indicate length of time in the community, place of employment, amount of family income, and religion—none of which at the time may be important to meeting the client's immediate need. Furthermore, revealing so much that may be negative (e.g., failed marriage, evictions, and lost job) reinforces the client's sense of personal deficiency, which is often already a dysfunctional aspect of the personality of the African American client. The helping process becomes part of the problem rather than part of the solution.

In order to counteract the problem, a guiding principle of social work practice from an empowerment perspective is to ask no questions that do not have direct bearing on the problem-solving work. This may mean that the social worker does not even ask the client for his or her telephone number. If arrangements have been made for a future appointment, the client may be asked, "In case anything happens and the appointment has to be changed, is there a way I can reach you?" Then the client has the option to give the telephone number, to indicate that he or she will call the agency to confirm the appointment, or to take his or her chances. In such a case, clearly the client rather than the social worker will control the flow of information.

A client's sense of power over his or her life situation is also enhanced when the relationship with the social worker is a peer relationship. Each party brings a degree of expertise to the problem-solving process; that is, knowledge and/or skills that are necessary but not sufficient to reach a solution. For example, the client brings to the process firsthand knowledge of the problem he or she is experiencing, the strengths and weaknesses of the key actors (family members of the support network), and the consequences of past attempts at reaching a solution. The social worker brings to the process an understanding of human behavior and how people create problem situations, as well as how they can be influenced to change or modify them. It is the blending of separate areas of expertise that makes possible the eventual solution.

Because the problem-solving process is by definition a collaborative one, the client or client system must take responsibility for bringing about whatever change is sought. For example, if the problem is inability to maintain employment, the underlying reasons may include a variety of systemic forces (poor educational opportunities and discrimination in hiring, for example). If these forces are to be overcome, the client must take specific actions to counteract the negative impact of a hostile environment. These actions may be directed toward changes in the oppressive social institutions, such as the utilization of the legal and court systems to reduce discrimination or compensate for past discrimination. The social worker who is skilled in facilitating change at both the individual and larger system levels will have much more utility in African American communities than the one who is skilled and comfortable in dealing only with individuals or small groups.

The social worker's role with African American clients in the problem-solving process often is one of consciousness-raising so that the multiple forces that created problem situations can be acknowledged in order to relieve the demoralizing powerlessness stemming from an unconscious or conscious sense of personal deficiency. The questions may be asked, "Why am I unable to make it when other people seem to be able to do so very well?" This question has become particularly problematic in more recent years, when the reduction in legalized discrimination has meant that some African Americans have been able to take advantage of what Billingsley has referred to as "screens of opportunity." It is still necessary to educate many African Americans about the systemic factors that mitigate against "winning" if one is poor and black in this society.

Concluding Comment

There are unique issues involved in social work practice with African American clients. Most African Americans who come to social work agencies for help have been sent by schools, correctional authorities, or other agents of social control and do not have faith that the social worker has skills that can help in solving their social and emotional problems. It is not enough for the social worker to have an appreciation for cultural diversity; he or she must have basic knowledge regarding the life-styles, communication patterns, and characteristic problems encountered by African American individuals and families. This knowledge is required for accurate assessment of the client's strengths, resources, support network, and potential for collaborating in a problem-solving process. The preoccupation of social work practice with *person* variables rather than *system* variables is a particular obstacle in developing effective intervention strategies with African American clients. Their problems are characteristically intertwined with the behavior of the oppressive institutions with which they come into contact. However, these institutions are not monolithic and invariant in the application of oppression; therefore, skills can be enhanced in order to deal with them. The goal of increasing a client's sense of control in the problem-solving process and in his or her life situation characterizes the approach to social work with African American clients that has been identified as *empowerment*.

KEY WORDS AND CONCEPTS

African Americans

Social inequality

Gemeinschaft

Empowerment

Ethnosystem

Gesellschaft

Underclass

African American culture

SUGGESTED READINGS

Billingsley, A. *Black Families in White America.* Englewood Cliffs, NJ: Prentice Hall, 1968.

Billingsley, A. *Climbing Jacob's Ladder: The Enduring Legacy of African Americans.* New York: Simon and Schuster, 1993.

Bowles, D. D. "Development of an Ethnic Self-Concept among Blacks," in C. Jacobs and D. D. Bowles, eds., *Ethnicity and Race: Critical Concepts in Social Work.* Silver Spring, MD: NASW, 1988.

Gary, L. E., ed. *Black Men.* Beverly Hills, CA: Sage Publications, 1988.

Glasgow, D. G. *The Black Underclass.* San Francisco: Jossey-Bass, 1980.

Landrine, H., and Klonoff, E. *African American Acculturation: Deconstructing Race and Surviving Culture.* Thousand Oaks, CA: Sage Publications, 1996.

Leashore, B. R. "African Americans Overview," and Fariyal, R. S., "African Americans: Immigration," in R. L. Edwards, ed., *Encyclopedia of Social Work,* 19th Edition. Washington, D.C.: NASW Press, 1995.

Morales, A. "Social Work with Third-World People," *Social Work* 26 (January 1981).

Pinderhughes, E. *Understanding Race, Ethnicity and Power.* New York: Free Press, 1989.

Solomon, B. B. *Black Empowerment: Social Work in Oppressed Communities.* New York: Columbia University Press, 1970.

White, B. W., ed. *Color in A White Society.* Silver Spring, MD: NASW, 1984.

ENDNOTES

1. Lawrence Rosen, "Policemen," in Peter I. Rose, Stanley Rothman, and William J. Wilson, eds., *Through Different Eyes: Black and White Perspectives on American Race Relations* (London: Oxford University Press, 1973), pp. 257–290.

2. Signe I. Wetrogan, "Projections of the Population of States by Age, Sex and Race," *Current Population Reports* P25-1053 (Washington, D.C.: U.S. Bureau of the Census, 1989), pp. 15–22.

3. George Gilder, *Wealth and Poverty* (New York: Bantam Books, 1981), p. 160.

4. Douglas G. Glasgow, *The Black Underclass: Poverty, Unemployment and Entrapment of Ghetto Youth* (San Francisco: Jossey-Bass, 1980).

5. Guichard Paris and Lester Books, *Blacks in the City: A History of the National Urban League* (Boston: Little, Brown and Co., 1971), p. 78.

6. Ben J. Wattenberg and Richard M. Scammon, "Black Progress and Liberal Rhetoric," *Commentary* (April 1973): 35–44.

7. Gilder, *Wealth and Poverty*, pp. 155–156.

8. Robert Hill, "The Illusion of Black Progress," *Social Policy* (November–December 1978): 14–25.

9. William A. Darity, Jr., and Samuel L. Myers, Jr., "Racial Earnings Inequality into the 21st Century," in *The State of Black America, 1992* (New York: National Urban League, 1992), pp. 119–138.

10. D. H. Swinton, "The Economic Status of African Americans: Limited Ownership and Persistent Inequality," in *The State of Black America, 1992* (New York: National Urban League, 1992).

11. M. Kaus, *The End of Equality* (New York: Basic Books, 1992).

12. Swinton, p. 106.

13. H. Landrine and E. Klonoff, *African American Acculturation: Deconstructing Race and Surviving Culture* (Thousand Oaks, CA: Sage Publications, 1996).

14. A. A. K. Shapiro, E. Sturening, E. Shapiro, and H. Barten, "Prognostic Correlates of Psychotherapy in Psychiatry," *American Journal of Psychiatry* (1976): 802–808.

15. R. R. Carkhuff and R. Pierce, "Differential Effects of Therapist Race and Social Class upon Patient Depth of Self-Exploration in the Initial Clinical Interview," *Journal of Consulting Psychology* 31 (December 1967): 632–634.

16. Carolyn B. Block, "Black Americans and the Cross-Cultural Counseling and Psychotherapy Experience," in Anthony J. Marsellia and Paul B. Pedersen, eds., *Cross-Cultural Counseling and Psychotherapy* (New York: Pergamon Press, 1979), p. 183.

17. Barbara Lerner, *Therapy in the Ghetto: Political Importance and Personal Disintegration* (Baltimore: Johns Hopkins University Press, 1972), pp. 159–161.

18. W. M. Banks, "The Black Client and the Helping Professionals," in R. James, ed., *Black Psychology* (New York: Harper & Row, 1972), p. 210.

19. See particularly Jacquelyne Johnson Jackson, "Family Organization and Ideology," in Kent S. Miller and Ralph Mason Dreger, eds., *Comparative Studies of Blacks and Whites in the United States* (New York: Seminar Press, 1973); and Jerold Heiss, *The Case of the Black Family: A Sociological Inquiry* (New York: Columbia University Press, 1975).

20. See Robert Staples, "Toward a Sociology of the Black Family: A Theoretical and Methodological Assessment," *Journal of Marriage and the Family* 2 (February 1971): 119–138.

21. Barbara Bryant Solomon and Helen A. Mendes, "Black Families from a Social Welfare Perspective," in Virginia Tufte and Barbara Myerhoff, eds., *Changing Images of the Family* (New Haven, CT: Yale University Press, 1979), pp. 285–289.

22. Andrew Billingsley, *Black Families in White America* (Englewood Cliffs, NJ: Prentice Hall, 1968), p. 28.

23. Elaine Pinderhughes, "Family Functioning of Afro-Americans," *Social Work* 27 (January 1982): 92.

24. Elmer P. Martin and Joanne Mitchell Martin, *The Black Extended Family* (Chicago: University of Chicago Press, 1978), pp. 5–16.

25. James W. Leigh and James W. Green, "The Structure of the Black Community: The Knowledge Base for Social Services," in James W. Green, ed., *Cultural Awareness in the Human Services* (Englewood Cliffs, NJ: Prentice Hall, 1982), pp. 106–107.

26. Diane K. Lewis, "The Black Family: Specialization and Sex Roles," *Phylon* 36 (Fall 1975): 222.

27. Pinderhughes, pp. 92–94.

28. Leigh and Green, pp. 103–104.

29. C. Eric Lincoln, *The Black Church Since Frazier* (New York: Shocken Books, 1974), p. 121.

30. Leigh and Green, pp. 103–104.
31. Robert Joseph Taylor and Linda M. Chatters, "Religious Life," in James Jackson, ed., *Life in Black America* (Newbury Park, CA: Sage Publications, 1991), pp. 46–83.
32. Jacquelyne Johnson Jackson, "Urban Black Americans," in Alan Harwood, ed., *Ethnicity and Health Care* (Cambridge, MA: Harvard University Press, 1981), p. 117.
33. Leigh and Green, pp. 97–99.
34. Barbara Solomon, *Black Empowerment: Social Work in Oppressed Communities* (New York: Columbia University Press, 1976), p. 17.
35. Ibid., p. 19.
36. Ibid., p. 26.
37. William H. Grier and Price M. Cobb, *Black Rage* (New York: Basic Books, 1969), pp. 200–213.
38. Leon Chestang, *Character Development in a Hostile Environment*, Occasional Paper No. 3 (Chicago: School of Social Service Administration, University of Chicago, 1972), pp. 7–8.
39. Barbara Jones Draper, "Black Language as an Adaptive Response to a Hostile Environment," in Carel B. Germain, ed., *Social Work Practices, People, and Environments* (New York: Columbia University Press, 1979), p. 279.

CHAPTER 22

Social Work Practice
with Puerto Ricans

Gloria Bonilla-Santiago

Prefatory
Comment

Dr. Gloria Bonilla-Santiago, Professor in the Department of Public Policy and Urban Studies, Rutgers University, New Jersey, is one of the nation's premier scholars on social work research and the Puerto Rican population on the mainland. Puerto Ricans are the nation's second largest Hispanic group, having over 2 million persons living on the mainland. They are perhaps the most heterogeneous of them all. For example, in spite of being a traditional, Catholic culture, Puerto Ricans divorce and separate more frequently than Anglo Americans. Dr. Bonilla-Santiago reports that Puerto Ricans come in many forms, structures, and colors, reflecting extended families whose appearance range from black skin, dark hair, and dark eyes, to blond hair, blue eyes, and white, freckled skin.

Among the Hispanic groups, tragically, they are the poorest and have the highest poverty, alcoholism, and drug addiction rates. And, of all Hispanic groups, Puerto Ricans are truly the only "colonized" group. This legal status may be contributing to their social problems.

Understanding the diversity of the Hispanic family requires a fundamental understanding of the different Hispanic subgroups in the United States. Each group has a particular history with the United States that has effected the manner in which the family and its supportive institutions have been expressed. Only one group, Mexican Americans/Chicanos, originates in the area that is now the continental United States, but the bulk of the Hispanic population, like Puerto Ricans, Cubans, Dominicans, and Central and South Americans, immigrated into this country. Puerto Ricans are the only "colonized" group that has migrated and settled in the United States in mass. Significantly, Puerto Ricans are U.S. citizens and move freely between the island of Puerto Rico and the mainland. The adaptation of the Puerto Rican population in both urban and rural settings stems from the socioeconomic and historical relations between their home country and the United States, and migration continues to be based primarily on labor needs, and, to varying degrees, a continued relationship with home regions.

Current Demographics

POPULATION

Mainland Puerto Ricans are the second largest Hispanic group in the United States. More than 2.7 million live in the United States, and 3.5 million live in the Commonwealth of Puerto Rico. They constitute 10.3 percent or about one-eighth of the U.S. Latino population. They are relatively youthful, highly urbanized, and primarily concentrated in a few states in the Northeast and Midwest, although their numbers are increasing in western and southeastern states. In 1990, the ten states with the largest concentration of Puerto Ricans as a percentage of total population were New York, New Jersey, Florida, Massachusetts, Pennsylvania, Connecticut, Illinois, California, Ohio, and Texas. While Puerto Ricans live in many parts of the United States, they continue to live mostly in northeastern states (U.S. Bureau of the Census, 1991).[1]

Puerto Ricans became citizens of the United States on passage of the Jones Act in 1917. They began a northward migration in the late 1940s and 1950s as part of "Operation Bootstrap," a plan to establish a yearly migration of thousands of Puerto Ricans to the agricultural farmland of the Northeast corridor. As a result of this plan, an Economic Development Administration that brought industrial incentives designed to develop and diversify the economy was created in Puerto Rico. That plan is responsible for what is today a relatively stable, growing middle class of Puerto Ricans on the island and a growing underclass of Puerto Ricans on the island and mainland experiencing the most serious socioeconomic problems of any minority including Native Americans. For example, as of 1994, 38.7 percent of Puerto Rican families lived below the poverty level; of these, 74 percent were headed by females. Zavala-Martinez attributes this to four social and historical processes that have had a direct impact on Puerto Rican women's reality: (1) the political and economic relationship between Puerto Rico and the United States, that is, colonialism; (2) the development of capitalism in Puerto Rico and the economic transformation from an agricultural to an industrial society; (3) the role and social status of women in Puerto Rico and in the class society; and (4) the emerging forms of consciousness and struggle among Puerto Ricans, given the political relationship with the United States.[2]

EDUCATION

Although Puerto Ricans have made modest gains in educational attainment over the past ten years and have a higher median income than other Latinos, Puerto Ricans continue to have the lowest socioeconomic status of any Hispanic subgroup, as defined by poverty and employment data. Recent research illustrates that this economic disadvantage has persisted for several years. Major changes in family structure, as well as serious challenges to labor market participation in the previous two decades, have influenced their already severely disadvantaged social and economic position and prompted community, research, and policy attention.[3] The information that follows presents a current socioeconomic profile of Puerto Ricans in the United States with an emphasis on Puerto Rican poverty.

SOCIOECONOMIC CHARACTERISTICS OF PUERTO RICANS: 1980–1990

Puerto Ricans made significant gains in educational attainment between 1980 and 1990; however, the educational attainment gap between Puerto Ricans and non-Hispanics remains wide. In the early 1980s about two in five Puerto Rican adults aged twenty-five years old and over were high school graduates (42.2%). By 1994, more than half of all Puerto Ricans in this age group had completed high school (59.4%). In comparison, four-fifths of non-Hispanics aged twenty-five and over (84.9%) had completed high school in 1990, up from 42.2 percent in 1980.[4] In terms of higher education, Puerto Ricans who are college graduates remains low compared to the non-Hispanic population. Although the college completion rate steadily increased during the early part of the 1980s, the rate grew stagnant in the latter half of the decade. One in ten Puerto Ricans have completed college (9.7%), whereas more than one in five non-Hispanic have four-year college degrees (24.3%).[5]

Poverty rates for white heads of household who had not completed high school in 1990 (17.6%) contrast in comparison to African American householders (40.6%) and Latino householders (34%). A significant finding suggests that 54 percent of Puerto Rican householders without a high school diploma, aged twenty-five years and over, live in poverty.[6]

Another interesting phenomena in the data about Puerto Ricans is that the labor force participation rates of Puerto Rican men have registered negative changes over the past two decades. Puerto Rican males in the workforce have the lowest labor force participation rates of any ethnic/racial group and the lowest of any Hispanic subgroup. Fewer than seven in ten Puerto Rican men aged sixteen years old and over (65.8%) were participating in the labor force in 1994, compared to four-fifths of all Hispanic men (77.6%) and three-quarters of non-Hispanic men (73.9%).[7]

CHARACTERISTICS OF POVERTY

During the mid-1980s when most families experienced economic recovery, Puerto Rican families continued to experience extremely high poverty rates. The 1990s began with the Puerto Rican poverty rate at the same level at which it peaked in the 1980s. Almost two-fifths of all Puerto Rican families (38.7%) lived below the poverty level, compared to fewer than one-tenth of white families (10%), slightly more than one-fourth of all Hispanic families (30.8%), and three-tenths of all African American families (33.1%). Poverty for Puerto Rican children continues to climb, making Puerto Rican children the poorest of any major racial/ethnic group in the United States. For example, more than half of all Puerto Rican children under age eighteen (52.2%) were poor in 1994, compared to almost two-fifths of all Hispanic children (47.7%), more than three-sevenths of all African American children (47.1%), and about one-sixth of white children (33.1%).[8] Thus, the poverty rate for Puerto Ricans is four times the rate of white families and slightly higher than the rate for African American families.

According to a recent "Household and Family Characteristics Report," living in a single-mother family more than triples the chances of being poor for a Puerto Rican child. In 1989 almost three-fourths of Puerto Rican children living in a family maintained by a woman were poor (74.4%). In contrast, the poverty rate of Puerto Rican children living in two-parent or male-headed families was 20.3 percent.[9] In comparison to other Latinos, poverty in the Puerto Rican community has been especially persistent and severe and has been both a result of and a contributing factor to other social problems affecting Puerto Rican children and youth.

Puerto Rican female-headed families are likely to be poorer than other female-headed households. Almost two-thirds (64.4%) of Puerto Rican female-headed families were poor in 1990, compared to one-half of African American female-headed families (51.2%) and almost three-tenths of white female-headed families (28.4%). In contrast, only 16.8 percent of Puerto Rican married couple families were poor that same year. Almost three-quarters of all poor Puerto Rican families (74.4%) are maintained by single mothers.

Among some factors associated with Puerto Rican poverty are low educational attainment, concentration in low-wage work, growth in single-mother families, immigration, and discrimination, but these factors only partially explain the persistence of high Puerto Rican poverty. According to research, six principal factors underlie and help to explain the persistent poverty of Puerto Ricans. These include industrial and economic changes; changes in skill requirements; gaps in educational attainment between Puerto Ricans and non-Hispanics; growth in women maintained households; unstable participation in the labor force; and geographical location and concentration.

INDUSTRIAL ECONOMIC CHANGES.   Industrial and economic changes in the economy during the 1960s and 1970s greatly affected the Puerto Rican community. Specifically, U.S. cities lost thousands of low-skilled, well-paid manufacturing jobs when the shift from a manufacturing to a service economy began. The "deindustrialization" of cities, especially in the Northeast where Puerto Ricans were heavily concentrated at that time, eliminated jobs filled by Puerto Ricans with limited levels of education.[10,11]

CHANGES IN SKILL REQUIREMENTS.   The demands of the growing service sector economy increased the labor market demand for higher literacy and numeric skills, displacing low-skilled segments of the population. Since 1979, almost nine out of every ten new jobs created have been in industries like business and health services that require high levels of education and for which many Puerto Ricans are not qualified.

GAPS IN EDUCATIONAL ATTAINMENT BETWEEN PUERTO RICANS AND NON-HISPANICS. Over the past two decades, Puerto Ricans have made gains in their educational attainment, as measured by median years of school completed. However, examination of high school dropout rates and high school and college completion data show that there are still wide educational disparities between Puerto Ricans and non-Hispanics that put Puerto Ricans at a disadvantage when competing for jobs.

GROWTH IN WOMEN-MAINTAINED HOUSEHOLDS. The proportion of Puerto Rican female-headed households increased during the 1980s but has been decreasing since 1989. Such families experience higher rates of family and child poverty than do two-parent families; Puerto Rican single mothers tend to have limited work experience and to rely heavily on public assistance.

UNSTABLE PARTICIPATION IN THE LABOR FORCE. The labor force status of Puerto Ricans has changed dramatically since the major migration of Puerto Ricans to the United States during the early 1950s. Upon their arrival, Puerto Ricans, including women, were more likely to be working or looking for work than their non-Hispanic counterparts. For economic reasons highlighted in this chapter, forty years later both Puerto Rican men and women lag behind non-Hispanics in labor force participation and they experience higher unemployment rates than whites, other Hispanics, and, in some cases, African Americans.

GEOGRAPHICAL LOCATION AND CONCENTRATION. Recent research has begun to examine the labor market experiences of mainland Puerto Ricans based in the area of the country in which they reside—primarily the Northeast and Midwest, which have been especially affected by economic changes and which offer Puerto Rican workers poor employment opportunities.

Health and Mental Health Risk Factors

The 1980s had seen significant growth in the mental health literature addressing cultural, socioeconomic, clinical, and developmental issues of Puerto Ricans in the United States.[12] In addition there was more cross-cultural therapy and counseling literature concerning Puerto Ricans.[13] However, a gap seemed to exist between the valuable information being published and the application of that knowledge. The "pathologization" of Puerto Ricans and other minority groups in the United States continues to be a problem of significant proportion, as are the blaming, judgmental, and moralistic attitudes of many service providers. Furthermore, some authors still offer heavily stereotyped descriptions of Puerto Ricans, presenting a static rather than an evolutionary, dynamic, transactional view of the culture.[14]

Cultural awareness in therapy must include awareness of class differences, an awareness often absent in family therapy literature and practice. Socially disempowered families or individuals cannot be assessed separately from the position they occupy in the power structure of the society in which they live. Behaviors labeled as "mental illness" or "dysfunction" may actually be survival strategies in response to poverty, racism, sexism, or other types of oppression. In such instances, the victims end up being blamed.

Even when therapist and client share the same ethnic background, if issues related to poverty and migration are not considered, therapy is not likely to be successful. Values and belief systems usually differ significantly across classes, and ideology is usually linked to one's position in the social hierarchy. Having a common national origin or language does not mean that significant class differences will disappear inside the therapy room; in fact, they may be exacerbated.[15]

The scarcity of bilingual professionals available to offer mental health services to Puerto Ricans increases the difficulties in therapy. Although recruitment of Puerto Ricans by U.S. agencies is becoming common, it seldom includes basic orientation and training sessions about the characteristics and socioeconomic environment of the population these professionals are to serve. It is often incorrectly assumed that a common national origin will automatically increase the quality of services.

In mental health clinics, newly arrived clinicians from middle-class backgrounds often feel overwhelmed, frustrated, and impotent when they face the types of problems that migrant Puerto Rican clients present. Clients may far outnumber available bilingual practitioners; thus, clinicians may be assigned large case loads with no backup support system provided by the clinic. During their years of study, these practitioners may have never dealt with mental health issues related to poverty and migration.[16]

It is imperative that orientation and training be provided to practitioners and that they engage in clinical practice with Puerto Ricans. Comas-Diaz states that cross-cultural mental health training is not only useful where racial and ethnic differences exist between patient and clinician, but is also needed when the clinician and the patient are racially and ethnically similar but have different socioeconomic backgrounds and/or different value systems.[17] This is seen in the following cases.[18]

CASE ONE

The G family comprised both parents Pedro (49 years old) and Teresa (41), plus seven children. Carmen, the oldest, was 23, and Papo, the youngest, was 10. Pedro, Jr., Jaime, Fernando, Margarita, and Flor ranged in ages from 14 to 21 years. An eighth child had died five years previously at age 4. The circumstances of her death are described below.

The request for mental health and medical services was initiated by the father, who for six years had been the "identified patient." He attended the first therapy session with his older daughter, Carmen. He arrived tearful, head hung low, and depressed. Carmen did most of the talking during the initial stage. She reported that her father's symptoms included depression, crying spells, social withdrawal, insomnia, irritability, lack of appetite, excessive cigarette smoking (two packs a day), and continuous coffee drinking.

To get Pedro to talk, I asked him questions about the history of his present emotional state. Highlights of his report are as follows:

Six years previously, he had suffered an accident while working in Puerto Rico. The accident occurred while Pedro was driving a trailer. The fellow worker who was with him died instantly. Pedro spent three months hospitalized with head and back injuries, the first three weeks of which he was unconscious.

Upon discharge he went back to work, still experiencing visual and memory problems in addition to back pain. A year later he had a second accident while driving. The company laid him off with a total compensation of less than $2,000. (He had worked for the company for more than twenty years.) Pedro requested help from the Legal Services Corporation (a U.S. federal agency with offices in Puerto Rico), but in his opinion the services offered were not adequate and an appeal of the company's decision never reached the court.

Pedro began experiencing mood swings from severe depression to rage. This created crisis situations for the entire family, who, according to their report, had a fairly normal life up until then. During this time Pedro underwent eye surgery for lesions caused by the accidents.

Shortly after his layoff, his four-year-old daughter was hospitalized with a high fever of unknown origin. She died of a generalized infection caused by an infected intravenous tube administered at the public hospital. His daughter's death increased Pedro's depression, sense of despair, and feeling of powerlessness. Moreover, his wife Teresa also experienced severe depression as a result of their child's death.

Three years ago the family started to break up. The oldest daughter, Carmen, moved to the East Coast of the United States, followed gradually by her older siblings. Two years later Pedro's wife, Teresa, left him and also migrated to the United States with the two younger children. According to Pedro, she could no longer deal with his mood swings and outbursts of anger. Pedro reported that he often became very irritable, could not tolerate noise, and screamed and threw things when he got very upset. He stated that he had never become physically violent with his family.

Pedro remained in Puerto Rico, living alone in the family's house. Shortly after Teresa left, Carmen was contacted by an uncle who requested that she visit her father because his depression was getting worse and he was becoming physically ill. Carmen complied. She went to see her father and decided to bring him back to the United States with her.

When I started working with the Gs, Pedro and Teresa did not speak to each other and lived in separate apartments. Pedro was living with Carmen and her husband. Margarita, who had already been "adopted" by her older sister, also lived with them. Teresa lived with Papo and Flor in an apartment next to one of the older sons.

Jaime and his wife, who was pregnant, were estranged from the rest of the family. Carmen explained that she thought they avoided the family because her brother's wife, although Puerto Rican, did not speak Spanish and didn't feel comfortable with the family because of the language barrier. (This was a vague response, but I respected their apparent wish to maintain areas of privacy at that point.)

Fernando lived with friends and was also in conflict with his parents. Pedro explained that Fernando had a tendency to get himself in trouble (for example, borrowing more money than he could possibly repay) and then rush to his father requesting help. These requests, Pedro said, made him feel even worse because it made it more obvious that he could no longer "support or even help his family economically."

Pedro had "given up." The changes in the family structure from how they lived and functioned in Puerto Rico to their circumstances in the United States were too much for him to handle. Having lost his role as the family provider, he declared himself "terminally disabled" and allowed Carmen to "mother" him by taking care of all his needs except for personal hygiene. His depression continued, and the crying spells occurred more frequently. However, his outbursts of anger, which appeared to have been the only expression of power he had left, disappeared. Carmen even became his "voice" as a result of the language barrier.

The living arrangements gave Teresa a "break" from dealing with Pedro's depression as well as space to let her own depression be expressed. Teresa described herself as being "sick of her nerves" since her daughter died. The younger children, all of whom described Pedro as having been a "very strict father," found themselves liberated from his "law and order," as well as from his anger, while still maintaining physical closeness to both parents.

The family was experiencing turmoil when they started therapy: the sudden separation and lack of communication of the parents after more than twenty years of marriage; the migration of all family members to the United States, with the consequent difficulties of adaptation to a new land (the parents did not speak English); the organization of the family in the United States; the older daughter as the focus of support for the entire family system; the humiliation of having to request welfare support from local agencies (expressed by both parents in tears in one of the sessions); and the two teenage daughters having to work as waitresses for the first time due to economic difficulties.

The family's expressed goal in therapy was to get the parents back together: "If father could get his nerves cured!" I interpreted their request for therapy as a sign of readiness to assume control of their lives again. They needed me to facilitate the process by "legitimizing" their emotional reactions to the tragedies they had experienced and by helping them obtain financial aid from the disability, welfare, and rent-subsidy programs. Pedro was ill with a kidney infection; as a result of his accident, he still had visual problems and severe back pains. Teresa had never worked outside the home. In addition, their lack of skills in English reduced their job opportunities. Nonetheless, Pedro wanted to be recognized as the family provider, even at the cost of being declared "officially disabled."

Part of the work during therapy was to reframe their sense of shame at having to ask for help from Puerto Rican immigrants already established in the community while they reestablished themselves as a new immigrant family. A series of family rituals, such as collective dinners and presenting the history of their family through photographs and role playing, were incorporated into the treatment process.

In addition, throughout the process I shared with them my interpretations of their situation and development stages while requesting their feedback. I made it clear that therapy required teamwork and that their input and expertise about themselves were of utmost importance. I have found emphasizing teamwork to be very effective for empowering families: they are the experts, and I am the facilitator.

Family therapy lasted five months, at the end of which Pedro and Teresa were back together, had been granted the diverse financial aids for which they had applied, and had a support system in the community to help them deal with ongoing challenges.

CASE TWO

In the late 1970s, at age 16, Javier migrated to the United States from a slum in metropolitan San Juan. He had dropped out of school prior to completing the seventh grade because he felt he "wasn't learning anything, and it was a waste of time." He learned auto mechanics while helping a friend who had a garage. His father had left home when Javier was 10 years old, and they seldom saw each other. His mother had migrated to the United States the previous year with two younger children. Javier joined them with the intention of getting a job quickly as a mechanic and moving into his own apartment. He acquired basic English language skills within several months.

After a year of searching unsuccessfully for a job, he started to drink and get into fights. In one fight, he mortally stabbed another Puerto Rican. While in prison, he was diagnosed as "schizophrenic" by the consulting psychiatrist, apparently due to his continuous expression of anger, and was transferred to a psychiatric prison. After four years, during which he was medicated with antipsychotic drugs, he was released on probation. He returned to his mother's apartment and resumed his search for a job. Four months later he got a job at a gas station working for minimum wage. He lasted three weeks at this job. Someone informed the owner that Javier had been in a psychiatric prison, and he was fired. Once again, he turned to drinking to work out his frustrations.

Javier was 23 when I first saw him in therapy. He was seeking to be declared "disabled" so that he could get financial assistance. He was willing, he said, to "act crazy if that was necessary—he was already carrying the label anyway." Therapy lasted six months and consisted of several components: individual work with Javier on rebuilding self-esteem; and family work, which meant including his mother in some of the sessions in an effort to establish additional support and to plan strategies that could help Javier deal with the stigma of "madness." Together, they decided that moving to another community would help them in obtaining a fresh start.

During therapy, we contacted various agencies until we located one that was willing to train and certify Javier as an auto mechanic. With the certification in hand, Javier started his own business of fixing cars in front of his apartment (not uncommon in Puerto Rican *barrios*). He soon earned a solid reputation; staff from the clinic and other related agencies began going to him with their cars.

DISCUSSION OF CASES

These two cases are typical of the low-income migrant Puerto Rican situation in the United States. In both cases, disability was regarded as the solution to economic difficulties that the identified patients were facing.

Understanding these phenomena requires knowledge of the impact of socioeconomic conditions on people's lives. Without such knowledge, it is difficult, if not impossible, to understand how illness, either physical or mental, may become an asset. Low income and poor families confront the therapist with issues of economic survival, compared to the more existential or other clinical issues commonly addressed in graduate training programs.

The loss of jobs or absence of jobs poses a severe problem for male and female heads of households. Moreover, a significant number of employed Puerto Rican migrants continue to work at low-paying jobs. The fact that women receive even lower salaries than do men complicates the economic survival of the Puerto Rican family.

Clinicians need to be aware of these environmental circumstances and be sensitive to the particular situations of the family. Making generalizations about the unwillingness of a people to work helps no one. The quality of the clinician's interaction with the clients is essential to how the family reality is constructed, interpreted, and dealt with. It is important when working with families who are disempowered within societal structures that an ecosystemic assessment be conducted for the family.

General Data on Health Care and Puerto Ricans

The data concerning Puerto Ricans' national health status provide several overall findings. In general, the major national killers—heart disease, stroke, and cancer—are also the major causes of death among Puerto Ricans. Rates may be distorted, however, by the population's relative youthfulness. Among Puerto Rican families, the leading cause of death is heart disease; the second leading cause of death is AIDS; and the third leading cause is violence, including accidents, suicides, and homicides. Health status is significantly affected by lifestyle and behaviors. For example, improper diet, smoking, and excessive alcohol consumption are known to increase the risks for developing significant health problems such as diabetes, cardiovascular disease, and cancer.

Data from the National Health Interview Survey of 1988 suggest that the overall rate of smoking among Puerto Ricans is 54 percent higher than that of other groups, largely because of its low incidence among females in general. Prevalence of smoking also was highest for Puerto Rican men and women (35%) compared to any other Hispanic subgroup.[19]

Puerto Rican families are under considerable stress as they adapt to a different culture and way of life, as they cope with low income and poor housing, and as they experience exploitation and mistreatment from both individuals and institutions. For some people, such stressors increase the risk for somatic and functional illness, depression, organic disease, and interpersonal tensions.[20] Indeed, Puerto Ricans have been identified as a high-risk group for mental health problems, particularly depression, anxiety, and substance abuse.[21] Health professionals and social work providers working with Puerto Rican populations need to be aware that many Puerto Ricans believe in the interaction between mental health and physical health—that the physical affects the mental and vice versa.[22] Thus, it is important to understand mental health issues prevalent among Puerto Ricans in order to better address their specific needs and to design relevant preventive modalities.

Migration and subsequent culture shock are thought to engender anxiety and depression.[23] People in transition often experience feelings of irritability, anxiety, helplessness, and despair. They must mourn the loss of family, friends, language, and culturally-determined values and attitudes. Some Puerto Ricans respond to migration with a "hangover depression" that may include suicide attempts.[24] Puerto Rican women are particularly vulnerable to depression. Severe psychiatric disorders are sometimes diagnosed incorrectly when practitioners are not aware of prevalent cultural beliefs and practices. This is further exacerbated by the use of psychological tests that have not been standardized for bilingual populations.

In general, babies born with low birth weights are at highest risk for neonatal illness and death. Teenage mothers tend to have less prenatal care and to bear a larger percentage of low-birth-weight babies than do mothers in their twenties. Puerto Ricans bear children at about the same rate as African Americans, and their incidence of low-birth-weight infants (9–10%) falls between that of non-Hispanic whites and African Americans.[25] Puerto Rican women also tend to have the lowest levels of early prenatal care (55%) and the highest levels of delayed or no care (17%).[26]

Beliefs and Practices That Influence Puerto Ricans' Health

Factors such as economic status, level of education, and length of time in this country (recent arrivals, first or second generation, etc.) may influence individuals' health behavior more than cultural factors. Thus, among Puerto Ricans in the United States, there is not one predictable "Puerto Rican response." For example, traditional Puerto Rican diet is high in fiber, relying heavily on beans and grains, rather than on meats, for protection. However, Puerto Rican diets reflect many current dietary recommendations and also play a key role in some illnesses.

Healthy practices can be encouraged through use of traditional cultural sayings. The "health beliefs model" postulates that, in order for people to make changes in their lifestyle, they must believe that they are susceptible to a disease, that the disease is serious, and that prevention can be helpful. Some commonly known Puerto Rican sayings suggest that events in one's life result from luck, fate, or other powers beyond an individual's control: *Que sera* (What will be will be); *Que sea lo que Dios quiera* (It's in God's hand); *Esta enfermedad es una prueba de Dios* (This illness is a test of God); and *De algo se tiene que morir uno* (You have to die of something). Indeed, persons with acute or chronic illness may regard themselves, and often are regarded by others, as innocent victims of malevolent forces. In such cases family and friends expect support throughout the healing process. Similarly, when receiving traditional health services, Puerto Ricans may become passive, expecting the provider to "take charge" of them—a stance that doesn't fit with the active participation required to prevent or heal much disease.

Balance and harmony also are considered important to health. A person's sense of *bienestar* (well being) is thought to depend on balance in emotional, physical, and social arenas. Imbalance may produce disease or illness. For example, some Puerto Ricans attribute physical illness to *los nervios* (nerves), believing that illness results from having experienced a strong emotional state. Thus, they try to prevent illness by avoiding intense rage, sadness, and other emotions.

In the absence of adequate access to health care, some Puerto Rican families seek the services of folk healers instead of, or simultaneously with, mainstream health care. However, Puerto Ricans' reliance on folk medicine is minimal—fewer than 4 percent of any group consult a folk healer over a twelve-month period.[27] Belief in folk healers assumes that one can have contact with God and the supernatural without intervention of the traditional church; indeed, the traditional church and folk healing coexist. The following briefly describes the folk healing systems used by Puerto Ricans: *Santeria* combines the African Yoruban deities with Catholic saints; *Santeros/santeras* are both priests/priestesses and healers.

Among Puerto Ricans, a belief in *espiritismo* holds that the world is populated with spirits, including religious figures, who intervene in the lives of individuals. These *espiritistas* can communicate with the spirits and have the power of healing. These persons may know about different types of home remedies, herbs, and so on, and have skills in treating certain physical conditions (such as joint deviation) or have other special powers.

The extent of Puerto Ricans' reliance on folk healers is a subject of some controversy in research. Perhaps, because the belief systems and practice are so interesting, many people have studied and reported on them. Their prevalence in the literature, however, does *not* reflect its very modest use among Puerto Ricans.

In other Hispanic groups, one observer found the use of folk healers to be common though ancillary to a health care system among Mexicans in southern California. Apparently, they used them when they were pressured by family or friends, they disagreed with a physician's diagnosis, or when they were disappointed with the quality of care provided by a physician.[28]

Folk healers and some home remedies cause no harm and may well be helpful, but such remedies or practices may be harmful when they are used as substitutes for needed medical care. In such instances, social workers and other social service providers must carefully consider what approach to take so that clients are not "driven underground." It usually does not help to ask people if they use folk healers or folk medicine. People don't think of what they do in those terms. It does help to ask routinely, "Which prescription medications, over-the-counter medicines, or herbs are you taking now?" If you want to know something specific, ask a specific question. For example, pediatric health providers in certain areas routinely ask, "What do you do when your child has *empacho* (lack of appetite, stomachache, diarrhea, and vomiting)?

Respecting and affirming your patients' efforts to stay or become healthy will enhance your ability to influence them through positive education. Opportunities abound to educate through one-to-one interaction, culturally-sensitive program posters, pamphlets, and other displays in your waiting room, and so on.

Ecosystems Perspective

The practice of social work focuses on the interaction between the person and the environment. The goal of social work practice is to enhance and restore the psychosocial functioning of persons or to change oppressive or destructive social conditions that negatively affect the mutually beneficial interaction between persons and their environment.[29] In assessing Puerto Ricans' needs for services, the social worker should seek to understand the clients' feelings and attitudes about those oppressive and destructive factors and to ascertain their negative impacts.

The ecosystems model of practice developed by Morales and Sheafor[30] is adopted for analysis of psychological factors impacting Puerto Ricans. The ecosystem consists of five interconnected levels: (1) historical; (2) environmental-structural; (3) cultural; (4) family; and (5) individual. An analysis of each level as it affects the lives and social conditions of Puerto Ricans follows.

HISTORICAL INFLUENCES

Puerto Ricans, the second-largest Hispanic group in the United States, have been migrating to the mainland United States since the turn of the twentieth century. In 1917, the Jones Act granted all Puerto Ricans born on the island U.S. citizenship. This is a striking difference from all other Latino immigrants to the country, as Puerto Ricans can move freely between their country of origin without the legal restrictions and entanglements of U.S. immigration law.

Migration to the continental United States became a viable alternative to living in the deteriorating economic and social situation on the island. Economic changes on the island, brought about by foreign control of land for sugar and coffee plantations and tobacco, created high unemployment and a steady stream of emigrants to the United States that has continued to the present. One of the first casualties of this economic change was the incremental decline of family patterns based on subsistence. High unemployment coupled with gradual industrialization caused both increased unemployment and dependence on outside commodities. This imbalance created surplus labor at a time when jobs in New York City and elsewhere on the mainland needed to be filled. Puerto Ricans began migrating to the United States and, in particular, to New York City.

The decades before 1945 are considered the period of the "Great Migration" and pioneer migration. Many of the people emigrating from Puerto Rico were contract laborers who came to work in industry and agriculture. These individuals were the basis for many of the Puerto Rican communities that currently exist outside of New York City. By 1940, there were a total of almost 70,000 Puerto Ricans in the United States; more than 87 percent, or almost 61,000, were living in New York City.

By 1960, a total of 887,662 Puerto Ricans had migrated to the mainland; 69 percent of these people, or about 612,000, resided in New York City. Like other Hispanic immigrants, Puerto Ricans did not travel together in family groups at the beginning of the migration. Usually, young men immigrated to find work then began sending for spouses and families. But the social conditions in the United States, especially in New York where new communities were established, set parameters that changed family patterns and continued the adaptation of Puerto Ricans to the city.

Poverty became a significant factor in the lives of families in both Puerto Rico and the United States. It is impossible to discuss the Puerto Rican family in the United States without discussing the extreme conditions that have pervaded the Puerto Rican community here. From a historical perspective, Puerto Ricans have never recovered from the early colonial period when U.S. capital interest took over the ownership of the majority of land on the island and created a labor force that was dependent on cash crops. Puerto Rico had one of the highest infant mortality rates in the world and one of the lowest rates of average income per worker during the early years of U.S. jurisdiction over the island. Consider, for example, that in 1899 Puerto Ricans maintained ownership of 93 percent of all farms, but by 1930 foreign (U.S.) interest controlled 60 percent of sugar cultivation, 80 percent of tobacco lands, 60 percent of all banks, and 100 percent of maritime lines that controlled commodities entering and leaving the island.[31]

Although migration between Puerto Rico and mainland United States has been described as a primary reason for the poor socioeconomic status of Puerto Ricans in the United States, migration as a contributor to Puerto Rican poverty is difficult to confirm because Puerto Rican migration data is not regularly, or scientifically, collected. Moreover, little research exists on the demographic characteristics of migrants and the effects of migration on the socioeconomic status of mainland Puerto Ricans. The limited research that has been done has examined the number of Puerto Ricans migrating and the reasons behind their migration.

Significant Puerto Rican migration to the United States continued into the late 1940s and the early 1950s. As economic opportunities on the mainland increased during the post–World War II economic boom, low airfares between New York and Puerto Rico were introduced, thereby facilitating migration between Puerto Rico, where there was a surplus of low-skilled labor, and the mainland. According to the Bureau of Applied Research on the Puerto Rican Population in New York City, Puerto Rican migrants in the early 1950s included both men and women of all ages. The data showed that about four in ten were men between the ages of fifteen and forty-five; the Bureau noted that Puerto Rican migration, compared to foreign immigration, was characterized by family, as opposed to individual, movement.

At the end of the 1960s and into the early 1970s, what has become known as "revolving door" migration began. This is a back and forth stream of people moving between the United States and the island. It is no longer focused in New York, although a majority of Puerto Ricans continue to migrate and settle in the Northeast.

Since those early dates of migration to the mainland, the economies of both the United States and Puerto Rico have undergone serious changes. Instead of leaving the island because of economic opportunities in the United States, many Puerto Ricans are now leaving the island because of the lack of economic opportunity in Puerto Rico. Therefore, in addition to the promise of jobs, a wider range of employment options, and higher salaries on the U.S. mainland, the lack of economic opportunity in Puerto Rico also influences migration. Shifts and trends in the mainland economy also have consequences for the Puerto Rican economy, causing some islanders to migrate when they cannot find employment.[32] Migration to and from Puerto Rico between 1982 and 1988 showed that over 151,000 more Puerto Ricans left the island than moved to it.

ENVIRONMENTAL–STRUCTURAL FACTORS

Puerto Ricans have had a history of being victims of exploitation and racism in the United States. Unlike mainstream culture, which is predominantly Western European, the ancestral roots of the Puerto Ricans are Indian (indigenous to Puerto Rico), African, and Spanish. In the past a number of publicly accepted practices excluded people of color, and in particular Puerto Ricans, from many institutions and positions of influence. Jobs were advertised in separate categories (male or female, white or "colored") allowing organizations to exclude people who were viewed as undesirable. Puerto Ricans were largely confined to low-paying jobs and perceived as being inferior in intellect, training, and motivation to white men, women, and African Americans in the workplace.

When affirmative action legislation started to take hold, it did little to address the underlying assumptions and stereotypes that plagued nontraditional managers and created the barriers to advancement that persist today in views about Puerto Ricans. When the law forced them to hire and promote nontraditional employees, some responded with "malicious compliance" deliberately appointing nontraditional candidates who were weak or ill suited to the jobs available so that they would have little chance of succeeding.

BARRIERS TO ADVANCEMENT FOR PUERTO RICANS.   The most significant barriers today are the policies and practices that systematically restrict the opportunities and rewards available to Puerto Ricans and other Hispanics. This is a fundamental finding in Bonilla-Santiago's[33] study wherein managers agreed that prejudice is still a serious problem and the number one employment barrier.

Prejudice is defined here as the tendency to view people who are different from some reference group in terms of sex, ethnic background, or racial characteristics, such as skin color, as being deficient. For example, prejudice is the assumption (without evidence) that nontraditional individuals are less competent or less suitable than white males.

Ethnic and sex differences are sometimes used, consciously or not, to define "inferior" groups in a caste system. For example, Puerto Ricans were labeled as "unassertive people"—they "sit back" in meetings while others hurl and debate ideas. Some whites consider Puerto Ricans and Latinos "too polite" (and, consequently, as lacking in conviction), perhaps because of their concern for showing respect or maintaining cooperative teamwork.[34] There is also a trust barrier. Puerto Ricans and Latinos are perceived as dishonest and corrupt by individuals from the dominant culture. The prevailing stereotypes of African Americans are that they are lazy, uneducated, and incompetent. Women are often assumed to be indecisive and unable to be analytical. A 1990 survey by the University of Chicago's National Opinion Research Center, along with other research findings, shows that these stereotypes are still prevalent. This survey revealed that whites believe that people of other ethnic backgrounds are less intelligent, less hard working, less likely to be self-supporting, more violence prone, and less patriotic than whites.[35]

Restrictions against Puerto Ricans consist of additional discrimination in housing, employment, educational opportunities, and access to social services. Such structural, social, and psychological barriers are prevalent in the Puerto Rican culture today.

PUERTO RICAN CULTURE

Social workers need to focus on understanding the cultural values, belief systems, and societal norms of U.S. culture as Puerto Rican culture. In an attempt to understand the Puerto Rican client and to work effectively with this population, the following describes several important cultural values operating among Puerto Ricans: importance of the family; familism versus individualism; and the values of *respeto* and *personalismo,* styles of communicating that will continually affect your interaction with the client. To the extent that you can appreciate and respond to the client's values and language needs, you will be more effective. A further look at these cultural values follows:

1. Importance of the Family: Traditionally, Puerto Ricans include many relatives as "family," not only parents and siblings but grandparents, aunts, uncles, cousins, close family friends (who are often considered honorary uncles or aunts), and *padrinos* (godparents). All may be involved in an individual's health. During illness, people frequently consult other family members and often ask them to come along on medical visits.

2. Familism versus Individualism: Familism emphasizes interdependence, affiliation over confrontation, and cooperation over competitions.[36] Within familism, important decisions are made by the family, not by the individual alone. Thus, family members expect to be involved in treatment plans that require a shift in life-style; for example, a change in diet, if the family network is involved in providing and preparing food. Migration and geographic mobility may put stress on Puerto Ricans' values of familism. For example, a young family that has recently moved into your area may have left behind its extended family support system. Similarly, teen-agers who are quickly adopting the manners of their peers in the U.S. culture may be in marked conflict with their parents who maintain traditional values and customs.

3. *Respeto* Requires Deference: The way Puerto Ricans show respect to one another, establish rapport, express caring, treat each other as males and females, and communicate nonverbally to one another is different from that of the dominant culture. *Respeto* dictates appropriate deferential behavior toward others on the basis of age, sex, social position, economic status, and position of authority. Elders expect to receive respect from younger individuals, adults from children, men from women, teachers from students, employers from employees, and so on. Social work providers, by virtue of their treating functions, education, and training, are seen as authority figures and as such are awarded *respeto*.

Respeto Establishes Rapport: *Respeto* further implies that relationships are based on a common humanity, wherein one is required to establish—not simply assume—rapport, decency, and respect.[37]

As like the general population, positive interactions between social workers and the Puerto Rican client require providing information about the examination, diagnosis, and treatment; listening to the client's concerns and taking individual needs into consideration in planning treatment; and treating the client in a respectful manner. For example, Puerto Rican clients can be shown *respeto,* even by providers with limited Spanish, by always using the formal *"usted"* (Sir) for "you" until the patient explicitly offers the use of the informal *"tu"* (you). Address Puerto Ricans formally as *Señor* (Mr.) or *Don* (Sir), *Señora* (Mrs.) or *Doña* (Madam); and greet clients in Spanish with *buenos dias* (good morning) or *buenas tardes* (good afternoon).

4. *Personalismo*—Warm, Friendly, Personal Relationships: Younger social workers, even though they will be awarded *respeto* as authority figures, are expected to be especially formal in their interactions with older Puerto Rican clients. Formality as a sign of respect, however, should not be confused with distance. Puerto Ricans tend to stress the importance of *personalismo*—personal rather than impersonal or institutional relationships. Thus, many Puerto Ricans expect social work providers to be warm, friendly, and personal, and to take an active role in the client's life. For example, a social worker might greet a client, *"Buenos dias, Señora* Santiago. How are you today? How is your family feeling after the accident?" or "How are the children doing at school?" Such a greeting acknowledges *personalismo,* conveying to the client that the provider is interested in her as a human being. *Personalismo* also stipulates that the client's relationship is with the individual provider, not with the institution. When asked where they receive medical care, Puerto Ricans often respond with the name of the provider: "I am seeing Doctor (nurse)" rather than with the name of the institution.

5. Communication Styles Guided by *Respeto* and *Personalismo:* Verbal communication among Puerto Ricans tends to be structured, guided by the cultural values of *respeto* and *personalismo*. When interacting with social work providers, many Puerto Rican clients tend to avoid confrontation and conflict by not disagreeing, not expressing doubts about the treatment, and, often, by not asking questions. Many would rather not admit that they are confused about their instructions or treatment.

Communication Style Includes Nonverbal Communication and Expressiveness: Many Puerto Ricans communicate intense emotion and may appear quite animated in conversations—behavior that is sometimes misperceived by non-Puerto Ricans as being "out of control."

Physical Touching: Puerto Ricans tend to physically touch others. Many expect the provider to shake hands when greeting; males often hug family members and friends to express their affection, and they may express their gratitude to providers and other health care personnel by kissing or giving gifts.

Expression of Pain: Similarly, Puerto Ricans may express pain more openly than is expected among other cultural groups. For example, some Puerto Rican patients moan when in pain.

Eye Contact: Traditionally, Puerto Ricans have been taught to avoid eye contact with authority figures (such as health or mental health providers) as a sign of *respeto*; such behavior should not be misinterpreted as disinterest in the communication. Conversely, the provider is expected to look directly at the client, even when communicating through an interpreter.

Closeness versus Distance: When interacting with others, Puerto Ricans typically prefer being closer to each other in space. Overall, Puerto Ricans tend to be highly attuned to others' nonverbal messages. Non-Spanish-speaking providers must be particularly sensitive to this tendency when establishing relationships with patients who speak only Spanish.

6. *Fatalismo* (Fatalism): Fatalism and Puerto Rican values need to be examined in the context of Catholicism and colonialism. The notion of a "colonialist personality" is found throughout a good part of the literature. A few may see life's events as inevitable ("*Lo que Dios manda*"—What God wills). They feel themselves at the mercy of supernatural forces and are resigned to their fate. This fatalistic attitude of some Puerto Ricans has partly contributed to their unwillingness to seek outside professional help.

FAMILY STRUCTURE

The Puerto Rican family is not monolithic. The traditional Puerto Rican family is no longer the norm. Although the family continues to be central in Puerto Rican lives, it has taken on a variety of forms to meet changing personal and social conditions. The high unemployment of the 1980s and the change in the American economy from one based on manufacturing to one based on information and services has had staggering consequences on the Puerto Rican family. In fact, the Puerto Rican family is changing as the world around them changes. Family size, geographical distribution, and other characteristics in U.S. society have had obvious effects on the Puerto Rican family. Still, the Puerto Rican family tends to be family-oriented with strong kin networks, and fertility rates are about 50 percent higher than in the rest of the U.S. population. These relatively high rates result from a combination of traditional Catholic beliefs and relatively low family income and individual educational attainment. Because of profound psychological stressors caused by poverty and white racism, Puerto Rican families are also more likely to divorce or separate than Anglos.

Puerto Rican families come in many forms, structures, and colors. Extended families may have members whose appearances range from black skin, dark hair, and dark eyes to blonde hair, blue eyes, and freckled white skin. Within one family, all or some may speak Spanish, all or some may speak English, all may be bilingual, and in some families members may speak three or more languages. They also vary in social class. Many are poor and uneducated, and others are middle class in income and education; however, Puerto Ricans are the poorest of any Hispanic subgroup. Puerto Ricans tend to be mostly urban. They usually cluster together in communities where they can preserve their language, customs, and tastes. Generally, there are three types of Puerto Rican families: recently arrived families, return migration families, and second-generation descendant families.

Intervention Strategies

Social workers who provide direct service, or microlevel social work intervention, and indirect service, or macrolevel societal intervention, with Puerto Ricans need to have firsthand knowledge of how this unique ethnic minority group has traditionally responded to mental health and social services.

Puerto Rican families for the most part retain values, attitudes, and behaviors that can be used constructively in the context of mental health services. Such strengths include the affective bonds among extended family members, the value placed on the community in providing diverse types of support to its members, and *personalismo* as a commonly shared character trait. The willingness of the Puerto Rican family to be warm and sharing in relationships allows the social worker to approach and intervene. Open discussion among family members can resolve many problems, some of which may be related to conflicts caused by the closed bonds of the extended system. Knowledge of the family's specific cultural, socioeconomic, and religious background, together with sound intuitive skills, help clinicians use the strengths of Puerto Rican families.

Concluding Comment

When working with Puerto Rican families, social workers need to possess personal qualities that reflect genuineness, empathy, nonpossessive warmth, and the capacity to respond flexibly to a range of possible solutions. It is important that an acceptance of and openness to differences among people be respected. Willingness to learn to work with clients that are ethnically different is also important.

The social workers' articulation and clarification of their personal values, stereotypes, and biases about their ethnicity and social class, as well as those of others, and ways they may accommodate or conflict with the needs of the Puerto Rican client are essential in any process of intervention. Understanding the culture (history, traditions, values, family systems, and artistic expressions) of Puerto Rican clients is very important. It is important that the impact of ethnicity on therapists' and clients' behavior, attitudes, and values is understood.

When helping Puerto Rican families, the social worker must always consider cross-cultural issues and account for multiple components beyond those that pertain specifically to "culture." Issues related to socioeconomic class are particularly important to consider, as affluent Puerto Ricans have, for example, far more resources than impoverished Puerto Ricans, whose poverty becomes an additional psychosocial stressor. Social workers must always be clear about their professional practice role and intervention methods, being careful not to promote conformity and dependence in their clients. A cross-cultural micro and macro practice will achieve the best results.

KEY WORDS AND CONCEPTS

Puerto Ricans	Jones Act
Colonialism	Island Puerto Ricans
Espiritismo	Independence
Mainland Puerto Ricans	Puerto Rican culture
Statehood	

SUGGESTED READINGS

Bonilla-Santiago, G. *Breaking Ground and Barriers: Hispanic Women Developing Effective Leadership.* San Diego, CA: Marin Publications, 1993.

Comas-Diaz, L., and Griffith, E. H., eds. *Clinical Guidelines in Cross-Cultural Mental Health.* New York: John Wiley & Sons, 1988.

Facundo, America. "Sensitive Mental Health Services for Low-Income Puerto Rican Families," in Marta Sotomayor, ed., *Empowering Hispanic Families: A Critical Issue for the 90s.* Milwaukee: Family Service America, 1991.

Garcia-Coll, C. C., and Mattei, M. L., eds. *The Psychosocial Development of Puerto Rican Women.* New York: Praeger, 1989.

Mizio, Emelicia. "The Impact of Macro Systems on Puerto Rican Families," in Armando T. Morales and Bradford W. Sheafor, *Social Work: A Profession of Many Faces,* 6th Edition. Boston: Allyn and Bacon, 1992.

Zavala-Martinez, Iris. "En La Lucha: The Economic and Socioemotional Struggles of Puerto Rican Women," in Lenora Fulani, ed., *The Politics of Race and Gender in Therapy.* New York: Haworth Press, 1987.

ENDNOTES

1. U.S. Bureau of the Census, *Current Population Survey: 1994* (Washington, D.C.: U.S. Government Printing Office, 1994).
2. Ibid.
3. U.S. Bureau of the Census, "Household and Family Characteristics: March 1994," *Current Population Reports* (Washington, D.C.: U.S. Government Printing Office, 1994).

4. Institute for Puerto Rican Policy, *Puerto Ricans and Other Latinos in U.S.: March 1994* IPR Datanote No. 17 (New York: August 1994).

5. Ibid.

6. Ibid.

7. Ibid.

8. Ibid.

9. U.S. Bureau of the Census, "Household and Family Characteristics: March 1992," *Current Population Reports* P20-467 (Washington, D.C.: U.S. Department of Commerce).

10. Edwin Melendez, Clara Rodriguez, and Janis Barry Figueroa, eds., *Hispanics in the Labor Force, Issues and Policies* (New York: Plenum Press, 1991).

11. Douglass T. Gurak and Luis Falcon, "The Puerto Rican Family Poverty: Complex Paths to Poor Outcomes," in *Puerto Ricans: Breaking Out of the Cycle of Poverty* (Washington, D.C.: National Puerto Rican Coalition, June 1992).

12. C. C. Garcia-Coll and M. L. Mattei, eds., *The Psychosocial Development of Puerto Rican Women* (New York: Praeger, 1989); L. Comas-Diaz and E. Griffith, eds., *Clinical Guidelines in Cross-Cultural Mental Health* (New York: John Wiley, 1988); C. Falicov, ed., *Cultural Perspectives in Family Therapy* (Rockville, MD: Aspen Press, 1983); M. McGoldrick, J. K. Pearce, and J. Giordano, eds., *Ethnicity and Family Therapy* (New York: Guilford Press, 1982); I. Canino and G. Canino, "Impact of Stress on the Puerto Rican Family," *American Journal of Orthopsychiatry,* Vol. 50 (1980).

13. P. B. Pedersen, "Ten Frequent Assumptions of Cultural Bias in Counseling," *Journal of Multicultural Counseling and Development,* Vol. 15 (1987); I. Ibrahhim and P. M. Arrendondo, "Ethical Standards for Cross-Cultural Counseling: Counselor Preparation, Practice, Assessment and Research," *Journal of Counseling and Development,* Vol. 64 (1986); C. Falikov, ed., *Cultural Perspectives in Family Therapy* (Rockville, MD: Aspen Press, 1983); D. Sue, *Counseling the Culturally Different* (New York: John Wiley, 1981).

14. J. M. Dillard, *Multicultural Counseling: Toward Ethnic and Cultural Relevance in Human Encounters* (Chicago: Nelsen-Hall, 1983).

15. America Facundo, "Sensitive Mental Health Services for Low-Income Puerto Rican Families," in Marta Sotomayor, ed., *Empowering Hispanic Families: A Critical Issue for the 90s* (Milwaukee: Family Service America, 1991), p. 124.

16. G. Bernal and I. Flores-Ortiz, "Latino Families in Therapy: Engagement and Evaluation," *Journal of Marital and Family Therapy* 8 (1982): 357–365.

17. L. Comas-Diaz and E. Griffith, eds., *Clinical Guidelines in Cross-Cultural Mental Health.*

18. These cases are reprinted from America Facundo, *Empowering Hispanic Families: A Critical Issue for the '90s,* Marta Sotomayor, ed., pp. 126–130. © 1991, Family Service America. Used with permission.

19. S. Haynes, B. Cohen, C. Harvey, and M. McMillan, "Cigarette Smoking Patterns Among Mexicans and Puerto Ricans" (paper presented at the 113th Annual Meeting of the American Public Health Association, Washington, D.C., November 19, 1985).

20. W. A. Vega and M. R. Miranda, "Stress and Hispanic Mental Health: Relating Research to Service Delivery" (Rockville, MD: U.S. Department of Health and Human Services, National Institute of Mental Health, Public Health Service, 1985).

21. L. Comas-Diaz and E. Griffith, *Clinical Guidelines.*

22. A. Padilla and R. Ruiz, *Latino Mental Health: A Review of the Literature* (Rockville, MD: National Institute of Mental Health, 1973).

23. A. C. Garza-Guerrero, "Culture Shock: Its Mourning and Vicissitudes of Identity," *Journal of the American Psychoanalytic Association* 22 (1974): 408–429.

24. E. Trauatman, "Suicidal Attempts of Puerto Rican Immigrants," *Psychiatric Quarterly* 35 (1961): 544–554.

25. S. J. Ventura, "Births of Hispanic Parentage, 1983 and 1984," National Center for Health Statistics, Monthly Vital Statistics Report, 36 (4) Supplement (PHS), 87–1120 (Public Health Service, National Center Statistics, 1987).

26. Ibid.

27. N. Garcia-Preto, "Puerto Rican Families," in M. McGoldrick, J. K. Pierce, and J. Giordano, eds., *Ethnicity and Family Therapy* (New York: Guildford Press, 1982), pp. 164–186.

28. S. E. Keefe, "Acculturation and the Extended Family," in A. Padilla, ed., *Acculturation* (Boulder, CO: Westview Press, 1980).

29. "Social Work Practice with Asian Americans," in Armando Morales and Bradford W. Sheafor, *Social Work: A Profession of Many Faces,* 6th Edition (Boston: Allyn and Bacon, 1992), pp. 535–550.

30. Morales and Sheafor, 1992.

31. J. Jennings and Monte Rivera, *Puerto Rican Politics in Urban America* (Westport, CT: Greenwood Press, 1984).

32. I. Perez-Johnson, "Industrial Change and Puerto Rican Migration to the United States, 1982–1988" (Paper presented at conference on Puerto Rican Poverty and Migration, New School for Social Research, New York, May 1, 1992).

33. G. Bonilla-Santiago, *Breaking Ground and Barriers: Hispanic Women Developing Effective Leadership* (San Diego, CA: Marin Publications, 1993).

34. Bonilla-Santiago, 1993.

35. T. W. Smith, "Ethnic Images," National Opinion Research Center, GSS Topical Report No. 19 (Chicago: University of Chicago, December 1990).

36. Falicov, 1983.

37. R. Maduro, "Curanderismo and Latino Views of Disease and Curing," *Western Journal of Medicine* 139 (1983): 868–874.

The Social Worker in Action

When the seventh edition of this text was going to press, the nation was celebrating Martin Luther King Jr. Day on Monday, January 17, 1994. At 4:31 AM, a major earthquake struck southern California, with the epicenter in the San Fernando Valley. This 6.8-force earthquake took sixty lives, injured 7,839 persons of whom 216 were in critical condition, and caused billions of dollars worth of damage, leaving 185,000 homeless and countless more without food, electricity, gas, or water. The final estimate of injuries and psychological trauma caused by this disaster, are still being measured.[1]

When the eighth edition was being prepared, new tragedies struck the nation in different parts of the country. There was the Oklahoma City bombing, TWA Flight 800, which mysteriously exploded and crashed into the ocean near Long Island, the 1996 Olympic Games bombing in Atlanta, and Hurricane Fran with its 115-mph winds, which tore through North and South Carolina, flooding beach towns, causing $1 billion in damage, leaving 4 million people without electrical power, and killing 17 people.[2]

Now, as the ninth edition was being prepared, again major tragedies with accompanying traumas visited this nation and other parts of the world. Foremost in the United States for the year 1999 was the Trench Coat Mafia gang massacre at Columbine High School on April 20 in Littleton, Colorado, resulting in the death of 13 students and one teacher, followed by the immediate suicide of the two adolescent perpetrators, Eric Harris and Dylan Klebold. America still has not recovered from this violence, which is also so prevalent thoroughout the nation in poor, inner cities.

On August 17, 1999, a 7.4 earthquake struck Turkey, killing at least 7,000 people.[3] A few weeks later in Fort Worth, Texas, Larry Gene Ashbrook started a shooting spree outside Wedgewood Baptist Church, killing two church goers, and then walked into the church and killed an additional five defenseless worshippers and wounded seven.[4] And on September 20, still another human catastrophe was experienced in Taiwan when a 7.6-magnitude earthquake leveled 6,000 buildings, killing 2,000 people, and leaving over 100,000 homeless.[5]

These disasters make life even more difficult for those who are already vulnerable and are struggling economically and emotionally. Some exploit the situation through looting or illegal business practices such as overcharging for their services. Yet others, for some reason, are deeply touched by these tragic circumstances and events, and their latent feelings of empathy seem to rise to the occasion. They become good neighbors to their "fellowmen" and help their neighbors with the most basic tasks such as cleaning their homes, and, in some instances, actually to save their neighbors' lives. The majority of these "good samaritans" are not trained helping professionals. Their good deeds are generally unplanned and spontaneous.

As four-year-old Amy Tyre-Vigil was being laid to rest during funeral services following the 1994 Los Angeles earthquake in which her home collapsed around her, her father commented, "Nature gave her to us, and nature took her away."[6] Perhaps people become more philosophical and more understanding when "nature" follows its plan of action as it has for millions of years, totally ignoring humans in its destructive path. How can one get angry at nature's motive or specific intention for causing natural disasters? It can all be scientifically explained.

"Man-made disasters" elicit many of the same feelings as natural disasters, such as fear, anxiety, depression, and stress disorders such as posttraumatic stress disorder (PTSD) but, in addition, they invoke a significant amount of anger because of the specific *intention* by the perpetrator or perpetrators to cause harm to fellow humans. For example, with very few exceptions, people calling in to talk shows to share their feelings regarding the "L.A. Quake of '94" stated that they were more frightened and threatened by the Los Angeles riots in April 1992, which claimed sixty lives, than by the earthquake because of the *deliberate* killing of persons by armed citizens during the riots. People feared that they might also be assaulted and killed.

A national poll in December 1993 reported that 70 percent of the people favored stricter gun-control laws. Politicians have received the message from the people that they no longer feel safe and they want to see violence prevention as the number 1 issue on the political agenda.[7] Americans probably feel even stronger about this issue as we go into the twenty-first century.

How would social workers respond to these natural and man-made disasters? Would they follow in the path of good neighbors and Samaritans as described above? Or, armed with their professional knowledge and macro and micro intervention skills, would they be expected to do more? Do their education, values, knowledge, and skills really make a difference? The final chapter in the text, "The Social Worker in Action," gives some answers to these questions. A high school homicide incident—one of hundreds across the nation—finds one social worker in action responding to this crisis. The intervention model presented is very applicable to other "Columbines" occurring around the nation.

ENDNOTES

1. "Earthquake: The Long Road Back," *Los Angeles Times,* January 23, 1994, p. A-8.
2. *Newsweek,* September 16, 1996, p. 52.
3. *Los Angeles Times,* Part One, Friday, August 20, 1999, p. 1.
4. David Van Biema, "Terror in the Sanctuary," *Time,* September 27, 1999, pp. 42–43.
5. Jeffrey Kluger, "Tears and Trembling," *Time,* October 4, 1999, pp. 80–81.
6. "Earthquake: The Long Road Back," *Los Angeles Times,* Valley Section, January 22, 1994, p. 1.
7. Nancy Gibbs, "Up in Arms," *Time,* December 20, 1993, p. 19.

CHAPTER 23

The Social Worker in Action: A High School Homicide Case

Prefatory Comment

The "Social Worker in Action" is an original chapter written especially for this volume for the purposes of showing how the profession and the schools of social work can be more relevant to the nation's great need for knowledge and practice intervention as it involves ever-increasing violence and homicide among youths. The country is threatened and intimidated by this rising tide of random violence occurring at shopping malls, fast-food restaurants, schools, and other public places.

Knowledge about violence and who is predisposed to violence, and even homicidal behavior, can be gained either through a scientific deductive process, that is, by drawing conclusions from a large number of cases obtained through a random sample, or through an inductive process, that is, drawing conclusions from a scientific, in-depth analysis of one case and then generalizing to many cases. The latter, in-depth approach was adopted for this chapter; it concerns a school homicide. It has applicability to Columbine High types of school homicide.

"The Social Worker in Action" is based on a case composite, re-created to convey important concepts, underlying theories of violent and homicidal behavior and details the multiple micro and macro roles of an advanced social work practitioner in addressing this problem.

Background to the Case

Bob Pla, MSW, was making his usual fifteen-minute morning drive to work on a sunny, yet windy, clear day. Bob was singing along with his favorite "Oldies but Goodies" radio station. He was happy and felt very fortunate to be living in Olas,* California, a moderately sized, predominantly middle-class beach community of

---

*In Spanish, *olas* means ocean waves.

nearly 200,000 people. It had a small minority population of mostly working class people, which included 5 percent African Americans, 7 percent Asian Americans, and 12 percent Latinos. Bob thought it was a good place to raise a family because of the community's outstanding schools and very low crime rate, ranked fourth in the nation as to the least ratio of crime per population. Although there were a few gangs in the community, Bob knew from prior street gang group work in violent, crime-ridden Los Angeles that they were not the violent type. They were more like "wanabes" (want-to-bes), trying to impress their peers in school. Bob smiled as he reflected that Olas was a relatively safe, crime-free community.

HOMICIDES ARE IN EVERY COMMUNITY

Actually, there *had* been four to five homicides each year in Olas, but Bob had blocked them out of his mind. Bob was seduced by the media into believing that violence and homicide were predominantly a poor "black and brown inner-city" common event. Olas did have about thirty, mostly minority-group, gangs, and, even though they had committed some burglaries and minor and serious assaults, they had not committed any homicides in the past ten years.

Bob also reminded himself, from providing forensic court testimony in violent crimes cases in Los Angeles, that nationally, out of nearly 25,000 annual homicides, two-thirds to 70 percent involved a family member killing another; spousal homicides, a parent, usually a mother, killing her child under four years of age;[1] a homicide resulting from conflicted hetero- or homosexual relationships; or killings of friends or close acquaintances. These are called *criminal* homicides, where the primary intent is to kill another human being.

CRIMINAL VERSUS FELONY HOMICIDES

The majority of public media attention, however, focuses on *felony* homicides, which involve the killing of another person during the commission of a felony crime such as a robbery, burglary, or "carjacking." "We're in greater danger from being killed by someone we know well rather than by a complete stranger," concluded Bob, recalling the very recent love-triangle killing in San Diego, adjacent to Olas. This multiple murder, a criminal homicide, involved three Navy officers in which Alton Grizzard, a former star quarterback from the Naval Academy, killed his rival, George P. Smith, a nuclear submarine engineer, and ex-girlfriend, Kerryn O'Neill, a former track star at the Naval Academy. Immediately thereafter, with the same gun, Lt. Grizzard committed suicide.[2] Emotions and passions *can* humble even the most upstanding, moral citizens. Desperate women sometimes kill when they are trying to get away from a bad relationship, and some possessive men kill to keep "their" woman from getting away from them.

THE OLAS FAMILY SERVICES CENTER

Bob continued on his way to work, and he began to collect his thoughts in preparation for the Monday morning staff meeting. He had been Executive Director of the Olas Family Services Center for nearly four years. He enjoyed his job and believed he had a very competent staff, comprised of ten MSW-licensed clinical social workers, four BSW-level social workers, a quarter-time psychiatrist, and five administrative and clerical staff. The music on his radio was suddenly interrupted. Danny Jones, the popular Olas DJ, stated:

> Sorry folks. We have to take a time out. I just received a bulletin. There was a possible homicide at Olas High School. Details are not yet confirmed, but police report that a twelve-year-old girl was shot several times by an unknown assailant, in what appears to be a gang "drive-by" shooting. Three ambulances are on the scene, but so far only one person is confirmed injured. Hundreds of students entering the campus on their way to their first class witnessed the tragic event. Many are hysterical.

Bob resisted the impulse to drive to the school to see if he could help. He wondered if some of his staff had had the same thought and had already gone to the school. Using his cellular telephone, he called his office from his car and asked his secretary to notify all staff to remain at the office for a staff meeting. The agency had to coordinate an appropriate response to this crisis at Olas High. Danny Jones again interrupted the music on the radio, and said:

> I have just been handed some current information concerning that shooting at Olas High. The twelve-year-old white female victim died at the scene. She has been identified, but this information will remain confidential until her parents have been notified.

A SCHOOL HOMICIDE SHOCKS ANY COMMUNITY

Bob turned off his radio. He was shocked and saddened and did not wish to hear any more music. He arrived at the Olas Family Services Agency promptly at 9 AM and quickly went into the conference room where most of the staff were congregating. They appeared to be upset and angry and wanted to go immediately to the school to help. Two staff members were arguing with each other. One member stated that Olas was a fine, safe community until Mexican immigrants and L.A. African Americans moved into town. The other staff member, a Hispanic female social worker, argued that, had it not been for the racism in Olas, there would not be any problems in the community. Two social workers demanded that Bob cancel the staff meeting so that they all could go to the school to help the distraught students.

Others were numb with shock and did not say anything. Mrs. Scott, a social worker, asked for permission to take time off and go to the school to look after her two children who were students there. She was the only staff person with children at Olas High. Her request was granted as she now was functioning as a parent and not as a representative of the agency. Bob also knew that her anxiety and emotional state of mind would interfere with her attempts to help others at the school. Several thoughts ran through Bob's mind. His professional staff was in chaos given the current high school crisis. Anxiety, guilt, anger, and feelings of helplessness were quite prevalent. He wondered how his staff could go out and help others given their current states of mind. He had to assume leadership for the staff and to develop an overall strategy to address the problem and its various manifestations.

Social Work Psychosocial Intervention

Bob Pla knew that, with input from his staff, he had to develop several levels of intervention for them in order to be most effective. He organized the tasks into three levels of intervention, going from a micro- to a macrolevel perspective:

First-Level Tasks (Micro Practice)

1. Encourage sharing and venting of feelings among agency staff prior to contacting the school.
2. Attend to the emotional needs of the agency's most vulnerable clients.
3. Obtain agency board permission for overtime and weekend work to deal with the crisis.
4. Develop a team strategy for providing assistance to the school and obtain authorization to work with the school and their counselors.
5. Contact and coordinate resources with other mental health agencies and professionals in the community in providing mental health services to the school, especially those students most affected by the school homicide.

Second-Level Tasks (Micro Practice)

1. Provide clinical assistance for deceased victim's family.
2. Provide clinical and mental health consultation to students as needed.
3. Provide clinical and mental health consultation to school faculty and administrators as indicated.
4. Provide clinical and mental health consultation to paramedics and law enforcement personnel as needed.

Third-Level Tasks (Macro Practice with a Prevention Goal)

1. Meet with the media to encourage calm, brief reporting to avoid provoking fear, anger, anxiety, and hysteria in the community by dramatic, sensationalistic reporting.
2. Provide mental health consultation to the Mayor and Board of Supervisors Chair to call for calm in the community and discourage minority-group scapegoating and vigilantism.
3. Provide mental health consultation to the informal leaders of the minority communities, appealing to "cool heads" during this crisis period.
4. Spearhead the creation of a multidisciplinary, multiethnic task force to investigate the causes of the campus violence and develop recommendations for the prevention of such incidents.

MOBILIZING THE AGENCY AND STAFF FOR ACTION

The First-Level Tasks 3 and 4 had to be dealt with immediately. Bob had his secretary phone the president of the board. He gave Bob permission for staff overtime and weekend pay. Bob personally called the school principal, who was familiar with the agency's work because the school often referred students with behavioral problems. The principal appreciated the agency's offer to provide assistance because his two school counselors were trained in psychometrics and educational counseling rather than treating emotional crises. In addressing task 2, Bob asked the staff to assess the ego strengths of their clients and to anticipate how they would respond to the current crisis. Special consideration would be given to those clients who themselves had been victims of violence as the campus homicide may cause a relapse among some clients.

CRISES BREED MIXED EMOTIONS

Before Bob could continue on the remaining first-level tasks pertaining to the community, he had to give the staff the opportunity to vent their feelings (First-Level Task 1). The staff responses to the tragedy were not predictable. Some minority staff believed they had worked very hard to advance themselves and their families to get out of the *barrio* and ghetto, and now their safety was being threatened. They wanted to see schools built in the poor minority communities so that these children would not have to travel into the affluent areas. Some staff members strongly objected, stating that this thinking was racist and would take them back to segregated schools such as they had prior to the 1950s. Mrs. Smith, one of the senior social workers, wanted to see metal detectors installed in all schools and police stationed on campuses. Others argued against this, pointing out that the perpetrator of the homicide was in a vehicle and not on campus when the incident occurred. Miss Garcia asserted that the availability of guns was the main "culprit." Many agreed, but Mr. Karls, an NRA member and hunter, strongly disagreed, stating that "people, not guns, kill people!"

BUILDING STAFF COHESION

Bob seemed very surprised by the varied responses and the divisiveness among his staff. He had been under the impression that he had a cohesive staff. "Social workers are no different from the general public," he reflected, "and represent the many faces not only of social work, but of the society at large." He decided to try and unify them around a common goal. He assumed control of the meeting by stating:

> I can see that we have several conflicting viewpoints, reflecting the general views of society. There is not one single answer or cause of this problem. The causes are many as are the solutions. We have to agree on a common strategy and intervention as social workers. We have to do our best for our clients—the students, their families, and the general community, which includes the minority communities. We really do not have a lot of facts concerning this homicide, other than that "someone" fired a weapon from a vehicle into a crowd of students on campus, resulting in the death of a white, twelve-year-old female student. Things are still rather sketchy, and we really do not know whether the perpetrator was a minority-group person or even whether the crime was gang-related. These incidents are not uncommon in the inner cities of Los Angeles, New York, Chicago, or Detroit, but the general public in Olas does not become too alarmed because many believe in their minds: "Thank God it doesn't happen here." But it did happen here, in our "nice" community, and this time the victim was a white girl from an affluent family. We feel rage and guilt, and we project blame onto many people and factors. But we all carry a lot of fear because, on some level, we do not feel safe—it's just like living in the poor, minority community. We're feeling powerless, just like the poor. As professionals,

we need to go to our strength and look at the total psychosocial situation. Let us bring our micro and macro skills to the tasks that must be accomplished in order to reduce the anger, guilt, anxiety, frustration, and fear in our clients. Our clients are the students, their families, the high school faculty and administrators, the minority communities, the police, and the general community. We are all in a crisis. We must be challenged by that crisis and respond with the best that social workers have to offer. We must work together toward that goal and not lose sight of that goal. This campus homicide was a "wake-up call" for all of us.

SOCIAL WORKERS RESPOND TO THE CHALLENGE

There was initial silence in the group. Then Mrs. Smith remarked that she felt proud to be a social worker and that they all had a professional role to play. Another social worker responded that this was like a natural disaster and that usually people respond accordingly and pitch in to help. Yet another social worker commented, "I feel overwhelmed. What are we supposed to do?"

Bob took this opportunity to explain in detail the three levels of micro and macro tasks previously outlined. Knowing that people do their best in activities suited to their skills, he asked the staff to volunteer for their choice of activities within these three levels of tasks. The staff began to show some enthusiasm and believed they could accomplish their goals now that the tasks were outlined.

Applying Crisis Theory to the Tasks at Hand

Bob asked the group to review the literature related to crises. He reminded them that a crisis can occur at any point in a person's life and that some people react to a greater degree than others to the emotional hazards inherent in certain events. The *crisis* is the *emotional state*, the reaction of the individual, family, or community to the hazardous situation, not the hazardous situation *per se*. A hazardous event calls for a solution new to the individual, group, family, or community in relation to that life experience.[3]

There are three broad types of crisis situations that may enrich or endanger people's functioning: (1) those that are "biologically tinged," such as adolescence or menopause, and therefore may be anticipated by all people as part of the life cycle; (2) those that are "environmentally tinged," such as a change of job or retirement, and hence are somewhat less inevitable but are usually anticipated; and (3) those that are "adventitious," such as disasters, floods, and fire, which are attributable to chance and cannot be anticipated.[4]

NATURAL VERSUS MAN-MADE DISASTERS

Floods, fires, and earthquakes are *natural disasters*. Wars, mass killings, and public homicides such as the Olas High student killing are *man-made* disasters. Victims of the latter often have more difficulty getting over their symptoms because they were *intentionally* caused by another human being, who, if not apprehended, could strike again. People feel especially vulnerable. Bob Pla had learned that during the crisis period an individual is in a state of acute anxiety. Feelings of helplessness and hope-lessness are evident.

In this situation, ego patterns are more likely to be open to influence and change. Because defenses are lowered during this temporary period of disequilibrium, the client is usually more accessible to therapeutic influence than prior to the crisis or following establishment of a new equilibrium with its accompanying defense pat-terns.[5] During this period of upset, there are emotional symptoms such as tension, anxiety, shame, guilt, and even hostility. Past conflicts that may or may not have been satisfactorily resolved may be reactivated because the stresses of a crisis may be viewed as a threat, either to "instinctual" needs or to one's sense of integrity; as a loss of either a person or something else causing a feeling of acute deprivation; or as a challenge.[6]

THE UNIQUE, SUBJECTIVE PERCEPTION AND RESPONSE TO A CRISIS

Each of these states is usually accompanied by a typical emotional effect. If the crisis situation is primarily experienced as a threat, it will be accompanied by a great deal of anxiety. If the crisis is experienced primarily as a loss, it will involve depression and mourning. If viewed as a challenge, it will be accompanied by some anxiety or drive for problem solving.[7] In many respects, a crisis presents a new opportunity for change that might result in a higher level of psychosocial functioning.

BIOPSYCHOSOCIAL CONSIDERATIONS IN RESPONSES TO CRISES

Crisis intervention strategies should also take into consideration the biopsychosocial development stages of the persons being helped. For example, Olas High included grades seven through twelve, hence, these youths ranged in age from twelve to eigh-teen years. The deceased victim, Tammy Rowan, was twelve, therefore it would be anticipated that those students most affected would be her peers, particularly those who might have witnessed the shooting. Twelve-year-olds are usually growing out of the latter developmental stages of latency and the security of childhood experi-enced in the family and grammar school. They are now entering a period of greater independence coupled with increased anxieties spurred on by physical development and hormonal changes. In addition, they are in the less secure social and physical environment of a high school that has significantly more students than the previous elementary school. In this respect, then, the random killing of a peer can traumatize seventh graders who are already psychologically vulnerable.

Mobilizing Related Mental Health Disciplines

In working to fulfill First-Level Task 5—coordinating mental health resources to help the school—Bob Pla called the local NASW Chapter, the Olas Community Mental Health Center, the Olas Psychological Association, and the Olas Psychiatric Associ-ation. As an executive, he knew the directors of these professional bodies when they pooled their resources three years previously in response to a severe wind and rain storm. This storm, called "Super Olas" (Super Waves), left more than one hundred families homeless when their beach front homes were completely destroyed by the constant battering of massive waves. Bob volunteered to coordinate the helping effort of these professional groups, and their first meeting was held the first evening at the Olas Community Mental Health Center, which was closest to the school.

DEVELOPING A SCHOOL-BASED INTERVENTION STRATEGY

The twenty-member mental health group called itself the "Olas High Crisis Team" and appointed Bob Pla Chairperson. The majority of assistance would be provided at the school. They agreed to divide their consultation services based on the targeted population (Second-Level Tasks 1, 2, 3, and 4). The highest priority would go to those students who actually witnessed the killing, irrespective of age or grade level.

Second in priority would be all of the seventh graders, followed by eighth and ninth graders. A crisis team member would visit each classroom for one period. With the tenth-, eleventh- and twelfth-grade students, the approach would involve inviting them, via the public address system, to meet with the crisis team in the auditorium after school. Still another identified high-risk group would be those students who were too frightened or "stressed out" to attend school. With this latter group, it is possible that the traumatic event reactivated preexisting, unresolved conflicts or severely impacted a fragile, vulnerable individual. A special outreach effort would have to be made in their behalfs.

REACHING OUT TO RELATED HIGH-RISK GROUPS

Another targeted group would be the school parents and their other children who were not students of Olas High. Evening and weekend meetings would be provided for them. Consultation services would also be available for administrators and teachers, either individually or in groups. Similar offers were made to law enforcement agencies and paramedics involved in handling the case.

DEVELOPING AN APPROPRIATE CLINICAL INTERVENTION

To minimize the traumatic effects of the school homicide on all affected parties described above and reduce any long-term psychiatric consequences related to the event such as posttraumatic stress disorder (PTSD) and adjustment disorder symptoms, the Olas High Crisis Team developed the following psychosocial intervention model. The goal of the model is to help people return to their previous level of functioning:

1. The team makes assessments of symptom responses, being particularly sensitive to *physical* changes such as eating, sleeping, headaches, and other somatic symptoms, and *psychological* changes such as anger, irritability, anxiety, frustration, poor concentration, preoccupation, depression, and increased family dependence or withdrawal.

2. The crisis team attempts to diffuse and neutralize some of these feelings through group and individual counseling. Calm listening, venting, and assisting the consultees to "problem solve," make decisions, and refocus has been found to be helpful in these crisis situations.

3. The crisis team will teach persons to use their inner strengths and to develop techniques for managing stress.

4. The crisis team is prepared to make referrals in those cases that are found to require more intensive, in-depth treatment. They will develop a list of licensed clinical social workers and psychologists in private practice who will be able to see clients on a reduced fee, or no-fee (pro bono) basis. The victim Tammy Rowan's parents and siblings were already being seen by a social worker in private practice (fulfilled Second-Level Task 1).

Dealing with the Media

The first of the Third-Level tasks concerned dealing with the media. The Chief Executive Officers (CEOs) representing the various mental health disciplines decided to meet with representatives of the media. The CEOs, however, felt that it was important to also involve the Chief of Police and the County Sheriff in order to present a united front. A press conference was called the third day after the homicide, and by this time rumors were rampant. Some media were reporting that L.A. gangs were fighting for the "turf" around Olas High in order to sell drugs. Others were saying that the killing was an "initiation rite" by "Crips" (African American gang members). Other media reports were that local Olas minority group gangs were attempting to establish a reputation so that big city gangs would respect them. These media reports, all unfounded but fed by the typical bravado of nongang- and gang-member adolescents, caused the white community to begin patrolling their neighborhoods in the evening hours. There were also rumors that some of these residents were armed and were planning to go into the minority communities to "teach them a lesson" to stay on their side of town.

CONFRONTING RUMORS

The Chief of Police and the County Sheriff opened the meeting stating that they had the license number of the vehicle involved and were very close to apprehending the suspects, who were local adolescents. They did not know whether they were gang members but asked the media not to print the speculative stories because this might cause retaliation and conflict between gangs. Representatives of the press replied that they had a First Amendment right of freedom of speech to report the news (including speculation) as they saw fit.

FEARS IMMOBILIZE SCHOOLCHILDREN

Bob Pla joined in the discussion, identified himself as representing the Olas High School mental health crisis team, and commented that the speculative reporting was causing a significant amount of unnecessary fear and anxiety in the community and that even small children were reluctant to attend school. Some parents were also prohibiting their children from going to school. Mr. Pla pleaded for more restrained reporting to keep the incident in perspective. He reminded the news reporters that this was the first homicide at a school in Olas since the founding of the town in 1888—a little more than one hundred years ago. The reporters had not done their homework, hence, did not know how to respond. One of the reporters asked Reverend Hudson, who was eighty-seven years of age and born in Olas, if Mr. Pla's statement was true. The Reverend confirmed Bob's statement.

PRESENTING ACCURATE FACTS

Bob Pla also pointed out that, even if the killing had been gang-related, Olas gangs had not committed one homicide in the past ten years. "*There* is your story," replied Bob. "We have a fine community that really is very safe. The killing of Tammy Rowan *was* an aberration—an extremely rare occurrence! The odds of this happening in Olas are forty million to one." Some members of the press thought that people really did not want to hear about statistics, rather, they feared that their community was "going down the tubes," and many wanted to move out of Olas.

Sensing that what the media really wanted was a "story," the law enforcement representatives again called for restrained, factual reporting, promising that, if they would pursue a policy of discretion in reporting, the media in Olas would be the first to know who the suspects were once they were apprehended. Representatives of the media were very responsive to this suggestion and agreed to cooperate.

INVOLVING THE ELECTED OFFICIALS

Bob Pla, representing the crisis team, contacted the Mayor and the Board of Supervisors Chair (Third-Level Task 2) to apprise them of the importance of their exercising their formal influence as elected officials of the community to call for calm, rational thinking and to ask the public to wait for actual facts evolving from the ongoing law enforcement investigation to avoid prejudging or jumping to conclusions. Both elected representatives thought it was a helpful suggestion. The Mayor, however, decided to reach the public through a prepared five-minute television announcement, to be aired several times a day. The Board of Supervisors Chair decided to call a press conference and to have his staff prepare a brief article for the local newspapers.

CONTACTING THE MINORITY COMMUNITIES

Mr. Pla asked his BSW minority-community liaison staff to contact the informal leaders in the African American, Latino, and Asian American communities to assess their current thoughts regarding the school homicide (Third-Level Task 3). The Asian Americans, especially those of Japanese descent, believed that Americans were too violent as a people and very trigger-happy, calling the United States a land of "sick shooters." They recalled the slaying of sixteen-year-old Yoshihiro Hatori on his way to a 1992 Halloween party in Baton Rouge who made the mistake of knocking on the door of the wrong house and was killed by the homeowner who thought the youth was an intruder. The perpetrator was acquitted of manslaughter, which generated 1.6 million petition signatures in Japan urging the removal of guns from

U.S. homes.[8] (In Japan, in one year, handguns claimed forty-six lives, compared with the United States where handgun homicides numbered 8,092.)[9] The Asian community representatives did not want any involvement in the current crisis and just wanted to be left alone to manage their own community, which they felt was the safest in Olas.

Reacting to the vigilante threats emanating from the Olas white community, the African American and Latino communities promised retaliation if any minorities were attacked in the white community. Latinos were particularly worried about a resurgence of anti-immigrant sentiment among whites and an escalation of U.S. Immigration and Naturalization Services "raids" into their *barrio*. These two minority communities also threatened violent retaliation if armed white vigilantes invaded their communities. This was primarily the position of the veteran gang members.

Bob hoped that all of this posturing was simply rhetoric to frighten off the white community. Nevertheless, he presented this information to law enforcement intelligence officials, urging them to be especially alert to armed or unarmed whites entering the minority communities. He also asked law enforcement to be particularly careful in making any arrests in the minority communities during this tense climate, because even a routine arrest could trigger a riot, as had been the experience in other communities that rioted in the 1960s and 1970s.

COOPERATION BY THE MEDIA IS REWARDED

A week later, as promised, law enforcement representatives and the District Attorney contacted the Olas media for a special press conference. The suspects had been identified. At the press conference, the District Attorney announced that he had in custody an eighteen-year-old female adolescent, Rita Gomez, who admitted to the police that she had been in the moving vehicle and had fired the shots that struck Tammy Rowan. Police did not believe the incident was gang-related, because Ms. Gomez was not a gang member. She was a resident of Olas, living in *Barrio Town*, the poor, Latino section of Olas. She did not know the victim. After waiving her rights to an attorney, she confessed to the police that she had fired the semiautomatic weapon at the students merely to "scare them." She was not intending to injure anyone.

ONE SUSPECT ELUDES ARREST

The co-defendant, who was driving the vehicle, was thirty-three-year-old Michael Webster, a native of Olas and an unemployed school dropout and laborer. He was residing with his parents in the white, affluent section of Olas at the time of the murder. He had a long history of substance abuse and heroin and cocaine addiction, both as a juvenile and as an adult. He had just completed a five-year prison sentence for selling drugs and was on parole. According to Ms. Gomez, he left the state the same day of the shooting. A warrant for his arrest was issued. First-degree murder charges with "special circumstances" were filed against Ms. Gomez, who, if convicted could result in the death penalty.

A Town Tries to Heal

After the announcement by the media of the primary suspect's being in custody and confessing that she had fired the weapon that had killed Tammy Rowan, the community appeared quite relieved and more secure. The mental health crisis team consultation groups and services continued for a few more weeks, with most of the groups disbanding by the eighth week. Several of the students who actually witnessed the slaying continued in individual treatment, as many of their PTSD symptoms were still in the acute stage. A few needed psychiatric medication to calm symptoms such as insomnia and nightmares, as the memories of violence were interfering with their school functioning.

A RIGHT TO A SPEEDY TRIAL

Daily television and newspaper interviews of Olas residents kept asking the same question: "Why did Rita Gomez kill Tammy Rowan?" Even the police did not understand the motive. Rita Gomez was relatively unknown in Olas. She did not attend high school, and some rumored that she had dropped out of school in the seventh grade. The court appointed an attorney on her behalf, Eddie Falls, a new resident of Olas, who, like Bob Pla, had left Los Angeles to enjoy a healthier and safer environment for his family. Mr. Falls wanted to change Ms. Gomez' plea to "not guilty," but Ms. Gomez insisted on pleading "guilty" because she wanted to "get it over as soon as possible."

The defense attorney attempted to plea bargain with the District Attorney to have the charge reduced to manslaughter or even second-degree homicide with a guilty plea, but to no avail. The community was angry and wanted "the book thrown at her." "Nothing less than first-degree murder and the death penalty," argued the District Attorney representing the people of California. Attorney Falls finally was able to persuade Ms. Gomez to enter a "not guilty" plea hoping to have the jury reduce the charge to second-degree murder or manslaughter to avoid the death penalty. The determining factor for Ms. Gomez was that she wanted to avoid being executed because she wanted to be able to see her two children, aged two and four, grow up.

During the following weeks a jury was impaneled. It comprised six middle-class non-Hispanic white women and six non-Hispanic white men. All were from the Olas community. In a ten-week period, the jury completed its work and went into deliberation. In one day, they returned a unanimous "guilty" verdict of first-degree homicide with "special circumstances." (All thirty-seven states with death penalty statutes have special circumstances criteria, such as the killing of a police officer or a judge, which, if found present in a homicide, could warrant the death penalty.)[10] In California, Penal Code Section 190.2 specifies nineteen special circumstances, of which only one of those that have been charged need to be found to be true.[11] In Ms. Gomez' case, the jury found the following two special circumstances to be true:

#14. The murder was especially heinous, atrocious, or cruel, manifesting exceptional depravity. As utilized in this section, the phrase *especially heinous, atrocious, or cruel manifesting exceptional depravity* means a conscienceless, or pitiless crime which is unnecessarily torturous to the victim.

#16. The victim was intentionally killed because of his or her race, color, religion, nationality, or country of origin.

The jury determined that eight 9-millimeter bullets struck and killed an innocent, unsuspecting, twelve-year-old child in the upper chest, heart, neck, and head, and that this was a heinous and atrocious violent act manifesting exceptional depravity on the part of the perpetrator. Second, because the victim was a white Anglo-American and the perpetrator a person of a different nationality (Mexican descent), the jury concluded that the homicide had a racial and nationality motive.

THE DEATH PENALTY PHASE OF THE TRIAL

Following the guilty verdict with special circumstances, the jury now had to deliberate the death penalty phase of the case to decide whether there were any mitigating factors (for or against) that might justify life imprisonment without the possibility of parole rather than execution by the state. While in his office reading the newspaper concerning the Rita Gomez Case, Bob Pla received a telephone call from attorney, Eddie Falls. The attorney asked Bob whether he would be willing to participate in the death penalty phase of the Gomez case by evaluating Ms. Gomez, writing a report with accompanying recommendations, and thereafter testifying in court.

Bob's evaluation would have to address two central questions before the jury and the court: (1) Are there any mitigating factors in the case justifying life imprisonment without the possibility of parole rather than execution? and (2) Of what value is Ms. Gomez' life to society that she should not be executed? Initially Bob felt overwhelmed by the proposed assignment, stating that he had not been trained to play God. The attorney stated that he had read about Bob's testimony in a legal newspaper concerning a few homicide cases in Los Angeles in which he had evaluated defendants prior to sentencing.

Bob admitted he had done this and had established expertise in testifying in assault, suicide, riot, gang violence, police brutality, and homicide cases, but never in a death penalty case. The attorney argued that, because of these experiences, he would be in the most advantageous position to "educate" the judge and jury about what factors would lead a teenaged girl to commit such a heinous crime. "How can Olas learn from this experience? How can we prevent this from happening again?" demanded the attorney.

Bob decided to do it. "You've just convinced me. You are correct! How else are we going to learn? And you used the magic word—*prevention!* There might be dozens or even hundreds of persons like Rita Gomez out there. As social workers, we are trained to look at the interface of the person and the environment and the transactions occurring between the person and the environment. What *are* the biopsychosocial factors relevant to this case? *What went wrong?*" Bob agreed to take the case contingent on receiving authorization from his agency board.

He was later granted permission by the board because they saw this as an opportunity for the agency to make a contribution to the community in reducing tension and learning more about factors that contribute to violence. The board felt honored that one of its employees was being asked to participate in a very high-profile case that was in the news daily. Bob felt proud that, as a representative of the social work profession, he was being asked to use his micro and macro knowledge and skills in the comprehensive assessment of a case extremely important to the welfare of the community and to the eighteen-year-old Hispanic female whose life was at stake.

PREPARING FOR THE CASE.   The attorney submitted a written request to Superior Court Judge William Banks who was presiding in the Rita Gomez case, asking him to appoint Bob Pla, MSW, as an expert defense witness. The Judge approved and signed the order, defining Bob Pla's role as an expert in violence and homicide. Bob was given a copy of the order, which permitted him to visit Ms. Gomez in the Olas County Jail. The attorney also gave Bob several boxes of case materials that included the police investigation reports, the medical autopsy report, all school, health, and employment records, a record of the defendant's prior contacts with law enforcement, her psychiatric and psychological evaluations, numerous witness accounts, videotapes showing a four-hour taped confession with an accompanying typed copy of the confession, and selected court transcripts of the murder trial including testimony by various forensic, medical, and law enforcement experts.

PLANNING A CASE STRATEGY.   A "strategy conference" was also held with the defense team led by Attorney Falls, his assistant attorney, and the chief investigator. At this conference, Attorney Falls set forth his theories related to causation, which would form the foundation of mitigating factors that, if accepted by the jury, would warrant life imprisonment without the possibility of parole rather than death. The attorney believed that the strongest mitigating factor was that Ms. Gomez was a drug addict and, while under the influence of drugs, her judgment had been impaired, leading to the killing of Tammy Rowan. Bob agreed to this approach, stating that he would look carefully into the drug problem as well as the possibility of *other* mitigating factors presently unknown. The attorney believed that any additional mitigating factors could "score points" with the jury.

THE JAIL VISIT.   Visiting someone in jail is a sobering experience, even for Bob Pla who has worked with jail and prison populations for many years. The suspicious, skeptical looks from jail personnel that one receives even after presenting the appropriate documents, authorization, and identification, is something one never gets used to. This discomfort was further exacerbated by having to go through a metal detector and having one's briefcase searched for hidden weapons or contraband such as drugs. "Don't personalize it," Bob thought to himself. "It's just a part of their job for security reasons." Then the female Sheriff's Deputy cautioned Bob that he was entering the women's jail at his own risk and that the Sheriff had a policy of not recognizing or responding to demands if he were to be taken hostage by the inmates. "Thanks a bunch," responded Bob in a somewhat sarcastic tone. "I'm only doing my job," responded the Deputy in a defensive manner. "Now I'm going to pay for it," Bob reflected. "They're really going to make me wait a long time."

INTERVIEWING A "KILLER."   Bob was sitting in the empty attorney's room, which was filled with about thirty stalls. "I guess attorneys do not work on Sundays like social workers," mumbled Bob. After waiting only thirty minutes rather than the usual hour to an hour-and-a-half, Bob was pleasantly surprised when Rita Gomez was led into the interview room by a deputy. She did not look mean or hard and actually was quite cooperative, friendly, and soft-spoken. She was an attractive, slim, eighteen-year-old Mexican American Catholic female, born and raised in Olas. Bob already had a psychosocial framework in mind as to the information he was seeking that related to her early childhood, family, marital, educational, and social history, and health, drug, and delinquency history.

He did not want to delve into the specific offense during the first interview. He preferred to wait until a subsequent interview when she would have more trust in him. He explained to her that this would be the first of three interviews, and that, with her permission, he was also planning on interviewing her parents, grandparents, aunts and uncles, husband, and children. Bob also explained the reasons why it was important to interview all these family members. She approved of this plan. She warned Bob that he was going to hear a lot of bad things about her and that she had worn out the welcome mat with her immediate family as well as with other close relatives. "What did you do?" asked Bob.

Rita rolled her eyes, smiled, and stated, "What *didn't* I do?" She went on to say that she was a "junkie" and had stolen from the family to support her habit and had lied to everybody, including her husband, to get money for drugs. "I even was turning tricks for money to buy drugs," she confessed. She became emotional and began to cry, stating that, most of all, she missed her children, aged four and two. "And that poor little girl who I killed. I can imagine the pain her mother is in. I didn't mean to shoot her. I've never physically hurt nobody. I'm an alcoholic and an addict, but not a violent person," she cried. She seemed very remorseful, and Bob recalled that in the videotapes she was crying nonstop for nearly four hours. Bob decided to change his plan of not going into the specific offense because Rita seemed comfortable with him and was herself leading the interview into this painful area.

"Why do you think you killed her?" inquired Bob. "I did not know her and was not planning on hurting anyone," replied Rita. "Mike (Michael Webster, second suspect, at large) and me were slamming several times that morning (injecting heroin and cocaine), and then Mike said 'Let's go cruising in my car.' We got in his car and then he showed me a gun. It was real heavy. I don't know what kind it was. I've never held a gun in my life. Then Mike said 'Let's go by the school and scare the squares. I'll drive by, and you just wave the gun at them and watch them run and drop.' Mike was laughing and I thought it was funny, too. We drove by the school once and I waved the gun out of the window and some of the students saw us and started running, yelling 'Drive-by, drive-by!!!' That was a real trip. Then we went around the block a second time and I waved the gun again and we were laughing real hard. Then Mike said 'Pull the trigger, pull the trigger!' I did and the gun went off a lot of times, like a machine gun. I was so loaded that I could hardly aim the gun. I aimed above their heads and didn't think I hit anyone. Then we sped away. We were still laughing. Then later we heard on the radio that someone had been shot at the school. I got real scared. Mike dropped me off at home and then took off. I haven't seen him since. A few days later I was arrested at home after someone at school ID'd me."

The Report: A Psychosocial Evaluation

Bob Pla followed through with his plan of interviewing Rita's family members, spouse, children, and significant relatives who could provide an insight into Rita's personality and behavior. There was one area of common agreement; during periods of complete abstention from drugs and alcohol, that is, in a state of remission, she was a sensitive, responsible, loving, and caring daughter, mother, wife, and person. But when using drugs and alcohol, she became a completely different person, doing anything short of violence to get money or things of value to use to purchase her drugs. Sometimes she would exchange sex for drugs. In addition to the interviews described above, Bob relied on various reports and documents to arrive at his conclusions and recommendations. He then prepared a report for the attorney, who in turn, would present it to the judge and prosecutor for their consideration. The report initially highlights Bob Pla's area of expertise, because, as in most cases, the prosecutor will challenge and oppose the appointment of Bob Pla because the prosecutor, who represents the people of the State of California, wants to see Rita Gomez executed. By law, the jury comprises only persons who support the death penalty. All opponents of the death penalty are excluded as jurors. The following is Bob Pla's evaluation.

> Olas Family Services Agency
> 2301 N. Pacific Coast Highway
> Olas, California 92133

December 1, 2000

Eddie Falls
Attorney at Law
321 South Oak Street
Olas, California 92134

Re: Rita Gomez, Case #C-93187

Dear Mr. Falls,

On November 7, Superior Court Judge William Banks signed an order appointing me as a violence, homicide, and psychosocial evaluation expert for the Defense in the case of Rita Gomez, case #C-93187. The information in this report should assist the jury in resolving the issue of the appropriateness of life without the possibility of parole *versus* execution by the state.

By way of professional credentials, I received my master's degree in social work from the University of Southern California and thereafter had twenty years of professional experience in probation, parole, community mental health, and, later, as a faculty member at the UCLA Department of Psychiatry, establishing the first psychiatric clinic in the University of California system specializing in the assessment and treatment of Spanish-speaking patients. For the last four years, I have been directing the Olas Family Services Agency where I supervise a staff of fifteen persons and where I continue to treat clients.

I have given numerous presentations at professional conferences concerning the assessment and treatment of suicidal and homicidal patients and homicide perpetrators. Additionally, I have had over twenty years' experience in working with juvenile and adult male and female criminal offenders, including many who abused drugs and alcohol. For the last ten years I have been providing mental health consolation to parole officers concerning the management of parolees.

PSYCHOSOCIAL EVALUATION

What follows is my psychosocial evaluation of Ms. Gomez, which is based on three interviews with her in the Olas County Jail, totaling five hours, and fourteen hours of interviews with her parents, maternal grandparents, four aunts and uncles, and her husband and two children. In addition, I analyzed numerous reports and documents related to her medical, psychological, psychiatric, and juvenile history, and her law enforcement investigation, including a lengthy videotaped confession. This psychosocial evaluation has two major functions:

1. to provide the court with a comprehensive analysis to understand what factors contributed to making a Hispanic adolescent female (18.2 years of age at the time of the offense) commit such a violent crime, and
2. to assess whether this youthful lady has any value to society as a human being that might warrant a life sentence rather than execution by the state as the result of her conviction for first-degree murder with special circumstances.

This report will not be prepared in a traditional psychiatric or psychological report format primarily emphasizing the *individual*. Rather, this social work–oriented psychosocial evaluation will focus not only on the individual, but also on the interface of Ms. Gomez with her total environment, which includes her family, relatives, and other groups in the community. This psychosocial evaluation will have two major sections: Part one will concern six "predisposing factors" within a relevant topic framework, followed by an analysis. Part Two will focus on Ms. Gomez' value to society.

PART ONE: DATA AND DIAGNOSIS

I. IDENTIFYING DATA

Rita Gomez is a slim, attractive, dark-haired, eighteen-year-old, bilingual, bicultural Hispanic female of Mexican descent born at the Olas County General Hospital. She is the mother of two male children, aged two and four. She married the father of her children, Pedro Gomez, age twenty-two, when she was fourteen years of age. He works six days a week at a gas station during the days and as a parking lot attendant during the evenings. The marital relationship has always been conflictual due to his wanting to know her whereabouts during his long working hours. Having one child by age sixteen, let alone *two* children by that age, and being uneducated and unemployed, places a young adolescent female at even higher risk for additional problems.

2. PERTINENT GENETIC-BIOLOGICAL FAMILY HISTORY

There is a strong genetic factor for alcoholism that is seen to run in families. Children of alcoholics become alcoholic four times more often than children of nonalcoholics. Studies report higher rates for alcoholism among twins than among nontwin siblings.[12] Ms. Gomez is an alcoholic in remission, as well as a drug addict, also in remission. She continues to be addicted to the nicotine in cigarettes and has been a chronic smoker of one to two packs per day since she was twelve years old.

Rita Gomez comes from a traditional, male-dominated, hard-working, religious, Catholic Mexican family originally from Puebla, Mexico. Her great-grandfather on her maternal grandfather's side, was a ranch-hand and died at age eighty due to cirrhosis of the liver. He was an alcoholic. His wife had died two years previously due to heart disease. She had been a chronic smoker. Ms. Gomez' great-grandmother on her maternal grandmother's side was also a nicotine addict who smoked three to four packs of cigarettes per day. She died of lung cancer at age seventy, and her husband, a general construction worker, was an alcoholic, and died of cirrhosis of the liver at age forty. Ms. Gomez' biological father is also an alcoholic, as is his mother. Both of her parents are chronic smokers.

Ms. Gomez' maternal grandparents, ages sixty and sixty-two, report good health, with the exception of the grandmother who suffers occasional anxiety attacks related to stresses brought on by her granddaughter's murder case. The grandparents, as well as Ms. Gomez' mother, are employed at the local Sears Department Store, where the mother is head of the shoe department and the grandparents are in the janitorial department. Combining their modest incomes, they purchased and reside in their home located just inside the lower-middle-class area of Olas. They moved here because the area had better schools. This area, which is near *Barrio Town,* is 90 percent non-Hispanic white.

With the exception of Ms. Gomez, no member of the family dating back to the great-grandparents, has received psychiatric treatment, been hospitalized for mental illness, or been arrested for any violent or criminal acts. Ms. Gomez' maternal grandparents had eight children, currently ranging in age from twenty-three to forty-two, with her mother being the second oldest of these children. In turn, her mother had four children with Ms. Gomez being the second oldest child. Her older brother graduated from college and is a high school teacher in a neighboring community. The other two siblings are attending high school. Ms. Gomez has two male children of her own, aged two and four, who reportedly are in good health. According to her mother, Ms. Gomez was drug-free during her pregnancies, with only occasional light alcohol consumption.

3. EARLY CHILDHOOD DEVELOPMENTAL FACTORS

Ms. Gomez was a seven-pound, four-ounce natural-birth baby who was bottle-fed by family members because the mother had to work to support the family. She always had a healthy appetite but was always thin. She was quite active as an infant and began walking rather early, at ten months of age. Ms. Gomez slept well, had a calm demeanor, and did not present behavioral problems as a child. She was a very affectionate, trusting child and bonded well with her mother and other family members residing in the home, especially her maternal grandmother. Her first and primary language was Spanish, but this did not handicap her in kindergarten, or first and second grade at Olas Tree Elementary School located in *Barrio Town,* which had 85 percent Latino students. As they improved their economic circumstances, the family moved to a more affluent area where they currently reside. She transferred to Cherry Lane Elementary, which had only 3 percent Latino students, and the rest were non-Hispanic white students.

At this school she began to experience stress, as students mimicked and made fun of her Spanish accent and her very slim appearance, calling her "toothpick," "ostrich legs," and "dirty Mexican." Quite often she would cry at home because she did not want to go to school. She developed various somatic complaints and on occasion would vomit, causing her mother to keep her home from school, thinking her ill. The mother often complained to school officials but "nothing was done about it," and the insults continued. In spite of frequent absences and the prejudice and scapegoating she was suffering, she still was able to maintain above average grades, such as a few As, a few Bs, and the rest Cs. She began to resent school because it had become a very negative experience. She felt not only rejected, but also that she did not fit in. Her academic performance suffered and was reflected in poorer grades in the fourth, fifth, and sixth grades. Rejection during these important, formative years can lead to a child's low self-esteem at a critical time in his or her life, when the psychosocial developmental task is learning to become industrious in an atmosphere of validation by the school and peers.

4. FAMILY EMOTIONAL ENVIRONMENT

A warm, secure, loving, home environment is extremely important for a child to develop healthy emotions, emotional security, confidence, and self-esteem. According to the parents and grandparents, this happened for Ms. Gomez during her first five years of life in spite of the negative experiences she was having in school. The loving validation provided by her warm, very traditional Hispanic family helped her feel that, at least somewhere in her life, she was valued. This was reflected in her being a loving child who reached out to and established close relationships with her siblings, immediate relatives, and playmates. This emotional foundation and empathic capacity still exists, according to all of her relatives, except when she is under the influence of drugs and/or alcohol when she becomes a totally different person who is emotionally distant and cold and exploits people for her own benefit.

During these initial developmental years, her hard-working father was a light-to-moderate drinker of alcohol. However, as she approached seven years of age, his drinking escalated because he had been laid off from a few low-skilled jobs. His arguments with her mother evolved into physical battering in the presence of little Ms. Gomez, which caused her a significant amount of anxiety. Sometimes she was afraid of leaving her mother at home and would not go to school.

5. CHILDHOOD PSYCHOLOGICAL TRAUMA

It is very traumatic for children to observe their parents in violent confrontation, especially when it occurs frequently. On one occasion when Ms. Gomez was nine years old, she attempted to protect her mother from the father's abuse by stepping in between them, but this was met with physical retaliation against her. Thereafter, these physical beatings that the father thought was his right as a husband and a father also began to include Ms. Gomez. The beatings lasted for a few years until the father left home when she was almost twelve years old. Ms. Gomez cannot recall these beatings even though she had a few scars on her arms that her mother stated had been caused by them. This "blocking out" of painful trauma is not uncommon for post-traumatic stress disorder (PTSD) victims, especially children.

Ms. Gomez did recall one painful episode when she was ten years old and "glue-sniffing" with friends in a neighbor's garage. She was raped by two fifteen-year-old boys. Fearing that she would be blamed for this incident, she did not tell anyone. Such a traumatic event could also cause PTSD.

In my assessment of Ms. Gomez, she clearly had several psychiatric symptoms that met the criteria for a PTSD diagnosis. These symptoms of acute anxiety, hypervigilance, fear, and depression were never treated. In such situations, some people, especially when they are poor and do not have the resources to obtain professional treatment, have been known to "treat" themselves. No doubt this motivated her to seek her own self-prescribed medication with chemical substances such as paint, gasoline, "glue-sniffing," marijuana, PCP, heroin, cocaine, and alcohol. These substances help numb the person from psychological pain and, while in the intoxicated state, help suppress painful memories at least temporarily until the next "high." A psychological and physical dependence upon this "solution" reinforces its repetition.

6. SEARCHING FOR A SUBSTITUTE FAMILY

When children are rejected by the school and their families as they approach early adolescence (which is a developmental period of wanting to be part of a social group), they begin to gravitate to and are attracted to other youths having similar experiences and needs. These are the seeds that give growth to gangs. As Ms. Gomez was approaching age thirteen, she began to absorb some of the nonviolent aspects of adolescent female gang culture. She avoided school even more to be with her new friends. Michael Webster, the "at-large" co-suspect in this case, introduced her to heroin at age thirteen when he was twenty-eight years of age.

She quickly developed a psychological and physical dependence on this drug and had a new group of friends that she called "street junkies." In her frequent association with this group, she began to incorporate the subculture and lifestyle of the lower-class female street addict. She was now in a "retreatist gang" (a group in society that "retreats" into drugs and alcohol consumption). To support her drug habit, she stole from her family and friends, lied, and manipulated people in her pursuit of drugs. She was nicknamed "Bandit" by her group, and she had this name tattooed on her left arm when she was fourteen. Female street addicts rarely, if ever, are violent. Instead, they prey on potential victims whom they might be able to exploit for drugs, particularly recently paroled ex-convicts who are potential sources for drugs with their "gate money" (prison release money). In the street drug culture, they are labeled "Black Widows" for this behavior.

Ms. Gomez has no formal criminal history other than the current homicide offense. Her record indicates only one petty theft arrest as a juvenile when she stole cosmetic items at a Thrifty Drug Store. She did not have to appear in court because no petition was filed. She simply was counseled and released by the police.

7. PSYCHOSOCIAL ANALYSIS AND DIAGNOSIS

In analyzing the above six predisposition factors, any one of these factors could place a child, adolescent, or adult at a high risk for emotional, behavioral, criminal, or substance abuse and dependence problems. In the case of Ms. Gomez, her primary strength was the foundation of her relatively normal early childhood up until the age of five. The six factors were: (1) beginning motherhood before the age of 16, being unemployed, having only a seventh grade education, and being in a conflicted marriage; (2) having inherited four generations of a biological vulnerability to alcoholism addiction, which also made her biologically vulnerable to other addictions such as drugs and nicotine; (3) language and cultural difficulties in elementary school, further complicated by discriminatory rejection by non-Hispanic white students; (4) being raised in an unstable family after age five, which progressively deteriorated due to her father's alcoholism and physical abuse of her mother; (5) the traumatization of Ms. Gomez' rape at age ten by two fifteen-year-old males while all were glue-sniffing, compounded by beatings by her father until age twelve; and (6) her increased involvement with a "surrogate family" (the street addict subculture), which met her needs for companionship, affection, and drugs.

Throughout her young life from age five to eighteen, the dynamics of these six interacting, predisposing factors negatively impacted her psychosocial development and functioning, thereby contributing to her offense, which occurred while she was under the influence of heroin, cocaine, and alcohol. In this intoxicated state, her judgment was impaired and, being with an older, more experienced ex-convict and drug addict—who often enjoy respect and status among the younger, less experienced "junkies"—she was more vulnerable and prone to influence.

Being the victim of sexual and physical assaults as a child severely traumatized this adolescent. To this day, these emotional scars remain untreated. These symptoms demanded calming and, through self-medication beginning at the tender age of ten when most little girls are still playing with dolls, she began to ingest mood-altering chemicals (sniffing paint, gasoline, and glue). Four generations of a dormant, chemical genetic vulnerability toward addiction surfaced. In a relatively brief time after graduating to heroin and cocaine use, she became an addict and joined the street addict culture.

Ms. Gomez' career as a female street drug addict did not follow the usual pattern of most female drug addicts, that is, continued use with the possibility of death due to AIDS resulting from prostitution and/or using infected needles, suicide evolving from major depression, or "burning out" as an aging addict and then becoming an alcoholic. A few are able to leave drugs and assume a normal life. In the case of Ms. Gomez, however, she did not have the maturity nor the physical and emotional strength to alter her eight-year-old street drug addict pattern, which culminated in the death of a twelve-year-old child, and which now may even result in her own death.

DIAGNOSIS

In my interviews with Ms. Gomez, it is my diagnostic impression that she definitely is depressed. Following arrest she was suicidal but did not make any attempts. A year ago when her husband was threatening to leave her and take her children, she made a suicide attempt by slashing her wrists with a broken bottle. It was a serious attempt while intoxicated and required emergency room treatment and seventy-two hours of hospitalization. She did not receive treatment following release due to lack of insurance and financial resources. Such attempts are not uncommon among very depressed female adolescents. Her depression, in part, is also *reactive,* that is, it is an emotional reaction to being separated from her children, husband, family, and friends. Her depression may also be a long-term *dysthymic* (chronic low to moderate) depression arising from untreated PTSD symptoms since age ten. In addition to four generations of genetic factors predisposing toward alcoholism in the family history, there might also be an underlying *endogenous* (biological) depression having a genetic origin. With regard to the latter, a careful, extensive psychiatric evaluation would have to be made of the defendant and selected family members. The following is my diagnostic impression of the defendant:

DSM IV, 312.8. Adolescent Conduct Disorder (stealing, lying, running away), severe, present since age twelve to date arrested in present offense.
DSM IV, 309.81. Post Traumatic Stress Disorder, chronic type, present since age ten.
DSM IV, 303.90. Alcohol Dependence, in full remission since arrested in present offense.
DSM IV, 304.80. Polysubstance Dependence, in full remission since arrested in present offense.

PART TWO: THE DEFENDANT'S VALUE TO SOCIETY

1. In complying with the social work profession's ethical responsibility to promote the general welfare of society and to respond to this nation's great need for new and current knowledge to advance its understanding of violence and homicide, it becomes

imperative that Ms. Gomez be permitted to live in order to assist social and psychiatric scientists toward that end. This tragic case presents a unique opportunity to advance our current state of knowledge concerning the nature versus nurture debate and the relationship between American and Mexican culture. The Gomez case represents five generations of genetic vulnerability to addiction in one family, from the great-grandparents to and including Ms. Gomez' two children. Where this genetic vulnerability to alcohol and drug addiction coexists with too-easy access to firearms in the context of a violent Anglo-American culture, many young women with similar characteristics are being transformed into agents of violence and homicide. Ms. Gomez may simply be a female "pioneer" in this regard.

2. From this case we can also learn about the specific points of the process of early adolescent decision making, which lead a troubled youngster to choose a gang or a street addict group, to become a "loner," a criminal offender, a homeless, runaway youth, or some other alternative. All this information is valuable to society in the identification of genuine high-risk youths and their families in order to prevent these excessively violent crimes, by either young females or young males.

3. There is sufficient research information that documents the severe emotional impact upon immediate family members when there is a suicide in the family. This impact places each of them at very high risk for suicide, because, in periods of major depression, they tend to identify with the "solution" adopted by the dead family member.[13]

   In those cases in which a family member was a victim of a homicide, similar emotional vulnerabilities occur. Furthermore, it is a fact that *any* child who has lost a parent "by any means before the age of thirteen," has a higher risk for affective disorders and suicide than does a child who has not experienced such a loss.[14] In the defendant's case, the execution of Ms. Gomez by the state would place both of her children at a very high risk for possible homicidal and/or suicidal behavior in later years, because they would have to live with the emotions and the label of having been given birth by a mother who was so "evil" she had to be executed by the state. The defendant is a classic case of a victim of childhood sexual and physical abuse who later becomes a perpetrator of violence. Her execution would perpetuate this cycle of violence in her children.

4. Ms. Gomez would become the first woman and mother with minor children to be executed in the United States and in the world. Granting her a life sentence without the possibility of parole will spare her children this overwhelming, high-risk burden. When sober, Ms. Gomez can be an affectionate, nurturing mother, and she can continue her mothering responsibilities with her children through weekly and even once-a-month, weekend prison visits available to mothers with minor children.

5. She is quite remorseful and accepts full responsibility for all her actions in the homicide. All her statements to me have been corroborated by her family and other secondary sources. Her attitude was very positive, and this was quite evident in reading unsolicited letters shown to me by her relatives. Over the last few months, she has written letters to several of her younger cousins, nieces, and nephews, advising them to do well in school and listen to their parents. Her misfortune can be of a continuing educational benefit to other youths. Her death would end that important communication link.

Sincerely,

Bob Pla, MSW
Executive Director

The Report Is Challenged by the People

After the report was read by the judge and the District Attorney representing the people of the State of California, the District Attorney exercised his option to call for a "402 Hearing" without a jury being present. This special disclosure hearing permits the District Attorney to challenge Mr. Pla's credentials as an "expert" in a specific area and, secondly, to challenge parts, or even all, of Mr. Pla's report if the District Attorney is of the opinion that it might undermine his efforts in obtaining a death penalty verdict. The District Attorney challenged Bob Pla's MSW degree, stating that a social worker's training did not qualify him to be an expert on violent and homicidal behavior. The defendant's attorney, Eddie Falls, granted that Mr. Pla's graduate training and education did not in itself qualify him as a violence expert, but that, following graduation, one of Mr. Pla's specialty areas had become the assessment and treatment of violent offenders as well as murderers who had been released on parole. Attorney Falls added that Mr. Pla had testified in juvenile and superior court on at least fourteen occasions and had been accepted as an expert witness in these violence-related cases. The judge ruled that he was satisfied that there was sufficient evidence to show that Mr. Pla had earned expert witness status in previous trials.

SOCIAL WORKERS CAN'T DIAGNOSE

The District Attorney also challenged Mr. Pla's "psychosocial evaluation" report and diagnosis, stating that only a licensed physician, psychiatrist, or psychologist, was qualified to render a diagnosis, *not* a social worker. "Therefore," shouted the District Attorney dramatically, "this report is worthless!" Rita Gomez seemed stunned. Attorney Falls calmly showed a current copy of Mr. Pla's LCSW, his professional license, which originally had been granted twenty-six years previously, and stated to the Judge that Division 2, Chapter 14, of the California Business and Professions Code, authorized licensed clinical social workers not only to diagnose a patient or client but also to provide that person psychotherapy of a nonmedical nature. The judge ruled that the Business and Professions Code permitted Mr. Pla to diagnose patients, and *that* section of the report would be admissible evidence for the trier of fact (the jury). Rita Gomez smiled at Mr. Pla and her attorney.

THE DISTRICT ATTORNEY SCORES MAJOR RULINGS

Being cognizant of the fact that a four-generation genetic vulnerability for alcoholism in the defendant's family could be construed as a favorable mitigating factor and a foundation for a life sentence rather than the death penalty, the District Attorney attempted to strike out factor 2 in the report. He argued that the family history was based on "hearsay," there were no medical records to prove the existence of alcoholism, and that the great-grandparents were deceased, hence, could not testify as to their addictions. Attorney Falls argued that the grandparents could testify as to their parents' addictions if permitted. The judge inquired of Mr. Pla whether the genetic alcoholism studies pertained to males or females. Mr. Pla responded that so far, all of the studies concerned males, but that in 1971 China had discovered the same genetic link from mothers to daughters and fathers to daughters. The judge ruled that scientific knowledge on this point had to be restricted only to research in the United States, and because there was no evidence to show the specific genetic link to daughters, the mitigating factor of genetic inheritance of alcoholism could not be heard by the jury. This was a major setback for Ms. Gomez in fighting for her life.

REPORTED HISTORY VERSUS CORROBORATION

The District Attorney accepted predisposition factors 3 (early childhood developmental) and 4 (family emotional environment) in the report. However, in factor 5 (childhood psychological trauma), the District Attorney accepted the physical abuse history because this had been corroborated by the defendant's mother under oath on the witness stand. The District Attorney, however, did not accept the rape experience at age ten, because Ms. Gomez had not reported the incident to anyone, including the police. The judge supported the District Attorney in this request to keep the jury from hearing this information.

CLINICAL HIGH-RISK VERSUS COURTROOM HIGH-RISK PERCEPTION

The District Attorney mounted his strongest challenge to Mr. Pla's assertion that the execution of Ms. Gomez would place both of her children at very high risk for subsequent suicidal or homicidal behavior in later years. Mr. Pla quoted from the most recent research that concluded that the death of a parent increased suicide risk twenty-fold for a child thirteen and under, and that violent and homicidal behavior in family members placed youth at very high risk for modeling that violent behavior. The judge calculated that, since the suicide rate was on the average twelve per 100,000 according to Mr. Pla's figures, increasing the rate twenty-fold would result in a figure of "only" 240 per 100,000. The judge concluded that the fact that 99,760 persons would *not* commit suicide following the death of a parent was statistically a stronger argument.

The judge further inquired of Mr. Pla whether there was any research to indicate that the execution of a mother resulted in suicide and/or homicidal behavior on the part of her children. Mr. Pla replied that, although there were many women on "death row" in the nation, there had not been any specific research to address that question. Mr. Pla restated the documented argument, however, that the death of the parent for *any* reason—including execution by the state—placed a child thirteen and under at very high risk for suicide. The judge ruled that the jury would not be permitted to hear the argument that Ms. Gomez' execution would place her children at risk for either suicide or homicidal behavior. Ms. Gomez' mouth dropped open as she nodded her head from side to side in disbelief. Her attorney protested but was firmly silenced by the judge.

THE DEFENDANT'S VALUE TO SOCIETY?

The District Attorney argued that he did not want to see Ms. Gomez kept alive for the benefit of social and psychiatric scientific curiosity at the expense of taxpayers. He stated that the taxpayers and voters of California wanted to see the prompt execution of criminals committing heinous crimes, especially the killing of a child on her way to school. The judge ruled that the jury would not be able to hear Mr. Pla's testimony concerning Ms. Gomez' value to social science. The arguments presented by Mr. Pla of Ms. Gomez' value to her own children if kept alive for mothering–nurturing purposes and her value to young, extended family members and other potential youths she might be able to impact in a positive way because of her tragic story, were accepted by the judge over the opposition of the District Attorney.

THE COMPETITION

Bob Pla testified for two days before the jury under a barrage of challenging, often cynical questions advanced by the People's legal representative. Attorney Falls made a valiant effort in his *direct* (initial testimony) examination of Mr. Pla, which was followed by a lengthy *cross* (challenging the initial testimony) examination of Mr. Pla by the DA. The factual premise of each of Mr. Pla's statements in his report (minus all of the sections withheld from the jury as the result of the "402 Hearing") was challenged by the District Attorney as to its source, research methodology, and conclusions. Bob Pla was well prepared and defended each position with confidence and a presence of authority, hoping to impress the jury. This competitive interaction reminded him of his one-on-one boxing ring experience or perhaps preparing for and taking his LCSW oral examinations. Attorney Falls fought to retrieve any "points" scored by the District Attorney during his *redirect* (further clarification of initial testimony provided during the direct examination) examination of Mr. Pla.

Finally, following two days of the direct, cross, and redirect testimony of Mr. Pla, the defense rested its case. The attorneys were given two days to prepare their closing arguments for the jury.

THE VERDICT

As dictated by law, the prosecution was first to present its closing argument on behalf of the people of the state of California, followed by the closing argument of the defense. The District Attorney's tough law and order delivery calling for the death penalty was followed by the closing statement of the defense. Attorney Falls pleaded to the jury that, because Ms. Gomez was an adolescent and a mother with no prior criminal convictions whose judgment was gravely impaired because she was under the influence of alcohol and drugs at the time of the commission of the crime, these mitigating factors should warrant a sentence of life imprisonment without the possibility of parole, rather than execution.

The prosecution then was permitted to rebut the defense's closing arguments. The District Attorney argued that, in California, an eighteen-year-old is legally an adult, not an adolescent, and the fact that she is a mother had matured her far beyond her age. The prosecutor granted that Ms. Gomez was an alcoholic and a heroin and cocaine addict, but that there was no factual evidence to prove that she was intoxicated at the specific moment that she fired the gun at the victim. The District Attorney further advised the jury that, even though there were no criminal convictions in her history, by her own statements she had admitted stealing items from home to sell in order to purchase her drugs. The closing arguments ended after two days.

The all-white jury that consisted of six women and six men who had already convicted Ms. Gomez of first-degree murder with special circumstances deliberated the death penalty phase of the trial for two days. The jury was called back into the courtroom because they had reached a verdict. The courtroom was filled to capacity, and media cameras were running. The judge asked the jury whether it had reached a decision. The jury foreman stood up and replied, "Yes we have, your honor." The verdict, which was written on a piece of paper, was given to the judge by the bailiff to be read. The bailiff then returned it to the foreman who read the verdict in a rather businesslike voice, stating:

> Based upon the court instructions given to us, we the jury can find no mitigating factors or circumstances which would warrant life imprisonment without the possibility of parole for the defendant. We are unanimous in our opinion that her criminal actions involved in the taking of a child's life, warrant the death penalty.

After the first sentence had been read, the victim's family and supporters were crying and cheering, drowning out the second sentence. Ms. Gomez held her head down, crying, and loudly stated to the victim's family, "I'm sorry! I'm sorry!" Her attorney, who also had tears in his eyes, attempted to comfort his client by patting her on the shoulder.

A Social Worker's Work Is Never Finished

It had been a little over a week since Bob Pla had testified in the Rita Gomez case. It was the noon hour, and Bob was driving to the local In & Out Burger for his favorite double-burger and fries. He was again tuned in to Danny Jones and his "Oldies but Goodies" program. He pulled up to the speaker and placed his order and was waiting in the long line of cars. It was 12:05 and, in the middle of "Misty," Danny Jones cut in stating:

> Well folks. The verdict that you've all been waiting for has just come in. It looks like one of our Olas residents is going to fry! I guess what goes around, comes around. It's too bad that we'll be losing two beautiful young ladies. Catch you later. . . .

Bob was immobilized until the car in back of him honked its horn, waking him out of his preoccupied trance. He pulled up and paid for his order and received his lunch. As he drove away he could not recall whether he was given change—or even whether he had change coming. By habit he reached for the hot fries, but they seemed tasteless. "Maybe they forgot to put salt on them," he thought. For some reason, he had lost his appetite. He could not believe the verdict. He felt that he had done his very best given the unfair circumstances of having to spar with two, rather than one, opponents, the District Attorney *and* the judge. He thought that Eddie Falls was a good attorney who had also given his best. Danny Jones' words "what goes around, comes around," kept interfering with his thoughts about the case. "That's it! That is what all of this is about. What goes around, comes around. Rita was abused, and in turn, she abused!" Bob reasoned. She was subjected to physical punishment, and she had easy access to weapons; she killed, and now the state is going to kill her. "As social workers out to improve the human condition," Bob reflected, "we need to stop physical punishment, reduce easy access to firearms, and end capital punishment."

REGENERATING INTEREST AFTER A CRISIS IS OVER

Bob recalled that, in the original micro and macro psychosocial intervention strategy he had developed, all tasks had been addressed and completed except for the last task, no. 4. This final task was a macro Third-Level Task with a prevention goal. It involved the creation of a multidisciplinary and multiethnic task force to investigate the causes of the campus violence and develop recommendations for the prevention of such incidents. After making at least two dozen phone calls to social workers and other professionals, school representatives, and minority community people to work on this project, he found very little interest. Most believed that the case was closed and that everyone should move beyond it and "heal."

Others felt that Olas was still a safe community and the Gomez case was just an aberration and would never happen again. "I guess communities are just like people," thought Bob. "As soon as the crisis is over, everything cools off, and *denial* once again darkens our path so we don't have to see how dangerous it really is— and then we're more likely to get injured." Some minorities advised Bob, "Let sleeping dogs lie, man. Don't wake up the white monster (racism in Olas). Don't you remember how they wanted to come into our neighborhoods and shoot us?" Bob was becoming a little discouraged and had to remind himself that, just because he had been so intimately involved in practically all aspects of the case and understood clearly its wide-ranging implications to Olas and other communities, others did not seem to share his concerns. He also knew, however, that one can always find others who share one's concerns.

Bob decided to begin "at home," that is, with other social workers. He asked to be placed on the agenda for the following month's Olas NASW chapter meeting. At the meeting he explained his concerns regarding the growing youth violence problem, not only in Olas but throughout the nation, stating that the Gomez case was *not* an abnormality, rather that there were literally hundreds of persons in Olas with similar predispositional factors and dynamics, just waiting to explode. Many of the social workers agreed, because they had also observed these factors in the caseloads of the county Department of Children's Services.

Early childhood experiences of physical and sexual abuse were not uncommon in many families. "They should outlaw corporal punishment of children by parents as they did in the schools," exclaimed one of the social workers, with others quickly joining in and nodding agreement. "Corporal punishment starting with children is just at the beginning of a continuum of punishment," commented Ms. O'Leary, "that ends with the ultimate punishment—death!" "Maybe we need to get rid of the death penalty too," remarked still another social worker. Others thought that more social welfare services were needed for the poor as a violence prevention measure, rather than building more prisons.

One of the recent MSW graduates set forth what she believed was a progressive thesis, stating: "Perhaps we can look at the death sentence of Rita Gomez as 'progress for women,' as they are now really being treated as equal to men who commit horrendous crimes. I for one favor the death penalty and believe that women should also be executed for the same behaviors for which men are executed." Initially, the group of twenty-five social workers stared at one another in silence, some having surprised expressions.

Ms. O'Leary then spoke and agreed with the philosophical premise of equality in her colleague's statement. "It reminds me of the positions we used to take in the sixties and seventies as young student feminists and, that is that in our political protests and demonstrations, we did not wish to be protected and treated in any special way because we were women. We strongly believed that if we were demanding equal pay and treatment, we also had to be ready to assume the consequences of our new assertiveness, including being jailed like the male protestors. We fought against special treatment, better food, and far less crowded housing accommodations provided for women in prisons and jails. Our black and brown brothers and sisters 'doing time' brought it to our attention that, unlike young white feminists, they were quite overrepresented in correctional institutions, and that, if we *really* wanted to help, we should advocate 'up' rather than 'down.' They believed that the quality of living standards in institutions should rise to a higher standard of decency as women's were, rather than going down to the almost barbaric level found in many overcrowded men's prisons and jails. So, perhaps we shouldn't be executing a Rita Gomez, nor a mother, nor a married or single woman, nor *any* woman *or* man." "Amen to that and I second the emotion, sister," responded Bill Kennon from the Black Social Workers' Union, "and let's not forget guns. Everybody seems to have a gun, and a lot of people are using them."

Bob was sensing a certain enthusiasm in the group, often generated when people got together to discuss a particular issue. No longer were they feeling isolated or powerless. Indeed, social workers like to work together. People can be good medicine for one another. The group wanted to develop strategies related to violence prevention, agreeing that what was most needed was the massive social welfare needs of people with very few resources in society. NASW, through its national committees, commissions, and local chapters, was already working on these social welfare issues. The group did not see any reason to involve itself in that area, nor in the discussion of capital punishment since NASW already had a policy statement favoring its abolition. Rather, the group wanted to enter those violence-related areas not currently on the "front burner" of the profession. The group decided to develop a position paper for the profession and other private and government entities on the topic area of corporal punishment, with a special emphasis on youths. The following represents the concept paper they developed:

AMERICA'S DEPENDENCE ON CORPORAL PUNISHMENT

Corpus is the body of a person, and *corporal punishment* is the physical punishment of the person's body. For the purposes of this position paper, *physical punishment* and *corporal punishment* as it pertains to children is a legally permissible physical attack on children granted to all parents in the United States and to many teachers. The most common forms of physical punishment are hitting, slapping, spanking, grabbing, and roughly shoving a child. Any one of these acts would be legally considered a criminal assault if carried out by someone who is not the parent or in a custodial relationship to the child.[15]

The right to use corporal punishment is a cherished American value which begins at and is first learned and experienced in the home. Physical force is the ultimate measure to keep subordinate groups in their place, and for centuries physical punishment has been used against women to keep them in their place.[16] Wives were seen as the property of men, and as recently as 1867 in North Carolina husbands were permitted to physically punish their wives as long as the stick they used to administer the beatings was not larger than the husband's thumb, hence, "the rule of thumb."[17]

Even though the *right* to physically punish wives by husbands has disappeared from common law, the *practice* is still quite prevalent. Corporal punishment of women by men they live with in an intimate relationship is still "valued" by many men considering that 24 million women have experienced this at least once in those relationships.[18] Many men, therefore, find it difficult to give up a practice that represents power and control over women. Mothers, much like husbands, are also finding it difficult to give up power and control over their children. This power and control may be addictive.

The American heritage and tradition of corporal punishment for children is far worse than for women, as *both* parents participate in this practice to maintain dominance over their children. In colonial times in 1672, for example, the *General Laws and Liberties of the Massachusetts Colony* provided for corporal punishment of "diverse" children who were disobedient and disorderly toward their parents. The court, upon complaint and upon the child's conviction of such misdemeanors, " . . . shall be sentenced to endure such Corporal punishment, by whipping or otherwise, as in his judgment the Merit of the fact shall deserve, not exceeding ten stripes for one offense."[19]

Today, every state in the United States attempts to protect children through child abuse laws. An unbelievable contradiction exists, however, as physical punishment of children by parents is legal in *all* states! *Who* can best distinguish between physical child abuse and corporal punishment? Can a two-, three-, four-, or five-year-old child distinguish between corporal punishment and child abuse? This question was posed to child psychoanalyst, Lawrence Hartman, M.D., President of the American Psychiatric Association by NASW Board Member Armando T. Morales, DSW, at the Joint Commission of Interprofessional Affairs (JCIA) Presidents (of American Psychiatric Association, NASW, American Psychological Association, and American Nurses Association) Conference, held on Kiawah Island, South Carolina, in April 1992. Dr. Hartman agreed with Dr. Morales that a child at that age could *not* make the distinction, that either was traumatic for the child. In an issues paper titled "Children and Adolescents who Commit Homicide" presented to the four presidents, Dr. Morales recommended that for the purpose of violence prevention, the four major helping professions assume a leadership role for the nation and advocate for the adoption of laws that make it illegal for parents to physically punish their children.[20] The presidents refused to act on the recommendation. Perhaps the timing then was premature—it certainly is not today!

Is corporal punishment based on politics, geographic area, or historical era? In 1979, only four states considered corporal punishment in the schools as physical abuse of children and prohibited it—the rest did not. Ten years later, corporal punishment prohibition states increased slightly, from four to eleven. However, there is even greater support for corporal punishment for parents than in the schools. The strongest advocates include fundamentalist Christians, teachers' organizations, and school boards.[21] Research findings report that the more corporal punishment is authorized, the higher the rate of school violence and the higher the adult homicide rate. Straus argues that violent teachers produce violent students, and violent parents produce violent children.[22]

A national random sample of American families revealed that 97 percent of parents of three- and four-year-old children used corporal punishment that year. A replication of the study ten years later, which included children under three years of age, found that 20 percent of parents began hitting their child *before* the age of one.[23]

Corporal punishment by parents also extended to older children, by parents as the national sample revealed that 33 percent of children fifteen to seventeen years old were still being hit by their parents. This might have been underreporting by the parents. When these same adolescents were interviewed by the researchers, 50 percent reported that their parents were still hitting them when they were in high school.[24]

Straus believes that much corporal punishment administered by parents for misbehavior is in a context of "love," but it might also be teaching the child undesirable lessons and consequences such as

1. the association of love with violence;
2. the establishment of the moral "rightness" of hitting other persons who do something which is regarded as wrong; and
3. in observing their angry and frustrated parents attempting to restrain themselves from hitting the child, the child unintentionally learns that anger and frustration justify the use of physical force.[25]

There is precedent for a nation making it illegal for parents to physically punish their children. Such a law was passed in Sweden in 1978. The law was greeted with outrage, as 70 percent of the people opposed it according to a survey that first year. Offenders were given parenting classes, similar to "traffic school" in many states. Ten years later, Swedish citizens appreciate the law and recognize its benefits.[26] The homicide rate in the United States for males fourteen to twenty-four is 24 per 100,000; in Sweden, it is 1 per 100,000.[27]

According to Straus and other national experts, physical punishment by parents toward their child is the greatest single risk factor for the victim of this abuse later becoming a violence perpetrator. If social workers are going to have an impact on reducing violence and homicide in this country, we have to adopt measures which *prevent* and curtail its early formation. As was the experience in Sweden, the United States must be consistent in eradicating *all* forms of child physical abuse, whether labeled physical punishment, corporal punishment, physical force, battering, or other methods, which have the primary intent of causing physical pain to a child. To the child, the result is the same—psychological and, at times, physical trauma.

RECOMMENDATION

On behalf of the social work profession, which strives to become more relevant to the nation in its hour of need as it concerns the enormous and devastating psychological, physical, social, and economic costs brought on by the death of 25,000 Americans of all ages each year, it is therefore recommended that the professional body of social work (NASW) representing 155,000 members adopt as one of its major goals the complete abolition of corporal punishment in the United States by the year 2000.

The Olas NASW Chapter adopted the above recommendation which was then forwarded to the California NASW Chapter for its consideration, adoption, and approval. A legislative committee of the California Chapter plans to look into state statutes, rules, and regulations covering child abuse, physical punishment, and corporal punishment and thereafter make recommendations to the appropriate legislative elected bodies. The developing strategy is to also apprise the California member on the NASW Board of Directors of the issue for inclusion as an agenda item for the next Board meeting. California NASW Delegate Assembly representatives plan to introduce the issue in other states and at the next Delegate Assembly meeting for general membership approval.

(It could happen!)

Concluding Comment

The profession of social work is indeed a profession of many faces as seen in the high school homicide case. The "social worker in action" in the Olas tragedy possesses a repertoire of micro- and macrolevel intervention skills based on a foundation of biological, psychological, social, and community social work–related knowledge obtained through graduate school education, training, and subsequent experience.

Whereas psychiatrists rely primarily on the strengths of their biological training in medicating and treating *individuals,* and psychologists rely heavily on their psychological testing instruments in assessing their patients, social workers are trained to have the potential for macro- as well as microlevel intervention.

In the high school homicide case, Bob Pla, MSW, was an advanced professional practitioner involved in various *direct service* (micro) tasks and competencies, such as assessment and treatment of individuals, couples, families, and nonfamily groups. His in-depth, comprehensive assessment skills were evident in the Gomez case where he uncovered a generational alcoholism genetic link and identified other predispositional factors related to Ms. Gomez becoming a homicide perpetrator. Additionally, he was the chief administrator and director of a social work family services agency and was part of a team in identifying and organizing resources in the community to deal with the Olas crisis to help hundreds of residents in need. In short, he displayed numerous direct service competencies spelled out in Chapter 8.

Bob Pla also undertook various *indirect service* (macro) tasks and competencies utilizing prevention theories to help create conditions that would result in a safer community. During a period of heightened community tension and anger, he deployed staff members into the minority communities to help them vent their frustrations in response to being scapegoated by the dominant white community. Simultaneously, he was working with law enforcement and community groups in the majority community to discourage any vigilante-type retaliation.

Another *indirect service* prevention task to create a safer community directly evolving from the Rita Gomez case concerned the increasingly easy access to guns by youths and the dependence on capital punishment to "solve" problems of violence in the United States. The nation's obsession with firearms and its continued commitment to capital punishment with its powerful "modeling" impact for the country could have been other prevention issues and tasks Bob Pla and his colleagues could have undertaken, but there were simply not enough hours in a day—even for social workers. Instead, one issue—corporal punishment—became the focus of attention.

From the Gomez case, Bob learned most intimately the psychologically crippling effects of corporal punishment on victims and how this places abused children at extremely high risk for becoming future perpetrators of violence and homicide. In this regard, he was able to facilitate professional collaboration among peers, create a committee to review relevant literature pertaining to the topic, and assist in the production of a position paper concerning corporal punishment, along with local and national strategies for its dissemination.

It may be that one social worker *can* make a difference, as was seen in the Gomez case. It is also possible that *many* social workers *can* make more difference. Join the profession and make a difference.

KEY WORDS AND CONCEPTS

Homicide

Natural disasters

Pro bono

Man-made disasters

Criminal homicide

Dysthymia

Corporal punishment

Child abuse vs. corporal punishment

Felony homicide

DSM IV, 312.8

Endogenous depression

SUGGESTED READINGS

Andrews, Arlene Bowers. "Social Work Expert Testimony Regarding Mitigation in Capital Sentencing Proceedings," *Social Work* 36 (May 1991): 440–445.

Beckerman, Adela. "Mothers in Prison: Meeting the Prerequisite Conditions for Permanency Planning," *Social Work* 39 (January 1994): 9–14.

Blashfield, Jean F. *Why They Killed*. New York: Warner Books Inc., 1990.

Burman, Sondra, and Allen-Meares, Paula. "Neglected Victims of Murder: Children's Witness to Parental Homicide," *Social Work* 39 (January 1994): 28–34.

Ewing, Charles Patrick. *Kids Who Kill*. Lexington, MA: Lexington Books, 1990.

Hotaling, Gerald T., and Straus, Murray A. "Intrafamily Violence, and Crime and Violence outside the Family," in Lloyd Ohlin and Michael Tonry, eds., *Family Violence, Crime and Justice,* Vol. 11. Chicago: University of Chicago Press, 1989, pp. 315–375.

Loftus, Elizabeth, and Ketcham, Katherine. *Witness for the Defense*. New York: St. Martin's Press, 1991.

Mones, Paul. *When a Child Kills*. New York: Pocket Star Books, 1991.

Morales, Armando. "Homicide," in Richard L. Edwards, ed., *Encyclopedia of Social Work,* 19th Edition. Washington, D.C.: NASW Press, 1995, pp. 1347–1358.

Norris-Shortle, Carole, Young, Patricia A., and Williams, May Ann. "Understanding Death and Grief for Children Three and Younger," *Social Work* 38 (June 1993): 736–742.

Schwarz, Donald F., ed. *Children and Violence.* Report of the Twenty-Third Ross Roundtable on Critical Approaches to Common Pediatric Problems. Columbus, OH: Ross Laboratories, 1992.

Straus, Murray A. "Children as Witness to Marital Violence: A Risk Factor for Life Long Problems Among a Nationally Representative Sample of American Men and Women," in Donald F. Schwarz, ed., *Children and Violence.* Report of the Twenty-Third Rose Roundtable on Critical Approaches to Common Pediatric Problems. Columbus, OH: Ross Laboratories, 1991, pp. 98–109.

Straus, Murray A. "Discipline and Deviance: Physical Punishment of Children and Violence and Other Crime in Adulthood," *Social Problems* 38 (February 1991): 133–154.

ENDNOTES

1. Homicides of children four and younger number about 2.5 per 100,000 in the United States. Mothers are the most frequent perpetrators, followed by fathers, mother's boyfriends, and caretakers. See "Children's Safety Network," in *A Data Book of Child and Adolescent Injury* (Washington, D.C.: National Center for Education in Maternal and Child Health, 1991).
2. Fern Shen and Christine Spolar, "Three Lives Once Full of Great Hope," *Washington Post,* Friday, December 3, 1993, p. 1.
3. Lola G. Selby, "Social Work and Crisis Theory," *Social Work Papers* 10 (1963): 3.
4. See John Cummings and Elaine Cummings, *Ego and Milieu* (New York: Atherton Press, 1962), as cited in Howard J. Parad, "Crisis Intervention," in Robert Morris, ed., *Encyclopedia of Social Work* 1, No. 16 (New York: National Association of Social Workers, 1971), pp. 196–202.
5. See Gerald Caplan, *Principles of Preventive Psychiatry* (New York: Basic Books, 1964); Erich Lindemann, "The Meaning of Crisis in Individuals and Family Living," *Teachers College Record* 57 (February 1963), as cited in Howard J. Parad, "Crisis Intervention," pp. 198–199.
6. Lydia Rapoport, "Crisis-Oriented Short-Term Casework," *Social Service Review* 41 (March 1967): 35.
7. Ibid., p. 37.
8. "They Think We're a Land of Sick Shooters," *U.S. News and World Report,* June 7, 1993, p. 9.
9. L. A. Fingerhut and J. C. Kleinman, "International and Interstate Comparison of Homicide Among Young Males," *Journal of the American Medical Association* 263, No. 24, June 27, 1990.
10. Arlene Bowers Andrews, "Social Work Expert Testimony Regarding Mitigation in Capital Sentencing Proceedings," *Social Work* 36 (May 1991): 440.
11. "1992 Penal Code," Abridged California Edition (San Clemente, CA: Qwik-Code Publications), pp. 44–46.
12. Harold I. Kaplan and Benjamin J. Sadock, *Synopsis of Psychiatry,* 5th Edition (Baltimore, MD: Williams and Wilkins, 1988), p. 222.
13. Kaplan and Sadock, p. 456.
14. Ibid., p. 456.

15. Murray A. Straus, "Discipline and Deviance: Physical Punishment of Children and Violence and Other Crime in Adulthood," *Social Problems* 38 (February 1991): 134.

16. Murray A. Straus, "Sexual Inequality, Cultural Norms and Wife Beating," *Victimology* 1 (1976): 45–76.

17. Elizabeth Gould Davis, *The First Sex* (New York: Putnam, 1971).

18. Lenore E. Walker, *The Battered Woman* (New York: Harper & Row, 1979).

19. Sol Chaneles, ed., *Prisons and Prisoners: Historical Documents* (New York: Haworth Press, 1985), p. 6.

20. Armando T. Morales, "Children and Adolescents Who Commit Homicide," unpublished paper presented by JCIA Commissioner Morales before the Presidents of the American Psychological Association, American Psychiatric Association, American Nurses Association, and the National Association of Social Workers, at the Joint Commission of Interprofessional Affairs (JCIA) Eleventh Annual Leadership Conference, Kiawah Island, South Carolina, April 26–28, 1992, p. 4.

21. Irwin A. Hyman, *Reading, Writing and the Hickory Stick* (Lexington, MA: D.C. Heath Lexington Books, 1990).

22. Murray A. Straus, "Why Are American Youth so Violent? Some Clues to Causes and Prevention from an Analysis of Homicide Rates," Family Research Laboratory, University of New Hampshire, Durham, May, 1991, p. 12.

23. Ibid., p. 11.

24. Murray A. Straus and Richard J. Gelles, "Societal Change and Change in Family Violence from 1975 to 1985 as Revealed by Two National Samples," *Journal of Marriage and the Family* 48 (August 1986): 469.

25. Straus, 1991, p. 11.

26. Murray A. Straus, "Children as Witness to Marital Violence: A Risk Factor for Life Long Problems Among a Nationally Representative Sample of American Men and Women," in D. F. Schwarz, ed., *Children and Violence*. Report of the Twenty-Third Ross Roundtable on Critical Approaches to Common Pediatric Problems (Columbus, OH: Ross Laboratories, 1992), p. 105.

27. Straus, 1991, p. 23.

NAME INDEX

This is a continuation of the copyright page.

PHOTO CREDITS